Alan Howe

J

20 . vi . 1988

THE RECORD SOCIETY OF LANCASHIRE AND CHESHIRE

FOUNDED TO TRANSCRIBE AND PUBLISH
ORIGINAL DOCUMENTS RELATING TO THE TWO COUNTIES

VOLUME CXXVI

The Society wishes to acknowledge with much gratitude
the financial support from Mrs Diana Barraclough which has made possible
the publication of this extra volume in the Society's
series of texts.

ISBN 0 902593 17 X

Produced by Alan Sutton Publishing Limited, Gloucester
Printed in Great Britain

THE CHARTERS OF THE ANGLO-NORMAN EARLS OF CHESTER, c. 1071–1237

Edited by the late Professor
Geoffrey Barraclough

PRINTED FOR THE SOCIETY
1988

CONTENTS

GENERAL EDITOR'S INTRODUCTION

This very substantial 'extra' volume in the series of publications of the Record Society of Lancashire and Cheshire represents the final contribution to historical scholarship of Professor Geoffrey Barraclough, who died in December 1984 having virtually completed the text of his long-awaited *Charters of the Anglo-Norman Earls of Chester*.[1] Professor Barraclough had not begun to write the introduction to his edition, and there was nothing in the notes which he left to suggest the form which he intended his introduction to take. It was certainly not within the general editor's competence to attempt to write the full introduction which Professor Barraclough would have wanted, and it did not in any case seem appropriate for anyone else to add an 'outsider's' contribution to a work which was distinctively his own. The limited purpose of this short introduction is thus to set Professor Barraclough's work in its immediate perspective and to outline the nature of such editorial work as has been necessary to bring the original manuscript text to publication.

Half a century of active scholarship has made Geoffrey Barraclough one of the best known and most highly regarded of twentieth-century historians among students, fellow teachers of history, and academic writers. He is perhaps best remembered for his studies on the history of medieval Europe, and more especially of the Holy Roman Empire and the Papacy, in such standard works as *Papal Provisions* (1935), *Medieval Germany* (1938), *The Origins of Modern Germany* (1946), *The Medieval Empire* (1950), and, somewhat later, *The Medieval Papacy* (1968). His later career was characterised by a leap of six centuries and more to the modern era, where he brought his insight into the foundations of Europe to topical questions of European unity and contemporary world affairs in such works as *European Unity in Thought and Action* (1963), *An Introduction to Contemporary History* (1964), *Turning Points in World History* (1979), and *From Agadir to Armageddon* (1982). He will also be remembered for his editing of the best-selling *Times Atlas of World History* (1978) and *The Times Concise Atlas of World History* (1982). It was in what might be regarded as a 'middle period' between these two phases of his writing that he established his reputation as an authority on the history of medieval Cheshire. From 1945 to 1956, he was Professor of Medieval History at Liverpool University. In 1951 he published an important article entitled 'The Earldom and County Palatine of Chester' in the *Transactions of the Historic Society of Lancashire and Cheshire*. It was here that he observed that 'It may perhaps be true that a definitive account of the formative period in the history of the palatinate, from the Norman Conquest to 1237, must await the publication of a critical edition of the charters of the Anglo-Norman earls, which are the primary and only surviving "official" source for Cheshire history before the thirteenth century'.

---

1. Strictly speaking, not every document in this volume is a charter, but this edition has been anticipated for many years as 'Barraclough's Charters', and it seemed unduly pedantic to assign it any other title.

The Record Society of Lancashire and Cheshire has a long history of close relations with the University of Liverpool, and it was thus fitting that Professor Barraclough's *Facsimiles of Early Cheshire Charters* should be published for the Society in 1957 in honour of the 89th birthday of William Fergusson Irvine, who had been President of the Society since 1923. In acknowledging Fergusson Irvine's pioneering work on Cheshire medieval history in the *Cheshire Sheaf*, including his critical studies in that publication of certain charters of the Norman earls, Professor Barraclough noted that he had not included any examples of such charters in his own volume of facsimiles. His reasons for this omission included the fact that many facsimiles of the earls' charters were already published elsewhere, and he also considered that it would not have been possible to do justice to these records without destroying the balance of the volume as a whole. His main reason, however, was that he was in the process of preparing his own critical edition of the earls' charters 'which it is hoped shortly to publish'. By the time of the publication of the volume of facsimiles, however, Professor Barraclough had already left Liverpool, and a series of professorial appointments in London, the United States and Oxford removed him from the academic environment which had evidently stimulated his interest in local historical studies, and led him in the direction of broader projects in national and international history. During the years of his retirement from full-time academic duties, the work was revived, and its appearance was eagerly awaited by medieval and local historians. Professor Barraclough was aware, however, as he embarked on the intensive labour of preparing the text for publication, that he could not expect to live to see the finished edition in print. Defying the worst prognosis of his condition, his dedication and determination enabled him to complete all but a small fraction of the work he had set himself in checking references and queries, revising the texts of the charters, and seeking advice and information for his critical assessments. He was still corresponding with his fellow medievalists in the week before his death.

In September 1984, Professor Barraclough had written to Brian Redwood, then Secretary of the Record Society, expressing his intention of making a donation of £6,000 to the Society towards the publication of the volume if he were able to complete it. His widow, Mrs Diana Barraclough, most kindly affirmed her husband's very generous offer, which has enabled this volume to be published as an additional volume to the usual annual Record Society publications. Professor Barraclough had also expressed the wish that his working notes, and a set of photocopies of many of the charters, should be given to Cheshire Record Office, and this material will have been lodged there by the time that this volume appears in print.

As has been noted, Professor Barraclough had completed his work of editing virtually all the charters and other 'Acta' of the earls which he had been able to discover. The main exceptions are the Scottish charters (nos. 464–469), where the text is merely based on an earlier printed edition with the addition of Professor Barraclough's own footnotes. He had also intended that there should be substantial critical notes to the spurious Whitby charter (no. 5): his working notes record printed sources which he hoped to use for this purpose, and the reader is referred to these works in a brief note after the text of the charter. He had been particularly anxious to discover the original of an item from the 'Greenwell Deeds' (no. 278), but had already virtually given up hope of tracing it. With these few exceptions, his working notes suggest that he regarded his editing of the charters as completed.

The paradox that, while this was indeed the case, a certain amount of 'editorial' work remained to be done, was largely due to the fact that while each individual charter was completed, and while there was considerable cross-referencing from one charter to another, Professor Barraclough did not live to edit his very extensive text as a single unit. This has led, for example, to a slight tendency to repetition in the critical studies, since each charter remains treated, to a significant degree, as an independent item. There has been no attempt to 'remedy' this situation beyond adjusting a very small number of accidental inconsistencies: any attempt at rewriting would not have reduced the text significantly, and there are instances where the reader may be saved the trouble of consulting cross-references or the index.

The most obvious area of sub-editing has concerned the order in which the documents are presented. Professor Barraclough numbered his charters at an early stage in his work, but these original numbers appear to have had no significance, probably representing the order in which the items were 'collected'. There seems no reason to suppose that they have ever been used in scholarly referencing, but they may be readily traced in the working notes lodged in Cheshire Record Office. To retain this order would have been in no way meaningful, and two alternatives were considered. Of these, the idea of arranging the charters by the main places referred to (e.g. Dieulacres Abbey, St Werburgh's Abbey, etc) was rejected on the ground that once these had been placed in order, a considerable amount of material would remain outside this scheme. It was therefore decided to attempt, as far as possible, a chronological arrangement. A strict chronological sequence might have been most appropriate if all or most of the exact dates of the charters were known; but any student of the period is aware of the problems of dating these documents, and many can only be traced to the time of a particular earl, or to a ten- or twenty-year period of his tenure of the earldom. The charters have thus been arranged, in the first instance, in order of the earls.[2] Charters 1–5 are those of Hugh of Avranches (Hugh I), earl from 1071[3] to 1101, and nos. 6–9 those of his son Richard (1101–20), who was drowned in the sinking of the White Ship. Richard was succeeded by his first cousin Ranulf 'Le Meschin' (Ranulf I), who appears to have died early in 1129 (nos. 10–14). He was survived by a widow, the Countess

2. Charters granted by countesses during their husbands' lifetimes, or by countesses in association with their husbands, are incorporated in the appropriate earl's sequence with due acknowledgment in the abstract.
3. There is no firm proof that Hugh was granted the earldom in this year, but Professor Barraclough's opinion has been followed here.

Lucy, who granted nos. 16–19 in her own right during the earldom of her son Ranulf 'de Gernons' (Ranulf II), in whose time (1129–53) nos. 15–118 were granted. Ranulf's widow Matilda granted nos. 119–122 at the beginning of the earldom of her son Hugh (II), who died in 1181 (nos. 123–201). His son Ranulf 'Blundeville' (Ranulf III) held the earldom from 1181 to 1232, and documents from these years represent almost exactly half of the whole of this collection (nos. 202–437): two charters of Ranulf's mother Bertrada appear at appropriate points in the sequence at nos. 251 and 331. Ranulf was succeeded by his nephew John 'the Scot', earl of Huntingdon, who was responsible for nos. 438–469 with the exception of nos. 442–444, which were granted by Ranulf III's second wife and widow Clementia. John died without issue in 1237, and the earldom passed to the Crown.

Within the years of each earldom, an attempt at chronological order has been made, but in view of the impossibility of providing exact dates, and of the obviously close consecutive relationship of certain items to one another, a degree of arrangement by 'place' (and in some instances by person) has been introduced. Thus, for instance, the first charter relating to St Werburgh's Abbey under Ranulf III is entered at the appropriate chronological place, and is followed by subsequent grants relating to St Werburgh's under that earl, in as near chronological order as possible. It is hoped that this arrangement combines the best of both principles. Readers needing to consult *all* charters relating to a particular place or person will, of course, find all the references they need in the index, which has been compiled by the general editor.

The arrangement of the critical edition of each charter is a particularly full version of the standard format for such studies, as follows:

i)   An abstract of the text of the charter, in English, followed by the place of issue of the document, where known, and the (usually approximate) date. The grantor of the document, or the 'he' or 'she' referred to in the abstract, is the earl or countess whose name appears at the head of that group of documents, unless there is a clear statement to the contrary.

ii) References to the whereabouts of all known manuscript texts and printed versions. These include statements as to whether the manuscript is an original, a facsimile, a transcript, a full text, an abbreviated version, an abstract, a fragment or a short notice. Bibliographical references to printed versions may indicate whether the charter is reproduced in Latin or English, in facsimile, in calendared or abstract form, or whether it is merely the subject of a short notice or incidental mention. While Professor Barraclough generally intended 'Ed.' to denote full printed editions in the original language (almost invariably Latin), this cannot be guaranteed to be the case in every instance: readers are recommended to check the works cited in order to be certain of the precise format in which the charter has been presented in print.

iii) The full text of the document. Where there are variations between the texts referred to in (ii), these are recorded in footnotes.

iv)   Information on the seal, if one exists, or if there is a record of its existence.
v)   Critical analysis and comments, sometimes very detailed. These include information relevant to dating, remarks on the careers of persons mentioned in the text, especially the witnesses to the document, and general remarks on historical context. There is frequently an assessment of the document's authenticity, as Professor Barraclough included many items which are irrefutably spurious as they stand, or which give reason for varying degrees of scepticism.

Footnotes have been sited at the end of the appropriate section of the edition of each charter, rather than gathered together at the end of the whole study and assessment of the document. Apart from some work in rationalising the text in keeping with this 'principle', most of the sub-editing of the text has concerned section (ii). As mentioned above, Professor Barraclough was not able to collate the full text, and thus locational references for charters, and to some extent bibliographical data, appeared in the manuscript in a variety of formats. A concerted attempt has been made to impose consistency of format in these references: in the (hopefully few) instances where this may not have been achieved, it is unlikely that the validity of the reference has been materially affected. A similar approach has been taken in the case of Professor Barraclough's abbreviations of references to printed works. Where it was felt that an abbreviation was merely a 'working reference' which would have been modified at a later stage, and especially where the form of letters in an abbreviation might cause confusion, I have taken the liberty of modifying it, usually in the direction of expansion: in most instances, however, the abbreviations remain in the form in which they appear in the manuscript. As a result of the imposition of greater consistency of format in referring to printed works, full bibliographical references (e.g. authors' forenames, dates, and places of publication) are not incorporated in the main text. This information may be found in the bibliography, which is prefaced by a comprehensive list of abbreviations.

Where Professor Barraclough has referred to printed texts of charters, the number given by an earlier editor is frequently cited instead of, or as well as, the page number of the relevant text. While some consistency has been imposed here, it should be noted that both forms of reference are adequate for tracing the individual charters within a volume. Where documents are cross-referenced within this edition, the numbers are printed in bold type for greater emphasis, and to distinguish them from references to charter numbers in other works.

While it is to be expected that the charters of the earls of Chester should contain much information relating to Cheshire, rather less than 40% of the material in these documents relates to that county.[4] Nearly 20% relates to Lincolnshire, a

4.   More exact figures for percentages or other statistics have not been provided, as it would be virtually impossible to take account of the different sizes of individual items, and of the fact that several refer to more than one county or theme.

reminder of Ranulf III's title of earl of Lincoln from 1217 to 1232. Warwickshire (nearly 10%, much of which relates to Coventry), Staffordshire (c. 7–8%, especially Dieulacres Abbey) and Leicestershire (c. 5–6%) are also strongly represented. The c. 5% of documents relating to France reflects the fact that the earls had major interests in Normandy, and were affected by the loss of that duchy to Philip II of France in 1204. There are smaller numbers of items relating to Berkshire, Buckinghamshire, Derbyshire, Dorset, Essex, Gloucestershire, Hertfordshire, Huntingdonshire, Lancashire, Middlesex, Northamptonshire, Nottinghamshire, Oxfordshire, Rutland, Shropshire, Wiltshire, Worcestershire and Yorkshire, as well as North Wales (mainly Flintshire) and Scotland. This wide geographical range emphasises that the 'honour' of Chester extended into over twenty English counties and across the Channel, and that it was this greater unit, rather than the 'special status' of Cheshire, which gave the earls their eminent standing in English society and in political life.

This eminence is reflected in many of the charters. Ranulf II was constantly involved in the politics of the troubled reign of Stephen, and has earned the dubious distinction of being the subject of an article primarily devoted to assessing the number of times he changed sides in the civil wars of that reign.[5] His son Hugh II suffered temporary disgrace after his rebellion against King Henry II in 1173. Ranulf III was believed in 1199 to be the greatest landowner in England after King Richard I's brother John, and he was predictably prominent in the political events of the reigns of John and Henry III, when he was a consistent, if not uncritical, servant of the Crown in the face of baronial opposition and civil unrest. His rewards included the title of earl of Lincoln in 1217.[6] By right of his first wife Constance, Ranulf held the titles of duke of Brittany and earl of Richmond from 1189 to his divorce in 1199. His second wife Clementia, whom he married in the following year, survived him.[7] It was doubtless at least partly as a result of Ranulf's good relations with the Crown during his long tenure of the earldom that he was able to consolidate the peculiar status of Cheshire along lines which paralleled contemporary developments in the royal administration. This development was illustrated by the growing importance of the office of justice of Chester (analogous to that of justiciar of England) during the tenure of Philip of Orreby (c. 1206/7–1229).

Relations between Crown and baronage, England's involvement in Normandy and Wales, relations between the earls, their families, and other members of the aristocracy, the careers of the earls' retainers and servants, and the rôles of local office-holders and administrators, all figure prominently in the charters. Land transactions are obviously abundantly represented, providing primary material for the study of social, economic and agricultural history, the latter being

5. See R. H. C. Davis, 'King Stephen and the Earl of Chester Revised', *E.H.R.*, lxxv, pp. 654–60; also H. A. Cronne, 'Ranulf de Gernons, Earl of Chester, 1129–1153', *T.R.H.S.*, 4th Ser. xx, pp. 103–34.

6. See e.g. B. E. Harris, 'Ranulph III, Earl of Chester', *J.C.A.S.*, lvii, pp. 100–114.

7. Also known as Clemence or Clemency; see above, p. x.

illustrated, for instance, by Ranulf III's schemes for the reclamation of the Lincolnshire fens (nos. 417–421). Where these transactions involve the Church, there is a wealth of evidence for the student of ecclesiastical history, including material relating to the foundation of religious houses, the continuing grants of lands, liberties and privileges, and relations between ecclesiastical and lay authorities and individuals. There is information on such diverse subjects as the fisheries of the Dee, the holding of markets and fairs, the Cheshire salt industry, and the keeping of horses and falcons. The whole collection surely fulfils Professor Barraclough's aim of producing a substantial and important resource for the study not only of medieval Cheshire, but of English society as a whole in the twelfth and thirteenth centuries.

Professor Barraclough was assiduous, in his earlier publications, in his acknowledgment of the assistance given to him by fellow scholars and by libraries, record offices and similar institutions, as well as by private owners of primary material. It is much to be regretted that those who may have been particularly helpful cannot receive special mention here. The formidable list of repositories cited in the bibliography clearly represents a considerable amount of personal contact, and the Society's thanks are here gratefully added to those which Professor Barraclough must have offered to these institutions and their staff over thirty years of research. Every effort has been made to ensure that the law of copyright, and the conventions of securing permission for the reproduction of hitherto unpublished material, have been duly observed, and apologies are offered for any inadvertent omissions. In the case of certain items which have been published very recently (notably a series of Coventry charters published by Dr Peter Coss in 1986)[8], the text is for copyright reasons not reproduced here, and the reader is referred to the appropriate publication. The appearance of this study, and other work which is known to be in progress, is evidence of a resurgence of scholarly interest in this period of history. The Society is confident that Professor Barraclough's volume will make a major contribution towards sustaining and promoting this interest.

Peter McNiven
July 1987

8. *The Early Records of Medieval Coventry*, ed. and introd. by P. R. Coss, pp. 1–27.

THE CHARTERS OF THE ANGLO-NORMAN EARLS OF CHESTER

HUGH (I), EARL OF CHESTER(1071–1101)

1. Confirmation of Hugh I's gifts to the abbey of St. Evroul of land and tithes in Little Pillerton (Warws.) and in Brickhill and Sauley (Bucks.), and of the gifts of Robert of Rhuddlan, given with the earl's consent, of West Kirby (Wirral), the church of St. Peter in Chester, and the churches of Marston and Byfield (Northants.), and the gifts of other of the earl's men, viz. Roscelin of Stainton, Osbern son of Tesson of Newball, Baldric of Farforth, Roger of Milly and Brisard (all in Lincolnshire), and of Robert Pultrel in Leicestershire.

    [1071–1081]

    Ord. Vitalis, iii. 26–28; *Mon.*, vi. 1078–9 (from Orderic, the only surviving text). Noted: Baker, *Hist. of North-ants.*, i. 484, 639; *Regesta*, i. no. 140.

. . .Hugo autem Cestrensis comes filium suum nomine Rodbertum in Uticensi ecclesia ad monachatum dei obtulit et eidem ecclesie dedit unam hidam terre in Parva Pilardentona et decimam ac unum rusticum in villa que dicitur Brichella decimamque de Sauleia in Buccingehamscira. Rodbertus vero de Rodelento, prefato Hugone Cestrensi comite domino suo concedente, dedit sancto Ebrulfo Cherchebiam cum duabus ecclesiis, una scilicet que in ipsa villa est et alia prope illud manerium in insula maris, et ecclesiam sancti Petri apostoli et quicquid ad eam pertinebat in Cestrensi urbe, et in Merestona, que est in Northamtonescira, ecclesiam sancti Laurentii et quicquid ad eam pertinet, et in eadem provincia ecclesiam de Bivella cum duabus terre carucatis. Alii quoque homines Hugonis comitis Uticensi ecclesie decimas suas dederunt, in Nicholescira Rozscelinus de Estentona, Osbernus Tezsonis filius de Neubela, Baldricus de Farefort decimam cum uno rustico, Rogerius de Millai et Brisaud, et Robertus Pultrel in Legrecestrescira. Omnes hi decima suas sancto Ebrulfo dederunt, et predictus comes gratanter concessit.

William I's charter of 1081 for St. Evroul, or Utica, in Normandy, from which the present excerpt is taken, is clearly a product of the monks. Whether it is genuine or not as it stands, there is no reason to question the grants of Hugh I, which it recites. With only two exceptions, its terms are reproduced in Ranulf I's charter of 1123–28 (**no. 11**). The exceptions are the omission in the latter of Robert Pultrel's gift of tithes in Leicestershire, which had presumably been lost in the interval, and the attribution of the gift of the church of Byfield, here stated to have been a gift of Robert of Rhuddlan, to Earl Richard. Here again, we must assume a resumption some time after 1081. The date of Hugh I's gifts cannot be closely fixed, but must fall between 1071 and 1081. Later, probably between

1

1137 and 1140 (*Chart. St. Werburgh*, p. 290, no. 505), St. Evroul disposed of West Kirby to St. Werburgh's abbey for an annual payment of 30s. (**no. 132**). According to *Sanctorum prisca* (**no. 3**), Robert Pultrel later gave a carucate of land at Macclesfield to St. Werburgh's, but I have not otherwise been able to trace him.

2.   Letter to Rainald abbot of Abingdon agreeing, after consulting his wife and barons, to hand over the land (Shippon, Berks.) for which the abbot had petitioned, on condition that he should receive £30 from the latter and be treated as one of the brethren in prayers and other religious ceremonies.

[1089–90]

B.L. Cott. MS. Claudius C. 9, f. 136v.--137; printed Orm., i. 11.

Hugo Cestrensis comes Rainaldo venerando abbati et carissimo amico suo salutem. Mando tibi, quod de terra, quam erga mei petiisti, locutus sum cum uxore mea et cum meis baronibus, et inveni in meo consilio quod concedam eam deo et sancte ecclesie, de qua pastoralis cura super te imposita est, tali pacto quod dones mihi xxx. libras denariorum de tua pecunia, et ut frater vester sim, et uxor mea et pater meus et mater mea in orationibus vestris, et ita ut simus scripti omnes in libro commemorationum, et ut sit factum tale obsequium pro nobis quale debet fieri pro uno fratre de ecclesia, ubicunque moriamur. Quicquid itaque pro illa terra exactum est, nil fieri relictum, nam et pecunia data et cetera quesita omnino impensa.

According to the *Abingdon Chronicle* (ii. 19–20), Earl Hugh completed this transaction on 31 March 1090 in the sanctuary of the church at Abingdon by laying a knife on the altar, as a token of livery of seisin. The above letter, laying down the conditions for completion, evidently preceded the actual transaction, but probably by no more than a few weeks.

3.   The so-called foundation charter of St. Werburgh's abbey (Sanctorum prisca). [Spurious]

[1093]

Bodleian Library, MS. Engl. Hist. c. 242, ff. 72–3 (A) (formerly Gurney MS., in Dugdale's hand 'ex ipso authographo penes Decanum et Capitulum ecclesie cathedralis Cestrie, August. anno 1640', some words written in facsimile, with drawing of seal); Dodsworth MS. 31, ff. 6–9 ('Originale huius copiae remansit penes Willelmum

Brereton de Brereton militem') (B); Chester, Booth of
Twemlow, Liber D, f. 39–41 (also 'penes Wm. Brereton
de Brereton') (C); B.L. Harl. MS. 1965 (St. Werburgh's
register), ff. 1–1v, (new f. 4–4v.), abbreviated text,
without witnesses (D); St. George's Chapel, Windsor,
MS. xi. E.5 (*inspeximus* by Guncelin de Badlesmere,
1280) (E); P.R.O., C.53 (Chancery Charter Rolls), no.
73, m. 11 (F). Ed.: *Mon.*, ii. 385 (from Dugdale's MS.);
Orm., i. 12 (Sir Peter Leycester's copy of Badlesmere
inspeximus); *Chart. St. Werburgh*, pp. 15–22 (Tait's fully
collated edition).

Sanctorum prisca auctoritate patrum, qui in nomine patris et filii et spiritus
sancti in sancta ecclesia regiminis gubernacula hactenus tenuerunt, quique suos
adiutores sancteque ecclesie fundatores sua nobis industria suorumque scrip-
torum longa traditione cognitos reddiderunt, admoneri videmur, ut ea que a
temporaneis nostris in sancte ecclesie matris exaltatione facta sunt, presentibus
per nos manifestentur posterisque dinoscenda, nobis scribentibus reserventur.

Nos igitur, maiorum imitantes exempla, iam quedam pietatis opera referamus,
que in Anglica terra gesta sunt a Hugone Cestrensi comite anno ab incarnatione
domini millesimo nonagesimo tercio, regnante potentissimo rege Willelmo atque
in archiepiscopatu Cantuariensi pontificante Anselmo atque in Eboracensi
pontificante Thoma. Volumus vero ut religiosi atque fideles Christiani cognoscant
quia iccirco nobis ista describere placuit, ut qui ea relegerint vel audierint deum
supplicabiliori affectu pro sancte ecclesie fundatorum salute implorent, et ut
presentes ad regna celestia tendentes etiam inter etatis huius primates, quos
sequantur, inveniant. Igitur ad honorem et gloriam summe et individue trinitatis
atque incomprehensibilis divinitatis iam proferamus que nos dicere spopondimus.

Hugo comes Cestrensis atque Ermentrudis comitissa, devotioni religiose pia
mente subditi piissimaque dei visitatione inspirati, in quadam ecclesia, que
constructa est in honore sancte Werburge virginis in civitate Cestrie, monachos
religiose viventes posuerunt, concedente rege Willelmo, qui deum assidue
exorarent tam pro utilitate anime regis Willelmi et Willelmi patris eius nobilissimi regis et matris eius Mathildis regine fratrumque et sororum eius atque regis
Edwardi, quam pro animarum suarum salute et pro animabus patrum et matrum
et antecessorum heredumque et parentum et baronum suorum, omniumque
Christianorum tam vivorum quam defunctorum. Huic vero ecclesie sancte
Werburge Hugo supradictus comes et Ermentrudis comitissa possessiones
priores liberas in perpetuum[1] et quietas concesserunt et de suis augmentaverunt,
habitationique monachorum habilem reddiderunt, eamque abbatiam nulli
omnino abbatie subditam fecerunt. Postea in ea monachos et abbatem deo
donante et supradicto rege Willelmo concedente constituerunt.

Hanc etiam et quicquid ad eam pertinet abbati et monachis dederunt, videlicet Ynes (*Ince*),[2] Salthonam (*Saighton*), Suttonam (*Sutton*), Cheveleiam (*Cheveley*), Huntithonam (*Huntington*), Bocthonam (*Boughton*), Wervenam (*Wervin*), Croctonam (*Croughton*), Trochford (*Trafford*), Clifthonam (*Clifton*), Estonam (*Middleton Grange*), Wisdeleth (*Lea by Backford*), Hodisleiam (*Hoseley*), Weapram (*Wepre*), et dimidiam Rabi (*Raby*), et terciam partem de Nestona (*Neston*), et terciam partem de Leche (*Lache*), et unam carrucam terre ad Pulford (*Pulford*), et terciam partem de Berewardesleia (*Burwardsley*), et Edinchale (*Iddinshall*) et Sotewica (*Shotwick*). Insuper dederunt huic ecclesie in ipsa civitate de suo dominio vicum a porta de North (*Northgate*) usque ad ecclesiam et locum unius molendini ad pontem civitatis, et duo maneria in Anglisi (*Anglesey*), unum autem in Ros (*Rhos*), unum in Wirhalle (*Wirral*), Erberiam (*Irby*), et in Lindesei (*Lindsey*) terram decem boum, et post obitum comitis vel comitisse Westonam (*Weston-upon-Trent*) cum appendiciis suis in Derbesira, et ad presens decimam ipsius manerii et ecclesiam de Estona (*Aston-upon-Trent*) et terram duarum carrucarum, et rectam decimam non solum de annona verum etiam de pullis et vitulis, de porcis et agnis, de butiro et caseo, et de omnibus rebus de quibus debeat decima dari, in his meis maneriis, scilicet Etthona (*Eaton*), Frodesham (*Frodsham*), Weveresham (*Weaverham*), Lech (*Leek*), Roccestra (*Rochester*), Haurdina (*Hawarden*), Coleshul (*Coleshill*), Bissopestred (*Bistre, co. Flint*), Uppetuna (*Upton*), Campedena (*Chipping Campden, Gloucs.*), Esteham (*Eastham*), et rectam decimam piscatoriarum de Frodesham (*Frodsham*), de Rodelant (*Rhuddlan*), de Anglesheia (*Anglesey*), non solum de dominio suo sed etiam de navibus ibi, et in omnibus aquis suis piscantibus et decimam de piscatoria Etthone (*Eaton*) et de omni pisce qui accipitur in De (*Dee*), et unum batellum ab omni re liberum. Adhuc vero dederunt ecclesiam et terram ecclesie et decimam de molendinis et de omnibus rebus que decimari debent in Denefordia (*Denford, Northants.*)

Quin etiam baronibus suis principalibus concesserunt ut unusquisque daret prefate abbatie centum solidatas terre, alii autem secundum suum posse et velle. Insuper constituerunt ut singuli barones et milites darent deo et sancte Werburge post obitum suum sua corpora et terciam partem totius substantie sue. Et non solum hec constituerunt de baronibus et militibus sed etiam de burgensibus et aliis hominibus liberis suis. Teste Anselmo archiepiscopo, Herveio episcopo, Baldwino monacho, Eustachio monacho, Heldebaldo monacho, Roberto filio Hugonis, Willelmo constabulario, Willelmo Malbanc, Rannulfo dapifero, Hugone Normanni filio, Radulfo dapifero, Hugone filio Osberni, Hamone de Maci, Gileberto de Venables, Ricardo de Vernun, Ricardo de Rullos, Bigod de Loges, Ricardo filio Nigelli, Roberto filio Serli, Rannulfo venatore, Erneiso venatore, aliisque quamplurimis.

Willelmus Malbanc dedit huic abbatie sancte Werburge Witebiam (*Whitby*) et terciam partem Weupre (*Wepre, co. Flint*) et ecclesiam et decimam de Tatenhala (*Tattenhall*) et unam salinam in Wicho (*Nantwich*) et terram duobus bobus et decimam de Salchale (*Saughall*) et de Claitona (*unidentified*) et de Yraduc (*unidentified, probably in commote of Rhuddlan*). Teste comitissa, Ricardo Banaste, Hugone Osberni filio, Bigod de Loges, Ricardo pincerna, Sirardo.

Robertus filius Hugonis dedit capellam Cristentune (*Christleton*) et terram capelle et terram cuiusdam rustici ipsumque rusticum, et quoddam molendinum terramque ipsius molendini, et chotam Ordrici ipsumque Ordricum et quendam campum iunctum huic chote, et Cryu (*Crewe by Farndon*), et quandam salinam in Fulewich (*Fullwich*), et duas mansuras in civitate, et paululum terre iuxta Bochtunestan (*unidentified*). Hoc donum concessit Hugo comes. Teste Willelmo Nigelli filio et fratre eius Ricardo, Rannulfo dapifero, Bigod, Hamone de Maci, Hugone Osberni filio, Hugone Normanni filio, Fulcone de Baiunvilla, Unfrido de Costentin, Willelmo de Berneres, Acardo, multisque aliis.

Hugo filius Normanni et Radulfus frater eius dederunt partem suam de Lostoch (*Lostock*) et ecclesiam de Cotintuna (*Coddington*) et terram ecclesie et decimam illius ville et de Lay (*Lea-cum-Newbold*) similiter. Teste Willelmo Malbanc multisque aliis.

Ricardus de Vernon dedit decimam Estone (*Ashton*) et Pichetone (*Picton*). Ricardus de Rullos dedit ecclesiam et decimam Wavertone (*Waverton*) et Hettone (*Hatton*) et Clotone (*Clotton*) et molendini Clotone. Billeheld uxor Baldrici dedit Pecfortunam (*Peckforton*), teste Normanno de Arretio multisque aliis.

Radulfus venator dedit terram trium carrucarum in Brochetuna (*Broughton by Hawarden*). Hugo de Mara dedit Reddeclivam (*Redcliff in Chester*) concedente comite. Teste comitissa, Willelmo Nigelli filio, Rannulfo dapifero, Gileberto Venables, multisque aliis.

Hugo comes, dum habuit in suo dominio Calders (*Great Caldy*), dedit inde decimam de omnibus que decimari debent, quod etiam concessit et confirmavit Robertus filius Serlonis, quando villa data est ei. Item comes Hugo, quando habuit in suo dominio Stortonam (*Storeton*) et Gravesbiri (*Greasby*), dedit inde decimam de omnibus que decimari debent, sicut antea dederat in suis propriis maneriis, que omnia confirmavit Nigellus de Burceio veniens in hereditatem, augens etiam ex sua parte terram octo bobus in Gravesbiri (*Greasby*). Teste Rannulfo et Garacino fratre eius, multisque aliis.

Radulfus Ermewini filius et uxor eius Claricia dederunt terram ad octo boves in Wudechirche (*Woodchurch*) et decimam de Berlestona (*Barnston*) in Wirhala (*Wirral*) et de Wervelestona (*Worleston*) in Wichesfeld (*i.e. the district of Nantwich*) de equabus omnibus, ubicunque sint, et de omnibus que decimari possint. Teste Godefrido mercatore, Roberto Anglico, Fulberto, multisque aliis.

Robertus de Tremouz dedit Tidelvestan (*Tilstone Fearnall*), teste Ranulfo fratre suo, Roberto dapifero, Ricardo de Briceio.

Wacelinus nepos Walteri de Vernon dedit quendam agricolam et terram quatuor boum in Nessa (*Ness*), et decimam de omnibus rebus suis que decimari possint in Prestona (*Prenton*), in Levedesham (*Ledsham*), et terciam partem totius substantie sue et uxoris eius. Teste Gileberto multisque aliis. Scirard dedit capellam de Bebintone (*Bebington*) et terram quatuor boum et decimam illius manerii, et decimam de Bromhale (*Bromhall*) et de Walei (*Wallasey*) et de Maynes (*Little Mayne and Friar Mayne, Dorset*) et de Westona (*Weston-upon-Trent*) et de Wilne (*Wilne, co. Derby*), et post obitum suum omnem substantie sue et sue mulieris terciam partem de Cestresira et de Maynes. Teste Willelmo constabulario, Hugone Osberni filio, et Wimundo de Colonciis.

Gillebertus de Venables dedit deo et sancte Werburge ecclesiam de Esteburi (*Astbury*) cum medietate bosci et plani et omnium que pertinent ad Neobold (*Newbold in Astbury*). Galfridus de Sartes dedit decimam suam de Withtrichestun (*Wightreston*). Teste Willelmo filio Gud, et ipso domino suo Willelmo Malbanc.

Ricardus de Mesnilwarin dedit decimam de Blachenot (*Blacon*) de annona, de piscatoria, et de omnibus de quibus decima debet dari. Teste Rogero fratre suo et Rannulfo Beurello, et Rannulfo de Walbruno.

Robertus Pultrel dedit terram unius carruce ad Masclesfeld (*Macclesfield*). Teste Walerano de Baro, et Nigello de Rapentune, et multis aliis.

Walterius de Vernon dedit decimam equarum suarum. Comes dedit navim unam cum decem retibus ad piscandam in Anglisi in perpetuum liberam et quietam. Teste comitissa, Willelmo pincerna, Hugone camerario.

Item ad festum sancte Werburge in estate dedit comes Hugo theloneum omnesque redditus et exitus nundinarum trium dierum, precipiens ut si aliquis forisfecerit in nundinis, omnia placita pertractentur in curia sancte Werburge ad opus monachorum. Concessit etiam ad honorem virginis, ut sive latro sive aliquis malefactor venerit ad solempnitatem, habeat firmam pacem dum fuerit in nundinis, nisi forte in illis aliquid forisfecerit.

Hec sunt itaque dona data abbatie sancte Werburge, que omnia ego comes Hugo et Ricardus filius meus et Ermentrudis comitissa et mei barones et mei homines dedimus abbatie sancte Werburge. Et concessimus ut hec omnia predicta et abbatia et omnia ad eam pertinentia essent libera et pacata et quieta ab omni consuetudine et ab omni re, nichil retinentes in hiis omnibus nisi orationes et beneficia monachorum in hoc loco commanentium, et tam liberum et quietum honorem sancte Werburge dedimus et constituimus pro salute anime regis

Willelmi et omnium nostrum, ut nullus post nos aliquid libertatis vel quietis addere possit. Et quando nos hanc cartam confirmavimus, nullum opus, nullum servitium, nullam consuetudinem, nullam omnino rem preter orationem in terra sancte Werburge retinuimus, preter hoc solum quod, si abbas huius loci superbia inflatus nollet facere rectum vicinis suis, comes constringeret eum ad rectum faciendum, et hoc in curia sancte Werburge, quia volumus ut sancta Werburga habeat per omnia curiam suam, sicut comes suam.

Et ut hec omnia essent rata et stabilia in perpetuum, ego comes Hugo et mei barones confirmavimus ista omnia coram Anselmo archiepiscopo, non solum sigillo meo sed etiam sigillo dei omnipotentis, id est signo sancte crucis + , ita quod singuli nostrum propria manu in testimonium posteris signum in modum crucis facerent. + Signum Hugonis comitis. + Signum Ricardi filii eius. + Signum Hervei episcopi. + Signum Ranulfi nepotis comitis. + Signum Rogeri Bigod. + Signum Alani de Perci. + Signum Willelmi constabularii. + Signum Ranulfi dapiferi. + Signum Willelmi Malbanc. + Signum Roberti filii Hugonis. + Signum Hugonis filii Normanni. + Hamonis de Masci. + Signum Bigod de Loges.

> SEAL:[3] fragmentary, on cord, no inscription remaining,
> haunch of horse standing, and legs of knight on horseback
> in surcoat.

1. *E reads* inperpetuum; *A, B, C* imperpetuum.
2. Modern forms of place-names adapted with acknowledgements from Tait's edition, inserted in round brackets for reference.
3. From drawing in Bodl. MS. Engl. Hist. c. 242, f. 69.

Sanctorum prisca (as it is usually called) is probably the most famous, and certainly one of the more difficult, of all Cheshire charters. As such, it requires a lengthier consideration than most others, particularly as a re-examination suggests conclusions at variance with those of James Tait, whose elaborate critical analysis of 1920 appears to have been accepted without criticism by all subsequent historians.[1]

Sanctorum prisca belongs to the category of document known as a *pancarte* or *pancarta*. This takes the form of a list drawn up by the monks of a monastic foundation, usually in the third person, of gifts of land, tithes and liberties, normally including witnesses and often opening with an account of the circumstances of the foundation, followed by a solemn confirmation, usually in the first person, by the founder or one of his successors. Such documents are not infrequent and are always problematical. The best known examples in England, apart from this and **no. 28**, are the so-called foundation charters of Shrewsbury abbey, which are particularly important in the present context because they include one which also opens with the *Sanctorum prisca* introduction and has other striking similarities to the so-called foundation charter of St. Werburgh's abbey;[2] but Earl Richard's charter for Troarn (**no. 9**) belongs to the same category and raises similar problems of interpretation.

Such documents, produced by the monks in their own interest, provide ample opportunities for manipulation and falsification, and it is not surprising that they have a bad reputation. The so-called foundation charter of St. Werburgh's abbey, alleged to have been granted by Hugh Lupus in 1093, is no exception. Tait had no difficulty in proving that it could not be, as it purported to be, the original foundation charter of 1092 or 1093, the inclusion among the signatories of Earl Hugh's son, Richard, who was only born in 1094, being itself sufficient to disprove that claim. Tait nevertheless believed that it represented, perhaps with interpolations, a genuine charter of 1096–1101. His argument (p. 28) rested on two assumptions: (i) that the Shrewsbury *Sanctorum prisca* charter, which dates from 1121, was copied from the Chester version; (ii) that the grant of liberties by Earl Hugh of Shrewsbury (d. 1098), which is incorporated in the Shrewsbury charter and which is echoed almost verbatim in the Chester charter, was 'faithfully reported', i.e. that it is the actual text of a genuine grant made between 1094 and 1098. Neither assumption is compelling. It is hard to think of any reason why Shrewsbury, which was the senior foundation (1083), should have borrowed from Chester;[3] but if the borrowing was the other way round, the Chester charter cannot date from before 1121. As for Earl Hugh of Shrewsbury's alleged grant of liberties, which Tait believed was taken from the Chester charter some time before 1098, it is at least doubtful whether it ever existed at all and 'more probable' that it was fabricated and 'incorporated when the Shrewsbury *Sanctorum prisca* was made', i.e. in or about 1121.[4]

These considerations, if they have any validity, clearly militate against Tait's arguments for dating the Chester *Sanctorum prisca* between 1096 and 1101, and still more for accepting it as a genuine charter of Hugh Lupus. Tait was, of course, well aware of the anomalies – e.g. the attribution (p. 4) to William Malbank of the gift of a salthouse in Nantwich, which was in reality given by his son Hugh in the time of Earl Richard – which make it difficult to accept *Sanctorum prisca* at face value. But he tried to save the credit of the charter, in this and in other instances, by dismissing the passage in question as 'a later interpolation'.[5] This may be true; but the interpolations are an integral part of the text as it stands and cannot simply be left out of account when we attempt to establish its date.

This is almost certainly considerably later than Tait suggested, and perhaps not earlier than the reign of Stephen. Just as the monks of Shrewsbury falsely attributed the grant of a 3-days' fair to their founder, Earl Roger of Montgomery, although it dates at earliest from the reign of Henry I,[6] so the monks of Chester included in *Sanctorum prisca* grants which almost certainly belong to a later period. Thus Earl Hugh is credited (p. 4) with the gift of the tithe of all fish caught in the Dee, but this gift was in reality made by Ranulf II 'ex meo proprio dono' (p. 44), and the charter, dating from 1141 to 1150, in which Ranulf made the gift, still survives (**no. 26**). It is also evident, as Tait pointed out (p. 23), that the passage in which Earl Hugh is said to have granted the monks a fair of three days (p. 6) is an addition or interpolation, and the same is probably true of his concession that they shall have their own court, 'as the earl has his'. Significantly, the former is not mentioned at all in the charter of Earl Richard (**no. 8**), while the grant of a court is recorded (p. 15) as Richard's own gift, with no suggestion that it had previously been made by his father. The implication is that both grants belong to a later period than *Sanctorum prisca* would have us believe, the former perhaps to the time of Earl Ranulf I, and if this is the case, the document must be adjudged, by its own standards, as a forgery, or at best as a later fabrication.

Other considerations support this view. First is the surprising fact, if the charter was by then sixty or seventy years old, that the earliest independent evidence we possess of its existence occurs in a charter from the time of Hugh II, which Tait dates 1154–58, but which is almost certainly later in date.[7] Secondly, there is the evidence, tenuous but not insignificant, of the copy, unknown to Tait, which Dugdale made of the 'autograph' in Chester cathedral in 1640.[8] Tait was sceptical of the existence of this 'so-called original', and wrote it off (p. 26) as 'an interpolated copy of the fourteenth century or later'. But the fact that Dugdale provides facsimiles of the handwriting and a drawing of the seal is clear evidence that it actually existed. The important fact, however, is that the writing, so far as Dugdale's copy enables us to judge, is a monastic book-hand not earlier than the middle of the twelfth century, and the seal, whatever else, is certainly not a seal of Hugh I. It is, of course, possible that a later seal was attached to the charter at some time unknown, but there is no doubt that the long pleated surcoat, which is virtually all that remains, closely resembles that of Hugh II's first seal, in use after he attained his majority in 1162.[9] If it is genuine, and not a later attachment, it puts the date of the charter after the middle of the twelfth century.

Finally, there is the complicated question of the relationship between *Sanctorum prisca* and Ranulf II's 'great charter' (**no. 28**), which certainly does not date from before 1150 and is probably later. Tait paid a good deal of attention to this question, seeking to establish the 'priority' of *Sanctorum prisca*.[10] Without re-opening the question in detail, it is fair to say that the evidence Tait assembled makes it far more likely that both texts were put together about the same time from a common body of material in the abbey muniments. Considering that the monks of Shrewsbury put together three different versions of their alleged charter of liberties[11] and the monks of Troarn three different versions of **no. 9**, it is credible enough that the monks of Chester should have produced two versions of their foundation charter or charters. Certainly, if we compare *Sanctorum prisca* and Ranulf II's charter, there is no compelling evidence of priority. On most points of substance their recitals overlap; but each contains important information supplementing the other, and there is no reason to suppose that one preceded the other in point of time.

The conclusion to which these considerations point is that *Sanctorum prisca*, far from being a genuine charter of Hugh I, was probably compiled, like **no. 28**, towards the end of Ranulf II's tenure of the earldom, or even during the minority of his son, Hugh II. This would explain, among other things, why there is no mention of it before 1162.[12] On the other hand, it does not mean that the information it contains is valueless. In particular, its recital of the gifts of the barons is clearly derived from authentic charters or notices in the abbey's possession, and Tait, who was particularly concerned with identifying these gifts and their donors, and thus providing a solid foundation for the feudal history of Cheshire under the Anglo-Norman earls, was fully justified in claiming that, even if *Sanctorum prisca* and the charters of Richard and Ranulf I 'proved to be fabrications, the genuineness of the grants confirmed by them would remain unaffected' (p. xliii). With rare exceptions, this is true.[13] It is also possible, though this is less certain, that *Sanctorum prisca* contains in its opening section, ending with the long list of witnesses on p. 4, the substance of a genuine confirmation by Hugh I. But the charter as it stands, however much authentic material it contains, is clearly a twelfth-century compilation. We can only guess why it was made at this time, but presumably it had something to do with the disorders of Stephen's reign and Ranulf II's notorious high-handedness. That alone would be reason enough to make sure that the abbey had a full record of its lands and rights. Some of its possessions were certainly alienated not only by Ranulf II himself (**no. 34**), but also by his constable (**no. 21**) and steward (*Chart. St. Werburgh*, no. 527), and a solemn charter, allegedly from the founder, was at least a reasonable precaution against further depredations.

1.　*Chart. St. Werburgh*, pp. 13–37.
2.　There is now an extremely thorough critical edition of the Shrewsbury charters by Una Rees, *The Cartulary of Shrewsbury Abbey*, which supersedes all earlier work. The Shrewsbury *Sanctorum prisca* is no. 35. The other immediately relevant charter is no. 4, which purports to be Earl Hugh's charter of liberties, but dates from c.1150. Significantly, its text differs considerably in detail from that in no. 35.
3.　The one piece of positive evidence that the Chester charter was derived from the Shrewsbury charter – namely, the incorrect reading *temporaneis* in the former (p. 3) for the correct *contemporaneis* in the latter – is rather cavalierly dismissed by Tait (p. 28, n. 1) as insignificant.
4.　Cf. Rees, p. xvi. In any case 'if there was an original charter granted by Earl Hugh, it was not necessarily identical with the version preserved in *Sanctorum prisca*' (p. xvii).
5.　Cf. pp. xlii, 24, 32.
6.　Rees, pp. xii, 6, 260.
7.　*Chart. St. Werburgh*, no. 329 (pp. 217–8). Tait's dating rests on the identification of the witness William of Warenne with King Stephen's son, William count of Mortain. But Tait himself agrees that this is most unlikely. In fact William of Warenne is more likely to be the same man as witnesses nos. 342 and 344. Furthermore, the preceding witness, Hugh de Lacy, only succeeded after 1158 (Tait, p. 77). Without pursuing this question further, the list of witnesses as a whole points strongly to a date after, and probably some time after, Hugh II's majority in 1162.

8. This is the copy, formerly in the Gurney muniments, now in the Bodleian Library, MS. Engl. Hist. c. 242, ff. 72–3 (old ff. 68–9).
9. For a reproduction of Hugh II's seal, see the facsimile in Warner and Ellis, plate xxxiii. The long surcoat does not seem to have been used on earlier seals; cf. the seal reproduced in Orm., i. 20.
10. *Chart. St. Werburgh*, pp. xl, 22, 24, 26–7. Tait was attacking a certain Dr. Robson, who argued that *Sanctorum prisca* was fabricated from Ranulf II's charter. He successfully destroyed Robson's case; but the controversy perhaps misled him on the main issue.
11. Cf. Rees, p. xvi.
12. It also explains why the earliest papal confirmation of it (*Chart. St. Werburgh*, no. 61) dates from no earlier than 1188–91.
13. Tait's meticulous examination of the baronial grants retains its validity, and historians will always refer to this remarkable piece of work. For that reason it was decided not to discuss these grants here, since nothing would be added to Tait's account.

4. Gift of Atherstone (Warws.) to the abbey of Bec.

[1086–1101]

> P.R.O., C.53 (Chancery Charter Rolls), 12 Henr. III, m.11. Ed.: *Mon.*, vi. 1068 (from Charter Roll); mentioned *Cal. Ch. Rolls*, i. 66 (no text).

. . .De dono comitis Hugonis Cestrie in Anglia manerium quod vocatur Aldredestone.

In view of Hugh I's close relations with St. Anselm, abbot of Bec, and the latter's active role in the foundation of Chester abbey (*Chart. St. Werburgh*, pp. xxiii–xxv), it is surprising that this is his only known donation in England to the important Norman abbey of Bec, though the loss of the archives of Bec during the French Revolution may conceivably have destroyed evidence of other gifts. It is only known from the above terse entry in Henry III's confirmation of Henry II's charter of 1171 (Eyton, p. 157), but Atherstone remained in the possession of Bec until the suppression of alien monasteries (Morgan, *The English Lands of the Abbey of Bec*, p. 144), and there is no reason to question the authenticity of the gift. We do not know when it was made, but as Atherstone with other of the former lands of the Countess Godeva was still part of the royal demesne at the time of the Domesday survey (*H.K.F.*, pp. 6, 280), it must have been after 1086.

5. Notification to Thomas archbishop of York, William Percy and the sheriff of York of his confirmation to Prior Reinfrid and his convent of the church of St. Peter at Whitby and his gift of the church of Flamborough with the tithes of French and English. [Spurious]

[1086–1100]

> Whitby cartulary, in possession of Strickland family of

Whitwell, Yorks, f. 7. From cartulary, Bodleian Library,
Dodsworth MS. 105, f. 39v. Ed.: from cartulary: *Mon.*, i.
412; J.C. Atkinson, *Cartularium abbathiae de Whiteby*
(*Surtees Society*, vol. lxix) no. 25; Farrer, *Early Yorkshire
Charters*, ii. 193.

Hugo Cestrensis comes Thome archiepiscopo de Eboraco et Willelmo de Perci
et H.[1] vicecomiti Eboraci, prepositis et ministris meis et omnibus fidelibus
salutem. Sciatis me concessisse Renfrido priori et conventui eius ecclesiam sancti
Petri Whitbyensis et omnia que ad eam pertinent, ipsisque et predicte ecclesie
dedi ecclesiam de Fleinesburgh, cum omnibus decimis Francigenis et Anglicis, in
elemosinam perpetuam. Teste Alano comite et Radulfo Paganello et Aschetillo
de Bulmer et Roberto de Bruis et Gisleberto Adeladi filio, cum aliis.

1.   *sic Farrer*; Henrico *Atkinson*; H̄ *Dodsworth*.

[Professor Barraclough was still compiling the notes for a critical assessment of
this charter when he died. His rough notes included general references to Farrer,
op. cit., pp. 194–7; Knowles & Hadcock, pp. 58, 80; and *Heads of Religious
Houses*, pp. 77–78. For William de Percy he noted *Complete Peerage*, x. 436–38;
for Count Alan, Farrer, *op. cit.*, iv. 86–87, 94.]

RICHARD, EARL OF CHESTER (1101–1120)

6.   Confirmation by Earl Richard and Countess Ermentrude, his mother, of
Drogo of Andely's gift to the church of Abingdon of one hide of land at
Woodmundslea (South Weston, Oxfordshire), and quittance of Roger son
of Ralph of all service due therefrom. Abingdon, 13 May 1106.

B.L. Cott. MS. Claudius C. 9, f. 147; Cott. Otho D. 4, f.
15 (mutilated fragment); Harl. 2044, f. lv. (new foliation
26v.) from the Cotton MS; printed *Abingdon Chronicle*,
ii. 69; Orm., i. 16.

Ricardus Cestrensis comes et Ermentrudis comitissa, mater eius, Nigello de Oilli
et Rogero filio Radulfi et omnibus baronibus de Oxenefordscira salutem et
amicitiam. Sciatis quia pro amore dei et anima patris mei et remissione[1]
nostrorum peccatorum concedimus hidam illam, quam Droco de Andeleia dedit
ecclesie Abbendonensi, que est in loco qui dicitur Wdemundeslai. Nos eidem
ecclesie concedimus et auctorizamus perpetuo habendam, solidam et quietam ab
omni nostro servitio. Et Rogerus filius Radulfi et successores eius sint quieti in[2]
nostro servitio, quantum ad illam hidam pertinet, et defendimus ut nullo modo
Rogerus vel alius per eum inquietet habitantes in terra illa. Hoc autem fecimus[3]

testimonio nostrorum baronum, scilicet Willelmi filii Nigelli et Hugonis filii Normanni et Ricardi Balaste et Willelmi filii Anskitilli et Ricardi filii Nigelli et domini Goiffridi[4] capellani et aliorum. Hoc actum est in sexto anno regni Henrici regis in mense maio in die pentecostes.

1. remissionem *MS.*
2. *sic MS*; *for* de?
3. *add* et *MS. except Otho D. 4.*
4. *sic MS*; Goisfridi *in printed texts.*

The circumstances in which this charter was issued are explained at length in the Abingdon Chronicle. The land in question was held by Nigel de Oilli of the honour of Chester, and held of Nigel by his knight Drogo. The latter, falling sick, took the habit at Abingdon, and gave the land to the monastery. His gift was confirmed by Nigel and, probably in October 1105, by King Henry I (*Regesta*, ii. no. 693), but confirmation from the earl of Chester seems to have been outstanding. In 1106, however, Richard with his mother and 'the best of his barons' came to Abingdon, where he was received by Abbot Faritius, who besought him, with the support of Countess Ermentrude, to issue a confirmation. The outcome was the present charter, which also acquitted Roger son of Ralph, who had married Drogo's daughter, of the service due from the land in question. However, since Earl Richard was still a minor and not yet knighted, the charter was attested with his mother's seal, which no doubt explains why it was issued in her name, as well as his.

7. Confirmation of Nigel of Stafford's gift to St. Alban's abbey of the church of Norton by Twycross (Leics.).

[1115–1120]

Belvoir Castle, Rutland MSS., Belvoir cartulary, f. 66v.
Cal.: *Hist. MSS. Comm.*, *Rutland MSS.*, iv. 143.

Notum sit omnibus tam presentibus quam futuris, quod ego Ricardus gratia dei Cestrensis comes pro redempcione anime atque uxoris mee et patris mei necnon matris mee concedo ecclesiam de Nortuna cum terra, quam Nigellus de Stadfort dedit deo et sancto Albano, et precipio omnibus hominibus meis et fidelibus ut eandem elemosinam manuteneant et custodiant, et huius concessionis testimonium deo et sancto Albano eternaliter perhibeant.

The present gift refers to Belvoir priory, which was founded c.1076–88 by Robert of Tosny as a cell of St. Alban's abbey. Earl Richard's confirmation is irregular in form (most noticeably the addition of *gratia dei* to his title), but Nigel of Stafford's charter survives (*Mon.*, ii. 210), and there is no reason to question the authenticity of the confirmation. As Richard married in 1115 (*Ann. Cestr.*, p. 18), it must fall between then and his death in 1120.

8.   Confirmation of the gifts of the earl and his barons and those of Earl Hugh and his barons to St. Werburgh's abbey, and grant of a court for all pleas and wrongdoings, exactly as the earl has his, so that the abbot shall not have to plead against anyone in any matter except in his own court. [? Spurious]

Greetham, [1119]

> P.R.O., C.53 (Chancery Charter Rolls), no. 73 (inspeximus of 1285), m. 11; St. George's Chapel, Windsor, MS. xi. E5 (inspeximus of 1280); B.L. Harl. MS. 2071, f. 44v. (old f. 30), from 1280 inspeximus; Harl. MS. 1965, f. 5 (old f. 2) and Harl. 2062, f. 25 (copies of register of St. Werburgh, both heavily abbreviated); Chester, Booth of Twemlow, Liber K, f. 30 (source not known). Ed: *Mon.*, ii. 387 (from Charter Roll); Orm., i. 17 (from Sir Peter Leycester's transcript of the charter 'among the evidences' of St. Werburgh's, 1644, 'removed thence' 1648); *Chart. St. Werburgh*, pp. 39–42 (no. 5).

Anno ab incarnatione domini MCXIX., regnante potentissimo rege Henrico, ego comes Ricardus meique homines communi consilio confirmavimus sigillo meo omnes donationes, que date sunt a me vel a meis in meo tempore ecclesie sancte Werburge Cestrie.

Ego itaque comes Ricardus post obitum patris mei dedi pro salute anime sue et mee terram Wlfrici prepositi foris portam de North, prius per unam spicam frumenti, deinde per unum cultellum super altare sancte Werburge, et molendinum de Bache, et tres mansuras quietas et ab omni re liberas, duas in civitate et unam extra portam de North. Testibus Willelmo constabulario, Waltero de Vernun, Radulfo dapifero, et multis aliis.

Willelmus constabularius dedit Neutonam (*Newton-juxta-Sutton*) simul cum servicio Hugonis filii Udardi de quatuor bovatis, et cum servicio Wiceberni de duabus bovatis.

Hugo filius Normanni dedit Gosetre (*Goostrey*) et Lautonam (*Lawton*), teste Hugone de Lasci et Radulfo et Rogero filiis Normanni multisque aliis.

Ricardus de Praers dedit Cnoctirum (*Noctorum*), testibus Willelmo et Adam filiis suis. Corbinus dedit unam carucam terre in Werewelle.

Hamundus de Masci concessu heredum suorum et Roes uxor Pigoti concessu

Rogeri fratris sui dederunt Norwrdinam (*Northenden*) et ecclesiam cum omnibus que ei pertinent, concedentibus et testibus filiis eorum.

Rogerus de Melinguarin dedit Plumleiam (*Plumley*) cum Widone filio suo, quando factus est monachus, testibus Willelmo et Rannulfo filiis suis.

Rannulfus venator dedit Bradeford et unam salinam in Nortwich, concessu Ricardi comitis et Hugonis de Vernun domini sui.

Item Ricardus comes dedit decimam salmonem de ponte et locum unius molendini citra pontem et decimam illius molendini ultra pontem.

Burel dedit ecclesiam de Haliwella (*Holywell*) et decimam de molendino suo et de omnibus rebus suis.

Herebertus wambasarius dedit terram quatuor boum in Hole (*Hoole*). Ricardus pincerna dedit ecclesiam sancti Olavi et terram iuxta ecclesiam et duas mansuras in foro. Rogerus de sancto Martino dedit terram duorum boum in Bebintona.

Willelmus de Punterleya dedit Buttavari (*Bodfari*) cum omnibus appendiciis suis, id est ecclesiam et totum manerium solutum et quietum, et silvam Lectone ad rogum faciendum et ad communem usum domestici operis, concessu et testimonio Hereberti filii sui et Aluredi domini sui et Ricardi comitis.

Hugo de Vernun concessu Ricardi comitis dedit unam mansuram in civitate, solutam et quietam ab omni re et consuetudine.

Hiis ita descriptis, ego comes Ricardus meique barones et mei homines confirmavimus non solum ista sed et illa omnia que comes Hugo pater meus et barones sui confirmaverunt, constituentes, sicut illi constituerunt, ut hec omnia sint stabilia, soluta et quieta et ab omni re ita libera ut nichil libertatis possit eis addi ulterius. Nichil enim retinemus preter orationem in rebus sancte Werburge virginis.

Concedimus etiam ut beata virgo Werburga habeat suam curiam de cunctis placitis et forisfactis, sicut comes habet suam, ita vero quod abbas illius loci non exeat neque placitet contra aliquem de aliquo placito vel de aliqua re extra curiam suam. Testibus Ranulfo Meschin et Willelmo fratre suo, Willelmo constabulario et Ricardo fratre suo, Hugone Malbanc, Osberno Meschin, Hugone filio Osberni et Willelmo fratre eius, multisque aliis apud Graham.

Earl Richard's charter for St. Werburgh's is a sequel to *Sanctorum prisca* in the sense that the latter lists the gifts of Earl Hugh I and his barons and men and Earl Richard's charter continues with his gifts and those of his men. It is a shorter and simpler document, but it also is not without problems and difficulties. The first, curiously unnoticed by earlier commentators, is the document itself. It is surely surprising that a young man of 25, who had no inkling that he would die by drowning in the following year, should have decided in 1119 to draw up a list of donations made 'in my time', but by no means surprising that the monks of Chester should have drawn up such a list after the event. Secondly, the date of the charter, though not impossible, is not easily reconciled with the fact that Richard, who was in Normandy in October 1118 (*Regesta*, ii.no. 1183) is known to have been there for most of 1119 (Ord. Vitalis, iv. 346) and in 1120 as well (**no. 9**). The charter also contains a number of inconsistencies, or apparent inconsistencies, noted by Tait, one of the more striking being the omission of Hugh Malbank's gift of a salthouse at Nantwich, easily explained as an oversight by a later copyist, but highly unlikely in a contemporary document. The most suspicious feature, however, is the insertion among the baronial grants of the earl's gift of the tenth salmon taken at the bridge in Chester. This is referred to, once again almost certainly as an interpolation, in Ranulf II's charter (**no. 26**) granting St. Werburgh's a tenth of his rents in Chester; but it does not appear in his general confirmation (**no. 28**) of his predecessors's gifts. It may, of course, be a later interpolation in an otherwise genuine charter; but it is difficult to quarrel with Tait (*Chart. St. Werburgh*, p. 43) when he says of Richard's charter that 'the number of features which demand explanation is disquieting'. On the other hand, the initial dating, though unusual, is not impossible in monastic charters of this period, the witnesses are not incompatible with the date, and there is no reason to question the genuineness of the baronial grants listed in the charter.

9.   Grant by Earl Richard and King Henry I to St. Martin of Troarn of the church and tithes of the castle of Vire, and confirmation of the gifts of Ranulf de Praers in Normandy and England, of Alured de Combray, Ralph *vicecomes* of Vire and William de Milly.

[c.1120]

MS. Paris lat. 10086 (cart. de Troarn), f. 65v.–66; printed *Regesta*, ii. 328.

Ego Henricus rex Anglorum et dux Normannorum Ricardusque Cestrensis consul damus et concedimus pro nostrarum animarum salute nostrorumque antecessorum animarum requie ecclesiam de castello Vire cum omnibus rebus ad eam pertinentibus ac decimam omnium reddituum ad idem castellum pertinencium – damus, inquam, et concedimus ecclesie ac monachis sancti Martini Troarni.

Rannulfus quoque de Prateriis eodem pacto dedit quicquid habebat in Mansiolo Berherii eidem ecclesie sancti Martini, scilicet ecclesiam cum tota terra, et quod suum erat in ecclesiis de Burceio et Prateriis, et dimidiam partem eiusdem ville molendini terramque Hucemanie ac unam mansuram, quam in Calvinolis habebat. Dedit eciam dimidiam ecclesiam de Moscans ac landam, que est iuxta ecclesiam, criptamque Burnelli, que est iuxta pontem, cum II. acris,[1] et mansuram Avice, omniumque suorum molendinorum ac pecorum, caseorum, vellerum decimam. In Anglia vero apud Dalbeiam et Olosbeiam dedit duas partes decime de[2] segetibus et firma sua pecoribus, caseis, velleribus, ac mansuram sewardi bracheatoris. In nemoribus autem suis concessit ligna comburenda et faciende materiei et pasuagii decimam.

Porro Alverelus de Combraio, nepos eiusdem heresque Rannulfi, hec predicta dona concessit. Dedit eciam anno MCXV. in dedicatione sancte Marie Celle et sancto Martino Troarni decimam tocius panis, qui de sua annona[3] fit, et decimam precii sui frumenti et annonarum que vendentur. Radulfus vero vicecomes dedit ecclesiam de Campegnolis et totam decimam, tali pacto, quod unus suorum filiorum monachus Troarni fieret; quod quidem factum[4] est. Hoc ipsum filius eius Guillelmus totum laudavit et concessit. Et Guillelmus de Milleio dedit ecclesiam eiusdem ville cum xl. acris[5] terre in Milleio, et ecclesiam de Calvoloco et totum Lessardbois cum ecclesia et molendinis et memore eiusdem ville; quod totum filii eius, Alveredus et Robertus, bono animo concesserunt. Et Rannulfus de Prateriis et eius homines dederunt xx. acras.[6]

Hec omnia predicta ego Henricus dei gratia rex Anglorum duxque Normannorum libera et quieta sancti Martini Troarnensis ecclesie et eius monachis donamus et concedimus, ego et Ricardus Cestrensis consul, signisque nostrarum manuum confirmamus.

Signum   +   regis. Signum Ricardi   +   comitis.

1. agris *MS.*
2. in *MS.*
3. ainona *MS.*
4. *om. MS.*
5. agris *MS.*
6. agros *MS.*

Two other versions of this charter exist, and are in *Regesta*, ii, 327–9, and Sauvage, *L'Abbaye de Saint-Martin de Troarn* (*Mémoires de la Société des Antiquaires de Normandie*, vol. xxxiv), pp. 366-7. Their relationship – and, indeed, the question of their authenticity – raises complicated and difficult problems, similar to those raised by the series of charters (**nos. 3, 8, 13, 28**) alleged to have been granted by Earl Hugh I and his three immediate successors to the monks of St. Werburgh in Chester. Of the two other versions, the former, which is fuller and longer (but omits the English grants at Dalby and Ulceby in Lincolnshire) is issued in the name of King Henry alone; but it includes a confirmation by Earl Richard, said to have been executed at Troarn by placing the text of the gospels on the altar, and concludes with Richard's *signum*, as well as the king's. The other is a much abbreviated text in narrative form, without *signa*, ending 'Hec igitur omnia ego Ricardus etc.' But this also includes material, notably the donation of the church and tithe of Vengeons (dép. Manche, canton Sourdeval) by Ralph Guz and his nephew, Robert Guz, not found in either of the other two versions. The version printed here is also anomalous. It opens ('damus, inquam, et concedimus') with a statement in direct speech which perhaps echoes the actual words spoken by Henry I on behalf of himself and Earl Richard in conveying their grant to the monastery. In any case, it is not in normal charter form.

Two conclusions appear to follow: (i) none of the three versions is derived from either of the others; (ii) all three were evidently compiled by the monks of Troarn from deeds in the abbey's possession and not drawn up by the king's or earl's clerks. That does not necessarily imply that they are spurious. We do not know why it was thought desirable to draft three different versions; but it is at least plausible that one or other was laid before the earl and the king for approval and received their formal sanction. On the other hand, it is possible that they were prepared *ex post facto* as a basis for the confirmation issued by Henry II in 1155 (Sauvage, pp. 376–83; cf. Eyton, p. 11; Round. *C.D.F.*, no. 480).

Even if the latter was the case, there is no reason to doubt the genuineness of the transactions enumerated in the charter. The ostensible occasion of the grants of Henry I and Earl Richard was the dedication in 1115 of the cell or priory of Le Désert (known also as 'ecclesia sancte Marie Celle'), a dependency of Troarn, and it is not impossible that Henry I (who was in Normandy from December 1114 to July 1115) and Earl Richard were present on that occasion, and made a joint gift of the church and tithes of the castle of Vire, of which the earl of Chester was hereditary castellan. The site of the new priory, at Mesnil-Bréhier in wild wooded country near Presles (dép. Calvados, canton Vassy), had been given towards the close of the eleventh century by Thurstan de Presles, or Praers (*de Prateriis*), a tenant of the honour of Chester, of whose family a branch settled at Barthomley (Cheshire), and was confirmed by his son Ranulf, with the assent of Ranulf's own son Hasculf, at the beginning of the twelfth century (Sauvage, p. 155). Other deeds record the donation of most of the other gifts specified in the charter: Burcy (canton Vassy) by Radulf de Prateriis and Gautier and Joel de Mayenne at the beginning of the twelfth century, the remainder by Otto de Tilly in 1101 (Paris lat. 10086, ff. 54v., 57–57v.); half the church of Montchamp (dép. Calvados, canton Vassy) by Otto de Tilly in 1101 (Sauvage, p. 131) and the other half by Ranulf de Praers about the same time (Paris lat. 10086, f. 62–62v.); Lessardoisbois by Engeran de Vassy in 1107 (Sauvage, p. 132), and the church of Chaulieu (dép. Manche, canton Sondeval) by William of Milly in the time of Abbot Arnoul, i.e. before 1112. In addition, there is a charter of Henry I (*Regesta*, ii, no. 1023a) in which he confirms the gifts already made or to be made in future by his barons 'in the territory of Presles' for the building of a monastery in the name of the Holy Trinity and St. Mary (i.e. Notre-Dame du Désert), at the same time adding his own gift of one tithe (but not the church) of the castle of Vire. This charter, which makes no mention of Earl Richard, evidently belongs to an earlier stage in the history of the new foundation, probably during Earl Richard's minority, and may possibly have been issued during King Henry's visit to Normandy in either 1106–7 or 1108–9.

It is entirely credible that these earlier donations were in a single document assembled and confirmed by King Henry and Earl Richard in 1115 at the time of the dedication of Notre-Dame du Désert, and were supplemented, to celebrate the occasion, by the addition of the church of Vire. Nevertheless, it is evident that the present charter cannot date, in any of the versions, from 1115. In the first place, the gift of tithes by Alured de Combray, nephew and heir of Ranulf de Praers, at the time of the dedication in 1115, is definitely recounted as a past event. Secondly, a copy of Ralph the viscount's gift of the church of Campagnoles (dép. Calvados, canton Saint-Sever) survives in the cartulary of Troarn (f. 209–209v.) and is there dated 1120. If this date is correct, the present charter cannot fall before that year. In fact, Henry I was in lower Normandy in the early months of 1120, proceeding in about May to Rouen, and it is quite possible that he and Earl Richard, who was also in Normandy (*Regesta*, ii. no. 1233), issued a joint confirmation at that time. In any event, the actual composition of the charter must fall after 1115, although the intention evidently was to provide a record of the endowment of the new foundation of Le Désert which took place in that year.

RANULF (I), EARL OF CHESTER (1120–1129)

10. Grant to the abbey of St. Evroul of the church of St. Martial at Croisilles, as previously granted by Earl Richard.

[1121–1125]

MS Paris lat. 11056 (Cart. de St. Evroul, pars II),
f. 26. Cal.: Round, *C.D.F.*, no. 635.

Rannulfus comes de Cestria[1] omnibus sancte ecclesie filiis salutem. Sciatis me dedisse abbatie sancti Ebrulfi ecclesiam sancti Martialis de Crusillis in elemosina cum omnibus rebus eidem ecclesie pertinentibus in perpetuum preter regale servicium, scilicet pro amore dei et pro me et pro anima avunculi mei Hugonis et pro anima Ricardi,[2] qui ante me illam dedit, necnon et pro animabus omnium antecessorum meorum. Testes: Rotbertus de Avrincis, Radulfus dapifer, Robertus Carbonel, Ricardus de Colonciis, Robertus de Dusi, Gislebertus de Avrincis,[3] Rogerus Baneista, Ricardus de Giznai. Ex parte monachorum:

Rogerus de Millai, Richerius de Nucerio, Alveredus de Solengi, Rogerus pectinatus. Ego Rannulfus comes +

1. Cestra *MS.*   2. R. *MS.*
3. Avric[is] *MS.*

Earl Richard's grant is recorded in **no. 11**, also the grant of tithes in Leicestershire by Roger de Milly, but his charter has not survived. The present charter almost certainly precedes the blanket confirmation of earlier gifts in **no. 11**. Robert and Gilbert of Avranches witnessed an agreement between Thomas de St. Jean and the abbey of Mont-Saint-Michel in 1123 or 1124 (*Regesta*, ii. no. 1422) and Robert Carbonel a lawsuit at Caen of unspecified date but before 1129 (ibid., no. 1593). Ralph of Montalt, the steward (*dapifer*), was dead by 1130 at latest (*Chart. St. Werburgh*, p. 50), and Richard de Coulances was dead by 1125, when he was succeeded by his son Hugh (Ord. Vitalis, iii. 17–18). Roger *pectinatus* (with combed hair?) does not appear to be otherwise mentioned. The present charter may conceivably be abbreviated, but it is noticeable that there is no mention of a seal and that Ranulf attests with the sign of the cross.

11.   Confirmation to the abbey of St. Evroul in Normandy of the gifts of Earl Hugh and his tenants in England; also of Earl Richard's gift of the churches of Byfield (Northants.) and of Croisilles, Orgères and Touquettes in Normandy, and of the church of Tarentan given by Earl Ranulf's man, Goit.

[1123–1128]

MS. Paris lat. 11055 ('cartularius maior' of St. Evroul), f. 30. Cal.: Round, *C.D.F.*, no. 636.

Ranulfus comes Cestrensis omnibus fidelibus suis salutem. Noverit universitas vestra me pro salute anime mee et omnium antecessorum meorum donasse et concessisse et presenti carta mea confirmasse abbati et monachis sancti Ebrulfi in perpetuam elemosinam liberam et quietam in Anglia ecclesiam de Bifeilt, quam eis donavit antecessor meus Ricardus comes Cestrensis, cum omnibus pertinentiis suis et unam carucatam terre in liberam et quietam elemosinam ab escuagio et tallalio[1] et omni alio terreno servicio. Item in Anglia de donis Hugonis comitis Cestrensis in parva Pilardentana unam hidam terre, et decimam de Brichella et ibidem unum rusticum, et decimam de Sauleia in Bochingehamscira. De donis Roberti de Roelento, hominis sui, villam que Cherchebeia dicitur, cum duabus ecclesiis ad eandem villam pertinentibus; ad Merestonam ecclesiam cum tota decima et octo hospitibus et ibidem duas carucatas terre; ad Cestriam[2] ecclesiam sancti Petri de mercato et tres burgenses. De dono Roscelini hominis eiusdem comitis totam decimam garbarii angnorum[3] et porcorum de Stantona. De dono Osberni filii Ceuxonis[4] decimam de Neobotha, decimam quoque de Forefort et

Oxtcunde quam dedit Baldricus de Lindissi sancto Ebrulfo, et decimam⁵
Brisardi ad Lindissi cum decima terre Rogeri de Millaio. In Normannia
ecclesiam de Croissiles, quam ipsis donavit Ricardus comes Cestrensis,⁶ cum
omnibus pertinentiis suis, ecclesiam quoque de Orgeriis⁷ cum omnibus pertinentiis suis, Willelmo de Verreis cum Agnete uxore sua, Thoma de Clara cum
Ysabeth uxore sua, et Odone de Ciseio atque Willelmo de Belvesmaria
consentientibus et condonantibus, ecclesiam de Tolqueta cum decimis et terris
aliisque pertinentiis suis, hermitagium de Rupe⁸ cum nemore et terris et pratis
aliisque pertinenciis suis, ecclesiam sancti Petri de Tarentana de dono Goit
hominis mei. Testibus Hugone Maubaent, Morado de Liveriz, Ricardo filio
Baldrici de Lindissi, Rogero de Combraio et aliis multis.

1. *sic MS.*
2. Cestram *MS.*
3. *sic MS.*
4. *sic MS for* Teszonis.
5. after decimam *three letters, faint and probably erased, probably* Rog., *i.e. Roger of Milly, whose name follows.*
6. Cistrensis *MS.*
7. Orgiis *MS.*
8. Ruppe *MS.*

For the grants of Earl Hugh, Robert of Rhuddlan, Roscelin, Osbern fitz Tesson,
Baldric of Lindsey, Brisard and Roger of Milly see **no. 1.** For an earlier
confirmation of Earl Richard's gift of the church of Croisilles, dated 1121–1125,
see **no. 10**. The present charter is almost certainly later in date. An alleged
confirmation of Henry I (*Gallio Christ.* [*sic.*] xi, App., p. 208), which, however,
is not included in the cartulary, is usually dated 1123–1128 (*Chart. St. Werburgh*,
p. 289). The present charter probably dates from the same period.

12.   Confirmation of Earl Hugh's gift to St. Werburgh's abbey of a three-days'
fair and the revenues accruing from it.

[1121–1129]

> Bodleian Library, MS. Top. Cheshire b. I, p. 80 (from
> MS. of John Arden of Stockport); Chester, Booth of
> Twemlow, Liber K, f. 31; Shakerley MS. 1 (*penes* Sir
> Arthur Bryant), f. 181. Ed.: *Chart. St. Werburgh*, p. xvii
> (from the Shakerley MS.)

Ranulfus comes Cestrie *etc.* Notum sit vobis quod comes¹ Hugo meus avunculus
a² fundacione abbatie dedit deo et sancte Werburge theolonium omnesque
redditus et exitus nundinarum trium dierum. Quapropter confirmo illud *etc.*

Teste Willelmo constabulario, Radulfo dapifero, Ricardo filio Nigelli, Hugone Malbanc, Gaufrido capellano, Normano clerico multisque aliis. Valete.

1. *om. Shakerley MS.*
2. in *Shakerley MS.*

It is difficult to pass judgement on this charter in the abbreviated form which is all that survives. Tait (*Chart. St. Werburgh*) evidently doubted its authenticity. As he points out, all the witnesses except Norman the clerk also witnessed Ranulf's general confirmation (**no. 13**), and it is possible that it is simply an abstract from the corresponding passage of that charter. On the other hand, it is also possible that the compiler of **no. 13** took over the passage referring to the three-day fair from the present charter, incorporating it in his recital, but omitting the witnesses.[1] On the whole, it seems possible that this is a genuine charter of Ranulf I.

It should be noted, however, that the statement that Earl Hugh granted the monks a fair of three days 'from the foundation of the abbey' is not correct, if we are to believe *Sanctorum prisca*, where the gift is said to have been made 'on the festival of St. Werburgh in the summer' (i.e. 21 June); but, as noted previously (p. 9), it is doubtful whether the passage in *Sanctorum prisca* can be taken at face value. Unfortunately there is no means of dating Ranulf's charter accurately. William the constable almost certainly refers to William fitz Nigel, who died shortly before 1130, but may conceivably refer to his son of the same name. Richard fitz Nigel was his brother. Ralph the steward and Hugh Malbank witnessed Ranulf I's charters (**nos. 10, 11**) for St Evroul. Norman the clerk witnessed the charter (**no. 14**) which Ranulf and his wife Lucy gave to Spalding some time after 1123.

1.   This would be parallel to his omission of the witnesses (listed p. 43) of Earl Ranulf's own gift of Upton. The witness lists of many of the baronial grants (e.g. those of William Meschin and Matthew of Rhuddlan) are also abbreviated.

13.   Gift to St. Werburgh's abbey of Upton, near Chester, to take effect on the earl's death, and confirmation of Earl Hugh's grant of a fair on the day of the translation of St. Werburgh and the day before and after, also confirmation of the gifts, individually specified, of the earl's men and those of his predecessors, and of the exclusive jurisdiction of the court of St. Werburgh in all matters concerning the abbey, to impress which upon posterity Earl Ranulf himself had appeared in the abbey court and received judgement from the abbot's doomsmen. [?Spurious]

[1121–1129]

Bodleian Library, MS. Engl.Hist. c. 242 (formerly Gurney MS.) f. 74 (old f. 71), copied in Dugdale's handwriting, the opening sentence in facsimile, 'ex autographo penes predictum decanum et capitulum apud Cestriam remanente'; St. George's Chapel, Windsor, MS. xi. E.5 (inspeximus of 1280); P.R.O., C.53 (Chancery Charter Rolls), no. 73 (inspeximus of 1285), m. 11; B.L. Harl. MS. 2071, f. 44v. (old f. 30), apparently from Charter Roll: other copies in Lansdowne MS. 229, f. 121v., and Lansdowne MS. 447, f. 7v., and, heavily abbreviated, in the register of St. Werburgh's (Harl. MS. 1965, f. 5). ed.: *Mon.*, ii. 387 (from Charter Roll); Orm., i. 18 (from Leycester's copy of 'an ancient charter among the evidences' of St. Werburgh's, not identical with Dugdale's text); *Chart. St. Werburgh*, pp. 47–50 (no. 6). The present edition is based on Dugdale's text (D), as being apparently nearest to the original. It is also the only one with a fascimile of the (alleged) seal.

Universis matris ecclesie filiis Rannulfus comes Cestrie salutem.[1] Notum sit vobis pariter me concessisse, quando feci transferri corpus Hugonis comitis mei avunculi a cimiterio in capitulum, ut in die mee mortis darem simul cum corpore meo ecclesie sancte Werburge Vptunam[2] (*Upton*) solutam et quietam ab omni re ut elemosinam liberam, sicut ego ipse in illa die haberem eam in terris, in hominibus, in planis, in pascuis, in pratis, in placitis, et in omnibus pertinentiis suis, pro anima ipsius Hugonis comitis et pro salute anime mee et animarum omnium parentum meorum.

Item, quoniam comes Hugo concesserat antea ecclesie sancte Werburge theloneum et omnes redditus nundinarum trium dierum, id est a nona vigilie sancte Werburge usque ad vesperam sequentis diei post solennitatem, ego comes Rannulfus illud idem concedo et confirmo constituens, sicut ipse constituerat, ut sive latro sive robbator sive aliquis malefactor venerit ad solennitatem, habeat firmam pacem dum fuerit in nundinis, nisi forte forisfecerit in illis. Et si forte aliquis forisfecerit in nundinis, omne placitum et forisfactum et iustitia a ministris abbatis et a vicecomite civitatis tractabuntur in curia sancte Werburge virginis. Et ut vicecomes intentius et fidelius hoc agat, computetur et tallietur ei a meis camerariis in suam firmam quicquid monachi ex hiis omnibus acceperint.

Willelmus Meschinus frater meus dedit deo et ecclesie sancte Werburge ecclesiam de Dissart (*Dyserth*) cum omnibus pertinentiis suis, concensu[3] Rannulfi comitis et Rannulfi filii sui, teste Willelmo clerico de Ruelant, Willelmo Flandrensi, multisque aliis.

Matheus de Ruelant dedit ecclesiam de Tursteinestun (*Thurstaston*) cum suis pertinentiis, quando Simon frater eius factus est monachus, teste Roberto de Petraponte multisque aliis.

Hugo filius Osberni dedit unam mansuram in Cestria et unum pratum quod vocatur Kingeseia.

Suuein de Wethenhale (*Wettenhall*) factus monachus dedit duas bovatas in Wethenhale, concedentibus filiis suis.

Ricardus de Cruce dedit unam mansuram in Cestria in vico apud pontem et partem terre quam habuit in Morsetun (*Moston*), cum vellet monachus fieri, teste Normanno filio suo multisque aliis.

Leticia de Malpas dedit deo et sancte Werburge unam mansuram versus portam Clippe, teste et concedente Ricardo domino suo et fratre suo Ricardo Mailard, Nigello Chaldel, multisque aliis.

Willelmus filius Andree dedit cum filio suo monacho facto unam magnam soppam inter domum Winebaldi et Hamund[4] in foro.

Hec sunt itaque dona que data sunt a me et a meis hominibus ecclesie sancte Werburge in meo tempore. Quapropter concedimus et confirmamus tam ego quam homines mei non solum hec supradicta sed et ea omnia, que comes Hugo meus avunculus vel Ricardus comes eius filius aut eorum homines dederunt ecclesie sancte Werburge, deprecantes et precipientes cunctis nostris amicis et hominibus tam presentibus quam futuris, quatinus ea omnia sint stabilia, soluta et quieta, et ut elemosina ab omni re ita libera ut nichil libertatis possit eis addi ulterius, quia nichil retinemus in his exceptis orationibus.

Adhuc etiam concedimus et confirmamus, sicut predicti comites et eorum homines antea confirmaverunt, ut beata Werburge habeat de cunctis rebus curiam suam, ita quod abbas illius loci non placitet usquam contra aliquem de aliqua re ad ecclesiam pertinente extra curiam suam. Et ut ego comes darem exemplum posteris, veni ipse propter unum placitum in curiam abbatis, audiens et suscipiens ibi meum iudicium, non a meis sed a iudicibus abbatis, ut in omnibus haberet beata Werburge ius sue dignitatis imperpetuum.[5]

Ut igitur sic sint omnia, sicut supradictum est, libera, confirmamus ea hinc sancte crucis signo + , hinc meo sigillo, hinc horum virorum testimonio, scilicet Willelmi Meschini, Willelmi constabularii, Radulfi dapiferi, Hugonis Malbanc, Ricardi Banastre, Hugonis filii Osberni, Osberni filii Hugonis, Roberti de Maci, Roberti filii Bigot, Ade de Praieres, Gaufridi capellani, Turgisii doctoris, Ricardi filii Nigelli. Signum + Rannulfi comitis. Signum + Willelmi Meschini. Signum + Willelmi constabularii. Signum + Roberti[6] de Palmas. Signum + Radulfi dapiferi. Signum + Hugonis Malbanc. Signum + Ricardi Banastre. Signum + Hugonis filii Osberni. Signum + Osberni filii Hugonis. Signum + Roberti de Maci.

SEAL[7] on cord: equestrian, horse standing with left foreleg raised, knight without shield or surcoat; legend missing.

1. *To here in facsimile E.*
2. *sic D.*
3. *sic D.*
4. *sic D.*
5. *sic D and all other texts, save Ormerod's printed edition.*
6. Ricardi *D.*
7. *Seal only noted in D.*

This is the third in the series of charters listing the gifts to St. Werburgh's abbey in the time of the first four earls, and like the two preceding charters cannot easily be accepted as authentic. The curious intrusion of the word *pariter* (in like manner, at the same time) at the very beginning suggests that it may have formed part of a longer document, perhaps, like **no. 28**, beginning with a recital of the gifts of the earl's predecessors. The appearance in all manuscripts (but not in Ormerod's edition) of the neologism *imperpetuum* (p. 24), if not due to the different copyists, which seems unlikely, points to a date nearer to Ranulf III than to Ranulf I. The short address, though common enough in everyday charters fifty or more years later, is, to say the least, unusual at this time and in a document of this importance. But the most disquieting feature is the fact that it omits no less than five out of a total of only eleven gifts attributed to Ranulf I's tenants.[1] One or other of these, but scarcely all five, may possibly have been donated after the earl's confirmation was issued; but it is noteworthy that his charter, like Earl Richard's, purports to set out all the gifts made in his time (*in meo tempore*). There is also, in one instance discussed at length by Tait (*Chart. St. Werburgh*, p. 50), an apparent incompatibility in the name of one of the witnesses. Finally, there is the evidence (unknown to Tait) of the seal which Dugdale copied from what he called 'the autograph'. This is undoubtedly identical with the seal of Ranulf II attached to Rylands Charter 1807 (**no. 35**), which is discussed at length by Stewart-Brown (*H.S.L.C.*, lxxxvii, pp. 104 sqq.),[2] and different in substantive ways from the seal sometimes attributed to Ranulf I, reproduced by Ormerod, i. 20. The possibility cannot be excluded that Ranulf II's seal may have been attached to the so-called autograph at a later date; but cumulatively the evidence seems to indicate that Ranulf I's charter should be viewed, like Richard's, with considerable caution. The probability is that both, like **no. 3**, were put together by the monks of Chester from genuine material during the reign of Stephen. Tait was surely right when he observed (*Chart. St. Werburgh*, p. xliii) that 'the very completeness of the series' is itself 'a suspicious circumstance'.

1. The other five are listed in **no. 28**, (pp. 43–4) Three, admittedly, are of only minor importance, but two (William of Mold's gift of Lea-cum-Newbold and Leticia de Malpas' gift of Little Christleton and Bache) were substantial.
2. There is also a photograph in Taylor, *Selected Cheshire Seals*, plate 1.

14. Grant to Spalding priory of the churches of Belchford, Scamblesby and Minting.

[1123–1129]

> B.L. Add. MS. 35296 (Spalding register), f. 386; Add. MS. 5844 (Cole's transcript of preceding), f. 429 (new f. 218). Ed.: *The Genealogist*, N.S. v, p. 68 (no. 15).

Sciant tam presentes quam futuri quod ego Ranulphus comes Cestrie et Lucia comitissa uxor mea dedimus et concessimus ecclesie dei et sancte Marie et sancti Nicholai de Spaldingis et monachis ibidem deo servientibus ecclesiam de Beltisforda et ecclesiam de Scamelisbi et ecclesiam de Mintingis, et omnia que ad ecclesias pertinent, pro animabus patrum et matrum et antecessorum nostrorum et pro nobismet ipsis. Et volumus quod eas bene et in pace teneant. Hoc donum dedimus Alexandro Lincolniensi episcopo concedente et teste existente, et Willelmo capellano Barba Aprilis, Normanno clerico, Hascullo dapifero et aliis.

The priory of Spalding was founded in the time of William the Conqueror by Ivo Taillebois, the first husband of Countess Lucy, as a cell of St. Nicholas, Angers. It remained her favourite foundation, even after her marriage to Earl Ranulf, and she was buried there. The places mentioned were all part of her inheritance in Lindsey. The present charter must fall after the accession of Bishop Alexander of Lincoln in 1123. It was confirmed by Henry I at the request of Ranulf and Lucy (**no. 44**), but unfortunately the surviving text of the confirmation (Add. MS. 35296, f. 386v) lacks both witnesses and dating-clause. Norman the clerk witnessed Ranulf I's charter for St. Werburgh's, Chester (**no. 12**). Hasculf the steward does not occur elsewhere in Cheshire charters; he was probably steward of Lucy's Lincolnshire estates and is certainly not connected with the Cheshire family of Stewards of Mold. William 'Barba Aprilis' is evidently not the same man as witnessed charters of Hugh II (**nos. 173, 194**) as late as 1180; rather we may identify him with the William *capellanus*, who witnesses **no. 59** with his son Ralph *capellanus*. The latter was the father of the younger William, who was active under Hugh II (**no. 123**) and the present William his grandfather.

RANULF (II), EARL OF CHESTER (1129–1153)

15. Confirmation to Hugh son of Odard of the lands he held of the earl's father and his predecessors.

[1129–1130]

> Tabley MSS., Sir Peter Leycester's Liber C, f. 154, from the originals of Lady Kilmorey; Chester, Booth of Twem-

low, Liber K, f. 38 ('This is a coppie verbatim of a deede remayning in the hands of the heires of Dutton'); B.L. Harl. MS. 2077, f. 181 (new f. 92v.); Bodleian Library, MS. Top. Cheshire b. I, p. 111. Ed.: *Stenton Misc.*, p. 36 (no. 7)

Ranulfus comes Cestrie omnibus baronibus suis et omnibus ministris suis et suo vicecomiti salutem. Sciatis me reddidisse Hugoni filio Udardi quicquid tenuit de patre meo et de omnibus antecessoribus meis, ita libere et quiete sicut unquam melius tenuit de illis. Et nolo quod aliquis ei aliquam contumeliam faciet de Uttlet nomine et de pueris suis et de femina sua, et Algaro et pueris suis et femina sua. Testibus Ranulfo venatore et Roberto Grevesac.

Hugh son of Udard or Odard was the son of the Domesday tenant of the earl in Dutton (*D.S.C.*, p. 211) and of William fitz Nigel the constable in Halton and Weston (*ibid.*, p. 169, 171). The terms of the present charter, restoring or re-granting the lands Hugh held of Ranulf I, suggest that it was given shortly after the latter's death in 1129, when, according to the views of the time, all fiefs reverted to the heir; and a remarkable charter (Orm., i. 690), which recounts how the constable and his son visited Hugh son of Odard on his deathbed at Keckwick and enfeoffed his son, another Hugh, with his father's lands, provides another limit of date. This was not later than 1130 (*E.H.R.* lvii, p. 448), in which year the death of William fitz Nigel himself probably occurred (*Book of Seals*, p. 354). The present charter can therefore safely be dated 1129–1130.

[LUCY, WIDOW OF RANULF I.]

16. Gift to the monks of Spalding of the manor of Spalding (Lincs.) with all the liberties with which she held it in the time of Ivo Taillebois, Roger fitz Gerold and Earl Ranulf.

Pontefract, [c.1135]

> P.R.O., C.53 (Chancery Charter Rolls), no. 117, m. 37; B.L. Add. MS. 35296 (Spalding register), f. 9, and Add. MS. 5844, f. 147 (new f. 76), the two latter with abbreviated witness-list. Ed.: *Mon.*, iii. 217; *Cal. Ch. Rolls*, iv. 165; *The Genealogist*, N.S. v, p. 68 (no. 19); Farrer, *Early Yorkshire Charters*, iii. 184.

In nomine sancte et individue trinitatis notum sit omnibus tam presentibus quam futuris quod ego Lucia cometissa[1] Cestrie concedo et dono ecclesie et monachis sancti Nicholai de Spallingis[2] manerium de Spallingis[2] cum socha et sacha[3] et thol et them, cum omnibus consuetudinibus suis et libertatibus, cum quibus melius tenui et liberalius tempore Ivonis de Thallebos[4] et Rogeri filii Geroldi et cometis[1] Rannulfi, in elemosina anime mee pro redempcione anime patris mei et matris mee et dominorum meorum et paurentum[1] meorum. Quare volo ut bene et in pace teneant cum omnibus appenticiis suis. Teste priore Martino de Pontefracto et Ilberto[5] de Laceio, Richardo de Foliot, Iurdano et Pagano fratribus suis, Hugone filio Gileberti, Willelmo de Semervilla, Richardo filio Guobolt, Widone de Russedene, Petro filio Bugardi, Radulfo de Wenervilla, Richardo Russel.

1. *sic Ch. Roll.*
2. Spalding *Add. MSS.*
3. soca et saca et tol *Add. MSS.*
4. Tayleboys *Add. MSS.*
5. *All MSS have* Gilberto, *but* Ilberto *is correct.*

Ivo Taillebois, Roger fitz Gerold and Earl Ranulf I were the three husbands of Countess Lucy. The grant of the manor of Spalding was originally made by Ivo, the founder of the priory (*Mon.*, iii. 216), and was confirmed by William II (*Regesta*, i. no. 386). Lucy herself died c.1138, and this gift was made in her widowhood. It seems evident that it was made at Pontefract. The honour of Pontefract was restored to the great northern baron Ilbert of Lacy by Stephen in 1135 after Henry I had taken it from his father Robert the founder of Pontefract priory (Richard of Hexham, *Chronicles of the Reign of Stephen*, iii. 140), and most of the witnesses of the present charter are Ilbert's tenants or associates. Farrer (*loc. cit.*) dates it c.1135; it must at least fall within the period 1135–38.

[LUCY, WIDOW OF RANULF I.]

17.   Grant to the monks of Spalding of the tithes of her demesne, i.e. of Belchford, Scamblesby, Stenigot, Normanby, Tetney, Donington and Hautebarge.

[c.1135]

> B.L. Add. MS. 35296 (Spalding register), f. 388v., and Add. MS. 5844 (Cole's transcript of preceding), f. 432 (new f. 219v.). Ed.: *The Genealogist*, N.S. v, p. 68 (no. 18).

Omnibus sancte matris ecclesie filiis tam presentibus quam futuris Lucia comitissa Cestrie salutem. Noverit universitas vestra quod ego Lucia comitissa in mea libera potestate dedi et concessi et hac presenti carta mea confirmavi deo et beate Marie et beato Nicholao de Spaldingis et monachis ibidem deo servient-

ibus pro anima domini mei Ivonis Talbos et pro salute anime mee et antecessorum et heredum meorum in puram et perpetuam elemosinam omnes
decimaciones et obvenciones de dominico meo, scilicet de blado de estauramento de pecuniis meis, in villa de Beltisford et in villa de Scamelisbi et in
Stenighou et in Normanbi et in Tetenei et in Donigtona et in Hautebarge,
ubicumque sint infra metas et limites parochiarum predictarum villarum seu
quicumque tenuerint vel teneant. Hiis testibus Ilberto[1] de Laceio, Ricardo de
Foliot, Iordano et Pagano fratribus suis, et aliis.

1.   Gilberto *MSS.*

Although here, as there, the cartulary abbreviates the witness list, there can be
little doubt, if any, that this charter is contemporaneous with **no. 16**, which see
for the date.

[LUCY, WIDOW OF RANULF I.]

18.   Grant to the nuns of Stixwould of all her land in Stixwould, *etc.*

[c.1135]

P.R.O., C.47 (Chancery Miscellanea), Bundle 19, File 3,
no. 16.

Lucia comitissa Cestrie omnibus *etc.* Sciatis me concessisse et dedisse et hac
presenti carta mea confirmasse deo et sancte Marie et sanctimonialibus de
Stikeswold pro dei amore et pro salute anime mee et omnium parentum meorum
etc. in liberam possessionem sancte ecclesie totam terram meam in Stikeswold
etc.

The nunnery of Stixwould (Lincs.) was founded c.1135 by Countess Lucy. This
abbreviated text is unfortunately all that remains of her foundation charter, but
its terms are repeated verbatim in her notification to her two sons, Earl Ranulf
and William of Roumare (**no. 19**). It can safely be dated c.1135.

[LUCY, WIDOW OF RANULF I.]

19.   Notification to her sons, Ranulf earl of Chester and William of Roumare,
of her gift to Stixwould nunnery of her land at Stixwould and at
Honington and Bassingthorpe (Lincs.), and begging them to uphold her

gift, because it will be very useful to them all when they come before the throne of God.

[c.1135]

B.L. Add. MS. 46701 (Stixwould cartulary), f. 1.

Lucia comitissa Rannulfo comiti Cestrie et Willemo de Romara, karissimis filiis suis, salutem. Sciatis me concessisse et dedisse et hac mea presenti carta confirmasse deo et sancte Marie et sanctimonialibus de Stykeswold tam futuris quam presentibus in puram et perpetuam elemosinam, liberam et quietam ab omnibus secularibus serviciis et consuetudinibus et exaccionibus et in liberam possessionem sancte ecclesie, totam meam terram de Stykeswold et totam meam terram de Hundintuna et totam meam terram de Torp cum omnibus pertinenciis suis in ecclesiis, in bosco et plano, in villis et extra, in aquis, piscariis et molendinis, pratis et marescis, et in omnibus locis eisdem terris pertinentibus. Et hoc feci pro salute anime mee et animarum vestrarum, quare precor vos, sicut meos carissimos filios, quatinus istam meam elemosinam et vestram pro dei amore et pro salute anime mee et animarum vestrarum manuteneatis et custodiatis, nam utillimum erit mihi et vobis ante deum. Huius mee concessionis et donacionis isti sunt testes: prior de Spalding, prior de Pontefracto, *etc.* Et ita ut xxx. liberate terre sint.

For Lucy's foundation charter, see **no. 18**. This letter to her sons is almost certainly of the same date. For another of her charters witnessed by the prior of Pontefract, see **no. 16**.

20.   Confirmation to the nuns of Stixwould of the seat of their abbey, which is in his fee, and of the lands in Stixwould, Honington and Bassingthorpe already given by Countess Lucy, his mother.

[1140–1150]

B.L. Add. MS. 46701 (Stixwould cartulary), f. 1. Short notice in P.R.O., C.47 (Chancery Miscellanea), Bundle 19, File 3, no. 16, and thence in Bodleian Library, Dodsworth MS.89, f. 88v.

Ranulfus comes Cestrie constabulario, dapifero,[1] baronibus et omnibus ballidis et ministris et omnibus hominibus Francis et Anglis[2] clericis et laicis tocius Anglie salutem. Sciatis quod ego dedi et concessi et hac carta mea confirmavi deo et sancte Marie et sanctimonialibus de Stykeswold pro dei amore et pro salute anime mee[3] et omnium parentum meorum in puram et perpetuam elemosinam liberam et quietam ab omni seculari servicio et consuetudine et exaccione sedem abbacie de Stykeswold cum tota terra plenarie et integre, que est de feodo meo in eadem villa cum ecclesia et cum omnibus aliis pertinenciis suis, et totam terram de Hundintuna de meo feodo cum ecclesia et cum omnibus pertinenciis suis, et totam terram de Torp de meo feodo cum ecclesia et cum omnibus aliis pertinenciis suis, habendam et tenendam in puram et liberam possessionem sancte dei ecclesie in perpetuum, in ecclesiis, in bosco et plano, in villis et extra, in aquis et piscariis et molendinis, in pratis et pasturis, et in omnibus aliis locis, cum omnibus libertatibus et consuetudinibus eisdem terris pertinentibus. Quare precor omnes amicos et homines meos, quatinus pro dei et meo amore illas manuteneant[4] et adiuvent et custodiant. Et bene sciatis quod ego et heredes mei warantizabimus illis omnes predictas terras in puram et liberam possessionem sancte ecclesie in perpetuum, et prohibeo quod nullus inquietacionem vel molestiam eis inferat. Testibus *etc.*

1.   dab. *MS.*
2.   Anglie *MS.*
3.   om. *MS.*
4.   manuteant *MS.*

It may safely be assumed that this charter was issued after (probably some time after) the death of Countess Lucy (1138), the founder of Stixwould. It was also issued before Whitsuntide (7 June) 1153, when it was confirmed, together with Countess Lucy's foundation charter (**no. 18**), by Henry, duke of Normandy, at Leicester (*Cal. Pat. Rolls, 1405–1408*, p. 218). Owing to the omission of witnesses, a more exact date within this period is impossible. It is curious, and unusual, that Ranulf makes no mention of his mother and her gifts; his charter nevertheless follows fairly closely the wording of hers.

21.   Confirmation of William the constable's restoration to St. Werburgh's abbey of Raby in pursuance of an agreement made by his father with Abbot Richard.

[1135–1140]

P.R.O., C.53 (Chancery Charter Rolls), no. 73, m. 10; a second copy m. 15. Ed.: *Chart. St. Werburgh*, p. 235 (no. 352).

Notum sit omnibus fidelibus sancte ecclesie et constabuloni et dapifero et baronibus et ministris meis Francis et Anglis, quod ego Randulfus comes Cestrie concedo et confirmo terram Rabbi, quam Willemus constabulo reddidit deo et ecclesie sancte Werburge, solam et quietam de omnibus placitis et causis, sicut prebendam antiquitus illi ecclesie adiacentem. Et sciatis quod nolo quod alicui respondeat, nec pro brevi meo nec pro nuncio, de aliqua causa, set ita liberam eam habeat sicut aliquam prebendam ecclesie illius habet liberiorem. Testibus Ricardo de Aquila et Normanno de Verdun et Olivero de Manners et Ivone filio Anschetilli et Willelmo de Amundevilla et Radulfo de Melinguarim.

William the constable's charter is printed *Chart. St. Werburgh*, no. 351, but cannot be accurately dated. William himself succeeded his father as constable c.1130, and was succeeded by Eustace fitz John at latest in 1146, but probably died two or three years earlier (*Stenton Misc.*, pp. 25, 27–8, 34). It is unlikely, if not impossible, that Ranulf II's confirmation followed William's death, in which case the present charter falls within the period 1130–1143. This is consonant with the little that is known of the witnesses. Richer de Aquila and Oliver de Manners were fathers of the witnesses of **no. 26**, Roger son of Richer and Hugh son of Oliver. Richer had been granted Bonsmoulins by Stephen as the price of his support in 1137, but was taken prisoner in Normandy by Robert of Bellême on 8 September 1140 and not released until the following year (Ord. Vitalis, v. 83, 130–132). William de Amundeville was constable of Alexander bishop of Lincoln (Stenton, *First Century of English Feudalism*, p. 78), who died in 1148, and Ivo son of Anschetil witnessed two charters of Ranulf for Coventry priory (**nos. 113, 114**). On the whole the evidence seems to point to a date before 1140, and after 1135 or 1136, the year of succession of Robert of Montalt (*Chart. St. Werburgh*, p. 287), the first witness of William the constable's charter. The circumstances of William's restoration of Raby to St. Werburgh's are not clear, but it looks as though he may have resumed the gift after his father's death, and only been persuaded to make restitution some years later.

22.   Confirmation to St. Werburgh's abbey of his predecessors' grant of a fair, with all the profits and the right to try any cases arising in the abbey court, also the privilege that any thief or malefactor coming to the fair shall have peace, unless he commits an offence while there.

[1130–1150, probably c.1140]

B.L. Harl. MS. 2060, f. 62 (old f. 116), from original with facsimile of witness-list; Harl. 2071, f. 18 (old f. 5), also from original with drawing of seal. Ed.: *Chart. St. Werburgh*, p. 68 (no. 10) (from Harl. 2071).

Ranulfus comes Cestrie constabulario, dapifero et maxime vicecomitibus atque burgensibus omnibusque ministris suis Cestrie salutem. Notifico vobis me concessisse, sicut comites Hugo et Ricardus et Ranulfus pater meus concesserunt, ecclesie sancte Werburge omnes, redditus et exitus nundinarum ab hora nona vigilie sancte Werburge usque ad noctem sequentis diei post festum, in thelonio, in forisfactis, et in omnibus rebus que acciderint in nundinis in his tribus diebus, ut si aliqua causa interveniat, omne placitum et iusticia in curia sancte Werburge ad opus monachorum pertractetur. Adhúc vero concessi, sicut antea concessum est ad honorem virginis, ut sive latro sive aliquis malefactor venerit ad festum, habeat firmam pacem dum fuerit in nundinis, nisi forte forisfecerit in illis. Teste Normanno de Verdun, Ricardo pincerna, Iohanne capellano, Philippo camerario.

> SEAL: equestrian, figure to right with uplifted sword in right hand; reverse, an antique gem with two wrestlers or gladiators fighting. Legend   +   COM. SIGILLUM. COM. DE CESTRE.

This charter is a straightforward confirmation and contains nothing new. The grant of a three-day fair occurs in the so-called foundation charter of Hugh I (**no. 3**), and was confirmed, with a specification of the hours of opening and closing (not found in **no. 3**) by Ranulf I (**no. 13**); but there is no charter of Earl Richard dealing with the fair, unless it has been lost. The present charter is also much fuller and more specific than Ranulf II's own 'great charter' (**no. 28**), which makes only a brief reference to the fair, and its wording (e.g. the phrase 'ad honorem virginis') indicates that it was derived from **nos. 3** and **13**. Unfortunately it is impossible to establish at all accurately when it was drawn up, but if Norman de Verdun died some months before Ranulf II (**no. 26**), it was presumably before 1153. It also seems likely that it precedes **no. 24**, in which case it would date from the earlier years of Ranulf's tenure of the earldom. It is noteworthy that it is addressed specifically to the burgesses and officials of Chester and to the sheriffs, presumably the sheriff of the county and the sheriff of the city. In **no. 23** the sheriff of the city is charged with policing the fair.

23. Grant to St. Werburgh's abbey of a fair and stalls for traders and a market before the abbey gate, the monks to put up the stalls and let them to traders for the profit of the church, and no trader or leather-dresser or shoemaker or other artisan is to buy or sell elsewhere as long as the fair lasts. The sheriff of the city is to arrest offenders and detain them with their goods, until they find sureties for their appearance in the court of St. Werburgh.

[1129–1153]

> P.R.O., C.53 (Chancery Charter Rolls), no. 73, m. 11.
> Abstracts: B.L. Harl. MS. 1965, f. 5, and Harl. 2060, f. 68
> (old f. 128). Ed.: *Mon.*, ii. 388; *Chart. St. Werburgh*, pp.
> 52–53 (no. 7).

Rannulfus comes Cestrie constabulario, dapifero, iusticiaris, et nominatim vicecomitibus atque ministris suis Cestrie tam presentibus quam futuris, et omnibus hominibus suis Francis et Anglis salutem. Universitati vestre notum facio me concessisse in elemosina imperpetuum deo et sancte Marie et monachis ecclesie sancte Wereburge pro salute anime mee et pro salute animarum omnium meorum antecessorum nundinas et mentoria mercatoria atque forum omnium venalium fieri ante portam eorum monachorum, ita vero quod ipsi monachi faciant ex suo mentoria mercatorum, conducentes ea postea mercatoribus, in quantum poterint, ad proficuum ecclesie eorum. Quapropter prohibeo super amorem meum, ut nec mercator nec institor nec permentarius nec corvesarius nec ullus minister volens vendere vel emere non vendat nec emat aliquid alicubi nisi ibi, quamdiu nundine duraverint. Et si quisquam deprehensus fuerit vendere vel emere aliquid alias extra hunc locum, precipio vicecomiti civitatis, quicumque fuerit, super amorem meum et forisfactum meum ut ipsi et ministri abbatis cum eo eant et accipiant ipsum mercatorem cum sua mercatione, retinentes eum donec inveniat fideiussores faciendi rectum in curia sancte Werburge. Volo etiam atque firmiter precipio, ut super omnia hec elemosina bene et integriter manuteneatur, ne mea oblacio, quam ego ipse optuli super altare sancte Werburge coram meis baronibus, in aliqua re disturbetur. Ego enim optuli eam propria manu mea super altare coram testibus.

In the St. Werburgh's register (Harl. MS. 1965) this grant is attributed to Ranulf I, but the Charter Roll attributes it to 'Ranulf the son of Ranulf Meschin', and it is claimed for Ranulf II in **no. 28**. Unfortunately, like **no. 22**, there is no means of dating it accurately, but it is perhaps unlikely that it precedes Ranulf's general confirmation (**no. 22**) of his predecessors' grant of a fair. The permission for the monks to set up stalls and a market before the abbey gate is new, and Ranulf states that he had offered it himself on the altar of St. Werburgh in the presence of his barons. There is no reason to doubt the genuineness of the gift.

24.   Earl Ranulf pledges his peace to all coming to the fair of St. Werburgh, and forbids any of his merchants or men of Cheshire to buy or sell elsewhere, as long as the fair is in session.

Thorney, [1143–1146]

B.L. Harl. MS. 2060, f. 62v. (old f. 117) (A); Harl. 2071, f. 19v. (old f. 6v) (B), both from original, with some attempt at facsimile. Ed.: *Chart. St. Werburgh*, p. 69 (no. 11) (from B).

Ranulfus comes Cestrie dapifero et Aluredo de Combrai et omnibus baronibus suis de Cestresira[1] et militibus et omnibus mercatoribus de quocumque orbe terrarum venerint, salutem et pacem. Concedo et affido meam firmam pacem, et vos illam ex parte mea affidatis, omnibus venientibus ad feriam sancto Wareburge, et salvum ibi stare et recedere. Prohibeo etiam super forisfacturam meam ne aliquis mercatorum vel hominum meorum Cestresire vel Cestrie quecumque[2] vendant vel emant nisi[3] in feria sancte Wareburge, quamdiu feria duraverit. Et vos barones mei et amici illud integriter fieri faciatis, ne clamorem audiam. Testibus Ricardo pincerna et W. capellano, apud Tornehagh.[4]

> SEAL: fragment of equestrian seal, figure facing right, brandishing a sword in right hand.

1. suis de Cestresira *om. B.*
2. quicunque *A, B.*
3. nihil *B.*
4. Toinehag' *B.*

The claim of the monks of St. Werburgh to a three-day fair on 20–22 June is included in Hugh I's alleged foundation charter (**no. 3**) and was confirmed by Ranulf I (**nos. 12, 13**), and also by Ranulf II in a charter (**no. 22**), which presumably precedes the present document. The grant of peace to all coming to the fair is new, and was perhaps necessitated by the disturbed state of the country at the time, but Ranulf had already issued a charter prohibiting merchants from buying or selling elsewhere 'quamdiu nundine duraverint' (**no. 23**). The second clause of the present charter is therefore a repetition. But whereas the sheriff of the city had been charged with enforcement in the earlier charter, the duty of enforcement was now extended to all the barons of Cheshire, and specifically to the steward (Robert of Montalt) and to Alured de Combray, who appear to have had some joint responsibility for policing the fair. Alured de Combray was a newcomer to Cheshire, on whom Ranulf II conferred Nether Whitley about 1143–44 (**no. 67**), and the present charter can scarcely be earlier than that. The only other indication of date is the fact that it was issued at Thorney (Notts). This suggests that it belongs to the period between 1141 and 1146 when Ranulf was busy consolidating his position in the midlands, in which case it may tentatively be dated 1143–1146. Richard the butler attested no fewer than 33 of Ranulf II's charters; he was particularly close to the earl, and accompanied him regularly on the various expeditions and campaigns of his stormy career (*Stenton Misc.*, p. 4).

25. Confirmation of his predecessors' gifts of tithes to St. Werburgh's abbey, and gift of the tithes of all his mills in Cheshire and of Leek mill in Staffordshire.

[1143–1153]

P.R.O., C.53 (Chancery Charter Rolls), no. 73, m. 11.
Ed.: *Mon.*, ii. 388; *Chart. St. Werburgh*, p. 76 (no. 20).

Notum sit tam futuris quam presentibus quod ego Ranulphus comes Cestrie concedo et confirmo donationes omnium decimarum quas Hugo comes, Ricardus filius eius, aut Ranulphus pater meus dederunt ecclesie sancte Wereburge. Et insuper ego ipse do predicte ecclesie pro salute anime mee et pro animabus predictorum comitum decimas omnium molendinorum meorum Cestresire et molendini de Leec, precipiens omnibus ministris meis et omnibus hominibus meis[1] super amorem et hominium michi debitum, quatinus reddant predicte ecclesie per singulos annos hanc meam elemosinam, ne audiam inde super forisfactum querimoniam. Et si quis fecit de dominio terram tributariam, sive sit rusticus sive sit firmarius qui teneat eam, precipio ut reddat sancte Wereburge decimam suam, ita vero quod nec clericus nec laicus faciat eis[2] inde iniuriam. Testibus Hugone Osturcario, Ricardo,[3] Gaufrido dispensatore, Aluredo de Cumbrai, Radulfo capellano.

1. hominibus meis *om. MS.*
2. *om. MS.*
3. *Almost certainly* Ricardo pincerna, pincerna *omitted by oversight in MS.*

The list of tithes granted by Hugh I is recited in **no. 3**, but there is no evidence that any were given by Earl Richard and Ranulf I, apart from Richard's alleged gift of a tenth salmon from the Dee (**no. 26**). Ranulf II's own grant is new and was confirmed by his son, Hugh II (**no. 130**), though without mention of Leek. The reason for the omission may be that Henry II resumed possession of Leek, at least temporarily, after Ranulf II's death (*H.K.F.*, p. 256). There is no reason to question the genuineness of the present charter. It presumably falls after Alured de Combray acquired the manor of Nether Whitley (**no. 67**) but the date is otherwise uncertain. Ranulf's gift of the tithe of his mills in Cheshire is recorded in **no. 28**, but here again there is no mention of Leek.

26.   Gift to St. Werburgh's abbey, of one-tenth of his rents from the city of Chester, including the tenth penny of the ninepence received from the bridge and other fisheries, except for salmon, since the abbey had already been given the tenth salmon by Earl Richard. The earl's chamberlains were instructed to deduct the sum involved from the sheriff's farm.

[1141–1150]

B.L. Harl. MS. 2060, f. 61v (old f. 115), from original, with a facsimile of the witness list; Harl. 2071, f. 19v (old f. 6v), also from original; St. George's Chapel, Windsor, MS. xi. E.5 (inspeximus of 1280); P.R.O., C.53 (Chan-

cery Charter Rolls), no. 73, m. 10, and m. 15. Ed.: *Chart.
St. Werburgh*, pp. 70–71 (no. 12); *Mon.*, ii. 388 and Orm.,
i. 25 (both incomplete).

Ranulphus comes Cestrie constabulario, dapifero, baronibus, iusticiario, vic (ecomiti) Cestrie, tam presentibus quam futuris, et omnibus hominibus suis Francis et Anglis clericis et laicis salutem. Universitati vestre notam facio me dedisse in elemosinam in perpetuum deo et sancte Marie et ecclesie sancte Werburge et Radulfo abbati et conventui predicte ecclesie pro salute anime Hugonis comitis, prefate ecclesie fundatoris, ac pro salute anime Ranulfi comitis patris mei et antecessorum meorum, et pro salute anime mee et Christianorum omnium, omnem decimam integriter et plenarie omnium reddituum meorum civitatis Cestrie, videlicet de denariis, et nominatim decimum denarium de illis novem denariis qui accipiuntur de ponte et de aliis piscationibus, quia habuerunt antea decimum salmonem ex dono Ricardi comitis. Eapropter volo et firmiter precipio ut predicta elemosina sit stabilis et firma, et ut computetur et talliatur vicecomiti meo in firmam suam a camerariis meis. Prohibeo etiam ne aliquis vestrum contra deum et sanctam Mariam et contra beatam Werburgam, et super amorem et forisfactum meum, prefatam elemosinam temerarie disturbare, celare vel aliquo modo minuere presumat. Si quis autem vestrum infelix hanc elemosinam a me manu mea super altare sancte Werburge oblatam forte disturbare vel minuere presumpserit, precor episcopum Cestrie et obnixe requiro, et iusticiam meam Cestrie super amorem meum et meorum precipio, quod illum iusticiet, donec ad dignam satisfactionem veniat. Testibus Roberto dapifero, Normanno de Verdun, Turstano Banastre, Willelmo filio Dunecani, Willelmo capellano, Ricardo capellano, Ricardo pincerna, Rogero filio Ricardi de Aquila, Spilemanno camerario, Hugone filio Oliveri, Dunn(ing) filio Wlmari, et multis aliis.

SEAL: 'The Seale is broke away'.

Ranulf II's gift of one-tenth of his rents from the city of Chester is new, and so almost certainly is the grant of a tithe of the fish taken at the bridge in Chester or in other fisheries. The latter, it is true, occurs in Hugh I's so-called foundation charter (**no. 3**), where the abbey is given 'decimam . . . de omne pisce qui accipitur in De' (p. 4), and Earl Richard's alleged gift of every tenth salmon is found in his reputed charter of 1119 (**no. 8**). Neither gift, however, is mentioned in the recital of the gifts of earlier earls in Ranulf II's so-called 'great charter' (**no. 28**). Here (p. 44) the tithe of the rents of the city and the tithe 'de omni pisce qui capitur in aqua de De' are specifically attributed to Ranulf himself 'ex meo proprio dono'. This is almost certainly the truth of the matter, and in that case Hugh I's alleged gift must be rejected as spurious. The same is true of Earl Richard's gift of every tenth salmon. This, as Tait pointed out (*Chart. St. Werburgh*, p. 43), has all the appearance of an interpolation in his own charter, and here also it looks like a clumsy addition. Probably the two interpolations were made at the same time. In any case, there is little doubt that the present charter is the original grant, and we can only speculate why the monks thought it necessary to carry it back to the early days of the abbey's history.

Although the somewhat inflated style of the present charter suggests that it was produced by the monks, there is no reason – except, perhaps, for the passage about Earl Richard's gift, which may be an interpolation – to doubt its authenticity. The fact that the grants it conveys are briefly recorded in **no. 28** indicates that it falls before that, but otherwise its date is not easily determined. Norman de Verdun predeceased Earl Ranulf (*H.K.F.*, p. 215), as did Spileman the chamberlain (**no. 93**). William son of Duncan, nephew of King David I of Scotland, who also is among the witnesses of **no. 28**, probably died in 1152, if not earlier (*Chart. St. Werburgh*, p. 71). Roger, the son of Richer de l'Aigle (*Aquila*), a relative of the earl through Judith, sister of Hugh I, witnessed Ranulf II's charter of 1144–45 for Eustace fitz John (**No. 73**), as did Thurstan Banastre and Norman de Verdun. The present charter must fall after the accession of Abbot Ralph (1141), and probably before 1150, but any date can only be approximate.

27.   Confirmation of the gifts and liberties bestowed on St. Werburgh's abbey by his predecessors and by their barons and his own, with special mention of the exclusive jurisdiction of the abbey's court.

Chester, [1136–1153]

St. George's Chapel, Windsor, MS. xi, E.5; B.L. Harl. MS. 2071, f. 45 (old f. 31); abbreviated text ('This I had from Mr. Leicester'), *ibid.* f. 18 (old f. 5). Ed.: Orm., i. 25 (from abbreviated text); *Chart. St. Werburgh*, pp. 67–8 (no. 9).

Rannulfus comes Cestrie constabulario dapifero, iusticiario, baronibus, vic (ecomiti), ministris et ballivis et omnibus hominibus suis, Francis et Anglis, clericis et laicis, tam presentibus quam futuris salutem. Sciatis me concessisse et confirmasse in perpetuam elemosinam pro salute anime mee et parentum meorum ecclesie sancte Werburge Cestrie et monachis ibidem deo servientibus omnes donaciones et dignitates et libertates quas comites antecessores mei, scilicet Hugo comes et Ricardus filius eius et Rannulfus pater meus, et barones in tempore illorum vel in meo eis dederunt. Quapropter volo et heredibus meis et omnibus amicis et hominibus meis precipio, ut omnia ad abbatiam pertinencia in burgo et extra, in bosco, in plano, in villis et extra, in viis et semitis, in pratis et pasturis, in aquis et molendinis, in piscariis et in omnibus aliis locis, sint soluta

et quieta et ita libera, ut nichil libertatis possit addi illis ulterius, quia ego nichil
retineo, in rebus sancte Werburge nisi oraciones tantummodo. Et insuper
concedo, sicut alii comites ante me concesserunt, ut sancta Werburga habeat
plenarie cursam suam de omnibus rebus. Teste Roberto dapifero, Normanno de
Verdun, Rannulfo vicecomite, Hugone hostricario, Ada de Praers, Ricardo
Pain, Willelmo Grisille, apud Cestriam.

This is a normal confirmation and calls for little comment. There is no equivalent
confirmation by Hugh II, but the present charter was repeated in almost
identical words by Ranulf III (**no. 227**). The evidence unfortunately does not
permit a precise dating, but it presumably falls after the succession of Robert the
steward (c.1136) and before the death of Norman de Verdun (1152 or 1153).
Adam de Praers witnessed Ranulf's charters for Basingwerk abbey (**no. 38**) and
for Alan Silvester (**no. 35**). William of Gresley witnessed his deathbed charters
for St. Werburgh's and for Trentham abbeys (**nos. 34, 118**). Ranulf the sheriff
was one of the witnesses of the famous treaty between Earl Ranulf and the earl
of Leicester (**no. 110**). As indicated below, the present charter is almost certainly
earlier in date than Ranulf's confirmation of **no. 28**, supposing the latter to be
genuine; in which case it probably falls before 1150 at latest.

28. Ranulf II's 'great charter', confirming in detail the gifts made to St.
    Werburgh's abbey by his predecessors and their barons and other donors,
    followed by a statement of his own gifts, and those of his barons.
    [Spurious]

[1151–1152]

> Original: Eaton Hall, Chester, Grosvenor MSS. no. 1.
> Transcr.: Bodleian Library, Dodsworth MS. 31, ff. 1–5v.
> Other transcripts, including the cartulary of St. Wer-
> burgh's (B.L. Harl. MS. 1965), omit the confirmations
> and include only Ranulf II's own gifts and attestation.
> Ed.: *Chart. St. Werburgh*, pp. 53–61. Facsimile: *J.C.A.S.*,
> N.S. vi, frontispiece.

IN NOMINE PATRIS et filii et spiritus sancti, amen.

Sanctorum prisca auctoritate patrum, qui in nomine patris et filii et spiritus
sancti in sancta ecclesia regiminis gubernacula hactenus tenuerunt, quique suos
adiutores sanctęque ecclesię fundatores sua nobis industria suorumque scrip-
torum longa tradicione cognitos reddiderunt, admoneri videmur, ut ea que a
temporaneis nostris in sanctę ecclesię matris exaltatione facta sunt, presentibus
per nos manifestentur posterisque dinoscenda nobis scribentibus reserventur.

Nos igitur maiorum imitantes exampla iam quedam pietatis opera referamus, quę in Anglica terra gesta sunt a HUGONE Cestrensi comite anno ab incarnatione domini millesimo nonagesimo tercio, regnante potentissimo rege Willelmo atque in archiepiscopatu Cantuariensi pontificante Anselmo atque in Eboracensi[1] pontificante Thoma. Volumus vero, ut religiosi atque fideles Christiani cognoscant, quia iccirco nobis ista describere placuit, ut que ea relegerint vel audierint deum supplicabiliori affectu pro sanctę ecclesię fundatorum salute implorent, et ut presentes ad regna cęlestia tendentes etiam inter ętatis huius primates, quos sequantur, inveniant.

Igitur ad laudem et gloriam summe et individue trinitatis atque incomprehensibilis divinitatis iam proferamus quę nos dicere spopondimus. HUGO Cestrensis comes atque Ermentrudis cometissa, devotioni religiose pia mente subditi piissimaque dei visitatione inspirati, in quadam ęcclesia, quę constructa est in honore sanctę WERBURGĘ virginis in civitate Cestrę, monachos religiose viventes posuerunt, concedente rege Willelmo, qui deum assidue exorarent tam pro utilitate animę regis Willelmi et Willelmi patris eius nobilissimi regis et matris eius Mathildis reginę fratrumque et sororum eius atque regis Edwardi, quam pro animarum suarum salute et pro animabus patrum et matrum et antecessorum heredumque et parentum et baronum suorum, omniumque Christianorum tam vivorum quam defunctorum.

Huic vero ecclesię sanctę Werburgę HUGO supradictus comes et Ermentrudis cometissa possessiones priores liberas imperpetuum et quietas concesserunt, et de suis augmentaverunt, habitationique monachorum abilem reddiderunt eamque abbatiam nulli omnino abbatię subditam fecerunt. Postea in ea monachos et abbatem deo donante et supradicto rege Willelmo concedente constituerunt. Hanc etiam et quicquid ad eam pertinet abbati et monachis dederunt, videlicet Ynes, Saltonam, Suttonam, Ceveleiam, Huntitonam, Bostonam, Wevenam, Crostonam, Trochfort, Clistonam, Estonam, Vuisdeleth, Hodesleiam, Weupram, et dimidiam Rabbi, et terciam partem de Nestuna, et terciam partem de Salhala, et terciam partem de Staneia, et dimidiam partem de Leche, et unam carrucam terre ad Pulforth, et terciam partem de Burewardesleia, et Edinchale, et Sotewica.

Insuper etiam dederunt huic ęcclesię in ipsa civitate de suo dominio vicum a porta de North usque ad ęcclesiam et locum unius molendini ad pontem civitatis, et duo maneria in Anglisi, unum autem in Ros, unum in Wirhalle, Erberiam, et in Lindesei terram decem boum; et post obitum comitis vel cometissę Westonam cum appendiciis suis in Derbesiria; et rectam decimam de piscatorio Etone et omnium quę ei pertinent, et decimam de Frodesham, de molendino de piscatoria et de pullis equarum, et de Weverham, et de Vfre, et de Lech, et de · Roecestra, et de Haurdina, et de Colesul et Bissopestred, et de Uppetuna, de Estham, et de Campedene, et decimam piscatoriarum de Ruelent, et decimam Anglisi de dominio suo, etiam de navibus; ęcclesiam et terram ęcclesię et

decimam de dominio de Danefort et de molendinis. Horum omnium supradict-
orum maneriorum rectam decimam in omnibus dederunt, in pullis, in vitulis, in
ovibus, in porcis, in lana, in caseis, et in aliis rebus quę decimari debent.

Donum Westunę Ermentrudis cometissa[2] iussu comitis HUGONIS posuit super
altare coram domno Anselmo archiepiscopo Cantuarię et baronibus suis. Ea die
seiserunt[3] santam Werburgam de Westona per decimam eiusdem Westonę et
per ęcclesiam et terram ęcclesię Estonę et per terram unius carruce[4] quam tunc
presenter exhibuerunt. Reliquam vero partem omnem liberam et quietam in
elemosina semper in posterum post discessum illius, qui prius obiret, concesserunt. Quin etiam baronibus suis concesserunt, ut unusquisque post obitum
suum rectam partem omnis substantię suę prefatę abbatię daret, et centum
solidatas terrę, aliis autem secundum posse suum. Teste reverendo domino
Anselmo archiepiscopo, Harveio episcopo, Balduino monacho, Rodberto filio
Hugonis, Willelmo constabulario, Willelmo Malbanc, Rannulfo dapifero,
Radulfo dapifero, Hugone filio Osberti, Ricardo Banastro, Hamone de Maceio,
Gilleberto de Venables, Ricardo de Vernon, Ricardo de Rullos, Bigod des
Loges, Rannulfo venatore, aliisque quam plurimis.

Willelmus Mabeench dedit huic abbatię sanctę Werburgę Witeberiam et terciam
partem Weuprę et ecclesiam et decimam de Tatenhala et terram duobus bobus,
et decimam de Salchale et de Claituna et de Yraduc. Teste cometissa, Ricardo
Banaste, Hugone Osberti filio, Bigod des Loges, Ricardo pincernario, et
Sirardo.

Rodbertus filius Hugonis capellam Cristentunę et terram capellę et terram
cuiusdam rustici ipsumque rusticum, et quoddam molendinum terramque ipsius
molendini et Chotam Ordrici et ipsum Ordricum, et quendam campum iunctum
huic cotę, et Cryu, et quandam salinam in Fulewic, et duas masuras in civitate, et
paululum terrę iuxta Bochtunestan. Hoc donum concessit HUGO comes. Teste
Willelmo Nigelli filio et fratre eius Ricardo, Rannulfo dapifero, Bigod,
Hammone de Maceio, Hugone Osberti filio, Hugone Normanni filio, Fulcone de
Baiunvilla, Unfrido de Costentin.

Hugo filius Normanni et Radulfus frater eius partem suam de Lostoch et
ęcclesiam de Cotituna et terram ęcclesię et decimam, et de Lay. Teste Willelmo
Malbeench multisque aliis. Ricardus de Vernon decimam Estonę et Pichetonę.
Ricardus de Rullos ęcclesiam et decimam Waveretonę et Hottone et Clotonę, et
molendini Clotonę. Billeheld uxor Baldrici Pecfortunam. Teste Normanno de
Arrecio multisque aliis.

Radulfus venator terram trium carrucarum in Brochetuna. Hugo de Mara
Reddeclivam, concedente comite. Teste cometissa, Willelmo Nigelli filio, multisque aliis. Nigellus de Burceio decimam de Stortuna et de Gravesbyri et

quartam partem de Gravesbyri tam de luco quam de plano. Teste Garatin fratre eius, Ricardo de Rullos, Willelmo filio Huberti, Gisleberto de Blayne.

Radulfus Ermuini filius et uxor eius Claricia terram in Odecerce ad octo boves et decimam de Berlestona in Wirhale et de Verulestane in Wicesfeld et de equabus suis, ubicunque sint. Teste Godefrido mercatore et Nigello multisque aliis. Rodbertus de Tremouz Tidelvestan. Teste Rannulfo fratre suo, Rodberto dapifero. Wascelenus nepos Walterii de Vernon quendam agricolam et terram quatuor boum in Nessa et decimam de Prestona et terciam partem tocius substantię sue et uxoris eius. Teste Gisleberto, Wulmaro archidiacono.

Sirard capellam de Bedintone et terram quatuor boum et decimam illius manerii, et decimam de Bromhale et de Waleie et de Maynes et de Westone et de Wille, et post obitum omne substantię suę et uxoris suę de Cestresyra et de Mannis. Teste Willelmo constabulario, Hugone Osberti filio, et Wimundo de Col.

Ricardus de Mesnilwarin decimam de Blachenoth, de annona, de piscatoria, et de omnibus de quibus decima debet dari. Teste Rogero fratre suo et Rannulfo de Beurello et Rannulfo de Walebruno. Rannulfus filius Gocelini concessit decimam suam sicut pater suus dedit eam. Rodbertus Putrel terram unius carrucę a Maclesfeld. Teste Waleranno de Baro et multis aliis. Walterius de Vernon decimam equarum suarum.

Comes navim unam cum decem retibus ad piscandum in Anglisi imperpetuum liberam et quietam. Ad festum sanctę Werburge in estate concessit feiriam trium dierum. Teste cometissa, Willelmo pincerna, Hugone camerario, Willelmo Malbeenc, Ricardo Banastro.

There follows here the so-called testimony of Archbishop Anselm confirming Earl Hugh's foundation of the abbey. It is printed in Chart. St. Werburgh, *p. 38, and omitted here as not directly relevant. A break between the sections dealing with the different earls has been introduced for convenience of reference; such breaks are not found in the original text.*

Post obitum HUGONIS comitis Ricardus comes filius eius dedit pro anima illius deo et sanctę Werburgę terram Wlfrici prepositi foris portam de North, et molendinum de Beche, et tres mansuras quietas et pacatas, duas in civitate et unam extra murum. Teste Willelmo conestabulario, Walterio de Vernona, Radulfo dapifero et aliis multis.

Willelmus constabularius dedit Neutonam, teste Radulfo dapifero et aliis multis. Hugo Malbeench dedit unam salinam in Wico suo, teste Adaliza matre sua, Ricardo de Praeres et Gutha, et aliis multis. Hugo filius Normanni dedit Gosetro et Lautonam, teste Hugone de Laci et Rogero filio[5] Normanni et Sirardo, et aliis multis. Ricardus de Praieres dedit Cnoctyrum, teste Willelmo et Adam filiis suis, et Lamberto. Corbin dedit unam carrucam terre in Wirwella. Roes uxor Pigoti et Hamundus de Maci dederunt Norwrdinam et ecclesiam cum omnibus que ei pertinent, concedentibus et testibus filiis eorum.

Rogerus de Mannilwarini dedit Plumleyam cum Widone filio suo, teste Willelmo, Rannulfo filiis suis. Ricardus pincerna dedit ęcclesiam sancti Olafi et duas mansuras in civitate. Rannulfus venator dedit Bradefort et unam salinam in Norhtwich, concessu Ricardi comitis et Hugonis de Vernon. Bourel dedit ęcclesiam de Haliewelle et decimam suam et de molendino suo. Herbertus wombasarius dedit terram iiii. boum in Hole. Rogerus de sancto Martino dedit terram duorum boum in Bebintona.

Willelmus de Punterleya dedit Butavari cum omnibus appendiciis suis, id est ecclesia[4] et totum manerium solidum et quietum, et silvam Lestone ad rogum faciendum et ad communem usum domestici operis, concessu Herberti filii sui et Alveredi domini sui et Ricardi comitis. Teste Willelmo constabulario, Ricardo Banastro, Willelmo pincerna, et aliis multis. Hugo de Vernon unam mansuram in Cestra, solidam et quietam.

Rannulfus comes, nepos Hugonis comitis, dedit Uppetunam cum omnibus appendiciis suis et omnibus ad eam pertinentibus solidam et quietam pro anima Hugonis avunculi sui, et pro anima sua et uxoris suę Lucię et pro Rannulfo filio suo, et pro animabus omnium antecessorum et successorum suorum, concessu Rannulfo filii sui. Teste Willelmo fratre eius, Willelmo constabulario, Rodberto dapifero, Warino Banastro, Hugone filio Osberni, Osberto filio Hugonis, et aliis multis.

Willelmus Meschinus dedit deo et sanctę Werburgę ęcclesiam de Dissart, concessu Rannulfi filii sui, teste Willelmo clerico de Ruelent, Willelmo flandrensi, Willelmo pincerna, Matheo de Ruelent, Ricardo filio Berlei, et aliis multis. Matheus de Ruelent dedit ęcclesiam de Thurstanestona cum omnibus quę ad eam pertinent, teste Rodberto de Petra Ponti, Rodberto Banastro, Ricardo filio Berley.

Hugo filius[6] Osberti dedit unam mansuram in Cestra et unum pratum quod vocatur Kingeshei. Suein dedit duas bovatas in Wetenhala, concedentibus filiis suis. Ricardus de Cruce dedit unam mansuram in Cestra, et Morsetonam. Willelmus de Muhald deo et sanctę Werburgę Le Lay dedit pro anima sua et parentum suorum, teste Hugone Malbeenc, Ricardo Pagano, et aliis multis qui affuerunt.

Leticia de Malpas dedit deo et sanctę Werburgę Parvam Cristentonam et Bechiam et unam mansuram in civitate, teste et concedente domino suo Ricardo et fratre suo Ricardo Mailardo, Rodberto Grefesac, Nigello Chaldel, et aliis multis. Sweinus faber dedit unam mansuram ante ęcclesiam sanctę Werburgę.

Hugo filius Osberti dedit aliam iuxta illam pro dimidia Wereburtuna. Willelmus filius Andree dedit cum Andrea filio suo deo et sancte Werburgę magnam sopam, scilicet inter domum Winebaldi vicecomitis et Hamundi. Utredus Walensis dedit unam mansuram cum crophtis liberam et quietam ab omni re.

In nomine domini nostri Ihesu Christi, ego secundus Rannulfus comes Cestrie concedo et confirmo has omnes donationes, quas mei antecessores vel barones eorum dederunt, dans etiam ex meo proprio dono pro salute animę mee parentumque meorum decimum denarium universi redditus mei de civitate et de omni pisce qui capitur in aqua de De. Adhuc concedo deo et sancte[4] Werburge[4] ut loges mercatorum fiant ante[7] portas monachorum, ita quod monachi accipiant inde redditus, precipiens super meum forisfactum, ne aliquis emat vel vendat aliquid in nundinis sancte Werburge[4] nisi ibi. Do etiam ecclesiam[4] sanctę Marie[4] de Castello et duas mansuras ante portas monasterii, unam scilicet Hugonis presbiteri, qui vocatur le Leure, et alteram Suargari pelliparii, et terram Haagne de Chel, et decimam molendinorum meorum de Cestrasiria. Teste Roberto dapifero, Normanno de Verdun, Roberto Banastro, Gileberto de Venables, Willelmo Malbanc, Willelmo filio Dunecan, Chatwaladro rege Nortwaliarum, Willelmo de Mannilwarini,[8] Roberto de Maci et Simone fratre eius,[9] et Roberto filio Picod, et aliis multis.

Robertus de Maci et Simon frater eius dederunt deo et sancte[4] Werburge[4] octo bovatas in Bacfort cum omnibus rebus illis bovatis pertinentibus, solutas et quietas ab omni servicio et ab omni re. Simon filius Willelmi dedit decimam molendini sui, de Bretebi, testibus et concedentibus filiis suis et Hugone de Petraponte. Alanus de Vilers dedit deo et sancte[4] Werburge[4] Litegade cum omnibus rebus[7] eidem ville pertinentibus, solutam et quietam ab omni servicio et omni re, teste Ricardo pincerna et Ricardo Fitun et Willelmo filio Duning.

Et sciant tam presentes quam futuri, quod ego iunior Rannulfus comes Cestrie, tum pro utilitate et honore ęcclesię, tum pro abbatis et monachorum fratrum nostrorum prece, tum, quod maximum est, pro salute anime[4] mee,[4] confirmo et corroboro mea auctoritate et meo sigillo quecumque continentur in hac carta, scilicet omnes donationes quas mei anticessores[8] comites et barones vel milites vel burgenses dederunt deo et sancte[4] Werburge.[4] Et hanc confirmationem in tesauris ęcclesię in testimonium posteris repono. Et precor amicos et precipio super fidem mihi debitam meo heredi omnibusque meis hominibus tam futuris quam presentibus, quantinus hec omnia, tam mea quam antiquorum dona, sint stabilia, integra et rata, et ita ab omni re et consuetudine libera, sola et quieta ut nichil liberatis nec in[7] placitis nec in consuetudinibus vel in aliquibus rebus possit eis addi ulterius. Valete. Valeant omnes fideles in Christo.

There follows, in a different handwriting, a confirmation of Archbishop Theobald, which has no apparent connection with the preceding charter and is omitted here.

SEALS: on the left, below first column, on parchment tag, seal missing. On the right, below fifth column, attached by red and green cords, an equestrian seal, legend   +   SIGILL [UM . . .] BERTI . . .. N ..

1. Eboriacensi *orig.*
2. comissa *orig.*
3. *Corr. from* sesierunt, *orig.*
4. 'e' *not tagged, orig.*
5. filius *orig.*
6. *Corr. from* Hugone, *but leaving* felius, *orig.*
7. *Added above line, orig.*
8. *sic orig.*
9. Simon frater eius *orig., evidently in error for succeeding entry.*

This remarkable document, which has survived among the muniments of the duke of Westminster at Eaton Hall, is the oldest existing original charter of St. Werburgh's abbey. Its form is unusual, if not unique, and immediately arouses suspicions about its authenticity. The opening invocation of the Holy Trinity, the invocation of the name of our Lord Jesus Christ at the beginning of Ranulf II's confirmation, and the concluding valediction ('Valeant omnes fideles in Christo'), all betray its clerical origin. But there are many other charters produced by the recipients, which were endorsed or confirmed by the grantor and must be regarded as authentic. The question is whether the present charter falls into this category.

The document belongs, like **no. 3**, to the category usually known as a *pancarte*, or *pancarta*, and is written in five columns (the lower half of the fifth column left empty) on a large sheet of parchment (approximately 23 inches long and 16 inches wide) in a twelfth-century book-hand. It is followed in a different handwriting by a confirmation of Archbishop Theobald of Canterbury which has no apparent connexion with the main text. The first (and longest) part of the document recites, sometimes with substantial differences in detail, the charters of Hugh I (**no. 3**), Richard (**no. 8**) and Ranulf I (**no. 13**), and these are followed, beginning in the lower half of column four, by Ranulf II's confirmation of his predecessors' gifts and a recital of his own and those of his men. The confirmation is added in a narrower, more compressed handwriting with differences in spelling (e.g. Roberto for Rodberto, and Malbanc for Malbeenc) and in orthography (notably the infrequent use of the tagged 'e'). The suggestion seems to be that the first part was prepared in advance by the monks of Chester for submission to Ranulf II, and the concluding section added when he confirmed the preceding sections.

The earl states at the end that he has deposited the document in the abbey's treasure-chest (*thesaurus*). If so, it remained there – another remarkable feature – unused and unknown until after the dissolution, when it was copied by the seventeenth-century antiquaries, Roger Dodsworth and Randle Holme, but it only finally came to light in 1849. Unlike **nos. 3, 8** and **13**, it was never submitted for royal confirmation, and the conclusion we must draw is that the monks, who produced it, decided that it was more advantageous to rely on the separate charters of the three preceding earls. As Ranulf's own gifts were recorded in separate charters (**nos. 23, 25, 26, 31, 33**), the more important of which were inspected and confirmed by the Crown, and as he also issued a general confirmation of a normal type (**no. 27**), the present document had little, if any, practical use. Hence, no doubt, the decision to leave it in obscurity.

It is a more difficult question, even allowing for the fact that it was drawn up for the monks, whether it can be regarded as a genuine charter of Ranulf II. Tait did his best to save it, but clearly had serious doubts. The writing is certainly compatible with a date c.1150, plus or minus ten years, but no experienced palaeographer would wish to be more specific than that. The use of tagged 'e's would be unusual, but by no means impossible, later. More disturbing is the appearance on two occasions (pp. 40, 42) of the ugly neologism *imperpetuum* (for *in perpetuum*). This to the best of my knowledge is unprecedented in original charters of Ranulf II's time (though it may be introduced by copyists in later transcripts) and points to a considerably later date. Also unusual and irregular in a genuine charter of Ranulf II is the use of the phrases 'Ego secundus Rannulfus', and 'Ego iunior Rannulfus', though it would not be surprising to find them in a monastic compilation (e.g. *Chart. St. Werburgh*, no. 13). On the other hand, the witnesses of Earl Ranulf's confirmation are compatible with the date 1151–52 usually assigned to the charter. William son of Duncan, nephew of King David I of Scotland, witnessed **no. 26**. The Welsh prince Cadwaladr, who also witnessed **nos. 64** and **84**, is known to have taken refuge with Ranulf when he was expelled from Wales in 1151 or 1152 (Lloyd, ii, 490–91). It is more difficult, as Tait pointed out (*Chart. St. Werburgh*, p. 66), to accept the statement in the charter that Ranulf's own gifts (a tenth of the rents of Chester, the right to erect and let booths for traders outside the monastery gate, and the tithes of his mills) were made on the occasion of his confirmation of the gifts of his predecessors. All are recorded in separate charters (**nos. 23, 25, 26**), and though unfortunately none can be closely dated, there can be little doubt that all three precede the present charter. Finally, there is a confirmation in regular form (**no. 13**), with a different set of witnesses, which was re-confirmed in almost identical words by Ranulf III (**no. 227**).

(The surviving seal is irregularly attached, and is certainly not one of the original seals. When and why it was attached, we do not know; but as a later addition it does not directly affect the question of authenticity and there is no need to discuss it here. It is discussed at some length by Tait in *Chart. St. Werburgh*, pp. 63–64).

These facts would seem to point to the conclusion that this remarkable document was compiled by the monks for their own purposes, perhaps at the very end of Ranulf's life, perhaps after his death. A clue to the date may perhaps be found in the concluding passage, where Ranulf admonishes his heir (born in 1147 and therefore only five or six years old at the time) to maintain all the gifts set out in his charter. This suggests that it may have been drawn up as a precaution during Hugh II's minority (1153–1162) to safeguard the abbey's position in case of any attack on its rights and possessions after he came of age. As, in point of fact, Hugh II showed no hostility to St. Werburgh's – on the contrary, he is known on occasion to have restored possessions which had been lost under his father (*Chart. St. Werburgh*, no. 354) – the precaution proved unnecessary; which may explain why the present charter was allowed to lapse for all practical purposes. This is, of course, only surmise; but, whatever the explanation, it is extremely dubious whether we should accept it as a genuine charter of Ranulf II. In this respect it falls into line with the corresponding charters of Hugh I, Richard and Ranulf I. This does not mean that the contents of any should be rejected out of hand. This was a time when, in response to rapid legal developments, monasteries everywhere were anxious to establish their titles on a sound footing and obtain written confirmation of grants which in many instances had probably been made by oral tradition and without charter. The series of St. Werburgh's charters should be viewed in this light. They were not forgeries in the ordinary sense; but equally they were not regular grants of the earls to whom they were attributed.

29–33. Various gifts, confirmations and privileges for St. Werburgh's abbey, Chester.

[1129–1153]

B.L. Harl. MS. 1965, ff. 5v, 6v, 7v, 12, 26 (old ff. 2v, 3v, 4v, 9, 23); P.R.O., C.53 (Chancery Charter Rolls), no. 73, m. 25. Ed.: *Chart. St. Werburgh*, nos. 13, 37, 51, 146, 499.

29. Secundus Rannulfus comes Cestrie confirmavit donacionem de Uptona, quam Rannulfus pater suus dedit ecclesie sancte Werburge, quando fecit transferri corpus Hugonis comitis de cimiterio in capitulum.

30. Ranulphus dudum comes Cestrie, per cartam suam quam inspeximus, concessit Radulpho tunc abbati Cestrie hanc videlicet libertatem, quod ipse et successores sui imperpetuum per totam Cestreshiriam fugare possent cervos et omnes alias feras iuxta genus suum.

31.   Ranulphus comes Cestrie dedit ecclesie sancte Werburge Cestrie terram que fuit Hagene de Chel, cum omnibus pertinenciis in bosco, in plano, in pratis, in aquis, solutam et quietam.

32.   Ranulphus comes Cestrie confirmavit monachis Cestrie donacionem Roberti venatoris super quatuor bovatis terre in Weston.

33.   Ranulphus comes Cestrie dedit ecclesiam[1] sancte Marie de Castro Cestrie in puram elemosinam.

1.   ecclesie *MS*.

Except for **no. 30**, which is also briefly recited in a charter of Edward I, the gifts and confirmations listed above are only found in abbreviated abstracts in the cartulary of Chester abbey. They have no witnesses and, except for **no. 30**, which (if genuine) must fall in the time of Abbot Ralph (1141–1157), cannot be dated more closely than 1129–1153. It therefore seems appropriate to group them together. The gifts of the church of St. Mary of the Castle (later known as St. Mary on the Hill) and of the land of Hagene de Chel (**nos. 31** and **33**) are recorded in Ranulf II's 'great charter' (p. 44), which they must precede. Ranulf I's gift of Upton nr. Chester is the first item of **no. 13**, and is briefly recited in **no. 28**, but the present notice (**no. 29**) is the only evidence that it was confirmed by his son; it seems clear from the wording that it was derived directly from **no. 13**. Robert the hunter's gift of land in Weston-upon-Trent, which is confirmed in **no. 32**, is recorded in the cartulary (*Chart. St. Werburgh*, no. 189), where it is described as the land which belonged to Erneis the hunter. Erneis appears as witness in **no. 3** (p. 4), which makes it fairly certain that this is a charter of Ranulf II, though it could conceivably be a charter of Ranulf I. Weston was conferred on St. Werburgh's by Earl Hugh and Countess Ermentrude (pp. 3, 4), of whose dower it was probably a part.

34.   Grant of Eastham and Bromborough to St. Werburgh's abbey on his death, as compensation for injuries inflicted by him.

Gresley, [December 1153]

P.R.O., C.53 (Chancery Charter Rolls), no. 73 (13 Edw. I), m. 11 (another copy m. 15) (A); D.L. 39/1/19 (Forest Pleas), m. 26 (B); CHES 33/4 (Forest Rolls 20–21 Edw.

III), m. 26 (from royal confirmation); St. George's Chapel, Windsor, MS. xi. E.5 (inspeximus of 1280) (C); B.L. Harl. MS. 2060, f. 61v. (D), and Harl. 2071, f. 45v. (E), (both from inspeximus). Ed.: *Mon.*, ii. 388; Orm., ii. 405; *Chart. St. Werburgh*, pp. 231–2 (no. 349).

Ranulphus comes Cestrie episcopo Cestrie, archidiacono, omnibusque sancte ecclesie filiis, necnon et constabulario, dapifero, iusticiario, baronibus, vicecomitibus, ministris et balivis,[1] et omnibus hominibus et amicis suis salutem. Nostis quidem, karissimi, quanta mala feci[2] rebus sancte Werburge, quorum omnium[3] in fine penitenciam agens, dedi deo et sancte Werburge pro salute anime mee et pro satisfactione[4] malorum predicte ecclesie a me illatorum Estham et Brumburgh in perpetuam elemosinam cum cunctis suis adiacentiis[5] in hominibus, in ecclesiis, in[6] terris, in aquis,[7] in silvis, et in omnibus consuetudinibus, sicut ego habui eas die qua ego fui vivus et mortuus. Quapropter volo et firmiter precipio super fidem et amorem mihi debitam,[8] ut hec mea elemosina pro salute et absolucione[9] mea data sit, sicut decet, ab omni re soluta et libera, et si quisquam eam diminuerit in aliquo,[10] ipse deus eum diminuat et destruat.[11] Testibus Waltero episcopo,[12] Willelmo abbate Rademore, Roberto priore de Calke,[13] Iohanne capellano, Eustachio filio Iohannis, Simone filio Willelmi, Willelmo de Greille,[14] Ricardo pincerna, Hugone aucipite, Roberto de Buschervilla, Roberto filio Hugonis, Simone filio Osberni, apud Greselegam.

1. ballidis *A*.
2. *For* Nostis . . . feci, *A, B and D have* Notum est vobis quod multum forisfeci.
3. Unde *for* quorum omnium, *A, B, D*.
4. *add* omnium *B, C, E*.
5. pertinenciis *A, B, D*.
6. et *B, C, D, E*.
7. *add* et piscationibus *C, E*.
8. *C and E read* firmiter cunctis meis super fidem mihi debitam precipio.
9. satisfactione *A, B, D*.
10. *B, C, E have* et si quisque vestrum, sive heres sive alius, diminuerit eam in aliquo.
11. *C and E add* et destructum cum diabolo condempnet.
12. Waltero episcopo *om. A, B. D*.
13. *This witness omitted C, E*.
14. *This witness omitted C, E*.

The great manor of Eastham, by far the largest in Cheshire, which at that time comprised Bromborough, had been part of the earl's demesne from the time of Domesday (*D.S.C.*, p. 110), but the tithes had been given to St. Werburgh's abbey, with those of his other manors, by Hugh I (**no. 3**). It included some of the best land in Cheshire, and was a major accession to the abbey's possessions. The gift was one of those made by Ranulf II on his deathbed at Gresley (Derbys.) to atone for his sins, and shares many witnesses with others (**nos. 117 and 118**) made at the same time, but we know of no 'evils' inflicted by Ranulf which would demand compensation on so generous a scale. As the textual variants indicate, his charter appears to have existed in two versions, a shorter one preserved on the Charter Roll and a more elaborate version in the Windsor manuscript. I have on the whole preferred the former, but the differences do not affect the substance. The grant was confirmed by Henry II in 1155 (*Chart. St. Werburgh*, no. 350) and about the same time by Bishop Walter of Coventry and by Archbishop Theobald of Canterbury (*ibid.*, nos. 100, 101).

35.   Grant to Alan Silvester of Storeton and Puddington in Wirral.

Chester, [1130–1140]

> Orig.: J.R.U.L.M., Rylands Charter 1807. Transcr.: B.L. Harl. MS. 139, f. 206v. (old f. 237v.); Harl. 2074, f. 158v.; Harl. 2079, f. 7v. (old p. 15); P.R.O., D.L. 39/1/19, m. 27; CHES 33/4 (Forest Rolls), m. 31v.; London, College of Arms, MS. 1 D., f. 182; Bodleian Library, Dodsworth MS. 31, f. 101v; MS. Top. Cheshire b. 1, p. 136; Chester, Booth of Twemlow, Liber D (94, A591), f. 149. Ed.: Stewart-Brown, *H.S.L.C.*, lxxxvii, pp. 97–8 (with facsimile); Tyson, *Handlist of Charters, Deeds and Similar Documents in the possession of the John Rylands Library*, ii. 127; Irvine, *Ches. Sheaf*, no. 5137. Abstract: Orm., ii. 445.

R. comes Cestrie constabuloni et dapifero et omnibus baronibus suis et hominibus et amicis Francis et Anglis et Walensibus salutem. Sciatis me dedisse et concessisse Alano Silvestri meo homini et ministro Stortunam et Pudican in feudo et hereditate sibi et suis heredibus pro suo servicio, scilicet pro dimidio milite. Et volo et precipio quod supradictas villas habeat et teneat cum omnibus adiacentibus in bosco et in plano et ubique libere et honorifice et quiete. Testibus Willelmo de Romara, Willelmo de Perci, Ricardo de Haia, Willelmo constabulone, Willelmo[1] monaco, Roberto Grevesac, Roberto de Treveres, Serlone venatore, Willelmo meschin de Romara, Gaufrido dispensatore, Beringero falcunario, Rogero de Verdun, Spilemanno camerario, Ricardo pincerna, Philippo camerario, Adam de Praheres, Hugone filio Anschetil, Roberto filio Walteri, Willelmo pincerna, Iohanne clerico qui hanc cartam fecit ad Cestriam precepto comitis.

> SEAL, on tongue, an equestrian figure facing right, bearing a sword in the right hand. Legend [SIG]ILLVO RANNVLFI C[OMITIS CEST]RIENSIS.

1.   W°*MS.*

Although not stated in the charter, later evidence indicates that Storeton and Puddington were given to Alan Silvester (or Savage) as an endowment for his position as master forester of Wirral. As the former had been held by Nigel de Burcy and the latter by Hamo de Mascy at the time of Domesday (*D.S.C.*, pp. 181, 209), it is not clear how they came to be in the earl's hands; the latter at least may have escheated on the death of Hamo de Mascy I. Stewart-Brown (*op. cit.*, p. 101) thinks the grant to Alan Silvester was made in 1129–1130, 'probably nearer the latter year than the former'. It cannot have been earlier if, as generally held (*H.K.F.*, p. 64, *Stenton Misc.*, pp. 25, 35) William the constable did not succeed his father until 1130, possibly later.[1] On the other hand, since Earl Ranulf's uterine brother, William of Roumare, does not have the title earl of Lincoln, it cannot be later than Christmas 1140 or early 1141, when he was given the earldom. The other witnesses do not help to limit the date. William Monk (*monacus*) was accidentally killed in Normandy in 1145 (Robert of Torigni, *Chron.*, p. 150); Spileman the chamberlain died c.1150 (*H.K.F.*, p. 173). Richard de Haia, who was *dapifer Normannie* in the time of Geoffrey of Anjou, survived until 1169 and Serlo the hunter until 1179.

1. *Regesta*, ii. 438, places his death in 1133; Beamont, *A History of Halton and Norton*, p. 9, in 1134, but Beamont is unreliable.

36. Grant to the abbey of Basingwerk of the manor of Fulbrook with all its rights and possessions including specifically a silver mine on its land.

Rhuddlan, [c.1135]

P.R.O., C.53 (Chancery Charter Rolls), no. 18, m. 6.
Ed.: *Cal. Ch. Rolls*, ii. 289.

Notum sit omnibus sancte matris ecclesie filiis, tam presentibus quam futuris, quod ego Ranulphus comes Cestrie do et confirmo deo et sancte Marie et monachis de Basingwerk unam maneriam, scilicet Fulebrok, cum omnibus libertatibus et pertinentiis suis in campis, in silvis, in aquis et in omnibus aliis aisiamentis, et nominatim mineriam argenti que est super terram prefatam. Hanc ergo donacionem do deo et sancte Marie et monachis de ordine Saveneie pro salute anime mee et domini mei regis Henrici et omnium antecessorum meorum. Quare volo et firmiter precipio ut hanc prefatam elemosinam liberam et quietam absolutam ab omni seculari actione teneant et possideant. Testibus Willelmo constabulario, Roberto dapifero, Normanno de Verdun, Turstano Banastre, Ricardo pincerna, Serlone venatore, Gaufrido dispensatore, Ricardo filio Aluredi, cum ceteris pluribus apud Rueland.

The abbey of Basingwerk in Flintshire was founded by Ranulf II in 1131 as a house of the order of Savigny and became Cistercian in 1147. Fulbrook was situated nearby in the vicinity of Holywell (*D.S.C.*, p. 235), which was given to Basingwerk with Ranulf's consent by Robert Pierrepont (*Cal. Ch. Rolls*, ii. 290). The formulation of the reference to Henry I in the present charter suggests strongly that it was issued before his death on 1 December 1135. If so, it cannot have been much earlier, since Robert the steward only succeeded his father Ralph about this time (*Chart. St. Werburgh*, p. 287). Apart from the present charter and the gift of Caldy in Wirral (**no. 37**), it is known from a confirmation of Henry II (*Mon.*, v. 263) that Ranulf II also gave land at Lache in Marlston (*Orm.*, ii. 822), 100s. from the rents of Chester, and the chapel of Basingwerk 'in which the monks originally remained'. The latter was presumably the foundation charter of 1131; but unfortunately it has not survived.

37.   Grant to the abbey of Basingwerk of the manor of Caldy in Wirral with all rights, excepting only his warren and the pleas of the warren which he will hear in the abbey's court.

Chester, [19 November 1135–1140]

P.R.O., CHES 33/4 (Forest Rolls, 20–21 Edw. III), m. 30v. (A): CHES 33/6 (Forest Rolls, 27–31 Edw. III), m. 47 (B): D.L. 39/1/19 (Forest Pleas, 21 Edw. III) m. 27 (C)

Stephano regi Anglie, archiepiscopis, episcopis et omnibus sancte dei ecclesie filiis Ranulfus comes Cestrie, et constabulario suo et dapifero et omnibus baronibus suis et hominibus Anglie et Normannie et Wallie salutem. Sciatis me dedisse et concessisse ecclesie sancte Marie de Basyngwerke et monachis[1] ibi deo servientibus unam maneriam,[2] in Wyrhale Caldhers nomine cum omnibus rebus eidem ville pertinentibus in terris et in aquis et omnibus consuetudinibus libere et quiete in liberam elemosinam, ut eodem modo habeant et teneant eandem elemosinam quo habui die qua eam eis dedi, proxima die ante festum sancti Edmundi. Et nichil inde excipio preter warennam meam et placita warenne, que concedo et volo ut per me tractentur in curia sancte Marie ibidem, et hoc pro salute anime mee et uxoris mee et antecessorum meorum. Et omnes excommunicentur de deo et sancte Maria et sancte ecclesia, qui hanc elemosinam minuent aut decrescent de aliqua re. Teste Matillida comitissa et Roberto dapifero, Gaufrido de Nosburc et Gaufrido dispensatore, Roberto de Petrapunt et Willelmo filio Serlonis et Henrico Pultrell et Ricardo pincerna, Willelmo albo[3] et Hugone de Ardena et Spileman camerario et Meino capellano et Iohanne magistro et aliis quam pluribus, apud Cestriam.

1.   *om. MSS.*
2.   *sic MSS.*
3.   abbo *B.*

This charter has only previously been known from a brief entry in a confirmation of Henry II (*Mon.*, v. 263) and from mention in a lawsuit between Basingwerk and St. Werburgh's in 1287 (Orm., ii. 485). Since neither includes address or witnesses, it is impossible to determine the date of the grant. In fact, the address to King Stephen shows that it is later in date than Ranulf's grant of Fulbrook to Basingwerk (**no. 36**). It also shows that it was issued at a time when relations between Ranulf and Stephen were good, and at latest before the open breach between them in 1140. Of the witnesses Meinus the chaplain witnessed Ranulf's charter of 1141–45 for his wife, the Countess Matilda (**no. 59**) and William *albus* (White) witnessed a charter of approximately the same date for Belvoir priory (**no. 50**). Robert de Pierrepont granted Holywell to Basingwerk with Earl Ranulf's consent (*Cal. Ch. Rolls*, ii. 290). For Henry Pultrel, see **nos. 84** and **85**, and for Hugh of Arden (rather a surprising witness to find at Chester) see *Book of Seals*, p. 33 (no. 46). Unfortunately none of the attestations helps to narrow the limit of date, nor is it clear whether the date of Ranulf's gift – the day before the feast of St. Edmund, or 19 November – is also the date of his charter, though that is probably the case.

38. Grant of a salthouse in Northwich to the abbey of Basingwerk.

[c. 1140–1150]

P.R.O., CHES 2/36 (Recog. Rolls, 26–27 Edw. III), m. 3v.[1] Cal.: *36th Rep. D.K.P.R.*, p. 25.

1. In bad condition, and only legible with ultra-violet ray.

Ranulphus comes Cestrie constabulario suo et omnibus ministris suis salutem. Sciatis me dedisse et concessisse abbatie mee de Basingwerk unam salinam in Northwych cum omni tolneto et consuetudine, libere et quiete sicut ego meas possideo. Et precipio ne aliquis de meis ministris de hac elemosina se intromittat contra voluntatem illorum quibus dedi predictam salinam, scilicet monachis de Basyngwerk. Teste Adam de Praeriis, Serlone venatore,[1] Willelmo Blundo, Spileman camerario, Hugone filio Oliveri.[2]

1. Sexlnen *for* Serl. ven. *MS.*
2. Ov[er]i *for* O[li]v[er]i *MS.*

This charter is not easy to date, but appears to be later than **nos. 36** and **37**, though Adam de Praers, reputed founder of the family of Praers of Barthomley (Orm., iii. 299), is already found as a witness before 1119, if Earl Richard's charter for St. Werburgh's (**no. 8**) can be trusted, and does not appear after c.1145. William *blundus* is probably identical with William *albus* of Ranulf's charter granting Caldy to Basingwerk (**no. 37**), and also witnessed his charter of 1136–38 for Geva Ridel (**no. 39**). For Hugh son of Oliver, who witnessed Robert

Pierrepont's gift of Holywell to Basingwerk (*Cal. Ch. Rolls*, p. 290), see **no. 98**. He was still alive under Hugh II and witnessed two of his charters (**nos. 157, 158**) for Poulton. On the whole, a date c.1140–1150 seems to be indicated, but the evidence is inconclusive.

39.   Confirmation to Geva Ridel, daughter of Earl Hugh, of Drayton Basset (Staffs.), as given her in free marriage by her father.

'Sainzona', [1135–1138]

> B.L. Harl. MS. 294, f. 248v.; Harl. 380, f. 27; Harl. 2044, f. 1 (new f. 26); Harl. 2060, f. 39 (new f. 23v.); Bodleian Library, Dugdale MS. 15, f. 11. All copies are from the Basset cartulary in Arundel House in 1638. Ed.: *Hist. Coll. of Staffordshire*, iii. 187; Orm., i. 15.

Ranulfus comes Cestrie Willelmo constabulario et Rodberto dapifero et omnibus baronibus suis et hominibus Francis et Anglis totius Anglie salutem. Sciatis me dedisse et concessisse Geve Ridel filie comitis Hughez[1] Draitunam cum pertinentiis in libero coniugio, sicuti comes Hughez ei in libero coniugio dedit et concessit. Et teneat bene et in pace, honorifice et libere, ut melius et liberius tenuit tempore Hugonis comitis et aliorum meorum antecessorum, eisdem consuetudinibus et libertatibus. Testibus Gileberto filio Ricardi et Adeliza sorore mea, et Willelmo Blundo, et Alexandro de Tresgoz, et Rogero de Bellocampo, et Willelmo de Sais et Rodberto de Sais, et Ricardo filio Aluredi, et Hugone filio Osberti, et Henrico de Chaldri.[2] Apud Sainzonam.[3]

1.   Hughes, *Harl. 2044 and 2060*; Huez, *Dugdale 15*.
2.   Chalder, *Harl. 2044 and 2060*.
3.   Saintonam, *Harl. 2044 and 2060*.

Geva, one of the illegitimate children of Hugh I, married Geoffrey Ridel (who perished in the White Ship in 1120), and received Drayton as her marriage settlement. She survived at least until 1145, when she founded the priory of Canwell in Staffordshire (*Mon.*, iv. 105), but must have died shortly afterwards, as there is a later charter (**no. 40**) of Earl Ranulf conferring Drayton on her grandsons, Geoffrey Ridel and Ralph Basset, the children of her daughter Matilda, who had married Richard Basset in 1123 (*Regesta*, iii. no. 1389). The present charter has erroneously been attributed to Ranulf I and dated 1120 or soon after (Orm., i. 15). If Robert the steward only succeeded his father shortly before 1136 (*Chart. St. Werburgh*, p. 287), it must fall between then and 1138, when the first witness Gilbert fitz Richard, the son of Ranulf II's sister Adeliza, acquired the title of earl of Clare or Hertford. Adeliza had married Richard fitz Gilbert of Clare, who was killed in an encounter with the Welsh in 1136. The present charter indicates that she and her son then took refuge with Ranulf. Unfortunately, it has not proved possible to identify the place where the charter was issued. In the margin of Harl. MS. 2044 'Suttoniam' (presumably Sutton Basset in Northamptonshire) has been added in a different handwriting, but does not seem very plausible. Sandon (Staffs.) seems more likely, but is also not easily acceptable on etymological grounds.

40. Grant of Drayton Basset (Staffs.) to Geoffrey Ridel and Ralph Basset, the latter to hold of the former, with all the liberties with which Geoffrey Ridel, their grandfather, and Geva Ridel held it before them.

Castle Donington, Leics., [c.1150]

B.L. Harl. MS. 294, f. 248v.; Harl. 380, f. 27; Harl. 2060, f. 39 (new f. 23v.); Bodleian Library, Dugdale MS. 15, f. 11 (all from the Basset cartulary, in the possession of the earl of Arundel, 1638). Ed.: *Hist. Coll. of Staffordshire*, iii. 192.

Ranulfus comes Cestrie constabulario et dapifero, iusticiariis, baronibus, vicecomitibus, ministris et ballivis, et omnibus hominibus suis totius Anglie Francis et Anglicis clericis et laicis salutem. Sciatis me dedisse et reddidisse Galfrido Ridello et Radulfo Basset fratri suo ad tenendam de Galfrido Ridello Draitunam cum omnibus pertinentibus eidem manerio, illis et heredibus eorum ad tenendam de me et de meis heredibus iure hereditario, solutam et quietam et libere et quiete et cum omnibus libertatibus que eidem manerio pertinent et cum quibus libertatibus Galfridus Ridellus avus eorum et Geva Ridel uxor sua illum manerium tenuerunt una die et una nocte, et ita quod Galfridus Ridel et Radulfus Bassat debent mihi facere et heredibus meis servitium unius militis de manerio de Draituna, cum soc et cum sac et cum tol et cum tem et cum infrangenthef, in bosco et in plano, in villa et extra villam, in viis et in semitis, in pratis, in pascuis, in pasturis, in rivis, in aquis et molendinis et in omnibus locis. Testibus Hugone Wak, Simone filio Willelmi, Roberto dapifero,[1] Radulfo Manselle, Roberto Bassat, Roberto Banaster, Ranulfo vicecomite, Willelmo Bacun, Roberto filio Hugonis, Beringero falconario,[2] Willelmo Malbanc, Pagano de Cherera,[3] Roberto filio Hugonis vicecomitis, Ricardo filio eius, Rogero Pula, Ricardo de Clottona,[4] Radulfo de Ouvile.[5] Apud Dununtone.

---

1. *all the MSS (except Dugdale, where all the words are abbreviated, and Harl. 2060 which reads* dapifero) *have* Simone, Willelmo, Roberto dapiferis. *This makes no sense, and it seems clear that the first witness should be* Simone filio Willelmi (*of Kyme*), *a frequent witness of Ranulf II's charters.*
2. 'Folc' *MSS.*

3. Clierera [?] *Harl. 2060; almost certainly stands for* Cheverchi (*or an equivalent form*), *i.e.* Chaworth.
4. Dottona *Harl. 2060.*
5. Donvile *or* Sonvile, *Harl. 380.*

Geoffrey Ridel and Ralph Basset were the grandsons of Geva Ridel who was given Drayton by her father, Earl Hugh I. She was still alive c.1145 (**no. 39**), and the present grant must have followed her death, but its exact date is uncertain. Most of the witnesses appear in other charters of Ranulf II. Ranulf the sheriff, who attests half-a-dozen other charters, was one of the earl's three representatives who concluded the famous agreement between Ranulf II and the earl of Leicester (**no. 110**), dating from 1149 to 1153. Ralph Mansell and Pain Cheverchi (clearly identical with the Pain, or Paganus, of the present charter) together attest a writ for Calke (**no. 46**), dated 1142–1153. Robert Basset witnessed the grant of the constableship of Chester to Eustace fitz John in 1144–45 (**no. 73**), as did Simon fitz William of Kyme, a well-known figure who administered Cheshire on behalf of the Crown during the minority after Ranulf II's death. William Bacon appears in **no. 67**, probably issued in 1143–45, and Robert Banastre witnessed Ranulf's charter to Lancaster priory in 1149 (**no. 88**). William Malbank, who survived until 1176, as did Hugh Wake (*H.K.F.*, p. 170), and Robert the steward (*dapifer*) both succeeded in or about 1136. But if most of the witnesses are well attested, others are not. Robert son of Hugh witnessed Ranulf II's gift of Eastham and Bromborough to St. Werburgh's, in all probability in 1153 (**no. 34**), but *Robertus filius Hugonis vicecomitis*, if it is the same person, is otherwise unknown, and it is difficult to explain the double appearance, unless there was a mistake in copying, as there certainly was in the case of Simon fitz William (cf. note 1). The charter has been dated c.1150 (*Hist. Coll. of Staffordshire*, iii. 192), a suggestion which is borne out by the names of the witnesses and the style and formulation of the charter, which is matched in other grants of the period (**nos. 69, 89**).

41.   Grant to Garendon abbey of a boat on the river Dee.

[1135–1145]

Facsimile of the original deed in the collection of William
Hamper, in Nichols, *Leicestershire*, IV, plate lxi, p. 411.

R. comes Cestrensis constabuloni et dapifero et omnibus baronibus suis et hominibus Francis et Anglis, et nominatim iusticie[1] et vicecomitibus[1] suis Cestriȩ salutem. Sciatis me dedisse et concessisse sanctȩ Mariȩ et suis monachis Gerodoniȩ, unam naviculam in perpetuum elemosinam liberam et quietam pro salute animȩ meȩ et antecessorum meorum ad piscandum ad pontem Cestriȩ et ubicumque voluerint in aqua Cestrensi. Teste Matildide comitissa et Willelmo constabulone et Serlone venatore et Ricardo monacho et magistro Iohanne.[2]

SEAL: on strip from left-hand side of charter, missing.

1. *sic original.*
2. *The use of the 'e' caudata in this charter is noteworthy.*

Ranulf is said to have married Matilda, daughter of Robert earl of Gloucester, before 1135. William the constable died before 1146, probably in 1143 or 1144 (*Stenton Misc.*, pp. 27, 30, 34). A closer dating seems to be impossible. Serlo the huntsman is a frequent witness of Earl Ranulf's charters (see **nos. 35, 36, 38, 43, 55, 56, 59, 85, 90, 113**), in the case of **no. 59** together with Master John. Richard Monk (*monachus* is in this instance a patronymic) was sheriff of the land of the earl of Chester in the island of Guernsey in 1156 (Robert of Torigni, *Chron.*, p. 335). The earl of Chester's interests in Guernsey are occasionally referred to in the cartulary of Mont Saint Michel (Bibl. Avranches, 210), but nothing more specific appears to be known, and no charters have survived. Among tenants of the earl of Chester, Baldwin Wake and Robert Patric both held lands on the island (*Rot. Scacc. Norm.*, ii, 385; MS. Paris lat. 10072 and 5430A, p. 281).

42.   Confirmation of a grant by the countess of Chester to Poyns her servant of lands near Chester castle.

[1135–1150]

Abstract (in English) from a charter formerly in the archives of the earl of Shrewsbury, Orm., i. 356 and ii. 546.

Earl Ranulf confirms the gift to Poyns, the servant of the countess, of 'lands between the bridge gate and the castle and a messuage, held by the service attached to these lands, which had been given by the countess'. Witnesses Fulco de Bricasart, Benedict brother of the earl, William pincerna, Philip the chamberlain, and others.

It is surprising that no other copy of this interesting charter exists. It was in the possession of William Hamper in 1807 but disappeared subsequently, possibly in the fire at the Birmingham Reference Library in 1879, when most of Hamper's collection perished, or more probably, if it was still among the Shrewsbury muniments, in the fire at Ingestre in 1883. It has been variously attributed to Ranulf I and to Ranulf III, but, as the list of witnesses shows, it was indubitably a charter of Ranulf II. Fulk de Briquessart, who also witnesses **nos. 88** and **98**, may have been an illegitimate son of Ranulf I, who was also known as Ranulf de Briquessart, but was more probably his nephew. William the butler (*pincerna*) of the earl of Chester died c.1150 (*E.C.C.*, p 3). Philip the chamberlain (*camerarius*) witnessed at least four other charters of Ranulf II (**nos. 22, 35, 55, 59**). For Benedict brother of the earl, an illegitimate son of Ranulf I, see **no. 153**. This is the only mention of Countess Matilda's servant, Poyns, but W.F. Irvine has traced the history of the piece of land conferred on him, known variously as 'Punciescroft', 'Ponssus croft' and 'Poyntz's croft' (*Ches. Sheaf*, nos. 9544, 9550). The present document was obviously issued after Ranulf II's marriage (c.1135), but otherwise could fall at any time before the death of William the butler.

43.   Grant of Gawsworth to Hugh son of Bigod.

> London, College of Arms, MS. 1 D. 14, p. 269 ('ex evidenciis Edwardi Fyton de Gouseworth militis'); Bodleian Library, Dodsworth MS. 31, f. 102; MS. Top. Cheshire b. I, p. 136; B.L. Harl. MS. 2074, f. 184v. (new f. 81v.); Harl. MS. 2079, f. 16 (new f. 8); Chester, Booth of Twemlow, Liber D, f. 150; Shakerley MSS. Liber C, f. 247v. Ed: *Stenton Misc.*, p. 31 (no. 3).

Ranulfus comes Cestrie Willelmo constabulario et Roberto dapifero et iusticie sue de Cestrescira salutem. Notum sit vobis me concessisse et in feodo et hereditate dedisse Hugoni filio Bigodi et heredibus suis tenendum de me et heredibus meis Gouswurth cum pertinentiis suis in planis et nemoribus, in pratis et pascuis, in viis et semitis, in aquis et molendinis, et tac et tem et curiam suam ita libere et quiete et in pace et honorabiliter habeat et teneat ut alicui homini, et nominatim erga prefectos de Macclesfeldia non placitet nec respondeat. Hec omnia concessi ipso mihi donante quendam apreciatum equum in meo talamo Cestrie, hiis autem existentibus testibus Waltheuo filio Wlfrici et Hugone filio Osberti et Serlone venatore et Ricardo Bacone et Ranulfo venatore et Galfrido hostiario et Roberto filio Gocetalini.

[1136–45]

Hugh son of Bigod was a son, probably a younger son, of Bigod des Loges, the Domesday tenant *inter alia* of North Rode, Nether Alderley and Siddington (*D.S.C.*, pp. 53, 185), all in the immediate vicinity of Gawsworth, and two of the witnesses, Waltheof son of Wulfric and Robert son of Joscelin, were also sons of Domesday tenants. The date of Ranulf II's charter must fall between 1136, when Robert the steward had succeeded his father Ralph (*Chart. St. Werburgh*, p. 287), and the death of William the constable in 1144 or 1145 (*Stenton Misc.*, p. 27). Richard Bacon was the founder, c.1142–3, of Rocester abbey; his mother was apparently a natural daughter of Ranulf I, and he referred to Ranulf II as his uncle (*H.K.F.*, pp. 257–8).

44. Confirmation of Ranulf I's and Countess Lucy's gift of the churches of Belchford, Scamblesby and Minting to Spalding priory.

[1138–1141]

> B.L. Add. MS. 35296 (Spalding register), f. 386; Add. MS. 5844 (copy of preceding), f. 429 (new f. 218).

Ego Ranulphus iunior comes Cestrie hac mea carta presenti confirmo et in perpetuam elemosinam concedo donacionem ecclesiarum de Lindesei, de Beltisford, de Scamelisbi, de Mintingis, cum omnibus earum appendiciis monachis ecclesie beate Marie et beati Nichalai de Spaldingis, qui ibidem deo servient, sicut Ranulphus comes Cestrie pater meus et Lucia comitissa mater mea dederunt eis et concesserunt in presencia Alexandri Lincolniensis episcopi et postea a domino H. rege optinuerunt quatinus predicta donacio ipsius sigillo confirmaretur. Hiis testibus Willelmo de Romara fratre meo, Roberto Marmioun, Anketino barbato, et aliis.

This charter is a confirmation of **no. 14.** Although a little irregular in form (probably due to the copyist of the cartulary), there is no reason to question its authenticity. It was presumably issued before William of Roumare became earl of Lincoln in 1141 and after the death of Countess Lucy which occurred c. 1138. Robert Marmion II died in 1144. *Anketinus barbatus* may be identical with Anschetil the serjeant, who is mentioned in Ranulf II's gift of Waddington to Hugh Bardulf (**no. 66**).

45. Confirmation to the canons of Calke of the gifts which Earl Richard made for the restoration of their buildings, of land in Ticknall and the chapel of Smisby given by Nicholas the priest, and of Geva Ridel's gift of a messuage in Tamworth; also his own gift of a boat on the river Dee and of the land of Loftcote, and of a court as fully as the earl holds his court in Repton.

Castle Donington, [1138–1147]

> Cambridge Univ. Library, Add. MS. 3917 (Blore Collection), f. 26 (from original). Ed.: *Stenton Misc.*, pp. 32–3.

+ Domino Rogero gratia dei Cestre si episcopo universoque clero tocius Cestrensis episcopatus et omnibus sancte ecclesie filiis Rannulfus comes Cestrie, insuper et constabulario, dapifero, iustic(ie), vicecom(iti), ministris, balivis, necnon et omnibus hominibus suis Francis et Anglis salutem. Notum sit omnibus Christiane religionis fidelibus me concessisse et confirmasse donacionem ecclesie sancti Egidii de Calc et dominis canonicis ibidem deo servientibus cum omnibus incrementis et elemosinis, quas Ricardus comes eum locum ad restaurandum et edificandum donavit, videlicet silvam in quam habitant inter Seggburgebroc et Alrebroc, et parvam gillibergam, et culturam inter Alrebroc et Sudwde, et parvum molendinum Rapendone, et iiii. bovatas terre in Tichehale, et ex dono Nicholai sacerdotis ii. bovatas in eadem villo, et capellam Smithesbi. Insuper et ex dono Geve Ridel unam mansuram terre in Tamwurtha. Et ex meo dono cum omnibus supranominatis concedo eis pro salute anime mee et anime patris mei et matris et antecessorum meorum i. batum in piscatura Cestrie, ubicumque voluerint,[1] ad piscandum, et hoc cum una mansura terre ad opus eorum piscatoris, et nominatim terram Lofdcot, videlicet[2] sicut via descendit[3] de Rapendona ad fontem Neuhathewelle, et sicut idem fons descendit[3] usque ad metas Meeltone, et ex altera parte sicut terminus Meeltone est, usque ad capud Loftesco. Insuper ad honorem dei et supradicte ecclesie dono eis eorum curiam, tam plenariam quam habeo meam in Rapendona, cum tol et tem et infag-genthef, cum omnibus consuetudinibus quas ego vel aliquis antecessorum meorum eis melius et plenarius eis[4] concedere potuerit. Et wolo[5] et precipio quod teneant libere et honorifice et quiete in bosco et in plano, in pratis et aquis, in viis et semitis, in foro et mercato, in molendinis et in omnibus locis et omnibus rebus, et nominatim volo quod de bosco meo habeant copiam ad omnia sua edeficia et ad ignem. Et precipio omnibus meis ne aliquis presumat impedire eis in aliquo. Precor etiam vicinos et hominibus meis precipio per fidem quam mihi debent, eos et omnia sua protegere et defendere et manutenere et diligere ut corpus et animam meam. Et inde sunt testes: Radulfus capellanus comitis et Ricardus capellanus, Iohannes capellanus, Willelmus capellanus, Nicholaus sacerdos Rapendone, Gilbertus comes de Clara, Willelmus[6] de Ferreres, Ricardus pincerna, Rogerus nepos comitis, Robertus Basset, Robertus pincerna de Hegglebi, et pluribus aliis apud Dunigtunam.

> SEAL: obverse, equestrian, head and hands wanting; legend . . . ANNUL[F]I . . . ITI . . . Reverse: an oval counterseal, perfect; a female figure facing to dexter, resting on pillar; legend CONTRASIGILLUM DOMINI CESTRIE

1. voluerit *MS*.
2. inde licet *MS*.
3. decendit *MS*.
4. *sic MS*.
3. *sic MS*, W *underlined*.
6. Willelmo *MS*.

The Augustinian priory of Calke in Derbyshire is usually stated to have been founded c.1130–36. This charter shows that it was already in existence in the time of Earl Richard (1101–1120). Its date must fall between 1138, when Gilbert of Clare was made earl of Hertford, and May 1147, when Bishop Roger Clinton of Chester departed on crusade. The witness William Ferrers was presumably the son of Robert Ferrers, earl of Derby, who succeeded his father in 1160, and later confirmed the church of East Leake (Notts.) to Calke (*Book of Seals*, no. 34). Roger, nephew of the earl, was the brother of Earl Gilbert, and succeeded to the title on the latter's death in 1152. For the two butlers, Richard and Robert, see *E.C.C.*, pp. 3–5; for Geva Ridel, an illegitimate daughter of Hugh I, see **no. 39**.

46.   Order that the prior and canons of Calke are to have sufficient charcoal from Southwood for one forge.

[1142–1153]

> Cambridge Univ. Library, Add. MS. 3917 (Blore Collection), f. 27 (from original). Ed.: *Stenton Misc.*, p. 33 (no. 5).

Ranulfus comes Cestrie conestabulario, dapifero suo, omnibus ministris suis, omnibus baronibus, omnibus hominibus suis Francis et Anglis salutem. Sciatis me dedisse et concessisse priori de Calc et canonicis licentiam facere et parare et habere carbones in Sutwde satis et sufficienter ad unam forgam. Quare mando vobis et precipio, quod nullus eis vel alicui suorum aliqua causa impediat. Testibus Hugone austrecario et Galfrido dispensatore et Pagano Cheverchi et Ricardo pincerna et Radulfo Mansello.

For the approximate date of this writ and the witnesses, see *Stenton Misc.*, pp. 32–3.

47.   Writ to Richard de Veim and other vavasours of Bisley (Gloucs.) ordering them to do their service henceforth to Miles the constable of Gloucester.

[?1140]

> Orig.: P.R.O., D.L. Ancient Correspondence, no. 1. Ed.: Stenton, *First Century of English Feudalism*, p. 257.

R. comes Cestrie Ricardo de Veim ceterisque vavassoribus suis de Biseleia salutem. Precipio vobis quod amodo intendatis servicium vestrum Miloni constabulario, ita benigne sicut umquam melius fecistis. Valete.

> SEAL: on tongue, equestrian; fragmented and indecipherable.

Bisley had been part of the Chester fee since the time of Domesday, and the turning over of it to Miles of Gloucester is hard to explain except in relation to the civil wars following the arrival in England of the Empress Matilda in the late summer of 1139. Miles of Gloucester was one of the first to go over to her, and she eventually created him earl of Hereford on 25 July 1141. The present writ must date from before then; the question is how long before. Stenton (*loc. cit.*) cautiously dates it 1129–41. Farrer (*H.K.F.*, p. 51) thinks it was issued soon after 1130, but without advancing any reason. Any dating must be tentative, but it is hard to think of any reason for such a grant until Ranulf himself deserted to the Angevin cause and joined forces with Miles and Robert of Gloucester. This would have been in 1140, and that is the most probable date for the writ. In any case, the alienation was only temporary, as is shown by Earl Hugh's charter restoring Bisley to Miles of Gloucester's son-in-law, Humphrey de Bohun (**no. 180**); it was presumably a temporary arrangement for the conduct of the war, which ceased with the restoration of peace, or even with Miles' death in 1143.

48.   Gift to the abbey of Louth Park of land and pastures in Tetney (Lincs.)

[1140–1153]

> P.R.O. C.53 (Chancery Charter Rolls, 10 Edw. III), m.
> 17. Ed.: *Mon.*, v. 414 (from preceding); *Cal. Ch. Rolls*,
> iii. 247. see also *H.K.F.*, p. 93.

. . . ex dono Ranulfi comitis Cestrie terras et pasturas quas dedit eis in Teteneia, cum ceteris adiacentiis in aquis et salinis, in mariscis, in pratis.

This monastery was founded by Bishop Alexander of Lincoln in 1137 and transferred to Louth Park in 1139. The above brief notice from a confirmation by Henry II in 1155, recited in an *inspeximus* of Edward II (*Cal. Ch. Rolls*, iii. 247), is the only evidence of Ranulf II's gift, but there is no reason to doubt its authenticity. The date of his grant falls between 1140 and his death in 1153. There is also mention of a gift by Ranulf earl of Chester of his meadow in Huttoft (*Cal. Ch. Rolls*, iii. 265), but the context suggests that this was Ranulf III.

49.   Writ to his men of Wiltshire, notifying them that he has given the tithe of his fee, which Richard de Cruce used to hold and which is held by Richard Pasturel of the fee of the earl of Lincoln, to the chapel of Wilsford and to Roger, subcantor of Salisbury.

[1140–1153]

Orig.: Dean and Chapter of Salisbury, Fourth Press, Box
E.5. Ed.: *Hist. MSS. Comm., Report on Various Collections*, i. 371; W.H. Rich Jones, *Register of St. Osmund*, i.
265; *Ches. Sheaf*, no. 2900 (from *H.M.C.* report).

Comes Rannulfus Cestrie omnibus hominibus suis de Wiltescira salutem. Sciatis
quoniam dedi et concessi in elemosinam perpetuam capelle de Wivelesford et
Rogero subcantori Sarum decimam feodi mei, quod Ricardus de Cruce tenere
solebat, et quod Ricardus Pasturel tenet de feodo comitis Lincolnie, ad hostium
grangie semper recipiendam decimam garbam et plenariam decimam de agnis et
porcellis et omnibus rebus unde decima dari debet. Et ideo precipio quod eam
amodo in pace teneant. Valete.

SEAL: on tongue cut from foot of parchment, missing.

Very little is known of the earl of Chester's landholdings in Wiltshire, and the
present document is no exception. It is dated 1129 by the editor of the Register
of St. Osmund, and in the reign of Stephen in the Report of the Historical
Manuscripts Commission. The reference to the fee of the earl of Lincoln
indicates a date after 1140, but how the land in question came to be transferred
to the earl of Lincoln (presumably Ranulf II's brother, William of Roumare) is
not known. Richard de Cruce gave land in Chester to St. Werburgh's abbey
during the time of Ranulf I and apparently became a monk there (**no. 13**); it
would seem that his son Norman did not succeed to his Wiltshire estate.

50. Notification that he has made himself advocate and defender of the monks
of Belvoir, and has given them the same rights as St. Werburgh's abbey in
Chester.

[? 1141]

Belvoir Castle, Rutland MSS., small cartulary of Belvoir
priory, f. 57.

R.[1] comes Cestrie archiepiscopis, episcopis et omnibus fidelibus sancte ecclesie
clericis et laicis salutem. Notum vobis sit me recepisse monachos de Belveer cum
rebus eorum in mea advocatione et defensione sicuti meam propriam
elemosinam. Precipio igitur ut ipsi monachi omnium rerum suarum curam
habeant et dominium, scilicet in ecclesiis, decimis et omnibus aliis rebus, sicut
melius habuerunt temporibus antecessorum meorum, et ita libere et quiete
teneant[2] sicut tenet abbas sancte Werburge Cestrensis ecclesie. Precipio etiam
ne aliquis eos sub aliqua occasione nisi ante me placitare faciat aut in aliquo

vexare presumat super forisfacturam meam. Teste Radulfo abbate Cestrie, Rodberto dapifero et Gaufrido dispensatore et Willelmo Albo. Valete.

1. *Blank space for initial; small 'r' in margin MS.*
2. teneneant *MS.*

This hitherto unknown charter is mainly interesting for the light it throws upon Ranulf II's aims and ambitions in the Midlands. The priory of Belvoir, together with the honour and castle, had passed, apparently towards the end of Henry I's reign, to William d'Aubigny *Brito* in marriage with the granddaughter of the founder of Belvoir priory, Robert de Tosny (*Hist. MSS. Comm., Rutland MSS.,* iv. 106–7). Some time after 1140, in circumstances which have not been clarified, Ranulf II laid hands on William's inheritance, and the present charter shows him deliberately assuming William's rights as patron of Belvoir priory. The date must be after 22 January 1141, when Ralph became abbot of Chester. Unfortunately, it is not possible to limit the date more closely, but the implication is that Ranulf was already in full control of Belvoir when this charter was issued. Such other evidence as is available (*T.R.H.S.,* 4th Ser. xx, pp. 118–19) suggests that this occurred in the months following the battle of Lincoln (2 February 1141), and it would certainly be in character if Ranulf wasted no time in asserting his alleged rights.

51.   Notification that he has taken the monks of Belvoir under his protection and order for them to have their manor of Horninghold (Leics.) and other possessions as freely and peaceably as they ever held them.

[? 1141–1142]

Belvoir Castle, Rutland MSS., Belvoir cartulary, f. 58v. (A), and small cartulary, f. 57 (B). Cal. (from A): *Hist. MSS. Comm., Rutland MSS.,* iv. 136–7.

R.[1] comes Cestrie omnibus ministris et fidelibus suis salutem. Notum vobis sit me recepisse monachos de Belvedeir cum omnibus rebus suis in mea advocacione et defensione sicuti meam elemosinam. Precipio igitur ut ipsi monachi[2] in sua cura et dominio habeant manerium suum de Horningwald[3] necnon et omnia, que ad ecclesiam illorum pertinent, et ita libere et quiete teneant sicut unquam melius tenuerunt temporibus antecessorum meorum, et nullus sub aliqua occasione se intromittat[4] super eos de rebus eorum, nisi per me. Precipio etiam et concedo ut Heldewinus homo illorum se intromittat de Horningwald[3] sic firmiter, libere et quiete sicut fecit tempore Willelmi de Albineio,[5] si tamen concesserint monachi. Valete.

1. *space for initial*; small r *in margin B.*
2. *om. A.*
3. Horningwold *A.*
4. *Followed in A by* de Horningwold sed firmiter, *but these words deleted by points.*
5. Albeneio *B.*

The date of this charter is probably a little later than that of **no. 50**, the wording of which it follows closely, but not much later. Like **no. 50**, it asserts Ranulf II's rights as advocate of Belvoir priory, this time with specific reference to Horninghold, and the phrase 'in the time of William d'Aubigny' explicitly indicates that Ranulf had taken William's place as lord of Belvoir. This, as suggested in the note to **no. 50**, probably occurred in the course of 1141, and the present charter is unlikely to be much later in date.

52. Notification to the bishop of Lincoln, the archdeacon of Leicester and the whole convent of St. Mary of Lincoln that the church of Redmile (Leics.) is founded in the land and fee of Robert Basset, and confirmation of his gift of it to the monks of Belvoir.

[1141–1147]

Belvoir Castle, Rutland MSS., Belvoir cartulary, f. 71v.
Cal.: *Hist. MSS. Comm., Rutland MSS.*, iv. 147.

A. dei gratia Lincolniensi episcopo et Waltero archidiacono Legrecestrie ac toti conventui sancte Marie Lincolnie et omnibus filiis sancte ecclesie Ranulfus comes Cestrie salutem. Noverit universitas vestra ecclesiam de Redmild esse fundatam in terra et feudo Roberti Basset, et sua est, et concedo quod voluntatem suam in racione faciat. Preterea confirmo donacionem quam ille fecit monachis de Belveir in elemosinam. Teste Gaufrido Malebisse et Ricardo Bacun.

The church of Redmile had been given to Belvoir priory by William d'Aubigny (Belvoir cart., f. 71v). It would appear that, after William's dispossession by Ranulf II (**no. 50**), the latter enfeoffed Robert Basset with Redmile, who then granted, or more accurately re-granted, the church to the monks of Belvoir 'by consent of his lord Earl Ranulf for the redemption of that earl's soul' (Belvoir cart., *loc. cit.*) The present charter is a confirmation of Robert's gift. It must fall before the death of Bishop Alexander of Lincoln on 20 February 1148, perhaps before 1145 (*T.R.H.S.*, 4th Ser. xx, p. 120), but an accurate date is impossible. Richard Bacon, Earl Ranulf's nephew, was the founder of Rocester abbey (**no. 68**).

53.   Grant to Belvoir priory of a bovate of land in Woolsthorpe (Lincs.)

[1141–1147]

Belvoir Castle, Rutland MSS., Belvoir cartulary, f. 98v.
Cal.: *Hist. MSS. Comm.*, *Rutland MSS.*, iv. 167.

Matilda comitissa Cestrie constabulario, dapifero, baronibus, castellanis, ius-
tic(iario), vic(ecomiti), ministris et ballidis, et omnibus hominibus suis Francis et
Anglis salutem. Sciatis me dedisse in elemosinam monachis sancte Marie de
Belvario i. bovatam terre quam Kocscelinus tenet in Wulstorp cum servitio
ipsius Kocscelini et uxoris sue. Eapropter precipio quod ipsi monachi predictam
elemosinam teneant bene in honorem dei pro salute anime comitis[1] Cestrie
domini mei et mee. Teste comite Willelmo Lincolnie et Willelmo de Colevilla et
aliis.

1.   comitiss[e] *MS.*

This is another of the grants made after Ranulf II took possession of the honour
of Belvoir (**no. 50**). It cannot be dated very closely. William de Colville was one
of the witnesses of Ranulf's grant of Wheatley to his brother, William earl of
Lincoln (**no. 70**) and the present charter may date from approximately the same
time.

54.   Confirmation of Countess Matilda's grant to Belvoir priory of a bovate of
land in Woolsthorpe (Lincs.)

[1141–1147]

Belvoir Castle, Rutland MSS., Belvoir cartulary, ff. 98v.–
99. Cal.: *Hist. MSS. Comm.*, *Rutland MSS.*, iv. 167.

Rannulfus comes Cestrie constabulario, dapifero, baronibus, iusticiario, castellanis, vic(ecomiti), ministris et ballidis, et omnibus hominibus suis Francis et
Anglis salutem. Proculdubio sciatis me concessisse et carta mea confirmasse
donacionem illam quam Matilda comitissa mea Cestrie fecit pro salute anime
mee deo et sancte Marie et monachis ecclesie sancte Marie de Belvario de una
bovata terre quam Kocscelinus tenet in Wulstorp cum servicio ipsius Kocscellini
et uxoris sue. Quare volo et firmiter precipio quod ipsi monachi prefatam
elemosinam bene et honorifice et libere et quete teneant, ne aliquis eos super
amorem dei et meum honorem temere inquietet. Teste comite Willelmo
Lincolnie et Willelmo Colville et aliis.

Ranulf's confirmation has the same witnesses as Countess Matilda's gift (**No. 53**) and almost certainly was issued on the same occasion.

55. Gift to Robert Fumichon, his butler, of the land in Thorley (Lincs.) which Ralph of Claxby held, for the service of mewing one hawk a year when he left the court and went to his own home, but as long as he was in the earl's court, performing his duties there, he was to be free of that and all other services; for which gift Robert had given the earl a roan war-horse in the earl's house at Lincoln in the presence of his barons.

Lincoln, [1141–1143]

Orig.: P.R.O., D.L. 36/2 (Cart. Misc.), f. 74: Transcr.: D.L. 42/2 (Coucher Book II), ff. 252–252v. Ed.: Stenton, *Danelaw Charters*, pp. 362–3.

R. comes Cestrie constabulario, dapifero, baronibus vic(ecomitibus), ministris et ballidis et omnibus hominibus suis de Lindesia Francis et Anglis salutem. Sciatis me dedisse in feodo et hereditate Roberto de Folmuc(hon) pincerna et heredibus suis pro servicio suo, quod patri meo et mihi postea fecit, totam terram et tenuram de Tortlaia, quam Radulfus de Clachesbia ibi tenuit et habuit, in villa et extra, in hominibus et pecuniis, in bosco et plano, et in omnibus aliis rebus, ad tenendam de me ipse et heredes sui et de heredibus meis. Eapropter volo et firmiter precipio, quod predictus Robertus et heredes sui ita bene et honorifice predictam tenuram teneant cum omnibus libertatibus et consuetudinibus, sicut aliquis de baronibus meis Lindesie melius et honorabilius tenuram suam tenet, pro omni servicio mutando mihi singulis annis i. osturium, cum ad domum suam, sicut homo liber, a curia mea disscesserit.[1] Et quamdiu in curia mea ipse et heredes sui in mysterio mihi, sicut iustum fuerit, servierint, de illo et de omnibus aliis serviciis sint quieti. Et teneant bene et honorifice in villa et extra, in foro et mercato, in bosco et plano, in pratis et pascuis, in molendinis et aquis, in piscariis et stagnis, et in omnibus aliis locis, cum soca et saca et tol et theom et infangethef, ne super forisfactum meum ei vel suis iniuria vel contumelia fiat. Et pro hac concessione et donatione dedit mihi predictus Robertus i. falvum dextrarium bonum in presentia baronum meorum apud Lincolniam in domo mea. Testibus Normanno de Verdun et Rogero filio Ricardi, nepote comitis, et Roberto Grevesac et Gaufrido Malebisse et Mainone capellano et Ricardo pincerna et Gaufrido dispensario et Hugone osturcario et Serlone venatore et Roberto filio Hugonis et Willelmo pincerna et Waltero de Hambia et Willelmo de Costenciis et Philippo camerario et Spileman et Willelmo de Bovilla et Roberto de Boivilla et Ranulfo ostiario et Radulfo iusticia et Gaufrido nepote Bocardi et Gaufrido nepote Ricardi Bacun et

Turgerro Lincolniensi et Willelmo ac Ricardo capellanis et Herberto coco. Apud Lincolniam.

1. sic *orig.*

Fumichon is 6 kms. south-east of St. Lô on the road to Torigni. The family, variously described as Foumucon, Foumuzum and Folmuzum, occurs frequently in the cartulary of St. Evroul (MS. Paris lat. 11055), but there is no evidence that the recipient of the present charter had any contact with Normandy. He was evidently a minor officer, probably a younger son brought over from Normandy by Ranulf I, in the earl's Lincolnshire household, on a par with Spileman the chamberlain (for whom see **no. 93**) and Wimund the cook (**no. 80**), and Thorley was a small estate in Minting. It was still held in 1212 by serjeanty tenure by Robert's son, or possibly grandson (*H.K.F.*, p. 173), but there is no sign that the family prospered. Ranulf II's charter is nevertheless interesting for its precise definition of the terms of Robert's tenure, and also for its reference to the earl's house in Lincoln. This points to a date after 1140 and before 1146, when Ranulf had to surrender Lincoln to the king. Within these limits, it must be earlier than the grant of his father's lands to Wimund, son of Herbert the cook (**no. 80**), since Herbert, the last witness, was still alive when it was issued. As it is witnessed also by Robert Grevesac, who seems to have died or at least ceased to function by 1144 (**no. 70**), it probably falls within the period 1141–43. It is written by the same hand, almost certainly that of William (Barbe d'Averill) the chaplain, as **no. 66** (and also **nos. 56** and **82**), also given at Lincoln, but the witnesses are almost entirely different, and the present charter is probably a little earlier in date.

56.   Grant of Weekley (Northants.) to William the falconer, his man, as freely as he had held it from Ralph de Péronne.

Thorney, [1141–1143]

Orig.: Northants. Record Soc., Weekley Charters, Box 7, no. 3. Mentioned: Bridges, *Hist. and Antiq. of Northants.*, ii. 344.

Rannulfus consul Cestrie constabulario, dapifero, baronibus, iusticiario, vic(ecomiti), ministris et ballidis et omnibus[1] hominibus suis Francis et Anglis salutem. Scitote me reddidisse Willelmo osturcario homini meo Wichelaiam cum omnibus pertinenciis suis, sicut rectum suum. Eapropter volo et precipio quod ipse Willelmus et heredes sui de me et de heredibus meis predictam tenuram teneat ita bene et honorifice sicut tenere solebat de Radulfo de Perona, in villa et extra, in foro et mercato, in bosco et plano, in pratis et pasturis, in viis et semitis, in aquis et molendinis, et in omnibus aliis locis, cum soca et saca et tol et theom et cum infangetheof, et cum omnibus aliis libertatibus et consuetudinibus omnibus. Et si aliquo modo forte eveniret, quod ipsi Willelmo predictam tenuram warantizare non possem, escambium ei darem ad valens et ad warandum suum. Testibus Willelmo Coleville, Willelmo de Veci et Serlone venatore et Gaufrido dispensatore et Willelmo de Ferrariis et Hugone de Longo Campo et Gaufrido Barreido et Willelmo capellano, apud Thornehagh.

> SEAL missing, but tongue to which it was applied remains.

1. *repeated orig.*

For another charter given at Thorney (Notts.), see **no. 24.** The present charter, written, like **nos. 55** and **66,** in the hand of William (Barbe d'Averill), the earl's chaplain, is of approximately the same date, i.e. 1141–43, when Ranulf II, profiting from his victory at the battle of Lincoln, was busy consolidating his position in the Midlands (*T.R.H.S.*, 4th Ser. xx, p. 120). Ralph de Péronne, a prominent baron of the Vermandois, was one of the foreigners who joined Stephen as an auxiliary in 1138 (Ord. Vitalis, v. 109) and presumably lost his land after the battle of Lincoln. Geoffrey Barreidus is probably identical with the Geoffrey Barre who accounted for 5 marks in Notts. and Derby in 1176–77 (*P.R.S.*, xxvi, p. 59). William Ferrers witnessed Ranulf II's charter for Calke (**no. 45**); he was the son of Robert, earl of Derby, and succeeded to the earldom in 1162. This is the only occasion on which William the falconer is mentioned in Ranulf's charters, and it looks as though his appearance as the earl's 'man' was a temporary occurrence in the short period when Ranulf was building up adherents in the Midlands; he occurs later on the Northamptonshire Pipe Roll in 1155–6 and again in 1166–7, when the sheriff rendered account for 'Weekley of William the falconer' (*P.R.S.*, xi, p. 118).

57.   Gift to Thorney abbey of the toft and carucate of land in Stoke Albany, which was Robert the forester's and which William d'Aubigny gave to the monks.

Rockingham, [1141–1144]

> Cambridge Univ. Library, Add. MSS. 3021 (Thorney cartulary), f. 205v., no. 4; Northants. Record Soc., Brudenell MS. c. i. 20, f. 14 (abbreviated text from cartulary).

Ranulfus comes Cestrie constabulario, dapifero, baronibus, vicecom(iti), ministris et ballivis, et omnibus hominibus suis Francis et Anglis salutem. Sciatis me dedisse pro salute anime mee et in remissione peccatorum meorum et antecessorum meorum abbati et monachis sancte Marie et sancti Botulphi de Thorneia totam toftam que fuit Roberti forestarii in Stokes, cum carrucata terre quam Willelmus de Albeneio eis in elemosinam dedit, cum prato eidem terre pertinenti et cum aisiamento bosci, et illam donationem confirmo et concedo. Et monachi vel monachorum ministri predictam elemosinam custodientes meam firmam pacem in Stokes et ubique in balliva mea habeant, ita ne aliquis eos inquietet super forisfactum meum nec disturbet. Testibus Roberto Grevesaca et Gaufrido dispensatore et Willelmo capellano, apud Rokingham.

This charter follows Ranulf II's acquisition of William d'Aubigny's honour of Belvoir (**no. 50**) and may be compared with his charter for Pipewell (**no. 95**), also granting land in Stoke Albany. The attestation of Robert Grevesac, who does not appear as a witness after c.1144 (**no. 70**), suggests a fairly early date, certainly earlier than **no. 58**. Rockingham, a royal castle, was presumably appropriated by Ranulf during his conflict with Stephen, but we do not know when; like Belvoir, it became one of his strongholds in the Midlands.

58. Gift to Thorney abbey of the land which Hugh of Redmile held in Pipewell, and the toft of Robert the forester and other land in Stoke Albany, which William d'Aubigny Brito had given them.

Stamford, [1145–1146]

> Cambridge Univ. Library, Add. MS. 3021 (Thorney cartulary), f. 205v., no. 5; Northants. Record Soc., Brudenell MS. c. i. 20, f. 14 (abbreviated notice from cartulary). Ed.: *Mon.*, ii. 603.

Ranulfus comes Cestrie constabulario, dapifero, baronibus, vicecom(iti), ministris et ballivis, et omnibus hominibus suis et omnibus fidelibus sancte ecclesie Francis et Anglis salutem. Sciatis me dedisse pro salute anime mee deo et sancte Marie et ecclesie Thornensi et abbati et conventui totam terram et tenuram, quam Hugo de Rademelde habuit in Pipewelle in hominibus, in agris, in bosco et plano, et in omnibus aliis rebus, et unam carucatam terre in Stokes cum prato eidem terre pertinenti, et preter hoc totam toftam que fuit Roberti forestarii in Stokes cum omnibus aisiamentis bosci, sicut Willelmus de Albeney Brito eis concessit et carta ipsius testatur. Eapropter volo et firmiter precipio quod monachi Thornensis ecclesie predictam terram et tenuram solam et quietam de omni servicio et consuetudine teneant in villa et extra, in foro et mercato, in bosco et plano, in pratis et pascuis, et in stagnis et molendinis, et in omnibus aliis locis sicut elemosinam sancte ecclesie, ne aliquis ab eis super forisfactum meum quicquam requirat, sed eos sicut corpus meum manuteneatis. Teste Rogero de Molbrai et Balduino filio Gileberti et Waltero de Reinervilla et Gaufrido filio Gaufridi et Gaufrido dispensatore et Willelmo capellano et Hugone Wake, apud Stanfordiam.

This charter repeats the grant of the lands in Stoke Albany already made in **no. 57**, but adds the lands of Hugh of Redmile in Pipewell, and is therefore presumably the later of the two. The Thorney cartulary has a notification by William d'Aubigny (**no. 103**), addressed to Alexander, bishop of Lincoln, informing him of his gift to Thorney of 'the land of Pipewell, which is of the fee of Belvoir, which the knight Hugh held', as well as of the various tenements in Stoke Albany. As Bishop Alexander died on 20 February 1148, this sets an outside limit to the date of the present charter. It would be tempting, but perhaps hazardous, to attribute it to the same time as the famous meeting between Ranulf and King Stephen at Stamford, usually attributed to the end of 1145 or the beginning of 1146. Nevertheless, as Roger of Mowbray and Baldwin fitz Gilbert both fought for the king at the battle of Lincoln (February 1141) and were taken prisoner, it would be a little surprising to find them attesting a charter of Ranulf, except at a time when he was on good terms with Stephen. Redmile lies about 2 miles north of Belvoir, and Hugh was evidently one of the knights of the Belvoir fee.

59. Confirmation of Earl Robert of Gloucester's gift of Chipping Campden (Gloucs.) to his daughter Matilda, countess of Chester, and gift of the same to her on the same terms.

Lincoln, [27 October 1141–1145]

Orig.: P.R.O., D.L.25 (Ancient Deeds, Series L), no. 36.
Ed.: *35th Rep. D.K.P.R.*, App., p. 7. Cal.: *Trans. Bristol and Gloucs. Arch. Soc.*, ix., p.139.

Rannulfus comes Cestrię episcopo suo Bangoriensi et constabuloni et dapifero et omnibus baronibus suis et hominibus Francis et Anglis et Walensibus et omnibus amicis suis salutes. Sciatis Robertum comitem Gloucestrię dedisse et concessisse Matilli filię suę comitissę Cestrię Campadenam et omnia eidem villę adiacentia et in bosco et in plano cum omnibus consuetudinibus, ita libere et honorifice sicut ipsemet eam unquam melius et liberius tenuit. Et sciatis quod ego eam eodem modo sibi concedo et firmiter do. Et precipio omnibus meis hominibus, per fidem quam mihi debent, hoc donum manutenere ad posse suum in vita mea et post descensum[1] meum, et quicumque hoc fecerint benedictionem dei et mei inde consequantur. Hoc donum fuit confirmatum apud Lincolniam in vigilia apostolorum Simonis et Iude, et inde sunt testes: Willelmus constabulo et

Robertus dapifer et Robertus Grevessac et Robertus de Treveres et Galfridus dispensator et Serlo venator et Ricardus pincerna et Willelmus pincerna et Pillippus[1] camerarius et Spileman camerarius et Willelmus capellanus et Radulfus capellanus eius filius, et Mainnus capellanus et Rogerus capellanus et magister Iohannes, et pluribus aliis.[1]

> SEAL: on tag threaded through tongue, yellow wax;
> obverse missing; reverse blank (no device or other mark).

1. *sic orig.*

Ranulf II married Matilda, daughter of Robert of Gloucester, about or before 1135. Farrer (*H.K.F.*, p. 53) and others have dated the present charter 1148, on the assumption that it was probably given after Robert's death on 31 October 1147. But if Eustace fitz John had succeeded William as constable of Chester by 1146 at latest, as seems certain, and if, as is also possible, William died in 1143 or 1144 (*Stenton Misc.*, pp. 27, 29, 34), this date is impossible. Furthermore, it is virtually certain that Ranulf was never in possession of Lincoln between his arrest at Northampton on 29 August 1146 and 1153. The probability, therefore, is that the present charter falls between Ranulf's notorious seizure of Lincoln towards the close of 1140, or more probably after the battle of Lincoln on 2 February 1141, and 1146, but the evidence does not permit us to say to which year in this period it belongs.

The charter, which is written in a large, upright book-hand, with tagged 'e's, has other puzzling features. It has not been explained why a document issued at Lincoln and concerned with land in Gloucestershire should be addressed specifically to the bishop of Bangor and to Welsh as well as French and English. More important, it is hard to account for Robert of Gloucester's interest in Chipping Campden, since Campden had been part of the honour of Chester since 1086. There is, moreover, no reference to it in the surviving charters of the earls of Gloucester (ed. R.B. Patterson), nor any other grant to Matilda, though it is reasonable to assume that she was given a *maritagium* at the time of her marriage to Ranulf II. The assumption must be that the manor of Campden passed temporarily into Robert's hands during the civil wars following the landing of the Empress Matilda in England in the autumn of 1139. There is other evidence (**nos. 47, 49**) that Ranulf had difficulty in maintaining the more distant possessions of the honour of Chester in the south of England, from which he was separated by a wide band of territory in the Midlands in the hands of hostile families (*T.R.H.S.*, 4th Ser.xx., p. 112). Campden was probably affected in the same way. If it was seized by Robert of Gloucester, it was probably in 1139 or 1140, when Robert had declared for the Empress and Ranulf was still loyal to Stephen. The present charter makes it clear that Ranulf had no intention of surrendering his rights, and in fact the earl of Gloucester's tenure terminated with Robert's death, if not sooner.

60. Grant to John Malyn of sixteen acres in Helweyn (Hellinhall, now Kingshill, Warws.) and remission of the payment of one bezant a year, owing to him and his predecessors by gift of King Henry I, reserving to himself one virgate of land at Hulle.

Coventry, [1141–1146]

Stratford-upon-Avon, Shakespeare's Birthplace,
Gregory-Hood Leger Book, p. 172.

Ranulphus comes Cestrie constabulario, dapifero et omnibus hominibus suis Francis et Anglis salutem. Sciatis me dedisse Iohanni Malyn sexdecem acras terre in Helweyn et remisisse illi totum servitium unius bizantei, quod mihi solebat reddere singulis annis et antecessoribus meis ex dono Henrici regis, salvo reliquo feodo meo, videlicet una virgata terre apud Hulle. Quare volo et precipio firmiter, quatenus predictus Iohannes predicta queque teneat libere et quiete. Apud Coventrie, testibus Lydulfo de Coventrie, Alexandro capellano meo, Iohanne camerario, Iordano clerico, et aliis pluribus.

This grant appears to illustrate the confusion of tenures arising from the civil wars of Stephen's reign. Earlier in the Leger Book (p. 171) there is a charter of Helen Malyn, witnessed among others by Henry of Arden, granting her son Henry the manor of Helanhulle in Stoneleigh to hold of King Stephen, quit of service except for the bezant due to the king ('salvo bizanteo predicto regi forinsecus spectante'). The implication seems to be that, after Ranulf's breach with Stephen in 1140 or possibly in 1146, the earl stepped into the king's place as chief lord, claiming in justification that the bezant, which had been paid to Stephen, had been granted to him or his predecessors by Henry I. Unfortunately, the present charter cannot be dated accurately. Liulf of Coventry, or Liulf of Brinklow, was granted land at Coventry and the vill of Bisley by Ranulf II (**nos. 145, 146**), but Ranulf's charter has not survived, and we do not know the date of the grant. If the present charter falls after 1146, its date cannot be before 1153, as Ranulf lost control of Coventry during the intervening years, but it may well have been given earlier. Ranulf is known to have been at Coventry between 1144 and 1146 (**no. 73**), and this is a likely time; but there were undoubtedly other possible occasions after 1141.

61. Grant to the monks of Shrewsbury of freedom from toll in the city and county of Chester, even in time of war or discord between Shropshire and Cheshire, provided that the monks of Chester have the same liberty in Shrewsbury.

[1141–1149]

Nat. Lib. Wales, MS. 7851 D (Cart. S. Petri de Salopes-
beria), p. 285, no. 312; from the cartulary, B.L. Add. MS.
30311, f. 525 (new f. 260). Ed.: *Chart. St. Werburgh*, p. 73
(no. 15); Rees, *Cartulary of Shrewsbury Abbey*, pp.
288–9.

Ranulfus comes Cestrie constabulario suo atque dapifero et omnibus baronibus,
vicecomitibus, ministris et omnibus fidelibus suis totius Cestresire salutem.
Sciatis quod ego condonavi monachis Salopesberie theloneum suum in civitate
Cestrie et in toto comitatu meo solutum et quietum, et omnes consuetudines et
libertates et quietancias suas concessi eis, sicut melius habuerunt tempore
Hugonis comitis et patris mei Rannulfi. Quapropter firmiter precipio super
decem libras de forisfactura, ut nec propter guerram nec propter discordiam
aliquam, que possit contingere inter Salopessiriam et Cestresiram, ullo modo de
hac re disturbentur, nisi forte monachi mei de Cestria fuerint disturbati[1] de
huiusmodi re apud Salopesberiam. Hac enim conditione concessi eis hanc
quietationem, ut monachi mei habeant consimilem apud Salopesberiam.
Testibus Radulfo abbate, Roberto dapifero, Turstano Banastre, et multis aliis.

1.   distubati *MS.*

This charter reflects the conditions of the civil war of Stephen's reign. After the
abortive revolt of William fitz Alan, the sheriff and constable, in 1138 (**no. 85**),
Shrewsbury was firmly in the hands of the king. Ranulf II, on the other hand,
was committed to the Angevin party after the battle of Lincoln in February 1141,
if not before. There was therefore always the possibility of open conflict between
Shropshire and Cheshire. The date of the present charter must be later than the
election of Abbot Ralph of Chester on 22 January 1141, but it is not possible to
relate it to any specific event. It may conceivably relate to the breach between
Ranulf and Stephen in 1146, and the ensuing warfare, but it is not likely to be
much later in date than that.

62.   Confirmation of William fitz Alan's gift of the chapel of Trafford and four
       bovates of land to Shrewsbury abbey.

[1144–1148]

Nat. Lib. Wales, MS. 7851 D (Cart. S. Petri de Salops-
beria), p. 340, no. 377; from the cartulary, B.L. Add. MS.
30311, f. 632 (new f. 313v.). Ed.: Rees, *Cartulary of
Shrewsbury Abbey*, p. 342.

Ranulfus comes Cestrie omnibus fidelibus suis sancte ecclesie et omnibus ministris suis omnibusque baronibus suis et omnibus hominibus suis Francis et Anglis totius honoris sui salutem. Sciatis quod concedo et confirmo donationem, quam Willelmus filius Alani fecit deo et abbatie et monachis Salopesberi, scilicet suam capellam de Trocford et quatuor bovatas terre; et firmiter precipio quod predicti monachi firmam meam pacem ibidem habeant et omnes sue res. Testibus Willelmo filio Alani et Normanno[1] de Verdun et abbate Cestrie et Rodberto Staffordie et aliis.

1. Ifornam *MS.*

For William fitz Alan, see **no. 85**. The place concerned is Wimbolds Trafford (Cheshire), held by the fitz Alans as lords of Dunham on the Hill (Orm., ii. 34). William's gift of the church was confirmed by Bishop Roger Clinton of Chester, who died in the Holy Land on 16 April 1148 (Rees, *op. cit.*, pp. 298–9, no. 328), and Ranulf II's confirmation is not likely to be much later in date. As the gift was not included in the Empress Matilda's confirmation of the possessions of Shrewsbury abbey (ibid., pp. 47–8, no. 40), it probably dates from after 1144, but the evidence does not permit a closer dating.

63. Grant to Shrewsbury abbey of the manor of Garston, the church of Walton, the tithe of Newton-in-Makerfield, the vills of Woolston and Poulton, a moiety of the Mersey fishery, and the third part of Thelwall, as previously given by Count Roger of Poitou.

[1146–1147]

Nat. Lib. Wales, MS. 7851 D (Cart. S. Petri de Salopes-beria), p. 285, no. 311; from the cartulary B.L. Add. MS. 30311, f. 524 (new f. 259v.). Short abstracts: P.R.O., C. 66 (Chancery Patent Rolls), no. 174, m. 14; B.L. Harl. MS. 2063, f. 110v. (old f. 230); B.L. Add. MS. 30323, f. 48b. Ed.: *L.P.R.*, p. 277; Rees, *Cartulary of Shrewsbury Abbey*, p. 288.

Rannulfus comes Cestrie episcopo Cestriensi, abbati Cestrie totique clero, constabulario Cestrie, dapifero, baronibus, iusticie,[1] vicecomitibus, ministris et omnibus fidelibus suis Francis et Anglis salutem. Sciatis me reddidisse pro salute anime mee et antecessorum meorum deo et sancte Marie et abbati et monachis beati Petri ecclesie Salopesberie manerium de Gerstan cum omnibus que ad illud pertinent, in plano et in bosco et in aquis, ecclesiam etiam de Waletona cum terris et ceteris rebus que ad eam pertinent, decimam quoque de Niwetona de dominio et villas duas Ulsitonam et Pultonam et dimidiam piscariam in Merse, terciam etiam partem de Thelewelle in terris et in aquis et in bosco. Quare volo et firmiter precipio, ut bene et in pace et libere teneant et habeant ista omnia in bosco et plano et pratis et pasturis et aquis et in omnibus rebus cum omnibus libertatibus et quietanciis et consuetudinibus, cum quibus melius tenent alias terras suas; nec aliquid ibi retineo nisi orationes pro me. Qui vero hoc temerare ausus fuerit vel imminuere, sententia anathematis veniat super eum, que scripta est in carta Roggeri comitis, qui Pictavensis dictus est, qui ista omnia sancto Petro prius dedit, et sentencia que confirmata est per cartam regis Henrici coram archiepiscopis et episcopis in consilio Anglie. Testibus Rogero episcopo Cestrensi, Radulfo abbate,[2] Willelmo archidiacono, Normanno de Verdun, et multis aliis.

1. iustic. *MS.*
2. abbato *MS.*

All the places mentioned, except Thelwall, are in Lancashire, and were granted by Ranulf II as successor to Roger of Poitou, brother of Earl Hugh and Earl Robert of Shrewsbury. But when did he succeed? Roger had been invested with the lands between the Ribble and the Mersey by the Conqueror, probably in 1068, but he lost them and all his English estates as a result of his involvement in Earl Robert's revolt in 1102, and the lands reverted to the Crown, until they were bestowed by Henry I on his nephew Stephen, count of Mortain. Stephen continued to hold them after his succession to the throne in 1135, but at some date unknown, presumably to purchase the earl's support, he conferred them, with other major territorial concessions, on Earl Ranulf of Chester. There appear to be only two possible dates for this grant, 1140 or 1146. Most earlier authorities have attributed it to 1140, but the weight of the evidence, though circumstantial, favours 1146 (*Regesta*, iii. no. 178). If that is the case, the present charter must fall between 1146 and the departure of Bishop Roger Clinton for the Holy Land in May 1147, where he died in April 1148.

The statement that all the places listed had previously been given to Shrewsbury abbey by Roger of Poitou is not literally true. The third part of Thelwall was given by William the constable of Cheshire between 1121 and 1130 (Rees, *op. cit.*, p. 291, no. 316). Henry I's confirmation (*op. cit.*, pp. 31–36, no. 35) was issued at the Council of London in 1121. The use of the word *vicecomites* (sheriffs) in the plural is interesting, indicating that Ranulf had a separate sheriff for the lands between Ribble and Mersey, distinct from the sheriff of Cheshire.

64.   Order to the earl's officers to leave the abbot and convent of Shrewsbury in peaceful possession of their land between Ribble and Mersey, particularly of Garston and of the service of their tenant there.

Chester, [1147–1148]

Nat. Lib. Wales, MS. 7851 D (Cart. S. Petri de Salopes-
beria), p. 286, no. 313; from the cartulary, B.L. Add. MS.
30311, f. 526 (new f. 260v.). Brief abstracts: Bodleian
Library, Dodsworth MS. 135, f. 91v.; Ashmole 799, f. 99.
Ed.: *L.P.R.*, p. 278; Rees, *Cartulary of Shrewsbury
Abbey*, p. 289.

Rannulfus comes Cestrie iusticie sui[1] de inter Riblam et Mersam, quecunque
fuerit,[2] et omnibus baronibus et ministris suis et omnibus hominibus[3] suis
salutem. Precipio quod abbas et conventus sancti Petri de Scropesberia habeant totam tenuram suam de inter Riblam et Mersam, quam de me tenent, bene
et in pace, libere et quiete, sicut elemosinam sancte ecclesie, et nominatim
Gerestanam, sicut carta illorum testatur, quam de me habent; et ita quod
Ricardus filius Multonis eis integriter et plenarie servicium de predicta Gerestana[4] faciat, sicut amat amorem meum, et ita quod nullus meorum quicquam
de ipso Ricardo requirat quod ad predictam Gerestanam pertinuerit. Clamo
enim[5] Ricardum ex toto quietum de omnibus que ad predictam Gerestanam[6]
pertinent, quoniam nichil inde nisi orationes requiro. Testibus comite de Clara
et Cadwaldro rege Waliarum et Roberto Basset et Gaufrido dispensario, apud
Cestriam.

1. iustic. suis *MS*.
2. *sic MS*.; quicunque fuerint *ed*.
3. *om. MS. (clearly in error)*
4. *add* servicium *MS*.; servicere *ed*.
5. eum *MS*.
6. predicta Gerestana *MS*.

This charter is clearly later in date than **no. 63**, to which it makes reference, but
probably not much later. Cadwaladr, who witnesses two other charters of Ranulf
II (**nos. 28, 84**), was a younger brother of Owen ap Gruffydd, or Owen the
Great, the ruler of Gwynedd. He had married a sister of Earl Gilbert of Clare,
the first witness of the present charter, who was a son of Ranulf's sister, Adeliza,
and when he was driven out of Anglesey in 1151 or 1152 he took refuge with
Ranulf (Lloyd, ii. 490–91). For this reason, the present charter has been dated
1151–52, but, as Tait points out (*Chart St. Werburgh*, p. 65), he had fought for
Ranulf at the battle of Lincoln in 1141 (Lloyd, p. 489), and there is no reason
why he should not have been at Chester at an earlier date. Farrer (*L.P.R.*, p.
280) places his meeting with Earl Ranulf and Earl Gilbert in 1142, but that is
certainly too early. The most probable date is 1147–48, when other relatives of
Ranulf and leading members of the Angevin faction foregathered in Chester
(**nos. 84 and 85**).

65.   Grant of two pieces of land in Middlewich to the monks of Shrewsbury as compensation for the injuries he had frequently done to the abbey.

Newcastle-under-Lyme [c. 1153]

P.R.O., CHES 29/18 (Plea Rolls, 35 Edw. III), m. 8v.; brief abstract Orm., iii. 173.

Ranulphus comes Cestrie constabulario, dapifero, baronibus, iusticie, ministris, ballivis et omnibus hominibus suis salutem. Sciatis me dedisse et in puram et perpetuam elemosinam concessisse deo et sancto Petro et monachis Salopesburiensis ecclesie duas mansuras terre in Midelwico in satisfacionem pro iniuriis, quas prefate ecclesie sepe intuli, liberas et quietas a theloneo et omni consuetudine et exaccione et omni seculari servicio. Quare volo et firmiter precipio, quod predicti monachi habeant et teneant bene et in pace hanc meam elemosinam, nec aliquis heredum vel successorum meorum ab eis ulterius exigat aliquid preter oraciones. Testibus Roberto de Stafford, Thoma de Verdun, Roberto de Buschervilla, Willelmo Burdet, apud Novum Castellum.

This charter must fall after Stephen's grant of Newcastle-under-Lyme to Ranulf II (*Regesta*, iii. no. 178), presumably in 1146, but otherwise it is not easy to date. Ranulf made a number of grants towards the end of his life or on his deathbed to religious houses in compensation for injuries inflicted (**nos. 34, 117, 118**), and this charter probably belongs to the same period. It probably follows Duke Henry's Devizes charter to Ranulf in the spring of 1153, in which he reaffirmed Ranulf's position in Staffordshire (*Regesta*, iii. no. 180).

66.   Gift to Hugh Bardulf for his service of the whole demesne of his manor of Waddington (Lincs.), except for the lands already held by the Knights of the Temple, Spileman the earl's chamberlain, Anschetil the serjeant and William Becdaw, to be held by the service of three knights.

Lincoln, [1142–1146]

Orig.: P.R.O., D L 36/2 (Cart. Misc.), f. 61.[1] Transcr.: D.L. 42/2 (Coucher Book II), f. 475v. Ed.: Stenton, *Danelaw Charters*, p. 361.

1.   Original mutilated and partly illegible; readings in square brackets supplied from Coucher Book, where available.

Ranulfus comes Cestrie constabulario, dapifero, baronibus, castellanis, const[abulariis], vic(ecomitibus), ministris et omnibus hominibus suis Francis et Anglis, clericis et laicis, salutem. Sciatis me [dedisse] H[ugoni] Bardulfo pro servicio suo totum dominicum meum de manerio meo Wadintonie, excepta [terra mili]tum sancti Templi Ierussalem, videlicet c. solidatas terre et x., et excepta terra Spilemani camerarii mei, scilicet ploxlaudam unam, et excepta terra Anschetilli servientis et Willelmi Becdaw, in feodo et hereditate sibi et heredibus suis. Et nisi ibi de dominio meo xl. librate terre fuerint, alibi ei perficiam de hereditate mea iuxta warandum meum et suum in Lindesia. Eapropter volo et firmiter precipio, quod ipse Hugo et heredes sui de me et de heredibus meis predictam tenuram teneat per fra[nc]um servicium trium militum bene et hon[orifice in vil]la et extra, in foro et mercato, in bosco et plano, in pratis et pascuis, in viis et [sem]itis, in aquis et molendinis, in stagnis et piscariis, cum soca et s[aca et] tol et [th]eom et infangetheof, et cum omnibus aliis consuetudinibus et libertatibus. Testibus comite Willelmo L[in]colnie [et R]adulfo de Haia et Normanno de Verdun et Roberto Grevesac et Simone filio Willelmi et [Hugone o] sturcario et Gisleberto Neiville [et Willelmo C]oleville et Willelmo [p]i[ncerna] et Ricardo pincerna et R[oberto de] Treveris et Willelmo Bacun et [Rogero de] Tu[rribus] et Willelmo [Bar]d[ulfo] et Hame[lino] Bardulfo et [Ro]berto Englebie et Willelmo capellano, [apud Lincolniam].

Hugh Bardulf was the son of Hamelin Bardulf (*H.K.F.*, p. 234). As he seems to have survived until 1200 (*P.R.S.*, N.S. xvi, p. 103), this was the beginning of a long career, much of it spent in royal service. His tenure of Waddington was not untroubled. In 1185 it was part of the dower of Countess Matilda and later his heir, Robert, arraigned an assize of novel disseisin against Earl Ranulf III, apparently successfully (*H.K.F.*, p. 199), but the matter was settled by an agreement c.1200, under which Robert Bardulf surrendered the present charter and received back half of the manor, excluding the advowson of the church, for the service of one-and-a-half knights' fees (D.L. 42/2, p. 476). The present charter is not easy to date accurately, but a comparison with the witnesses of other charters dated at Lincoln (**nos. 55, 59, 77, 111**) indicates a date between 1142 and 1146. As Ranulf's brother, Earl William of Lincoln, appears to have been in Normandy in the earlier part of this period (**no. 70**), it probably dates from 1144–46, but, assuming that it marks Hugh's entry into Ranulf II's service, it is probably earlier than other charters of the earl (**nos. 77, 82, 93, 111**) which Hugh attests.

67. Grant of (Nether) Whitley in Haltonshire to Alured de Combray for the service of one-half of a knight's fee 'until I have seen or heard what it can bear'.

Greetham, [1143–1144]

B.L. Add. MS. 6032, f. 201 (new f. 100v.); Harl. MS. 2022, f. 140v. (new f. 93v.); Bodleian Library, Dodsworth

MS. 31, f. 141v.; MS. Top. Cheshire b. I, p. 136; Chester, Booth of Twemlow, Liber D, f. 189; Warrington, Beamont MSS., Transcripts I. Ed.: Orm., i. 659 (abbreviated and inaccurate); *Stenton Misc.*, p. 34 (no. 6).

Ranulfus comes Cestrie constabulario, dapifero, iustic(ie), baronibus, ministris et ballivis Cestrescire, et omnibus hominibus suis Francis et Anglis salutem. Scitote me dedisse in feodo et hereditate Aluredo de Cumbrai Witteleiam cum omnibus pertinentiis suis in Haltonscira, et illam ei admensuravi ad servitium dimidii militis, donec viderim et audierim quid possit pati. Eapropter volo et firmiter precipio quod ipse Aluredus et heredes sui predictam tenuram teneant de me et de heredibus meis bene et honorifice per admensuratum servitium in villa et extra, in foro et mercato, in bosco et plano, in pratis et pascuis, in viis et semitis, in aquis et molendinis, et in omnibus aliis locis cum secca et sac et tol et tem et infangthefe et cum omnibus aliis consuetudinibus et libertatibus. Testibus Radulfo abbate Cestrie et Normanno Verdun et Ricardo pincerna et Turstano Banaster et Willelmo Bacun et Willelmo capellano, apud Graham.

> SEAL: 'sealed with a great seale, the impression upon the one side being a man on horsebacke, on the other side a naked woman, a piller standinge at her backe'.

Alured de Combray (canton of Thury-Harcourt, Calvados) was not a Cheshire man, but the son of Reginald de Combray of Lee Gomery, Shropshire (Orm., i. 659). He was introduced to Cheshire by Ranulf II by this charter, and the frequent references to him show that he was closely in the confidence of the earl. As Whitley had been part of the constable's fee since 1086 and was subsequently held of the constable's honour of Halton, his enfeoffment by the earl was irregular. Tait (*E.H.R.*, lvii, p. 450) suggested that, on the death of William II the constable, Ranulf may have treated the constableship as an escheat and, before re-granting it to Eustace fitz John (**no. 73**), may have used the opportunity to confer Whitley on one of his followers. In this case the grant probably took place in 1143 or 1144. For Haltonshire, see *E.C.C.*, pp. 41–2.

68.   Confirmation of the gift which Richard Bacon, his relative, gave to Rocester abbey.

[1143–1144]

B.L. Harl. MS. 818, f. 38; Harl. 1424, f. 98v. (new f. 96v.); Harl. 1988, f. 14 (new f. 25); Harl. 2043, f. 184 (old f. 202): Bodleian Library, Dodsworth MS. 96, f. 36v. (all apparently 'ex cartis ostensis per Thomam Trentham de Rouecester armigerum').

Rogero Cestrensi episcopo *etc.* Ranulfus comes Cestrie salutem. Notum vobis omnibus facio me confirmasse proprio sigillo et carta mea donationem quam Ricardus Bacun, cognatus meus et familiaris, donavit deo et sancte Marie et canonicis de Roucestria *etc.* Testibus Hugone Wac, Willelmo constabulario de Donintona, Turstano Banaster, Willelmo Bacun, Roberto Basset *etc.*[1]

1. *Harl. 1988 has* testes ut supra, *i.e. the witnesses of Richard Bacon's charter, continuing* Willelmo de Colevile, Ricardo pincerna, Willelmo de Boyvil, Galfrido dispensatore.

Rocester abbey (Staffs.) was founded in or shortly after 1143 by Richard Bacon, who probably married an illegitimate daughter of Ranulf I (*H.K.F.*, pp. 257–8). His foundation charter (*Mon.*, vi. 411) is certainly not genuine as it stands, but there is nothing suspicious about the witness-list, and it is probably an inflated version of a genuine charter. As the witnesses of Ranulf II's confirmation are the same as those of the foundation charter, they were presumably issued at the same time, and the date is set by the appearance (in Richard's charter) of Archbishop William of York, who was consecrated on 26 September 1143, and (in both) of William the constable, who was succeeded by Eustace fitz John in 1144 or 1145 (*Stenton Misc.*, pp. 26–28). There appears to be no intrinsic reason to reject the present charter, except that, according to a drawing by Randle Holme in Harl. MS. 2043, it has a seal (a shield of three garbs surmounted by a visor supported on either side by lampreys) which is evidently not authentic. If the charter is genuine, it must be assumed that the seal was appended later; but it is certainly a suspicious circumstance. On the other hand, there is a confirmation of Pope Eugenius III, given at Autun on 27 September 1147 (Harl. 4028, p. 231), which seems to vouch for the authenticity of the original grant of Rocester and its appurtenances.

69.   Grant of Lowdham and East Bridgeford (Notts.) to Henry de Lacy.

Lincoln, [c.1143–1144]

P.R.O., D.L. 42/2 (Coucher Book II), f. 71. Transcr. (abbreviated): B.L. Harl. MS. 2063, f. 240 (new f. 115v.); Central Reference Library, Manchester, Towneley MS. 8, p. 1077. Ed.: Farrer, *Early Yorkshire Charters*, iii. 190–1; Stenton, *First Century of English Feudalism*. pp. 270–1.

Ranulphus comes Cestrie constabulario, dapiferis,[1] vicecomitibus,[1] ministris et ballidis et omnibus hominibus suis Francis et Anglis salutem. Scitote me dedisse Henrico de Laceio in feodo et hereditate Ludeham et Brigeford cum omnibus pertinenciis suis sibi et heredibus suis ad tenendum de me et de heredibus meis pro servicio suo imperpetuum. Quare volo et firmiter precipio, quod ipse Henricus et heredes sui de me et de heredibus meis ita bene et honorifice teneant sicut teneo meam hereditatem propriam, in villa et extra, in foro et mercato, in boscis et planis, in pratis et pascuis, in stagnis et molendinis, in aquis et piscariis, in viis et semitis, cum soca et saca et tol et theom et infangetheof, et cum omnibus aliis libertatibus et consuetudinibus. Testibus comite Willelmo Lincolnie et Baldewino filio Gisleberti et Willelmo Coleville et Turstano Banastre et Ranulfo vicecomite et Hugone osturcario et Willelmo filio Haconis et Ricardo pincerna et Willelmo Malebisse et Willelmo capellano et Blundo marescallo, apud Lincolniam.

1.   *Plural in MS.*

Henry de Lacy, founder of Kirkstall abbey, was the brother of Ilbert de Lacy (**no. 16**), one of Stephen's active supporters who was taken prisoner at the battle of Lincoln in 1141 and died shortly afterwards, and succeeded him as lord of the honour of Pontefract. The present charter, witnessed by Ranulf II's half-brother, William of Roumare, and Baldwin fitz Gilbert, the brother-in-law of his sister Adeliza, probably dates from not much later, and in any case from before 1146. The grant of Lowdham and Bridgeford in return for his service may have been intended to win over Henry to Ranulf's side in his conflict with Stephen. It is at least noteworthy that Henry was later engaged in warfare with one of Stephen's foremost supporters, Gilbert of Gant, whom Stephen made earl of Lincoln in place of William of Roumare in 1149 (Stenton, *op. cit.*, p. 244). His alliance would have been invaluable in 1143 and 1144 when Ranulf was busy harassing Stephen's supporters in Yorkshire (*T.R.H.S.*, 4th Ser. xx. p. 122), and the present charter may well date from that time.

70.   Gift to his brother, William earl of Lincoln, on his return from pilgrimage to Compostela, of Watteleia (Wheatley, Notts.?) for the service of his knights.

15 September, [? 1144]

> P.R.O., D.L. 42/2 (Coucher Book II), f. 445. Transcripts from Coucher Book (all abbreviated): B.L. Harl. MS.2044, f. 2v. (new f. 27v.); Lansdowne 229, f. 108v.; Bodleian Library, Dugdale MS. 18, f. 19; Rawlinson B 140, f. 73.; Central Reference Library, Manchester, Towneley MS. 8, p. 108v. Ed.: Dugdale, *Baronage*, i. 39–40; Orm., i. 25 (both from Coucher Book, abbreviated).

Ranulphus comes Cestrie constabulario suo et dapifero et cunctis baronibus suis et hominibus, Francis et Anglis, et amicis et vicinis tam clericis quam laicis salutem. Sciatis me dedisse et concessisse Willelmo comiti Lincolnie fratri meo Watteleiam in feudo et hereditate sibi et heredi suo ad tenendam de me ac de meis heredibus, et ita uti eam habui die qua sibi eam donavi, et cum omnibus suis pertinentiis libere et quiete et honorifice, inde reddenti[1] servicium duorum militum in singulis annis. Hec autem donatio facta est in eodem anno quo ipsemet Willelmus comes Lincolnie redivit de itinere sancti Iacobi apostoli in crastina die post festum sancte Crucis, quod celebratur mense Septembri. Et inde sunt testes ex mea parte: Willelmus de Colevilla, Robertus Gravissacca, Gaufridus Malabisse. Ex parte vero comitis Willelmi: Hadewisa comitissa Lincolnie Wido de Povilla.

---

1. *sic MS. Transcripts have* reddendo.

Compared with other leading persons of Stephen's reign, we have tantalisingly little information about Ranulf II's elder half-brother, William of Roumare, who was created earl of Lincoln in 1141 or possibly towards the end of 1140. As is well known, he participated with Ranulf in the seizure of Lincoln castle at the end of 1140, but thereafter, except for occasional mention in charters which are difficult to date with any degree of accuracy, the sources are silent until 1146 or 1147, and it does not appear that he took part in the battle of Lincoln (2 February 1141), at which Stephen was made captive. The probability is that he withdrew to Normandy and came to terms there with Duke Geoffrey. His pilgrimage to Compostela has been placed, for no evident reason, in 1152 or 1153 (*Complete Peerage*, vii. 669). This suggestion has little to recommend it. Although it is impossible to determine the year with certainty, a careful examination of the witnesses makes it virtually certain that the present charter is a good deal earlier in date. The countess Hadewisa and Guy (Wido) de Poville (Potville) witnessed William of Roumare's confirmation of land to the Premonstratensian abbey of Newhouse. This was c.1144 (Warner and Ellis, no. 24). Robert Grevesac, who appears as early as 1130 on the Pipe Roll of 31 Henry I (*H.K.F.*, p. 22) and who witnessed a charter of Ranulf II in 1129–30 (**no. 15**), does not occur much, if at all, after this date. He appears with Geoffrey Malebisse (**no. 55**) and with Earl William (**no. 66**) in charters which fall between 1141 and 1146, and Geoffrey Malebisse and William Coleville witnessed Ranulf II's charter for Hartsholme (**no. 77**). William Coleville and Earl William were also the witnesses of the charters (**nos. 53, 54**) of Earl Ranulf and Countess Matilda for Belvoir priory. All this suggests that the present charter falls in the period 1141–45, and if the suggestion that Watteley (which has not hitherto been identified) is Wheatley, Notts., is correct, this would fit well with the proposed date. Waleran of Meulan, earl of Worcester, is known to have gone on pilgrimage to Compostela in 1144 (*Complete Peerage*, xii. 833). It might not be fanciful to suggest that Earl William went at the same time. In that case the date of the present charter would be 15 September 1144. William is known to have been in England about this time, when he witnessed Ranulf's charter for Eustace fitz John (**no. 73**) at Coventry.

71.   Grant to Hugh son of Pincon of 100s. worth of land from the fee which Halenald of Bidun held of the earl in Lincolnshire.

Lincoln, [1144–1145]

P.R.O., D.L. 42/2 (Coucher Book II), f. 255; B.L. Lansdowne MS. 205, f. 185v. (abbreviated notice from Coucher Book).

Rannulfus consul Cestrie constabulario, dapifero, baronibus, iustic(iario), vicecom(iti), ministris et ballidis et omnibus hominibus suis Francis et Anglis salutem. Scitote me dedisse in feodo et hereditate Hugoni filio Pincon[1] centum solidatas terre de feodo Halenaldi de Biduun, quam de me tenebat in Lincolnescira. Eapropter volo et firmiter precipio, quod ipse Hugo et heredes sui de me et de heredibus meis predictam tenuram teneat bene et honorifice per servicium dimidii militis in villa et extra, in foro et mercato, in bosco et plano, in pratis et pasturis, in molendinis et aquis, in stagnis et mariscis, et in omnibus aliis locis, cum soca et saca et tol et teom et infangethef, et cum aliis consuetudinibus et libertatibus omnibus. Et si forte eveniret, quod ipse Halenaldus vel heredes sui terram illam recuperarent, predicto Hugoni escambium darem ad valens ad warandum suum de propria hereditate mea. Testibus Radulfo de Haia, Normanno de[2] Verdun, Hugone osturcario, Waltero de Hambia, Roberto filio Hugonis, apud Lincolniam.

1. Pineon *MS.*
2. *om. MS.*

Hugh son of Pincon, like his father before him, was steward of the bishop of Durham, and a substantial landholder in Lincolnshire, who obtained considerable notoriety in 1144 when he abandoned his lord, Bishop William de Ste.-Barbe, and went over to William Cumin, the Empress's nominee to the see of Durham (*Book of Seals*, p. 28). It would not be surprising if this switch of allegiance won him the present grant. Halenald de Bidun, a considerable landholder in Buckinghamshire and Norfolk (Farrer, *Honors and Knights' Fees*, i. 1), presumably remained loyal to King Stephen and forfeited his Lincolnshire fee as a result, but it is an interesting indication of the unstable situation that Ranulf envisages the possibility of his recovering his lands. In fact, he withdrew from secular life and became a monk at St. Andrew's, Northampton, but we do not know when.

72.   Grant to Robert of Barrow of the mill he had built at the fishpond of Coventry and of the house which had belonged to Duisset the park keeper, quit of service for the first year and thereafter paying half a mark of silver for the earl's oblation.

Coventry, [1144]

B.L. Harl. MS. 7, ff. 101v.–102. Ed.: *Langley cart.*, no. 189.

Ranulfus comes Cestrie constabulario Cestrie, dapifero, baronibus, ius-tic(iariis), vic(ecomitibus), ministris et ballidis castellarii de Coventre, quicum-que fuerit, et omnibus hominibus suis Francis et Anglis salutem. Sciatis me concessisse Roberto de Barow molendinum quod fecit apud vivarium de Coventre, ad tenendam de me et de heredibus meis in isto primo anno quietum de omni servitio, et exinde singulis annis[1] reddendo mihi inde dimidiam marcam argenti ad oblationem meam faciendam, perinde tenendo ei mansio[2] que fuit Duisset[3] parcarii ad se hospitandum. Et volo quod ipse Robertus et heredes sui de me et de heredibus meis predictum molendinum cum omnibus pertinentiis suis ad feufirmam bene et honorifice tenent, ne aliquis ab eo quicquam inde requirat. Testibus comite Willelmo Lincolniensi, Turstano[4] Banaster, Hugone osturcario, Ivone constabulario, Radulfo capellano, Philippo, Spileman camerariis, apud Coventre.

1.   *om. MS.*
2.   mansiones *MS.*
3.   *Almost certainly miscopied for* Duillet *MS.*
4.   Lurst(ano) *MS.*

The date of this charter is almost certainly 1144, when Earl William of Roumare is known to have been at Coventry with Thurstan Banastre and Ivo the constable of Coventry castle (**nos. 70, 73**), during the hostilities with Robert Marmion, when Earl Ranulf and Thurstan Banastre, with the assent of Bishop Roger (d. 1148), ordered the populace to take refuge in the nearby cemeteries of Ansty, Allesley and Wyken (Coss, no. 12). Robert of Barrow, who witnessed a charter of Earl Hugh (**no. 145**) not many months after Ranulf II's death, subsequently disposed of this holding to Simon, son of Liulf of Brinklow (**no. 156**), but Earl Hugh retained the house and land of William Duillet, which he then gave to Bishop Walter Durdent (**no. 124**).

73.   Conferment on Eustace fitz John of the whole honour of William fitz Nigel, constable of Chester, thus constituting him constable and chief counsellor after the earl himself over all the magnates and barons of his whole land.

Coventry, [1144–1145]

> Orig. (much damaged): B.L. Cott. Charter xvi, 36; collated, where mutilated, with Bodleian Library, Dugdale MS. 17, p. 82 ('ex ipso autographo') and P.R.O., D.L. 42/1 (Coucher Book I), f. 41. Ed.: Orm., i. 52 (from Coucher Book); *Stenton Misc.*, pp. 28–9.

Rannulfus comes Cestrie episcopo Cestrie, dapifero, baronibus, iusticiariis, castellanis, vicecomitibus, ministris et ballivis, et omnibus hominibus suis Francis et Anglis, clericis et laicis, salutem. Proculdubio scitote me reddidisse et dedisse Eustachio filio Iohannis totum honorem, qui fuit Willelmi filii Nigelli constabularii Cestrie, in rebus et dignitatibus omnibus, et ipsum Eustachium constituisse hereditarie constabularium et supremum consiliarium post me super omnes obtimates et barones totius terre mee. Eapropter volo et firmiter precipio, desicut ei rectum suum reddidi et donavi et concessi constabulariam et honorem integrum constabularie Cestrie et totius terre mee, quod in omnibus rationabiliter ei intendatis sicut corpori meo. Proinde precipio quod ipse Eustachius et heredes sui de me et de heredibus meis predictum honorem et terram et tenuram totam pertinentem eidem honori, scilicet constabularie, teneat ita bene et honorifice et libere et quiete sicut unquam Willelmus Nigelli filius melius et liberius tenuit, et sicut Willelmus constabularius eius filius in vita sua honorabilius tenuit, et die qua fuit vivus et mortuus. Teneat etiam ita libere et quiete sicut unquam Willelmus filius Nigelli tenebat in tempore comitis Hugonis et comitis Ricardi et tempore patris mei Rannulfi, in villa et extra, in foro et mercato, in bosco et plano, in pratis et pascuis, in viis et semitis, in forestis, in molendinis et aquis, in piscariis et stagnis, et in omnibus aliis locis, cum socca et sacca et tol et theom et infangetheof, et cum sciris et hundredis et cum omnibus consuetudinibus et libertatibus omnibus et quietanciis. Testibus Willelmo comite Lincolnie et Willelmo de Perceio et Turstano Banastre et Simone filio Willelmi et Normanno de Verdun et Ricardo pincerna et Roberto Basset et Simone de Tuschet et Gaufrido dispensatore et Ivone constabulario de Coventre, Ricardo de Vernun, Walchelino Maminot, Hugone de Nueris, Rogero de Maletot et Willelmo Malebisse, Hugone de sancto Paulo et Willelmo de Veci et Huberto de Muntchanesi et Rogero Flamangville et Willelmo filio Guerini et Raginaldo Basset et Willelmo capellano et Herveo filio Willelmi et Willelmo capellano comitis Cestrie et Rogero filio Ricardi et Gisleberto de Aquila, apud Coventriam.

SEAL: missing.

The constableship, here conferred on Eustace fitz John, one of the 'new men' who rose to prominence under Henry I, was the highest office in rank of the earldom. Eustace married as his second wife Agnes, the elder sister of William, constable of Chester, who succeeded his father, William fitz Nigel, in the constableship and the barony of Halton in or shortly before 1130. William died childless, probably in 1143 or 1144 (*Stenton Misc.*, p. 27). The present charter suggests that Ranulf II may have hesitated some time before conferring the inheritance on Eustace, but Eustace was definitely constable when Stephen issued his Stamford charter for William of Roumare (*Regesta*, iii. no. 494) at Easter 1146. The evidence suggests that his promotion probably occurred in 1144, when Earl Ranulf is known to have been at Coventry. The long witness-list provides a valuable picture of Ranulf's entourage at this time.

74. Grant to Robert Marmion of the fee of Osbert of Arden, together with his service, reserving only the service due to the earl.

[1144–1146]

> Bodleian Library, Dugdale MS. 13, p. 268 (copied in facsimile from original 'penes Joh. Ferrers de Tamworth arm., anno 1636'); briefly mentioned Dugdale, *Warwickshire*, p. 761.

Rannulfus comes Cestrie cunestabulario suo et dapifero et omnibus hominibus suis Francis et Anglis salutem. Sciatis me dedisse Roberto Marmion feodum Osberti de Ardena et eius servitium cum omnibus pertinentiis in feodo et hereditate sibi et heredibus suis tenendum de me[1] et de meis heredibus in bosco et plano, in aquis, in viis, in semitis, et in omnibus aliis rebus, salvo servitio meo. Testibus Normanno de Verdun et Simone filio Willelmi et Olivero de Malnuier et Hugone de Cuilli et Roberto Potario.

1. *MS. reads* de me tenendam (sic).

Osbert of Arden was the tenant of Kingsbury in Coleshill hundred (Warws.), which came to the earl of Chester with the manor of Coventry in the time of William II (*H.K.F.*, p. 6). Ranulf II's decision to grant Osbert's fee and service to Robert Marmion is not easily accounted for, since his relations with the Marmions were notoriously bad, and Robert Marmion II, a lawless and pugnacious character, who had seized Coventry, lost his life in 1144 defending it against the earl (William of Newburgh, *Hist. Rer. Angl.*, i. 47). Nevertheless the present charter, unlike Ranulf's alleged gift of Coventry to Robert Marmion (no. 75), appears to be genuine, but it is difficult to date accurately, except that almost certainly it falls before 1146, when Osbert of Arden left England to take part in the Second Crusade (Warner and Ellis, no. 12). Of the witnesses, Norman de Verdun died at about the same time as, or a little before, Earl Ranulf (*H.K.F.*, p. 215). Hugh de Cuilli (Quilli, Calvados, arr. Falaise) and Robert Potarius were known tenants of Marmion (*E.H.R.*, lxxxvi, p. 536).

Oliver de Malnuier is clearly identical with the Oliver de Manners who witnessed Ranulf II's confirmation of William the constable's restoration of Raby to St. Werburgh's abbey c.1135–40 (**no. 21**), and whose son Hugh witnessed another charter for St. Werburgh's (**no. 26**), probably nearer 1150 in date, suggesting that Oliver himself had died in the interval. These sparse indications do not greatly help, but, so far as the evidence goes, it seems reasonable to conclude that the present charter falls between 1144 and 1146. In that case it may perhaps be regarded as an act of reconciliation with Robert Marmion III or of atonement for his father's death.

75. Grant of Coventry to Robert Marmion and his heirs, to hold of the earl and his heirs. [Spurious]

[1144–1146]

> Orig.: Stratford-upon-Avon, Shakespeare's Birthplace, Gregory-Hood Deeds. Ed.: *E.H.R.*, lxxxvi, p. 534; Coss, no. 1.

For a full text of this document, see Coss, *The Early Records of Medieval Coventry*, p. 11 (no. 1).

> SEAL: on tongue, much repaired, knight on horseback with sword raised in right hand; legend wanting.

This charter should be compared with Ranulf II's grant of the fee of Osbert of Arden to Robert Marmion (**no. 74**), with which it has three witnesses in common. If it is genuine, it must fall after 1144, when Ranulf II and Robert Marmion II were engaged in open warfare for possession of Coventry, resulting in the death of the latter, and before Ranulf's arrest on 28 August 1146, after which he had to hand over Coventry, among other places, to King Stephen, and was in no position to dispose of it, even if he had been so minded. But there are a number of features which make it difficult, if not impossible, to accept the charter at face value. (1) The seal is certainly not a genuine seal of Ranulf II, and appears to date from the late thirteenth century. (2) The text has been tampered with, and another, later hand, for reasons unknown, has substituted the anachronistic formula *quod mihi serviat contra omnes homines et omnes mulieres* over an erasure. (3) The parchment on which the charter is written is quite unusually thin by the standards of the mid-twelfth century, suggesting that it may have been rubbed clean and re-used, or that it dates from considerably later. (4) The most disturbing feature is the language. The word *iubeo* (for *precipio*) might conceivably occur in a monastic concoction of the eleventh century (though I do not recollect having seen it), but is quite unprecedented in any genuine charter of Ranulf II; so also the word *constanter* (standing presumably for *in per-petuum*). These irregularities alone are sufficient to condemn the charter as spurious.[1] (5) Finally, the writing is commonplace and undistinguished, and the most that can be said of it is that it bears no discernible resemblance to that of any of Earl Ranulf's surviving original charters.[2] Its date could conceivably be c.1150, but equally conceivably it could be twenty or thirty years later. The difficulty, supposing it to be later, is to think of any reason for a forgery in the period after Ranulf II's death, since there is no evidence that Robert Marmion III showed any interest in Coventry and there are no Marmion documents involving the city or lands in the city.[3] On the other hand, it is equally difficult to think of any reason why Ranulf II should have divested himself of Coventry within a few months of recovering it from Robert Marmion II. Like Chester in the north and Lincoln in the east, it was a pivot of his territorial power (*T.R.H.S.*, 4th Ser. xx., pp. 127–8) and of great strategic value; hence his efforts to recover it in 1147 (*Gesta Stephani*, pp. 198–200). These would make little sense, if he had handed it over to Robert Marmion III. Perhaps the most likely explanation of the charter is that it was forged by, or on behalf of, Robert Marmion II in 1143–44 after his seizure of Coventry, in order to provide some sort of legal justification for his possession. If so, it did him no good. One of the first acts of Ranulf II in 1153 was to recover possession of Coventry, and the charter disappeared from view until it was briefly brought to light in the 1580s in the course of a minor local dispute (*E.H.R.*, lxxxvi, p. 546). No copies were made, no confirmation sought; and even Dugdale, the indefatigable collector of Warwickshire material, knew nothing of its existence.

1. J. Lancaster (*Medieval Coventry – a City Divided?* pp. 33–35) has drawn attention to some other minor peculiarities, to which I would add an obtrusive use of *ac* for *et*.
2. The nearest is Ranulf's charter for Alan Silvester (**no. 35**), given at Chester c.1130–40 and written by a clerk named John, but even here the similarities are superficial.
3. Robert Marmion's grant of land at Checkendon (Oxon.) to Coventry priory as compensation for the injuries inflicted by his father (*Oxford Hist. Society*, lxxxviii, pp. 4, 8) can hardly be considered an exception.

76. Gift to the monks of Hartsholme of one mark annually from his mill of Bracebridge.

Lincoln, [1144–1146]

P.R.O., C.53 (Chancery Charter Rolls), no. 118 (5 Edw. III), m. 3; B.L. Cott. MS. Vesp. E. xx (Bardney cartulary), f. 207v. (old f. 202v.) Ed.: *Cal. Ch. Rolls*, iv. 235 (no. 5).

Rannulfus comes Cestrie universis Christi fidelibus salutem. Sciatis me dedisse et hac carta confirmasse ecclesie sancte Marie Magdalene de Hertesholm unam marcam argenti recipiendam annuatim ad Pascha de molendino meo de Bracebrigge in liberam et puram et perpetuam elemosinam pro salute anime mee et antecessorum meorum. Et ego et heredes mei hanc elemosinam ei in perpetuum warantizabimus. Testibus Bertram de Verdun, Willelmo filio Rogeri, Berengero, et pluribus aliis apud Lincolniam.

This charter was attributed by the editor of *The Calendar of Charter Rolls* to Ranulf III, presumably because of the presence as a witness of Bertram de Verdun, but it must be a charter of Ranulf II and should be compared with **nos. 77** and **78**. Logically it should precede **no. 77**, and the appearance of Berengar, or Berengar the falconer, who occurs in half-a-dozen charters of Ranulf II between c.1130 and c.1150, is compatible with such a date. It has also been suggested that William son of Roger was the son of Roger Mainwaring who witnessed his father's grant of Plumley to St. Werburgh's c.1119 (**no. 8**), and was mentioned on the Pipe Roll of 1130 (*H.K.F.*, pp. 227–8). The difficulty is Bertram of Verdun, the well-known justiciar of Henry II, who died on crusade in 1192. Bertram was the son of Norman de Verdun, who died in 1153 (**no. 106**), and this is by far his earliest known appearance. He witnessed an agreement between William de Verdun and the monks of Mont St. Michel in 1155 (Robert of Torigni, *Chron.*, (Appendix), p. 333), but his earliest known mention in England is on the Staffordshire Pipe Roll of 1158–9. If the present grant precedes **no. 77**, as appears to be the case, it cannot be later than 1146, and this puts back our knowledge of Bertram by approximately ten years. This is not impossible, but he must at that time have been a very young man at the beginning of his long career.

77.   Gift to the monks of Hartsholme of 2 marks yearly, one mark from the mill of Bracebridge and one mark from the mill of Waddington (Lincs.)

Lincoln, [1144–1146]

P.R.O., C.53 (Chancery Charter Rolls), no. 118, m. 10; B.L. Cott. Vesp. E.xx (Bardney cartulary), f. 202v. (new f. 207v). Ed.: *Cal. Ch. Rolls*, iv. 235 (no. 4).

R. comes Cestrie constabulario, dapifero, baronibus, vic(ecomiti), ministris et ballidis, et omnibus hominibus suis Lincolnscire Francis et Anglis salutem. Scitote me dedisse in elemosinam pro salute anime mee monachis et ecclesie sancte Marie Magdalene de Hertesholm duas marcas argenti singulis annis, videlicet in molendino de Bracebrige unam marcam argenti ad Pascha et alteram marcam argenti de molendino de Wadingtona ad terminum quo inde firmam accipere et recipere solebam. Quare volo et firmiter precipio quod predictum redditum plenarie et integre singulis annis ad terminos constitutos habeant.

Quicumque autem eos inde disturbare proposuerit, in forisfactum meum decidat et peccatum super eum veniat. Testibus Radulfo de Haia et Willelmo Coleville[1] et Simone filio Willelmi et Hugone Bardulf et Gaufrido Malebisse et Willelmo Haconis[2] filio et Willelmo capellano, apud Lincolniam.

1. *remaining witnesses omitted, Cart.*
2. Hiconis *MS.*

St. Mary Magdalene at Hartsholme, nr. Lincoln, was a cell of Bardney abbey. Ranulf II's gift is not easily dated, but the witnesses suggest that it falls between 1144 and 1146. For Hugh Bardulf, see **no. 66**. William son of Hacon, who had been granted land in Cuxwold (Lincs.) by Henry I as early as 1115–18 (*Linc. Rec. Soc.*, xix, p. 247), witnessed William of Roumare's foundation charter for Revesby abbey in 1142 (*Northants. Rec. Soc.*, iv, p. 3).

78. Notification to the bishop of Lincoln that he has given to the monks of Hartsholme an annual rent of one mark from the mill of Bracebridge and one mark from the mill of Waddington and the whole mill of Braidwood, and reminding him to do ecclesiastical justice on anyone who exercises force or violence against them.

[1149–1153]

B.L. Cott. MS. Vesp. E. xx (Bardney cartulary), f. 208.

Roberto divino munere episcopo Lincolnie et toti capitulo Lincolniensis ecclesie Ranulfus comes Cestrie salutem. Notificetur vobis me concessisse atque dedisse iamdudum ecclesie sancte Marie Magdalene de Hertesholm et monachis ibidem deo famulantibus in molendino de Bracebrige unam marcam argenti et in molendino Wadingtonie unam marcam et totum molendinum de Braidewad, sicut carta mea testatur, quam habent, queque etiam apostolico confirmatur privilegio, detestans anathematizansque omnes illos, qui eis inde violenciam fecerint, auferendo aut ullo modo diminuendo iura sua. Ideoque vobis commemorare non indignum arbitror, quatinus plenarie faciatis ecclesiasticam iusticiam super hiis omnibus, qui eis vim aut violentiam fecerint. Testibus Ricardo pincerna *etc.*

The use of the word *iamdudum* in this document indicates that the earl's gifts were not recent, and in fact they were confirmed by Pope Eugenius III in a privilege issued at Autun on 14 August 1147 (Vesp. E. xx, f. 14). This is presumably the 'apostolic privilege' to which Ranulf II refers. As the only witness recorded is Richard the butler (*pincerna*), an exact date is impossible, but the whole tone of the letter suggests that the earl was drawing the attention of the new bishop of Lincoln (consecrated 19 December 1148) to his donations and asking him to support them with ecclesiastical penalties. The relation to **no. 96** is not clear, but it looks as though the present charter may be a little later in date.

79.   Confirmation to the leper hospital of Lincoln of Earl Ranulf's gift of 2½ marks of silver from the mills of Bracebridge.

[? 1140–1153]

P.R.O., C.53 (Chancery Charter Rolls), no. 23, m. 1.
Ed.: *Mon.*, vi. 628; *Cal. Ch. Rolls*, ii. 111.

H. dei gratia rex Anglie et dux Normannie et Aquitanie et comes Andegavie . . . Sciatis me concessisse et presenti carta confirmasse leprosis hospitalis Lincolnie . . . ex dono comitis Rannulfi Cestrie duas marcas argenti et dimidiam de molendinis de Brascebrige . . .

The foundation of the leper hospital of the Holy Innocents, or the Malandry, on the outskirts of Lincoln is variously ascribed to Henry I and to Bishop Remigius (1072–92); it was certainly in existence in the early years of the twelfth century (Hill, *Medieval Lincoln*, p. 343). Earl Ranulf's gift is only known from Henry II's confirmation, given at Nottingham, perhaps in 1175 (Eyton, p. 193), and cannot be dated accurately, but is likely to be later, rather than earlier, in his tenure of the earldom, probably after 1140 and perhaps at the time of his grant of one mark from the mill of Bracebridge to St. Mary Magdalene of Hartsholme (**no. 77**), i.e. 1144–46.

80.   Grant, to Wimund, son of Herbert the cook, of the land his father held in Little Minting (Lincs.) and of his office of cook in the earl's kitchen.

Lincoln, [1144–1146]

B.L. Add. MS. 35296 (Spalding register), f. 411; Add. MS. 5844 (transcript of register), f. 448 (new f. 227v.).
Ed.: Stenton, *First Century of English Feudalism*, p. 271.

Ranulphus comes Cestrie constabulario, dapifero, baronibus, castellanis, ius-tic(iario), vic(ecomitibus), ministris et ballivis, et omnibus hominibus suis Francis et Anglis salutem. Scitote me reddidisse Wimundo filio Herberti coci totam terram, que fuit patris sui, et suum misterium in coquina mea, ut ibi sit cocus cum aliis sicut ius suum et hereditatem suam. Eapropter volo et precipio quod ipse Wimundus et heredes sui de me et heredibus meis predictam tenuram suam et rectum suum habeat integriter in coquina et extra in[1] Mintinga Parva in bosco et plano, in pratis et pasturis et omnibus aliis locis ita bene et libere sicut umquam pater suus melius habuit, cum socca et sacca et tol et them et infangenthef et cum omnibus aliis consuetudinibus et libertatibus omnibus. Testibus Normanno Verdun et Gilberto Neville, Ricardo pincerna, Hugone osturcario, Rogero Belchamp,[2] Roberto Folamenum, Hugone pistore, Radulfo iusticiario, Willelmo capellano, apud Lincolniam.

1. de *Add. MS. 35296 and ed.*
2. Bele hamp *MSS. and ed.*

This charter should be compared to **no. 55**, the grant of another minor office in the earl's household to Robert Fumichon or Folamenum, one of the witnesses of the present charter. As Herbert the cook, one of the witnesses of **no. 55**, was dead by the time his lands were conveyed to his son Wimund, the present charter must be the later of the two. On the other hand, it must be earlier than **no. 92**. Unfortunately, the witnesses do not help to narrow the date, but 1144–46 seems probable.

81. The priory of Norton is freed from all the aids the earl is accustomed to levy in his lands, and from giving hospitality to his serjeants beyond what the canons wish; they are to maintain and protect them and their possessions, whatever they may be.

Frodsham, [1144–1153]

P.R.O., CHES 29/62 (Plea Rolls, 24 Edw. III), m. 2v.; CHES 34/4 (Quo Warranto, 15 Henr. VII), m. lv., from which B.L. Harl. MS. 2060, f. 75v., Harl. MS. 2115, f. 140v., Add. MS. 19517, f. 5v. and Bodleian Library, Dodsworth MS. 39, f. 155, derive. Ed.: *Stenton Misc.*, pp. 29–30 (no. 2).

Ranulfus consul Cestrie Roberto dapifero, iustic(ie) baronibus, vic(ecomitibus), ministris et ballidis et omnibus servientibus de Cestriscira, quicumque fuerint, Francis et Anglis, salutem. Super amorem dei et meum forisfactum et super oculos vestros precipio quod de talibus omnibus auxiliis, que solitus sum ponere in terra mea et hominum meorum, sit in perpetuum quietus prioratus et prior et omnes homines sui de Nortona, elemosina constabularii Cestrie, ita ne quicquam inde requiratis nec molestiam terris nec hominibus suis, ubicumque illas in mea ballida habuerint, inferatis, set solas in perpetuum illas de omnibus consuetudinibus et exactionibus et geldis et castellorum operacionibus pro me et heredibus meis possideant, sicut elemosinam sancte ecclesie, ita ne mihi pro ullo precepto nec mandato meo nec meorum nec servientibus meis respondeant, nisi de solis oracionibus et dei servicio pro salute omni faciendis. Insuper etiam prohibeo infestationem hospitalitatis servientium meorum apud illos vel homines suos, ita ne per consuetudinem ab eis quicquam supra velle illorum requirant, set illos et eorum possessiones attentius, ubicumque fuerint, manuteneant et protegant, ne inde queremoniam audiam. Testibus Eustachio constabulario Cestrie et Normanno de Verdun et Ricardo pincerna et Iohanne et Willelmo capellanis et Ricardo clerico de Frodesham, apud Frodesham.

The future priory of Norton was originally established at Runcorn by the constable of Chester, William fitz Nigel, about 1115, and transferred to Norton in 1134. Eustace fitz John succeeded to the constableship in 1144 or 1145 (**no. 73**), and the present charter falls between then and Earl Ranulf II's death in December 1153. Norman de Verdun died shortly before the earl (**no. 106**), but probably also in 1153.

82.   Grant to Robert, earl of Leicester, of Charley (Leics.) and the woods adjacent to Robert's forest of Leicester, except the park of Barrow-upon-Soar, and of anything he possesses in the city of Leicester, for which Robert pledged his faith to Earl Ranulf as the lord of whom he held. In the country between Leicester and Mountsorrel.

[1145–1147]

Orig.: Huntington Library, San Marino, Calif., Hastings MSS., Leicester and Charley no. 375 (HAD 3623). Transcr.: B.L. Lansdowne MS. 415 (Garendon cartulary), f. 41 (new f. 42); Bodleian Library, Dugdale MS. 11 ('ex vetusto chartulario Lirensis cenobii'), f. 66. Ed.: Nichols, *Leicestershire*, III. ii. 830; Dugdale, *Baronage*, i. 39; *Hist. MSS. Comm., Report on the MSS. of R.R. Hastings*, i. 66–67.

Ranulfus comes Cestrie constabulario, dapifero, ministris, vic(ecomiti) et omnibus ballidis suis Francis et Anglis salutem. Sciatis me dedisse et concessisse Roberto comiti Legrecestrie in feodo et hereditate sibi et heredibus suis de me et de heredibus meis Cerneleam et omnes boscos adiacentes iuxta forestam suam Legrecestrie, tam meos proprios quam eos de feodo meo, excepto parco meo de Barow, ad habendum eos in foresta de me ita bene et libere et plenarie sicut melius tenet forestam Legrecestrie de rege, excepto hoc solo quod retineo in boscis illis aisiamenta maneriorum iuxtapositorum sine wasto et sine venditione. Et preter hoc dedi ei hereditarie quicquid habeo in civitate Legrecestrie in dominio et feudo. Et de hac tenura fidem mihi fecit sicut domino de quo tenet. Quare volo et precipio quod bene et in pace et libere teneat, et prohibio ne quis ei quicquam de rebus istis forisfaciat. Testibus Alexandro episcopo Lincolnie et Rogero episcopo Cestrie, comite Willelmo Lincolnie et comite Symone Norhantonie et Radulfo de Haia et Hugone Waac et Willelmo Coleville et Symone filio Willelmi et Turstano Banastre et Hugone Bardulf et Hugone osturcario et Ricardo pincerna et Gaufrido dispensatore et Ivone fratre suo et Rogero de Turribus et Hugone Malebisse et Roberto filio Nigelli et Iohanne de Stutevilla et Willelmo Burdet et Roberto de Creft et Gaufrido abbate et Radulfo Normanville et Fulcone Trussell et Roberto Puher. In[1] agris deinter Legrecestriam et Monte Sorell.

1. *orig. reads* et, *clearly a mistake.*

Charley, which was part of Earl Hugh's extensive landholding in 1086, had been handed over to Henry I, together with the adjacent woods in the forest of Charnwood, by Ranulf I in 1129, and the king had granted them to Robert, earl of Leicester (*Regesta*, ii. no. 1607). How they subsequently came into the hands of Ranulf II, whether by grant from Stephen or by simple usurpation, is not known; but their occupation must have been a potent cause of friction between him and Earl Robert, particularly as the lands in question bordered closely on Robert's Leicester domain. The purpose of the present charter, which amounts to a one-sided act of restitution, was evidently to put an end to this friction. It must fall before the departure on crusade of Bishop Roger of Chester in May 1147 and presumably after Ranulf II's charter for Hugh Bardulf (**no. 66**), another witness. Otherwise the evidence is circumstantial. It has been surmised that the most likely date is 1145–6 (*E.H.R.*, lxxxvi, p. 538), but it is perhaps more likely that Ranulf would have sought reconciliation with the earl of Leicester at the time when he was rebuilding his position after his release following his arrest at Northampton in August 1146. In that case the present charter would date from late 1146 or early 1147; but no date is more than tentative.

83. Gift to the abbey of St. Mary de Pré, Leicester, of the church of Barrow-on-Soar and the chapel of Quorndon, with one carucate of his demesne in Barrow and Quorndon, and two carucates in Rothley.

[1143–1153]

Bodleian Library, MS. Laud misc. 625, ff. 6v., 19;[1] B.L. Cott. MS. Vitell. F. xvii, f. 11v.[2] Engl. abstract: *H.K.F.*, p. 55; Thompson, *Leicester Abbey*, p. 6.

1. This MS. is a rental of 1477, and has no texts of charters but refers to them where appropriate in abbreviated form.
2. Apparently a similar compilation to the Bodleian MS., but seriously damaged by fire in 1731, and only fragments, often barely legible, survive.

Habemus in Baro ex dono Ranulphi comitis Cestrie ecclesiam cum omnibus pertinenciis suis et cum una carucata terre in Querendona et in Barow de dominio dicti Ranulphi comitis Cestrie cum omnibus libertatibus et consuetudines, ut patet per primam cartam . . . Habemus capellam de Quorndon ex dono Ranulfi comitis Cestrie[1] . . . Ex dono Ranulfi comitis Cestrie duas carucatas terre in Roleia, que vocatur Baneclestoft, cum prato adiacente . . .

1. Further references to preceding gifts recur a number of times, but add nothing and have been ignored.

Leicester abbey was founded by Robert, earl of Leicester, in all probability in 1143. In view of the strained relations between him and Ranulf II, usually on different sides in the conflicts of Stephen's reign (**nos. 82, 89**), it is somewhat surprising to find the latter endowing Robert's foundation, and it would be tempting, but rash, to attempt to link Ranulf's gifts to the politics of the time. The date of his charter (of which the above notices are the only evidence surviving) must fall between 1143 and 1153, and probably in 1146 or 1147; but its genuineness is warranted by confirmations of King Stephen (*Regesta*, iii. no. 436) and Henry II (*Cal. Ch. Rolls*, iii. 380), both printed in *Mon.*, vi. 466–7.

84.   Gift to the monks of Lenton (Notts.) of the hamlet of Kersal (Lancs.) to build a place for the worship of God, with a pasture and the right to extend their estate by making assarts and fisheries.

Chester, [1147–1148]

B.L. Add. MS. 5860 (formerly Cole MS.), p. 188.[1] Ed.: *L.P.R.*, p. 326.

1. Cole's note: 'My worthy and much respected friend Dr. Farmer communicated the following papers to me in December 1780. The first is a very ancient deed, about Henry 2ᵈs reign, on a piece of parchment of 6 inches deep and 4 broad, which, being used as lining to the cover of an old book, has suffered a trifle by being worm-eaten.'

R. consul Cestrie episcopo Cestrie, archidiacono et omnibus ordinatis dei, et constabulario Cestrie, dapifero, baronibus,[1] iusticiis,[2] vicecom(itibus), ministris et ballidis, et omnibus hominibus suis clericis et laicis, Francis et Anglis, salutem. Sciatis me concessisse et dedisse deo et sancte Marie et monachis Sancte Trinitatis de Lentona in elemosinam Kereshalam, locum ad servicium dei edificandum, et pasturam, et ad se dilatandum de essartis et piscariis, et de rebus illis omnibus, quibuscumque se dilatari et aisiari poterint. Quare volo et firmiter precipio quod predicti monachi bene et honorifice predictam elemosinam solam et quietam et liberam de omni seculari servicio habeant, ne aliquis meorum super timorem dei et meum amorem temere perturbet. Testibus Mathilda comitissa Cestrie et Kadwalader rege Waliarum et Willelmo filio Alani et Symone Corbet et Roberto dapifero, Ricardo pincerna et Henrico Pultrell et Willelmo capellano, apud Cestriam.

1. B . . . *MS*, ('the other letters being eaten by worms').
2. *sic MS.*

Ranulf II is unlikely to have issued this charter until he was invested with the land between Ribble and Mersey, almost certainly in 1146 (**no. 63**). He had no known connection with Lenton priory, a foundation of William Peverel, and his charter, although cast in the form of a gift, is almost certainly a confirmation of an earlier gift by King Stephen. His charter has been attributed to the year 1142 by Farrer (*L.P.R.*, p. 327), but this, as Tait pointed out (*Chart. St. Werburgh*, p. 36, note 5), is certainly too early a date. The probable date is 1147 or possibly 1148, when there appears to have been a gathering of Angevin supporters at Chester, and it is likely that **nos. 63, 64** and **85** were issued at approximately the same date. For William fitz Alan of Oswestry and Clun, see **No. 85**, which he witnessed at Chester with four other witnesses of the present charter, viz. Henry Putrel or Pultrel, Robert the steward, Richard the butler and William the chaplain. For Cadwaladr, self-styled king of Wales, see **no. 64**. Both were related to Ranulf II by marriage.

85. Restoration to Henry Tuschet, as his heritage, of all the lands previously held by Henry his father and Joscelin his grandfather.

Chester, [1147–1148]

B.L. Add. MS. 6032, f. 200 (new f. 100); Bodleian Library, Dodsworth MS. 31, f. 142; MS. Top. Cheshire b. I, p. 136: Chester, Booth of Twemlow, Liber D, f. 190. (All have exactly the same description of the earl's seal, and must come from a common source, presumably the original charter, but source is not stated). B.L. Harl. MS. 2079, f. 24 (new f. 12); Bodleian Library, Dodsworth MS. 41, f. 118 (abbreviated); B.L. Add. MS. 19517, p. 184 (new f. 93v.). (These MSS. all have a note 'in dorso Tattenhall' indicating a common source, presumably the original charter). Ed.: *The Genealogist*, N.S. xxxvi, p. 20.

Ranulfus comes Cestrie constabulario, dapifero, baronibus, iusticiario, vic(ecomiti), ministris et omnibus hominibus suis de Cestreshira, et[1] Francis et Anglis, salutem. Sciatis me reddidisse Henrico de Tuschet totam terram suam, que fuit Henrici de Tuschet patris sui et Iocelini de Tuschet avi sui, sicut hereditatem suam. Quare volo et firmiter precipio quod ipse Henricus et heredes sui de me et heredibus meis predictam terram et tenuram teneant ita bene et honorifice et libere et quiete sicut unquam avus et pater suus melius in vita sua tenuerunt, in villa et extra, in foro et mercato, in bosco et plano, in pratis et pascuis, in viis et semitis, in forestis, in aquis, in stagnis et molendinis, et in omnibus aliis locis cum soca et saca et tol et them et infangthefe et cum omnibus aliis consuetudinibus et libertatibus, ita quod nec[1] aliquis et vel suis iniuriam vel molestiam faciat super meam forisfacturam. Testibus Rogero comite Herefordie et Willelmo filio Alani et Radulfo abbate Cestrie et Roberto dapifero et Hugone austricario et Serlone venatore et Roberto filio Iocerami et Henrico Putrell et Galfrido dispensatore et Ricardo pincerna et Willelmo archidiacono Cestrie et Hugone decano Derebie et Willelmo et Iohanne capellanis, apud Cestriam.

> SEAL: 'sealed with the earles great seale, the impression
> beinge a man on horsebacke very large'.

1. *sic MSS.*

This interesting charter has usually been dated 1143–49 (Tait, *Chart. St. Werburgh*, p. 123; Farrer, *H.K.F.*, p. 28). As the first witness, Earl Roger of Hereford, did not succeed until after the death of his father on 24 December 1143, it can scarcely fall before 1144. The later date is supplied by the mention of William, archdeacon of Chester from 1139 to 1149 (*L.P.R.*, p. 278), but the charter is almost certainly earlier than that. One of its notable features is the appearance together, as its first two witnesses, of two prominent Angevin supporters. William fitz Alan of Oswestry and Clun, who also witnesses **no. 84**, had rebelled in 1138 and held Shrewsbury castle against Stephen, but was forced to take flight, and is found with the Empress Matilda at Oxford in the summer of 1141, and then at Winchester and Devizes. He had married a niece of Robert of Gloucester, Matilda's brother and the leader of the Angevin party, and probably took refuge with him. Roger of Hereford, like his father Miles of Gloucester, was an adherent of the empress who gave active support to the earl of Gloucester almost immediately after his succession in 1144 (*Gesta Stephani*, p. 172). The presence of these two men in Chester is significant, and should be considered also in connection with the presence there of Gilbert fitz Richard of Clare, earl of Hertford, the son of Ranulf II's sister Adeliza, and of Cadwaladr, so-called king of Wales, who had married a sister of Earl Gilbert (**no. 64**). It appears that Ranulf, who had been up in arms ever since his arrest at Northampton on 28 August 1146 (*Gesta Stephani*, p. 198), took over the leadership of the Angevin faction after the death of Robert of Gloucester on 31

October 1147, and it is safe to assume that this charter, like **nos. 64** and **84**, which were also given at Chester, belongs to this period.

The political situation at the end of 1147, when the Angevin cause was at a low ebb (*T.R.H.S.*, 4th Ser. xx, p. 128), probably also explains the terms of the charter. Tattenhall in south-west Cheshire, the 'land' to which it refers, had been in the hands of the Tuschets since the eleventh century.[1] Evidently Ranulf II had refused at some stage, presumably after his father's death, to recognize Henry Tuschet's right of succession. If he now reversed his position and gave him back (*reddidisse*) the land which had been his father's and his grandfather's 'as his inheritance' (*sicut hereditatem suam*), the reason may well have been the need to secure the loyalty of his Cheshire tenants at a critical moment in his struggle with Stephen. The right of hereditary succession was a leading issue during Stephen's reign (David, *King Stephen*, pp. 154–5), and the present charter is an unusually explicit recognition of it.

1. This is the accepted view (Orm., ii. 717). It was contested by Tait and Farrer (*loc. cit.*) on the ground that the charter mentions neither Tattenhall nor any other manor by name. This is true; but neither was aware that it is specifically endorsed 'Tattenhall', as three of the surviving manuscripts are careful to note. Although there are problems in the subsequent descent, it is safe to conclude that Ormerod's view is correct.

86. Grant of Fifehead (Dorset) to Robert fitz Harding and his son Maurice to hold in fee and heredity, in return for a payment of 23 marks and one falcon yearly, guaranteeing an equivalent tenure before they were disseised, if he could not warrant his gift.

[1147–1148]

Berkeley Castle, Gloucs., Cartulary of St. Augustine's, f. 29v.

Rannulfus comes Cestrie constabulario, dapifero, baronibus, iustic(iariis), vic(ecomitibus), ministris, ballidis, et omnibus hominibus suis Francis et Anglis salutem. Sciatis me dedisse Roberto filio Hardingi et Mauricio eius filio Fifhidam in feodo et hereditate cum omnibus pertinenciis suis. Quare volo et firmiter precipio quod ipse Robertus et Mauricius eius filius et heredes illorum predictam Fifhidam de me et de heredibus meis bene et honorifice teneant in villa et extra, in foro et mercato, in bosco et plano, in pratis et pascuis, in viis et semitis, in molendinis et in aquis, et in omnibus aliis locis, cum soca et sacca et tol et them et infangethef et cum omnibus aliis consuetudinibus et libertatibus. Scitote etiam quod, quando eis hanc donacionem feci, propter hoc dederunt mihi de recogni- tione xxiii. marcas, et ita quod pro omni servitio mihi singulis annis reddituri, sunt I. osturium. Et nisi eis istam tenuram de Fifhida warrentizare possem, escambium ad valens et ad eius warandum donarem, priusquam de predicta Fifhida dissaisirentur. Testibus *etc.*

Robert fitz Harding of Bristol was the paymaster, either voluntarily or under pressure from Earl Robert of Gloucester, who made Bristol his headquarters, (*Gesta Stephani*, p. 57), of the rebels against King Stephen, and in the end was handsomely rewarded by Henry II before and after he succeeded to the throne. It has been suggested that fitz Harding was grandson of Eadnoth the staller, who held Fifehead and other Dorset manors before the Conquest (*H.K.F.*, p. 286), and, if true, this might account for the present enfeoffment. Unfortunately, the enrolment of the present charter omits the witnesses, and it cannot be dated accurately. The only safe thing that can be said is that it is earlier than **no. 87**, which seems to date from 1149–50, probably 1149. The problem is that, apart from this charter and **no. 87**, there is no evidence that Earl Ranulf was ever at Bristol in this period; but if the suggestion that he may have gone to Bristol after the death of Robert of Gloucester on 31 October 1147 is acceptable, this would be the most likely date for the charter. This was a low point in the fortunes of the Angevin rebels, particularly in Wiltshire and Hampshire (*Gesta Stephani*, pp. 208–214), and this situation probably explains the last sentence of Ranulf's charter, i.e. the promise of an equivalent, if he could not guarantee possession of Fifehead. As the royalist forces were strong throughout the region in 1147 and 1148, this was a real possibility.

87.   Notification to Henry, son of the duke of Normandy and count of Anjou, of his gift to Robert fitz Harding, his man of Bristol, of Fifehead (Dorset), to be given in alms to the canons of St. Augustine's, Bristol; he himself with Robert had offered it on the altar of St. Augustine.

[June 1149–March 1150]

Berkeley Castle, Gloucs., Cartulary of St.Augustine's, ff. 29v.–30.

Rannulfus comes Cestrie Henrico filio ducis Normannorum et comitis Andegavorum domino suo, et archiepiscopis, episcopis, et omnibus baronibus suis, hominibus et amicis, et universis sancte dei ecclesie filiis salutem. Notum vobis facio, me pro salute anime mee et animarum predecessorum meorum concessisse Roberto Hardingi filio, homini meo de Bristolio, terram meam de Fifhida, donandam in elemosina ecclesie sancti Augustini de Bristolio et canonicis regularibus ibidem degentibus, quam ego prius eidem Roberto in feodo dederam. Et sciatis, quia ego ipse predictam terram cum Roberto super altare sancti Augustini optuli. Et ideo volo atque precipio[1] quatinus predicti canonici eandem terram bene et pacifice et liberam et quietam ab omni servitio et exactione de me et de meis heredibus in perpetuum teneant. Testibus *etc.*

1. prepio *MS.*

This interesting charter casts new light on the career of Ranulf II, and it is a pity that the only surviving copy omits the names of the witnesses. As Henry is still described as son of the duke of Normandy, it must fall before March 1150, by which time Geoffrey of Anjou had handed over the duchy to his son. On the other hand, Ranulf's description of Henry as 'his lord' (*dominus suus*) points to a date after the famous meeting at Carlisle on 22 May 1149, when King David of Scotland knighted the sixteen-year-old youth in Ranulf's presence and received him 'cum regio honore' (*Gesta Stephani*, p. 216). This was the first occasion when Henry was formally recognized as a king, and it is a fair assumption, though direct evidence is lacking, that Ranulf may have used the opportunity, as the phrase *dominus suus* implies, to do homage to him. Another interesting point is the statement that Ranulf, together with Robert fitz Harding, had personally placed his gift of Fifehead on the altar of St. Augustine's church. This points to a hitherto unknown visit by Ranulf to Bristol. He had previously granted Fifehead to fitz Harding as a fief (**no. 86**), and as a result fitz Harding became Ranulf's man (*homo meus*). The grant was now varied to permit fitz Harding to give it in alms to the abbey of St. Augustine's, which he had probably founded c.1148 (Knowles and Hadcock, p. 130). Although it can only be a suggestion, it seems possible that Ranulf may have gone to Bristol, as the headquarters of the insurgents, after the death of their leader, Robert of Gloucester, on 31 October 1147. There are other indications (**no. 85**) that he took over the leadership of the Angevin party around this time, and such a visit would have been an obvious move.

88. Confirmation to Lancaster priory of the liberties conferred by Roger of Poitou.

Lancaster, [27 July 1149]

B.L. Harl. MS. 3764, f. 1d; printed *Chetham Soc.*, N.S. xxvi, p. 31 (Roper, *Materials for the History of the Church of Lancaster); L.P.R.*, p. 296.

Ranulphus comes Cestrie archiepiscopo Eboracensi omnibusque sancte ecclesie fidelibus, insuper et suis baronibus, vic(ecomitibus), ministris et omnibus hominibus suis tam clericis quam laicis tocius terre sui, salutem. Sciatis me reddidisse et confirmacione presentis sigilli concessisse ecclesie sancte Marie de Lanc(astre) et monachis ibidem deo servientibus, quod habeant ita bene et in pace, libere et quiete, ecclesias et terras et consuetudines et rectitudines et res suas, et omnes illas libertates quas Rogerus comes Pictavensis predicte ecclesie dedit et concessit, sicut melius et liberius tenuerunt et habuerunt suo tempore, in redditibus et decimis et aliis elemosinis et beneficiis, in bosco et in plano, in viis et semitis, in aquis et molendinis, pratis, pascuis et pissinis.[1] Praeter hoc concessi eis Arnoay cum sua domo et mansione et cum suo servicio eis faciendo, et super hec omnia omnes sancte ecclesie fideles deposco eis et omnia sua protigere et adcrescere et manutenere ut elemosinam racionabiliter constitutam. Hiis testibus Normano de Verdun, Willelmo filio Gilberti, et Rodberto Banastre, Ricardo pincerna, Fulcone de Brichelhert, Michaele flandrensi, Iohanne capellano, Rogero capellano, Rogero filio Ravenchil,[2] Rogero[3] Gernet, Willelmo capellano qui hanc cartam scripsit sexto Kalendis Augusti, apud Lancastr(am).

1. *sic MS.*
2. *MS. has* Fravenchil *in error for* Ravenchil. *Roger is evidently the son of Ravenchil filius Raigenald of Roger of Poitou's charter.*
3. Rogero Willelmo *repeated MS.*

For the dating, see Farrer, *L.P.R.*, p. 297. Earl Ranulf met Prince Henry (the future Henry II) and King David of Scotland at Carlisle at Whitsuntide 1149, and was invested with the honour of Lancaster, including Lancashire north of the Ribble which David had held since 1138. The present charter was almost certainly executed, by virtue of his newly acquired rights, on the return journey from this meeting. Roger of Poitou's charter precedes Ranulf's in the cartulary, and is printed by Farrer (*op. cit.*, pp. 289–290) under the date 1094.

89.   Grant to Robert earl of Leicester, of the village and castle of Mountsorrel (Leics.) for his homage, and confirmation of the holdings already given, for which the earl of Leicester had pledged himself to the earl of Chester.

[1148–1149]

B.L. Lansdowne MS. 415 (Garendon cartulary), f. 41 (new f. 42). Ed.: Nichols, *Leicestershire*, III. ii. 830; Stenton, *First Century of English Feudalism*, p. 285.

Rannulfus comes Cestrie constabulario, dapifero, baronibus, iustic(iario), vic(ecomiti), ministris et baillivis et omnibus fidelibus suis Francis et Anglis salutem.[1] Sciatis me dedisse Roberto comiti Legrecestrie in feudo et hereditate pro homagio suo Muntsorell, villam et castellum desuper, cum omnibus pertinenciis suis. Et preter hoc dono ei hereditarie omnes tenuras de quibus erat meus affidatus, et sicut carta mea ei testatur. Eapropter volo et firmiter precipio, ut ipse comes Robertus Legrecestrie predictum castellum et villam de Muntsorell cum predictis tenuris bene et honorifice iure hereditario de me et de heredibus meis teneat in villa et extra et castro et foro et mercato, in bosco et plano, in pratis et pasturis, et in aquis et molendinis, in viis et semitis et forestis, et in omnibus aliis locis, cum soca et saca et thol et them et[2] infanganthef, et cum omnibus aliis consuetudinibus et libertatibus. Teste Gilleberto comite de Clara.

1. Anglis salutem *illegible in MS., which has deteriorated.*
2. *Barely legible in MS.*

As the cartulary omits the witnesses, except Gilbert of Clare, earl of Hertford, this important charter unfortunately cannot be dated accurately. Stenton (*loc. cit.*) dates it c.1148, presumably because it is earlier than **no. 110** and later than **no. 82**, to which it makes reference. As the castle of Mountsorrel was a strongpoint for the defence of Ranulf II's extensive interests in the Midlands, its surrender to the earl of Leicester, one of King Stephen's prominent supporters, is difficult to explain, unless at this time Ranulf was seeking to stabilize the position in the Midlands in order to turn his attention to the honour of Lancaster, which he had recently acquired (**no. 88**). In that case, the date of the charter would be 1149.

90.   Grant to the monks of Evesham of Howick (Lancs.), as they held it in the time of Count Roger of Poitou and of Earl Ranulf I.

Ravensmeols, [c.1149]

B.L. Cott. MS. Vesp. B. xxiv (Evesham cartulary), f. 75v.
Ed.: *Mon.*, iii. 420; *L.P.R.*, p. 319.

Rannulfus consul Cestrie constabulario, dapifero, baronibus, iust(iciario), vic(ecomiti), ministris et baillivis, quicumque fuerint, inter Ribbam et Mersam, et omnibus hominibus suis Francis et Anglis salutem. Sciatis me concessisse deo et sancte Marie et monachis de Evesham elemosinam suam de Hocwica ita bene et libere et quiete et honorifice sicut melius tenuerunt tempore comitis Rogeri Pictavensis et tempore Rannulfi comitis patris mei, et sicut decet elemosinam habere sancte ecclesie, ita quod nullus super monachos predictos se intromittat de predicta elemosina, nec de operationibus nec de aliis exactionibus, nec de occasione aliqua aliquis eos vel eorum elemosinam super timorem dei et super meum forisfactum inquietet, set honorifice teneant in terris et decimis et pasturis, et in bosco et in plano, et in aquis et molendinis et piscariis, et in omnibus aliis locis. Testibus Eustachio constabulario Cestrie et Hugone ostucario[1] et Serlone venatore et Ricardo Buissel et Ricardo pincerna, apud Molas Warini.

1. ostucarius *MS.*

This charter is subsequent to Earl Ranulf's investiture with the land between Ribble and Mersey, almost certainly in 1146 (**nos. 63, 84**). For the original grant by Roger of Poitou, of which the present charter is effectively a confirmation, see Farrer, *L.P.R.*, p. 318. As Tait pointed out (*Mediaeval Manchester and the Beginnings of Lancashire*, p. 165), it is just possible that Ranulf I was in possession of the land between Ribble and Mersey at some date after Roger of Poitou's forfeiture in 1102; but there is no other evidence, and it is highly improbable. Farrer dates Ranulf II's charter in 1149, on the assumption that he stopped off at Warin's Meols (later Ravens Meols) on his way to or from his meeting with King David of Scotland at Carlisle in that year; but Tait pointed out that this was not necessarily the case. Nevertheless the date may very well be correct. Howick lay in the parish of Penwortham, where Warin Bussel, who died c.1150 (*V.C.H. Lancs.*, i. 355), made gifts to Evesham c.1140–49 which subsequently led to the establishment of the cell of Penwortham (*L.P.R.*, pp. 320–1). As Ranulf's charter is witnessed not by Warin but by his son Richard Bussel, it seems likely that it was issued after Warin's death. For Eustace the constable, who probably succeeded in 1144, see **no. 73**.

91.   Confirmation to Evesham abbey of the lands and liberties granted by Warin, Richard and Albert Bussel, and grant of a court of Howick to be held as freely as the earl held his court in Penwortham. [Spurious]

[c.1150]

P.R.O., D.L. 41/3/29 (15th century roll of donations to Evesham); Chetham's Library, Kuerdon Folio MS., f. 74 (abbreviated text, source not stated).

Rannulfus consul Cestrie constabulario, dapifero, baronibus, iusticiar(io), vicecomit(i), ministris et ballivis, quicumque fuerint, inter Riblam et Mersam, et omnibus hominibus suis Francis et Anglis[1] salutem. Sciatis me omnes possessiones, terras et tenementa et omnes libertates abbati Evershamie et monachis ibidem deo servientibus a Warino, Ricardo, Alberto Bussell et heredibus suorum prius concessas concessisse et confirmasse in omnibus, et quod habeant curiam suam in Howyca de omnibus hominibus suis ita libere sicut ego habeo meam in Penwortham. Concedo insuper quod habeant in bosco et moscis de Penwortham pro se et omnibus tenentibus eorum husiboldam et hayboldam ad edificandum, comburendum et omnia alia negotia[2] sua faciendum sine conturbacione heredum meorum seu quorumcumque. Volo etiam et firmiter precipio quod nullus supradictos monachos de predicta concessione et confirmacione se intromittat[3] de occasione aliqua, exaccione seu[4] demanda super timorem dei et meum forisfactum, sed[5] honorifice et libere teneant in omnibus locis. Et ego

Ranulphus et heredes mei dictam concessionem et confirmacionem dicto abbati et conventui et successoribus eorum warantizabimus sine fine. Testibus etc.

1. Anglie *MS.*
2. necessitate *MS.*
3. intromittant *MS.*
4. et confirmacionem dicto abbati et conventui et successoribus eorum warantizabimus sine fine *inserted here MS.*
5. scilicet *MS.*

This charter is a gross forgery, probably fabricated by the monks at the cell of Penwortham, which Warin Bussel had given to Evesham c.1140–49 on condition that three brethren and a chaplain were sent there to conduct divine service (*L.P.R.*, pp. 320–1). Ranulf II's charter granting Howick to Evesham (**no. 90**) was clearly used as a model; but the warranty clause added at the end (with the extraordinary phrase *sine fine* for *in perpetuum*) is more appropriate to 1200 than to 1150, and a number of other anomalies (e.g., *tenentibus* for *hominibus*), betray its late date. As Warin Bussel died c.1149, Richard c.1164 and Albert c.1193 (*V.C.H. Lancs.*, i. 335–6), the forgery probably dates from the end of the twelfth century at earliest, but the putative date is c.1150. I have not been able to discover the reason for the forgery. There is no evidence that Ranulf II ever had a court in Penwortham, and Richard Bussel, who gave the court to Evesham, definitely stated that it was his and his father's before him (*L.P.R.*, p. 323). The main novelty of the charter is the claim to 'housebote' and 'haybote' in the wood and mosses of Penwortham, and it is possible that this had been denied, either by Albert Bussel's successor, Hugh, or, more likely, by Roger the constable of Chester, who purchased the barony of Penwortham from Hugh in 1205. The charter would then serve to establish an existing right; but firm evidence is lacking.

92. Notification to Bishop Robert of Lincoln and others of his gift to the abbey of St. Benedict-sur-Loire of the church of Gautby (Lincs.) and of lands of Wimund the cook and William the butler, and whatever he has in the two Mintings, except the land of Robert Fumichon and of Berengar the falconer.

Donington, [1149–1151]

B.L. Add. MS. 35296 (Spalding register), f. 410; Add. MS. 5844 (18th-century transcript from register) f. 447 (new f. 227).

Ranulphus comes Cestrie R. dei gratia Lincolniensi episcopo, R. archidiacono totique capitulo sancte Marie Lincolnie, dapifero, baronibus, iustic(iario), vic(ecomiti), et omnibus hominibus suis clericis et laicis, omnibusque prelatis et filiis sancte ecclesie salutem. Sciatis me concessisse et dedisse deo et sancte Marie et sancto Iacobo et sancto Benedicto et monachis eorum in perpetuam elemosinam pro dei dilectione et pro salute anime mee et pro animabus antecessorum meorum ecclesiam de Goutebi, que fuit Willelmi presbiteri de Segtrebroc, et duas bovatas terre et dimidiam Wimundi coci et unam bovatam terre Willelmi pincerne, et quicquid habui in duabus Mintingis, excepta tenura Roberti de Foumchun et Beringarii falconarii. Et concedo etiam quod predicti monachi et homines illorum habeant omnia aisiamenta sua in bosco meo de Mintingis ad edificia sua et pannagium eorum et ad alia negotia sua, sine vendicione vel donacione. Quapropter volo et firmiter precipio quod ipsi monachi supradictam elemosinam in rebus omnibus libere et quiete in perpetuum possideant, et ita honorifice sicut elemosina liberius dari potest. Testibus Radulfo abbate Cestrie, Widone abbate de sancto Severino, Iohanne capellano, Roberto Basset, apud Donigtonam.

The priory of Minting, Lincs., was founded as a cell or dependency of the abbey of St. Benedict at Fleury-sur-Loire, to which the gifts in the present charter are made. The charter must date after the succession of Robert Chesney to the see of Lincoln in December 1148, but is clearly earlier than no. 93. Whether the place at which it was issued was Donington-on-Bain (Lincs.) or Castle Donington (Leics.) is not clear, but the implication in either case is that Ranulf was not in possession of Lincoln. For Wimund the cook, see **no. 80**; for Robert Foumchun or Foumouzon, see **no. 55**.

93.   Notification to Bishop Robert of Lincoln and others of his gift to the abbey of St. Benedict-sur-Loire of the churches of St. Andrew of Minting and All Saints of Gautby, together with lands of Wimund the cook, William the butler and Spileman his late chamberlain, and whatever he possesses in the two Mintings, except the land of Robert Foumouzon and Berengar the falconer.

Lincoln, [1153]

MS. Paris lat. 12775 (from the cartulary of Fleury, now lost), p. 114; B.L. Add. MS. 35296 (Spalding register), ff. 409v.–410, and Add. MS. 5844 (transcript of register), f. 446 (new f. 226v.); P.R.O., C.53 (Chancery Charter Rolls), no. 123, m. 9 (inspeximus of Edw. III). Ed.: *Mon.*, vi. 1024; Prou et Vidier, *Receuil des chartes de l'abbaye de Saint-Bênoit-sur-Loire*, pp. 358–60; *Cal. Ch. Rolls*, iv. 378 (no. 1).

R. comes Cestrie Rotberto dei gratia Lincolniensi episcopo, Rotberto archidiacono, capitulo sancte Marie Lincolnie, constabulario, dapifero, baronibus,
iustic(iario), vic(ecomiti), ministris, ballivis et omnibus hominibus suis Francis et
Anglis, omnibusque prelatis et filiis sancte ecclesie salutem. Sciatis me concessisse et dedisse deo et sancte Marie et sancto Iacobo et sancto Benedicto et
monachis eorum in perpetuam elemosinam pro dei dilectione et pro salute
anime mee et pro animabus antecessorum meorum Mentingas et ecclesiam
sancti Andree de Mentingis et ecclesiam omnium sanctorum de Gouteby et duas
bovatas terre et dimidiam Wimundi coci et unam bovatam terre Willelmi
pincerne et terram Spilemanni, qui fuit camerarius meus, et quicquid habui in
duabus Mentingis, excepta tenura Rotberti de Fomuchun et Berengarii
falconarii. Et concedo quod predicti monachi et homines eorum habeant omnia
aisiamenta sua in bosco meo de Mentingis ad edificia sua et ad alia negotia sua,
et pannagium eorum sine venditione et donatione. Quapropter volo et firmiter
precipio quod ipsi monachi totam supradictam elemosinam in rebus omnibus ita
libere et quiete et honorifice in perpetuum teneant et habeant sicut elemosina
liberius et quietius et magis honorifice potest teneri et haberi et dari. Testibus
Waltero de Mundevilla, Normanno de Verdun, Radulfo de Haia, Hugone
Bardo[lf], Rotberto de Buschervilla, Rotberto Basset, Gaufrido Mansello, et
Willelmo capellano apud Lincolniam.

As Ranulf did not have access to Lincoln at any time between the consecration
of Bishop Robert in December 1148 and 1153, the present charter belongs to the
latter date. It is clearly later than **no. 92,** with which it should be compared.
There are three main differences: (i) the omission, in reference to the church of
Gautby, of mention of the former incumbent, William priest of Sedgebrook; (ii)
the additional gift of the church of St. Andrew of Minting; (iii) in addition to the
two and a half bovates of Wimund the cook and one bovate of William the
butler, the gift of the land of Spileman 'who was my chamberlain'. The third
change suggests that Spileman died between the grant of **no. 92** and the present
charter, in all probability in 1152 or 1153. The second is noteworthy because the
church of Minting (unless there was more than one) had been granted to
Spalding priory by Ranulf I (**no. 14**), and Ranulf II had previously confirmed his
father's gift (**no. 44**). It looks, therefore, as though its transfer to Minting priory
was another of the high-handed actions for which Ranulf II was notorious; but
Minting was one of the foundations he specially favoured (**no. 117**). Hence, no
doubt, his addition to new donations in a matter of a few months, which may be
compared with the doubling, at virtually the same time, of his compensation to
Lincoln cathedral (**nos. 104, 106**).

94. Confirmation to the abbey of Radmore of Osbert of Arden's gift of
Marston (nr. Kingsbury, Warws.)

[1149–1153]

Stratford-upon-Avon, Shakespeare's Birthplace, Stoneleigh Leger, f. 9; Gregory-Hood Leger, p. 221; Bodleian Library, Dugdale MS. 12, p. 36 (from Stoneleigh Leger). Ed.: Hilton, *Dugdale Society*, vol. xxiv, p. 13 (from Stoneleigh Leger).

Rannulfus comes Cestrie omnibus baronibus et castellanis suis et omnibus fidelibus suis, tam Francis quam Anglis, salutem. Notum sit vobis me concessisse et sigilli mei munimine confirmasse deo et sancte Marie de Rademore et Willelmo abbati et monachis ibidem deo servientibus in perpetuam elemosinam Merstonam cum omnibus appenditiis suis in bosco et plano et pascuis et rivis et omnibus rebus aliis, sicut Osbertus de Ardena eandem terram eis dedit et concessit et carta sua confirmavit. Unde mando et precor, ut dei et mei amore predictos monachos de Rademore diligatis et manuteneatis, nec aliquam iniuriam eis ab aliquo fieri, pro posse vestro eos defendendo, aliquatenus permittatis, quia abbatiam de Rademore cum omnibus pertinentiis in mea custodia retineo et dei adiutorio et materiali gladio eam defendere satago, et omnibus meis, ne predictis monachis aliquam iniuriam inferant, super amorem meum prohibeo. Valete.

Radmore was founded as a hermitage early in Stephen's reign, and converted into a Cistercian abbey probably c.1148. According to a charter of Henry duke of Normandy, which must date from 1153, Ranulf II had given the monks the village of Cannock 'to make their church and construct their offices'; but Ranulf's charter has not survived. The present document, which is more in the nature of a writ than of a charter, nevertheless indicates clearly that he regarded the abbey as under his special protection. Its date is uncertain. The charter of Osbert of Arden and his wife Matilda, which it confirms, is in the Stoneleigh Leger (f. 11v.), and was witnessed by Bishop Walter of Chester, who succeeded on 2 October 1149. It is dated 1153–56 by Hilton (*op. cit.*, p. lix), which is impossible, as it must precede Ranulf's confirmation. The latter must fall between 1149 and 1153. The unusual address, to his barons and castellans, and the general tone of the document, implying that the new house was under constant threat, suggest a time of warfare and upheaval in the Midlands, but it is impossible to pin it down more closely.

95.   Grant to Pipewell abbey, which he has taken under his protection, of the wood of Miclehaue in his fee of Geddington (Northants.), in which the abbey is built, and the wood of Stoke Albany which William d'Aubigny gave them, which he claims as his hereditary right.

[1149–1153]

B.L. Add. MS. 37022 (Pipewell cartulary), f. 7; Cott. MS.
Calig. A. xii (second, later cartulary), f. 10 (new f. 10v);
Bodleian Library, Dodsworth MS. 10, f. 190 (source not
stated); Northants. Record Office, Finch Hatton MS. 145,
f. 9 (probably from Cottonian text).

R.[1] Lincolniensi episcopo et omnibus sancte matris ecclesie filiis tam presentibus quam futuris, prelatis et subiectis, Rannulfus comes Cestrie, salutem. Notum sit omnibus hanc cartam videntibus et audientibus me dedisse et concessisse et presenti scripto confirmasse deo et abbatie de Pipewelle et monachis ibidem deo servientibus terram illam et boscum, scilicet Miclehaue,[2] que est de feodo meo de Geitentona, in qua predicta abbatia constructa est, et terram illam et boscum de Stokes, quam Willelmus de Albeneio eis dedit, et ius hereditarium quod in ea clamo, in elemosinam puram et perpetuam, liberam et quietam ab omni seculari servitio et exactione pro salute anime mee et predecessorum meorum et uxoris mee et liberorum meorum. Et sciant omnes quod ego predictam abbatiam sub manu et protectione mea habeo, et omnes res eidem ecclesie pertinentes sub tuitione mea suscepi. Quare volo ut firmiter et quiete sine alicuius vexatione et violentia omnes possessiones suas in perpetua pace tanquam monachi mei teneant, nec ullam molestiam ab aliquo sustineant. Huius donacionis hii sunt testes: Radulfus capellanus, Iohannes capellanus, Ricardus capellanus, et ceteri.[3]

1. *All MSS. except Add. 37022 have* T., *which is impossible.*
2. Mikelehai, *Dodsworth MS.*; Michlehae, *Cott. Calig.*
3. *sic Dodsworth MS*; *all others read* etcetera.

This charter is clearly a monastic production and slightly irregular in form, but there is no reason to question its authenticity. It is one of a number issued to religious houses, including Belvoir priory (**nos. 52, 54**) and Thorney abbey (**nos. 57, 58**), after Ranulf II had taken possession of the fee of Belvoir and claimed the succession to William d'Aubigny, the former lord of Belvoir (**no. 50**). It must fall after the consecration of Robert de Chesney as bishop of Lincoln on 19 December 1148, but cannot be dated more closely. Ranulf's claim to hereditary right in Stoke Albany should not be taken too seriously. There is no evidence that previous earls of Chester had ever exercised rights there, and the claim was presumably made to legitimise, so far as possible, his seizure of William d'Aubigny's lands. He made a similar claim in regard to Lancashire, asserting that his father, Ranulf I, had held the lands between Ribble and Mersey before him (**no. 90**); for which, as Farrer pointed out (*L.P.R.*, pp. 319–20), there was not a scrap of justification.

96.   Notification to the bishop of Lincoln that he has given the mill of
Braidwood to the abbey of Bardney for the injuries inflicted on it, and
request for him to take his gift under his protection.

[1149–1153]

B.L. Cott. MS. Vesp. E. xx (Bardney cartulary), f. 99v.
(new f. 104v).

Roberto dei gratia Lincolniensi episcopo Rannulfus comes Cestrie salutem.
Sciatis me dedisse et presenti carta confirmasse deo et monachis sancti Oswaldi
de Bardneio in liberam elemosinam molendinum de Bradewad cum pertinenciis
suis pro salute anime mee et antecessorum meorum et pro dampnis ecclesie
illorum illatis. Unde precor vos quatinus hanc meam elemosinam sub vestra
protectione suscipiatis et episcopali auctoritate manuteneatis. Testibus Hugone
Wach, Simone filio Willelmi, Roberto filio *etc.*

This can hardly be the original grant of the mill of Braidwood, since it was
confirmed by Pope Eugenius III in August 1147 (**no. 78**), and Bishop Robert of
Lincoln only succeeded in December 1148. Moreover, the reference to compensation for injuries inflicted points to a date nearer the end of Ranulf's life. Perhaps
he was notifying the new bishop of his gift and soliciting his support. Unfortunately the abbreviated witness list makes a close dating impossible.

97.   Grant to the nuns of Clerkenwell (Middlesex) of land across the bridge of
Chester from 'Betha de Bureswelles' to the Pulford road and thence to the
river and from the river to the houses of the sons of Huniz.

[1129–1150]

B.L. Cott. MS. Faustina B. ii (Clerkenwell cartulary), ff.
8, 10v. Ed.: Hassall, *Camden Society*, 3rd Ser. lxxi, pp. 6,
12.

Ex dono Randulfi comitis Cestrie transpontem Cestrie de Betha de Bureswelles
usque ad viam que venit de Pulfordia et de hac usque ad aquam et de aqua usque
ad domos filiorum Huniz.[1]

De dono Ranulfi comitis Cestrie locum in quo manent moniales Cestrenses cum
pertinentiis suis.[2]

1.   From a confirmation of Henry II, 1176 or 1178–9 (printed *Mon.*, iv. 85). The reading Buuiz (=
Hughes?) is doubtful and may be Huniz.
2.   From a confirmation of Richard I, dated 20 March 1190.

These tantalizing fragments are important for the origins and early history of St. Mary's nunnery in Chester. It seems that Ranulf II at some uncertain date imported nuns from Clerkenwell to set up a nunnery, and that their original site lay outside the city across the river, probably in the hide and a half 'ultra pontem' referred to in Domesday Book (*D.S.C.*, p. 78); but I have failed to find any other mention of Burwell. Ranulf's grant is also referred to in a privilege of Pope Urban III dated 19 October 1186 (*E.H.R.*, lvii, p. 97), but these are the only existing references. Hassall (*J.C.A.S.*, N.S. xxxvi, pp. 178–9) surmised, almost certainly correctly, that Henry II's confirmation and Richard I's confirmation of Ranulf II's gift of 'the place in which the nuns of Chester reside' refer to the same grant. It also seems reasonable to surmise that when the nuns received a site across the river to build their church (**no. 98**), the early arrangements lapsed and the relationship between St. Mary's and Clerkenwell quickly disappeared. At any rate there is no further evidence of Clerkenwell's interest in Chester. Unfortunately, it is impossible to set a date on Ranulf II's donation, but it evidently precedes **no. 98** and probably by a fairly considerable time.

98. Grant to the nuns of Chester of the crofts which Hugh son of Oliver released in the presence of the earl and countess and many barons as a site for building their church, and grant to them of their court and of freedom from tolls and all secular exactions.

Chester, [c.1150]

> P.R.O., C.66 (Chancery Patent Rolls), no. 360, m. 19. Transcr. (all from enrolment): B.L. Harl. MS. 2060, f. 18 (old f. 28); Harl. 2101, f. 180 (new f. 18) and f. 182 (new f. 20): Bodleian Library, Dodsworth MS. 39, F. 154; Rawlinson MS. B. 144, f. 141v. (brief abstract). Ed.: *Mon.*, iv. 313–14 (no. 1); Orm., i. 346; *Cal. Pat. Rolls, 1399–1401*, p. 296; *J.C.A.S.*, N.S. xiii, pp. 91–2 (from Ormerod).

Ranulfus comes Cestrie episcopis, archidiaconis, decanis, abbatibus, constabulario, dapifero, iusticiario, baronibus, vic(ecomitibus), ministris et ball-ivis et burgensibus suis, et omnibus hominibus suis Francis et Anglis clericis et laicis, universisque sancte dei ecclesie filiis tam futuris quam presentibus salutem. Sciatis me dedisse et in perpetuam elemosinam concessisse deo et sancte Marie et monialibus Cestrie, nostris in Christo sororibus, illas croftas quas Hugo filio Oliveri de dominio meo tenuit, concessione et bona voluntate ipsius Hugonis, ita quod illas clamavit quietas coram me et comitissa et plurimis baronum meorum liberas et immunes ab omnibus secularibus serviciis et omnimoda subieccione, ad edificandam ibi ecclesiam in honore dei et sancte Marie in remissionem peccatorum meorum et ad fundamentum sui edificii. Volo igitur et precipio quod ecclesia ista in elemosina mea fundata de tolneto et omni exaccione seculari libera sit et quieta, et curiam suam et dignitatem ac libertatem in omnibus et per omnia, prout libera exigit elemosina, habeat. Quare vobis mando diligenter et in domino obsecro, quatinus predictam ecclesiam et moniales ibidem deo et sancte Marie iugiter servientes cum omnibus ad illas pertinentibus pro deo et communi salute mee videlicet anime et vestrarum manuteneatis et protegatis, et ne patiamini quod elemosina mea depravetur neque moniales in ea manentes ab aliquibus vexentur. Testibus Iohanne et Rogero capellanis, Matilde comitissa, Hugone filio comitis, Fulcone de Brichsard, Radulfo Mansell, Ricardo pincerna, apud Cestriam.

This frequently printed document is commonly regarded as the foundation charter for St. Mary's nunnery in Chester, but this is not the case. The original body of nuns had apparently been brought from Clerkenwell some years earlier (**no. 97**), and the most that can be said of the present charter is that it may mark a re-foundation of the existing nunnery. Hugh son of Oliver, who quitclaims the land for building their church, witnessed a charter of Ranulf II for St. Werburgh's (**no. 26**), probably shortly before 1150. He was the son of Oliver Manners (**no. 21**) or de Malnuier (**no. 74**), and he also witnessed a gift of Richard the butler (*pincerna*) for the nunnery (*J.C.A.S.*, N.S. xiii, pp. 93–4). As Ranulf's son Hugh was only born in 1147, the present charter must be somewhat later in date, even if his presence in the witness list is only nominal. Fulk of Brichsard (Briquessart, s. of Bayeux, between Caumont-l'Evente and Villers) witnessed Ranulf's charter for Lancaster priory in 1149 (**no. 88**); Ralph Mansell charters c.1150 (**nos. 40, 104**). The present charter is also dated c.1150 by Fergusson Irvine (*J.C.A.S.*, loc. cit.), and this appears to be as accurate a date as possible.

99.   Grant to the nunnery of St. Mary, Chester, of a boat for fishing above and below the bridge of Chester and at Eaton.

Chester, [1150–1153]

P.R.O., C.66 (Chancery Patent Rolls), no. 360, m. 19.
Ed.: *Cal. Pat. Rolls, 1399–1401*, p. 297; Engl. abstract: *J.C.A.S.*, N.S. xiii, p. 92.

Ranulfus comes Cestrie constabulario, dapifero, iusticiario, baronibus, vic(ecomiti), ministris et ballivis, et omnibus hominibus suis Francis et Anglis clericis et laicis tocius terre sue salutem. Sciatis me dedisse et concessisse in elemosinam deo et sancte Marie et dominabus Cestrie batellum unum in aqua Cestrie ad piscandum ubicumque voluerint, et de supra pontem et de subtus pontem et in Hetun, in dreinet, in flotnet, in stalnet et in qualicumque rete voluerint, libere et quiete ab omni seculari servicio preter orationes, ita quod nulli inde respondeant, nec iusticiario nec alicui meorum ballivorum, et precipio camerariis meis, quod illud computent et talliant in firma mea coram vicecomite et ballivis meis. Hiis testibus Matilda comitissa, Iohanne capellano, Rogero et Andrea capellanis, Ranulfo vicecomite, Ricardo pincerna, Gaufrido dispensatore, apud Cestriam.

This grant of a boat is almost certainly later than the so-called foundation charter (**no. 98**), but the evidence does not permit an exact dating. The instruction to the chamberlains to make allowance for the concession in rendering account for the earl's farm is paralleled in **no. 26**.

100.   Notification by Walter, bishop of Chester, of Ranulf II's gift of the land of Combe (in Chipping Campden, Gloucs.) to the monks of Bordesley.

[1150–1152]

Orig.: P.R.O., E.326 (Exchequer Aug. Office, Ancient Deeds, Series B), no. 9226.

W. dei gratia Cestrensis episcopus omnibus sancte matris ecclesie filiis tam futuris quam presentibus salutem et eterne salutis interminabilem iocunditatem. Notum sit caritati vestre, fratres dilectissimi, quod R. comes Cestrie pro salute sua et patris et matris sue et omnium amicorum suorum preteritorum, presentium et futurorum, concessit et in perpetuam elemosinam dedit monachis de Bordesleia terram illam que dicitur Cumba cum omnibus pertinentiis suis, adeo liberam et quietam ab omni consuetudine et servicio sicut ipse eandem unquam liberius vel quietius vel aliquis antecessorum suorum iure hereditario tenuit ac possedit. Huic quidem donationi cum aliis religiosis personis quam plurimis, tam monachis et clericis quam laicis, interfuimus et pro hac eadem elemosina predictum comitem obnixe interpellavimus, et eius donationem predictis fratribus pro deo factam, quantum ad nostri officii spectat dignitatem, confirmamus et illam sigilli nostri munimine et impressione in perpetuum corroboramus. Quicumque igitur hanc de qua loquimur elemosinam prefate ecclesie fideliter conservaverit, in perpetuum conservet illum dominus, et nostre benedictionis et orationum necnon et omnium beneficiorum nostrorum participem illum sua gratia Christus efficiat.

SEAL on tongue: missing.

The Cistercian abbey of Bordesley in Worcestershire was founded in or about 1138 by Waleran count of Meulan and earl of Worcester. The text of Ranulf II's charter granting Combe has not survived, but seems to be recited almost verbatim in the opening sentence of Bishop Walter's letter, after the address. It was confirmed in 1153 in a charter of Countess Matilda (**no. 102**), issued apparently while Ranulf was on his death-bed. Walter Durdent succeeded to the see of Chester on 2 October 1149. As his letter states specifically that he was present when Ranulf made his gift, and indeed was instrumental in securing it, it must have occurred after that date, but we cannot say precisely when. Chipping Campden, in which Combe was situated, was part of the original endowment of the earls of Chester. It may have been temporarily alienated during the troubles of Stephen's reign (**no. 59**), but was again in Ranulf's hands by 1148 at latest.

101.   Restores to the brothers Maurice, Geoffrey and Thomas their heritage in Combe (Gloucs.), and begs the abbot of Bordesley to protect and maintain them in their right.

Gloucester, [April–May 1153]

B.L. Harl. MS. 2079, f. 63 (new f. 32); Bodleian Library, Dodsworth MS. 31, f. 93; MS. Top. Cheshire b. I, p. 135; Chester, Booth of Twemlow, Liber D, f. 141 (all 'ex rotulo cartarum antiquarum vocata Domesday').

Ranulfus comes Cestrie constabulario suo, dapifero, omnibusque aliis suis, iusticiario, vic(ecomiti), ministris, ballivis et omnibus hominibus suis clericis et laicis salutem. Sciant tam posteri quam presentes me reddidisse istis tribus fratribus, videlicet Mauricio, Gaufrido et Thoma, hereditatem suam in Cumba, sicut unquam aliquis antecessorum suorum melius tenuit. Quare volo et firmiter precipio quod teneant libere et quiete et honorifice per rectum servicium eorum. Et precor dominum abbatem de Bordeslee, quod eos protegat et manuteneat et custodiat. Testibus Rogero[1] pincerna, Warino dispensatore, Alano ostiario, apud Gloucestriam.

1.   Ricardo *Harl. MS.*

This charter was almost certainly issued when Ranulf II was at Gloucester in April–May 1153 (**no. 116**). He is unlikely to have asked the abbot of Bordesley to intervene on behalf of the three beneficiaries until after his donation of Combe to the Abbey, which was in 1150–52 (**no. 100**). A noticeable feature of this charter is that the three witnesses – the butler, dispenser and usher – were not members of Ranulf's household. The probability is that they belonged to Duke Henry's, or possibly to that of the abbot of Gloucester, but I have failed to identify them under either heading. The identity of the three brothers, who had been dispossessed, and were now restored, is also not known.

102. Confirmation by Countess Matilda and her son Hugh of Ranulf II's gift of Combe (Gloucs.) to Bordesley abbey.

[1153]

Bodleian Library, Dodsworth MS. 31, f. 93v.; MS. Top. Cheshire b. I, p. 135; Chester, Booth of Twemlow, Liber D, f. 141; B.L. Harl. MS. 2079, f. 63 (much abbreviated). Ed.: *Mon.*, v. 410 ('ex autographo in officio armorum').

+ Omnibus sancte matris ecclesie filiis tam prelatis quam subditis, tam presentibus quam futuris domini fidelibus, Matildis comitissa Cestrie et Hugo filius suus veram, que est in Christi, salutem. Notum sit vobis nos eandem donacionem dedisse et in perpetuam elemosinam concessisse H. abbati et monachis de Bordeslea, scilicet Cumbam, cum omnibus pertinenciis suis tam libere et quiete et plenarie uti dominus et sponsus noster R. comes Cestrie illam donacionem dederat et concesserat, pro redempcione animarum nostrarum et antecessorum nostrorum. Huius donacionis et concessionis testes sunt S. abbas de Sav(igneio), Iohannes abbas de Hoil., Ricardus de Bill., Willelmus de Redem(ora), R. capellanus, G. de Haud., R. filius H. ostrucarii. Valete in Christo.

For Ranulf II's gift, see **no. 100.** From the appearance of Serlo, abbot of Savigny (d. October 1153) as a witness, it appears that Matilda issued this charter shortly before her husband's death in December 1153 (*H.K.F.*, p. 53). I have failed to identify most of the other witnesses, but William de Redemora is presumably the first abbot of Radmore (**no. 94**), later removed to Stoneleigh. For Robert son of Hugh the falconer, see **no. 150**.

103. Confirmation to Kirkstead abbey of William son of Ivo's gift of land in Timberland (Lincs.)

[1145–1153]

B.L. Cott. MS. Vesp. E. xviii (Kirkstead cartulary), f. 34v. (old f. 62), no. 24.

Rannulfus comes Cestrie omnibus sancte dei ecclesie filiis salutem. Sciatis me concessisse et pro salute anime mee confirmasse donacionem, quam Willelmus filius Ivonis fecit deo et ecclesie de Kyrkested de quadam mansura sui dominii et tribus bovatis in Timberlund in perpetuam elemosinam, salvo meo servitio. Testibus Eustachio filio Iohannis, Hugone aucipitro, Roberto filio Hugonis, *etc.*

William son of Ivo's gift precedes the present confirmation in the cartulary as no. 23, but has no witnesses or dates. The present charter is also abbreviated and cannot be dated closely, but falls after the appointment of Eustace fitz John as constable of Chester, probably in 1144–45 (**no. 73**.) If the third witness is the son of Hugh the falconer, as seems likely, it is probably nearer to 1150–53 (**no. 150**).

104.   Gift to Lincoln cathedral of the church of Repton (co. Derby) in lieu of the fifteen pounds of rent he proposed to give annually in compensation for the injuries inflicted by him or his men.

[1150–1153]

> Orig.: Lincoln, Dean and Chapter, Dij/86/1/1. Transcr.: D. and C. A/1/5 (Registrum Antiquissimum), f. 35v. no. 201. Ed. (with facsimile): Lincoln, *Registrum Antiquiss-imum*, ii. (*Linc. Rec. Soc.*, xxviii), p. 7 (no. 316).

Rannulfus comes Cestrie omnibus sancte ecclesie fidelibus salutem. Sciant omnes tam presentes quam futuri, quod ego divina inspirente clementia proposui restituere sancte Marie Lincolniensi ecclesie xv. libratas redditus per annum in recompensationem dampnorum, que per me seu per meos sibi illata fuerant suisque pertinentibus. Unde bonorum virorum consilio concessi et dedi eidem ecclesie Lincolniensi ecclesiam Rappendone cum suis pertinentiis in perpetuam elemosinam, habendam et tenendam pro illis videlicet xv. libratas. Que si in valore illius ecclesie plene invente non fuerint, ego de meo supplere habebo ad valorem xv. librarum, et si ultra xv. libras ecclesie valor superhabun-daverit, illud quod supererit reddet ecclesia[1] Lincolniensis, ubi illud disposuero idonee persone reddendum. Testibus Simone filio Willelmi, Hugone ostriciarius,[1] Roberto Basset, Roberto de Calz, Roberto de Belmes, Radulfo Mansel, Philippo de Chima, Roberto filio Walteri, Gisleberto filio Hugonis, Rannulfo vicecomite.

SEAL on tongue: missing.

1. *sic MS.*

The injuries inflicted by Earl Ranulf and his men may have occurred during the sacking of the city of Lincoln after the battle of Lincoln in 1141, but more probably during the abortive assault in 1149. It is doubtful whether the present gift ever took effect, for shortly after Ranulf's death, the church of Repton was given by his widow, Countess Matilda, to the canons of Calke with the consent of her son, Earl Hugh (**no. 120**.) The probability is that it was superseded by the grant in 1153 on similar terms of the equivalent of thirty pounds of land (**no. 106**), in effect a doubling of the compensation.

105. Grant to the church of Repton of the tithe from the Countess Matilda's manor of Repton and from her parks, and the tithe of her rents and profits of justice from the same place, as the charter of Earl Ranulf witnesses.

[c.1150–1154]

Orig.: formerly with Sir Francis Burdett, not traced. Ed.:
The Topographer, ii, p. 252; Bigsby, *History of Repton,* p. 58; Jeayes, *Derbyshire Charters,* no. 1940.

Matilda comitissa Cestrie, uxor Ranulfi comitis, omnibus sancte matris ecclesie filiis salutem. Sciatis me concessisse et hac carta mea confirmasse totam decimam de manerio deo de Rapendon et de omnibus adiacentiis suis integre et de omnibus parcis meis Rapendon et . . . [et]¹ totam decimam meam de redditibus meis eiusdem ville et de placitis et querelis, deo et sancte Marie et ecclesie sancti Wistani de Rapendon, sicut carta domini mei testatur. Hiis testibus Willelmo capellano, Stephano clerico de Rapendon, Rogero Barbe Daverill, Reginaldo pincerna Simone nepote comitisse, Henrico, et multis aliis.

SEAL: 'broken; part of it the figure of a woman'.

1. All existing texts defective.

This charter has three of the same witnesses (Roger Barbe d'Averill, Stephen the clerk of Repton, and Reginald the butler) as **no. 122**, but it is hardly likely to be so late in date. The grant is still to St. Wistan, not (as in **no. 122**) to the Holy Trinity, and there is no suggestion (as in **nos. 119** and **120**) that Repton is to be the seat of a new monastic foundation. It is also noticeable that there is no reference, as in Matilda's other charters, to the assent of her son, Earl Hugh. From Matilda's description of herself as 'wife of Earl Ranulf', it almost looks as though her grant was made before Ranulf's death. It evidently had his approval, though his charter announcing it has not survived. Any date must be tentative, but the evidence suggests that this charter precedes **nos. 119** and **120**, and may be before Ranulf II's death in December 1153.

106. Notification by Duke Henry that Earl Ranulf, in the duke's presence, had given Marston and Wavercourt (Warkworth, Northants.), valued at 30 l. a year, to the church of Lincoln and Bishop Robert in compensation for the damages he had inflicted, and if they were not worth 30 l. a year, Ranulf would make up the deficit out of his own inheritance; furthermore, as Walter of Wahull had renounced his claim to any rights in the two manors, and Earl Ranulf had covenanted to cause the heirs of Norman de Verdun and of William Meschin to renounce any rights they might claim, the earl would warrant them to the bishop and church of Lincoln. But if Earl Ranulf did not keep his covenant, Duke Henry, desirous that the agreement should stand firm, had come in as surety and would make good the 30 l. of land out of his own demesne.

Stamford, [31 August 1153]

Orig.: Lincoln, Dean and Chapter, A1/1/40 (only a small fragment surviving); facsimile of same, *Linc. Rec. Soc.*, xxviii, pl. xvi. Transcr.: Lincoln, D. and C. A/1/5 (Registrum Antiquissimum), no. 166. Ed.: *Linc. Rec. Soc.*, xxvii, pp. 96–7 (no. 150); *Regesta*, iii. no. 492; brief English summary; *H.K.F.*, p. 214.

H. dux Normannorum et Aquitanorum et comes Andegavorum omnibus archiepiscopis, episcopis, comitibus, baronibus, vicecomitibus, iusticiis, et omnibus amicis et fidelibus suis Normannie et Anglie salutem. Sciatis quod Rannulfus comes Cestrie in presentia mea et assensu meo dedit deo et sancte Marie Lincolnie et Roberto episcopo eiusdem loci pro salute animarum patris et matris sui et aliorum predecessorum suorum et pro salute anime sue, et in recompensatione dampnorum que fecerat ecclesie sancte Marie Lincolnie, Merstonam et Wavercuurt cum appendiciis suis pro xxx libratas terre tenendas libere et quiete in perpetuam elemosinam, tali tenore quod si ville ille cum appendiciis suis xxx. libras annuatim non valuerint, quando episcopus eas recipiet, predictus comes Rannulfus de propria hereditate sua perimplebit sine frustratoria dilatione. Ibidem remisit calumpniam suam Walterus de Wahella in presentia mea et quicquid iuris habebat in maneriis predictis ulterius in eis nichil reclamaturus, et Rannulfo comiti eadem maneria reddidit, et ipse comes ecclesie et episcopo illa donavit. Conventionavit etiam comes Cestrie quatinus infra terminum proximi festi sancti Michaelis heredi Normanni de Verduno eadem maneria quieta clamare faceret et quicquid ad ea pertinet, nec aliquo tempore adversus ecclesiam Lincolnie vel episcopum calumpniam inde movebit. Similiter conventionavit legitime comes Rannulfus, quod si heredes Willelmi Meschini vel alius aliquid in predictis terris calumpniarentur, ipse adquietaret eas et warantizaret episcopo Lincolniensi et ecclesie sancte Marie Lincolnie; quod si non faceret comes Rannulfus vel heres suus, si post decessum comitis calumpnia ista fieret, de propria hereditate sua omni occasione remota illas xxx. libratas terre Lincolniensi ecclesie et episcopo restitueret de libera elemosina in perpetuum ab ipsis tenenda et possidenda, vel ipsis calumpniatoribus in escambium daret.

Ego autem, hanc conventionem firmam esse volens, interposui me fideiussorem, hac conditione quod si comes Rannulfus eam non teneret vel de ea exiret, de predictis libratis terre sic in liberam elemosinam date guarantum episcopi et Lincolniensis ecclesie non faciens, restituerem eas ecclesie Lincolniensi et episcopo de dominio meo in perpetuam et liberam elemosinam possidendas et ab omni seculari consuetudine quietas. Concedo etiam quod ille xxx. librate, quas Rannulfus comes dabit ecclesie Lincolnie, sint quiete ab omni exactione et secularibus consuetudinibus.

Facta fuit hec conventio quadam die Lune in vigilia sancti Egidii in obsidione Stanfordie. Testibus Ricardo de Hulmez, Waltero Herefordie, Waltero Wahelle constabulariis, Hugone Waac, Gervasio Paganell[o?], Walchelino Maminot, Roberto Dunestanvilla, Warino et Henrico filiis Geroldi, Willelmo de Coleville, Simone filio Willelmi, Iocelino de Bailoll', Gossumo castellano de Fines, Roberto filio Walteri, Pagano de Cheverci, Ricardo pincerna, Osberto Malebissa, Hugone Hameslap' clerico, apud Stanfordiam in obsidione.

Although not a charter of Earl Ranulf II, this document deserves inclusion, not least for the light it throws on Ranulf's character. A short time earlier, perhaps also in 1153, he had granted the church of Lincoln the church of Repton (Derbys.) in lieu of 15 l. of rent he proposed to give in compensation for the injuries inflicted by him or his men (**no. 104**). This gift probably never took effect, and was superseded by the arrangement set out here, in effect a doubling of the compensation to 30 l. per annum. We shall not be far wrong if we attribute this change to pressure from Duke Henry (soon to be King Henry II), anxious perhaps to pave the way for a surrender of Lincoln. Henry's present charter, given on 31 August 1153, was preceded by a shorter, more general charter, simply stating Ranulf's gift of 30 l. of land without further detail, which was issued in July or early August during the siege of Crowmarsh (ed. *Reg. Antiquissimum*, i., p.97 (no. 151), *Cal. Ch. Rolls*, iv. 144, no. 30; *Regesta*, iii. no. 491). It looks as though this agreement was not binding enough on Ranulf, and was therefore superseded by the present far more rigorous and specific document, which was re-issued after Henry became king (*Cal. Ch. Rolls*, iv. 108–9, no. 10; *Linc. Rec. Soc.*, xxvii, pp. 94–96, no. 149). Unlike the Crowmarsh charter, the present one specifically states that Ranulf made his undertaking in Henry's presence, presumably making it more difficult for him to break the agreement, but the cautious terms of the charter seem to indicate that even now he was not entirely trusted. A minor incidental point is the reference to the heirs of Norman of Verdun, indicating that he was dead by this time; the witness list is also an interesting indication of some of Henry's principal supporters.

107. Grant to the hospital of the Holy Sepulchre below Lincoln of 100 s. of land in his manor of Belchford, together with a tithe of all victuals of his corrody and of the countess's corrody, and a tenth of any brewing of ale if a brewing were made.

Lincoln, [1153]

P.R.O., Duchy of Lancaster, Ancient Deeds Series L
(D.L. 25), no. 3199;[1] D.L. 42/2 (Coucher Book II), f.
472v.–473.

1. Not an original deed, but a 14th-century copy, followed on a single sheet of parchment with a break of one line by **no. 108**. The copy appears to have borne a seal, the tag for which remains at the foot of the parchment; this may have been a seal authenticating the transcripts. The text in the Coucher Book is almost certainly a copy of L/3199.

R. comes Cestrie omnibus hominibus suis Francis et Anglis salutem. Sciatis quod ego dedi et concessi et hac carta mea confirmavi deo et sancte Marie et fratribus et pauperibus de sub Lincolnia, et pro amore magistri G. cognati mei eiusdem domus rectoris, centum solidatas terre in manerio meo de Beltesforde, scilicet molendinum meum de Randdennat et molendinum de Beltesforde et decem et septem bovatas et dimidiam terre in Beltesforde et in campis et unam mansuram in cultura mea iuxta villam, quam habent de dono meo, cum libero introitu et exitu per totum sibi et suis averiis, cum omnibus libertatibus et aisiamentis per totum cum suis pertinentiis, exceptis thoftis quos in manu mea retineo adhuc. Dedi vero eisdem pauperibus decimam partem omnis generis victus corrodii mei et comitisse mee et heredum meorum et comitissarum suarum sine omni retinemento. Et si contingat quod fieri debeat cervisia de brasio, omni tempore detur eis decima pars de ipso brasio. Et videatur bene quod nullus de meis amodo contra deum predictam domum vel aliquos de suis temere super forisfacturam meam inquietet. Hec vero omnia dedi eis in puram et perpetuam elemosinam, liberam et quietam ab omni servicio et seculari exactione. Quare volo et firmiter precipio quod ipsi fratres et pauperes habeant et teneant hec omnia bene et in pace, libere et quiete, honorifice per totum, in viis et semitis et in pratis et pascuis et pasturis et in omnibus locis, quoniam ego et heredes mei hec omnia ipsis fratribus et pauperibus garantizabimus et adquietabimus et defendemus de omnibus rebus in perpetuum. Hec vero facta fuerunt in presencia domini Roberti Lincolniensis episcopi, Alelmi decani, Unfridi subdecani, Willelmi archidiaconi, Hamonis cancellarii, Willelmi de Vescy, Iocelini castellani,[1] Ricardi pincerne, Ricardi filii Radulfi, Thome filii Willelmi, Iohanne et Rogero et Reginaldo servientibus, et multis aliis.[2]

1. castellu(m) *MSS.*
2. *Names in genitive as far as* Iocelini, *thereafter abbreviated*; servientibus *etc. in ablative. It may reasonably be presumed that this discrepancy goes back to the original charter.*

The hospital of the Holy Sepulchre, south of the city limits, just without the Bargate, was apparently founded by Bishop Robert I (1094–1123), but little is known of it, except for this charter, until shortly before 1165 (Eyton, p. 87), when Bishop Robert II placed it in the custody of the adjacent priory of St. Katherine's which he founded about this time (*Mon.*, vii. 969; cf. Hill, *Medieval Lincoln*, pp. 345–6). The present charter granted to St. Mary, i.e. the cathedral church of Lincoln, as well as the brethren and poor of the hospital, suggests that it was previously in the custody of the canons. Although the charter does not mention Holy Sepulchre by name, the identification is warranted by **no. 108**. The identity of Earl Ranulf II's relative 'G.', who was rector, has unfortunately not been established.

The authenticity of the charter in its present form is not above suspicion; in particular, the reference to easements (*aisiamentis*) and the warranty clause seem anachronistic. But the substance of the charter is certainly genuine, and the list of cathedral dignitaries, who witnessed it, is a valuable addition to our knowledge of the history of the church of Lincoln at this time. Their presence also makes it virtually certain that the charter was given at Lincoln, as does that of Joscelin the castellan, probably Joscelin of Engleby, or Ingleby (Hill, p. 98, no. 4). The date when Ranulf II recovered Lincoln, which he had surrendered to King Stephen in 1146, is not definitely known; but as he tried and failed to take the city in 1149 (*Gesta Stephani*, p. 220), at the same time devastating the suburbs, it was probably not until 1153. The clause in the charter ordering that none of the earl's men should molest the hospital in future (*amodo*) may well refer back to the devastation of 1149.

108. Notification to Robert bishop of Lincoln and the chapter of Lincoln of the gift to the hospital of Holy Sepulchre outside Lincoln of 100s. of land in Belchford.

[1153]

P.R.O., D.L. 25 (Ancient Deeds, Series L), no. 3199;[1]
D.L. 42/2 (Coucher Book II), f. 473.

1. See note to **no. 107**.

Rodberto dei gratia Lincolniensi episcopo et toti capitulo sancte Marie Lincolniensis ecclesie necnon universis sancte ecclesie filiis Ranulfus comes Cestrie obedientiam et salutem in Christo. Sciatis me dedisse deo et sancte Marie et fratribus hospitalis sancti Sepulcri extra civitatem Lincolnie C. solidatas terre de hereditate mea in manerio Beltesfordie, scilicet molendinum de Randenad et molendinum de Beltesfordia[1] et xviii. bovatas terre in campis eiusdem ville et mansuram in cultura iuxta villam, solas[2] et quietas ab omni terreno servicio in perpetuam elemosinam cum pratis et pascuis communibus. Teste episcopo Lincolniense Roberto secundo, Alelmo eiusdem ecclesie decano,[3] Umfredo subdecano et Willelmo archidiacono, Amundo cancellario et Willelmo de Veci et Iocelino castellano, Ricardo pincerna, Ricardo filio Radulfi.[4]

1. Beltesfordie *MSS.*
2. *sic MSS.*

3.   cap(itu)lo *MSS.*
4.   Witness list appears to be incomplete; cf. **no. 107**.

This letter refers to the grant made in **no. 107**; it has the same list of witnesses (here incomplete) and was presumably issued at the same time. However, the grant of 17½ bovates of land at Belchford is here rounded up to 18 bovates, and the name of the cathedral chancellor, Hamo in **no. 107**, now appears as Amundus (? Hamundus). It may seem remarkable that Bishop Robert II should appear as a witness to a letter addressed to himself; but the written notification was presumably made for future reference.

109.   Grant to the monks of Wenlock of a boat on the Dee and a house in Chester for a fisherman, and freedom of tolls throughout his land.

Wenlock, [1149–1153, probably early 1153]

P.R.O., CHES 34/4 (Plea Rolls, 15 Henr. VII), m. 3;
B.L. Harl. MS. 2115, f. 141 (old f. 167), from enrolment.

Ranulfus comes Cestrie constabulario, dapifero, iusticiario, baronibus, vicecomitibus, ministris et ballivis, et burgensibus suis Cestrie et omnibus hominibus suis Francis et Anglicis[1] tocius terre sue salutem. Notum sit tam presentibus quam posteris[1] me dedisse in perpetuam[2] elemosinam et concessisse deo et sancte Marie et sancte Milburge de Wenlok et monachis fratribus meis ibidem deo iugiter servientibus batum unum in Dhe aqua Cestrie ad piscandum ubicumque voluerint cum omni genere retium, sagenis, stalnettis et flotnettis, nocte et die subtus pontem ubicumque voluerint, et superius pontem usque Eatonam, sine omni inquietamento et alicuius contradictione. Super hoc dono et concedo eis hominem unum in Cestria cum domo et mansura sua ad sequendum batum suum et ad serviendum priori et monachis de Whenelok libere et quiete et plenarie, ita quod nulli respondeat de aliqua exaccione, neque de firma neque de tolneo neque de auxiliis neque de vigilia, nisi priori et monachis de Whenelok. Insuper dono eis et hominibus suis libertatem tolnei et omnium exaccionum per totam terram meam in burgis, in castellis et passagiis, et in omnibus locis, ne aliquis presumat eis forisfacere aut in aliquo inequitare vel contriscari[1] vel disturbare super decem libras forisfacturi vel membrorum suorum periculum illis aut hominibus suis. Precipio camerariis meis Cestrie quod illud computent et talliant coram vicecomitibus et ballivis meis in mea firma. Hanc quidem donacionem feci deo et sancte Milburge pro anime mee salute et pro animabus patris et matris mee et antecessorum meorum et incolumitate Matildis comitisse et filiorum meorum tempore domini Rainaldi prioris. Hiis testibus Ranulfo abbate Baldewas, Iohanne, Rogero et Andrea capellanis, Waltero fratre comitis Herefordie, Ricardo de Claro, Gilberto filio Baderoni, Ricardo Pincerna,

Matheo de Praeres, Willelmo filio Otuwi, Simone filio Osberti, et aliis quampluribus, clericis et laicis, apud Whenelok.

1. *sic MS.*
2. imperpetuam *MS.*

This is the only evidence of Ranulf's presence at Wenlock and it is not easy to
date, but the reference to the earl's sons – Hugh, born 1147, and his younger
brother Richard, who died early and was buried at Coventry (**no. 177**) – implies
a date after 1149. Walter, the brother of Roger earl of Hereford, a man of
somewhat unsavoury reputation (*Gesta Stephani*, p. 190), outlived his brother.
Richard of Clare was a younger brother of Gilbert of Clare, earl of Hertford
(*Complete Peerage*, vi. 499), and, like Gilbert, a nephew of Earl Ranulf, and
Gilbert *filius Baderoni* was the son of Baderon of Monmouth. It looks,
therefore, as though the charter belongs to a time when Ranulf linked up with
the Angevin forces in the west of England, probably on the way south following
Duke Henry's landing in England on 6 January 1153. Unfortunately, the little
that is known of the two prelates, Prior Rainald and Abbot Ranulf, does not
help; the date usually assigned to the latter, i.e. after 1155 (Knowles & Hadcock,
p. 129), must be wrong. For William son of Otuer, the natural brother of Earl
Richard, who was drowned in the White Ship in 1120, see **no. 127**; he was still
alive under Hugh II.

110.   Final peace and concord agreed between Earl Ranulf and Robert, earl of
Leicester.

[1149–1153, probably early in 1153]

Original cirograph: B.L. Cott. MS. Nero C. iii, f. 178.
Facsimile: *New Palaeographical Society*, ii. pl. 40. Ed.:
Orm., i. 23; Stenton, *First Century of English Feudalism*,
pp. 285–8; Engl. trans.: Nichols, *Leicestershire*, I. i. 27.

Hec est conventio inter comitem Rannulfum Cestrie et Robertum comitem
Legrecestrie et finalis pax et concordia, que fuit concessa et divisa ab eis coram
secundo Roberto episcopo Lincolnie et hominibus ipsorum, ex parte comitis
Cestrie Ricardo de Lovetot, Willelmo filio Nigelli, Rannulfo vicecomite, ex
parte comitis Legrecestrie Ernaldo de Bosco, Gaufrido abbate, Reginaldo de
Bordineo, scilicet quod comes Rannulfus dedit et concessit Roberto comiti
Legrecestrie castrum de Muntsorel sibi et heredibus suis tenendum de eo et
heredibus suis hereditarie, et sicut carta ipsius comitis Rannulfi testatur, et ita
quod comes Leecestrie receptare debet ipsum comitem Rannulfum et familiam
suam in burgo et baliis de Muntsorel ad guerreandum quencunque voluerit, ut

de feodo suo, et ita quod comes Leecestrie non potest inde forisfacere comiti Rannulfo pro aliquo. Et si necesse fuerit comiti Rannulfo, corpus ipsius receptabitur in dominico castro de Muntsorel, et ita quod comes Leecestrie portabit ei fidem, salva fide ligii domini sui. Et si oportuerit comitem Leecestrie ire super comitem Cestrie cum ligio domino suo, non potest ducere secum plusquam viginti milites, et si comes Leecestrie vel isti viginti milites aliquid ceperint de rebus comitis Cestrie, totum reddetur, Nec ligius dominus comitis Leecestrie nec aliquis alius potest forisfacere comiti Cestrie nec suis de castris ipsius comitis Leecestrie nec de terra sua, et ita quod comes Leecestrie non potest aliquam causam vel propter aliquem casum impedire corpus comitis Cestrie, nisi eum defideravit quindecim dies ante. Et comes Leecestrie debet iuvare comitem Cestrie contra omnes homines preter ligium dominum ipsius comitis Leecestrie et comitem Simonem. Comitem Simonem potest iuvare hoc modo, quod si comes Rannulfus forisfecerit comiti Simoni et ipse comes Rannulfus noluerit corrigere forisfactum propter comitem Leecestrie, tunc potest eum iuvare, et si comes Simon forisfecerit comiti Cestrie et noluerit corrigere se propter comitem Leecestrie, non iuvabit eum comes Leecestrie. Et comes Leecestrie debet custodire terras et res comitis Cestrie, que in potestate ipsius comitis Leecestrie sunt, sine malo ingenio. Et comes Leecestrie pepigit comiti Rannulfo quod castrum de Ravenestona cadet, nisi concessu comitis Rannulfi remanserit, et ita quod, si aliquis vellet illud castrum tenere contra comitem Leecestrie, comes Rannulfus auxiliabitur absque malo ingenio ad diruendum castrum illud. Et si comes Rannulfus fecerit clamorem de Willelmo de Alneto, comes Leecestrie in sua curia habebit eum ad rectum, quamdiu ipse Willelmus manserit homo comitis Leecestrie et terram tenebit de eo, et ita quod, si Willelmus vel sui recesserint a fidelitate comitis Leecestrie propter castrum prostratum, vel quia rectum noluerit facere in curia comitis Leecestrie, non receptabuntur in potestate comitis Cestrie neque Willelmus neque sui ad malum faciendum comiti Leecestrie. In hac conventione remanet comiti Leecestrie castrum de Witewic firmatum cum ceteris castris suis.

Et e converso comes Rannulfus portabit fidem comiti Leecestrie salva fide ligii domini sui. Et si oportuerit comitem ire super comitem Leecestrie cum ligio domino suo, non potest ducere secum plusquam viginti milites, et si comes Cestrie vel isti viginti milites aliquid ceperint de rebus comitis Leecestrie, totum reddetur. Nec ligius dominus comitis Cestrie nec aliquis alius potest forisfacere comiti Leecestrie nec suis de castris ipsius comitis Cestrie nec de terra sua, et ita quod comes Cestrie non potest propter aliquam causam vel aliquem casum impedire corpus comitis Leecestrie, nisi eum defideravit quindecim dies ante. Et comes Cestrie debet iuvare comitem Leecestrie contra omnes homines preter ligium dominum ipsius comitis Cestrie et comitem Robertum de Ferreriis. Comitem Robertum potest iuvare hoc modo. Si comes Leecestrie forisfecerit comiti de Ferreriis et ipse comes Leecestrie noluerit corrigere forisfactum propter comitem Cestrie, tunc potest eum iuvare comes Cestrie, et si comes Robertus de Ferrariis forisfecerit comiti Leecestrie et noluerit se corrigere propter comitem Cestrie, non iuvabit eum comes Cestrie. Et comes Cestrie debet custodire terras et res comitis Leecestrie, que in potestate ipsius comitis Cestrie sunt, sine malo ingenio. Et comes Cestrie pepigit comiti Leecestrie quod si aliquis vellet castrum de Ravenestona tenere contra comitem Leecestrie, comes Rannulfus auxiliabitur absque malo ingenio ad diruendum castrum illud. Nec comes Cestrie nec comes Leecestrie debent firmare castrum aliquod novum inter Hinchelai et Covintre, nec inter Hinchelai et Hardredeshellam, nec inter Covintre et Donintonam, nec inter Dunnintonam et Leecestriam, nec ad Gataham nec ad Cheneldestoam nec propius, nec inter Cheneldestoam et Belveeir, nec inter Belveeir et Hocham, nec inter Hocham et Rochingheham nec propius, nisi communi assensu utriusque. Et si aliquis in predictis locis vel infra predictos terminos firmaret castrum, uterque alteri erit auxilio sine malo ingenio, donec castrum diruatur.

Et hanc conventionem, sicut in hac carta continetur, affidavit uterque comes, videlicet Cestrie et Leecestrensis, in manu Roberti secundi Lincolniensis episcopi tenendam, et posuerunt eundem episcopum obsidem huius conventionis super Christianitatem suam, ita quod, si aliquis exiret ab hac conventione et nollet se corrigere infra xv. dies, postquam inde requisitus fuerit, sine malo ingenio, tunc episcopus Lincolniensis et episcopus Cestrensis facient iusticiam de eo tanquam de fide mentita. Et episcopus Lincolnie et episcopus Cestrensis tradent obsides, uterque duos, quos receperunt propter conventiones istas tenendas, illi videlicet qui conventiones istas predictas tenebit.

CIROGRAPHVM[1]

1. *The word* CIROGRAPHUM *cut through in straight line.*

This famous treaty has been much discussed by historians of English feudalism, notably Stenton, *op. cit.*, pp. 249–255. There had previously been two local agreements between Ranulf II and Robert of Leicester (**nos. 82, 89**), but this large-scale attempt to define their respective spheres of interest and limit the possibility of warfare between them is clearly an arrangement of quite a different magnitude. It was dated 'about the year 1151' by Sir Peter Leycester (Ormerod, *loc. cit.*), but without specific evidence. The date usually given (Stenton, p. 288) is 1148–1153. As Robert Chesney was not consecrated bishop of Lincoln until 19 December 1148, it is unlikely to be before 1149 at earliest. Furthermore, though we do not know when Ranulf did homage to the future Duke Henry as his 'liege lord', it is almost certain (as indicated with reference to **no. 87**) that it took place at their meeting at Carlisle in May 1149. A closing date is more difficult to establish, but the tenor of the agreement fits the situation in February–March 1153, when Robert of Leicester, without having yet openly abandoned Stephen, was busy hedging his bets. In this situation, when the leading barons on both sides were unwilling to pursue the conflict further, it would not be surprising if Ranulf and Robert agreed to limit their support for their liege lords, the one for Henry, the other for Stephen, and restore peaceful relations between each other, in anticipation of the general pacification that was to follow.

111.   Grant to Henry 'my falconer' of the lands of Turold son of Bernard of Humberstone (Lincs.) for the service of looking after his falcons.

Lincoln, [c. 1153]

> B.L. Lansdowne MS. 207A (Collections of Gervase Holles), f. 229v.; Harl. 6829 '(ex archivis Ger. Holles'), p. 10 (apparently from original).

R. comes Cestrie constabulario, dapifero, baronibus, vic(ecomiti), militibus, ministris, ballivis, et omnibus hominibus suis Francis et Anglis salutem. Scitote me dedisse Henrico falconario meo totam terram et tenuram Turoldi filii Bernardi de Hungrestain pro servicio suo, scilicet xl. et i. solidatas terre predicte. Quare volo et firmiter precipio quod ipse Henricus et heredes sui de me et heredibus meis in feodo et hereditate teneant ita bene et honorifice pro servitio aucipitrum meorum, sicut melius teneo terram meam propriam, in villa et extra, in foro et mercato, in bosco et plano, in pratis et pascuis, in viis et semitis, in stagnis et molendinis, in piscariis et salinis, et in omnibus aliis locis cum soc et sac et tol et theom et infangethef, et cum omnibus aliis consuetudinibus et libertatibus. Testibus Symone filio Willelmi et Hugone Bardulf et Willelmo filio Hacon et Hugone osturcario et Berengario falconario et Gisleberto Neivill et Radulfo filio Drogonis, apud Lincolniam.

> SEAL: 'that which belongd to ye Earle of Chesters lapt in Wooll & sowed up in a linnen bagge for ye better preservation of it, yet when I opened it, I founde it mowldred to dust'.

Henry the falconer is elsewhere described as 'Henry the falconer of Humberstone' and 'Henry Flamengs the falconer'. After the death of Earl Ranulf II he transferred his service to the king, and in a writ issued at Clarendon, probably in 1166, and witnessed by Alan Neville and Hugh Gundeville, Henry II wrote to 'all his faithful of Lincolnshire' ordering that the doves of Henry Flamengs, 'my falconer', should be left in peace, and no-one should presume to take them with nets or otherwise (Harl. MS. 6829, p. 11). He appears almost yearly on the Lincolnshire Pipe Roll from 1158 to 1192, and was clearly a young man at the time of the present grant. It seems possible that he was appointed falconer in place of Hugh the falconer (**no. 150**). The present charter cannot be dated accurately, as all the witnesses outlived Ranulf II; but the fact that it was given at

Lincoln suggests that it dates from the last year of Ranulf's life, since there is no evidence that he was ever in possession of Lincoln between 1146 and 1153. Moreover, it is perhaps significant that this is the only mention of Henry the falconer in Chester charters. If he was only enfeoffed in 1153, and then transferred his services to the king, this would explain why, unlike Hugh the falconer and Berengar the falconer, he does not appear elsewhere in charters either of Ranulf II or of Hugh II.

112. Alleged grant of liberties and free customs to the burgesses of Coventry, as recited in a confirmation of Henry II. [Spurious]

[1153]

> Orig.: Coventry Record Office, B.2. Ed.: *Archaeological Journal*, xv, pp. 243–4; *Cal. Ch. Rolls*, ii. 88; Coss, no. 11.

For a full text of this document, see Coss, *The Early Records of Medieval Coventry*, pp. 18–19 (no. 11).

> SEAL: missing.

No charter of Ranulf II for the burgesses of Coventry has survived, either in original or copy, but this document, abstracted from a confirmation of Henry II in the city archives, has long been accepted as authentic. Recently, however, a number of reservations have been made (Coss, *Midland History*, ii, pp. 144–5), and there is reason to think that the text submitted to Henry II for confirmation may have been either a forgery or, at best, an interpolated version of a genuine charter which no longer exists.

The reservations may be summarized under three headings. (1) The disappearance of the original charter, supposing one ever existed. Considering the pains taken by the corporation of Coventry to preserve its muniments, this itself is suspicious and suggests that the original charter may have been destroyed, if its terms conflicted with a later forged or interpolated version. (2) The long gap between the time when the charter was ostensibly issued and the date when it was first heard of. As Tait established (*E.H.R.*, xliii, pp. 383–5), the date of Henry II's confirmation was 1182, the putative date of Ranulf II's charter 1149–1153, or more probably 1153. If a genuine charter had existed, it would have been normal for Henry II to confirm it within a few years of Ranulf II's death, during the minority of Hugh II, rather than during that of Hugh's son, Ranulf III. Instead, we have 30 years' silence and no sign that Hugh II was aware of the charter's existence. The implication is that it did not exist, and was fabricated by the burgesses during the period following Hugh II's death. (3) The internal evidence supports these arguments. Overall, the effect of the alleged charter is to set limits on the rights of the earl and his officers. The most striking and unusual clause of all – that authorizing the burgesses to elect their own justice – appears to have cut out the earl's bailiff, leaving the elected official as the only intermediary between the burgesses and the earl, who does not even reserve the right to remove him, if unsatisfactory. Equally noteworthy is the clause limiting the amercement of anyone who fell into the earl's mercy to a maximum of 12d., or less if his neighbours testified that he could not afford so much. It is difficult to think of any circumstances in which Ranulf II would have consented to such limitations, and it is significant that Ranulf III, when he came to confirm the burgesses' privileges (**no. 311**), introduced substantial changes. In particular, he reaffirmed the position of his bailiff in the portmoot and dropped the clause limiting amercements to 12d., substituting the much more elastic provision that any delinquent should be 'reasonably amerced'. Other changes introduced by Ranulf III – e.g. omission of the clause freeing the burgesses from levies (*corredia*) for the earl's maintenance, except under strict guarantees – indicate a tightening of the earl's control and a rejection of the more extreme claims embodied in the confirmation of 1182. The implication is that the burgesses took advantage of the minority of Ranulf III, when the honour of Chester was in the king's hands, to stake out claims they would never have been able to substantiate otherwise. It was not the only forgery produced in Coventry at this time (see **nos. 114** and **178**), and it is perhaps significant that the men of Coventry paid 20 marks at Michaelmas 1182 for the king's confirmation of their liberties (*H.K.F.*, p. 281). No doubt they regarded it as a good bargain.

The possibility remains that the forgery was based on a genuine charter. There is nothing particularly unusual about the first half, confirming the existence of burgage tenure as in the time of Ranulf I, granting the customs of Lincoln, abolishing the jurisdiction the constable of Coventry castle had been exercising, probably irregularly, during the civil war, and granting the burgesses a portmoot, or portmanmoot. So far the contents of the confirmation might be genuine. But in the absence of direct evidence this can only be surmise, and does not affect the conclusion that the document as a whole, as it has come down to us in Henry II's confirmation, is a later fabrication, dating probably from 1181–1182. It cannot, in any case, safely be accepted as it stands as a genuine charter of Ranulf II.

113.   Grant to the monks of Coventry of the right to send two carts twice daily, except on feast days, to his wood to take what they need for repairs, fuel and hedging, by view of his foresters.[?Spurious]

[?1153]

P.R.O., C. 53 (Chancery Charter Rolls), no. 135, m. 4;

> B.L. Add. MS. 32100, f. 61. Ed.: *Cal. Ch. Rolls*, v. 103,
> no. 14; Coss, no. 3; noted Dugdale, *Warwickshire*, p. 101,
> and *Baronage*, i. 40; *H.K.F.*, ii. 281.

For a full text of this document, see Coss, *The Early Records of Medieval Coventry*, p. 12 (no. 3).

This charter is not easy to date, but as Ranulf II appears to have lost possession of Coventry between 1146 and 1153, it probably dates, if genuine, from the end of his career. But it is doubtful whether it is a genuine charter of Ranulf II. The interest of the monks in obtaining access to the earl's woods dates from the end rather than the middle of the twelfth century, and the probability is that they fabricated the present document about that time as an inducement to Ranulf III to grant them a charter (**no. 342**) in identical terms. If Ranulf II really made this grant, it is curious that it was passed over in silence by Hugh II and disappeared from view for half a century. On the other hand, it turned up very conveniently in the time of Ranulf III.

114. Restoration to Prior Lawrence and the monks of Coventry of the chapel of St. Michael in his fee at Coventry and of all other chapels, specified by name, within his fee and within their parish, with tithes, oblations and other parochial rights. [?Spurious]

[1153]

> P.R.O. E. 164/21 (Exchequer, King's Remembrancer, Misc. Books), f. 76 (register of Coventry priory): C. 53 (Chancery Charter Rolls), no. 135 (inspeximus of Edw. III), m. 5; B.L. Add. MS. 32100, f. 60 (from inspeximus); Bodleian Library, Dugdale MS. 12, p. 238, and Dodsworth MS. 65, f. 23v. (both from Register). Ed.: *Cal. Ch. Rolls*, v. 102 (no. 11); Coss, no. 2. Mentioned: Dugdale, *Warwickshire*, pp. 80–82, 106, 129, 130, 134, 148.

For a full text of this document, see Coss, *The Early Records of Medieval Coventry*, pp. 11–12 (no. 2).

This charter is not easy to evaluate. It has been suggested that it was one of the fairly numerous acts of restitution Ranulf II made at the end of his life, and it has therefore been dated 1153. The list of witnesses, so far as can be established, is compatible with this date. But the suspicion remains that it is not a genuine charter of Ranulf II.[1] It is evident from Hugh II's confirmation (**no. 177**) that

Ranulf issued another charter, unfortunately no longer extant, granting the chapel of St. Michael's to Coventry abbey, but without the elaboration and the list of subordinate chapels which is the substance of the present charter. We do not know the date of the earlier charter, but if the present charter is genuine, it seems to betoken an extraordinarily rapid development of the parochial system and of a network of chapels dependent on St. Michael's. This is, of course, not impossible, but it seems more likely that the present charter and the parallel charter of Earl Hugh (**no. 178**) were fabricated by the monks of Coventry at a later date, when the network of chapels had sprung up, to establish a specific claim to them, rather than rely on the general grant of St. Michael's and all its appurtenances. When the charters were fabricated, assuming them to be spurious, is a difficult question, but they were certainly in existence by the time of Bishop Gerard Pucelle (1183–84), who refers to Ranulf II's grant in an extremely interesting charter (Coss, no. 12). Furthermore, he states that he has seen a confirmation of his predecessor, Bishop Richard Peche (1161–82). It looks as though they may have been fabricated towards the end of Bishop Richard's pontificate, probably after the death of Earl Hugh on 30 June 1181 and during the minority of Ranulf III. Whether genuine or spurious, they were later presented to Ranulf, and were the basis upon which he conveyed the chapels to the church of Coventry in 1192 (**no. 219**).

1. If the original charter had the form 'imperpetuum' (for 'in perpetuum'), it would be fatal to so early a date as 1153. No original charter of Ranulf II uses 'imperpetuum', which creeps in under Ranulf III. It is found in all the surviving transcripts, but it may be due to the copyist of the Coventry Register and the compiler of the Charter Roll. If so, they introduced it independently of each other.

115.   Grant to Burton abbey of the islands of Willington and Potlock (Derbys.), which his officers had unjustly occupied, in satisfaction of the injuries he had done to the church.

Rocester, [November–December 1153]

> Orig.: Burton-upon-Trent, Museum and Art Gallery, Anglesey muniments, no. 14. Transcr.: B.L. Deposited MSS., no. 30 (Burton cartulary), f. 53 and f. 65 (abbreviated text, without witnesses). Ed.: *William Salt Arch. Soc.*, V. i, pp. 48, 58, and *Hist. Coll. of Staffordshire*, 1937, p. 11 (no. 14).

Ranulfus comes Cestrie omnibus hominibus suis tocius Anglie et Normannie necnon et omnibus sancte dei ecclesie filiis salutem. Sciatis me donasse et quietum clamasse a me et a meis heredibus deo et sancte Marie et ecclesie de Buretona quietum et solutum insulas de Wilintona et de Pollac, quas aliquando ministri mei preocupaverunt iniuste, in satisfactione omnium forisfactorum quecumque feci ecclesie sue. Testibus Iohanne capellano, Willelmo de Rademora, Albino abbate Derebi, priore de Calc, Eustachio filio Iohannis, Simone filio Willelmi, Willelmo filio Nigelli, Ricardo pincerna, Ricardo filio Radulfi, Roberto de Englebi, apud Rouecestriam.

This is another of the charters issued by Ranulf II at the end of his life to compensate for injuries inflicted on religious houses. Others (**nos. 34, 117, 118**) were issued at Gresley (Derbys.) where he died. The present charter has many of the same witnesses – notably the abbot of Radmore and the prior of Calke, Eustace fitz John the constable, Richard the butler, and Simon fitz William of Kyme – and it can safely be assumed that it was issued at approximately the same time, probably only a few days earlier on his way to Gresley after his attempted poisoning in the house of William Peverel of Nottingham. For Robert of Engleby, i.e. Robert *pincerna*, the founder of Poulton abbey, see *E.C.C.*, p. 4.

116. Gift to St. Peter's abbey, Gloucester, of an annual rent of 40s. from the mills of Olney (Bucks.), and confirmation of his sister Alice's gift of the mill of Tathwell (Lincs.), which she gave for the soul of her husband, Richard fitz Gilbert.

[April–May, 1153]

P.R.O., C. 150/1 (Cartulary of Gloucester), f. 44, no. 157.
Ed.: Hart, *Hist. et Cart. Monasterii S. Petri Gloucestrie* (Rolls Series), i. 240–1.

Ranulfus[1] comes Cestrie constabulariis suis et dapiferis suis, et omnibus baronibus suis Francis et Anglis, et omnibus ministris suis, et omnibus fidelibus sancte ecclesie salutem. Sciatis me dedisse in elemosinam ecclesie sancti Petri Gloucestrie et monachis eiusdem ecclesie quadraginta solidos in molendinis Olneye hereditario iure. Et ideo volo et precipio ut firmiter et in pace teneant, et ut nullus eis aliquam molestiam inde illis inferat. Confirmo etiam per presentem hanc cartam molendinum de Taddeswelle, quod dedit eis Aliz soror mea pro anima Ricardi filii Gileberti viri sui. Et ideo volo et precipio quod illud teneant in elemosinam perpetualiter de me et heredibus meis, et si quis eis aliquam iniuriam inde faciat, super excommunicationem faciat.

1. Rogerus *MS.*, but the correct name is given in the abbreviated notice in the history of the abbey (Hart, *op. cit.*, p. 104).

Henry, duke of Normandy and Aquitaine and count of Anjou, ordered Eustace fitz John and Joscelin *castellanus Fruarii* to enforce this gift (Hart, *op. cit.*, p.

241, no. 159). This must have been in 1153 or 1154 (*Regesta*, iii. no. 365), almost certainly in 1153, and this gives some indication of the date of Ranulf II's charter. Ranulf was at Gloucester with Henry in April–May 1153 (*Regesta*, iii. no. 840), and it is fairly safe to conclude that his charter was issued on this occasion. Richard fitz Gilbert was slain in 1136.

117.   Grant, in his 'infirmity', to Minting and Trentham priories and to the nuns of St. Mary, Chester, of that part of his tithe which he had not previously disposed of.

Gresley, [December 1153]

B.L. Add. MS. 35296 (Spalding register), f. 410v; Add. MS. 5844, f. 447 (new f. 227).

R. comes Cestrie episcopo Cestrie et omnibus sancte ecclesie filiis, insuper et heredi meo et omnibus hominibus meis tocius terre mee, salutem. Sciatis quod illam partem decime meorum reddituum, quam ante hanc meam infirmitatem ad nullam ecclesiam adturnavi, illam nunc michi valde necessariam statuo de omnibus maneriis meis dominicis, quecumque umquam habui vel umquam habere potero, in pace, si vixero, ad satisfaciendum ecclesiis omnibus quibus forisfeci; qua impleta, ad vestimenta fratrum et sororum abbaciarum trium vero, videlicet Minting(is) et Tengham[1] et sanctimonialibus sancte Marie Cestrie et pro anime mee salute imperpetuum remaneat. Testibus Willelmo de Larademora abbate Raucestrie, abbate Roberto de Grimmesbi, Iohanne capellano, Andrea clerico, apud Greseleiham.

1.   *sic MSS.*

This remarkable document, by which Ranulf II sought to make amends for the ills he had inflicted on the Church, was clearly executed on his deathbed at Gresley, as he lay ill as a result of poisoning by William Peverel of Nottingham. The three houses specifically mentioned were his own foundations. It has been suggested (*Chart. St. Werburgh*, i. 232) that **no. 34** was issued at approximately the same time.

118.   Gift of 100 solidates of his land in Staffordshire – from Trentham and its dependencies – to restore Trentham abbey.

Gresley, [December 1153]

Bodleian Library, Dodsworth MS. 10, f. 210; 110, f. 43 (both from original with Richard Leveson of Trentham, 1638); B.L. Harl. MS. 2060, f. 1 (new f. 4v.), also from original. Ed.: *Mon.*, vi. 397; *Hist. Coll. of Staffordshire*, xi. 300.

Ranulfus comes Cestrie episcopo Cestrie, archidiacono omnibusque prelatis et sancte dei ecclesie filiis, necnon et omnibus constabulariis, dapiferis, iusticiariis, baronibus, vicecomitibus, ministris et ballivis, et omnibus hominibus et amicis suis salutem. Sciatis me donasse centum soliditas terre mee Staffordisirie deo et sancte Marie et omnibus sanctis ad restaurandam quandam abbatiam canonicorum in ecclesia de Trentham in elemosinam, ad serviendum deo ibidem perpetualiter pro salute anime mee et antecessorum meorum; et eas assigno de Trenteham et de omnibus illis pertinentiis unde rex Henricus habuit C. solidos. Volo itaque et firmiter precipio quod prenominata ecclesia supradictam villam cum omnibus libertatibus et dignitatibus in bosco et plano, in aquis et molendinis et omnibus consuetudinibus teneat, sicut unquam eam melius tenui. Testibus Willelmo abbate Radmore, Roberto abbate Grimesbie,[1] Roberto priore de Calc, Eustachio filio Iohannis, Simone filio Willelmi, Willelmo de Gresele, Roberto filio Hugonis, Simone filio Osberti, Ricardo pincerna, apud Greselegam.

1. Gunesb., *Dodsw. 110*; Ginesburg, *Dodsw. 10*; Gunesb., *Harl. 2060*.

This is usually said to be the foundation charter of Trentham, though the indications are that the abbey was founded earlier, perhaps c. 1087–1100 by Hugh I, fell on evil times, and was restored or re-founded by Ranulf II at the end of his life (*H.K.F.*, p. 266). He obtained Staffordshire by grant of Duke Henry (Henry II) at Devizes early in 1153 (*Regesta*, iii. no. 180), and the present charter, as the witnesses indicate, was issued on his deathbed at Gresley in December of that year. Abbot Robert of Grimsby witnessed another charter (**no. 117**) on the same occasion. Among other charters given at approximately the same time, with many of the same witnesses, is **no. 34**.

MATILDA, WIDOW OF RANULF II

119. Notification to Walter, bishop of Coventry, that she has given the canons of Calke a quarry at Repton, together with the advowson of the church of St. Wistan of Repton, on condition that the convent is moved there when a suitable opportunity occurs, and that Calke is subordinated to it.

Repton, [1154–1160]

Orig.: Derby, Public Library, Bemrose Deeds, no. 192.
Ed.: *Mon.*, vi. 598; Bigsby, *History of Repton*, pp. 56–7;
Jeayes, *Derbyshire Charters*, no. 531.

Waltero dei gratia Coventrensi episcopo universisque sancte matris ecclesie filiis
Matillis comitissa Cestrie salutem. Vestra noscat sanctitas me concessu comitis
Hugonis filii mei dedisse deo et sancte Marie et canonicis de Calc in puram et
perpetuam elemosinam culturam quarerie de Rependona iuxta Trente simul
cum advocatione ecclesie sancti Wicstani de Rependona cum omnibus eidem
pertinentibus, conditione hac quod conventus ibi constet tanquam capiti, cum
oportunitas idonea hoc expetierit, cui Calc subiciatur membrum; eius etenim
diocesis semper permansit. Prece igitur multimoda vestram exoro dulcedinem,
quatinus hanc elemosinam consilio vestro caritative inceptam permanere faciatis
ratam. Teste ipso comite Hugone filio meo, Willelmo abbate Lilleshill, Helia
priore de Bredune, Rogero capellano, Turri clerico, Aluredo de Cumbrei, Luuel
de Hesbi, Nicholao de Mealtun, multis aliis, apud Rependonam. Vale.

This charter, which marks the first step in the transfer of the Augustinian priory
of Calke to Repton, dates from between 1154 and the death of Bishop Walter of
Coventry on 7 December 1160.

120.   Notification to Walter, bishop of Coventry, of her grant of the church of
Repton to the canons of Calke, on condition that the convent there shall
be the head, to which Calke shall be subject.

[1154–1160]

Orig.: formerly with Sir Francis Burdett, not traced. Ed.:
The Topographer, ii, p. 251; Bigsby, *History of Repton*, p.
57; Jeayes, *Derbyshire Charters*, no. 1939.

Waltero divina gratia Coventrensi episcopo universisque sancte matris ecclesie
filiis Matilda comitissa Cestrie salutem. Vestra noscat celsitas me concessu
Hugonis comitis filii mei dedisse deo et sancte Marie et sancto Wistano et
canonicis de Kalc ecclesiam de Rapendon cum omnibus eidem pertinentibus
liberam et quietam ab omni seculari servicio et ita liberam sicut aliquis ecclesia
ad religionem liberius potest dari, pro salute anime mee et pro anima Henrici
regis avi mei et Ranulfi comitis Cestrie domini mei et Roberti comitis Gloucestrie patris mei et Mabilie comitisse sue matris mee et pro animabus omnium
antecessorum meorum, conditione hac quod contentus ibi constet tanquam
caput, cui Calc subiiciatur membrum. Illius tamen persone ecclesiam illam et
eorum tenuram . . . comitante absque impedimento possideant . . . spontanea
voluntate demissi sibi sua largiti fuerint.[1] Prece ergo multimoda vestram exoro

dulcedinem, quatenus hanc elemosinam consilio vestro karitative inceptam permanere faciatis ratam. Teste ipso comite Hugone filio meo, Nicholao, Galfrido, Turch[oldo] illius ecclesie personis, Willelmo abbate de Lilleshull, Helia priore de Bredune, Rogero [capellano, Turri] clerico,[2] Aluredo de Cumbrei, Iuuel sacerdote de . . .,[3] Nicholao de Meltun, magistro Adamo, Ormo sacerdote de[4] Wilinton, Roberto filio suo, Benedicto Hugonis comitis avunculo, Roberto de Roppelei, Iordano de Rasur, Simone de Stantun. Tempore Roberti prioris nobis data fuit hec elemosina.

1. All transcripts defective. The sense is that the parsons in office (who witness as Nicholas, Geoffrey and Turchold) shall continue to enjoy their tenure, unless they voluntarily surrender it to the canons.
2. Last two witnesses om. Jeayes; names supplied from **no. 119**.
3. Almost certainly identical with Luuel de Hesbi of **no. 119**.
4. Three preceding witnesses om. Jeayes.

This charter has a similar wording to **no. 119**, and many of the same witnesses. Presumably the countess's decision to give the church of Repton to the canons of Calke, rather than just the advowson, followed later, but it looks as though the difference was a matter of days at most, perhaps a result of persuasion by the ecclesiastics surrounding the countess; otherwise it is difficult to see the need for two separate charters.

121. Notification to Richard, bishop of Coventry, of Earl Hugh's confirmation of Countess Matilda's gift of Repton church to the canons of Calke.

[c. 1162–1164]

> Orig.: formerly with Sir Francis Burdett, not traced. Ed.: *The Topographer*, ii, pp. 251–2; Bigsby, *History of Repton*, p. 58; Jeayes, *Derbyshire Charters*, nos. 535, 1941.

Ricardo divina gratia Coventrensi episcopo universisque sancte matris ecclesie filiis Hugo comes Cestrie salutem. Vestra [sanctitas],[1] sciatis me concessisse et confirmasse petitione matris mee comitisse Matildis deo et sancte Marie et sancto Winstano et canonicis de Calch elemosinam quam illis dedit comitissa mater mea, videlicet ecclesiam de Rapenduna cum omnibus pertinenciis suis, pro salute anime mee et sue et pro anima Ranulfi comitis Cestrie patris mei et Roberti comitis Gloucestrie avi mei et pro animabus omnium antecessorum nostrorum, liberam et quietam ab omni seculari servicio, sicut unquam tempore antecessorum nostrorum liberior extitit, tali conditione ut ibi constet conventus tanquam caput, cui Calc subiciatur membrum. Illius tamen persone ecclesiam illam et eius tenuram . . . absque impedimento possideant . . . spontanea voluntate demissi canonicis sua largiti fuerint.[2] Prece ergo multimoda vestram exoro dulcedinem, quatenus hanc elemosinam ammonicione et consilio beati Walteri episcopi predecessoris vestris karitative inceptam permanere faciatis ratam. Teste ipsa matre mea comitissa Matilda et Ricardo avunculo meo et Radulpho capellano meo et Willelmo et Herberto clericis meis et Galfrido de Costutino et Alvered de Conbrai, Willelmo Patric, Gilberto filio Picot, Ricardo de Luvetot, Rogero de Livet, Bertramo camerario, Iordano Rasur, et pluribus aliis.

> SEAL: 'a man on horseback, sword in hand and shield before him.'

1. Text defective; word supplied from **no. 119**.
2. Text defective; see note to **no. 120**.

This charter is a confirmation of **no. 120**, the wording of which it follows closely. Richard Peche succeeded Walter Durdent as bishop of Coventry in April 1161, and it is safe to assume that this request for his support for the new foundation, which had been begun with his predecessor's advice, followed shortly after his accession. Hugh II attained his majority in 1162, and this charter was probably issued in the following months.

122.   Grant to Repton priory of all her land in Gransden (Hunts.).

[1164–1172]

> Orig.: B.L. Stowe Charter 159. Ed.: Warner and Ellis, no. 52 (with facsimile); Jeayes, *Derbyshire Charters*, no. 1943.

Matillis comitissa Cestrie universis sancte matris ecclesie filiis et universis hominibus Francis et Anglicis tam presentibus quam futuris, et omnibus ad quos presens carta pervenerit, salutem. Sciatis me concessu filii mei Hugonis comitis Cestrie dedisse et hac presenti carta mea confirmasse deo et ecclesie Sancte Trinitatis de Rapendona et canonicis ibidem deo servientibus totam terram meam de Grandendena cum omnibus pertinentiis in puram et perpetuam elemosinam, in bosco et plano, in pratis et pascuis, in viis et semitis et silvis, in firmis et redditibus, in auxiliis et consuetudinibus, in serviciis et operibus, et in omnibus rebus mihi et heredibus meis pertinentibus, liberam et quietam de omnibus rebus que mihi et heredibus meis pertinent, pro amore dei et pro salute anime Henrici regis et heredum suorum et matris eius imperatricis amite mee, et pro salute Roberti comitis Gloucestrie patris mei et comitisse Mabillie matris mee, et pro salute comitis Ranulfi domini me, et pro salute anime mee et

Hugonis comitis Cestrie filii mei et omnium antecessorum et successorum nostrorum. Hiis testibus Alano clerico, Rogero Barbe de Averil, Stephano clerico de Rapendona, Reginaldo pincerna, Willelmo de Tilli, Thoma fratre Milonis.

> SEAL: brown wax, pointed oval, very imperfect; a lady in tight-fitting dress with long sleeves, standing; legend wanting.

This charter is dated 1162–67 on rather slender evidence by Warner and Ellis and by Jeayes. It is certainly later than **nos. 119** and **120**, granting the church of St. Wistan of Repton to the canons of Calke, and also later than Hugh II's confirmation of **no. 120**, dating probably from 1162 (**no. 121**). Now the transfer from Calke to Repton has taken place and the new priory has been re-dedicated to the Holy Trinity. Unfortunately the evidence does not permit a closer dating. The foundation of Repton is said to have been completed in 1172 (*Mon.*, vi. 429), and this must remain the outer date, but the grant is possibly some years earlier.

HUGH (II) EARL OF CHESTER (1153–1181)

123. Permission to his mother, Countess Matilda, to grant ten librates of land in Gransden (Hunts.) to the priory of Holy Trinity at Repton.

[1164–1172]

> Orig.: B.L. Stowe Charter 158. Ed.: Warner and Ellis, no. 51 (with facsimile); Jeayes, *Derbyshire Charters*, no. 1942.

Universis sancte matris ecclesie filiis Hugo comes Cestrie salutem. Notum sit vobis me concessisse domine matri mee Matildi comitisse, quod ipsa donet, quando sibi placuerit, in puram et perpetuam elemosinam decem libratas terre in Grantendene deo et Sancte Trinitati de Rapendona et canonicis ibidem deo servientibus, pro dei amore et salute patris mei Randulfi comitis Cestrie et pro salute anime sue et mee et omnium antecessorum nostrorum. Teste me ipso, Ricardo de Luvetot, Gileberto filio Picot, Radulfo vicecomite de Valle Vire, Rogero de Luvetot, Frembalt de Ridefort, Seer de Stoke, Henrico Mansel, Radulfo Barbe de Averil capellano meo et Willelmo filio suo, et pluribus aliis.

> SEAL: equestrian, brown wax; horse with left fore-leg

raised; ornamental saddle-cloth; knight with sword lowered in right hand, shield in left. Reverse: two impressions
of small oval gem seal of William Barbe d'Averill.
Legend: [SIG]IL[LUM HUG]ONIS COMITIS CESTRIE.

Hugh's charter precedes (at least logically) his mother's (**no. 122**), but they were
probably given at approximately the same time. The names of the witnesses do
not permit a narrower dating.

124.   Grant of Styshall (nr. Coventry) by Earl Hugh and Countess Matilda to
Bishop Walter of Chester in reparation for the injuries inflicted by Earl
Ranulf II.

[1154–1157]

Orig.: Stratford-upon-Avon, Shakespeare's Birthplace,
Gregory-Hood Deeds, no. 575.[1] Transcr.: Bodleian Library, Dugdale MS. 13, p. 127 (from an ancient copy 'in
quadam baga de diversis inquisitionibus penes thesaur-
arium et camerarium scaccarii' at Westminster); Ashmole
MS. 1527, f. 74v. (register of bishopric of Lichfield); MS.
Top. Warwick. O.6, f. 124v.; P.R.O., Confirmation Roll
17 (14 Eliz.) m. 1, no. 16. Cal.: Dugdale, *Baronage*, i. 40,
Warwickshire, p. 199; Orm., i. 25. Ed.: Coss, no. 4.

1.   Edited from original in monastic book-hand with tagged 'e's; episcopus *abbreviated* epc.

For a full text of this document, see Coss, *The Early Records of Medieval
Coventry*, pp. 12–13 (no. 4).

SEAL on tongue, slit from left side: equestrian, damaged
and repaired, legend perished.

Ranulf II is said to have been excommunicated by Bishop Walter Durdent
(1149–60) and died excommunicate. This charter is another example (cf. **no.
141**) of the efforts of his widow and heir to make amends for the wrongs he had
done to the church and others, and in this case more specifically to secure his
absolution. It must have been issued between December 1153 (death of Ranulf
II) and 1157 (death of Eustace the constable), and probably earlier in the period
rather than later; but as all the witnesses except Eustace were alive after 1157,
the evidence does not allow a closer dating. Styshall (Stiviehall) was part of the

extensive manor of Coventry, held by the earls of Chester since the time of William II (*H.K.F.*, p. 6). Duillet is clearly identical with William Duillec, rights in whose land Earl Hugh specifically reserved in another charter (**no. 156**).

125.   Confirmation to the priory of Minting of the gifts of his father.

Belchford, [1154–1157]

> P.R.O., C. 53 (Chancery Charter Rolls), no. 123, m. 9; B.L. Add. MS 35296 (Spalding cartulary), f. 411; Add. 5844 (transcript of Add. 35296), f. 447 (new f. 227). Ed.: Prou et Vidier, *Recueil des chartes de l'abbaye de Saint-Bênoit-sur-Loire*, pp. 366–7; *Cal. Ch. Rolls*, iv. 378. Cal.: *H.K.F.*, ii. 173.

Hugo comes Cestrie episcopo Lincollniensi totique presulatus eiusdem clero, necnon et constabulario Cestrie et dapifero et baronibus et famulis et hominibus omnibus suis Francis et Anglicis, clericis et laicis, salutem. Vos scire volo me concessisse et confirmasse in perpetuam elemosinam pro salute anime patris mei et matris mee et antecessorum meorum necnon et mee totam illam elemosinam, quam pater meus dedit, carta sua confirmatam, deo et sancte Marie et sancto Iacobo et sancto Benedicto et monachis de Mentinges. Volo igitur et precipio, quod monachi prefati elemosinam illam libere et quiete et honorifice possideant et teneant. Testibus Eustachio filio Iohannis, Roberto dapifero, Simone filio Willelmi, Hugone filio Hastacii, Rogero capellano, Terri clerico, Roberto de Buscarvilla,[1] Serlone[2] venatore, apud Beltesford. Valete.

1.   Botervile *ir the B.L. manuscripts.*
2.   Sal(one) *MSS.*

For the charter of Ranulf II, here confirmed, see **no. 93**. Earl Hugh's confirmation must date between 1154 and 1157 (death of Eustace fitz John). It is very similar in formulation to the confirmation for Greenfield (**no. 127**), which was also given at Belchford, and it is probable that both were issued on the same occasion. Robert of Montalt, the steward, and Simon son of William of Kyme accounted to the exchequer for the receipts of the county of Chester during Hugh II's minority, Robert of Buscherville is mentioned on the Pipe Roll of 1160–61, and Serlo the huntsman apparently survived until shortly before 1179 (*P.R.S.*, xxix, p. 104).

126. Confirmation of the grants made by his father, Ranulf II to the monks of Minting.

Belchford, [c. 1165–1170]

B.L. Add. MS. 35296 (Spalding register), f. 410v.; Add.
5844 (transcript of register), f. 447 (new f. 227).

Hugo comes Cestrie conestabulario, dapifero, baronibus, iusticiario, vic(ecomiti), ministris et ballivis et omnibus hominibus suis Francis et Anglis, omnibusque prelatis et filiis sancte ecclesie salutem. Sciatis me concessisse et hac carta mea confirmasse in perpetuam elemosinam pro salute anime patris mei et matris mee et antecessorum meorum et mee deo et sancte Marie et sancto Benedicto et sancto Iacobo et monachis eorum Mintinges et ecclesiam sancti Andree de Mintinges et ecclesiam Omnium Sanctorum de Goutebi et terram Spilemanni et duas bovatas terre et dimidiam Wimundi coci et unam bovatam terre Willelmi pincerne et quicquid pater meus habuit in duabus Mintingis, excepta tenura Roberti de Founchun et Berengarii falconarii. Et concedo quod predicti monachi et homines eorum habeant omnia aisiamenta sua in bosco meo de Mintingis ad edificia sua et pannagium suum sine vendicione et donacione. Quapropter volo et precipio quod supradicti monachi predictam elemosinam in rebus omnibus ita libere et quiete et honorifice in perpetuum teneant, sicut elemosina liberius et quietius et honorificius potest teneri. Testibus Simone filio Osberti, Radulfo filio eius, Ricardo de Lovetot, Frambaldo de Radefort,[1] Willelmo Bennibers,[2] Ricardo capellano, apud Beltisford.

1. Radefont *MSS.*
2. *sic MSS; probably for* Bennigwrd (Beningworth).

This charter recites almost word for word the charter of Ranulf II (**no. 93**), which it confirms. It is later in date than the general confirmation Hugh made soon after his accession (**no. 125**) and was probably issued because the latter was not specific enough for the monks; but it is not easy to date closely. Simon fitz Osbert died in 1184 (*Ann. Cestr.*, p. 33) and Frumbald about the same time (*H.K.F.*, p. 175). Richard de Lovetot was taken prisoner with Earl Hugh at Dol in 1173. On the whole a date around 1165–70 seems most likely, but any approximation is little more than a guess.

127. Notification to Robert, bishop of Lincoln, of his confirmation to the nuns of Greenfield of the land at Thoresby (Lincs.) given by William son of Otuer.[?Spurious]

Belchford, [1154–1162, perhaps 1155]

Orig.: B.L. Harl. Charter 52A 14; from the original (*penes Simonem Dawes militem et baronettum*, EE no. 4, in 1649); Tabley MSS., Sir Peter Leycester, Liber C, pars II, f. 15, and Harl. MS. 2060, f. 35v. (old p. 63). Ed.: Orm., i. 27; Stenton, *Danelaw Charters*, no. 151.

Roberto dei gratia Lincolniensi episcopo et capitulo sancte ecclesie Lincolniensis totique clero illius presulatus Hugo comes Cestrie salutem, necnon et constabulario et dapifero et baronibus et ministris et famulis et hominibus suis omnibus tam clericis quam laicis salutem similiter. Vos scire volo me concessisse et confirmasse sanctimonialibus de Grenefelt illam terram quam Willelmus filius Otuher eis in elemosinam perpetuam dedit, quam etiam pater meus comes Ranulfus eis concessit, carta sua confirmatam.[1] Eapropter volo et precipio, quod prefate sanctimoniales terram illam perhenniter bene et quiete et libere habeant et possideant. Testibus Matilla comitissa matre mea, Simone filio Willelmi, Rogero capellano,[2] Ricardo capellano, aliis multis. Apud Beltesfordam. Valete.

SEAL: missing, but still attached in 1649. 'A very fayre seale with the impression of the earle on horsebacke; and on the backe parte of the seale two lesser impressions of a man holdinge or settinge something on a form or stoole, inscribed about – Contra Sigillum Comitis Cestriae.

1. *illegible orig.: sic Liber C and Harl. 2060.*
2. Ro *only visible in orig.; Rest torn away. Name supplied from Liber C and Harl. 2060.*

William son of Otuer, whose gift is here confirmed, was the son of Otuer, a natural son of Earl Hugh I, who was drowned on 25 November 1120 with his brother, Earl Richard, in the White Ship. His charter for Greenfield is printed by Stenton, *Danelaw Charters*, no. 149A, and he also witnessed charters of Earl Hugh for Trentham (**no. 151**) and Poulton (**no. 157**), but the date of his death is not known. Simon son of William of Kyme, who accounted for the farm of Cheshire during Earl Hugh's minority (*R.S.L.C.*, xcii, pp. 1–2), probably died in 1162 (*H.K.F.*, p. 119), and the bishop of Lincoln in 1167. The present charter therefore falls between 1154 and 1162, but if, as seems likely, it was issued at the same time as **no. 125**, the date can be narrowed to 1154–57. Stenton (*op. cit.*) suggests c. 1155.

There is also a second, inflated version of this charter (printed *Danelaw Charters*, no. 150), of which the putative original still exists in the British Library (Harl. Ch. 52A 13). Unlike the text printed here, which is written in an unusually cursive charter-hand, this is written in a modified book-hand or 'diplomatic minuscule', and is evidently a version produced by or for the recipients. The main difference is that it reproduces more fully the terms of William son of Otuer's grant, viz. 'illam terram de Thoresbi, scilicet xxxii. acras'.

It also introduces an additional witness, Robert son of Hugh of Ropsley (Lincs.) Since the writing is roughly contemporaneous with that of Harl. 52A 14, and it appears to be sealed with an authentic seal of Earl Hugh (B.L. Seals, no. 5807), it is not impossible that this is a genuine charter, perhaps a re-issue ratified by the earl by the addition of his seal. But there are a number of suspicious features, e.g. the misplacing of 'baronibus' before 'constabulario' in the address, which would be impossible in a genuine charter, and the description of Countess Matilda as 'his mother' (*matre sua*) instead of the usual *matre mea*. On the whole, it seems safest to reject it as spurious.

128.   Confirmation of the grants of Helte de Boydell to the nuns of Sempringham.

[1154–1157]

B.L. Add. MSS. 6118, f. 747 (new f. 392).

Hugo comes Cestrie confirmat sanctimonialibus de Sempringham omnem donationem, quam illis dedit Heltho de Boydel, *etc.* Testibus Eustachio[1] filio Iohannis, Matildis comitissa mater Hugonis,[2] Rogero capellano, *etc.*

1.   *Blank in MS.*
2.   Mat. com. mater Hugonis *in nominative case.*

The charter, of which only this brief notice survives, must date between the death of Ranulf II in December 1153 and that of Eustace fitz John, the constable, in July 1157. It seems likely that it refers not to Sempringham itself, but to the Gilbertine priory of Bullington, which had been founded shortly before as a dependency of Sempringham by Simon of Kyme (*Mon.*, vi. 952), and to which Helte of Boydell and his wife Idonea are otherwise known to have made gifts (**no. 330**).

129.   Confirmation of the gift of Greasby in Wirral to St. Werburgh's abbey by Richard de Rullos.

[1154–1160]

P.R.O., C. 53 (Chancery Charter Rolls), no. 73, m. 10 and m. 15; St. George's Chapel, Windsor, MS. xi. E. 5; B.L., Harl. MS. 2060, f. 62 (old f. 116), and Harl. 2071, f. 45v. (old f. 31v.), both copied from preceding. Ed.: *Cal. Ch. Rolls*, ii. 317; *Chart. St. Werburgh*, p. 78 (no. 22).

Hugo comes Cestrie constabulario, dapifero, baronibus, iustic(iario), vic(ecomiti), famulis, hominibus suis omnibus tam clericis quam laicis, salutem. Vos vero scire volo, me in perpetuam elemosinam concessisse, in quantum ad me pertinet, Gravesbiam, ecclesie sancte Wereburge de Cestria in villa, in nemore, in pascuis, in aquis, in omnibus, quam Ricardus de Rullos eidem ecclesie in elemosinam dedit, carta sua confirmatam. Quapropter hominibus meis omnibus firmiter precipio, ne quis inde ecclesiam illam vexet, nec placitando nec alio modo ullo, set unusquisque pro sui posse elemosinam illam prefate ecclesie absque molestia ratam consistere faciat. Teste Matillde matre mea, Ricardo de Rullos et Roberto fratre suo, Roberto Basseat, Rogero capellano, Willelmo superbo, Alano Silvestri, et aliis multis.

For the family of Rullos, from Roullours, near Vire, Calvados, see *E.C.C.*, p. 12. One branch was established in Waverton (Broxton hundred), but it is not known how or when it came into possession of Greasby. The Richard who gave the township to St. Werburgh's appears to have survived until c. 1150, and was succeeded by Richard II, who witnesses the present charter. He and his brother Robert confirmed their father's grant about the same time as Earl Hugh's confirmation (*Chart. St. Werburgh*, no. 23). The present charter has some minor irregularities, but there is no reason to question its genuineness. The appearance of Hugh's mother, Matilda, as first witness, suggests that it was issued during his minority, but there is no means of fixing its date more exactly. The earl subsequently remitted all service due to him from Greasby, but only a brief notice of his concession survives (*Chart. St. Werburgh*, no. 348).

130. Confirmation of his precedessors' gifts to St. Werburgh's abbey of tithes of all his demesne lands in Cheshire and Staffordshire.

Chester, [1158–1177]

P.R.O., C. 53 (Chancery Charter Rolls), no. 73, m. 10; St. George's Chapel, Windsor, MS. xi. E.5 (inspeximus of Guncelin de Badlesmere, 1280); B.L. Harl. MS. 2060, f. 116 (new f. 62) and Harl. MS. 2071, f. 31 (new f. 45), from confirmation of bishop of Bath and Wells, 1283. Ed.: *Chart. St. Werburgh*, p. 77 (no. 21).

Notum sit tam presentibus quam futuris quod ego Hugo comes Cestrie concedo et confirmo donaciones omnium decimarum, quas Hugo primus comes vel Ricardus filius eius aut Rannulfus avus meus vel Rannulfus pater meus dederunt deo et ecclesie sancte Werburge Cestrie et monachis deo et prefate virgini ibidem servientibus, scilicet de omnibus dominiis meis in Cestrisira et in Staffordsira, de vacariis, pullis equarum, de molendinis, de bladis et de omnibus illis rebus, unde decima iuste dari debeat, precipiens omnibus ballivis meis et ministris et prepositis et omnibus hominibus meis super amorem meum et homagium quod mihi debent, quatinus reddant predicte virgini per singulos annos hanc elemosinam, ne audiam inde super forisfactum meum querimoniam. Et si quis de dominio meo fecerit terram tributariam, sive sit firmarius sive rusticus qui tenet eam, precipio ut reddat sancte Werburge decimas suas, ita vero quod nec clericus nec laicus faciat eis inde iniuriam, sicut carta patris mei testatur. Testibus Hugone de Lasci, Radulfo filio Warini, Hugone de Dutton, Willelmo capellano comitis, Willelmo de Haneford, et multis aliis apud Cestriam.

This confirmation is modelled closely on the corresponding charter of Ranulf II (**no. 25**), but omitting special mention of Leek mill. Unfortunately it cannot be dated closely, but the presence as witness of Hugh de Lacy, who succeeded to the lands of his father Gilbert after 1158, suggests that it probably falls before May 1177, when he was sent to Ireland and granted Meath and the custody of Dublin (Benedict of Peterborough, i. 161, 163–4).

131.   Confirmation of Robert Savage's gift to St. Werburgh's abbey of a bovate of land which Wulfric held in Storeton (Wirral).

Chester, in the abbot's chamber, [1162–1166]

> Orig.: J.R.U.L.M., Rylands Charter 1436. Abstract: Chester, Booth of Twemlow, Liber D, f. 109; *Chart. St. Werburgh*, p. 280 (no. 485); Tyson, *Handlist of Charters, Deeds and Similar Documents in the Possession of the John Rylands Library*, ii. 98.

H. comes Cestrie constabulario, dapifero, iusticiario, baronibus, vic(ecomite) et omnibus hominibus suis Francis et Anglis tam presentibus quam futuris salutem. Sciatis me concessisse et carta mea confirmasse donacionem quam Robertus Salvagius fecit deo et sancte Werburge et monacis ibidem deo servientibus, scilicet unam bovatam terre quam Wulfricus tenebat in Stortuna, liberam et quietam tenendam de me et de heredibus meis, salvo meo servicio. Testibus Ricardo de Luuetot, Radulfo filio Warneri, Rogero de Liuet, Frunbaldo, Roberto filio Gileberti, Hugone de Bosdel, Willelmo capellano comitis, et multis aliis in camera abbatis Cestrie apud Cestram.[1]

> SEAL on tag, fragmentary. Obverse, an equestrian figure in armour, to the right; reverse, a small oval counter-seal, an antique intaglio gem, subject uncertain; legend + SECRETUM ME . . . CHI.[2]

1. *sic MS.*
2. Cf. Taylor, *Selected Cheshire Seals*, p. 4.

Robert Savage was the son of Alan Silvester, or Savage, to whom Ranulf II gave Storeton about 1135 (**no. 35**). The present charter is not easy to date, but must fall before 1166, by which time Robert son of Gilbert was dead (*P.R.S.*, ix, p. 2, and xi, p. 40), and almost certainly after Earl Hugh's majority (1162).

132. Confirmation of agreement between the abbeys of St. Werburgh and St. Evroul regarding the vill and the church of West Kirby.

[1162–1172]

> Orig.: Alençon, Archives départementales de l'Orne, H. 901. Cal.: *Inventaire sommaire des archives départementales, Archives de l'Orne, Série H*; Round, *C.D.F.*, p. 225, no. 640. Ed.: *Chart. St. Werburgh*, no. 509 (from inaccurate transcript).

Notum sit tam presentibus quam futuris, quod ego Hugh[1] comes Cestrie concessi et presenti carta confirmavi convencionem inter ecclesiam sancte Werburge de Cestria et ecclesiam de sancto Ebrulpho, videlicet quod ecclesia sancte Werburge de Cestria reddet annuatim xxx. solidos argenti ecclesie de sancto Ebrulpho pro villa de Kircheby et monasterio, et pro omni rectitudine quam abbas et monachi de sancto Ebrulpho habuerunt in prefata possessione. Testibus Radulfo de Meinegarin, Conano, Ricardo de Luvetot, Ricardo de Cumbrai, Radulfo filio Warneri, Alveredo de Cumbrai, Rogero de Livet, et aliis multis.

> SEAL: missing.

1. Hogo *orig.*

Kirby (Wirral) had been given to St. Evroul by Robert of Rhuddlan in the time of Hugh I (**no. 1**) and his gift was confirmed by Ranulf I (**no. 11**). When and how St. Werburgh's acquired an interest in it is not definitely known. Ranulf II gave it, as appurtance to the manor of Caldy, to his new foundation of Basingwerk (**no. 37**), and it seems probable that the monks of St. Evroul, despairing of retaining possession, traded it to St. Werburgh's. This, as Tait has shown (*Chart. St. Werburgh*, p. 293), was in 1137–40, but it was clearly out of the question to get confirmation of the agreement until after the death of Ranulf II. Hence the present charter, which is not easy to date accurately, but seems to belong to the earlier part of Hugh II's tenure of the earldom. Richard de Lovetot and Richard de Combray were taken prisoner with the earl at Dol in 1173 (Benedict of

Peterborough, i. 57, 58). The confirmation probably falls between Hugh's majority and then. It did not end controversy. The abbot of St. Evroul laid a complaint against the abbot of Chester in or about 1205, and the claims and counter-claims of Chester and Basingwerk dragged on until 1287 before being decided in favour of the former (*Chart. St. Werburgh*, pp. xxxii, 295).

133.   Grant of the church of Prestbury to St. Werburgh's abbey.

[1178–1181]

> Orig.: Adlington Hall, Cheshire, Bundle 24, no. 1. Tran-
> scr.: Adlington inspeximus (1285), no. 2; St. George's
> Chapel, Windsor (inspeximus), MS. xi. E.5, no. 11;
> P.R.O., C.53 (Chancery Charter Rolls), no. 73, m. 11;
> abbreviated copy Bodleian Library, MS. Top. Cheshire,
> b. I, p. 80. Ed.: *Chart. St. Werburgh*, p. 79 (no. 24) from
> Charter Roll); Orm., i. 26–27 (abbreviated). Engl. trans.:
> *Ches. Sheaf*, no. 10111.

H. comes Cestrie constabulario, dapifero, iusticiario, baronibus, vic(ecomiti), baillivis, et omnibus hominibus suis clericis et laicis Francis et Anglis, tam presentibus quam futuris, salutem. Sciatis me dedisse cum corpore meo deo et sancte Wereburge ecclesiam de Presteburia cum omnibus pertinentiis suis ita libere et quiete sicut aliquis antecessorum meorum, aliquam elemosinam liberius et quietius eidem ecclesie sancte Wereburge unquam contulit, nichil omnino in hac elemosina retinens nisi orationes, nec etiam ius advocationis. Deo teste et omnibus sanctis, Iohanne priore de Trentham, Sansone canonico, Radulfo Barba Aprilis, Roberto clerico de Wico, Ranulfo de Lech, Radulfo de Meinil-warin, Radulfo filio Warneri, Gileberto filio Picoti, Roberto fratre eius, Frombaldo, Bertram camerario, Gileberto filio Helie. Hec carta facta fuit coram comitissa M. matre comitis et B. comitissa sponsa eius, et Ranulfo herede suo concedente.

SEAL, on tag: missing.

This charter is dated 1170–81 by Tait (*Chart. St. Werburgh*, p. 79) and c. 1178 by W. Fergusson Irvine (*Ches. Sheaf*, no. 10111). Seeing that Ranulf III, whose assent is specifically mentioned, was only born in 1170 (*Ann. Cestr.*, p. 24) and that Earl Hugh himself was in rebellion from 1173 to 1177, it can safely be dated 1178–81. Bishop Richard of Coventry's confirmation, dated 1181–82, is printed (with facsimile) in *E.C.C.*, p. 22, no. 10 (1). Ralph Mainwaring, the future justiciar, married Earl Hugh's daughter Amicia about this time (**no. 193**). For Bertram the chamberlain, see **no. 194**. Ralph Barbe d'Averill is elsewhere described as Earl Hugh's chaplain (**no. 123**); his son William performed the same function for Countess Bertrada (**no. 251**).

134–9. Various grants and confirmations for St. Werburgh's abbey, Chester.

[1153–1181]

B.L. Harl. MS. 1965, ff. 5v., 6, 7v., 20v., 25. Ed.: *Chart. St. Werburgh*, nos. 16, 17, 50, 348, 354, 482.

134. Hugo comes Cestrie dedit ecclesie sancte Werburge in die festivitatis eius firmam illam, scilicet xii. denarios, et omne servicium que quondam habebat in terris, quas Leoninus et Leonenth[1] sacerdotes et Willelmus le Palmer dederunt secum abbacie, quando fecerunt se monachos. Teste W. Patrick, etc.

135. Hugo comes dedit sancte Werburge et Roberto abbati omnes fugitivos servos vel nativos, ubicumque eos invenerit in terra sua vel hominum suorum, ut reducerentur cum omnibus catallis suis, nec ab aliquo detinerentur super forisfacturam x. librarum.

136. Hugo comes Cestrie concessit quod ecclesia sancte Werburge habeat unam masuram extra portam orientalem, quam Robertus de Moldeworthe coram ipso dedit.

137. H. comes Cestrie confirmavit donacionem Randulfi de Chingesleye de dimidia marca annuatim solvenda ad festum sancti Marci, et inde plegius fuit et ballivis suis precepit ut eum, si necesse esset, ad solucionem compellerent.

138. Hugo comes Cestrie dedit ecclesie sancte Werburge ecclesiam de Haliwelle cum omnibus pertinenciis in usus monachorum proprios, et unum mansum in dicta villa lx. pedum in latitudine et octaginta in longtitudine.

139. Hugo comes Cestrie remisit imperpetuum omne servicium quod Gravesby sibi facere debuit, ita quod omnino sit libera et soluta ab omni servicio sibi debito.

1. Emended by Tait (*Chart. St. Werburgh*, p. 73) to Leovinus (Leofwine) and Leoventh (Leofnoth?)

The six grants and confirmations listed above are only found in abbreviated abstracts in the register of St. Werburgh's abbey. Apart from **no. 134**, attested by William Patric (d. 1184), they have no witnesses. **No. 135**, authorising Abbot Robert and the monks to reclaim fugitive serfs wherever found on the earl's land or that of his men, must date from after the appointment of the first Abbot Robert in 1157. Otherwise, except for **no. 138**, they cannot be dated at all closely. Robert of Mouldsworth, whose gift of a tenement outside the Eastgate of Chester is confirmed in **no. 136**, witnessed two charters (**nos. 160, 161**) for Warin de Vernon, dating probably from 1162 to 1181. Ranulf of Kingsley (**no. 137**) was presumably the son of the Ranulf who is said to have been invested by Earl Ranulf I with the master-forestership of Mara and Mondrem by tradition of a horn (Orm., ii. 87, 90, 107); he died between 1190 and 1200 (*Ches. Sheaf*, no. 4704). Earl Hugh confirmed Richard de Rullos' gift of Greasby to St. Werburgh's c.1154–60 (**no. 129**); his remission of the services due from this manor (**no. 139**) presumably followed later, but the date cannot be established. The church of Holywell (**no. 138**) had been given to St. Werburgh's by one Burell in the time of Earl Richard, but was then conferred on Basingwerk abbey in the time of Ranulf II (**no. 36**). Hugh's gift, of which unfortunately only this short notice remains, appears to be an act of restitution. It must fall after 1157, when Owain Gwynedd, who had been in control of the whole district since 1152, was forced to hand it over to the English, and 1166, when he recaptured Basingwerk and recovered possession of the whole of Tegeingl (Lloyd, pp. 500, 519). St. Werburgh's enjoyment of Hugh's grant was therefore of very short duration.

140. Grant to St. Werburgh's abbey of pannage and common for its demesne pigs in his forests of Englefield and Cheshire. [Spurious]

> P.R.O., CHES 33/4 (Forest Rolls, 20–21 Edw. III), m. 30v.; CHES 34/1 (Quo Warranto, 31 Edw. III), m. 14; D.L. 39/1/19 (Forest Pleas, 21 Edw. III), m. 26v.

Hugo comes Cestrie constabulario, dapifero, iusticiario, baronibus, vic(ecomiti), ballivis et omnibus hominibus suis, clericis et laicis, Francis et Anglicis, tam presentibus quam futuris, salutem. Sciatis me concessisse et dedisse abbati et monachis sancte Werburge Cestrie, quod habeant pessonem et communam in forestis meis de Englefeld et de Cestresira porcis suis dominicis, habendam et tenendam sibi et successoribus suis libere et quiete, pacifice et honorifice, in puram et perpetuam elemosinam. Testibus Rogero de Lascy, constabulario

Cestrie, Philippo de Orreby tunc iusticiario Cestrie, Ricardo[1] dapifero de Monte Alto, Warino de Vernon, Willelmo de Venables, et aliis.

1. *sic MSS., for* Rogero. *There was no Richard* dapifer.

This charter is a gross forgery, adapted apparently from Ranulf III's charter containing the same concession (**no. 232**), the first five witnesses of which are identical with the witnesses of the present charter. It does not seem to have come into circulation before the fourteenth century. Given the existence of **no. 232**, it is hard to understand why it was needed. It is also hard to understand how so clumsy a forgery, with witnesses totally impossible in the time of Hugh II, could have been passed off as genuine; but it presumably served its purpose, since it was inspected and confirmed by Edward III in 1346–47.

141. Restoration to Walter of Vernon of the lands which his grandfather, another Walter of Vernon, held of the earl of Chester, and also of Harlaston (Staffs.), which Countess Matilda restores from her dowry.

London, [March 1155]

> Orig. now lost; printed by Stebbing Shaw, *The History and Antiquities of Staffordshire*, i. 399, from the original then in the possession of C. Chadwick.

Hugo comes Cestrie[1] constab(ulario), dap(ifero), baronibus, ministris et baillivis, secus mare et ultra, et omnibus hominibus suis salutem. Sciant omnes homines mei secus mare et ultra, quod reddidi Waltero de Vernun totam terram et honorem, quam Walterus de Vernun avus suus de comite Cestrie tenuit; et sicut ipse Walterus de Vernun avus suus tenuit de comite Cestrie, sic iste Walterus tenet[2] de me, et eodem servicio. Et sciant omnes, quod ego Matilda comitissa isti Waltero de Vernun reddidi Herlavestun, quod est de dote mea, tenendum de me. Testibus Ricardo filio comitis Gloecestrie,[3] Iohanne de Sulenhi, Eustacio filio Iohannis, Waltero Hose, Ricardo Pincerna, Serlone[4] venatore, Roberto dapifero, Alured de Culumberes,[5] Tancart, apud Lundun.[6]

1. Cestre *ed.*
2. tenuit *ed.*
3. Gloercestrie *ed.*
4. Stone *ed.*
5. *sic ed. for* Cumbrai.
6. *sic ed.*

The date of this charter must fall between the death of Ranulf II on 17 December 1153 and the death of Eustace fitz John, constable of Chester, during

Henry II's Welsh campaign in July or August 1157. If the dating *apud Lundun* is correct, the occasion was almost certainly Henry II's Great Council at Westminster in March 1155. Although he was only six years old at the time, it is entirely credible that Earl Hugh should have attended the council with his mother, along with the other great magnates of the realm. Furthermore, his charter is in line with Henry II's policy at the beginning of his reign of restoring orderly conditions. The elder Walter Vernon, who was a tenant of the earl of Chester in Staffordshire and Oxfordshire as well as in Cheshire at the time of Domesday (*H.K.F.*, p. 276; *D.S.C.*, pp. 142–5), was still alive in 1113 (*Regesta*, ii. no. 1022) and perhaps as late as 1119, if Earl Richard's charter for St. Werburgh's (**no. 8**) is genuine. He is said (*D.S.C.*, p. 47) to have died without issue, but in reality he was succeeded by a son, Richard (Robert of Torigni, *Chron.*, p. 172), who must, at some stage, have been dispossessed, presumably by Ranulf II. What happened to the Vernon lands in the meantime, we do not know; but by restoring Richard's son Walter to his heritage, Hugh was evidently seeking to normalize the situation resulting from his father's well-known high-handed actions.

142.   Confirmation of the donations of his grandmother, Countess Lucy, and his father, Earl Ranulf, to Stixwould abbey.

[1153–1181]

B.L. Add. MS. 46701 (Stixwould cartulary), f. 2.

Hugo comes Cestrie archiepiscopis, episcopis, abbatibus, iustic(iario), vic(ecomiti), ministris et ballidis, omnibus hominibus suis Francis et Anglis, clericis et laicis, tocius Anglie salutem. Notum sit vobis me concessisse et confirmasse deo et ecclesie sancte Marie de Stykeswold et sanctimonialibus que ibidem deo serviunt, donaciones quas fecerunt eis in elemosina Lucia comitissa ava mea et Rannulfus comes Cestrie pater meus et cartis suis et sigillis confirmaverunt, videlicet ex dono et elemosina L. comitisse totam terram quam habuit in Stykeswold et ecclesiam eiusdem ville, et totam terram quam habuit in Torp et ecclesiam eiusdem ville, et totam terram quam habuit in Hundingtuna et ecclesiam eiusdem ville. Hec dedit Lucia comitissa deo et sanctimonialibus predictis in perpetuam elemosinam, et Rannulfus comes Cestrie pater meus concessit et carta sua confirmavit. Ego quoque eandem elemosinam deo et eisdem sanctimonialibus concedo et per hanc cartam meam in perpetuam elemosinam confirmo pro salute mea et pro animabus antecessorum meorum, liberam et quietam ab omni seculari servicio et consuetudine, cum omnibus que pertinent eisdem terris et ecclesiis in bosco et plano, in villis et extra, in viis et semitis, in pratis et pascuis, in aquis et molendinis, et in omnibus aliis locis. Testibus *etc*.

This confirmation cannot be closely dated. For the charters of Countess Lucy and Earl Ranulf, see **nos. 18** and **20**.

143. Confirmation to the nuns of Stixwould of the gift of Robert, son of Sceidman of Barkworth, and his son William of the mill of Donington (Lincs.)

[?1153–1173]

B.L. Add. MS. 46701 (Stixwould cartulary), ff. 208v.– 209.

Hugo comes Cestrie constabulario suo, dapifero, iustic(iario), vicecom(iti) omnibus suis baronibus, omnibus hominibus suis Francis et Anglicis tam presentibus quam futuris salutem. Sciatis me concessisse et carta mea confirmasse sanctimonialibus de Stykeswold donacionem quam Robertus filius Sceidman de Barkwood et Willelmus eius filius predictis monialibus fecerunt, scilicet molendinum de Duningtuna et situm eiusdem molendini, sicuti carte predictorum testantur. Et hoc feci pro anima patris mei *etc.* Testibus.

The charters of Robert and William precede f. 208, but are undated; it is the mill, Robert says, which Ralph of Stixwould gave him in marriage with his daughter, Alice. Ralph of Stixwould appears before 1130 (*H.K.F.*, pp. 148, 169) and William of Barkworth in 1176 (*H.K.F.*, p. 121). This perhaps points to a fairly early date for the present charter, but the evidence is too slim for even a tentative attribution.

144. Notification that Ralph, son of Simon of Edlington, his man, had renounced his claim against the nuns of Stixwould, and confirmation of his gift to them of common pasture in the marsh pertaining to Edlington (Lincs.)

[?1155]

B.L. Add. MS. 46701 (Stixwould cartulary), f. 2.

Hugo comes Cestrie universis sancte matris ecclesie filiis salutem. Universitati vestre notum sit quod, anno primo post coronacionem Henrici regis secundi, Radulfus homo meus filius Symonis de Hederlingtuna dimisit se ab omni calumpnia quam habuit de terra de Stykeswold contra sanctimoniales ibidem deo servientes, et quietam clamavit a se et ab omnibus successoribus suis et ab omni parentela sua. Et preterea sciatis quod predictus Radulfus dedit et concessit in puram elemosinam deo et beate Marie et conventui de Stykeswold communem pasturam cum hominibus de Edelingtona per totam moram, que pertinet ad campum de Edelingtuna. Et illud donum concedo et confirmo ista presenti carta mea. Hiis testibus *etc*.

Henry II was crowned on 19 December 1154, so this charter probably belongs to 1155.

145.   Confirmation to Liulf of Brinklow of the lands in and outside Coventry which he held of Earl Ranulf II, and of the vill of Bisley, for an annual payment of half a mark.

Coventry, [? 1158–1160]

> Orig.: Stratford-upon-Avon, Shakespeare's Birthplace, Gregory-Hood Deeds, Coventry no. 1 (new numbering 257). Ed.: Coss, no. 8.

For a full text of this document, see Coss, *The Early Records of Medieval Coventry*, pp. 15–16 (no. 8).

Ranulf II's charter has not survived, and the date of the present charter can only be surmised, but the evidence indicates that it falls during Hugh II's minority. The witness list falls into two parts, the second half, beginning with the prior of Coventry, evidently being local men. The witnesses in the first half are almost exclusively associated with Ranulf II, and disappear shortly thereafter. Roger de Beauchamp witnessed Ranulf's charter for Geva Ridel (**no. 39**) as early as 1135–8 and another (**no. 80**) c. 1144–46. Hugh son of Anschetil (Haschat), who accounted for his father's land in 1130 (Pipe Roll, 31 Henr. I, p. 59), witnessed a charter (**no. 35**) not much later, and Ivo son of Anschetil witnessed Ranulf II's confirmation of William the constable's gift of Raby to St. Werburgh's c.1135–40 (**no. 21**). William son of Nigel witnessed Ranulf II's charter for Burton abbey (**no. 115**), and Ranulf the sheriff, obviously an important person, witnessed six charters between 1143 and 1153, but none, apart from the present charter, after Ranulf II's death. All this suggests an early date in Hugh II's minority. On the other hand, it has to be remembered that Hugh was only six years old when he succeeded in 1153, and not surprisingly most of his charters were issued jointly with, or witnessed by, his mother, Countess Matilda. Her absence, and that of Eustace fitz John (d. 1157), the constable and 'supremus consiliarius' (**no. 73**), from the list of witnesses militates against too early a date, and it may perhaps be suggested that the present charter falls between 1158 and 1160. In any case, there can be little doubt that it precedes **no. 146**.

146. Grant to Liulf of Brinklow of his tenements within and outside Coventry and of the vill and mill of Bisley, all of which Earl Ranulf II had granted him, and in addition quittance of pannage for 200 pigs, to be held for an annual payment of 14s. 6d.

Coventry, [c.1162]

> Orig.: B.L. Harl. Charter 83 F. 32. Transcr.: B.L. Harl. MS. 7 (Langley cartulary), ff. 102v.–103. Ed. from orig.: Nichols, *Leicestershire*, II, i., App. xv, p. 39 (with facsimile of seal, pl.xii.); Coss, no. 9.

For the full text of this document, see Coss, *The Early Records of Medieval Coventry*, pp. 16–17 (no. 9).

> SEAL: B.L. 5810. Bright red, pendent on lace, striped red and white, only centre remaining, about 3 ins. when perfect. Obverse: equestrian, knight in armour to dexter, hauberk of mail, helmet and sword, long pleated surcoat, shield ornamented with a bordure; horse galloping, saddlecloth diapered lozengy with small cross in each space and fringed ornamental breast-band with pendent pellets; legend wanting. Reverse: small oval counter-seal, $1\frac{1}{10}$ x $\frac{7}{10}$ ins.; impression of antique intaglio gem, a gryllus of two human faces conjoined, on left Silenus, on right Mercury; legend ＋ SIGILLUM WILELMI BARBE AVILL.

The relationship between this charter and **no. 145** is not entirely clear, but there are no grounds for questioning the genuineness of either. The simplest explanation for the issue of a second charter is probably that Earl Hugh, on reaching his majority, was dissatisfied with the terms of **no. 145** and, in addition to raising the annual rent from 6s. 8d to 14s. 6d. and getting an initial payment of 47 marks, took pains to emphasize that the lands in question, although originally given by Ranulf II, were now held *mea confirmatione et concessu*. In any case, the present charter is evidently later in date than **no. 145**, which it supersedes, and is attested in effect by a new generation of witnesses (William Patric, Richard Lovetot, William of Rhuddlan, Bertram the chamberlain). Thorold the earl's serjeant, who died c.1181–2 (*R.S.L.C.*, xcii, p. 8), witnessed charters c.1162–6 (**nos. 150, 151**), in one instance in association with Jordan Rasur, who also witnessed three charters for Calke and Repton (**nos. 120, 121, 173**) around this time. One of these charters (**no. 121**), dating from 1162 or perhaps a little later, has six witnesses in common with the present charter, in addition to Countess Matilda, and the latter may safely be assigned to the same period. Although the place of issue is not stated, the names of the last nine witnesses point unmistakably to Coventry, Gerard the vintner, Anschetil Locard and

William de Aula in particular being frequently named in Coventry charters, including **no. 195** below.

147.   Confirmation of the possessions and liberties of the priory of Calke, as specified in his father's charter, and also of the land of Eswin Esegar of Thringstone and the land and service of Nicholas, Earl Ranulf's squire.

Barrow-upon-Soar, [c.1162]

> *Mon.*, vi. 598 ('ex autographo penes Johannem Harpur de Calke anno 1664'; Bigsby, *History of Repton*, p. 59 (from *Mon.*); Jeayes, *Derbyshire Charters*, no. 536 (also from *Mon.*)

H. comes Cestrie constabulario, dapifero, iusticiariis, vicecomitibus, ministris, balivis, et omnibus hominibus suis Francis et Anglicis, tam presentibus quam futuris, salutem. Sciatis me concessisse et hac carta mea confirmasse omnes possessiones et omnes libertates ecclesie sancti Egidii de Calc et canonicis ibi deo servientibus pro anima patris mei et matris mee et pro salute anime mee et pro animabus antecessorum meorum in perpetuam elemosinam, sicut carte patris mei testantur et confirmant, videlicet silvam in qua habitant inter Sceggebroc et Aldrebroc, et parvam geilbergam, et culturam inter Alrebroc et Sudwude, et parvum molendinum de Rapindone, et quatuor bovatas terre in Tichehale. Et ex dono Nicholai sacerdotis duas bovatas in eadem villa, et capellam de Smithesbi. Et ex dono Geve Ridel unam mansuram terre in Tamwurtha. Et ex dono patris mei unum batum in piscatura Cestrie, ubicumque voluerint, ad piscandum, cum una mansura terre ad opus eorum piscatoris, et terram Loftescot, scilicet sicut via descendit de Rapindone ad fontem Neuhath-ewelle, et sicut idem fons descendit usque ad metas Meeltone, et ex altera parte sicut terminus Meeltone est, usque ad capud Loftescou. Et totam terram Eswini Esegar de Trengestona. Et precipio ut illa terra sit libera et quieta ab omni servicio et ab omnibus causis et querelis, ut debet esse elemosina. Et insuper precipio hominibus meis ne eos inquietent aut vexent aliqua re, sed ipsi canonici predictam terram teneant in bosco et in plano, in aquis et molendinis, et in omnibus locis ita plenarie, sicut unquam aliquis eam tenuit tempore meo et antecessorum meorum plenarius. Et Reginaldum filium Alfwini de Rapindone cum mansura sua et cum duabus bovatis terre eidem mansure adiacentibus, ipsum et suos heredes solum et quietem ab omni seculari servicio et de omnibus consuetudinibus, que pertinent meo[1] undredo Rapindone, et nominatim de placitis de halemote, et de omnibus querelis et occasionibus, ita quod quiete et libere possideant imperpetuum;[2] et precipue sit regi quietus de tolneio et pannagio et omni consuetudine imperpetuum.[2] Concedo etiam eidem prefate ecclesie terram et servicium Nicholai armigeri patris nostri, in bosco et in plano, in rivis et in pascuis, in foro et extra, et viis et semitis, libere et quiete sicut unquam melius vel quietius ante eum tenuit. Insuper ad honorem dei et supradicte ecclesie concedo eis eorum curiam tam plenariam quam habeo meam in Rapindona, cum tol et tem et infaggenthef, cum omnibus consuetudinibus, quas ego vel aliquis antecessorum meorum melius et plenarius eis concedere potuit. Et volo et precipio quod teneant libere et honorifice et quiete in bosco et in plano, in pratis et aquis, et viis et semitis, in foro et in mercato, in molendinis et in omnibus locis et omnibus rebus, et nominatim volo quod de bosco meo habeant copiam ad omnia sua edificia et ad ignem. Has autem possessiones et prescriptas libertates prefati canonici habeant libere et quiete, sicut carte patris mei testantur. Testibus Radulfo de Meidinwarin, Alfredo de Cumbrai, Alfredo de Suleini, Ricardo de Luvetot, Rogero de Livet, Giliberto filio Pigot, Roberto filio Giliberti, Willelmo clerico de Barva, Bertramo camerario, Sewalo, Alexandro fratre eius, Radulfo de Bricheshard, Roberto pincerna, Willelmo clerico Barba Aprilis, apud Barvam.

1.   me *Mon.*; *other texts have* mihi.
2.   *sic MSS.*

This charter is a confirmation of **no. 45** (with insertions), and like that a monastic product. As there is no suggestion of a transfer of the seat of the priory from Calke to Repton, it is probably earlier than **nos. 121** and **123**. It is dated c.1162 (i.e. shortly after Hugh attained his majority) by Jeayes, and what is known of the witnesses does not permit a closer dating. Ralph Mainwaring is unlikely to be the future justiciar, who survived until c.1210; but the early pedigree of Mainwaring (*Orm.*, iii. 226; *H.K.F.*, p. 228) is unsatisfactory and provides no reliable information.

148.   Confirmation to Bordesley abbey of the grant of Combe (Gloucs.) for the maintenance in perpetuity of six monks for the health of his soul and the souls of Earl Ranulf and his father, Robert earl of Gloucester his grandfather, his mother and all his ancestors.

[1162–1173, probably c.1162]

Bodleian Library, Dugdale MS. 17, f. 55 (from the original in the possession of William Sheldon of Beoley, copied in facsimile writing, with fine reproduction of seal). Ed.: Dugdale, *Baronage*, i. 41; *Mon.*, v. 407; brief notice Orm., i. p. 29, note a.

Episcopis, abbatibus, archidiaconis, decanis omnibusque sancte dei ecclesie filiis Hugo comes Cestrie salutem in Christo. Sciatis me concessisse et presenti carta in perpetuam elemosinam confirmasse deo et monachis de Bordleia Cumbe cum omnibus eius pertinentiis, ea conditione ut apud Bordeleam sustineantur vi. monachi in perpetuum pro salute anime mee et anime Ranulfi comitis patris mei et anime Roberti comitis Glocestrie avi mei et anime matris mee et animarum omnium antecessorum nostrorum, libere et quiete et plenarie sicut unquam aliqua elemosina liberius potest dari, in bosco, in plano, in aquis, in molendinis, in viis, in semitis, in pratis, in pascuis, in pasturis et omnibus locis, cum omnibus libertatibus que eidem terre pertinent.[1] Testibus Ricardo filio comitis Gloeces- trie, Radulfo filio Warini, Iohanne priore de Trentham, Radulfo capellano, Herberto et Willelmo clericis comitis, Ricardo de Luvetot, Gilberto filio Picot, Rogero de Livet, Aluredo de Cumbrai, et multis aliis.

> SEAL: equestrian, perfect; the earl with sword upheld in
> right hand, and shield in left hand; galloping horse.
> Legend SIGILLUM HUGONIS COMITIS CESTRIE.

1.   pertinet *MS.*

The hamlet of Combe in Chipping Campden (Gloucs.) was given to Bordesley abbey by Ranulf II (**no. 100**), and his gift was confirmed by Countess Matilda (**no. 102**). The indications are that the present charter was given between Hugh's majority (1162) and 1173, but the evidence does not permit a closer dating. It probably precedes **no. 149**. Hugh's uncle Richard, son of Earl Robert of Gloucester, died in 1175.

149.   Injunction to his bailiffs of Chester that the monks of Bordesley are to have their boat in his fishery at Chester as freely as when he first gave it to them.

Warwick, [c.1162–1164]

> Bodleian Library, Dodsworth MS. 31, f. 93v.; MS. Top.
> Cheshire b. I, p. 35; Chester, Booth of Twemlow, Liber
> D, f. 142; B.L. Harl. MS. 2079, f. 63 (new f. 32), all
> apparently 'ex rotulo cartarum antiquarum vocato
> Domesday'.

Hugo comes Cestrie constabulario et vicecomiti et ballivis de Cestria salutem. Precipio quod abbas et conventus de Bordeslea habeant et teneant battelum suum in piscaria mea Cestrie sicut illum[1] melius habere solebant quando illum eis donavi pro salute anime mee. Et videte ne ullo modo inde disturbentur. Testibus Ricardo pincerna et Hugone osturcario[2] et Willelmo capellano apud Warwicum.

1.   illam *in all MSS.*
2.   Ostiar[io] *MSS.*

This writ, presumably the result of a complaint made by the monks of Bordesley (Worcs.) to the earl while he was in Warwick, clearly indicates that Hugh had previously given them a boat on the Dee. The original grant has not survived, but it must have been shortly after his succession, since the present document cannot fall long after his majority. Both Richard the butler and Hugh the falconer had been frequent witnesses under Ranulf II, but both were at the end of their careers. Richard is not otherwise mentioned after 1159 (*E.C.C.*, p. 4), and Hugh the falconer passed on his lands to his son in a charter (**no. 150**) which dates from 1166 at latest. The present writ was probably issued not long after 1162.

150.   Grant to Robert, son of Hugh the falconer, at his father's instance, of all Hugh's land, for the service of one knight.

[1162–1166]

B.L. Harl. MS. 2059, f. 186 (new f. 105), from original, apparently with Mr. Brescy of Woodcote Heath.

Hugo comes Cestrie constabulario suo et dapifero et omnibus baronibus suis et hominibus suis Francis et Anglis tam futuris quam presentibus totius Anglie salutem. Sciatis me dedisse et concessisse Rodberto filio Hugonis accipitrum totam terram patris sui, quam de me et de meo feudo tenuit, peticione patris suis, in feudo et hereditate ei et heredibus suis ad tenendam de me et meis heredibus per servicium unius militis. Testibus Ricardo fratre comitis, Roberto filio Walteri et Gilberto filio Picoti et Iordano Rasur et Toroldo et Rodberto filio Gileberti et Radulfo capellano, qui hanc cartam iussu comitis fecit.

SEAL: 'Sealed with a great seale, a hand broad, wherein is printed the saide Earle on horsebacke armed at all points, in his right hand a speare, on his left arme a shild etc. SIG' HUG' COM. CESTR: roundabout.'

This charter must fall before the death of Earl Hugh's brother Richard (**nos. 175, 177**) and almost certainly in the early part of Hugh's tenure of the earldom. Robert son of Gilbert died in 1166 (*H.K.F.*, p. 107). Hugh the falconer was obviously an old man by this time, perhaps dying, and wished to pass on his inheritance to his son. He had witnessed no fewer than fifteen of Ranulf II's charters, but only one (**no. 124**) shortly after Ranulf's death, about which time his son also witnessed a charter of the Countess Matilda (**no. 102**). Furthermore, it seems evident that he had surrendered the position of falconer towards the close of Earl Ranulf's life, when it passed on to Henry the falconer (**no. 111**), he himself and Berengar the falconer witnessing the grant. The present charter can therefore safely be dated between 1162, the year of Earl Hugh's majority, and 1166, and probably nearer the earlier date.

151.   Grant to Trentham priory of a free boat and the right to fish on the river Dee.

Chester, [1162–1166]

P.R.O., CHES 2/26 (Recog. Rolls, 14–15 Edw. III), m.3.

Hugo comes Cestrie constabulario et dapifero suo, iusticiario, vicecomitibus,[1] baronibus, ballidis[1] et ministris suis et omnibus hominibus suis clericis et laicis tam futuris quam presentibus salutem. Notum sit omnibus me dedisse et in perpetuam elemosinam confirmasse pro anima Ranulfi[2] comitis patris mei et pro salute anime mee deo et ecclesie omnium sanctorum de Trentham et canonicis ibidem deo servientibus unam naviculam in Dee ad piscandum subtus et superius pontem cum omni genere retis, scilicet cum flotnet et stalnet et dreynet. Hanc naviculam liberam et cum omni libertate et adquietacione tenendam in perpetuum do et confirmo ecclesie de Trentham, et precipio, ut omnino quiete teneat. Ego enim warantizo naviculam ad sustentamentum canonicorum, et volo et precipio ut nullus meorum in aliquo impediat aut disturbet canonicos de hac elemosina, sicut diligant anime mee salutem. Huius rei sunt testes Robertus de Monte Alto, Randulfus de Belmis, Willelmus filius Otueri, Rogerus de Mainilwarin, Radulfus filius Warneri, Gilbertus filius Picot, Toraldus, Robertus filius Gilberti, Bertram camerarius, Rogerus camerarius, Robertus Fot[3] vicecomes, qui suo tempore clamavit quietam[4] naviculam ab omni consuetudine, et multi alii apud Cestriam.

1. *sic MS.*
2. Rand. *MS.*
3. *sic MS.*
4. qui . . . *(MS. torn).*

This charter was issued fairly early in Hugh's tenure of the earldom, probably shortly after he attained his majority in 1162. Of the witnesses Randulf de Belmis was dead by 1166 (*P.R.S.*, xii, p. 57), also Robert son of Gilbert (*H.K.F.*, p. 107). Robert of Montalt, the steward, died c.1177 (*Chart. St. Werburgh*, p. 302), Turold the earl's serjeant (*serviens*) by 1182 (*R.S.L.C.*, xcii, p. 8, and *P.R.S.*, xxxii, pp. 74, 152). Particular interest attaches to the mention of Robert Fot, the sheriff. The name Fot (perhaps the same as Foot) occurs more than a century later in the Cheshire Eyre Rolls (*Chetham Soc.*, N.S. lxxxiv,

p. 209), but (if correct) this is the only earlier instance I have seen. There is no other mention of a Robert the sheriff; in all probability he was a sheriff of the city, and not of the county, of Chester.

152. Notification that his gift of a boat to the monastery of Trentham should not be interpreted in such a way that his revenues from Chester are diminished, and his own fishing rights, particularly at Eaton, are to be maintained.

Chester, [1177–1181]

> Bodleian Library, Dodsworth MS. 31, f. 93v. 'ex rotulo cartarum antiquarum vocato Domesday' (A); MS. Top. Cheshire b. I, p. 135, 'from a MS. of John Arden intitled Baronagium Cestriae' (B); B.L. Harl. MS. 2079, f. 63 (new f. 32) (C); Chester, Booth of Twemlow, Liber D (94 A 591), f. 142v. 'ex Domesday' (D).

Hugo comes Cestrie constabulario, dapifero, iusticie, vicecomitibus et omnibus hominibus suis Francis et Anglis tam presentibus quam futuris[1] salutem. Notum vobis facio quod primum batellum quod dedi, illud dedi[2] elemosina[3] elemosine patris mei, scilicet ecclesie[4] de Trentham, pro anima patris mei et matris mee et pro me et pro comitissa et pro heredibus meis in perpetuam elemosinam, ita quod renta[5] mea Cestrie[6] non sit minuta plus amodo quam huiusque fuit, nec[7] vicecomites intromittant se de hac elemosina ut meus redditus comminuatur, et piscatum mihi voluerint [manutenere][8] desuper pontem et sub ponte et nominatim apud Hetonam cum stallnettis et flicnettis et omnibus modis. Et prohibeo ne aliquis in novam consuetudinem[9] illos ponat[10] quam unquam fecerint de terra[11] extra portam et de batello. Testibus Aluredo de Combrea,[12] Galfrido de Dutton,[13] Willelmo capellano, apud[14] Cestriam.

1. *For* et omnibus – futuris, *etc. C.*
2. *om.* illud dedi *C.*
3. *sic in all MSS.*
4. ecclesias *A*, ecclesia *B*, ecclesiam *D.*
5. beuta *A.*
6. de Cestria *C.*
7. *All the MSS. have* hec, *but this makes no sense.*
8. *There appears to be a verb omitted;* manutenere *is only one possibility among others.*
9. de nova consuetudine *C.*
10. ponant *B.*
11. terris *C.*
12. Cambrea *A*, Combra *B, C.*
13. *All MSS. have* Cottun; *in C it is corrected to* Dottun.
14. concessum apud *A, B, D.*

This unusual document, which evidently caused considerable difficulty for the copyists, is clearly a sequel to **no. 151**, and must be later in date. Geoffrey of Dutton, who occurs frequently as a witness under Ranulf III, mostly after 1200, married the heiress of Cheadle around 1199–1204 (**no. 261**) and can hardly have been active before the last years of Earl Hugh. The abrupt tone of Hugh's notification seems to suggest that there had been encroachments on his rights during the period between 1173 and 1177, when he was deprived of control of his earldom, and that he was determined to revoke the 'new customs' which had been introduced to his detriment. In that case, his charter falls between 1177 and his death in 1181, and probably not long after he resumed full control.

153.   Confirmation of his father's grant of land in Middlewich to Shrewsbury abbey.

Chester, [c.1162–1165]

> P.R.O., C.53 (Chancery Charter Rolls), no. 119, m. 17; CHES 29/67 (Plea Rolls, 34 Edw. III), m. 44v.; Nat. Lib. Wales, MS. 7851D (Cart. S. Petri de Salopesberia), p. 287, no. 315; B.L. Add. MS. 30311, f. 528 (new f. 261v.), from cartulary. Ed.: *Mon.*, i. 383; *Cal. Ch. Rolls*, v. 50 (no. 14); Rees, *Cartulary of Shrewsbury Abbey*, pp. 290–1.

Hugo comes Cestrie constabulario, dapifero, baronibus, iusticie, ministris, bailivis et omnibus fidelibus hominibus et amicis suis salutem. Volo vos scire comitem Ranulfum patrem meum dedisse deo et beato Petro et monachis Salopesberiensis ecclesie in puram et perpetuam elemosinam duas mansuras terre in Midelwicho in satisfactionem pro iniuriis quas prefate ecclesie intulerat, liberas et quietas a theloneo et omni consuetudine et exactione et omni seculari servicio. Volo igitur et precipio et concedo et confirmo hanc patris mei elemosinam firmam et ratam constare, et quicquid eis concessit et dedit carta sua corroboravit. Quare omnes fideles et amicos meos prece multimoda precor, quatinus hanc predictam elemosinam pro patris mei anima et salute mea et heredum meorum manuteneatis et protegatis et nullam iniuriam vel molestiam contra nostram donationem predictis monachis inferatis vel ab aliquo pro posse vestro inferre permittatis. Et hoc sciant omnes mei fideles, quia nichil retineo in honore sanctorum apostolorum Petri et Pauli nisi orationes et beneficium monachorum. Hiis testibus Aluredo de Combrai, Simone filio Osberti, Rogero capellano, Girardo, Benedicto fratre comitis, Tirrico clerico,[1] apud Cestriam.

1.   The witness is omitted in the cartulary.

This charter is a confirmation of **no. 65**, which in part it repeats verbatim. It may be assumed to have been issued fairly early in Hugh's tenure, but it is noticeable that, unlike similar confirmations, his mother, the Countess Matilda, is not involved. This may indicate a date after the end of Hugh's minority (1162). Alured de Combray died in 1186–7, Simon son of Osbert (or Osbern) in 1184. Terry the clerk witnessed at least three other charters in Hugh's early years (**nos. 119, 125, 173**), but disappears from view about 1170. Benedict the earl's brother was brother of Ranulf II (**no. 42**) and appears elsewhere as uncle of Earl Hugh (**no. 120**). He was presumably an illegitimate son of Ranulf I, in which case he probably did not long survive Ranulf II; but nothing else seems to be known about him. On the whole, the evidence suggests a date for the charter around 1162–65 and in any case before the rebellion of 1173 and Hugh's imprisonment.

154. Permission to Simon son of Liulf to make a mill at Heireneford (now Alderford) for an annual payment of one bezant.

[1162–1173]

B.L. Harl. MS. 7, f. 101v. Ed.: *Langley cart.*, no. 188.

Hugo comes Cestrie constabulario, dapifero, baronibus et omnibus hominibus suis Francis et Anglis, clericis et laicis, tam presentibus quam futuris salutem. Sciatis me concessisse et dedisse et hac carta mea confirmasse in feudo et in hereditate Simoni filio Lidolfi, ut faciat unum molendinum apud Heireneford sine detrimento molendinorum meorum, sic ut non amittam de firma mea. Et volo et precipio ut ipse Simon et heredes sui teneant supradictum molendinum de me et de heredibus meis libere et quiete et honorifice, pro omni seculari servicio reddendo mihi annuatim unum beisantum. Testibus Ricardo de Luvetot, Radulfo capellano, Alexandro capellano, Henrico Mansel, Gilberto filio Pycot, Roberto filio eius, Frumbalto Ridefordie, Lidulfo de Coventre, Villelmo de Aula, Adam filio Godrix, Nicholao filio Lidulfi, Rogero fratre eius, et aliis.

For other grants to Simon son of Liulf of Coventry, see **nos. 155** and **156**. Alexander the chaplain held land near Coventry (**no. 255**) and had been chaplain of Ranulf II (**no. 60**); he witnessed another charter of Earl Hugh with Henry Mansel and Gilbert son of Picot (**no. 169**). The date of the present charter is not easily determined, but seems to fall between 1162 and 1173.

155. Grant to Simon son of Liulf of the hillside between Helreneford (now Alderford) and the mill of Stifford.

[1162–1173]

B.L. Harl. MS. 7, f. 110. Ed.: *Langley cart.*, no. 213.

H. comes Cestrie constabulario, dapifero, baronibus et omnibus hominibus suis Francis et Anglis tam presentibus quam futuris salutem. Sciatis me dedisse Simmodo filio Liulfi pendentem terram, que est inter Helreneford et molendinum de Stifford et inter cheminum et aquam, tenendam illi et heredibus suis de me et de heredibus meis libere et quiete per unam libram piperis reddendo per annum pro omnibus serviciis. Testibus Radulfo capellano, Ricardo de Luvetot, Gilberto filio Picot, Roberto filio Gilberti, Filippo de Dive, et aliis.

This grant must be close in date to **no. 154**; whether earlier or later is impossible to say. Philip de Diva witnessed **no. 176**, which has been dated c.1166.

156.   Ratification of Simon son of Liulf's purchase of the mill in the earl's park at Coventry from Robert of Barrow, reserving his own right in the land and house of William Duillet.

Birmingham, [1154–1170]

B.L. Harl. MS. 7, f. 103v. Ed.: *Langley cart.*, no. 194.

Hugo comes Cestrie constabulario, dapifero suo, iusticiario, vicecom(iti), baronibus, ministris et ballivis, et omnibus hominibus suis Francis et Anglis tam futuris quam presentibus salutem. Notum sit omnibus me concessisse et presenti carta confirmasse Simoni filio Liulfi mercatum de molendino de parco meo de Coventre, quem idem Simon fecit erga Robertum de Barva, salvo iure meo de terra et mansura Willelmi Duillec. [Hiis testibus . . .][1] et Willelmo Patryk, Roberto Patrik, Gylberto filio Pycot, Matheo de Praeres, Henrico filio Philippi, Bertram camerario, apud Burmucham.

1.   *Omission in text following* Duillec.

Simon was one of the sons of Liulf of Brinklow, whose landholdings at Coventry were confirmed by Earl Hugh (**nos. 145, 146**). Robert of Barrow had received the mill in Coventry and the house of William Duillet from Ranulf II, probably in 1144 (**no. 72**). The present charter is not easy to date, particularly as the witness list appears to be incomplete, but the names are those usually found after Hugh II's majority (1162). On the other hand, the land of Duillet, which is here reserved to the earl, was given to Bishop Walter Durdent in a charter which cannot be later than 1157 (**no. 124**). Presumably this gift was subsequent to the present charter, but the evidence is confusing, and it is probably safest to leave a wide margin for the date.

157. Confirmation of Robert the butler's gift of a moiety of Poulton to found there an abbey of the order of Savigny.

Chester, [1162–1170]

> Bodleian Library, Dodsworth MS. 39, f. 154v. (from original); Dodsworth 61, f. 94; Chester, Booth of Twemlow, Liber D, f. 240 (from the register); P.R.O., C.53 (Chancery Charter Rolls), no. 117; C.66 (Chancery Patent Rolls), no. 421, m. 26, and no. 519, m. 20. Short abstracts: B.L. Harl. MS. 2060, f. 24 (old f. 40); Add. MS. 6032, f. 119 (old p. 240); Dodsworth 31, f. 165v. Ed.: *Mon.*, v. 628 (from the register); Orm., ii. 862 (from *Mon.*); *Cal. Ch. Rolls*, iv. 155 (no. 17); *D.C.*, p. 330 (no. 75) (abbreviated).

Hugo comes Cestrie episcopo Cestrensi et constabulario suo et dapifero suo et vicecomiti et ballivis et omnibus baronibus et omnibus hominibus suis Francis et Anglis tam futuris quam presentibus salutem. Scitote quod concedo et carta mea confirmo donacionem illam quam Ranulfus comes Cestrie pater meus concessit et carta sua liberam fecit, scilicet dimidiam partem de Pultona, quam Robertus pincerna eius fecit deo et ecclesie sancte Marie de Combremara ad abbatiam de ordine suo ibidem construendam. Hanc vero eandem donacionem, scilicet dimidiam partem de Pultona cum omnibus pertinentiis suis ad eam iuste pertinentibus, volo et firmiter precipio ut ipsa abbatia de Pultona et abbas et conventus eiusdem ecclesie in perpetuam elemosinam possidendam libere quiete et iuste ab omni servicio seculari habeant et teneant pro salute anime mee et predecessorum meorum in villa et extra, in bosco et plano, in pratis et pasturis, in piscariis et aquis et molendinis, et in omnibus aliis commoditatibus, que in eadem terra fieri poterunt. Et precipio atque prohibeo ne aliquis eis amodo ullam molestiam faciat neque disturbet super meam forisfacturam. Testibus Roberto dapifero et Aluredo de Cumbrai et Willelmo filio Otueri et Gileberto filio Pichot et Roberto filio Hugonis et Hugone filio Oliveri et Hugone sacerdote de Dodlestun et Geraldino[1] et Willelmo clerico de Aldefordia et Simundo de Bedfordia. Apud Cestriam.

> SEAL: sealed with a man on horseback; inscribitur SIGILLUM HUG' COM' CESTR'.

1. *sic Dodsworth 39; other MSS. read* Geralmo.

Poulton abbey was founded by Robert, the butler (pincerna) of Ranulf II in 1146; for his foundation charter, see *E.C.C.*, no. 1. Ranulf's charter, confirming the foundation, to which Hugh II here refers, has not survived. The date of Hugh's charter can only be surmised, but the names of the witnesses suggest that it was not long after his majority. Hugh son of Oliver gave the site for St. Mary's nunnery in Chester c.1150 (**no. 98**) and William son of Otuer witnessed Ranulf II's charter for Wenlock c.1153 (**no. 109**) and gave land to the nuns of Greenfield before 1155 (**no. 127**). Robert son of Hugh was present at Ranulf II's deathbed at Gresley in 1153 (**no. 34**). Robert de Montalt, the steward (dapifer) appears to have survived until c.1177 (*Chart. St. Werburgh*, p. 302), but the charter was probably given some ten years before his death.

158.   Grant to the monks of Poulton of the land around Gorstilowe (in Dodleston) and the meadow in the lower part of Calvesmoor, about which there had been a dispute between the abbey and the men of Eaton, according to the boundaries established on oath by the legal men of the neighbourhood on the king's orders.

[1177–1180]

> Orig.: Eaton Hall, Chester, Henr. II, no. 1. Transcr.: P.R.O., C.53 (Chancery Charter Rolls), no. 117; C.66 (Chancery Patent Rolls), no. 421, m. 26, and no. 519, m. 20. Ed.: *Cal. Ch. Rolls*, iv. 155 (no. 18); *D.C.*, p. 330 (no. 77) (abbreviated text).

Hugo comes Cestrie omnibus baronibus et hominibus suis Francis et Anglis tam presentibus quam futuris salutem. Sciatis me dedisse et hac presenti carta mea confirmasse deo et sancte Marie et abbati ac monachis de Pultona pro salute anime mee et patris mei et matris mee et omnium antecessorum et heredum meorum in puram et perpetuam elemosinam terram illam circa Gorstilanam et pratum in inferiori parte de Kalvemor, unde aliquando facta est controversia inter prefatos monachos de Pultona et homines de Ethuna, sicut homines legales vicinie ex mandato domini regis et meo assensu tactis sacrosanctis iurati perambulaverunt, videlicet incipientes paululum versus Dodleston sub Gorstilana, ab illo loco ubi campus de Eclestona et campus sibi adiunctus propior sub Gorstilana ex parte Pultone et campus ex parte Ethune ultra Gorstilanam versus Cestriam prius et propius sub Gorstilana conveniunt, pervenerunt iuxta locum qui dicitur Gorstilana, quem a dextris relinquentes secus culturam deforis versus Ethunam circuierunt campum illum circa Gorstilanam usque ad vallem, per quam in medio descendentes prope locum qui dicitur Saltpit, deflexerunt inter collem et pratum deorsum versus Ethunam usque ad inferiorem partem de Kalvesmor, et ita per transversum prati transeuntes pervenerunt ad vetus fossatum in inferiori parte de Kalvesmor, quod ibi desinit in flumine quod vocatur De, ubi ex altera parte fluminis pene econtra inferior pars nemoris de Aldeford terminatur versus piscariam de Ethuna. Concessi etiam predicto monasterio de Pultona et eiusdem loci monachis intuitu caritatis et pacis fossatum facere versus campum de Ethuna circa pratum suum per has autem divisas sicut in hac carta expresse sunt, et quicquid infra eas continetur ex dono Roberti pincerne circa abbaciam de Pultona. Ne quis contra eos aliquo modo materiam malignandi in posterum habeat, volo et firmiter precipio ut predicti monachi libere et quiete, plene et honorifice et sine ulla contradictione et absque omni terreno servicio et seculari exaccione, que ad me et ad heredes meos pertinent, teneant et in perpetuum possideant. Hiis testibus Aluredo de Combrei, Willelmo Patric, Radulfo filio Warneri, Ricardo de Pulford, Hugone filio Oliveri, Rogeri de Combrei, Roberto filio Ricardi de Pulford.

> SEAL on tag, missing.

The first four witnesses of this charter also witnessed **no. 159**, and it was probably granted at much the same time. The fact that the perambulation of the land in question was carried out on the king's orders indicates that it took place between 1173 and 1177, when the honour of Chester was in the king's hands, and Earl Hugh's confirmation probably dates from shortly after his restoration. The perambulation began below Gorstilowe, a little towards Dodleston, where the field of Eccleston and the adjoining field nearest below Gorstilowe on the side of Poulton and the field on the side of Eaton beyond Gorstilowe in the direction of Chester met below Gorstilowe. From there the jurors came almost to Gorstilowe, but leaving it on their right they went round the cultivated land around Gorstilowe towards Eaton until they came to the valley which they descended near the place called Saltpit. They then turned aside between the hill and the pasture running down towards Eaton as far as the lower part of Calvesmoor, and crossing the meadow, came to the old ditch in the lower part of Calvesmoor, which there emptied into the river Dee at the point where, on the other side of the river, almost exactly opposite, the lower part of the wood of Aldford terminated near the fishery of Eaton. The land within these boundaries appears to have been adjudged to the monks.

159. Grant to the monks of Poulton of the half of Poulton which they held in fee farm from Robert the butler (II), freeing them from the service due to the earl from that land.

Chester, [1177–1180]

> Orig.: Eaton Hall, Chester, Henr. II, no. 4. Transcr.: Bodleian Library, MS. Top. Gen. c. 26 (from Rudyard cartulary), p. 6; MS. Top. Cheshire b. I, p. 138. Brief abstracts: B.L. Harl. MS. 2060, f. 24 (old f. 40); Add. MS. 6032, f. 119 (old p. 240); Chester, Booth of Twemlow, Liber D, f. 56. Ed.: *Mon.*, v. 628; *D.C.*, p. 331 (no. 79) (abbreviated text).

H. comes Cestrie constabulario, dapifero, iustic(iario), vicecom(iti), baronibus, militibus, ministris, omnibus hominibus suis Francis et Anglicis tam presentibus quam futuris salutem. Sciatis me concessisse et hac mea carta in perpetuum confirmasse monachis de Pultona totam illam medietatem de Pultona cum omnibus pertinenciis suis, quam tenent in feudam firmam de Roberto pincerna, unde mihi servicium surgit. Et sciatis quod clamo eosdem monacos liberos et quietos ab omni servicio, quod ad me pertinet de eadem terra, et amodo ad Robertum pincernam de eodem servicio me tenebo. Et ideo volo ut nullo modo namum eorundem monacorum pro eodem servicio aliquis capere faciat, et precipio ut nullus omnino aliquam eis molestiam inde facere presumat. Testibus abbate Cestrie, Iohanne constabulario Cestrie, Willelmo Patric, Aluredo[1] de Cumbrai, Radulfo filio Warneri, Ricardo de Pulford, Willelmo capellano comitis, et multis aliis apud Cestriam.

SEAL (now in sack): 'a man on horseback'.

1. Aluedo *orig.*

Robert *pincerna*, the founder of Poulton abbey, had given half of Poulton to the new house (**no. 157**). The other half was given by his son, another Robert, who died in or about 1182 (*E.C.C.*, p. 5). It is this second grant which is confirmed by the present charter, which has been dated c.1176 (*Ches. Sheaf*, no. 7842). As Earl Hugh was still suspended from office at this time, it must fall a little later, but the evidence does not permit an exact dating. For Richard of Pulford, see *H.S.L.C.*, cvi, pp. 149–150.

160.   Notification that Warin of Vernon has made a fine of 4 marks with him for certain of his men, viz. Gamel, Hugh, Orm and Gerard of Shurlach, with their families, and he has quitclaimed them to Warin.

Middlewich, [1162–1173]

B.L. Harl. MS. 2077, f. 62 (from the collections of Sampson Erdwicke 'in parvo libro papiro de la ligne de le Vernons in manibus W. Dugdale', 1647); Bodleian Library, Rawlinson MS. B. 144, f. 77v. (Collections of the Vernons). Ed.: *Stenton Misc.*, p. 36 (no. 8).

H. comes Cestrie constabulario *etc.* Sciatis quod Warinus de Vernun fecit mecum finem de hominibus suis, scilicet de Gamelo filio Willelmi Magni et de fratribus suis et sororibus cum tota progenie, et Hugone et filiis et tota progenie sua, et Ormo et filiis suis et tota progenie sua, et Gerardo de Surlech et tota progenie sua, pro iiii. marcis argenti quas mihi dedit; et inde notifico vobis me istos homines clamasse quietos predicto Warino de Vernun et heredibus suis de me et heredibus meis. Testibus Willelmo Patric, Galfrido de Costentin, Aluredo de Cumbrai, Radulfo filio Warini, Gilberto de Venables, Radulfo de Mailnel-warin, Ricardo de Vernun, Roberto de Moldewrth, Hugone de Tiu, apud Middlewich.

This charter is discussed in *Stenton Misc.*, p. 35, where it is related to the practice of settling strangers, often fugitives from justice, later known as 'avowry men', on vacant land. The date cannot be fixed with precision, but seems to fall between 1162 and 1173.

161.   Grant to Warin de Vernon of the land within Wolfeld Gate in Chester on the left-hand side, which Hudard held.

Chester, [1162–1181]

B.L. Harl. MS. 2077, f. 95 (new f. 62); Bodleian Library, Rawlinson MS. B144, f. 78. Ed.: *Stenton Misc.*, p. 39 (no. 11).

H. comes Cestrie constabulario, dapifero, iusticiis,[1] baronibus, vicecomitibus,[1] et omnibus hominibus suis Francis et Anglicis tam presentibus quam futuris salutem. Sciatis me dedisse in feudo et hereditate Warino de Vernun et heredibus suis tenendam de me et heredibus meis terram intus Weflidegate[2] ad sinistram manum, quam Houdart tenuit, pro omnibus serviciis que ad terram pertinent, pro xii. denarios reddendo annuatim ad suum herbigagium ad festum sancti Iohannis Baptiste. Testibus Radulfo de Menulwarin, Ricardo Luvetot, Ranulfo Menulwarin, Frumbald, Ricardo de Cumbray, Roberto de Mollewrtha, Berteramo camerario, Bec, Willelmo clerico comitis, apud Cestriam.

1.   sic *MSS.*
2.   Wefeildsgate, *Harl. MS.*

This charter is of particular interest for the topography of Chester, as providing by a century or more the earliest known reference to the Wolfeld Gate, of Wolf's Gate, later called the New Gate, at the end of Pepper Street. Unfortunately it cannot be dated accurately, but probably falls before 1173.

162.   Notification that William Venables has made fine to hold Dilred Hog and Artusius and their progeny of the earl.

Chester, [1164–1173]

> Chester, Booth of Twemlow, Liber H, f. 69 (from
> original, in view of reference to the seal); B.L. Harl. MS.
> 2077, f. 9 (new f. 36), from an old parchment book in the
> custody of Henry Birkenhead of Huxley (witness list
> incomplete). Ed.: *Stenton Misc.*, pp. 36–7 (no. 9).

Hugo comes Cestrie dapifero, iustic(ie) suis Cestresire et omnibus hominibus suis Francis et Anglis tam presentibus quam futuris salutem. Sciatis Willelmum de Venables finisse mecum de Dilredo Hog et de filiis suis et de tota progenie sua et de Artusio et de filiis suis et heredibus suis, tenendis de me et de heredibus meis in feudo et hereditate. Testibus Radulfo dapifero, Willelmo Malbanc, Hamone de Maci, Roberto filio Nigelli, Radulfo de Mainwarin, Ricardo de Lovetot, Warino de Vernun, Ricardo fratre suo, Alured de Combrai, R. filio Warini, Frembald, Ricardo de Livet, Willelmo clerico comitis Cestrie, apud Cestriam.

SEAL: 'A bayre old deed without a seal'.

This charter may be compared with **no. 160**, and like that refers to the practice of settling strangers, often fugitives from justice, on vacant land. These were the *advocarii* or 'avowry men' of the Magna Carta of Cheshire of 1215 (**no. 394, §2**). The date of Hugh II's charter can only be approximately established, but falls before the death of William Malbank in 1176 (*E.C.C.*, p. 13), and therefore presumably before Hugh was deprived of his earldom from 1173 to 1177. As Ralph the steward appears to have succeeded his father not long after 1162, the approximate date is probably 1164–1173.

163.   Grant to Robert Grosvenor of Budworth, and a moiety of the earl's hunting rights in the forest of Mara and of the custody of his dogs.

Chester, [1162–1173]

> P.R.O., CHES 33/1 (Forest Rolls, 55 Henr. III – 24 Edw.
> I), m. 7; CHES 33/6 (Forest Rolls, 27–31 Edw. III), m. 49;
> D.L. 39/1/19 (Forest Pleas, 21 Edw. III), m. 29v. Printed:
> Orm., ii. 211 (from original, now missing, in possession of
> the earl of Shrewsbury, 1806, communicated by W.
> Hamper of Birmingham).

Hugo comes Cestrie constabulario et dapifero suo, iustic(iario), vicecom(ite), baronibus, ministris, ballivis, et omnibus hominibus suis tam Francis quam Anglis salutem. Notum sit omnibus me dedisse et concessisse et hac mea carta confirmasse Roberto Grosvenur et heredibus suis pro homagio et suo servicio totam villam de Buddeworth cum suis pertinenciis ad colendum et habitandum et ad alia bona sua facienda infra suas divisas illius ville, in bosco, in plano, in aquis, et in omnibus aliis locis. Preterea dedi et concessi illi et heredibus suis medietatem venerie mee in foresta de Mara et medietatem custodie canum meorum super custum meum libere et in feodo et hereditate, tenendas pro omni servicio dicte ville et dicte venerie pertinenti. Et super hoc clamavi quietos de me et heredibus meis illi et heredibus suis Acelinam uxorem Andree et eius successores, et Walterum et Gamel fratres Andree et Warnerum, qui sunt in terra Randulfi de Chingeslee, et Galfridum et Afward, quos omnes homines mei iuraverunt ad meum dominicum. Isti sunt testes: Ricardus filius comitis Glouces-trie, Willelmus Patric, Radulfus filius Warneri, Radulfus sacerdos de Boneburi, Gamel Peverel, Willelmus Malbanc, et multis aliis[1] apud Cestriam.

1. sic in all MS.

Earl Ranulf I is said to have conferred the master-forestership of Mara and Mondrem on Ranulf or Randulf Kingsley by delivery of a horn (Orm., ii. 87, 107), and the Randulf of Kingsley of the present charter was presumably his son. It is usually held that the effect of the present charter was to convey a moiety of the forestership to Robert Grosvenor, and that was certainly the view of his heirs in the thirteenth century (Orm., ii. 211).

This charter cannot be closely dated. It must fall after 1162, when Earl Hugh came of age, and before 1175, when Hugh's uncle, Richard son of the earl of Gloucester, died. Almost certainly it falls before the rebellion of 1173, as a result of which Earl Hugh forfeited his lands and was not restored until 1177. William Patric (d.1184) was among those taken prisoner with the earl at Dol in August 1173. William Malbank, who succeeded his father Hugh in 1135 (*Ann. Cestr.*, p. 20) died in 1176 (*Chart. St. Werburgh*, p. 94). Ranulf Kingsley, who survived until 1190 or later (Orm., i. 751), was granted land at Millington by John the constable at some date after 1178 for the service of training a hound annually to retrieve boars and deer (*E.C.C.*, no. 7). Of Robert Grosvenor, presumably the first of the family, nothing further appears to be known.

164. Quittance for Robert of Cheadle from the annual render of four pigs which he used to pay by an agreement made in love before the earl's barons.

[1162–1173]

B.L. Harl. MS. 1967, f. 67 (from original 'penes Ric. Buckley apud Chedle') (A); Harl. 2008, f. 129 (from William Vernon's Liber H, f. 261) (B); Chester, Booth of

Twemlow, Liber K, f. 21 ('a fayre deed under seale remayning in the hands of Richard Bulkeley of Chedle, knight') (C); Bodleian Library, MS. Top. Cheshire b. I, p. 109 (from MS. of John Arden) (D); Rawlinson MS. B.144, p. 141 (E). Short notice: Orm., iii. 621.

Hugo comes Cestrie constabulario et dapifero suo, iusticiario, vic(ecomiti), baronibus et ballivis et omnibus hominibus suis Francis et Anglis tam present-ibus quam non presentibus[1] salutem. Notum sit omnibus me in perpetuum clamare quietum de me et heredibus meis Roberto de Chedle et heredibus suis de quatuor porcis, quos annuatim ab eo exigebam per consuetudinem, quam ille mecum fecit in amore coram baronibus meis. Et[2] ideo volo et firmiter precipio, ut ille et heredes sui de me et heredibus meis[3] sunt[4] de illa consuetudine imperpetuum quieti. Testibus Ricardo filio comitis Glocestrie, Willelmo Patric, Hamone de Masci, Gilberto de Venables, Roberto de Aldfort, Radulfo filio Warneri, Rogero de Pelchinton, Thoma de Norburi, Lidulfo de Edislea, et Herberto[5] clerico comitis, qui hanc cartam scripsit.

SEAL: 'a fayre deed under seale'.

1.   non presentibus (*for* futuris?) *B*, *E*; *other MSS. have* etc. *after* Anglis.
2.   *This sentence omitted A, C, D.*
3.   *om. B, E.*
4.   tunc *B, E.*
5.   Huberto *A, E.*

This is the earliest surviving reference to Cheadle since the Domesday survey (*D.S.C.*, pp. 213–4). Since Earl Hugh's uncle Richard, the son of Robert earl of Gloucester, died in 1175, and Earl Hugh himself forfeited his earldom after the rebellion of 1173, its date must fall between 1162, when Earl Hugh came of age, and 1173. Robert of Cheadle was father, or possibly brother, of Jordan of Cheadle, whose daughter Helen married Geoffrey of Dutton about 1200 (**no. 261**). For Herbert the earl's clerk, i.e. Herbert Barbe d'Averill, see **no. 169**.

165.   Confirmation to Revesby abbey of the gift of Philip of Kyme and Matthew of Praers of a salt-pan at Wainfleet (Lincs.)

Greetham, [1162–1173]

B.L. Lansdowne MS. 203, f. 26 (partly written in facsimile).

Omnibus filiis sancte matris ecclesie Hugo comes Cestrie salutem. Sciatis me concessisse et hac mea presenti carta confirmasse deo et sancte Marie et monachis de sancto Laurencio in perpetuam elemosinam illam donationem, quam Philippus de Kime et Matheus de Pratariis illis dederunt, scilicet unam salinam cum quodam tofto eidem pertinente in territorio de Wainflet iuxta portum versus meridiem et eisiamenta maresci ad eandem salinam et liberum ingressum et egressum a salina ad grangiam suam de Seggedie per terram meam et hominum meorum. Volo ergo et precipio ut hanc elemosinam habeant predicti monachi bene et in pace liberam et quietam a me et heredibus meis, et solutam ab omni terreno servicio et seculari exactione, sicut carte predictorum donatorum testantur. Hiis testibus Simone filio Osberti, Galfrido de Costentin, Rogero de Maletoft, Radulfo de Mainilwarin, Roberto de Saltstorp, Simone filio Widonis, Ricardo capellano de Henbiggebi, Herberto et Willelmo clericis comitis, apud Graham.

> SEAL pendent on tag, equestrian figure brandishing a sword in the right hand; legend SIGILLUM HUGONIS COMITIS CESTR'. Reverse: oval, a gem showing a head to right.

The description of the seal is not full or accurate enough for certainty, but the indications are that it is Hugh's first seal, in use before the revolt of 1173, in which Matthew of Praers (who was taken prisoner with the earl at Dol) and Geoffrey de Côtentin supported Hugh, while Philip of Kyme was loyal to Henry II. Matthew of Praers belonged to the Norman family which founded the monastery of Le Désert (**no. 9**); he seems to have lived until about 1190 (*H.K.F.*, p. 143). Simon son of Osbert died in 1184 (*Ann. Cestr.*, p. 32). Ralph Mainwaring married Earl Hugh's natural daughter, Amicia (**no. 193**), and became justiciar of Chester towards the end of the twelfth century; he died about 1208 (*Ches. Sheaf*, no. 9394). The present charter may be dated tentatively between Hugh's majority (1162) and 1173, but the evidence does not permit more than an approximate dating.

166. Writ to the reeves and bailiffs of his soke of Belchford ordering them to see that the abbey of Spalding should receive its tithes as in the time of Ranulf I and Countess Lucy and to make sure he heard no more complaints.

[? 1162–1173]

B.L. Add. MS. 35296 (Spalding register), f. 390v.

H. comes Cestrie omnibus prepositis et ballivis suis de soka de Beltisforda salutem. Precipio vobis quod faciatis habere abbatie de sancto Nicholao de Spaldingis decimas suas de omnibus terris illis, de quibus illas habeant tempore

Ranulphi comitis avi mei et Lucie comitisse, et recipiant ad hostia horreorum sicut tunc temporis recipere solebant. Et tantum faciatis ut inde amplius clamium non audiam. Testibus Galfrido de Cestria, Philippo de Kima, Roberto filio Walteri, et aliis.

This writ cannot be dated accurately, but the context suggests that tithes had been withheld during the disorders of Stephen's reign, and that Earl Hugh was now restoring the position as it had previously been; in which case it probably dates from relatively early in his tenure of the earldom. Unfortunately, the witnesses do not help with the dating. Geoffrey of Chester was a younger son of John the constable of Chester (*E.C.C.*, p. 20), but he survived until 1205–6 (*P.R.S.*, N.S. xxii, p. 178), and the other two witnesses also outlived Hugh II.

167. Confirmation to the monks of Spalding of all tithes given by his ancestors, together with any tithes arising if he should open up uncultivated land, and the tithe of his new mill at Belchford.

[? 1177–1181]

B.L. Add. MS. 35296 (Spalding register), f. 388v., and Add. MS. 5844 (Cole's transcript of preceding), f. 432 (new f. 219v.). Ed.: *The Genealogist*, N.S. v, p. 71 (no. 40).

H. comes Cestrie constabulario, iustic(ie), baronibus, ballivis, ministris, militibus et omnibus hominibus suis tam presentibus quam futuris salutem. Sciatis me dedisse et concessisse et hac carta mea confirmasse deo et sancte Marie et beato Nicholao de Spaldingis et monachis ibidem famulantibus omnes decimaciones quas antecessores mei, scilicet Toraldus vicecomes et Lucia comitissa et Ranulphus comes avus meus et pater meus, dederunt ecclesie de Spaldingis, videlicet de blado de estauramento de pecuniis meis de Beltisforda et de Scamelisbi et de Stenighou et de Tetenei et de Donigtona. Et si forte in predictis villis frussuram aliquam fecero de terra que prius non culta fuit vel sartam de bosco, decimas monachis predicti loci similiter concedo cuicumque pater meus vel antecessores mei vel ego dederim illas terras seu quicumque tenuerint vel teneant. Et insuper dedi eis et concessi pro dei amore et pro salute anime mee decimam de meo novo molendino de Beltisforda. Hiis testibus Philippo de Kima, Roberto filio Hugonis, Simone filio Roberti, Ranulfo de Praeriis.[1]

1. Paeis, *MS. 35296*; Paris, *MS. 5844*.

For Countess Lucy's gift of tithes, see **no. 17**. Hugh II's confirmation is not easily dated, but as Philip of Kyme survived until 1189 at earliest (*H.K.F.*, p. 122), Robert son of Hugh until 1193 (*P.R.S.*, N.S. v, p. 26), and Ranulf de Praers until 1199 and probably later (*H.K.F.*, p. 144), it is unlikely to be very early. Simon son of Robert is mentioned on the Lincolnshire Pipe Roll in 1177 (*H.K.F.*, p. 127), and Ranulf of Praers was the earl's deputy in Avranches and St. James-de-Beuvron in 1180 (*Rot. Scacc. Norm.*, i. 40), and these dates perhaps indicate an approximate limit for the present charter.

168. Grant to Alan son of Liulf of Coventry of the land previously held by Richard Surrensis in Meriden (formerly Alspath), Warws.

[? 1162–1173]

B.L. Harl. MS. 7, f. 110v. Ed.: *Langley cart.*, no. 215.

Omnibus hominibus suis tam clericis quam laicis, tam Ballicys[1] quam Anglicis, H. comes Cestrie salutem.[2] Notum sit omnibus vobis me dedisse et hac mea carta confirmasse Alano filio Luufi de Coventre pro servicio suo totam terram et totam tenuram quam Ricardus Surrensis tenuit in Allespache in ridighes et in bosco et in plano, cum tacco et cum tollo et cum omnibus libertatibus, et excepta hac libertate concedo predicto Alano quadraginta foranos porcos in bosco meo quietos de pannagio quiete et libere, ipsi et heredibus suis[3] ad tenendam de me et de heredibus meis, reddendo annuatim pro omnibus serviciis unam libram comin.[4] Testes sunt hi: Gilbertus filius Picot, Radulfus de Busservilla, Iacob de Pakintona, Henricus de Coventre, Nigellus de Coventre, et multis aliis.[5]

1. *sic MS., presumably for* Gallicis (*for* Francis).
2. *The text of this charter is very corrupt. The address reads:* Omnibus suis H. comes Cestrie et Alexandro filio Geroldi et omnibus hominibus suis tam clericis quam laicis tam Ballicys quam Anglis Hyno filius Haskelli salutem. *It appears as though two addresses have been inadvertently run together.*
3. ipse et heredes sui *MS.*
4. *sic MS. for* cumin.
5. *sic MS.*

This document is extremely corrupt, but probably represents a genuine transaction. Nigel of Coventry witnessed **no. 146** for Liulf, the father of the grantee, and Ralph of Buscherville, who appears to have died by 1183 (*P.R.S.*, xxxiii, p. 90), witnessed another Coventry charter (**no. 178**). Nothing is known of Richard Surrensis. There is insufficient evidence for more than an approximate date, but the grant appears to fall between 1162 and 1173.

169. Grant to Herbert Barbe d'Averill, his clerk, of a virgate of land at Hulle (Hellinhull, now Kingshill, Warws.) for 6s. a year, to be paid to the monks of Stoneleigh in lieu of the boat which Ranulf II had given them.

Coventry, [1162–1173]

Stratford-upon-Avon, Shakespeare's Birthplace, Gregory-Hood Leger Book, p. 221 (in places defective; emendations in brackets).

H. comes Cestrie constabulario, dapifero et universis balivis suis, et omnibus hominibus suis Francis et Anglis, clericis et laicis, tam presentibus quam futuris salutem. Sciatis me atturnasse Herebertum Barbe Aprilis clericum meum et heredes suos ad redde[ndum] abbatie de Stanleia annuatim V. solidos pro tenemento, quod prefato Hereberto et heredibus suis dedi, id est quamdam virgatam terre apud Hulle, et hos predictos V. solidos [dedi] predicte abbatie in elemosinam pro escambio batelli, quod pater meus eis dederat. [Testibus Roberto] de Staphordia, Giliberto filio Pigot, Henrico Mansel, Willelmo Baschet, Henrico Tuschet, Willelmo de Verdun, Ingenulfo, Alexandro capellano, Willelmo Barbe Aprilis, apud Coventre.

The virgate of land here conveyed is evidently that which Ranulf II had reserved in his charter for John Malyn (**no. 60**). The boat given by Ranulf II was presumably a boat on the river Dee, as given to so many religious houses to enable them to lay in a stock of fish, but it cannot have been given to Stoneleigh, which was only founded after his death, and there is no evidence of such a gift to the preceding house at Radmore. Herbert Barbe d'Averill was a hitherto unidentified member of a family which provided a succession of clerks and chaplains for Ranulf I (**no. 14**), Ranulf II and Hugh II (**no. 194**), including William Barbe d'Averill, the last witness of the present charter. He was presumably the Herbert who witnessed Hugh II's charters for Repton (**no. 121**), Bordesley (**no. 148**) and Revesby (**no. 165**) in association with William, probably his brother, and who wrote Hugh's charter for Robert of Cheadle (**no. 164**). The date of the present charter is not easily determined, but as Henry Tuschet was dead by 1178 (*H.K.F.*, p. 28), it can fairly safely be placed before Earl Hugh's deprivation between 1173 and 1177. Alexander the chaplain witnessed Ranulf II's charter for John Malyn (**no. 60**) and held land in the vicinity of Coventry (**no. 255**).

170. Grant to William Neville and his wife Amabilia of the territory of Longdendale. [Spurious]

[1162–1173]

P.R.O., C.66 (Chancery Patent Rolls), no. 150, m. 13.
Ed.: *Cal. Pat. Rolls, 1317–21*, p. 245.

H. comes Cestrie constabulario, dapifero, iusticiario, vic(ecomiti), baronibus et omnibus ballivis suis et hominibus Francis et Anglicis tam presentibus quam futuris salutem. Sciatis me dedisse et concessisse et hac carta mea confirmasse Willelmo de Nevilla et Amabili uxori sue, et heredibus quod predicta Amabilia habuerit de predicto Willelmo, terram de Langedenedale libere et quiete in boscis et planis, et in omnibus libertatibus que pertinent eidem terre, tenendam de me et heredibus meis per servicium dimidii militis pro omnibus serviciis, cum soc et sac et tol et tem et infangenthef, et cum iusticia faciente de latronibus qui reprehensi fuerint in eadem terra de hominibus suis, cum igne et aqua et duello, quietus[1] de haiis faciendis in foresto meo apud Maclesfeld. Et de iudice quem invenire deberet de illa predicta terra apud Maclesfeld, sit ille quietus, ita[2] quod ille predictus Willelmus per rationabilem summonicionem, si presens fuerit in partibus illius provincie, apparebit in presencia domini comitis vel iusticie eius errantis apud Maclesfeld, et si forte predictus Willelmus non fuerit in illa provincia, dapifer suus in loco eius in presencia domini comitis vel iusticie sue errantis apparebit per eandem supradictam summonicionem. Hiis testibus Willelmo Malbanc, Radulfo dapifero de Monte Alto, Hamone de Mascy, Helia de Boisdele, Willelmo Venables, Radulfo de Mainewarin, Radulfo filio Warini, Roberto de Aldeford, Roberto Banastro, Rogero de Livet, Gilleberto filio Picoti, Heute de Boidel, Roberto filio Gilleberti, Henrico de Crui, Bertram camerario, Willelmo Barba Aprilis,[3] Roberto de Stokeport, Willelmo de Mainewarin, Petro clerico, et multis aliis.

1. *sic MS.*
2. per si *MS.*
3. Aprilis *om. MS.*

Apart from the witnesses, this charter is virtually word for word the same as the corresponding grant of Ranulf III to William Neville and his wife (**no. 321**). Its ostensible date must fall between 1162 when Ralph of Montalt succeeded to the seneschalship (*Ches. Sheaf*, no. 9394), and the death of William Malbank in 1176, and presumably before 1173 when Earl Hugh rose in revolt and was taken prisoner at Dol and deprived of his earldom until 1177. But the mere fact that William Neville did not marry Amabilia until shortly before 1202 (*L.P.R.*, p. 171) is sufficient proof that it is not an authentic charter of Hugh II. In view of the existence of Ranulf III's charter, it is hard to see what was gained by the forgery, but Ranulf's charter also is perhaps not above suspicion.

171.   Grant to William of Rhuddlan of (Little) Meols, as previously held by his father William and his brother Hugh.

[1163–1173]

J.R.U.L.M., Rylands Charter 1274a (fourteenth-century copy). Brief mention *Ches. Sheaf*, no. 6801.

Hugo comes Cestrie constabulario suo et dapifero suo et baronibus suis et ministris suis, omnibus hominibus suis Francis et Anglis tam futuris quam presentibus salutem. Sciatis me concessisse et dedisse Willelmo de Ruelant terram des[1] Meoles, ad tenendam de me et heredibus meis, sibi videlicet et heredibus suis[2] iure hereditario, libere et quiete cum omnibus pertinenciis suis in bosco et plano, in pratis et pascuis, in viis et semitis, et omnibus pertinenciis et libertatibus, eodem servicio quo Willelmus pater suus tenuit de patre meo et Hugo frater suus tenuit de me. Valete.Testibus Iohanne constabulario, Willelmo Malbanc, Willelmo Patric, Bertram de Verdun, Hamone de Maci, Helte de Boidile, Aluredo de Combrai, Hachet de Ridford, Henrico fratre suo, Radulfo filio Warini, Gileberto filio Picot, Stephano de Brexquesart,[3] Rogero del Quet, Cvioc filio David, et ceteris quam pluribus.

1. *sic MS.*
2. *MS. has* ad tenendam de me sibi videlicet et heredibus ad tenendam de me et heredibus meis.
3. Brexq̄ *MS.*; *presumably for* Briquessard.

Meols was part of the extensive Wirral estate of Robert of Rhuddlan, the famous lieutenant of Hugh I, at the time of Domesday (*D.S.C.*, p. 135). Its descent thereafter is obscure. Robert, who was killed in a Welsh campaign in 1088, is usually said to have left no legitimate issue (Orm., ii. 494, 503), and his estates to have reverted to the earl. In fact, he left a son William (Ord. Vitalis, v. 187). This could well be William, the father of the recipient of the present grant, who was in possession of Meols in the time of Ranulf II. He apparently was followed by his (elder) son Hugh, to whom his younger brother, the present William, succeeded. The facts seem at least to point to a continuous interest in Meols from 1086 onwards. William of Rhuddlan junior witnessed a charter of Earl Hugh for Richard of Davenport (**no. 176**), dating from 1162 to 1173, and another of land in Coventry for Godfrey the earl's homager (**no. 184**). He was among those taken prisoner with the earl in 1173 at Dol (Benedict of Peterborough, i. 36). As William Malbank died in 1176 and Earl Hugh was suspended until 1177, the present charter falls between 1163, when John the constable succeeded, and 1173. If we could assume that the Welsh witness Cuioc son of David was one of those who fled to Cheshire after Owain Gwynedd's victorious campaign in 1167 (*Ches. Sheaf*, no. 9406; cf. Lloyd, p. 520), the date could be narrowed still further.

172. Conveyance to John, constable of Chester, of the land held by Hugh Norris in Antrobus and of the homage of the aforesaid Hugh.

[1163–1181]

> P.R.O., D.L. 41/1 (inventory of Lacy charters), nos. 36 and 37.

Carta H. comes Cestrie facta eidem Iohanni et heredibus suis de illa terra quam Hugo Norreis tenuit in Antrebussa, et de homagio predicti Hugonis.

This brief notice in the inventory of Lacy muniments taken at Pontefract castle after the execution of Thomas, earl of Lancaster, in 1322, is the only surviving record of this charter. John must be the constable of Chester who succeeded in 1163. Antrobus had been part of the earl's demesne at the time of the Domesday survey (*D.S.C.*, p. 119) but disappears completely from view thereafter (Orm., ii. 656), and nothing apparently is otherwise known of Hugh Norris. By the time of Edward I, Antrobus was part of the constable's barony of Halton, probably as a consequence of this grant.

173. Notification to Gilbert, bishop of London, of his grant to Nicholas the prior and the canons of Repton of the advowson of the church of Great Baddow (co. Essex), as given by his mother, Countess Matilda.

Repton, [1164–1172]

> Original: B.L. Stowe Charter 153. Ed.: Jeayes, *Derbyshire Charters*, no. 1945.

G. dei gratia Londoniensi episcopo et omnibus sancte matris ecclesie filiis Hugo comes Cestrie salutem. Fidelis thesaurus memorie est scriptura, que rerum seriem incommutabili loquitur veritate. Huius itaque prospectu rationis presenti pagine commendare decrevi, me concessisse Nicholao priori de Rapendona et canonicis eiusdem loci ibidem Sancte Trinitati servientibus in puram et perpetuam elemosinam ius advocationis in ecclesia de Badewen, sicut mater mea Matillis comitissa concessit. Et ne concessio ista in posterum vacillaret, huius scripti munimine et sigilli mei appositione dignum duxi confirmare. Huic concessioni hii testes affuerunt: Radulfus Barba Aprilis, Umfridus sacerdos de Rapendona, Willelmus Barba Aprilis, Terricus clericus, Thomas clericus de Luhteburht, Lamfram sacerdos de Stoke, Alanus clericus, Ricardus clericus,

Willelmus sacerdos de Rapendona, Stefanus frater eius, Iurdanus Rasur, Seer de Stoke, Gilebertus filius Picot, Willelmus de Aula, Milo, Haldanus, Hugo Basset, Iurdanus, Thomas Rasur, Odo camerarius, Radulfus clericus, Walterus filius Levegar, Walterus Corb, Gilebertus filius Ricardi, Eilwinus, Gilebertus de Heige, Alexander sacerdos.

This charter is dated 1172–81 by Jeayes, but the reason is not very evident. Gilbert Foliot became bishop of London in 1163, and the charter probably falls between then and 1172, like **no. 123**. It can fairly be assumed that the advowson of Great Baddow was one of Countess Matilda's original endowments for her new foundation at Repton. The present charter is clearly a clerical product, both in writing and formulation, and it would not be surprising if it was produced at Repton. The unusual witness list seems to bear this out. Apart from Hugh's regular clerical attendants (Ralph and William Barbe d'Averill), the only regular secular witness is Gilbert son of Picot. All the others in the long list are local men, who do not otherwise appear in Hugh's charters.

174.   Confirmation of the gifts of his father and others to the nuns of St. Mary's, Chester.

Chester, [c.1165]

> P.R.O., C.66 (Chancery Patent Rolls), no. 360, m. 19. Transcr. (from enrolment): B.L. Harl. MS. 2060, f. 18 (old f. 28); Harl. MS. 2101, f. 18 (old f. 180), and f. 21 (old f. 183); Bodleian Library, Dodsworth MS. 39, f. 154: Abstract (without text): P.R.O., CHES 29/20 (Plea Rolls), m. 32. Ed.: *Mon.*, iv. 314 (no. 2); *Orm.*, i. 346. Engl. abstract (from *Cal. Pat. Rolls, 1399–1401*, p. 297): *J.C.A.S.*, N.S. xiii, p. 109.

Hugo comes Cestrie constabulario, dapifero, iusticiario, vic(ecomiti), baronibus et omnibus hominibus suis Francis et Anglis presentibus et futuris salutem. Sciatis me concessisse et hac carta mea confirmasse deo et sancte Marie et sanctimonialibus Cestrie omnes illas donaciones et tenuras quas comes R. pater meus vel alii eis caritative dederunt infra civitatem et extra, in redditibus, mansuris, domibus, terris, aquis, silvis, libertatibus, dignitatibus et omnibus modis donorum, que eis rationabiliter facta sunt, et quod ipse et terre sue libere sint et quiete de tolneto, vigilia, consuetudine omnique seculari servicio et exaccione. Et prohibeo quod nulli meorum in se vel sibi pertinentibus ullo modo manum extendant nec ab eis aliquid postulant nisi tantum preces et orationes, set pro deo et communi animarum nostrarum salute eas cum suis omnibus manuteneant et protegant, nichil vexantes nec ab aliquo vexari permittentes. Testibus Aluredo de Combrai, Radulfo filio Warneri, Rogero de Livet, Willelmo de Roelent,[1] Willelmo filio Ricardi, Bertramo camerario,[2] et aliis multis apud Cestriam.

1. Roil(ent) *MS.*
2. dain. *MS.*

Hugh II's confirmation of his father's charter for St. Mary's nunnery (**no. 98**) has been dated c.1165 (*J.C.A.S., loc. cit.*), and this is probably as close an approximation as possible. For William of Roelent, or Rhuddlan, see **no. 171**.

175. Conferment on the priory of Trentham of the church of Belchford (Lincs.) which William Barbe d'Averill now holds, on his death or removal.

Chester, [1165–1170]

> B.L. Harl. MS. 380, f. 29 ('transcripti ex ectypo, nec scio cuius iuris est autographum'); Harl. 2044, f. 1 (new f. 26) ('This coppy I had from Sir Simon d'Ewes'); Harl. 2060, f. 39 (new f. 23v.); Harl. 2079, f. 32 (old f. 63); Harl. 5855, p. 34 (old f. 21), with drawing of seal; Bodleian Library, Dodsworth MS. 31, f. 92v. ('ex rotulo cartarum antiquarum vocato Domesday'); MS. Top. Cheshire b. I, p. 135 (from MS. of John Arden); Chester, Booth of Twemlow, Liber D, f. 141 ('ex Domesday'). Ed.: *Hist. Coll. of Staffordshire*, xi. 316 (from Harl. MS. 2044); brief abstract Orm., i. 29 (from Sir Simon d'Ewes).

Omnibus sancte matris ecclesie filiis Hugo comes Cestrie salutem. Universitati vestre declaro me hanc libertatem concessisse priori et canonicis Trentham,[1] quod Willelmo Barba[2] Aprilis, qui modo possidet ecclesiam Bettesfordie per annualem pensam,[3] ab eadem ecclesia remoto sive defuncto,[4] eandem ecclesiam habeant et teneant integram ab ordinem suum sustinendum sine omni impedimento mei aut meorum heredum in perpetuam elemosinam pro anima patris mei et antecessorum meorum. Hiis testibus Ricardo filio comitis, Radulfo vicecomite, Radulfo filio Warini, Ricardo Lanceline. Apud Cestriam.

SEAL: 'Cerarium mutilatum, ita ut nullae literae in circumscriptione visae nec quicquid humanae figurae nisi crus et pes dexter cum toto pene equo' (Harl. 380). Harl. 5855: lower half of equestrian seal on tag showing horse galloping, but human figure and inscription perished.

1. de (Trentham) *om. in all MSS.*
2. *sic MSS.*
3. annuam pecuniam, *Harl. 380, 2044, 2060, 5855.*
4. *for* sive defuncto, dehinc, *MS. Top. Cheshire,* detunc *Dodsworth 31 and Booth's Liber D.*

For William Barbe d'Averill, one of the leading clerks in Earl Hugh's household, see **no. 194**. Hugh's younger brother, Richard, the first witness of the present charter, died early and was buried in Coventry abbey (**no. 177**). The date of his death is not known, but must have been before 1175 and possibly as early as 1165 or 1166. Of the other witnesses, Richard Lancelyn witnessed a grant to St. Werburgh's abbey, Chester, about 1153–60 (*Chart. St. Werburgh*, no. 23), and Ralph fitz Warin witnessed a number of charters of Earl Hugh in favour of the same foundation (**nos. 130, 132, 133**). *Radulfus vicecomes* was vicomte of Avranches in Normandy, and lived until shortly after 1200. The present charter has been dated c. 1155 (*Hist. Coll. of Staffordshire*, xi. 317), but this is certainly too early. The correct date is probably nearer to 1165–70.

176. Charter making Richard Davenport master-forester of the forest of Leek and Macclesfield, and conferring on him 'Anhus' for his service as forester; in return for which grant Richard gave the earl a 'kazzorium sor bauzan' and two marks of silver and the earl's uncle, Richard, a 'kazzorium ferrant'.

Leek, [c.1165–1170]

Orig.: J.R.U.L.M., Bromley-Davenport Muniments, Deeds, Davenports of Davenport (i). Transcr.: B.L. Harl. MS. 2074, f. 78v., and Harl. 2038, f. 86 (new f. 92); Bodleian Library, Dodsworth MS. 31, f. 53v. Ed.: Orm., iii. 61 (mutilated and inaccurate); *Stenton Misc.*, p. 38 (no. 10) (with facsimile); full English abstract, *Ches. Sheaf*, no. 9900.

H. comes Cestrie constabulario, dapifero, iusticie, vicecomiti, omnibus baronibus suis, omnibus hominibus suis Francis et Anglicis tam presentibus quam futuris salutem. Sciatis me dedisse et concessisse et hac carta mea confirmasse Ricardo de Deveneport et heredibus suis pro suo homagio et servitio Anhus cum omnibus pertinenciis, tenendam de me et de meis heredibus pro servitio foresterarii in feudo et hereditate libere et honorifice et quiete ab omnibus serviciis et consuetudinibus mihi pertinentibus vel meis heredibus, excepto predicto servitio foresterarii. Preterea dedi predicto Ricardo et heredibus suis foresterarium meum de toto meo foresto et de Lic et de Maclesfeld, tenendum de me et de meis heredibus in feudo et hereditate, ut sepedictus Ricardus sit meus supremus forestarius de toto meo predicto foresto iure hereditario. Pro hac autem hereditate iste idem Ricardus dedit mihi unum kazzorium sor bauzan et duas marchas argenti et Ricardo avunculo meo unum kazzorium ferrant. Teste Ricardo avunculo comitis, Roberto de Stafford, Radulfo filio Warneri, Radulfo vicecomite, Hugone de Duttun, Philippo de Diva, Rogero Malfillastre, Humfredo de Scovilla, Frembald, Rogero de Livet, Willelmo de Ruthelan, Bertramo camerario, Rondulfo del Lec, Ricardo de Lime, Ricardo le Large, Iurdano de Maclesfeld, Gamello filio Hardinc, Willelmo de Lec, Willelmo clerico, apud Lec.

SEAL: fragments, unidentifiable, in a bag.

This interesting charter marks the rise of the Davenport family. Its date lies between 1162, when Earl Hugh came of age, and 1175, the year of the death of his uncle, Richard, the son of Earl Robert of Gloucester and brother of Hugh's mother, Matilda. Roger Malfilastre also witnessed, c.1165–70, charters for Coventry priory (**no. 177**) and for Humphrey de Bohun (**no. 180**), and this probably gives the approximate limits of date. W.F. Irvine (*Ches. Sheaf*, no. 9900) identified Anhus with One House, 'an ancient stone mansion' in Rainow, 2 miles north-east of Macclesfield (Orm., iii. 771–2), and also suggested that 'kazzorium sor bauzan' is a sorrel skewbald hunter and 'kazzorium ferrant' an iron-grey hunter or possibly a blue roan. For William of Rhuddlan, see **no. 171**, and for Bertram the chamberlain **no. 194**.

177. Confirmation of Ranulf II's gift to St. Mary's abbey, Coventry, of the chapel of St. Michael in Coventry.

[1165–1170]

P.R.O., E.164/21 (Exchequer, King's Remembrancer, Misc. Books), f. 76 (Coventry Register); Bodleian Library, Dugdale MS. 12, p. 238, and Dodsworth MS. 65, f. 24 (both from the Register). Ed.: Orm., i. 27 (incomplete); Coss, no. 6.

For a full text of this document, see Coss, *The Early Records of Medieval Coventry*, pp. 14–15 (no. 6).

The chapel of St. Michael was long a subject of contention between the monks of Coventry and the earls of Chester, beginning with Ranulf II, if not earlier, and only brought to a conclusion when Ranulf III publicly recognized the monks' rights in 1192 (**no. 219**). It gave rise to considerable documentation, not all of which is genuine; but the present short charter, which should be compared with **no. 178**, has all the marks of authenticity. Noteworthy, and not mentioned elsewhere in the Coventry charters, is the reference to Earl Hugh's younger brother Richard, who is buried in the abbey church. The charter must date from before 1175, when Hugh's uncle, another Richard, died; but it is probably considerably earlier in date. John was prior of Trentham from 1155 (*Heads of Religious Houses*, p. 187), and Edmund the archdeacon of Coventry was active between 1161 and 1165. Roger Malfilastre, Hervey de Missi, Richard the earl's uncle and Ralph the *vicomte* together witnessed the earl's charter for Humphrey de Bohun (**no. 180**), which was also witnessed by John the constable of Chester, who succeeded in 1163, and Roger Malfilastre, Roger de Livet and Ralph the *vicomte* witnessed his charter for Richard Davenport (**no. 176**), which is dated c.1166. The present charter almost certainly falls in this period. It states that it was issued in confirmation of a previous charter of Ranulf II. This can hardly be **no. 114**, which was confirmed in **no. 178**, and, like that, is open to suspicion. It would seem, therefore, that Ranulf's original charter is lost, or, perhaps more probable, that it was suppressed when the expanded text of **no. 114** became available.

178.   Confirmation to Prior Lawrence and the monks of Coventry of the chapel of St. Michael, which his father Ranulf recognized to be their right, and of all other chapels, listed by name, in his fee of Coventry and in their parish. [? Spurious]

[1165–1173]

P.R.O., C.53 (Chancery Charter Rolls), no. 135, m. 4; B.L. Add. MS. 32100, f. 60 (from original inspeximus, 22 Edw. III). Ed.: *Cal. Ch. Rolls*, v. 102 (no. 12); Coss, no. 5. Mentioned: Dugdale, *Warwickshire*, p. 106.

For a full text of this document, see Coss, *The Early Records of Medieval Coventry*, pp. 13–14 (no. 5).

This charter follows closely the model of the parallel charter of Ranulf II (**no. 114**) and is open to the same suspicion. If it is compared with Hugh's earlier confirmation of his father's gift of the chapel of St. Michael to Coventry abbey (**no. 177**), to which no exception can be taken, a striking difference (also in **114**) is the emphasis placed on the abbey's position as 'mother church'. This does not figure at all in **no. 177**, nor, so far as can be established, in any earlier charters, forged or genuine,[1] and the obvious explanation is that it was introduced by the monks to establish their parochial rights over the fifteen chapels to which they laid claim, and, for good measure, over any others which might be established in future. If the present charter is compared with **no. 114**, the only substantial difference is in the final clause which now spells out in detail that none of Hugh's heirs or successors shall be entitled 'in any way or at any time' to claim 'any right' against the monks in respect of St. Michael's chapel. This suggests that the earlier donations were still being challenged in the time of Earl Hugh, and that the monks decided that they had better take steps to make their position as watertight as possible. When this decision was made, it is impossible to say. Possibly it was at the same time as **no. 114** was fabricated, i.e. 1181–82, but it may well be later. The putative date of the charter is before 26 August 1173, when William of Rhuddlan was taken prisoner with Earl Hugh at Dol (Benedict of Peterborough, i. 56). It clearly falls after **no. 177**, which seems to date from 1162 to 1165.

1. Cf. J. Lancaster, 'The Coventry Forged Charters', *B.I.H.R.*, xxvii, pp. 113–40.

179. Order to all his men and ministers not to interfere in the lands of the prior and monks of Coventry or to impede their market, setting out in detail the boundary between the church's fee and the earl's fee. [Spurious]

[1162–1179]

P.R.O., C.53 (Chancery Charter Rolls), no. 135, m. 5; B.L. Add. MS. 32100, f. 59 (17th-century transcript from original inspeximus dated 24 Oct., 22 Edw. III). Ed.: *Cal. Ch. Rolls*, v. 101 (no. 9); Davis, *Early History of Coventry*, p. 20; Coss, no. 7.

For a full text of this document, see Coss, *The Early Records of Medieval Coventry*, p. 15 (no. 7).

This charter has all the marks of forgery, beginning with the elaborate exordium, but it is not easy to establish the date of the forgery. It is clearly concerned with the much discussed division of Coventry into the 'prior's half' and the 'earl's half'.[1] This division was a fact by 1175 at latest (*H.K.F.*, p. 281), but that does not mean that the exact boundaries between the two halves were defined. The present document is best seen as an attempt by the prior and monks to fix the boundaries, no doubt to their advantage. Its ostensible date is before 1179, when

Edmund had ceased to be archdeacon of Coventry (*Hist. Coll. of Staffordshire*, 1924, p. 247), and the witnesses are compatible with this date; but, apart from Edmund, they are regular witnesses whose names could have been taken over from a number of charters. On the other hand, the names of the tenants in the body of the text, taken together, seem to reflect the situation under Ranulf III, rather than under Hugh II. It is true that Gerard the Vintner and Anschetil Locard attested charters of Hugh (**nos. 146, 195**), though the former also witnessed in 1192, as did Richard Fordwin (**no. 219**); but Robert Scot's land at Alwardsich was confirmed by Ranulf III after 1199 (**no. 316**), and Richard Beaufiz appears on the Warwickshire Pipe Roll in 1202–3 and 1203–4 (*P.R.S.*, N.S. xvi, p. 37, and xviii, p. 225). Although the evidence is inconclusive, it seems probable that the forgery may have been put together during the minority of Ranulf III, i.e. 1181–87. This was a particularly favourable opportunity for the monks to stake out claims, and other dubious or spurious charters (**nos. 113, 114, 178**) date from the same period.

1.   Cf. J. Lancaster, 'The Coventry Forged Charters', *B.I.H.R.*, xxvii, pp. 113–40. Her views were criticized by Davis, *E.H.R.*, lxxxvi, pp. 539–545. For her reply, cf. *Medieval Coventry – a City Divided*? pp. 31 sqq. It is unnecessary to pursue this question here.

180.   Grant to Humphrey de Bohun, restoring the fee of Bisley (Gloucs.), except for the fee of Philip de Belmis, which Hugh de Lacy held in chief of the earl, for the service of three of the five knights acknowledged to be there, and if there are found to be more than five, the earl is to have half the service from the increment.

[1165–1170]

Orig.: B.L. Cott. Charter x. 7. Ed.: Stenton, *First Century of English Feudalism*, pp. 257–8.

Hugo comes Cestrie constabuloni et dapifero suo, iustic(iario), vicecom(iti), baronibus ministris et ballivis, et omnibus hominibus suis Francis et Anglis tam futuris quam presentibus salutem. Sciatis me reddidisse Umfrido de Buhun et heredibus suis tenendum de me et de meis heredibus feodum de Biseleia ut suam hereditatem per servicium trium militum de quinque qui recognoscuntur. Et si contigerit quod plures milites quam quinque inveniantur in feodo vel per disratiocinationem vel per recognitionem, ego Hugo et heredes mei habebimus servicii dimidium de incremento. Et Umfridus et heredes sui per hoc teneant feodum de me et de meis heredibus sine feodo Philippi de Belmis, quod Hugo de Laci in capite tenet de me. Testibus istis: Ricardo filio comitis Gloecestrie, Iohanne constabulone Cestrie, Bertram de Verdun, Rogero Malfillastre, Radulfo vicecomite de Abricis, Herveio de Missi ex parte comitis, et Galfrido de

Costentin et Roberto filio Walteri; et ex parte Umfridi de Buhun, Engelger de Buhun, Waltero filio Roberti, Ricardo de Vehim, Ricardo de Abenesse, Waltero de Asseleia, Willelmo de Mineres, Olivero de Mara, Ricardo Bigot, Umfrido de sancto Vigor, Roberto de Vernun.

> SEAL: dark green, pendent on parchment tag, imperfect. Obverse: equestrian. Knight in armour, hauberk of mail, long pleated surcoat, sword raised in right hand, shield ornamented with bordure in left; horse galloping with saddle and saddlecloth diapered lozengy and fringed ornamental breast-band with pendent pellets. Legend: . . . CO[MITIS] . . .
>
> Reverse: two small counterseals, (i) heart-shaped, about 1 x ¾ ins.; impression of antique oval intaglio gem, a human face; legend indistinct; (ii) oval, slightly larger, impression of another oval antique intaglio gem, subject defaced, legend indistinct; beaded border.

Humphrey de Bohun married the eldest daughter of Miles of Gloucester, to whom Ranulf II had given the services of the vavasours of Bisley c.1140 (**no. 47**). In the meantime, perhaps after Miles' death in 1143, the fee reverted to the earl of Chester. It is now restored to Humphrey as his heritage. The date of the grant is not easily established. It must fall after the succession of John the constable in 1163, and almost certainly before 1173 when Humphrey de Bohun, Bertram de Verdun and Hugh de Lacy all adhered to the royal cause (Benedict of Peterborough, i. 51). Earl Hugh's uncle, Richard the son of the earl of Gloucester, died in 1175. With Roger Malfilastre, Hervey de Missi and Ralph the vicomte of Avranches, he witnessed Hugh II's grant of the chapel of St. Michael to Coventry priory (**no. 177**), and the present charter probably belongs to the same period. Humphrey de Bohun died in 1181 (*P.R.S.* xxxv, p. 5), and Engelger de Bohun apparently one or two years earlier (*Rot. Scacc. Norm.*, i. 38). Hugh de Lacy, to whom Henry II had granted the kingdom of Meath in 1172, was killed in Ireland in 1185 (*Ann. Cestr.*, p. 34).

181. General confirmation of the possessions of the abbey of St. Sever in Normandy and England.

[1165–1173]

> Rouen, Bibl. municipale, MS. 1235 (Cartulaire de Normandie), ff. 30v.–31v.

Quoniam per se labilis humana memoria monumentis litterarum et abolita recolit et nota custodit, ad posteritatis noticiam ego Hugo comes Cestrie[1] in presentia venerabilium patrum constitutus, Rothroudi scilicet Rothomagensis archiepiscopi et Henrici Baiocensis et Ricardi Constanciensis episcoporum necnon et Guillelmi sancti Stephani Cadomanensis et Victoris sancti Georgii abbatum et aliorum virorum religiosorum, quorum consilio et admonitione pro parvis magna pro caducis permanentia acquirere cupiens, redditus et dona, que antecessores mei in spe retributionis eterne et pro suaram animarum salute ecclesie beate Marie virginis et sancti Severi confessoris et monachis in eadem ecclesia deo servientibus contulerunt, omnia libere et quiete et absque ulla seculari reclamatione mei vel heredum meorum predictis monachis tam in Normannia quam in Anglia in perpetuum possidenda propter summi regis amorem et eterne beatitudinis retributionem concedo et, sicut in cartis super hoc confestis continetur, confirmo.

Dono igitur et concedo totam, ubi ipsa ecclesia sita est, villam et omnem loci illius silve decimam, venditionis scilicet arborum, herbagii animalium, pasnagii porcorum, decimam quoque porcorum meorum et ovium et vaccarum et equarum, decimam etiam venationum tam porcorum quam cervorum caprearumque, decimam quoque denariorum ex placitis foreste acquisitorum. Concedo etiam ut animalia monachorum, cuiuscumque generis sint, omni tempore quietam habeant pasturam in eadem silva. Concedo etiam ut inibi habeant monachi in perpetuum, qualescunque voluerint eligere, quatuor fagos in Nativitate Domini et totidem in Pascha totidemque in Pentechosten. Dono etiam et concedo ad omnem loci illius edificationem arbores sive vivas sive mortuas, sed et burgensibus mortuas ad domorum constructionem et ad aliarum rerum necessitatem. Concedo etiam ut omni tempore de eadem silva accipiant monachi per manum forestariorum meorum vivas arbores et mortuas ad focum suum sufficienter infra claustra abbacie faciendum.

Preterea dono et concedo decimam omnium molendinorum meorum de Valle Virie et de sancto Iacobo super Beuron.[2] Dono etiam et concedo decimam totius frumenti et avene tam in firmis quam in redditibus, quos habeo in Valle Virie; et si de residuo frumento panis mihi vel meis fiat, iterum monachi inde decimam habebunt, si vero vendatur, decimam iterum denariorum. Dono etiam decimam omnium valdarum mearum de Normannia. Concedo insuper et dono per totam Vallem Virie et per totum episcopatum Abrincensem decimam omnium victualium meorum, videlicet panis, carnium, piscium, cuiuscumque generis sint, caseorumque et ovorum.

Dono insuper et concedo predictis monachis ecclesiam sancti Germani de Talevenda cum omni decima et pertinentiis suis, ecclesiam sancti Martini de Torneor cum omni decima et pertinentiis, ecclesiam de Mansione Osoulphi cum omni decima et pertinentiis, ecclesiam sancti Mandici cum omni decima et pertinentiis, ecclesiam de Mesnill Chauceis cum omni decima et pertinentiis, ecclesiam de Morigni cum omni decima et pertinentiis, ecclesiam de Lucerna cum decima et pertinentiis suis, ecclesiam de Corchon cum omni decima, ecclesiam sancte Marie Osmondi cum omni decima et pertinentiis suis, ecclesiam de Ebrececo villa et decimam et silvam cum pertinentiis, medietatem ecclesie de Vallibus super Oram cum pertinentiis, ecclesiam de Campo Osberti cum decima et pertinentiis, ecclesiam de Gisneto cum pertinentiis, ecclesiam sancte Anastasie cum pertinentiis, tres partes ecclesie de Viarvilla cum pertinentiis.

In Anglis quoque dono et concedo Hacchan cum appenditiis suis et ecclesiam cum terra ecclesie pertinenti, ecclesiam de Cadvelle cum terra et decima ecclesie pertinenti, ecclesiam de Gretham cum decima et terra ecclesie pertinenti, ecclesiam de Barnetebi et decimam cum terra ecclesie pertinenti, decimam de Hantone et ecclesiam cum terra ecclesie pertinenti, ecclesiam de Watuthene et decimam cum terra ecclesie pertinenti, ecclesiam de Takobe et decimam cum terra ecclesie pertinenti, ecclesiam de Cesitone cum decima et terra ecclesie pertinenti, ecclesiam de Fisidan et decimam cum terra ecclesie pertinenti; apud Hengstric quatuor hidas terre.

Hec sunt, que ego Hugo comes Cestrie sancte Marie et sancto Severo et monachis ibidem sub abbatis imperio secundum regulam sancti Benedicti degentibus concedo et dono, et, ut ea monachi libere, quiete et pacifice in perpetuum possideant, sigilli mei munimine confirmo.

1. Cistrie *MS.*
2. Benron *MS.*

The abbey of St. Sever, near Vire, was the senior religious foundation of the earls of Chester, traditionally founded by Hugh I about 1085 (Orm., i. 15); but its archives were totally destroyed, and the present is the only surviving charter of any of the earls. It is clearly a product of the monks themselves, but there is no reason to reject it. Its date must fall between Rotrou's elevation to the archbishopric of Rouen in 1165, and 1173, but I have failed to narrow it more closely. The English churches given or confirmed are, in the order of their listing, Haugham, Tathwell, Greetham, Barnetby, Halton, Waddington, all in Lincolnshire, Tackley (Oxon.), Bickton (Hants.) and Fifehead (Dorset); in addition, the abbey received four hides of land in Henstridge (Somerset). The French churches (St. Germain-de-Tallevende, Le Torneur, Le Mesnil-Caussois, Morigny, Courson, etc.) lie in the immediate vicinity of Vire and St. Sever. Most of these donations, if not all, seem to go back to the original foundation by Hugh I, and were recited in a privilege of Pope Hadrian IV given in 1158 (Round, *C.D.F.*, p. 216, no. 615), but Hugh I's charter has not survived.

182.   Grant to the nuns of Bullington priory, Lincs., of his mill pond at Donington.

Belchford, [c.1166]

> Tabley MSS., Sir Peter Leycester's Liber C, pars II, f. 14v.; B.L. Harl. MS. 2060, f. 63 (new f. 35v.), both from original in archives of Sir Simon d'Ewes; B.L. Add. MS. 6118, p. 750 (new f. 393v.), short abstract from Bullington cartulary, now lost. Ed.: Orm., i. 27.

Hugo comes Cestrie constabulario suo, dapifero, omnibus baronibus suis, omnibus hominibus suis Francis et Anglicis tam futuris quam presentibus salutem. Concedo sanctimonialibus de Bolintona stagnum meum de Dunintona firmum terre mee, sicut fuit tempore Henrici regis, in perpetuam elemosinam pro anima mea et patris mei et meorum antecessorum. Et precipio omnibus hominibus meis quod habeant meam firmam pacem, ita quod nullus inde predictis sanctimonialibus iniuriam vel contumeliam faciat. Testibus Roberto dapifero de Monte Alto, Filippo de Kima, Simone filio Osberti, Willelmo Patric, Radulpho filio Warneri, Rogero de Maletot, Iohanne priore de Trenteham, Orm eius canonico, Rogero monacho de Hambi, Willelmo clerico comitis qui hanc cartam scripsit apud Beltesfort, et multis aliis.

> SEAL: 'a fayre seale with the impression of the earle on horsebacke, written about SIGILLUM HUGONIS COMITIS CESTRIE'.

The priory of Bullington was founded about the beginning of the reign of Henry II by Simon son of William, founder of the family of Kyme and one of Hugh II's important Lincolnshire tenants (*H.K.F.*, p. 119). Donington is presumably Donington-on-Bain, and the intriguing reference to the earl's land there 'as it was in the time of King Henry' (which must refer to Henry I) suggests that it may have been lost or otherwise affected during the civil wars of Stephen's reign. Hugh II's charter is unfortunately not easy to date. John prior of Trentham succeeded in 1154 or 1155 (*Heads of Religious Houses*, p. 187) and Robert of Montalt, the steward, was succeeded by his son Ralph in or about 1162 (*Ches. Sheaf*, no. 9394). Ralph son of Warner appears on the Pipe Rolls of 1165–66 and 1166–67, and that probably indicates the approximate date.

183.   Grant to the abbey of Montebourg of the gifts of his ancestors at Trévières and Galteville.

Trévières, [1168]

M.S. Paris lat. 10087, p. 63 (Cart. de Montebourg, no. 134).

Ego Hugo comes Cestrie concedo ecclesie sancte Marie Montisburgi donationem illam, quam dederunt antecessores mei eidem ecclesie pro se ipsis et pro antecessorum et successorum nostrorum animabus, scilicet decimam molendini mei de stagno de Treueris et decimam piscium eiusdem stagni, et illud, quod est de feudo Broc in ecclesia Gateville cum omnibus rebus eidem ecclesie de terra ipsa pertinentibus, sicut Galterus Broc dedit eidem abbatie concessu antecessorum meorum. Et ut donatio hec firma sit, signo sancte crucis + presens scriptum confirmo et auctoritate sigilli mei munio. Huius rei testes sunt Ranulfus de Grantval. Haket. Gaufridus de Costentin. Eudo de Aniseio. Rogerus de sancto Mauro. Robertus filius Adam. Freimbaut filius Haket. Gislebertus de Treueris et Iohannes frater eius, et multi alii. Hec concessio facta fuit apud Treueris anno ab incarnatione domini millesimo c°lxv°iii°.

Earl Ranulf II's gifts of the above were confirmed in 1381 by Charles VI, king of France (B.L. Add. MS. 15605, f. 3), but Ranulf's charter has not survived. Gatteville lies north of Barfleur on the Cherbourg peninsula, about 25 km. north of Montebourg. Walter Broc's gift of the church, with its lands and tithes, was confirmed by Henry I in 1107 (*Regesta*, ii. no. 825). If, as Earl Hugh's charter states, it was given with the consent of his predecessors, it must have been given with the consent of Earl Richard.

184. Grant of lands at Coventry to Godfrey his homager.

Chester, [1169–1173]

> Orm., i. 31, from original, now lost, in the possession of
> Mr Thomas Sharp of Coventry.

Grant to Godfrey his homager of 'duodecim numeratus terre' and two assarts at Coventry. Testibus istis: Bertreia comitissa Cestrie, Willelmo Patric, Alveredo de Cumbray, Galfrido de Costentin, Radulpho filio Warneri, Roberto Patric, Ricardo de Luvetot, Willelmo de Ruelent, Rogero de Livet, et Herberto clerico, qui hanc cartam scripsit, apud Cestriam.

> SEAL (reproduced by Ormerod), green wax, attached by
> silken cords of same colour; obverse, equestrian figure
> with sword in right hand, legend . . . VMITV . . . VS.;
> reverse, ancient gem, head (crowned with laurel wreath?)
> to right, surrounded by two inscriptions, the outer one
> Q'IS CVI Q'ID MANDET P'SENS MEA CARTULA

PAND'T, the last word at beginning of inner inscription
(indecipherable) in Norman French.

Unfortunately, this brief notice is the only surviving record of the original
charter, which perished in the fire at the Birmingham Public Library in 1879. Its
date must fall between the marriage of Earl Hugh and Countess Bertrada in
1169, and 1173. It has proved impossible to identify Godfrey the homager or his
holdings in Coventry.

185.   Grant to Andrew, the man of the countess, of a boat for fishing on the
Dee.

[1169–1173]

Orig.: J.R.U.L.M., Mainwaring MSS., Suppl. 1.
Transcr.: Bodleian Library, Ashmole MSS. 833, f. 42v.,
and 1137, f. 136 (both with sketches of seal). Ed.: *10th
Rep. Hist. MSS. Comm.*, App. pt. iv, p. 200.

H. comes Cestrie constabulario, dapifero, iusticiario, vic(ecomiti), ballivis et
omnibus hominibus suis Francis et Anglis salutem. Sciatis me concessisse et
dedisse peticione comitisse Andree homini comitisse et heredibus suis tenendum
de me et de heredibus meis unum batum ad piscandum in aqua de De
ubicumque voluerit, libere et quiete sicut unquam aliquis melius et liberius
habuit batum in De. Testibus comitissa B., Rogero de Livet, Ricardo de
Luvetot, Helia Avenel, Willelmo filio Ricardi, Willelmo Barba Aprilis clerico[1]
comitis, Picot de Lundris, Roberto Sarezeno, Godefrido camerario, Nicholao
capellano, qui hanc cartam scripsit.

> SEAL, on tag: obverse, knight on
> horseback, spear with banner in right
> hand, shield in left; all that remains of
> legend . . . OM . . . Reverse, a gem,
> upright male figure, legend: +
> SECRETVM [? HVCANICHI].

1. clerici *MS.*

This grant falls between 1169, when Hugh married Bertrada, daughter of Count
Simon of Evreux, and 1173. Unless he is identical with Andrew son of Mabel, to
whom Ranulf III granted fishing and other rights in Chester (**nos. 267, 268**),
nothing further is known of Andrew, the countess's man. Picot de Lundris was
possibly a member of the same family as Athelard de Lundris, who witnessed a

later Chester deed (*J.C.A.S.*, N.S.x, p. 18). For William Barbe d'Averill, see **no. 194**.

186. Confirmation to the abbey of St. Stephen, Caen, of the gifts of his ancestor, Ranulf *vicomte* of Bayeux, at Bretteville-l'Orgueilleuse and Biéville.

Chivilly, [June–July 1171]

> Orig.: Archives de Calvados, H.1854, no. 35. Transcr.: Rouen, Bibl. municipale, MS. 1235 (Cartulaire de Normandie), f. 10v. Cal.: d'Anisy, i. 276 (no. 35); Round, *C.D.F.*, p. 161 (no. 455).

Sciant tam presentes quam futuri, quod ego Hugo comes Cestrie concessu et assensu domini mei H. regis Anglie et ducis Normannie et Aquitanie et comes Andegavie concessi in perpetuam elemosinam et liberam et hac mea carta confirmavi, pro salute anime mee et antecessorum meorum, donationem quam Randulfus vicecomes Baiocensis antecessor meus fecit ecclesie beati Stephani de Cadomo et monachis ibidem deo servientibus de tota terra quam ipse habuit in Britevilla Orgoillosa, cum parte ecclesie ad illam pertinente et cum colonis et liberis hominibus ad eandem pertinentibus et cum omnibus aliis pertinentiis suis. Preterea donationem quam idem Randulfus predicte ecclesie fecit de ecclesia de Boevilla cum alodio et omni decima ad eam pertinente, sicut carta regis Willelmi Anglorum et principis Normannorum et Cenomannensium, quam inde habent, testatur. Quare volo et firmiter precipio quod predicta ecclesia et monachi eiusdem ecclesie habeant et teneant totam predictam terram cum parte predicte ecclesie et cum omnibus pertinentiis suis, et predictam ecclesiam de Boevilla cum alodio et omni decima ad eam pertinente, bene et in pace, libere et quiete, plenarie, integre et honorifice cum omnibus libertatibus suis. Testibus Gilleberto episcopo Lundoniensi, Ricardo archidiacono Pictaviensi, Walerano archidiacono Baiocensi, magistro Radulfo de Tamworth, Willelmo de Mandevilla comite de Essexia, Willelmo comite de Arundel, Hugone de Longo Campo, Reginaldo de Curtenai, Iohanne de Waureio, Hachet de Ridefort, Randulfo de Grandi Valle, Gaufrido de Costantiis, Rogero de Livet, Randulfo de Glanvilla, et Germano scriptore regis, et Willelmo clerico meo, et pluribus aliis. Apud Chivilli.

SEAL on tag on fold: missing.

Ranulf *vicomte* of Bayeux (or the Bessin) was father of Earl Ranulf I of Chester. His charter, witnessed by Archbishop Lanfranc, Odo of Bayeux, Roger of Montgomery and William of Semilly, is in Arch. Calvados, H. 1825, Côte 4, f. 3.

For the date of the previous charter see Eyton, p. 158, where its confirmation by Henry II is recorded. As both the royal confirmation and Earl Hugh's charter are dated at *Chivilli* and have identical witnesses, it can safely be assumed that they were issued on the same occasion. Richard of Ilchester, archdeacon of Poitiers, later bishop of Winchester, was a prominent royal servant (cf. *T.R.H.S.*, 5th Ser. xvi, pp. 1–20), and Master Ralph of Tamworth had been one of Henry II's envoys to the papal curia during the Becket controversy (Eyton, pp. 102–5). Geoffrey de Côtentin held the castle of Stockport against Henry II during the rebellion of 1173 (*Stenton Misc.*, p. 35); he appears to have died in 1179 or 1180.

187.   Confirmation to the Hospital of St. John of Jerusalem of the land at Wardle given to them by Simon Tuschet and Matthew of Newton, and of two halves of a salthouse in Middlewich, the gifts of Roger Mainwaring and Ralph Brereton, which are to remain in the hands of Gilbert the chaplain, who is also granted a perpetual vicarage in the church of Middlewich.

Leek, [1171–1173]

B.L. Harl. MS. 2099, f. 34 (old f. 307); Bodleian Library, MS. Top. Cheshire b. I, p. 80 and p. 109; MS. Top. Cheshire c.9, f. 16; Chester, Booth of Twemlow, Liber K, f. 4.

H. comes Cestrie constabulario, dapifero, iusticiario, baronibus et omnibus hominibus suis Francis et Anglis tam presentibus quam futuris salutem. Sciatis me concessisse et mea carta confirmasse deo et sancto Iohanni baptiste et pauperibus beate domus Ierusalem hospitalis donacionem quam Simon Tuschet et Matheus de Neuton dederunt predicto hospitali, scilicet totam terram de Warihall cum omnibus pertinenciis et cum omnibus libertatibus, et dimidiam salinam in Medio Wico ex donacione Rogeri de Meinilgarin, et dimidiam salinam ex donacione Radulfi de Brerton, quietas de telonio salis et omnibus teloniis et de omnibus secularibus exaccionibus, remanentes Gilberto capellano et heredibus quos ipse voluerit, concessu prioris et fratrum capituli totius Anglie, pro anima Ranulfi comitis patris mei et matris mee et sponse mee et puerorum meorum. Et confirmo huic predicto Gilberto capellano perpetuam vicariam in ecclesia de Medio Wico cum decimis et obventionibus, sicut Simon de Tuschet dominus fundi et Robertus persona eiusdem ecclesie concedunt et confirmant in cartis suis. Quare precipio vobis quatenus manuteneatis istam meam predictam elemosinam, nec patiamini quod aliquis vexet istam elemosinam super meum forisfacturum decem librarum. Testibus Roberto abbate Cestrie, Aluredo de Cumbrei, Radulfo Meinilgarin, Radulfo filio Garneri, Simone de Tuschet, Ricardo de Lunetho,[1] Frembaut, Hugone de Boisdel, Willelmo filio Ricardi, Henrico Bacun, Henrico Tuschet, Matheo de Neuton, Ranulfo clerico de Lehe, Ricardo de Davenport, fratre Godart hospitalis, apud Lehe. Valete.

> SEAL: obverse, fragmentary, equestrian; legend wanting.
> Reverse, two small seals, animal facing to sinister (lamb?)
> in beaded border, legend: . . . CH . . . ETU . . .

1. *sic MSS.: probably for* Luvetot.

Earl Hugh says his gift is made for the souls of his wife and (two) sons. As he married in 1169 and the elder son Ranulf (III) was born in 1170, it is safe to assume that Ranulf's younger brother Richard was not born before 1171. This sets one limit of date. As Henry Tuschet was dead by 1178, probably 1177 (*H.K.F.*, p. 28), this sets another, and Hugh himself was suspended between 1174 and 1177 for his part in the rebellion of Henry II's sons, when he was taken prisoner at Dol on 26 August 1173 (Benedict of Peterborough, i. 56–7). The likelihood, therefore, is that the charter was issued between 1171 and 1173, and this appears to be borne out by the seal which, so far as can be judged from the fragmentary remains, is Hugh's first seal, used before his imprisonment.[1]

In an original charter at Eaton Hall (Henry II, no. 5), dated 1184, Garner de Naplouse, prior of the Hospital of Jerusalem in England, confirmed the above grant to Gilbert the chaplain of Middlewich, for an annual payment of 2s. to the lord of the fee and half a mark of silver to the Hospital. At some date subsequently, Gilbert disposed of the half salthouses to Peter the clerk of the earl, and later, by an original deed extant among the Shakerley muniments, Peter the clerk disposed of them to Thomas of Croxton, the Hospital retaining a rent of 7s. 8d.; see the facsimile in *E.C.C.*, no. 20.

1. The fragmentary legend on the reverse (. . . [SECR]ETU[M] implies that it was the earl's secret seal. This he appears to have lost in 1173.

188. Gift to Alexander, tutor of the earl's son, of Storeton and Puddington on his marriage with Annabella, granddaughter of Alan Savage.

[1177–1181]

> B.L. Harl. MS. 2079, f. 15 (new f. 7) (A); London, College of Arms, MS. 1 D. 14, p. 182 ('ex cartis Rollandi Stanley militis, 1580' (B); Bodleian Library, Dodsworth MS. 31, f. 95v. (C); MS. Top. Cheshire b. I (from MS. of

John Arden, entitled 'Baronagium Cestriae'), p. 136 (D);
Chester, Booth of Twemlow, Liber D (94 A591), f. 143
('ex Domesday') (E). Ed. (incomplete): Orm., ii. 446.

Hugo comes Cestrie constabulario suo Cestrie et dapifero suo et universis
baronibus suis et omnibus hominibus suis salutem. Sciatis me dedisse Alexandro
magistro filii mei Anabellam[1] filiam filii Alani Salvagii cum tota sua hereditate,
videlicet cum Stortun et Pudintun et omnibus eorum pertinentiis, tenendam in
feodo et hereditate libere et quiete de me et heredibus meis illi et heredibus suis,
sicut carta patris mei testatur. Hiis testibus Bertramo de Werdon,[2] Iohanne
constabulario, Roberto Patric, Ricardo de Luuetot,[3] Radulfo vicecomite,
Roelein[4] de Werdun,[5] Willelmo Mansell.

SEAL: 'data sub magno sigillo dicti comitis'.

1. Amabilem *B, C, D, E*.
2. Verdon *C*.
3. Lunetot *A, C, E*.
4. Roelin *A, E*; Roeleni *D*.
5. Verdon *A, D*.

Annabella was the daughter and heiress of Robert Savage, who gave land in
Storeton to St. Werburgh's abbey (**no. 131**). As her marriage was in the earl's
gift, it must be assumed that Robert was dead by this time, but the date of the
present charter is not easy to establish. W.F. Irvine places it 'about the year
1180' (*Ches. Sheaf*, no. 9134). Stewart-Brown (*H.S.L.C.*, lxxxvii, p. 104) dated
it 'about 1170–81', but the earlier date is hardly credible, since Ranulf III was
only born in 1170 and Alexander (sometimes described as Alexander son of
Ralph) can hardly have been appointed tutor (*magister*) before 1175 at earliest,
and probably, since Earl Hugh was in the king's custody from 1173 to 1177, not
before 1177. Storeton and Puddington had been given to Alan Savage, or
Silvester, by Ranulf II, whose charter (**no. 35**) is referred to in the text. The
oxgang of land, which Robert gave to St. Werburgh's, was later restored to
Alexander for an annual payment of 12d. (*Chart. St. Werburgh*, no. 486).

189.   Confirmation of his father's gift to Grimsby abbey.

[1177–1181]

London, College of Arms, MS. Vincent 120, p. 74; Chetham's Library, Towneley MSS., transcripts from the
Vernon MSS., p. 539.

Hugo comes Cestrie omnibus baronibus suis et ministris et hominibus suis tam Francis quam Anglicis, et omnibus sancte ecclesie fidelibus tam clericis quam laicis tam presentibus quam futuris salutem. Sciatis me concessisse et hac presenti carta mea confirmasse ecclesie sancti Augustini de Grimsby et canonicis ibidem deo servientibus omnes illas elemosinas, quas Ranulfus comes Cestrie pater meus per cartam suam dedit *etc.* Testibus Ricardo filio comitis, Ranulfo de Ver, Hachet de Ridefort *etc.*

Ranulf II's gift to Grimsby of the church of Tetney (Lincs.) and land there and in Humberstone was confirmed in 1155–58 by Henry II (*Cal. Ch. Rolls*, iv. 311), but Ranulf's charter has not survived. As Earl Hugh's younger son, Richard, cannot have been born before 1171, the present (unfortunately abbreviated) charter presumably dates from after the earl's restoration in 1177, but a closer dating is not possible. Richard's appearance as a witness is very unusual.

190. Confirmation of John the constable's gift of Stanney to Stanlaw abbey, quitclaiming any service that might be owing to him.

[c.1178]

> B.L. Egerton MS. 3126 (Whalley cartulary), f. 32v.; P.R.O., E.132/7 (Exchequer Charter Rolls), m. 2 (unnumbered roll of Stanlaw charters), witnesses omitted. Ed.: *Chart. Whalley*, i. 8 (from Egerton MS.)

H. comes Cestrie universis sancte matris ecclesie filiis, et specialiter iusticiario, constabulario, dapifero, et omnibus baronibus suis et omnibus ballivis suis et omnibus hominibus suis Francis et Anglicis, tam presentibus quam futuris, salutem. Sciatis me concessisse et hac presenti carta mea confirmasse donacionem illam, quam Iohannes constabularius Cestrie dedit et concessit in puram et perpetuam elemosinam abbatie de Loco Benedicto et monachis ibidem deo servientibus, illum scilicet locum qui vocatur Staneya cum omnibus pertinenciis suis. Et si constet quod inde aliquod servicium habere debeam, hoc eis omnino remitto pro salute anime mee et omnium antecessorum et heredum meorum. Et prohibeo ne quis ballivorum meorum pro servicio, quod predictus constabularius mihi debeat, animalia vel aliquas possessiones illorum nullo modo capiat, sed alibi, ubicumque voluerint, in terra constabularii namum capiant. Testibus Radulfo de Menylwarin, Radulfo filio Warini, Aluredo de Cumbray, Willelmo Patrik, Willelmo clerico.

The monastery of Locus Benedictus, or Stanlaw, was founded between 1172 and 1178 by John the constable, who secured the land in Stanney for his foundation by an exchange with Richard of Moore (*E.C.C.*, no. 2). As Earl Hugh was suspended until 1177 as a consequence of his part in the rebellion of 1173, it is safe to date his charter 1178–1181, probably nearer the earlier than the later year.

191.   Grant of freedom from toll in Chester for the monks of Stanlaw for everything they buy there for the needs of their house.

Chester, [1178–1181]

> Tabley MSS., Sir Peter Leycester's Liber C, pars II, f. 11v. (from original in possession of Towneley of Carre); B.L. Harl. MS. 2064, f. 66 (probably communicated by Sir Peter Leycester to Randle Holme); B.L. Egerton MS. 3126 (Whalley cartulary), f. 33; P.R.O., E. 132/7 (Exchequer Charter Rolls), no. 2 recto, charter 10 (witnesses omitted). Ed.: Orm., i. 27, and ii. 401 (from Leycester's Liber C); *Chart. Whalley*, i. 9.

H. comes Cestrie iusticiario, constabulario, dapifero, vicecom(iti), et omnibus baronibus suis et omnibus ministris suis et omnibus hominibus suis Francis et Anglicis tam presentibus quam futuris salutem. Sciatis me dedisse et concessisse et hac presenti carta mea confirmasse in puram et perpetuam elemosinam pro salute anime mee et pro anima patris mei et pro animabus antecessorum meorum abbatie de Benedicto Loco de Stanlawa et monachis ibidem deo servientibus quietantiam de theloneo in villa mea Cestrie de omnibus que prefati monachi ibi emerint ad opus sue dominice domus de Stanlawa. Testibus abbate Cestrie, Iohanne constabulario, Radulfo filio Warini, Hugone de Duttona, Iohanne Burdun, Martino Angevino, Adam de Duttona, et multis aliis apud Cestriam.

> SEAL: 'a ffayre seale, the earle on horsebacke'; reverse, a small gem, a griffin facing to left, beaded border, no legend.

For the abbey of Locus Benedictus or Stanlaw, founded by John the constable between 1172 and 1178, see **no. 190**. The phrase of the present charter 'ad opus sue dominice domus' perhaps refers to goods bought for furnishing the new monastery. The date is 1178–1181, probably after **no. 190**. John Burdun was a fairly frequent witness of John the constable's charters (*E.C.C.*, p. 19), but is also found under his son, Roger.

192. Grant to Pain, nephew of Isold, of the land (in Chester), which belonged to Lander and which Pain the sheriff formerly held, with all the liberties any other citizen enjoyed.

[c.1178]

> B.L. Add. Charter 49968; Engl. trans. (with facsimile) *J.C.A.S.*, N.S. x, pp. 15–16.

Hugo comes Cestrie constabulario, dapifero, iusticiario et omnibus baronibus suis, vicecom(itibus) et omnibus baillivis suis, et universis hominibus suis Francis et Anglicis tam presentibus quam futuris salutem. Sciatis me dedisse et concessisse et hac presenti karta mea confirmasse Pagano nepoti Isold et heredibus suis in feudo et in hereditate ad tenendam de me et de heredibus meis terram que fuit Landri, quam Paganus vicecomes tenuit et que est inter terram Harn et Willelmi filii Holdeber, libere et quiete, reddendo annuatim xvi denarios pro omni servicio. Et volo et firmiter precipio quod idem Paganus sit liber custumarius ex hac terra et heredes sui post ipsum. Et habeat plenariam consuetudinariam libertatem in feudo et hereditate, et quietanciam a theloneis, a prisonibus capiendis et custodiendis, a namis capiendis, a brevibus portandis, a vigiliis nocturnis faciendis, et ab omnibus huiusmodi consuetudinibus et vexationibus, sicut aliquis civium meorum, liberius habet consuetudinariam libertatem in tota civitate mea. Teste Roberto abbate Cestrie et Iohanne constabulario, Willelmo Patric, Alwredo de Cumbrai, Radulfo filio Warneri, Ricardo de Luvetot, Toma dispensatore, Frumbaldo de Ridford, Bertram camerario, Willelmo clerico, et multis aliis.

> SEAL on tag: missing.

As Abbot Robert did not succeed until 1175 and Earl Hugh was suspended for rebellion from 1173 to 1177, the present charter probably falls c.1178. It seems probable that Thomas Despenser (father of the Thomas who died in 1218), who is last mentioned in 1175–1176, died about this time. Pain, the sheriff of the city of Chester, was dead by 1178 (*Ches. Sheaf*, no. 6661). The other witnesses outlived the earl. Frumbald died shortly before 1184, Alured de Combray in 1186 or 1187, and John the constable in 1190, while William Patric survived until 1199.

Nothing further is known of Pain, or Pagan, the nephew of Isold, but he was evidently a member of a Chester family. By this charter he is constituted a *liber custumarius*, or free customary tenant, and the liberties entailed are specified. The earliest surviving Chester borough charters (**nos. 256, 257**) date from the time of Earl Ranulf III, but they specifically confirm the liberties and free customs enjoyed by the citizens under his predecessors. Already at the time of Domesday, the churches of St. John and St. Werburgh had houses in the city *quietas ab omni consuetudine* (*D.S.C.*, p. 92). It looks as though, in course of time, these liberties were extended by charter to individuals, such as Pain, and their heirs. For another instance, cf. **no. 267**.

193.   Grant to Ralph Mainwaring in marriage with his daughter Amicia of the service of Gilbert son of Roger, i.e. of three knights, to be held for the service of two knights.

Leek, [1178–1180]

> Orig.: J.R.U.L.M., Mainwaring MSS., Suppl. 2. Transcr.: Shakerley MSS., Liber C, f. 206; Bodleian Library, MS. Top. Cheshire b. I, p. 135; B.L. Add. MS. 6032, f. 6 (old f. 9). Abbreviated texts: B.L. Harl. MS. 506, f. 46 (old f. 92); Harl. 2079, f. 32 (old f. 63); Add. MS. 19517, f. 23v. (old p. 46); Bodleian Library, Dodsworth MS. 88, f. 12v.; Chester, Booth of Twemlow, Liber D, f. 143. Ed.: Dugdale, *Baronage*, i. 41 (from original); Orm., iii. 226; *10th Rep. Hist. MSS. Comm.*, App. pt. iv, p. 200 (from original).

H. comes Cestrie constabulario, dapifero et omnibus baronibus suis et universis baillivis et hominibus suis Francis et Anglicis tam presentibus quam futuris salutem. Sciatis me dedisse et concessisse et hac presenti karta mea confirmasse Radulfo de Meinilwarin cum Amicia filia mea in libero maritagio servicium Giliberti filii Rogeri, scilicet servicium trium militum, faciendo mihi servicium duorum militum ille et heredes sui mihi et heredibus meis. Quare volo et firmiter precipio, ut nullus super hoc eum vel heredes suos vexet vel amplius quam servicium duorum militum de hoc predicto tenemento requirat. Testibus R. abbate Cestrie, Bertraya comitisse Cestrie, Simone Thuschet, Rogero de Livet, Giliberto filio Pigot, Roberto fratre suo, Frumbaldo de Ridford, Willelmo de Meinilwarin, Roberto filio Hamonis, Bertram camerario, Roberto de Meinil-warin, Ranulfo de Lec, Radulfo clerico, Petro clerico, qui hanc kartam fecit, et multis aliis apud hec.

SEAL, on tag: missing.

This is the famous Amicia charter, which gave rise in the seventeenth century to a fierce controversy (printed in full in vols. 78–80 of the first series of Chetham Society publications) between Sir Peter Leycester and Sir Thomas Mainwaring. Today, probably, no one questions that Amicia was an illegitimate daughter of Hugh II. As Hugh was born in 1147, it is not difficult to calculate that the date of the present charter must be c.1180, or conceivably a year or two earlier. The name of Amicia's mother is not known. Ralph Mainwaring went on to a distinguished career, including a period as justiciar, and another who rose to prominence was Peter the clerk, the writer of the charter. He is almost certainly identical with Peter the earl's clerk, who was to become a leading figure under Ranulf III. His subsequent career is briefly outlined in *E.C.C.*, pp. 45–46.

194. Grant to Bertram his chamberlain in marriage with Mabel, daughter of William Fleming, of her inheritance of (Great) Meols.

Chester, [c.1180]

> J.R.U.L.M., Rylands Charter 1274 (fourteenth-century copy); B.L. Harl. MS. 2059, f. 242 (new f. 133v.) (from original, apparently in possession of William Brereton of Brereton). Engl. abstract: *Ches. Sheaf*, no. 6801.

H. comes Cestrie constabulario, dapifero, iusticiario, vicecom(iti), et omnibus baronibus suis et omnibus hominibus suis Francis et Anglis tam presentibus quam futuris salutem. Sciatis me dedisse et concessisse Bertram camerario meo Mabiliam filiam Willelmi Flamenc cum tota hereditate sua, scilicet Moles cum omnibus pertinentibus suis in bosco et in plano, in pratis et in pascuis, et in omnibus locis, illi et heredibus suis, qui de prefata Mabilia uxore sua nascentur, ad tenendum de me et de heredibus meis libere et quiete, sicut unquam aliquis antecessorum suorum melius et liberius tenuit, salvo servicio meo, scilicet quinta parte unius militis, sicut karta patris mei testatur. Testibus Bertram de Verdun, Iohanne constabulario Cestrie, Radulfo dapifero de Monte Alto, Roolant de Verdun, Thoma dispensatore, Giliberto filio Pigot, Willelmo Barbe Aprilis, et multis aliis, apud Cestriam.

> SEAL: 'Sealed with a great seale of white wax appendant per labell of parchment, wherein is printed a man on horseback armed at all points, his horse trapped etc., a lance in his right hand with a banner at the upper end etc., a shild on his left arme etc. The writing is broken away. On the backe syd ys two litle seales etc., a man's head with necke to the sholders, with a helmet on the head with somwhat on the toppe of the helmet moche like to fethars. A writing about theme bothe of + SIGILLUM GWILELMV̄ DE WALE.

Like Little Meols (**no. 171**), Great Meols had been held at the time of Domesday by Robert of Rhuddlan. Nothing is known of its subsequent history, but the present charter shows that it was held, presumably by William Fleming, for the service of one-fifth of a knight's fee in the time of Ranulf II. A *William Flandrensis* occurs as a witness in Ranulf I's reputed charter for St. Werburgh's (**no. 13**), but whether he was identical with the father of Mabel Fleming is not clear. The origin of Bertram the chamberlain is also not known, but there is some slight indication (*E.C.C.*, p. 40) that he may have come from Brittany. He quickly became an important figure in Cheshire administration, and is a frequent witness of charters under Earl Hugh and Ranulf III, down to c.1210. His marriage with Mabel Fleming probably took place c.1180. He had a daughter Alice who married into the Walsh family between 1195 and 1200 (*E.C.C.*, no. 17), and was succeeded by his son Henry, from whom the family of Meols descended. Ormerod's pedigree (Orm., ii. 494–5) is inaccurate.

Some interest attaches to the very detailed description of the seal in the Harleian manuscript. It does not correspond exactly to any of the known seals of Hugh II, but the obverse is perhaps closest to no. 5809 in the British Library catalogue. William Barbe d'Averill, the last witness of the present charter, is elsewhere described as the son of the earl's chaplain, Ralph Barbe d'Averill (**no. 123**) and as the earl's clerk (**no. 185**). At this time, presumably as an absentee, he held the valuable living of Belchford (Lincs.), which he made over on his death or resignation to the canons of Trentham (**no. 175**). Later, after the death of Earl Hugh, he appears as clerk of Hugh's widow, Countess Bertrada (**no. 251**). He clearly played an important part in Hugh II's secretariat, perhaps in a rôle equivalent to that of chancellor (*Chart. St. Werburgh*, p. xlviii), and on more than one occasion his seal – an antique gem with a portrait of two male heads conjoined – is used as a counter-seal on the reverse of Earl Hugh's great seal (**nos. 123, 146**). It is tempting to regard the counter-seal of the present charter as his, and to identify him with the Gwilelmus de Wale of the inscription. But the subject-matter of the present counter-seal, which seems to be identical with that of **no. 165**, is quite different. Furthermore, there is no reason to identify William de Wale, who is otherwise unknown, with William Barbe d'Averill. He may conceivably be identical with the William *clericus comitis* who witnessed **no. 165**. In general, it seems possible that Earl Hugh, whose own counterseal (with two male athletes in combat) is well attested, may have lost or been deprived of it during his captivity between 1173 and 1177, and fallen back in its place on those of his clerical staff, but the difficult question of Hugh's seals requires further clarification. None of the existing accounts is entirely satisfactory.

195.   Grant to Nicholas son of Liulf in free burgage of all the lands his father held of the earl on the day he was alive and dead.

Coventry, [1181]

Bodleian Library, Dodsworth MS.31, f. 94; MS. Top.

Cheshire b. I, p. 135; B.L. Harl. MS. 2079, f. 15 (new f. 7); Chester, Booth of Twemlow, Liber D, f. 142 (all MSS. abbreviated and defective, and appear to come from same source). Ed.: Coss, no. 10.

For a full text of this document, see Coss, *The Early Records of Medieval Coventry*, pp. 17–18 (no. 10).

Liulf of Brinklow, also known as Liulf of Coventry, had received a grant of land at Coventry from Ranulf II, which was confirmed and renewed by Hugh II (**nos. 145, 146**) fairly early in his tenure of the earldom. The present charter falls towards the end of his life, probably in 1181. Liulf was in debt to the Crown in 1178 (*P.R.S.*, xxviii, p. 114), and his debt was only discharged in 1187 (*P.R.S.*, xxxi, p. 94). His son Nicholas still owed 9 marks in 1183–84 out of 13 marks due to the earl of Chester (*P.R.S.*, xxxiii, p. 23), and was not quit until 1186–7 (*P.R.S.*, xxxvii, p. 118). It is fair to assume that this sum represented a relief in respect of the grant of his father's lands in the present charter. Nicholas was evidently the eldest son, and was still witnessing Ranulf III's charters as late as 1206–1208 (**no. 342**), but he had two younger brothers, Simon and Alan, who also received grants (**nos. 154, 155, 156, 168**) from Hugh II. The preponderance of local names among the witnesses clearly indicates that the present charter was given at Coventry.

196. Grant of the manor of Fallibroome to Richard Fitton and his heirs.

[1153–1181]

Bodleian Library, Dodsworth MS. 39, f. 118v. (from a parchment cartulary in the muniments of Sir George Booth of Dunham, 1636); Shakerley MS. 3 (*penes* Sir Arthur Bryant), p. 155. Engl. transl.: Earwaker, *East Cheshire*, ii. 346.

Hugo iadys counte de Cestre dona le manour de Falibrome ove lez appurtenances a monsieur Richard Phiton et a sez heres, lequel monsieur Richard avait un fiz appele Richard, que ascun temps fust justice de Cestre plus de vynt ans et auxi fust seneschal del counte de Richmonde 18 ans en le temps le counte Randolf.

This Anglo-French notice, dating apparently from 1438, is somewhat hesitantly included as providing, if genuine, the earliest evidence of the settlement of a branch of the Fittons (allegedly originating in Leicestershire) in Cheshire. No charter or notice of a charter has survived, and the present memorandum should be viewed with caution. The grantee was certainly not *Sir* Richard Fitton, and his son, far from being justiciar for 'more than twenty years', was justiciar between 1233 and 1237. On the other hand, Fallibroome remained in the possession of the Fittons of Bollin until the extinction of the direct line in the time of Henry IV (Orm., iii. 702), which lends credence to Hugh II's alleged grant. This cannot be dated, but, as the younger Richard Fitton survived until 1246, it is likely to have been later, rather than earlier, in Earl Hugh's lifetime.

197. Grant of serjeanty in the forest of Macclesfield to Adam of Sutton.

[1153–1181]

> P.R.O., CHES 17/12 (Eyre Roll, 15 Edw. I), m. 7v. Engl. text: *Chetham Soc.*, N.S. lxxxiv, p. 233. Ref.: Orm., iii. 757.

Ricardus de Sutton summonitus fuit ad ostendendum qualiter tenet duas bovatas terre, que solebant esse de dominico istius manerii de Maclisfeld.

Et Ricardus venit et dicit, quod Hugo comes Cestrie, pater Ranulfi comitis Cestrie, feoffavit quemdam Adam proavum suum de predictis duabus bovatis terre tenendas de comite Cestrie sibi et heredibus suis per sergantiam forestarii.

Sutton is Sutton Downes, near Macclesfield. Richard of Sutton explained that Earl Hugh's charter had unfortunately been destroyed by fire in the house of John of Sutton at the time of the first Welsh war in the present king's reign, while the king was staying in the manor of Macclesfield. This was in 1277 (*Ann. Cestr.*, p. 104). The jurors accepted the truth of this statement. The grantee is said to have been Adam son of Onyt, but his dates are not known. He was presumably one of the nine subordinate foresters (Orm., iii. 538–9), as the master fore-stership was conferred by Hugh II on Richard Davenport (**no. 176**). Later, in the time of Ranulf III, his serjeanty was conferred on Vivian Davenport (**no. 409**).

198. The brethren of the leper hospital of St. Giles at Boughton outside Chester are freed from replying before the justiciar, sheriff or other officials.

[1153–1181]

> P.R.O., CHES 34/4 (Quo Warranto), m. 45 (torn); B.L. Harl. MS. 2115, f. 195v. (new f. 169v.), from preceding; noted Orm., i. 352.

. . .Quoad habendum libertatem quod non respondeant coram iusticiario, vicecomite sive ministris aliis quibuscumque, dicunt quod quidam Hugo quondam comes Cestrie per litteras suas patentes sigillo scaccarii sui Cestrie sigillatas absque data diu ante tempus memorie concessit et carta sua confirmavit predictis fratribus leprosis per hec verba: 'Deo et infirmis fratribus apud sanctum Egidium deforis Cestriam existentibus' libertatem predictam; virtute quarum litterarum iidem fratres seisiti fuerunt ut de feodo et de iure de libertate illa.

Nothing is known of the origin and early history of the leper hospital at Boughton and no original charters of any of the Anglo-Norman earls survive, though Ranulf III is known to have ordered that small gifts of 20d. a year should be paid to it by St. Werburgh's abbey and the sheriff of Chester (**nos. 234, 237**). It seems unlikely that it was otherwise ignored, but the present notice and **no. 222** are the only evidence of grants having been made. In neither case is the evidence very good, as so often in answers to Quo Warranto proceedings. In particular, the claim that the brethren had letters patent under the seal of the exchequer of Chester is hopelessly anachronistic, but may be due to a misguided attempt to make the best possible case at a much later date or simply to misunderstanding or ignorance. On the other hand, the address of Hugh II's alleged charter, as quoted, is plausible enough. If the claim is accepted as genuine, it casts new light on the date of foundation. This has traditionally been attributed to Ranulf III (*Chart. St. Werburgh*, p. 96), but, in view of Hugh II's charter, it must be considerably earlier, probably under Ranulf II; for, as Helsby observes (Orm., i. 352, note d), 'hospitals of this kind were founded at a very early period'. Certainly Earl Hugh's action in freeing the lepers from answering before the justiciar and sheriff and other ministers seems to suggest that the hospital was already in existence.

199. Confirmation to Stoneleigh abbey of the gift of Robert fitz Walter and his wife Mabel of 34 acres in the soke of Kinesby (Kingsbury, Warws.).

[1155–1181]

Orig.: P.R.O., E.326 (Exchequer Aug. Office, Ancient Deeds, Series B), no. 12437.[1] Transcr.: Stratford-upon-Avon, Shakespeare's Birthplace, Gregory-Hood Leger Book, p. 221.

1. Original torn; text completed from transcript.

Hugo comes Cestrie omnibus hominibus suis Francis et Anglis salutem. Sciatis me concessisse et carta mea confirmasse deo et ecclesie sancte Marie de Stanleia et monachis eiusdem loci pro salute mea et pro anima patris mei xxxiii. acras terre in soca de Kinesbi, quas Rodbertus filius Walteri et Amabilis uxor sua in puram elemosinam eis dederunt, et cum predicta terra homines qui eandum terram tenent, scilicet Ricardum Cotun et Reginaldum de Adhurst. Quare volo et firmiter precipio quatinus predicti monachi illam prenominatam elemosinam teneant ita libere et quiete cum omnibus pertinentiis suis in bosco et in plano et in omnibus aliis locis, sicut idem Rodbertus et uxor eius eis dederunt et carta sua confirmaverunt. Teste[1] Willelmo Patrich, Radulfo capellano, Willelmo clerico filio eius, Lidulfo de Coventre, Nicholao filio Lidulfi, Simone fratre eius, et alii plures.[2]

SEAL: on tag, missing.

1. Text in monastic book-hand; witnesses added in other, less formal diplomatic minuscule.
2. alii plures *in orig.*

This charter is not easy to date. Amabilis, or Mabel, wife of Robert fitz Walter, was grand-daughter of Osbert of Arden, who gave Marston to Radmore abbey (**no. 94**), and it has been suggested that she and her husband gave the present land at Kingsbury to Stoneleigh, whither the monks of Radmore had migrated in 1155, because they were unable to warrant Osbert's gift (*Dugdale Society*, xxiv, p. xxxii); but the date of their charter (recorded in the Gregory-Hood Leger, p. 224) is not known. As William Patric outlived Hugh II (see below, p. 255) and Liulf of Coventry was apparently still alive in 1180 or 1181 (*P.R.S.*, xxxi, p. 94), internal evidence for dating is lacking. If Robert fitz Walter was grandson of the Robert fitz Richard who died in 1136 (*Book of Seals*, p. 102), as seems possible (*H.K.F.*, pp. 395–6), the date is likely to be later, rather than earlier in Hugh II's tenure of the earldom; but whether Robert was a member of the well-known baronial house of fitz Walter of Dunmow is, unfortunately, not clear.

200.   Confirmation of gifts of Ranulf II to Leicester abbey and grant of three carts to take timber in Quorndon wood for the canon's fire.

[1156–1181]

Bodleian Library, MS. Laud misc. 625, f. 19; B.L. Cott. MS. Vitell. F. xvii, f. 11v.[1]

Habemus ex concessione et confirmacione Hugoni comitis Cestrie omnia contenta in predicta carta[2] nobis concessa et confirmata, ut patet in ii carta. Et preterea per eandem ii. cartam habemus ex dono illius Hugonis tres carettas errantes in bosco de Querndona in perpetuum ad capienda ligna ad focum nostrum, ut patet in ii. carta.

1. For these MSS. see notes 1 and 2 to **no. 83**.
2. i.e. **no. 83**.

Unlike **no. 83**, Hugh II's charter for Leicester appears to have been overlooked, but the repeated references in the manuscripts to the 'first charter' (i.e. Ranulf II's) and the 'second charter' (i.e. Hugh's) sufficiently warrant its existence. Its date cannot be established, but it must fall after Henry II's confirmation (*Mon.*, vi. 467) of 1156 (Eyton, p. 17), otherwise Hugh's grant would surely have been included there.

201. Confirmation to the monks of Crowland abbey (Lincs.) of Walter of Lindsey's gift of the churches of Fordington and Ulceby.

[? 1165–1181]

Spalding, The Gentleman's Society, Crowland cartulary f. 192.

Notum sit omnibus, ad quos littere iste pervenerint, quod ego Hugo comes Cestrie ratam habeo donacionem quam fecit Walterus de Lindeseye monachis sancti Guthlaci Crulandie, sicut eius carta testatur, super ecclesiis de Fordingtona et Ulsebya, que fundate sunt in feodo meo. Inde est quod easdem ecclesias predictis monachis concedo et in perpetuam elemosinam confirmo et presentis carte testimonio corroboro. Testibus istis *etc.*

For Walter of Lindsey, see *H.K.F.*, p. 377. He occurs between 1165 and 1185, but his dates do not help to date this charter.

RANULF (III), EARL OF CHESTER (1181–1232)

202. Confirmation of Earl Ranulf's gift of 40s. a year to the nuns of Westwood (Worcs.)

[1181–1183]

Orig.: Birmingham Reference Library, 473629 D.V. 737.

Ricardus dei gratia Cantuariensis archiepiscopus . . . universis sancte matris ecclesie filiis, ad quos littere presentes pervenerint, salutem . . . Nos dilectis in Christo filiabus monialibus de Westwude divino ibidem servicio mancipatis omnes possessiones, quas ex donatione virorum aut mulierum nobilium vel aliis

iustis titulis rationabiliter sunt adepte, nostri scripti auctoritate duximus confirmare, specialiter autem possessiones subscriptis nominibus designatas, super
quibus cartas et instrumenta donatorum contrectavimus et oculis propriis
inspeximus . . . Ex donatione comitis Ranulfi Cestrie singulis annis xl. solidos in
elemosinam . . .

The nunnery of Westwood in Worcestershire was founded as a cell of Fontev-
rault in or about 1158 (*Mon.*, vi. 1004; Eyton, p. 36). Richard of Dover, from
whose confirmation the above extract is taken, and who there claims to have
seen the earl's charter with his own eyes, was archbishop of Canterbury from
1174 to 16 February 1184. Ranulf III's gift,of which this is the only surviving
record, must therefore have taken place between his accession in 1181 and
(probably) 1183.

203.   Confirmation of the gifts of his grandfather, Ranulf II, to Minting priory,
adding a gift of the tithes of the assart in the woods of Minting.

Belchford, [1186–1200]

> P.R.O., C. 53 (Chancery Charter Rolls), no. 123, m. 9.
> Ed.: Prou et Vidier, *Recueil des chartes de l'abbaye de
> Saint-Benoît-sur-Loire*, VI ii., p. 137; *Cal. Ch. Rolls*, iv.
> 378 (no. 3).

Ranulfus comes Cestrie Hugoni dei gratia Lincolniensi episcopo et capitulo
Lincolniensis ecclesie et constabulario suo et dapifero et iusticiario et
vicecom(iti) et baronibus et ministris et ballivis, et omnibus hominibus et amicis
suis Francis et Anglicis, et omnibus prelatis et filiis sancte matris ecclesie
salutem. Noverit universitas vestra me pro amore dei et pro salute anime mee et
animarum antecessorum meorum concessisse et hac presenti carta mea confirmasse omnes donaciones et libertates, quas Ranulfus comes Cestrie avus meus
dedit deo et beate Marie et sancto Jacobo et sancto Benedicto et monachis
eorum in Mentinges. Volo itaque et firmiter precipio quod predicti monachi
bene et quiete et libere et honorifice imperpetuum teneant omnia illa que
predictus avus meus eis dedit in predicta villa, sicut in carta ipsius continetur et
in carta patris mei confirmatur, ita quod de bosco meo de Mentingis capiant
quod eis necessarium erit decenter per visum forestariorum meorum. Preterea
dedi et concessi et hac carta mea confirmavi deo et sancte Marie et sancto Jacobo
et sancto Benedicto et predictis monachis decimam assarti de bosco predicto de
Mentingis in perpetuum habendam, sicut puram et perpetuam elemosinam.
Testibus hiis Simone de Kyma, Thoma dispensario, Ranulfo de Praeriis,
Gaufrido et Willelmo Farsy, Ricardo de Croile, Hugone et Ricardo de Bordele,
Ricardo de Peissun, Simone de Dribia, Philippo de Thateshale, Ricardo de

Waringwurthe, Roberto filio suo, Hasculpho de Praeriis, Radulfo filio Simonis, Rogero de Maletot, Rogero de Estreby, Roberto clerico ballivo Bentefordie, Thoma clerico presencium scriptore, et aliis multis apud Bentefordiam.

Ranulf II's gifts are set out in **no. 93**, and Hugh's confirmation is **no. 126**. Bishop Hugh, to whom Ranulf III's charter is addressed, was bishop of Lincoln from 1186 to 1200, and in spite of the large number of witnesses, it seems impossible to narrow the date of the charter more closely. For Ranulf and Hasculf de Praers, see **no. 251**.

204. Write to his officials at Trévières instructing them to hand over to the abbey of Montebourg the tithes of his mill at the pond of Trévières and of the fish in the pond, which they had withheld, and the same tithes in future.

[? 1187–1189]

MS. Paris lat. 10087 (Cart. de Montebourg, no. 135), p. 63.

Ranulfus comes Cestrie Ade filio Hugonis et duci[1] et aliis ministris suis de Treveris salutem. Sciatis quod ego reddidi abbatie de Montisburgo decimam molendini mei de stagno de Treveris et de piscibus eiusdem stagni. Quare precipio vobis, quod bene reddatis ei decimas illas, quas non reddidistis ex eo tempore, ex quo tenuistis, et illas, que venture sunt, ita quod non audiam amplius inde clamorem recti.[2]

1. *sic MS.*
2. recte *MS.*

For Hugh II's charter conveying the above tithes, see **no. 183**. Ranulf's writ suggests that the tithes were withheld during his minority, in which case his order to make restitution was probably issued shortly after he came of age and before 1189 when he began to use the title duke of Brittany. The term *dux* is not found in English usage; it is presumably the equivalent of bailiff or reeve.

205. Confirmation to Croxden abbey of a salt house in Middlewich given by Bertram of Verdun.

[? 1187–1194]

P.R.O., CHES 29/20 (Plea Rolls, 2 Edw. I), m. 30.

Quidam Ranulphus quondam comes Cestrie, cuius statum dominus rex nunc habet, concessit et confirmavit deo et beate Marie et abbatie Vallis sancte Marie de Crokesdene et monachis ibidem deo servientibus unam salinam in Midelwich, quam Bertramus de Verdon eis dedit, in puram et perpetuam elemosinam, liberam solutam et quietam a teloneo et auxilio et consuetudine et ab omni seculari servicio.

The Cistercian abbey of Croxden in Staffordshire was founded by Bertram of Verdun, who removed his nascent foundation there from the original site at Cotton in the valley of the Churnet in 1179 (*H.K.F.*, p. 259). Although neither Bertram's nor Ranulf III's charter is enrolled, the wording of this notice clearly reflects the terms of a genuine confirmation. Its date cannot be established, but the probability is that it falls before the death of Bertram in 1194 and after Ranulf attained his majority in 1187.

206. Confirmation to Bordesley abbey of his predecessors' gift of Combe.

Coventry, [3 February 1188–15 November 1189]

> Bodleian Library, Dugdale MS. 17, f. 54 ('penes W. Sheldon de Beoley in com. Wigorn., anno 1637'), facsimile with fine reproduction of obverse of seal.

Ranulfus dux Britannie, comes Cestrie et Richmondie constabulario suo, dapifero, iusticiario, vicecom(iti), barronibus,[1] ballivis, ministris suis et hominibus universis, Francis et Anglis, tam presentibus quam futuris salutem. Sciatis me concessisse et presenti carta mea confirmasse deo et monachis de Bordesea Cumbe cum omnibus eius pertinentiis pro salute anime mee et antecessorum meorum omnino[2] libere et quiete et plenarie in puram et perpetuam elemosinam, secundum quod testantur carte antecessorum meorum. Testibus Bertrada comitissa Cestrie, Iohanne constabulario, Radulfo seneschallo de Monte Alto, Iohanne de Salignio, Radulfo de Mesnilwarin, Ranulfo de Praers, Gaufrido de Buxerea, Henrico et Stephano de Longo[3] Campo, Avuredo de Salignio, et aliis quam pluribus apud Coventriam.

> SEAL: on tag, perfect; knight on horseback to right with sword uplifted in right hand, shield with cross, helmet, sword and horse's legs protruding into legend circle. Legend: SIGILLVM RANVLFI COMITIS CESTRIE.

1. *sic MS.*
2. ōnī *MS.*
3. Longa *MS.*

For the grants of Combe, nr. Chipping Campden (Gloucs.), here confirmed, see **nos. 100, 102, 148.** The present charter must date after Ranulf III's marriage to Constance of Brittany on 3 February 1188 and before John the constable's departure in March 1190 for the Holy Land, where he died (*Ann. Cestr.*, p. 41); but as it was confirmed by Richard I on 15 November 1189 (Harl. MS. 258, f. 133v., 'ex evidentiis Clementis Throckmorton de Haseley armigeris, 1640'), it is possible to narrow the date still further. Although Ranulf is here styled duke of Brittany and earl of Richmond, it is noteworthy that the seal he uses, the same as that on **no. 227**, is that of the earl of Chester; perhaps he had not yet acquired a seal designating him duke of Brittany.

207. Grant to Bordesley abbey of freedom from toll and all other dues on all that the monks shall buy or sell for their own use in Chester.

[1207–1217]

> Tabley MSS., Sir Peter Leycester's Liber C, pars II, f. 14v. (from original in possession of Sir Simon d'Ewes, E.E. no. 11); B.L. Harl. MS. 2060, f. 63 (new f. 35v.), and Harl. 2074, f. 158v. (new f. 53v.); Bodleian Library, Dodsworth MS. 31, f. 94v., and MS. Top. Cheshire b. I, p. 135; Chester, Booth of Twemlow, Liber D, f. 142 (all apparently from Leycester's copy of original). Ed.: *Book of Seals*, p. 79 (no. 116).

Ranulfus comes Cestrie constabulario, dapifero, iustic(iario), vicecom(iti) et omnibus baronibus suis, ministris et baillivis, et omnibus hominibus suis presentibus et futuris presentem cartam inspecturis et audituris salutem. Sciatis me dedisse et concessisse et presenti carta mea confirmasse deo et beate Marie de Bordeslei et monachis ibidem deo servientibus in puram et perpetuam elemosinam pro salute anime mee et antecessorum meorum quietanciam tholneti et omnium consuetudinum de omnibus que predicti monachi et homines sui emerint aut vendiderint in villa Cestrie ad proprios usus ipsorum monachorum. Et prohibeo super forisfacturam meam decem librarum, ne aliquis predictis monachis aut eorum hominibus de predicta quietancia grav-amen aut disturbacionem inferre presumat. Hiis testibus Philippo de Orreby tunc iusticiario Cestrie, Roberto de Quinci, Petro clerico, Waltero de Dayvilla, Roberto fratre suo, Henrico dispensario, Aluredo de Sullingny, Willelmo de Haslewelle, Elya pincerna, Iohanne de Bartona, Alano capellano, et multis aliis.

> SEAL: on tag, green wax, lion seal; legend SIGILLUM RANULPHI COMITIS CESTRIE.

The monks of Bordesley had been given a boat on the Dee at Chester by Hugh II (**no. 149**). The present grant cannot be dated more than approximately, but falls after Philip of Orreby's appointment as justiciar and before Ranulf III became earl of Lincoln in 1217. Robert of Quincy is presumably the Robert who married Ranulf's sister, Hawise (**no. 308**); this is the only occasion on which he is known to have witnessed any of Ranulf's charters.

208.   Confirmation of the liberties and grants conferred on Stanlaw abbey by Earl Hugh, his father.

Chester, [1188–1190]

B.L. Egerton MS. 3126, f. 33 (Whalley cartulary); P.R.O., E.133/7 (Exchequer Charter Rolls), m. 2 recto, no. 15 (omitting witnesses). Ed.: Orm., i. 38, and ii. 401–2; *Chart. Whalley*, i. 10 (no. 8).

Ranulfus dux Britannie, comes Cestrie et Richemundie, constabulario suo, dapifero, camerario et omnibus ministris suis, et omnibus baronibus et militibus suis, et omnibus hominibus suis Francis et Anglis, clericis et laicis, tam presentibus quam futuris salutem. Notum sit vobis omnibus me concessisse et hac carta mea confirmasse deo et abbatie de Loco Benedicto de Stanlawa et monachis ibidem deo servientibus omnes illas libertates et donaciones, quas eis fecit comes Hugo pater meus et prout carta sua, quam habent monachi predicti, testatur. Testibus Iohanne constabulario Cestrie, Petro cancellario, Radulfo de Maynilwaringe, Hugone de Boidell, Ranulfo de Praeriis, apud Cestriam.

As Ranulf III married Constance of Brittany on 3 February 1188 and John the constable left for the Holy Land, where he died at the siege of Acre, in March 1190, the date of the present charter is narrowly circumscribed. It seems to imply that Earl Hugh had issued a general charter of confirmation for Stanlaw. If so, it has not survived, Hugh's only surviving charters being **nos. 190** and **191**, neither of which falls into this category. Peter the chancellor who witnesses the present charter is presumably identical with Peter the clerk, or the earl's clerk, who figures prominently under Ranulf III; but there is no reason to believe that his title *cancellarius* was official, and it is otherwise only found descriptively in a private charter of c.1220 (*E.C.C.*, p. 46). However, there is also a Thomas *cancellarius* (**nos. 247, 289**).

209.   Grant to the monks of Stanlaw of freedom from taking wild animals killed on their land to Chester; neither they nor their men are to be impleaded on account of any beast found dead on their land, unless a *sacreber* wishes to pursue the matter against them, and they are to be free from the earl's serjeants and foresters.

Frodsham, [c.1190–1200]

> B.L. Harl. MS. 2064, f. 66 (in Sir Peter Leycester's writing, from original with Towneley of Carre, with drawing of seal); Egerton MS. 3126 (Whalley cartulary), f. 33v.; P.R.O., CHES 33/4 (Forest Rolls, 20–21 Edw. III), m. 30; D.L. 39/1/19 (Forest Pleas, 21 Edw. III), m. 26; E. 132/7 (Exchequer Charter Rolls), m. 2 recto, no. 16 (omitting witnesses). Abbreviated texts: Harl. MS. 139, f. 237v. (new f. 206v.); Sloane 1301, f. 268v. Ed.: Orm., i. 38, and ii. 402; *Chart. Whalley*, i. 11 (no. 11).

Omnibus sancte matris ecclesie filiis, ad quos presens pagina pervenerit, Ranulfus comes Cestrie salutem. Notum sit vobis me dedisse et hac carta mea confirmasse deo et beate Marie et monachis de Stanlawa quietanciam de bestiis silvestribus occisis vel attinctis in terra ipsorum monachorum portandis usque ad Cestriam, et quod dicti monachi et eorum homines non incausentur propter aliquam bestiam aliquo casu mortuam et inventam in terra eorum, nisi fuerit aliquis sacreber, qui de hoc loqui voluerit adversus dictos monachos aut eorum homines, et quod sint quieti de servientibus et forestariis. Testibus hiis Rogero constabulario Cestrie, Warino de Vernon, Hamone de Mascy, Philippo de Orreby, Willelmo de Venables, Ricardo de Aldefordia, Adam et Hugone de Duttona, Petro clerico, Thoma dispensario, Colino de Quatuor Maris, Radulfo de Munfichet, Galfrido de Duttona, Adam de Byri, et multis aliis apud Frodesham.

SEAL: lion seal, legend gone save . . . CEST . . .

This exemption from the rigours of forest law is not easily dated, unless the appearance of Roger the constable without the surname Lacy points to the period 1190–1194. Colin de Quatremares witnessed the charter by which Roger acquired the Lancashire barony of Penwortham in 1205 (*L.P.R.*, p. 350) and a later charter (c.1208) for Stanlaw (*Chart. Whalley*, ii. 591). Like the Duttons, and probably Ralph de Munfichet, he evidently witnesses here as one of the Constable's men. The same is probably true of Adam de Byri (Bury, Lancs.), who appears on the Lancashire Pipe Roll of 1194 (*L.P.R.*, p. 77). As Philip of Orreby appears without the title of justiciar, the date is presumably before 1207. For the *sakeber* or sacreber, who pursued and inflicted summary justice on the 'hand-having' thief, or the man caught red-handed, see Pollock and Maitland, *History of English Law*, ii. 160, 496; by this time, as the charter indicates, this ancient procedure was exceptional and on the way out.

210. Writ to the justiciar of Cheshire, notifying him that he has freed the monks of Stanlaw from the forinsec service due from the land at Acton which they hold for a term of years from Richard of Aston.

Le Mans, [1194–1198]

B.L. Egerton MS. 3126 (Whalley cartulary), f. 167, no. 9.
Ed.: *Chart. Whalley*, ii. 392 (no. 9).

Ranulphus comes Cestrie iusticie sue de Cestrisiria salutem. Sciatis quod de terra de Actona, quam monachi de Stanlawa habent ad terminum de Ricardo de Estona, eis dedi quietantiam de servicio, quod ad me pertinet, scilicet de forinseco servicio, quamdiu monachi illi terram predictam tenebunt de eodem Ricardo. Teste me ipso apud Cenomanniam.

Richard of Eston or Aston appears fairly frequently as a witness of Roger the constable and others c.1190–1200 (*E.C.C.*, pp. 17, 18, 24, 35), and there is a charter of his granting land at Stockton Heath to Adam of Dutton, c.1190–99 (ibid., pp. 33–34). His grant for a term of years to Stanlaw has not survived, no doubt because it was superseded by his outright gift (*Chart. Whalley*, ii. 385–6); but there is a charter of Roger de Lacy, the constable (ibid., p. 393) quitclaiming the service due 'from the land of Acton which the monks have from Richard of Eston for thirty years'. This is obviously the counterpart of Earl Ranulf's quitclaim, which must have been issued about the same time. Ranulf accompanied Richard I to Normandy in 1194, and was there most of the time during the French wars which occupied Richard's last years. It is impossible to say exactly when he was at Le Mans, where his writ was issued; but it can safely be dated during the period 1194–98.

211.   Disafforestation of the abbey of Stanlaw and the grange of Stanney.

[1207–1211]

Tabley MSS., Sir Peter Leycester's Liber C, pars II, f. 12v. (from original with Towneley of Carre). P.R.O., D.L. 39/1/19 (Forest Pleas), m. 26; CHES 29/23 (Plea Rolls, 5 Edw. I), m. 3 (omitting witnesses); CHES 33/2 (Forest Rolls, 14 Edw. I), m. 3v.; CHES 33/4 (Forest Rolls, 20–21 Edw. III), m. 30; E.132/7 (Exchequer Charter Rolls), m. 2 recto, no. 14 (omitting witnesses); B.L. Egerton MS. 3126, f. 33v. (Whalley cartulary); Add. 10,374 f. 147v. (from Forest Pleas, 14 Edw. I); Harl. MS.

2064, f. 66 (Peter Leycester's copy). Ed.: Orm., ii. 402
(from Leycester's Liber C); *Chart. Whalley*, i. 10 (from
Egerton MS.)

Omnibus Christi fidelibus, ad quos presens scriptum pervenerit, Ranulphus
comes Cestrie salutem. Noverit universitas vestra quod ego pro salute anime
mee et omnium antecessorum meorum et successorum et dilecti mei Rogeri de
Laci constabularii Cestrie deforestavi abbatiam de Stanlawe et grangiam de
Staneia, que est de feudo predicti Rogeri constabularii Cestrie, cum omnibus
pertinenciis suis per certas divisas suas. Et sint omnino liberi et quieti de
omnibus causacionibus, querelis et placitis et serviciis ad forestam pertinentibus
in puram et perpetuam elemosinam. Hiis testibus Radulfo abbate de Pultona,
Guidone priore de Suwico, Philippo de Orreby tunc iusticiario Cestrie, Henrico
de Audeleye, Hugone Despensir, Thoma fratre suo, Hugone de Duttona,
Gaufrido fratre suo, Hugone de Pasci, et multis aliis.

SEAL: lion seal.

According to Ormerod (ii. 398) this grant was made during the first year of
Abbot Osbern, who succeeded after 24 August 1209; but he provides no
evidence. It must nevertheless fall within the period 1207–1211, and it appears
that it was given at the instance of Roger de Lacy, the patron of the abbey.
Stanlaw had already received a partial release from forest law a dozen or more
years earlier (**no. 209**). Stanney was part of the original foundation (*E.C.C.*, p.
6).

212. Grant to Stanlaw abbey of 20s. a year from the shrievalty of Chester, until
he has made better provision in land or otherwise.

[1207–1211]

Orig.: West Suffolk Record Office, Bury St. Edmunds, E.
18/710. Transcr.: B.L. Egerton MS. 3126 (Whalley
cartulary), ff. 33v.–34; P.R.O., E.132/7 (Exchequer Charter Rolls), m.2 recto, no. 17 (omitting witnesses). Ed.:
Chart. Whalley, i. 12 (no. 12).

Rannulphus comes Cestrie constabulario suo et dapifero, iusticiario, vicecomiti,
baronibus et ballivis suis, et omnibus hominibus et amicis suis salutem: Sciatis
me pro dei amore et pro salute anime mee et animarum antecessorum meorum
et successorum concessisse et dedisse et presenti carta mea confirmasse deo et
beate Marie et abbatie de Stanlawa et monachis ibidem deo servientibus in
puram et perpetuam elemosinam viginti solidos annuos in vicecomitatu meo de

Cestria sine dilatione vel retinemento percipiendos in vigilia Natalis domini per manum vicecomitis mei, quicumque sit vicecomes, nullo alio precepto inde expectato, quousque eis alibi melius providerim in terra vel in alio beneficio. Hanc autem elemosinam warantizabimus ego et heredes mei in perpetuum predicte abbatie et monachis. Hiis testibus Rogero de Lasci constabulario Cestrie, Philippo de Orreby iusticiario Cestrie, Hugone et Henrico dispensariis, Petro clerico de Cestria, Hugone et Gaufrido de Dutton, Rogero et Willelmo de Mesnilwarin, Iosceramo de Hellesby, Ricardo de Kyngesley, et multis aliis.

SEAL: on tag, lion seal.

This charter must fall after the appointment of Philip of Orreby as justiciar and before the death of Roger the constable, i.e. 1207–1211. The charge, it will be noted, falls on the sheriff of the city of Chester. Though there is plenty of earlier evidence of the existence of a separate sheriff for the city (*Chart. St. Werburgh*, pp. xlix–1), this is the first specific reference to a separate *vicecomitatus* (or shrievalty).

213.   Quittance of toll on salt and anything else the monks of Stanlaw buy or sell for their own use.

Chester, [1208–1211]

Tabley MSS., Sir Peter Leycester's Liber C, pars. II, f. 12 (from original of Towneley of Carre); B.L. Harl. MS. 2064, f. 66v. (copy provided by Leycester); B.L. Egerton MS. 3126, f. 33 (Whalley cartulary); P.R.O., CHES 29/59 (Plea Rolls, 22 Edw. III), m. 22v.; E.132/7 (Exchequer Charter Rolls), m. 2 recto, no. 18 (omitting witnesses). Ed.: Orm., i. 38; *Chart. Whalley*, i. 10 (no. 9).

Ranulfus comes Cestrie constabulario suo et dapifero, iusticie et vicecomiti, baronibus et ballivis suis salutem. Sciatis me pro dei amore et pro salute anime mee dedisse et hac carta mea confirmasse in perpetuam et puram elemosinam deo et sancte Marie et monachis Loci Benedicti de Stanlawa quietanciam de tolneio per totam terram meam de sale et de omnibus aliis rebus quas emerint vel vendiderint ad usus suos proprios tam per aquam quam per terram. Quare firmiter precipio ne aliquis ab eis tolneium exigat, nec propter tolneium eos vexare aut molestare presumat. Testibus hiis Rogero constabulario Cestrie, Philippo de Orreby tunc iusticiario Cestrie, Warino de Vernon, Willelmo de Venables, Petro clerico, Adam et Hugone de Dutton, Liulpho vicecomite, Alexandro filio Radulfi, Bertramo camerario, Iosceramo de Hellesby, et multis aliis apud Cestriam.

SEAL: 'a faire seale, the same with the former above mentioned', i.e. lion seal.

This charter must fall between Philip of Orreby's appointment as justiciar, probably in 1207, and the death of Roger the constable (1211). Bertram the chamberlain and Adam of Dutton probably died c.1210 (*E.C.C.*, pp. 22, 39), and Liulf may have ceased tó function as sheriff about this time (*ibid.*, pp. 46–7), but the evidence in all three cases is inconclusive.

214. Confirmation to Henry Despenser, his knight, of the vill of Wynlaton (Willington, Edisbury hundred), which William son of Henry, lord of Stapleford, had given him.

[1210–1215]

B.L. Egerton MS. 3126 (Whalley cartulary), f. 193v.; P.R.O., E.132/7 (Exchequer Charter Rolls), m. 2, no. 22 (witnesses omitted). Short notice: B.L. Harl.MS. 2060, f. 79. Ed.: *Chart. Whalley*, ii. 470 (from Egerton MS.)

Ranulphus comes Cestrie constabulario, dapifero, iusticiario, vic(ecomiti) et omnibus baronibus suis, ministris et ballivis, et omnibus hominibus suis Francis et Anglicis, presentibus et futuris, presentem cartam inspecturis et audituris, salutem. Sciatis me concessisse et presenti carta mea confirmasse Henrico dispensario militi meo et heredibus suis totam villam de Wynlatona[1] cum omnibus pertinentiis et aisiamentis et libertatibus suis, illam scilicet quam Willelmus filius Henrici, dominus de Stapelfordia ei dedit, habendam et tenendam ipsi Henrico et heredibus suis, sicut carta predicti Willelmi testatur, quam ipse Henricus de eo habet. Et ut illa donatio predicti Willelmi et hec mea concessio perpetue firmitatis robur optineat, eas presenti scripto et sigillo meo confirmavi. Hiis testibus Rogero de Monte Alto dapifero meo, Philippo de Orreby tunc iusticiario meo, Henrico de Aldithlea, Petro clerico meo, Warino de Vernon, Willelmo de Venables, Hugone et Thoma et Roberto et Galfrido dispensariis, Waltero de Daivilla,[2] Normanno Pantulf, Aluredo de Suligneio, Rogero de Meynilwarin, Iohanne de Arderna, Hamone de Mascy, Davide de Salopesberia, Ivone[3] de Caletot, Roberto de Say, Roberto de Daivilla,[2] Ricardo de Kyngesley, et multis aliis.

1. Winfletona, *Exch. roll.*
2. Danvilla *MS.*
3. Idone *MS.*

Henry Despenser was one of the brothers of Thomas Despenser, who held the adjacent manor of Barrow (**no. 357**) and died in 1218. William of Stapleford's charter, granting Henry Wynlaton (Orm., ii. 338), was witnessed by Earl Ranulf and many of the witnesses of the present charter, and is of approximately the same date. Henry Despenser then gave Wynlaton to the monks of Stanlaw (*Chart. Whalley*, ii. 467), which explains the presence of the present charter among the abbey's muniments. Its date can be fixed approximately by reference to Roger of Montalt who succeeded his brother Robert as seneschal before 1211 (*E.C.C.*, p. 17), and it is noticeable that no fewer than 11 of the 21 witnesses also witnessed Earl Ranulf's Charter of Liberties of 1215 (**no. 394**).

215.   Quittance for the monks of Stanlaw from the duty of feeding his serjeants and foresters in respect of their vill of Wynlaton (Willington in Edisbury hundred).

[1221–1229]

> P.R.O., CHES 33/4 (Forest Rolls, 20–21 Edw. III), m. 30; D.L.39/1/19 (Forest Pleas), m. 26; E.132/7 (Exchequer Charter Rolls), m. 2, no. 23; B.L. Egerton MS. 3126, f. 194. Ed.: *Chart. Whalley*, ii. 470 (no. 4) (from Egerton MS.)

Ranulfus comes Cestrie et Lincolnie omnibus presentem cartam inspecturis vel audituris salutem. Sciatis me pro deo et salute anime mee et antecessorum meorum concessisse et dedisse et hac presenti carta mea confirmasse abbatie de Stanlawa et monachis ibidem deo servientibus in puram et perpetuam elemosinam quietanciam de me et heredibus meis imperpetuum de pultura servientium et forestariorum meorum, scilicet de villa de Wynlaton.[1] Quare volo et firmiter precipio quod dicta abbatia et dicti monachi dictam quietanciam habeant imperpetuum pacifice et sine impedimento. Et in huius rei testimonium presentem cartam sigillo meo munitam eis habere feci. Hiis testibus Philippo de Orreby tunc iusticiario Cestrie, Fulcone filio Warini, Nicholao de Lettres, Galfrido de Duttona, Thoma de Orreby, Ricardo de Sondbache, Ricardo de Kingesley, Roberto le Gros Venour, Petro de Frodesham, Ranulfo de Thorintona, Simone et Petro clericis, et multis aliis.

1.   *sic Egerton MS.;   other MSS. have* Winfleton.

For the grant of Wynlaton to Stanlaw by Henry Despenser, see **no. 214**. The present charter is evidently a good deal later in date, to judge from the witnesses, nearer the end of Philip of Orreby's tenure of the justiciarship; but it cannot be dated accurately.

216. Confirmation to Stephen, clerk of Chipping Campden (Gloucs.), of the church of St. Mary of Campden, bestowed on him by Robert the abbot and the convent of Chester.

[1188–1194]

B.L. Harl. MS. 1965, f. 8 (new f. 11). Ed.: *Chart. St. Werburgh*, p. 138 (no. 120).

Ranulphus comes Cestrie confirmavit Stephano clerico de Campedena ecclesiam sancte Marie de Campedena, sicut carta Roberti abbatis et conventus Cestrie testatur, qui ei ecclesiam predictam contulerunt.

Chipping Campden belonged to Earl Hugh I in 1086, and its tithes were given to St. Werburgh's at the foundation, but there is no record that the advowson passed to the abbey. Campden appears to have been lost temporarily to Ranulf II during the troubles of Stephen's reign (**no. 59**), but was recovered by 1147 at latest, only to be forfeited to the Crown after Hugh II's rebellion in 1173 and given to Hugh de Gondeville, who was in possession as late as 1180, and perhaps until 1184 (*Trans. Bristol and Gloucs. Arch. Soc.* ix, pp. 139–141). It was still being tallaged with the royal demesne in 1187 (*H.K.F.*, p. 53) but appears to have been restored to Ranulf III shortly afterwards, probably on his majority and marriage in 1188. The present grant, of which this notice is the only evidence, therefore probably falls between 1188 and the resignation of Abbot Robert Hastings in 1194. The living of Campden later passed to Patrick, son of Peter the clerk, probably by 1208 (**no. 283**).

217. Confirmation of Robert fitz Harding's gift of Fifehead to St. Augustine's abbey, Bristol, with the consent of Earl Ranulf II.

[1188–1199]

Berkeley Castle, Gloucs., Cartulary of St. Augustine's, f. 30.

Rannulfus dux Britannie et comes Cestrie et Richemundie omnibus tam presentibus quam futuris, qui hanc cartam viderint et audierint, salutem. Sciatis me concessisse et hac mea carta confirmasse donationem illam de terra de Fifhida, quam Robertus filius Harding dedit ecclesie sancti Augustini de Bristolio et canonicis regularibus ibidem deo servientibus, concessu domini Rannulfi comitis avi mei. Et ideo volo et precipio quod predicti canonici eandem terram bene et pacifice liberam et quietam ab omni servitio et exactione de me et de meis heredibus in perpetuum teneant, sicut carta domini comitis Ranulfi avi mei testatur. Testibus *etc.*

For Ranulf II's charter, see **no. 87**. As the witnesses of the present confirmation are omitted, it can only be dated by reference to Ranulf III's title as duke of Brittany. There is also evidence, in a confirmation of John, count of Mortain, dating from 1189–91 (Patterson, p. 49, no. 31) that Ranulf II, in addition to Fifehead, had given the churches of St. Leonard, St. Nicholas and All Saints in Bristol, but no charter and no confirmation by any of Ranulf II's successors survives.

218.   Grant of the tithes of all his lands and rents in Coventry to the churches of St. Mary, St. Michael, St. Chad and St. Giles, and to his chaplain, Ralph, and his successors in the chapel of St. Michael and all the chapels pertaining to it. [? Spurious]

[1188–1192]

> P.R.O., C.53 (Chancery Charter Rolls), no. 135 (inspeximus of Edw. III), m. 5; B.L. Add. MS. 32100, f. 59v. (seventeenth-century transcript from original inspeximus, 22 Edw. III). Ed.: *Cal. Ch. Rolls*, v. 102 (no. 10); Coss, no. 14; brief mention, Dugdale, *Warwickshire*, pp. 102, 106.

For a full text of this document, see Coss, *The Early Records of Medieval Coventry*, pp. 21–2 (no. 14).

This rather unusual charter is not easy to evaluate, but there is little doubt that it is connected with the conflict between the bishop of Chester, or Lichfield, and the prior and monks of Coventry, which came to a head in 1189 when Bishop Hugh Nonant was empowered to appoint the prior and then, in 1190–91, brought the priory under his own control, expelled the monks and installed secular canons in their place (*V.C.H. Warws.*, ii. 53; *V.C.H. Staffs.*, iii. 24). It seems possible that the present charter was fabricated on the bishop's behalf in the course of this conflict. Its effect, as Coss pointed out, was to take the disposal of the tithes out of the hands of the prior and place it in the hands of the bishop. It also ensured that they should not go only into the coffers of the priory church (St. Mary's), but were to be shared with the cathedral church of Lichfield (St. Chad), St. Giles (conceivably the canonry of Calke and Repton in Derbyshire), and specifically with St. Michael's, the chapel of the earl's fee of Coventry, which the prior of St. Mary's had been endeavouring to reduce to dependence ever since the time of Ranulf II (**nos. 114, 177, 178**). All this was evidently in the bishop's interest. Furthermore, there are features which make it at least doubtful whether the charter is a genuine charter of Ranulf III. One is the appearance of Gilbert, son of Picot, as the first witness. Gilbert was a regular witness of Hugh II's charters, but under Ranulf III his place was taken by his brother Robert, and this is the only occasion after 1181 on which he occurs, a gap of approximately ten years which is difficult to explain.[1] More significant, perhaps, is the invocation, in the last clause of the charter, of the penalty of anathema, a spiritual penalty normally reserved to ecclesiastics, which has no place in a secular charter and seems to point to a clerical origin. Finally, its relationship to Ranulf III's charter of 30 July 1192 for Coventry priory (**no. 219**) casts further doubt on its authenticity. A striking feature of the present charter is the emphasis it places on the independent rights of the earl's chaplain, Ralph, and his successors at St. Michael's and its avoidance of anything suggesting the subordination of St. Michael's to St. Mary's. On 30 July 1192, on the other hand, Ranulf specifically recognized the right of the 'mother church' of Coventry over St. Michael's and its dependent chapels, including the right to the tithe. If the present charter were genuine, this would be a remarkable reversal, and the unlikelihood of such a sudden reversal is perhaps another indication that the present charter is not a genuine charter of Ranulf III. In any case, it is inconceivable that the present charter was issued after **no. 219**, and its approximate date, whether genuine or not, may therefore safely be placed between Ranulf III's marriage to Constance of Brittany in 1188 and 30 July 1192.

1. Gilbert son of Picot appears on the Warwickshire Pipe Roll every year from 1170 (*P.R.S.*, xvi, p. 95) to 1177 (*P.R.S.*, xxvi, p. 27), but then disappears. A Gilbert son of Picot is mentioned in 1189–90 under Northampton (*P.R.S.*, N.S. i, p. 30), and a Gilbert Pycot in Leicestershire (*H.K.F.*, p. 71), but it is unlikely that they were the same person. The name is not particularly unusual. Another Gilbert Picot gave land to Poulton abbey in Cheshire in 1210 (*D.C.*, nos. 89, 90).

219. Acknowledgement of the right of the church of Coventry in the chapel of St. Michael situated in his fee in the town of Coventry and gift of the other chapels pertaining to it, which gift he made publicly and solemnly in the church of Coventry, placing his charter on the altar and investing the church with a golden ring.

Coventry, 30 July 1192.

        P.R.O., C.53 (Chancery Charter Rolls), no. 135, m. 4; B.L. Add. MS. 32100 (transcript from inspeximus of Edward III), f. 60v. Ed.: *Cal. Ch. Rolls*, v. 102 (no. 13); Coss, no. 13. Brief reference: Dugdale, *Warwickshire*, p. 102, and Dugdale, *Baronage*, i. 44 (both from inspeximus).

For a full text of this document, see Coss, *The Early Records of Medieval Coventry*, pp. 20–21 (no. 13).

The authenticity of this charter is vouched for by an entry in the *Magnum Registrum Album* of Lichfield cathedral under the year 1238 (*Hist. Coll. of*

Staffordshire, 1924, p. 241, no. 500), settling a dispute between the bishop and the prior and convent of Coventry over the custody of the charter and the gold ring attached to it, in which the actual date (30 July 1192) is specifically mentioned. The charter itself falls into two distinct parts. In the first part Ranulf III recognizes in general terms the rights of the church of Coventry in the chapel of St. Michael and in other chapels already established or to be established in future, after receiving the testimony of a number of people and after inspecting the charters of Ranulf II and Hugh II 'who gave the aforesaid chapel of St. Michael to the church of Coventry in perpetual alms'. In the second part he specifies by name fourteen chapels and townships attached to St. Michael's, and says he has given them to the church of Coventry at the behest of Bishop Hugh Nonant. But these chapels had already been conveyed to Coventry in the reputed charters of Ranulf II (**no. 114**) and Hugh (**no. 178**), and it is a little unusual that Ranulf III makes no reference, in listing them by name, to the preceding grants, if the latter were genuine. In fact, he writes of them quite specifically as his own gift, and the probability is that his solemn act in the church of Coventry, when he conveyed them to the prior and convent with a gold ring, was the first specific grant of the chapels and places mentioned. In general terms Ranulf II and Hugh II had conveyed the chapel of St. Michael 'with all its appurtenances' (**no. 177**), but the specification by name of the 'appurtenances' comes almost certainly at a later stage, and the likelihood is that **nos. 114** and **178** were fabricated with this in view. The two charters were evidently produced for Ranulf III's inspection and approval, and he clearly accepted them at face value; but that does not imply that they should necessarily be regarded as authentic.

220.   Grant to David, earl of Huntingdon, brother of the king of Scotland, in marriage with Earl Ranulf's sister Matilda, of land to the value of £60, one half in Baddow (Essex) and the other half in Greetham, Goulceby, Hemingby and Asterby (Lincs.), together with the service of fifteen knights.

[August 1190]

Orig.: B.L. Cott. Charter xxiv, 15 (badly damaged by fire). Transcript: Bodleian Library, Dugdale MS. 18, f. 82v. Words in square brackets are supplied from the transcript.

Rannulfus comes Cestrie omnibus tam futuris quam presentibus, ad quos presens carta pervenerit, salutem. Notum sit vobis omnibus me dedisse et presenti carta mea confirmasse comiti David fratri regis Scottorum in libero maritagio cum Ma[ti]l[da] sorore mea s[exa]ginta [libra]tas terre, scilicet Badewennam in Esexa cum pertinenciis suis pro xxx. libratas terre, et G[raham] in Ly[nde]s[ei] et quicquam habui in Golgesby et in Emmungeby et in Cisterby cum ceteris terris et redditibus, quas ballivi mei ei assignabunt ad xxx. libratas terre perficiendas, et servicium quindecim militum, scilicet de Willelmo de Haringtona servicium duorum militum, de G[ilberto] de Thurs servicium trium militum, de Willelmo de Bracolo unius militis, de Ricardo de Lyndesei unius militis, et octo milites, qui ei desunt, ei perficere debeo: tenendum predicto comiti et heredibus suis, qui de predicta sorore mea pervenerint, de me et de meis heredibus tam libere et quiete sicud aliquod liberum maritagium melius et liberius tenetur in terra domini regis Anglie. Hiis testibus Willelmo comite de Ferrariis, Baudewino Wac, Radulfo de Mesnilwarin, Simone de sancto Lycio, Wakelino filio Stephani, Bartholomeo monacho, Henrico filio Wakelini, Rogero de Camvilla, Radulfo [vicecomite], Iuhello de Luvigneio, Philippo de Orreby, et multis aliis.

The marriage of Earl David and Matilda took place on 19 August 1190 (*H.K.F.*, p. 83). There is no reason to suppose that the present elaborate charter, with an illuminated initial and a red and gold border, was not issued at the same time, though no doubt it was preceded by negotiations over the dowry. The offspring of the marriage was John the Scot, who succeeded to the earldom on Earl Ranulf's death in 1232.

221. Confirmation to the hospital of St. John the Baptist outside the Northgate of Chester of the site of the house, which he takes under his protection, granting the brethren the right to preach and collect alms throughout Cheshire for the support of the poor.

Chester, [1190–1194]

P.R.O. C.66 (Chancery Patent Rolls), no. 102, m. 23; Ed.: *H.S.L.C.*, lxxviii, pp. 66–7.

Ranulfus dux Britannie et comes Cestrie et Richemundie constabulario, dapifero, iusticiis,[1] vicec(omitibus), baronibus, balivis et ministris suis et omnibus hominibus suis Francis et Anglis tam presentibus quam futuris salutem. Notum sit vobis me dedisse et concessisse et hac presenti carta confirmasse deo et sancte Marie et omnibus sanctis domum hospitalem et locum totum, in quo fundata est extra portam aquilonalem Cestrie ad suscepcionem pauperum, in puram et perpetuam elemosinam pro anima patris mei et animabus omnium antecessorum meorum, ita libere et quiete ab omni servicio, ab omni molestia et omni exaccione seculari ut in ea nichil michi retineam preter oraciones et elemosinas puras. Inde est quod universitatem vestram scire volo, quod predictam domum hospitalem in mea propria manu et in mea protectione suscipio ut puram et liberam elemosinam meam, et precipio ut nulli servituti sit subiecta, preterquam solo hospitalitati et suscepcioni pauperum Christi. Omnes eciam redditus eiusdem domus, omnes res et omnia iura et libertates, et cetera omnia ei pro Christi nomine racionabiliter collata, rata et firma habeo et sigilli mei municione confirmo, et firmiter precipio super forisfacturam meam ne quis sepedicti domui in aliquo detrahat aut aliquam ei molestiam inferat aut gravamen, set eam pro dei amore et nostro, in quantum poteritis, promovere studeatis. Et precipio quod per Cestresiram fratres predicti hospitalis ad predicacionem et ad elemosinarum collectionem ad pauperum sustentacionem honorifice suscipiantur. Testibus Radulfo de Menilgarin,[2] Rogero filio comitis, Rogero constabulario, Hugone de Bosco Ale, Alano de Bosco Ale, Henrico de Lungocampo[3] et Stephano fratre suo, Alexandro filio Radulfi, Bertram camerario[4], Bec et multis aliis, apud Cestriam.

1. *sic MS.*
2. Menilsar(in) *MS.*
3. Lungiap. *MS.*
4. *MS. has* Alexandro de Bertram, *an obvious running together of the names of the two well-known witnesses.*

This is usually described as the foundation charter of St. John's Hospital, but the text makes it evident that the community was already in existence. It is perhaps noteworthy that it is apparently the only charter the Hospital obtained from the earl. The witnesses are almost identical with those to **nos. 223** and **227**, and the date must be very similar. Roger, son of the earl, was an illegitimate son of Hugh II and appears in **no. 223** as Roger de Cestria.

222.   Grant to the brethren of the leper hospital of St. Giles at Boughton outside Chester of the right to collect one handful of flour, of corn, rye and barley and other foods from every sack brought into Chester for selling in a cart or on a horse's back, and of a boat for fishing above and below the bridge of Chester.

[1181–1232]

P.R.O. CHES 34/4 (Quo Warranto), m. 45; from which B.L. Harl. MS. 2115, f. 195v. (new f. 169v.) and Shaker- ley MS. 3, p. 32 (now *penes* Sir Arthur Bryant).

. . . Quoad habendum collectas quasdam de omnibus cibariis et de quibusdam aliis, que ad prefatam civitatem vendenda evenerint, videlicet de unoquoque sacco in biga et super equum et quocumque modo evenerint et cuiuscumque fuerint de farina frumenti, siliginis et ordei, videlicet manipulum cum una manu, ac alia similia in clameo predicto specificata, dicit quod Ranulphus quondam comes Cestrie diu ante tempus memorie per litteras suas patentes sigillo scaccarii sui Cestrie sigillatas sine data, quas iidem fratres hic in curia proferunt, dedit, concessit et carta sua confirmavit deo et sancto Egidio et fratribus leprosis nimis indigentibus extra civitatem Cestrie quod ipsi et successores sui libertates predictas modo et forma in clameo predicto inter alia specificatas haberent imperpetuum; virtute quarum litterarum patencium iidem fratres et predecessores sui de eisdem libertatibus seisiti fuerunt in dominico suo ut in feodo.

Et quoad habendum unum batum cum suo piscatore cum omnibus ea tangentibus supra pontem et subtus modo et forma in clameo predicto inter alia specificata, iidem fratres leprosi dicunt quod dominus Ranulphus diu ante tempus memoris per litteras suas patentes sigillo scaccarii sui Cestrie sigillatas absque data, quas iidem fratres hic in curia similiter proferunt, dedit et concessit imperpetuum fratribus predictis, per nomen infirmis fratribus apud sanctum Egidium deforis civitatem Cestrie in sancto hospitali existentibus, libertates predictas; virtute quarum litterarum patencium iidem fratres leprosi et predecessores sui de eisdem libertatibus seisiti fuerunt in dominico suo ut de feodo.

For the leper hospital at Boughton, see **no. 198**. As there, the claims of the brethren in answer to the quo warranto proceedings are not above suspicion, but Ranulf III's alleged grants are not inherently implausible, and the claims can probably be accepted as genuine, particularly as his charters are said to have been exhibited in court. Unfortunately they were not recited and it is impossible to put a date to either. The former, allowing the brethren to collect food, may perhaps be compared with Ranulf's charter authorizing the brethren of St. John's hospital to collect alms (**no. 221**).

223. Confirmation of the gifts of Ranulf II and Hugh II to the nuns of St. Mary, Chester, and grant of 40s. a year from his rents in Wich, a boat on the water of Chester, a free court and the rectory of Over which his father granted in frankalmoign.

(Middle)wich, [1190–1194]

P.R.O., C.66 (Chancery Patent Rolls), no. 360, m. 19.
Ed.: *Cal. Pat. Rolls, 1399–1401*, p. 297; Engl. abstract:
J.C.A.S., N.S. xiii, p. 96.

Ranulfus dux Britannie, comes Cestrie et Richemundie, constabulario suo, dapifero, iusticiario, vicecom(iti), baronibus, ministris, ballivis, et omnibus hominibus suis Francis et Anglis tam futuris quam presentibus salutem. Notum sit vobis omnibus me pro salute anime mee et animarum patris mei et matris mee et predecessorum meorum concessisse et presenti carta mea confirmasse deo et ecclesie sancte Marie apud Cestriam et monialibus ibidem deo servientibus omnes illas donaciones, quas ad edificandam ibidem ecclesiam et edificia sua dederunt et concesserunt predicte ecclesie Ranulfus comes avus meus et Hugo comes pater meus, et omnes illas tenuras quas ipsi eis concesserunt, et redditus infra civitatem et extra in toftis et croftis et mansuris et omnibusmodis donorum, que ecclesie sue rationabiliter facta sunt. Super hoc concedo predicte ecclesie et confirmo, sicut concesserunt avus meus et pater meus, ad sustentamentum monialium xl. solidos de redditibus meis de Wich annuatim et unum batellum in aqua Cestrie ad piscandum ubicumque voluerint de supra pontem et de subtus pontem et in Heatum, cum dreinetes et flotnettes et stalnettes et omni genere retium libere et quiete ab omni seculari servicio preter oraciones. Super hec concedo ecclesie sancte Marie et monialibus curiam suam liberam et quietam, sicut libera exigit elemosina, et prohibeo omnibus ballivis meis et hominibus meis, sicut diligunt salutem anime mee, ne ullo modo manum extendant in aliqua, que ad predictam ecclesiam pertineant. Concedo eciam ecclesie sancte Marie et monialibus ecclesiam de Huure, quam eis dedit comes Hugo pater meus in perpetuam elemosinam. Huius confirmacionis sunt testes Bertraya comitissa Cestrie, Radulfo senescallo de Monte Alto, Radulfo de Mesnilwarin, Gaufrido de Buxeria,[1] Rogero constabulario, Henrico et Stephano de Longo Campo, Hugone et Alano de Bosco Ale, Rogero de Cestria, Alexandro filio Radulfi, Bertram camerario, Ranulfo de Devenham, Roberto filio Gileberti, Roberto Lancelin, Willelmo fratre suo, Ricardo filio Radulfi, Lanc(elino) filio Andree, Ricardo clerico, et aliis quam pluribus apud Wich.

1. Buxia *MS.*

Ranulf III's confirmation dates from 1190–1194. Unlike Hugh II's general confirmation (**no. 174**), it enumerates and specifies the different grants confirmed, beginning with Ranulf II's so-called foundation charter, granting the land for the church and monastic buildings (**no. 98**), and his grant of a boat for fishing on the river Dee (**no. 99**). But it also refers to gifts for which there is no preceding evidence. These include Earl Hugh's gift of the church or rectory of Over, and Ranulf II's grant of 40s. a year from his rents in Wich. This has usually been regarded as an additional gift by Ranulf III, but the text of the charter is quite specific. It has also been assumed, for no very obvious reason, that Wich refers to Nantwich, but Nantwich at this time was in the possession of the heirs of William Malbank, who died in 1176 (*E.C.C.*, p. 13), and it seems more likely that Middlewich is intended. Ranulf III's enumeration of the gifts of his father and grandfather is, however, apparently not complete. According to a royal confirmation of 8 December 1246 (Charter Rolls, no. 39, m. 13) Ranulf II gave, in addition to the gifts already specified, a grant of one mark (*marcata*) of annual rents receivable from the county of Chester, and another royal grant, a few weeks earlier (7 November 1246), cites a charter of Hugh II giving a fourth part of the tithe of all victuals of the earl and his household, whenever and so often and as long as he was in residence in Chester (*Ches. Sheaf*, no. 3804). These charters have disappeared.

224. Grant to the nuns of St. Mary, Chester, of free multure of the corn for their table in his mills of Chester, to be milled first after his own corn and whatever might be in the hopper.

Chester, [1195–1199]

P.R.O., C.66 (Chancery Patent Rolls), no. 360, m. 19.
Ed.: *Cal. Pat. Rolls, 1399–1401*, p. 297; Engl. abstract,
J.C.A.S., N.S. xiii, p. 96.

Ranulfus dux Britannie et comes Cestrie et Richemundie omnibus tam present-ibus quam futuris, qui hanc cartam viderint et audierint, salutem. Sciatis me pro amore dei et pro salute animarum antecessorum meorum et mee dedisse et concessisse in puram et perpetuam elemosinam deo et beate Marie et monialibus de Cestria totam multuram de blado, quod ad mensam earum pertinet, quietam imperpetuum in molendinis meis de Cestria, ita quod bladum earum primo molatur in predictis molendinis meis post bladum meum proprium vel post illud quod erit in tremea. Et ut hec concessio rata inposterum et inconvulsa permaneat, presentis scripti auctoritate cum sigilli mei apposicione eam duxi roborandam. Testibus comitissa Bertraya, Radulfo de Meinilwarin,[1] Petro Reaaldo,[2] Galfrido Gernet, Patricio[3] de Madberlehe, Ranulfo de Praeriis, Hugone de Pascy,[4] Lidulfo de Twemlaw,[5] Betramo de camera, Roberto Sarraceno, Roberto filio Harding, Ricardo filio Radulfi, Ruald, Ricardo clerico, et multis aliis apud Cestriam.

1. Meisinbon *MS.*
2. *sic MS.*
3. Latricio *MS.*
4. Mascy *MS.*
5. Maulaw *MS.*

This charter can only be dated approximately. It is presumably later than Ranulf's confirmation of his predecessors' grants (**no. 223**), and in fact follows as the next item in the royal confirmation of 1246 (Charter Rolls, no. 39, m. 13). For Ranulf of Praers, see **no. 251**; for Geoffrey Gernet, see *L.P.R.*, pp. 134, 150, 153. The last five witnesses are members of local Chester families. Other witnesses' names are badly rendered, and have been appropriately emended. Bertram *de camera* is, of course, the well known Bertram *camerarius*, for whom see **no. 194.**

225. Gift of Wallerscote to the nuns of Chester, retaining only his forest rights.

Chester, [1200–1203]

P.R.O., C.66 (Chancery Patent Rolls), no. 360, mm.

19–17. Abstract: *Cal. Pat. Rolls, 1399–1401*, p. 297; *J.C.A.S.*, N.S. xiii, p. 96.

Ranulfus comes Cestrie omnibus tam futuris quam presentibus, ad quos presentes littere pervenerint, salutem. Notum vobis facio me pro amore dei et pro salute anime mee et animarum antecessorum meorum dedisse et presenti carta mea confirmasse deo et sancte Marie et monialibus Cestrie Wallerescote cum omnibus pertinentiis suis in puram et perpetuam elemosinam libere et quiete et plenarie in pratis, in pascuis, in viis, in semitis, in aquis, et in omnibus eiusdem ville pertinentiis, habendum et tenendum imperpetuum predictis monialibus sine omni servicio seculari et exaccione preter oraciones tantum, salva michi et heredibus meis foresta nostra, quod moniales aut servientes sui in ea non forisfacient, et si in ea forisfecerint, quod illud michi emendent. Hiis testibus Radulfo de Menilwarint,[1] Petro Roald, Roberto filio Pigoti, Petro clerico, Willelmo de Haselwalle, Ricardo de Kyngeslehe, Herberto de Pulfordia, Patricio de Modburleh, Rogero de Menilwarint,[1] Ranulfo fratre eius, Roberto Lancelyn, Thoma filio Willelmi, Ranulfo de Monte Alto, Albano Minur, et multis aliis apud Cestriam.

1. *sic MS.*

Wallerscote is a small manor in Delamere Forest. According to Ormerod (ii. 139) it was given to St. Mary's nunnery by a certain Adam of Wringle (otherwise unknown), but this identification is not very plausible, and if there had been a donor, it would have been usual for Ranulf III to have named him in confirming his grant. Ranulf III's charter has been dated c.1185 without any obvious reason (*Ches. Sheaf*, no. 2663). The witnesses indicate that it falls considerably later. Richard of Kingsley succeeded Ranulf Kingsley during the justiciarship of Ralph Mainwaring (c.1194–1204), when Ranulf's widow Leuca quitclaimed Barterton to him (Orm., i. 751). Ranulf Mainwaring and Robert son of Pigot are found together as witnesses to a charter of c.1200 (**no. 307**), and Thomas son of William witnessed (with Herbert of Pulford) Hugh Boydell's grant of Poulton and Bebington to Robert Lancelyn (Orm., ii. 440) and William Boydell's grant of a moiety of Winnington to Liulf of Twemlow (*Chart. St. Werburgh*, no. 553), about the same time. The evidence, as a whole, suggests that the present charter can safely be placed between October 1199, when Ranulf III ceased to be duke of Brittany, and 1204, when Pierre Rouaut went over to the allegiance of the king of France.

226.   Letters patent, notifying that the nuns of Chester had been unjustly disturbed in the advowson of the chapel of Budworth by Robert Grosvenor, and that he had caused the said Robert to appear before him in court and renounce his claim.

[1229–1232]

P.R.O., C.66 (Chancery Patent Rolls), no. 360, mm. 19–17. Ed.: *Cal. Pat. Rolls, 1399–1401*, p. 303.

Omnibus Christi fidelibus presentibus et futuris Rannulfus comes Cestrie et Lincolnie salutem in domino. Noverit universitas vestra quod, cum sanctimoniales Cestrie iniuste erant vexate super advocacione capelle sue de Buddeworth, que Robertus Grosvenor, dicens[1] illam ad se pertinere que ad me et antecessores meos omni tempore pertinebat, et dicte moniales ipsam capellam una cum sua matrice ecclesia de Oura ex donacione patris mei H. comitis et concessione mea et confirmacione in puram elemosinam habebant, feci illum coram me apparere, et rei veritate inde inquisita et cognita procedens coram me et baronibus meis et tota curia mea totam suam clamacionem inde habitam sepedictis monialibus concessit et quietam clamavit imperpetuum. Huius autem concessionis et quiete clamacionis sunt testes in primis ego ipse R. comes Cestrie et Lincolnie, Iohannes constabularius, Rogerus dapifer, Willelmus de Vernoun tunc iusticiarius, Philippus de Orreby, Warinus de Vernun, Willelmus de Seulant,[2] Hamondus de Mascy, Willelmus filius David, et tota curia mea.

1. dicente *MS.*
2. Seu' *MS.*

As the letters patent state, the church of Over had been given to the nuns of Chester by Hugh II (**no. 223**), and the chapel at Budworth, which was a dependency of Over, clearly went with it. Robert Grosvenor presumably claimed the advowson as going with the vill of Budworth, which had been granted to his ancestor, another Robert, by Hugh II (**no. 163**). The present Robert is almost certainly the Robert son of Ranulf involved earlier in a suit of mort d'ancestor (**no. 397**).

227. Confirmation of the gifts and liberties bestowed on St. Werburgh's abbey by his predecessors and by their barons and his own.

Chester, 30 June [1190–1194]

B.L. Harl. MS. 2071, f. 19 (old f. 6), from the original; Harl. MS. 2071, f. 46 (old f. 32), from inspeximus; Lansdowne MS. 229, f. 121v.; Lansdowne MS. 447, f. 8v.; Bodleian Library, MS. Engl. Hist. c.242, f. 75 (old f. 71),

Dugdale's copy 'ex autographo penes Decanum et Capitulum apud Cestriam remanente'; Ashmole MS. 860, f. 385 ('ex codice MS. misc. R. Gloveri'); P.R.O., C.53 (Chancery Charter Rolls), no. 73, m. 15; St. George's Chapel, Windsor, MS. xi. E.5 (Badlesmere's inspeximus, 1280); Adlington Hall, Cheshire, inspeximus of 1285, no. 5. Abbreviated texts in Bodl. Rawlinson MS. B.144, f. 141b, Top. Cheshire b. I, p. 80, and Chester, Booth of Twemlow, Liber K, f. 31. Ed.: Orm., i. 33 (incomplete), and *Chart. St. Werburgh*, pp. 74–75 (no. 18).

Rannulfus comes Cestrie constabulario, dapifero, iusticiario, baronibus, ministris et ballivis, et omnibus hominibus suis Francis et Anglis, clericis et laicis, tam presentibus quam futuris salutem. Sciatis me concessisse et confirmasse in perpetuam elemosinam pro salute anime mee et parentum meorum ecclesie sancte Wereburge Cestrie et monachis ibidem deo servientibus omnes donationes et dignitates et libertates quas comites antecessores mei, scilicet Hugo comes et Ricardus filius eius et Rannulfus comes et alius Rannulfus avus meus et Hugo pater meus, et barones in tempore illorum vel in meo eis dederunt. Quapropter volo et heredibus meis et omnibus amicis et hominibus meis precipio, ut omnia ad abbatiam pertinentia in burgo et extra burgum, in bosco et plano, in villis et extra, in viis et semitis, in pratis et pasturis, in aquis et molendinis, in piscariis et in omnibus aliis locis, sint soluta et quieta et ita libera, ut nichil libertatis possit addi eis ulterius, quia ego nichil retineo in rebus sancte Wereburge nisi orationes tantummodo. Et insuper concedo, sicut alii comites ante me concesserunt, ut sancta Wereburga habeat plenarie curiam suam de omnibus rebus. Hiis testibus Bertrada comitissa matre mea, Radulfo de Mesnilwarin, Hugone de Bosco Ale, Radulfo filio Simonis, Rogero fratre comitis, Rogero constabulario, Gaufrido de Buxeria, Stephano de Longo Campo, Alano de Bosco Ale, Bertramo camerario, Alexandro filio Radulfi, Iohanne clerico, Bech dispensario, Petro clerico, et aliis multis apud Cestriam in capitulo monachorum in aniversario die Hugonis comitis patris mei.

SEAL: appended on tag, equestrian, shield with cross, helmet, legs of horse and sword protrude into legend circle. Legend: +   SIGILLUM   R[ANUL]FI CO[MITIS C]ESTRIE. 'Nothinge on the indorse'.

This charter follows almost word for word the confirmation of Ranulf II (**no. 27**). Many of the same witnesses attested Ranulf's charters, issued while he was duke of Brittany, for the nuns of Chester (**no. 223**) and for the hospital of St. John outside the Northgate (**no. 221**). Tait (*Chart. St. Werburgh*, p. 75) dated the present charter after 1199, because of the absence of 'duke of Brittany and earl of Richmond' in the earl's title. But Ranulf's use of this title is too irregular to draw definite conclusions from it, and there is no reason to suppose that the present charter is later in date than **nos. 221** and **223**. Roger the constable succeeded his father, John, in 1190 and adopted the surname Lacy in 1194. Roger the earl's brother was an illegitimate son of Hugh II; he appears in **no. 221** as son of the earl and in **no. 223** as Roger de Cestria. The seal is that described by Planché (*Journal Brit. Arch. Assn.*, v, pp. 235–52) as Ranulf's second seal, and is reproduced in Orm., i. 33; the cross on the shield suggests (though there is no supporting evidence) that Ranulf may have taken the cross, with other 'chief persons', at Henry II's behest in 1188 (*Ann. Cestr.*, pp. 38–41). The Dieulacres chronicle states that he accompanied Richard I to the Holy Land (*Ches. Sheaf*, no. 10233), but the story is unconfirmed.

228. Confirmation of the gift of half a salthouse at Northwich to St. Werburgh's abbey by William de Venables.

Chester, [1191–1194]

Orig.: J.R.U.L.M., Mainwaring MSS., Suppl. 73. Transcr.: B.L. Add. MS. 19517, f. 139 (new f. 70v.) Ed.: *10th Rep. Hist. MSS. Comm.*, App. pt. iv. p. 201 (from original); *Chart. St. Werburgh*, p. 216 (no. 326) (from *Hist. MSS. Comm. Rep.*)

Rannulfus comes Cestrie omnibus tam futuris quam presentibus salutem. Notum sit vobis me concessisse et presenti carta mea confirmasse in puram et perpetuam elemosinam deo et ecclesie sancte Werburge in Cestria et monachis ibidem deo servientibus dimidiam salinam in Norwicho, que adiacet Wittonie, quam Willelmus de Venables eis dedit, liberam et quietam ab omni terreno servicio, sicut carta predicti Willelmi testatur. Quare volo et firmiter precipio quod predicti monachi predictam salinam in perpetuum habeant et teneant sicut liberam elemosinam absque omni vexatione et exactione et servicio seculari. Hiis testibus Rogero[1] constabulario Cestrie, Radulfo de Monte Alto senescallo Cestrie, Radulfo de Mesnilwarin, Roberto filio Picoti, Willelmo de Verdun, Petro clerico, Avveredo de Oreng(is), Roberto et Radulfo Sarracenis, magistro Hugone, Thoma clerico presencium scriptore, et multis aliis, apud Cestriam.

SEAL: repaired and fragmentary, different equestrian figures on obverse and reverse.

1. Rog[er]um *orig.*

For a brief notice of William Venables' gift, see *Chart. St. Werburgh*, no. 327. The present charter was dated 1200–08 in the Historical Manuscripts Commission report and by Tait, *Chart. St. Werburgh*, no. 326, but since Roger the constable does not use the name Lacy, which he adopted in 1194, it must fall a good deal earlier. Ralph of Montalt, the seneschal, died in 1199, probably during the Welsh attack on Mold on 6 January (*Ches. Sheaf*, nos. 9394, 10003), and William de Verdun probably in 1205 (**no. 337**). Alfred (Avveredus) de Oreng(is) or de Oreng(a) is a somewhat mysterious person, who does not otherwise appear in Chester charters. For Master Hugh, see **no. 231**. As Roger's father, John the constable, died in Palestine at the siege of Acre in 1190, the date of the present charter is probably 1191–1194.

229.   Confirmation of his father's gift of the church of Prestbury to St. Werburgh's abbey.

Walton [1194–1202]

Two originals: Adlington Hall, Cheshire, Bundle 24, no. 5 (A), and Bundle 17, no. 3 (B). Transcr.: Adlington inspeximus (1285), no. 3 (C); St. George's Chapel, Windsor, MS. xi E.5, no. 12 (D); P.R.O., C.53 (Chancery Charter Rolls), no. 73, m. 10, no. 38 (E). Ed.: Tait, *Chart. St. Werburgh*, p. 80 (no. 25) (from Charter Roll). Engl. trans.: *Ches. Sheaf.*, no. 10153.

Omnibus sancte matris ecclesie filiis tam presentibus quam futuris Rannulfus[1] comes Cestrie salutem in domino. Noverit universitas vestra me ratam habere donationem ab Hugone comite Cestrie patre meo factam deo et sancte Werburge[2] de Cestria[3] et monachis ibidem deo servientibus super ecclesia de Prestebirie cum omnibus eius pertinentiis in liberam et puram et perpetuam elemosinam illis concessa, sicut carta patris mei, quam ipsi inde habent, testatur, quam mihi oblatam presente corpore patris mei meminet me in ratihabitionem super altare sancte Werburge[4] posuisse. Et in huius confirmationis testimonium predictam donationem presenti scripto et sigilli mei munimine roboravi. Hiis testibus Philippo de Orrebi, Henrico de Aldidele, Waltero de Daivilla,[5] Iohanne de Pratellis, Roberto de Daivilla,[6] Thoma de Pleseleia, Thoma pincerna, Geroldo hostiario, Hugone de Pasci, et multis aliis apud Waltonam.

SEALED on tag; in both exemplars seal missing.

1.   Ranulfus *B*, *D*; Rannulphus *C*, *E*.
2.   Wereburge *B*, *C*, *E*.
3.   Cestrie *for* de Cestria, *B*, *C*, *D*, *E*.
4.   Wereburge *B*, *C*, *E*.
5.   Daivile *for* de Daivila, *B*, Daiville *C*.
6.   Daivila *for* de Daivilla *B*, Daiville *C*. *The readings of names in D, which are abbreviated, are omitted.*

Hugh II's charter (**no. 133**), which is here confirmed, dates from 1178–1181. As Ranulf III recalls in the present text how he had placed it on the altar of St. Werburgh in the presence of his father's corpse in ratification of his father's gift, the present charter evidently dates from considerably later than Earl Hugh's death in 1181. It was confirmed in a charter of Bishop Geoffrey of Coventry (*Ches. Sheaf*, no. 10160), who died in 1208, and must have been issued before 1206 or 1207, when Philip of Orreby became justiciar of Chester (**no. 296**); but the lower limit of date is not easily established. W.F. Irvine (*Ches. Sheaf*, no. 10153) dates the charter 'probably about 1200' on rather slender evidence, or 1194–1202 as the extreme limits. This is probably as close an approximation to the date as is possible.

The existence of two copies of the charter is not easily explained, though other instances (e.g. **nos. 334, 444**) have survived. Copy A, which is written in a flowing charter hand, presumably originated with one of the earl's clerks, and has been made the basis of the present edition. Copy B, of which the left-hand margin has perished, is written in diplomatic minuscule with elongated letters, as is common in episcopal documents of the period, and was probably drawn up by the monks of St. Werburgh's for their own purposes. The similarity of the variant readings shows that this was the copy submitted for the various confirmations C, D and E. On the other hand, the differences between A and B are purely orthographic. No new matter has been introduced, as in the spurious version of **no. 127**, and there is no question of forgery. The provenance of A is not known, but if, as seems possible, it comes from Prestbury, the simplest explanation of B is that the monks wished to have a second copy for their archives.

230.   Grant to St. Werburgh's abbey of freedom from providing food for the earl's serjeants in all its Wirral lands, except six foresters on foot, its four demesne manors of Sutton, Eastham, Bromborough and Irby not to be obliged to feed even these.

[1194–1208]

B.L. Harl. MS. 1965 (St. Werburgh's register), f. 17v.
(new f. 20); Ed.: *Chart. St. Werburgh*, no. 353.

Ranulphus comes sextus dedit monachis Cestrie imperpetuum quietanciam tocius terre sue de Wirallia de pultura servientium, exceptis tantum sex forestariis peditibus et sine sequela, ita tamen quod quatuor dominica sua maneria, scilicet Sutton, Estham, Bromburg et Irreby, quieta erunt tam de predictis forestariis pascendis quam de aliis. Et si forte, guerra urgente, oporteat plures servientes apponi, homines de terra sua in Wyrallia apponent quantum eos contiget ad servientes illos inveniendos et pascendos, exceptis dictis quatuor maneriis, que inde sunt libera et quieta.

This charter is the counterpart to the charter for the free men of Wirral (**no. 276**), and formulated *mutatis mutandis* in the same words. Like the latter, it may well be a later fabrication, but as it only exists in an abbreviated abstract in the St. Werburgh's register, it is impossible to pass a verdict. If it is genuine (and in that case probably the model for **no. 276**), it almost certainly dates from the time of Abbot Geoffrey (1194–1208), the first witness of **no. 276**; but its credentials should be viewed with circumspection.

231.   Licence to the abbot and convent of St. Werburgh's abbey to extend their buildings on the land next to that of Philip of Orreby, in the same way as Philip's houses are extended.

[1208–1210]

P.R.O., CHES 34/1 (Quo Warranto, 27–31 Edw. III), m. 16. Ed.: *Stenton Misc.*, p. 43 (no. 14).

R. comes Cestrie omnibus presentibus et futuris, ad quos presens carta pervenerit salutem. Sciatis me concessisse et dedisse et hac carta mea confirmasse dilecto et fideli meo Hugoni abbati Cestrie et monachis meis ibidem deo servientibus licenciam extendendi edificia, que vel ipsi vel alii per ipsos posuerint in terra sua, que iacet vicina terre Philippi de Orreby ante portam cimiterii sancte Werburge iuxta fabricas in antea usque ad viam preiacentes,[1] sicut domus dicti Philippi de Orrebi in terra vicina extense sunt. Concedo etiam eisdem, quod dicta terra cum habitantibus in ea sit quieta de vigiliis et theolonio et capcione cervisie ad opus meum vel ballivorum meorum et ab omni consuetudine. Et prohibeo super forisfacturam meam decem librarum, ne quis ipsos inde impediat vel ipsis aut suis inde iniuriam faciat aut gravamen. Testibus Philippo de Orreby tunc iusticiario Cestrie, Petro clerico, H. de Aldidelee, Thoma, Henrico dispensariis, David de Malo Passu, Willelmo de Venables,[2] Iohanne de Sancta Maria, magistro Hugone de Cestria, et aliis multis.

1.   preiacente *MS*.
2.   *Blank in MS.*

There is a brief uninformative abstract of this charter, without witnesses, in the abbey register (*Chart. St. Werburgh*, no. 395), but the poor and faded transcript in the Cheshire Quo Warranto enrolments is the only surviving record of the full text. It dates from shortly after the election of Hugh Grylle as abbot in 1208. Master Hugh of Chester (also referred to as Master Hugh of St. Werburgh) and

Master John of St. Mary appear together as witnesses to an agreement made in 1209 (*Chart. St. Werburgh*, no. 307), and Master Hugh was presented to the living of Coddington by Abbot Hugh's predecessor, Abbot Geoffrey, between 1194 and 1198 (*Chart. St. Werburgh*, no. 90). Philip of Orreby's house next to the cemetery of St. Werburgh was still in his family's possession after 1265 (*Chart. St. Werburgh*, no. 600).

232. Grant to St. Werburgh's abbey of the tithes of the earl's demesne in Rhuddlan and the tithes of the fishery and of the earl's mills in Englefield, together with a tenement in Rhuddlan on the road running from the castle to the fishery, and pannage and common for the monks' pigs in his forests of Englefield and Cheshire, restoring to the monks all the rights granted to them in Englefield by his predecessors or their men. [Spurious]

[1208–1211]

Adlington Hall, Cheshire, royal inspeximus of 1285, no. 4; P.R.O., C.53 (Chancery Charter Rolls), no. 73, m. 15, no. 46; CHES 33/6 (Forest Rolls, 27–31 Edw. III), m. 50; B.L. Harl. MS. 139, f. 207 (old f. 238), omitting witnesses. Ed.: *Chart. St. Werburgh*, p. 338 (no. 598).

Ranulphus comes Cestrie, filius Hugonis comitis, constabulario, dapifero, iusticiario, baronibus et militibus, vic(ecomiti) et ballivis suis et omnibus hominibus suis de Cestresira, et omnibus presentibus et futuris presentem cartam inspecturis vel audituris salutem. Noveritis me pro salute anime mee et antecessorum meorum concessisse et dedisse et hac mea carta confirmasse deo et sancte Wereburge Cestrie et monachis ibidem deo servientibus omnes decimas dominii mei de Ruelent ad proprios usus suos, tam in blado quam in aliis rebus universis, unde decima dari debet, et decimas piscarie de Ruelent, et decimas omnium molendinorum meorum de Englefeld. Dedi etiam unum mansum in villa de Ruelent, habens in latitudine sexaginta pedes et in longitudine quater viginti, in via que vadit a castello usque ad piscariam apud aquilonem. Concessi etiam et dedi dictis monachis quod habeant pessonem et communam in forestis meis de Englefeld et de Cestresira porcis suis dominicis. Insuper reddidi eisdem monachis omnia iura sua in Englefeld, tam in terris quam in ecclesiis et decimis, et in omnibus aliis rebus que antecessores mei aut illorum homines eis dederunt, habenda et tenenda libere et quiete, pacifice et honorifice, in puram et perpetuam elemosinam. Testibus Rogero de Lascy constabulario Cestrie, Philippo de Orreby tunc iusticiario Cestrie, Rogero dapifero de Monte Alto, Warino de Vernoun, Willelmo de Venables, Henrico de Aldidele, Rogero de Mainewarin, Roberto Patrik, Petro clerico domini comitis, Waltero Daiville, Aluredo de Suligni, Normanno Pantoft, Roberto de Coudrei, Henrico dispensario,

Bertramo de Verdun, Stephano de Segrave, Roberto de Ardredshill, Henrico de Longo Campo, Willelmo de Haselwello, David de Malo Passu, Willelmo filio suo, Leoffo vicecomite, magistro Alano, Ricardo vicecomite Cestrie, Ricardo de Kingesle, Hugone de Pascy.

If this were a genuine charter, it would date from 1208–1211, but the inclusion among the witnesses of Bertram de Verdun, the well-known judge who died on crusade in 1192, and of Alured de Suligny who died in 1204 at latest (*H.K.F.*, p. 41), is alone sufficient to condemn it, apart from minor stylistic peculiarities. Nor is it easy to see what the monks of Chester hoped to gain from a confirmation of their rights in Rhuddlan and Tegeingl (Englefield) at a time when the whole region was being overrun by Llywelyn the Great (Lloyd, pp. 638, 640). After Llywelyn's death in 1240, on the other hand, Tegeingl reverted to English hands for a few years (1247–56), but after 1256 the four cantrefs passed back to the Welsh, and Llywelyn ap Gruffydd's rights were formally recognized in the Treaty of Montgomery in 1267 (Lloyd, p. 740). It was only with the beginning of the Welsh collapse in 1277, when Llywelyn was forced to surrender all the lands between the Conway and the Dee (Lloyd, p. 759), that the monks of St. Werburgh's had any real prospect of realizing their claims in Rhuddlan and Tegeingl, and it is possible that this charter was fabricated at this time, perhaps to substantiate their case against the monks of Basingwerk, who had enjoyed the support of the Welsh princes (*Chart. St. Werburgh*, pp. 236–7). But it is more likely that it dates from the final English conquest of Wales in 1282. It first comes to light in Edward I's confirmation of 1285, and it is reasonable to suppose that it was fabricated about that time.

233.   Notification that he has taken into his protection all lands, tithes, rents etc. pertaining to the fabric of the church of St. Werburgh, and order to his bailiffs and other ministers to ensure that the clerk of the works receives due payment.

[? 1208–1217]

B.L. Harl. MS. 2060, f. 62v. (old p. 117). Harl. MS. 2071, f. 18 (old f. 5), both from original. Ed.: *Chart. St. Werburgh*, p. 72.

Rannulfus comes Cestrie constabulario, dapifero, iusticiario, vic(ecomiti), et omnibus baronibus suis, ministris et ballivis, et omnibus hominibus suis et amicis presentibus et futuris, ad quos presens scriptum pervenerit, salutem. Sciatis me suscepisse in protectione mea et custodia universa que pertinent ad opus sancte Werburge de Cestria, tam in terris et hominibus quam decimis et redditibus et aliis possessionibus universis. Quare volo et firmiter precipio ut ea in pace et securitate tanquam mea dominica protegatis et manuteneatis. Itaque nullus quidquam ex eis contra rectores eiusdem operis detenire presumat nec eis aliquatenus impedire, quominus omnia que ad opus pertinent memoratum libere et quiete percipiant, et de hiis, prout promotioni operis ecclesie sancte Werburge videtur expedire, disponant. Volo itaque et firmiter precipio quod, si aliquis in balliva vestra aliquos redditus ad opus illud pertinentes detinere presumpsit, eum ad solucionem compellatis et forisfacturam meam de detentore capiatis. Vale.

> SEAL: lion seal; nothing on reverse.

We do not, unfortunately, have any precise information about the building or rebuilding of the abbey church of Chester. Abbot Robert II (1175–84) drew up a schedule of the tithes and other income assigned to the fabric (*E.C.C.*, no. 3), and Abbot Hugh (1208–26) confirmed them (*Chart. St. Werburgh*, no. 488). There is evidence that work was in progress on the abbey buildings in his time, and Ranulf III's writ was probably issued at this period, in which case it falls between 1208 and 1217. The lion seal was in use throughout this period.

234–9. Various grants and confirmations for St. Werburgh's abbey, Chester.

[1181–1232]

> B.L. Harl. MS. 1965, ff. 7v, 12v, 19, 22, 24. Ed.: *Chart. St. Werburgh*, nos. 52, 53, 147, 315, 384, 440.

234.   R. comes Cestrie dedit abbatibus Cestrie in singulis maneriis suis tocius terre sue unam mansuram cum omnibus pertinenciis, ut cum abbates vel ceteri monachi ad curiam venerint, habeant de curia plenariam procuracionem et proprium hospicium cum ipso hospite et redditibus hospicii, et ipsum hospicium sit liberum a geldis et omnibus serviciis.

235.   Ranulphus comes Cestrie dedit dimidiam bovatam terre sancte Werburge in villa de Cibesey cum omnibus pertinenciis, solutam et quietam ab omni servicio.

236.   Ranulphus comes Cestrie dedit ecclesie sancte Werburge totum servicium et homagium quondam sibi debitum Galfridi filii Acke de Sibeseye, de terra quam de se tenuit in Sibesey, reddendo ei annuatim x. solidos, de quibus dicti monachi solvent annuatim leprosis de Bochtona xx. denarios et de residuo pascent c. pauperes in die anniversario sui patris H. infra abbaciam Cestrie.

237.   Ranulphus comes Cestrie dedit c. denarios habendos singulis annis de vicecomitatu Cestrie, erogandos in elemosina annuatim die anniversario sui patris H. infra abbaciam Cestrie per manus monachorum, ita ut leprosi Cestrie habeant exinde xx. denarios.

238.   Ranulphus comes Cestrie quiete clamavit monachis Cestrie clausuras de parco de Querendon, de Weston, Aston et de omnibus terris ad eos spectantibus in Derbisiria.

239.   Ranulphus comes confirmavit duas bovatas terre in Elton, quas Petrus clericus monachis dedit cum omnibus pertinenciis, et unam toftam in medio predicte ville, et vi. landas, quas Helias tenuit cum una predictarum bovatarum, cum omnibus libertatibus predicte ville.

The grants and confirmations set out above survive only in abbreviated abstracts in the register of St. Werburgh's abbey. The compiler of the register did not distinguish between Earl Ranulf's various titles (duke of Brittany, earl of Richmond, earl of Lincoln) and omitted the witnesses of his charters, thus making accurate dating impossible. But in some cases an approximate date can be established by internal evidence. Thus the grant of half a bovate of land (**no. 235**) and services (**no. 236**) in Sibsey (Lincs.) must fall after 1198, when Earl Ranulf succeeded the younger William of Roumare, as previously Sibsey had belonged to the Roumare honour of Bolingbroke (*H.K.F.*, p. 164). The confirmation (**no. 239**) of Peter the clerk's gift of two bovates and other lands in Elton (*Chart. St. Werburgh*, no. 396), falls after 1208–13 when Peter acquired Thornton-le-Moors (adjacent to Elton) from Richard of Aldford (**no. 285**), and before Peter's death c.1228. Unfortunately, the remaining grants cannot be even approximately dated. The leper hospital of St. Giles at Boughton, outside Chester, to which gifts of 20d. a year were assigned in **nos. 236** and **237**, claimed to have charters of Hugh II and Ranulf III (**no. 222**), but the actual texts have not survived. The gift of a house in every manor throughout the whole of the earl's territory (**no. 234**) so that the abbot or his representatives would have an appropriate residence when attending the earl's court, may conceivably have been made by one of the earlier Ranulfs, though in that case it is singular that it was not mentioned in their charters. In any case it is surprising that this is the only mention of what in total was a substantial grant, and we should perhaps look on the claim with a certain degree of suspicion.

240. Grant to Combermere abbey of a carucate of land in Wincle in Macclesfield Forest, with pasture for 2000 sheep, 24 cows, 2 bulls, 16 oxen, 6 horses and 10 mares, and their offspring, and with liberties and privileges for the monks and their men. [Spurious]

Macclesfield, [1190–1194]

> Orig.: B.L. Add. Charter 15771. Enrolments: P.R.O., CHES 2/50 (Recog. Rolls, various years Edw. III), m. 4; CHES 33/6 (Forest Rolls, 27–31 Edw. III), m. 48v. Transcripts from orig.: B.L. Harl. MS. 2060, f. 58 (new f. 33); Bodleian Library, MS. Top. Cheshire c. 9, f. 161. Briefly noted: Orm., iii. 769; Earwaker, *East Cheshire*, ii. 432; *36th Rep. D.K.P.R.*, p. 119.

Ranulfus comes Cestrie constabulario suo et dapifero, iusticiario, vicecomiti, baronibus et ballivis, et omnibus hominibus suis Francis et Anglis tam futuris quam presentibus salutem. Notum sit vobis omnibus me pro salute anime mee et omnium antecessorum meorum dedisse et concessisse in puram et perpetuam elemosinam deo et sancte Marie et monachis de Cumbermera et eorum successoribus unam carucatam terre in foresta mea de Maclesfeld, in loco qui vocatur Winchul, ad grangiam faciendam et ad prata circa terminos de Winchul, et in eadem foresta pasturam sufficientem duobus milibus ovium et earum exitui, quousque exitus earum sit unius anni, et viginti quatuor vaccis cum duobus tauris et exitui illarum vaccarum, quousque sint unius anni, et sexdecim bobus et sex equis et decem equabus cum exitu illarum trium annorum. Centenarius vero numerus ovium continet sexies xx. oves, ita quod, si mihi dictum fuerit predictos monachos in predicta pastura habere plures oves quam numerum hic eis concessum, per duos legales homines meos et per conversos suos numerabuntur, et si plures invente fuerint, a pastura ipsa sine forisfactura amovebuntur; si pauciores, addantur, si voluerint. Agni autem anni preteriti singulis annis infra octavas pasche removebuntur.

Locus vero, quem eis dedi, in quo habebunt carucatam terre et prata, hiis divisis distinguitur: a furno comitis, qui est iuxta viam que venit de Schiderford, per oraliam bosci usque Quernstanesich et per Quernstansich usque ad Withienlache et per Withienlache usque Gorsthul et inde per oraliam bosci usque Grenelache et per Grenelache usque in Winchulcloch et de Winchulcloch per oraliam bosci usque ad supradictum furnum. Et liceat predictis monachis predictum locum, et quicquid infra has divisas predictas continetur, claudere muro vel fossato vel sepi, et infra clausuram illam domos suas facere, ubicumque voluerint, et residuum loci illius exsartare et colere vel ad prata aut alias commoditates domus sue facere, quandocumque viderint expedire.

Do etiam et concedo predictis monachis et eorum successoribus in foresta mea prenominata de bosco meo sufficienter, quicquid eis necessarium fuerit, *ad edificia sua et caulas et sepes faciendas et ad focum suum capiendum,* quandocumque sibi viderint expedire. Concedo etiam predictis monachis et hominibus suis liberum transitum per totam forestam meam omni tempore anni, eundi, redeundi, afferendi et referendi omnia que necessaria habuerint.

Monachi vero predicti singulis annis reddent mihi et heredibus meis pro omnibus terrenis serviciis et consuetudinibus unam marcam argenti pro omnibus, *scilicet die sancti Petri ad Vincula, et remittent mihi predicti monachi tres marcas argenti, quas de elemosina mea singulis annis die illo eis dare solebam. Volo itaque et firmiter precipio quod predicti monachi et eorum successores sine omni contradictione habeant et teneant hec omnia per servicium prenominatum bene et in pace inperpetuum de me et heredibus meis ita libere, quiete et honorifice et absque omni terreno servicio et exactione seculari, sicut ulla elemosina melius et liberius teneri potest vel concedi.* Et habeant omnes commoditates, que ibi sunt vel que ibi fieri possunt, tam subtus terram quam super inperpetuum. Concedo etiam eisdem monachis quod nec ego aut heredes mei aut aliquis nomine nostro aliquod approviamentum faciemus aut aliquos homines recipiemus in predictam pasturam, qui sint illis ex nimia vicinitate sua ad nocumentum et districtionem predicte pasture quoquomodo, nisi de mera voluntate illorum monachorum. *Et ego et heredes mei hanc predictam donacionem contra omnes homines eisdem monachis warantizabimus et defendemus inperpetuum. Ut autem hec nostra donacio rata et firma* a me et heredibus meis inperpetuum *habeatur, scripti huius auctoritate et sigilli mei apposicione eam duxi confirmandam. Hiis testibus Rogero constabulario Cestrie, Radulfo de Monte Alto senescallo Cestrie, Thoma Basset, Radulfo de Masnilwarin, Petro Roeaud, Thoma dispensatore, Warino de Vernon, Radulfo filio Symonis, Hugone de Boydele, Ricardo et Rogero de Croylei, Gaufrido et Willelmo Farsi, Ricardo Pisce, Ricardo de Boydele, Reginaldo filio Archienbaldi, Patricio de Modberlegh, Thoma clerico comitis, Ricardo clerico de Roudestorn, et multis aliis apud Maclesfeld.*

> SEAL: on tag, through fold; obverse, lion seal, legend
> . . . GILLUM RAN . . .; reverse, gem seal, three figures,
> apparently naked, one upside down, central figure sitting,
> legend SECRETVM SIGILLUM.

The charters of Combermere abbey have deservedly a bad reputation (*Ches. Sheaf*, no. 3771), and the present charter, written in a handwriting that cannot possibly be earlier than the reign of Edward I, is no exception. A gross forgery, it is probably little earlier in date than the version of it in an inspeximus of 1285 enrolled on the Cheshire Recognizance Rolls (*36th Rep. D.K.P.R.*, p. 119). In all probability the forgery was undertaken in response to the vigorous attacks on forest rights and franchises carried out by Edward I's justices in the forest of Macclesfield (Stewart-Brown, *Calendar of County Court, City Court and Eyre Rolls of Chester*, pp. 235–9; Hewitt, *Medieval Cheshire,* pp. 12–15); such an eyre occurred in the period 1267–70 under the justiciar, Thomas de Boulton. The forgery may nevertheless be based on a genuine grant by Ranulf III of land and forest rights at Wincle, the forger's work being chiefly to specify, enlarge and clarify the rights of pasturage, assart, enclosure, etc., which Edward I's justices were challenging. The many similarities to the forged foundation charter of Hugh Malbank (*Mon.*, v. 325) and the alleged charter of Earl John (**no. 463**) suggest that these also may have been used as a source. The probable content of Ranulf III's original charter is indicated by italic. Its date must have been c.1190–94, and it seems that the forger transferred the original lion seal to his handiwork. No fewer than nine of the witnesses, including the two Farcys (from Pont-Farcy, north-east of Vire), Richard Pisce (Peissim), Richard de Croile, and the two Boydells, witnessed Ranulf III's charter for Minting in Lincolnshire (**no. 203**) some time between 1186 and 1200. Ralph son of Simon succeeded in 1184 (*H.K.F.*, p. 127). Thomas Basset, a younger son of the well-known Thomas Basset of Headington (*P.R.S.*, x, p. 108), married Philippa, the eldest surviving daughter and heiress of William II Malbank (*E.C.C.*, p. 13), and witnesses here as successor of the founder of Combermere, Hugh Malbank. The date of the marriage is not known, but may have been c.1190. Reginald son of Archenbald had served as seneschal of the barony of Wich Malbank in the time of William II (Orm., iii. 305), and received a messuage in Nantwich from Thomas Basset some time after 1190 (*E.C.C.*, no. 5. ii). For Patrick of Mobberley, founder of Mobberley priory, see *E.C.C.*, p. 36.

241. Confirmation to Combermere abbey of all the lands and liberties given by Hugh Malbank, the founder, and his son William, with a court, gallows, quittance of tolls and all other services. [Spurious]

Chester, [1230]

P.R.O., C.53 (Chancery Charter Rolls), no. 117, m. 3; CHES 29/43 (Plea Rolls, 6 Edw. III), m. 8; also CHES 29/50 (12 Edw. III), m. 8 (enrolled at request of abbot from an inspeximus of Edward I). Abbreviated transcripts (with witnesses): B.L. Harl. MS. 1967, f. 139v. (new f. 146v.), and Harl. 2072, f. 116v. (new f. 69v.) Ed.: *Mon.*, v. 325); Orm., iii. 402 (abbreviated); *Cal. Ch. Rolls*, iv. 208–9 (no. 6).

Ranulphus comes Cestrie et Lincolnie constabulario suo et dapifero et baronibus suis, iusticiario suo et ministris suis, et omnibus hominibus suis Francis et Anglis tam minoribus quam maioribus salutem in domino. Notum sit tam presentibus quam futuris quod ego Ranulphus comes Cestrie pro redempcione et salvacione anime mee et animarum omnium liberorum meorum et omnium antecessorum et successorum meorum concessi libertates, et confirmo omnes terras et tenuras ac etiam libertates cum omnibus pertinentiis suis, que et quas lictus Hugo Malbank et Willelmus filius eius eis dederunt et per cartas eorum eis confirmaverunt infra dominium meum Cestrisire, et nominatim locum illum qui vocatur Cumbermare, ubi dicta abbatia constructa est, cum omnibus pertinentiis suis per bundas et divisas, sicut in carta Hugonis plenius continetur, et etiam manerium de Wivelescle cum omnibus libertatibus et liberis consuetudinibus et pertinentiis suis, et ecclesias de Actona cum capellis suis, videlicet Wico Malbano et Wrennebury et Munshulle, cum communa bosci et cum omnibus pertinentiis suis. Et habeant et teneant omnia predicta in omnibus et singulis rebus per bundas et divisas libere et quiete et ab omni seculari exactione, sicut in cartis predicti Hugonis et Willelmi Malbank, quas dicti monachi inde habent, plenius testantur.

Concedo etiam dictis monachis et eorum successoribus quod habeant liberam curiam et tholneum et assisam panis et cervisie et uthesium et blodwite et catalla felonum, forisfacturas et felonias et omnes mensuras et omnimoda amerciamenta et emendas de omnimodis transgressionibus hominum et tenencium ipsorum vel aliorumcumque existencium infra terras vel limites seu bundas ipsorum monachorum nostrorum infra dominium meum Cestrisire, et habeant in predicto manerio furcas et infangenthef et utfangenthef in manerio predicto inperpetuum. Concedo etiam et confirmo pro me et heredibus meis dictis monachis et eorum successoribus et hominibus ac tenentibus ipsorum tam infra villam Cestrie quam extra infra dominium meum Cestrisire quietanciam de omni tholneo et de servientibus meis pascendis et de sectis comitatus et hundredorum, placitis et querelis, muragiis et pavagiis, passagiis et pontagiis, et de omni tholneo et operacionibus, et de scutagiis et de opere parci et custodia castelli, et de omni opere et genere servicii, cum omnibus libertatibus suis in hominibus et terris, in bosco et plano, in pratis et pascuis, in viis et semitis, in burgis, in aquis, in molendinis, in piscariis, et in omnibus locis, cum libertatibus et liberis consuetudinibus suis. Et prohibeo pro me et heredibus meis quod dicti monachi mei vel ipsorum successores aut homines seu tenentes ipsorum ponantur in placito de ulla re extra curiam dictorum monachorum, nisi tantum coram me aut capitali iusticiario meo. Similiter concedo pro me et heredibus meis eisdem monachis et eorum successoribus quod nullus escaetor vel vicecomes nec aliquis ballivus seu minister Cestrisire ingrediatur manerium ipsorum de Wivelescle vel alias terras infra limites seu bundas dictorum monachorum aliquo modo ad vexandum causa vacacionis monasterii vel ad distringendum seu gravandum ipsos monachos meos aut homines seu tenentes ipsorum sine speciali waranto meo vel capitalis iusticiarii mei, et hoc facient cum ballivo predictorum monachorum meorum super forisfacturam meam decem librarum ad levandum nobis et heredibus nostris, quocienscumque fecerint in contrarium, quia volo ex corde et animo quod monachi mei et eorum successores habeant et teneant omnia predicta in liberam, puram et perpetuam elemosinam eternaliter. Hiis testibus Willelmo constabulario, Roberto dapifero, Philippo de Horreby, Thoma dispensatore, Thoma filio eius, Ricardo Peysin, Reginaldo filio Erchebaldi, Liulfo de Twanlawe, Rogero Putrel, Herberto de Horreby, et multis qui hoc audierunt et viderunt apud Cestriam, anno domini M°CC° tricesimo.

Like **no. 240**, this supposed confirmation of the alleged charters of Hugh Malbank, the founder of Combermere abbey, and his son William, is a gross forgery. It is also a singularly clumsy one, from the address to all the earl's men 'small and great' to the concluding word of the text, 'eternally'.

It is hard to credit that anyone in 1230 would refer to Ranulf III's 'children', when he had been married since 1188 and had none. The forger made another mistake when he dated the charter, something possible in France, but quite out of place in Ranulf's English charters. Finally, the list of witnesses, beginning with William the constable, who died c.1143–44, and including the younger Thomas Despenser, who died in 1218, Reginald son of Archenbald, who was seneschal of Wich Malbank before 1176 (**no. 240**), and Liulf of Twemlow, sheriff c.1190–1215, appears to have been thrown together haphazardly; probably none of the alleged witnesses was alive in 1230. The purpose of the forgery probably lies in the long list of obsolete and obsolescent rights and privileges (*uthesium* or hue and cry, bloodwite, etc.), which were a favourite target of royal advocates in inquests *de quo warranto*, in which case it probably dates from the time of Edward I, or later.

242. Confirmation to the Hospitallers of St. John of Jerusalem of all gifts made to them, with extensive liberties. [Spurious]

Chester, [1190–1194]

P.R.O. CHES 29/59 (Plea Rolls, 21 Edw. III); Bodleian Library, MS. Lat. Misc. C. 66, f. 58.

Ranulfus dux Brittanie et comes Cestrie et Richemondie abbatibus, iustic(iariis), vic(ecomitibus), ministris et omnibus fidelibus suis Francis et Anglis salutem. Sciatis me concessisse et confirmasse deo et fratribus hospitalis Ierusalem omnes donaciones terrarum et elemosinarum que eis rationabiliter facte sunt, tam in ecclesiis quam in rebus et possessionibus mundanis. Quare volo et firmiter precipio quod predicti fratres et eorum homines omnes possessiones et elemosinas suas habeant et teneant cum soka et saka et tol et them et infangthef, et cum omnibus libertatibus et liberis consuetudinibus et quietanciis in bosco et plano, in pratis et pasturis, in aquis et molendinis, in viis et semitis, in stagnis et vivariis, in mariscis et piscariis, in grangiis infra burgum et extra, et in omnibus locis et in omnibus rebus, solutas, liberas et quietas de shiris et hundredis et placitis et querelis et murdro et wappentagio et scutagio et geldis et danegeldis et hidagio et assisis et operacionibus castellorum et pontium, et de fredwyta et de hengwythe et de flemenefrythe et de warpeni et averpeni et de blodwyte et de flutwyte et de hundredpeni et tethingpeni, et quietas de omni tolloneo salinarum et de omnibus aliis toloneis et passagiis et pontagiis et lastagiis et stallagiis, et de omni seculari servicio et exaccione et opere servili. Volo etiam quod predicti fratres et omnes eorum homines in terris eorum habitantes et in eis cubantes et bevantes quieti sint ex omni putura servientium meorum et similiter de eis hospitandis, et de omnibus aliis occasionibus et exaccionibus secularibus, excepta sola iusticia mortis et membrorum. Hec omnia eis concessi in puram et perpetuam elemosinam pro dei amore et pro anima patris mei H. comitis Cestrie et matris mee B. comitissa Cestrie et puerorum et heredum meorum. Hec omnia firmiter precipio ut ab omnibus fidelibus et hominibus meis illis integre teneantur super forisfacturam decem librarum sterlingorum. Hiis testibus R. abbate Cestrie, Iohanne abbate de Combermere, Roberto abbate de Pultona, S. abbate de Stanlawe, Rogero constabulario Cestrie, Roberto senescallo de Moalto, Roberto de Meinegaryn, Willelmo Patrico, Garino de Vernoun, Willelmo de Venables, Hugone de Boydel, Hugone de Wyco, Roberto de Praers, et multis aliis coram comite apud Cestriam.

This charter as it stands is a blatant forgery, but a genuine, shorter and more modest charter almost certainly lies behind it. The witnesses are entirely acceptable, and the date must lie between the succession of Roger the constable in 1190 and 1194, when Abbot Robert of Chester resigned and Roger took the surname of Lacy.

243.   Letter to Richard bishop of London, requesting him to aid the canons of Fougères to get possession of the church of Cheshunt (co. Herts.) which his predecessors the counts of Brittany had given them, or alternatively to ensure that they receive a pension from Master Osbert, who is in possession.

Martilly, [1190–1195]

Orig.: B.L. Cott. Charter xi, 44. Ed.: *Mon.*, vi. 1114; Clay, *Early Yorkshire Charters*, iv. 77. Abstract: Orm., i. 38.

Reverendo et karissimo patri in Christo dilecto [Ricardo]¹ Londoniensi episcopo, Rannulfus comes Cestrie salutem et debitam et devotam subiectionem. Paternitati vestre, de qua plene confido, preces porrigo affectuosas pro dilectis meis canonicis Fulgeriensibus, quanta possum rogans instancia, quod divine pietatis intuitu et mee peticionis interventu predictos canonicos iuvetis et promoveatis ad habendum ecclesiam de Cestrehunt, quam comites Britannie predecessores mei eis dederunt et cartis suis confirmaverunt, sicut vobis satis notum est. Et ipsos canonicos pro dei amore a iure suo nullo modo prolongare aut disturbare velitis, sed vestri gratia ipsos in possessionem eiusdem ecclesie mittatis, vel pensionem eis reddi faciatis a magistro Osberto, qui illam possidet. Et tantum super hoc, si placet, faciatis, quod me vobis et omnibus vestris obnoxium et devotum habeatis ad omnia, que pro vobis facere potero. Et sciatis quod, postquam egrotavi, sigillum meum penes me non habui, et ideo has litteras vobis destino sub sigillo domine matris mee. Teste me ipso, apud Martilli.

SEAL: missing.

1.　. . . *orig.*

It is unfortunate that we are unable to date more closely this interesting letter, which is the only evidence we have of Earl Ranulf's illness. However, it can safely be placed between March 1190, when Ranulf was in Normandy with Richard I (Landon, *Itinerary of Richard I, P.R.S.*, N.S. xiii, p. 30), and March 1196. It was evidently intended to reinforce a similar letter from Ranulf's wife Constance, duchess of Brittany and countess of Richmond, addressed specifically to R[ichard] bishop of London, also surviving among the charters in the British Library. As Richard was only consecrated on 31 December 1189, it cannot fall before 1190. On the other hand, the latest date must be before March 1196 when Ranulf seized Constance at Pontorson, while on her way to Richard I's court, and imprisoned her in his castle at St. James-de-Beuvron. Probably it is a good deal earlier than this, as the estrangement of Ranulf and Constance dated back many months previously. It is interesting that Constance does not describe herself here, or elsewhere, as countess of Chester, and that Ranulf does not use the titles duke of Brittany and earl of Richmond. It is therefore probably not safe to use Ranulf's description as a means of dating his charters at this period.

244. Grant to Robert Lancelyn of a boat on the river Dee, in exchange for which Robert has quitclaimed to the earl a house beside the South Gate of Chester and the land attached to that house.

Chester, [1190–1198]

Orig.: Eaton Hall, Chester, John, no. 7. Abstract: B.L. Harl. MS. 2022, f. 86 (new f. 65), from original with sketch of seal; Add. MS. 19517, f. 66; Bodleian Library, Dodsworth MS. 39, f. 117v. Engl. translation: *Ches. Sheaf*, no. 10003.

Rannulphus comes Cestrie constabulario suo et dapifero, iusticiario et vicec(omiti), baronibus et ballivis et omnibus hominibus suis Francis et Anglis tam futuris quam presentibus salutem. Notum sit vobis omnibus me dedisse et concessisse et presenti carta mea confirmasse Roberto Lancelin unum liberum batellum in aqua de De, tenendum illi et heredibus suis de me et de meis heredibus libere et quiete, sicut aliquis alius liberius habet aliquod batellum in eadem aqua, et ad piscandum subtus pontem Cestrie et supra pontem et nominatim apud Etonam, et ubique ubi aliquod aliorum liberorum batellorum piscatur, et cum flotnettis et draghenetis et stalnettis et cum omni genere retium, cum quibus alio libera batella piscantur. Hanc donationem feci predicto Roberto pro homagio et servitio suo. Et idem Robertus propter hoc mihi quietam clamavit ab illo et heredibus suis mihi et meis heredibus unam domum, que est iuxta portam australem Cestrie, cum terra que est in eadem pacia, que pertinet domui illi, ita quod nec predictus Robertus nec aliquis heredum suorum in domo aut terra predicta amodo aliquod rectum clamabunt. Testibus hiis Radulfo de Monte Alto senescallo Cestrie, Radulfo de Mesnilwarin, Philippo de Orrebi, Radulfo Recucon, Rannulfo Walense, Roberto filio Picoti, Warino de Vernun, Ricardo fratre constabularii, Roberto Patric, Roberto Sarraceno, Radulfo fratre suo, Roberto camerario, Roaudo, Hugone de Columbariis, et multis aliis apud Cestriam.

SEAL: damaged, on green and red silken cord; obverse, equestrian figure, sword raised, legend . . . SIGILL . . .; reverse equestrian figure with shield, sword lowered, legend . . . UNDIE . . .

The appearance among the witnesses of Richard the brother of the constable indicates that this charter cannot be earlier than 1190, when Roger the constable succeeded to the title. As Ralph of Montalt, the seneschal, was apparently killed at the beginning of January 1199, it cannot be later than 1198, but there is no way of deciding whether it is earlier or later than Ranulf III's second charter for Robert Lancelyn (**no. 245**). Of the witnesses Ralph Recuchon witnesses a Norman charter dated 1203 (**no. 333**) and a Lincolnshire charter a year or two earlier (**no. 324**) and Hugh de Colombers the charter granting Peter the clerk a boat on the Dee (**no. 280**). For Roaud or Rowald, not to be confused with the earl's Norman retainer Pierre Rouaut, see **no. 307**. The seal is evidently that used by Ranulf when he was duke of Brittany and earl of Richmond (see the facsimile in Orm., i. 37), which he presumably ceased to use on his divorce from Constance of Brittany in 1199. The fact that it is used on a charter with the simple title earl of Chester shows that little, if any, reliance can be placed on the earl's description, where no seal survives, for purposes of dating.

245. Grant to Robert Lancelyn of freedom from attendance at county and hundred courts in respect of his lands at Poulton and Bebington; he and his heirs are to pay 18d. a year to the earl's chamber in lieu of 'sheriff's stuthe' and streteward.

[1193–1203]

> P.R.O., CHES 29/42 (Plea Rolls, 5 Edw. III) m. 12; CHES 34/4, m. 27 (charter not recited in full); Bodleian Library, Gough Cheshire I, f. 30 (abstract in English, with full list of witnesses). English text: *Ches. Sheaf*, no. 2419; abstract: Orm., ii. 441.

Ranulfus comes Cestrie constabulario suo et dapifero, iusticiario, vic(ecomiti), baronibus et ballivis et omnibus hominibus suis Francis et Anglicis tam futuris quam presentibus salutem. Notum sit vobis omnibus me dedisse et concessisse et presenti carta mea confirmasse Roberto Launcelyn et heredibus suis, quod ipsi teneant terram suam de Pultona et Bebyntona liberam et quietam de shira et de hundredo et de iudicibus. Concessi etiam et presenti carta mea confirmavi predicto Roberto Launcelyn et heredibus suis quod ipse et homines sui non respondeant de aliquo forisfacto, si in aliquo delinquerint, nisi coram me vel coram capitali iusticiario meo. Et preterea concessi et hac mea carta confirmavi predicto Roberto et heredibus suis, quod ipsi annuatim redderunt camere mee xviii. denarios pro shirvestuth et streteward, et quod hoc sit talliatum vicecomiti meo. Et pro hac concessione dedit mihi predictus Robertus unum dextrarium falvum. Hiis testibus Radulfo de Mesnilwarin, Petro Roaud, Philippo de Orreby, Roberto filio Picoti, Liulfo vicecomite, Ranulfo de Davenham, Alano Muniro, Rogero de Mesnilwarin, Willelmo de Venables, Thoma clerico presencium scriptore, et multis aliis.

The Lancelyns are said to have held Poulton and Bebington as heirs of Scirard, who supposedly held them of the Domesday tenant Osbern fitz Tesson (Orm., ii. 440), but the descent is conjectural, and the first known member of the family is Richard Lancelyn, father of the recipient of the present grant, in the time of Earl Hugh II. Richard's tenure of Poulton and Bebington was confirmed to his son by Hugh Boydell about the time of the present charter, i.e. during the last decade of the twelfth century. The present charter, which assumes that Robert is in possession of Poulton and Bebington, is probably a little later in date, but cannot be dated more closely than 1193–1203. It is also impossible to say whether it precedes or follows **no. 244**.

246.   Confirmation of his father's grant to the monks of Poulton.

Chester, [1190–1199]

> Orig.: Eaton Hall, Chester, Richard I, no. 2. Transcr.:
> Bodleian Library, MS. top. Gen. c. 26, p. 2 (from
> Rudyard cartulary). Abbr. abstracts: B.L. Harl. MS.
> 2060, f. 24 (old f. 40); Chester, Booth of Twemlow, Liber
> D, f. 56. Ed.: *D.C.*, p. 330 (no. 76).

Ranulfus comes Cestrie constabulario suo et dapifero, iusticiario et vicecomiti et omnibus baronibus et ballivis suis et omnibus hominibus suis Francis et Anglis tam presentibus quam futuris salutem. Notum sit vobis omnibus me pro amore dei et pro salute anime mee et patris mei et antecessorum meorum concessisse et hac carta mea confirmasse deo et sancte Marie et monachis de Pultona donationem terre illius de Pultona quam pater meus eis dedit in puram et perpetuam elemosinam habendam, sicut continetur in carta patris mei, quam predicti monachi habent. Testibus hiis Rogero conestabulario Cestrie, Radulfo de Mesnilwarin, Roberto filio Picot, Iohanne de Cumbrai, Ricardo fratre conestabularii, Iohanne de Escaioel, Alexandro filio Radulfi, Bertramo camerario, Thoma clerico, Roaudo, Willelmo Gamberello tunc vicecomite, et aliis multis apud Cestriam.

SEAL: on tag, much damaged and indecipherable.

For Hugh II's charters, here confirmed, see **nos. 157** and **159**. The present confirmation must have been given before 1199, by when John de Combray was dead (*Chart. St. Werburgh*, p. 124). As Roger the constable does not use the surname Lacy, it may be before 1194. For John de Escaiol (or de Scagolo), see *E.C.C.*, p. 35. Alexander son of Ralph was Ranulf III's tutor, who married the heiress of Robert Savage c.1177–81 (**no. 188**). William Gamberell was almost certainly sheriff of the city, not of the county, of Chester. Richard the constable's brother witnessed a charter at much the same time for Robert Lancelyn (**no. 244**); he is more commonly known as Richard of Chester, and is said to have become a leper and been buried at Norton priory (Orm., i. 694).

247.   Grant to Poulton abbey of a free boat on the Dee at Chester with the right to fish above and below the bridge of Chester and at Eaton.

Chester, [c.1200]

Orig.: Eaton Hall, Chester; facsimile *J.C.A.S.*, iii, p. 237. Transcr.: B.L. Harl. MS. 2022, f. 65 (old f. 86), from original, partly in facsimile; P.R.O., C.53 (Chancery Charter Rolls), no. 117; C.66 (Chancery Patent Rolls), no. 421, m. 26, and no. 519, m. 20. Ed.: *Cal. Ch. Rolls*, iv. 156 (no. 19); *D.C.*, p. 331 (no. 80) (abbreviated).

Ranulfus comes Cestrie constabulario suo et dapifero suo, iust(iciario) et vicecom(iti) et barronibus[1] et ballivis[2] suis, et omnibus hominibus suis Francis et Anglicis tam presentibus quam futuris salutem. Sciatis me pro dei amore et pro animabus antecessorum meorum et pro salute anime mee concessisse et hac mea carta confirmasse deo et sancte Marie et abbatie de Pultuna et monachis ibidem deo servientibus in puram et perpetuam elemosinam unum liberum batellum in aqua Cestrensi in perpetuum, habendum sine omni impedimento et consuetudine liberum et quietum, et ad piscandum subtus pontem Cestrie et supra eundem pontem[3] et ubique ubi aliquod aliorum liberorum batellorum piscatur cum omni genere recium in aqua de De nocte dieque tam apud Etun quam alibi. His testibus Radulfo de Mainguarin, Philippo de Orrebi, Petro Rowald, Petro clerico, Thoma cancellario, Roberto Pigot, et aliis multis apud Cestriam.

SEAL: missing.

1. *sic orig.*
2. balliis *orig.*
3. ponte *orig.*

The date of this charter is approximately fixed by the appearance of Ralph Mainwaring and Philip of Orreby, both without the designation of justiciar, and also by the attestation of Pierre Rowald (Rouaut), who withdrew from the earl's service in 1203–4 (*Ches. Sheaf*, no. 2419). Particular interest attaches to the description of the clerk Thomas as chancellor. Tait (*Chart. St. Werburgh*, p. xlviii) thought this was a mistake for *camerarius* (chamberlain), but was unaware that Thomas appears as chancellor in another charter of Ranulf III a few years before 1200 (**no. 289**). The title is unusual, but at least points to the leading position which Thomas occupied. It has been usual to ascribe this position to Peter the clerk (Tait, *loc. cit.*; *E.C.C.*, p. 46), but Thomas witnessed some 20 charters of Ranulf III, usually as 'the clerk of the earl', between c.1195 and 1210, mostly c.1199–1203, and although Peter was active at the same period, it seems possible that his rôle has been exaggerated. There is no doubt that he rose rapidly in the favour of Ranulf III, who was godfather of his son (**no. 284**); but his rise to prominence seems to come after 1200 and should not obscure the leading position which Thomas seems to have occupied previously.

248.   Confirmation to the abbot and monks of Poulton of Richard of Aldford's gift of the vill of Byley (nr. Middlewich).

[1208–1213]

> Original: Shakerley Deeds (*penes* Sir Arthur Bryant), Y.
> iii. i. Transcr.: B.L. Harl.MS. 2060, f. 26 (old f. 44), and
> Harl. MS. 1967, f. 104v. (from original).

R. comes Cestrie omnibus presentibus et futuris salutem. Sciatis me concessisse et confirmasse Radulfo abbati et monachis de Pultona donum quod Ricardus de Aldeford fecit eisdem de villa sua de Biveleia cum omnibus pertinenciis suis, habendam et tenendam libere et quiete sicut liberam elemosinam, sicut carta ipsius R., quam dicti abas[1] et monachi habent, testatur. Et quia volo quod dicta donacio sit stabilis in perpetuum, eam presenti scripto et sigilli mei inpressione[1] roboravi. Testibus H. abbate Cestrie, A. abbate de Basigwerc, P. de Orrebi iusticiario Cestrie, Gualtero de Daivilla, Stephano de Segrave, Aluredo de Suligni, magistro Hugone, et multis aliis.

SEAL: green wax, pendent on tag, lion seal.

1.   *sic MS.*

For Richard of Aldford's grant, see *D.C.*, no. 97. It was given in the presence of Earl Ranulf and has, with one exception, the same witnesses as the present charter, and it can safely be assumed that the two charters were issued simultaneously. As Richard of Aldford died in 1213 (*Ches. Sheaf*, no. 10136), this sets an outside limit to the date. Abbot Hugh of Chester succeeded in 1208, and Stephen Segrave succeeded his father Gilbert about the same time (*H.K.F.*, p. 71).

249.   Confirmation to the monks of Poulton of the lands of Bradford and Wethull given to them by John of Arderne in exchange for the lands the abbey held in the manor of Aldford.

[1213–1214]

> Salt Library, Stafford, Dieulacres roll, no. 13; Bodleian
> Library, MS. Top. Gen. c. 26, f. 32 (transcr. of Rudyard
> cartulary). Brief abstracts: B.L. Harl. MS. 2060, f. 25v.
> (old p. 43); Chester, Booth of Twemlow, Liber D, f. 62.
> Ed.: *D.C.*, p. 339 (no. 106) (abbreviated).

Ranulfus comes Cestrie universis presentibus et futuris presentem paginam inspecturis et audituris salutem. Vestra noverit universitas me concessisse et presenti carta mea confirmasse abbati et monachis de Pultona totam donacionem terrarum, scilicet de Bradeford et Wetehull, in escambio terrarum quas idem abbas et monachi tenuerunt in manerio de Aldeford, tenendarum et habendarum in puram et perpetuam elemosinam libere et quiete, bene et pacifice, sicut carta Iohannis de Arderne domini de Aldeford testatur. Testibus hiis Philippo de Orreby tunc iusticiario Cestrie, Petro clerico, Ricardo de Perepunt tunc vicecomite Cestrie, Hugone de Pascy, Willelmo monacho, Bertrammo camerario, Ricardo de Rodestorne, Thurstano clerico, Ricardo de Sondbach, Ricardo clerico, et multis aliis.

John of Arderne is thought to have married the daughter of Richard of Aldford and to have succeeded to the great fee of Aldford in or possibly shortly before 1213 (*D.C.*, p. 338, note 3). If that is the case, the present charter can be narrowly dated, since it is highly unlikely that it was issued after Ranulf III decided to move the monks from Poulton to Dieulacres in May 1214. John of Arderne's charter for the monks is printed *D.C.*, no. 105, and has some of the same witnesses. For Ranulf's charter conferring Aldford on John of Arderne, see **no. 374**; for Richard of Pierrepont, who was almost certainly sheriff of the city of Chester, see **no. 372**.

250. Grant to Nicholas son of Robert of a boat for fishing on the Dee.

Chester, [1190–1199]

Orig.: J.R.U.L.M., Mainwaring MSS., Suppl. 3. Transcr.: Bodleian Library, Ashmole MS. 833, f. 43, and Ashmole MS. 1137, f. 136 (both from original). Ed.: *10th Rep. Hist. MSS. Comm.*, App. pt. iv, p. 201.

Rannulfus comes Cestrie constabulario suo et dapifero, iusticiario et vicecomiti, baronibus et ballivis suis et omnibus hominibus suis Francis et Anglis, et omnibus tam futuris quam presentibus salutem. Sciatis me dedisse et concessisse et presenti carta mea confirmasse Nicholao filio Roberti et heredibus suis pro homagio et servicio suo unum liberum batellum in aqua de De, tenendum de me et de heredibus meis libere et quiete et ad piscandum die ac nocte cum flotnettis et draghnettis et stalnettis et cum omni genere retium et subtus pontem Cestrie et supra pontem et nominatim apud Etonam et ubique ubi alia libera batella piscantur, reddendo annuatim mihi et heredibus meis ab illo et heredibus suis quatuor denarios in nativitate sancti Iohannis Baptiste. Et prohibeo super forisfacturam meam x. librarum ne aliquis predictum Nicholaum aut heredes suos inde disturbet, et quod faciant de piscibus quas capiant quod eis bonum fuerit. Hiis testibus Radulfo de Megnilwarin, Philippo de Orrebi, Iuhello de Luvingneio, Hugone et Ricardo de Boidele, Roberto filio Picoti, Roberto Sarraceno et Radulfo fratre suo, Rannulfo Dubbeldei, Ricardo filio Radulfi, Philippo filio Willelmi, Petro clerico, Thoma clerico presencium scriptore, et multis aliis apud Cestriam.

> SEAL: fragmentary, green wax on silken cord; on obverse
> and reverse a mounted knight.

Nicholas son of Robert witnessed with Ralph Saracen and Ranulf Doubleday a charter of the prioress of St. Mary's nunnery, Chester (*J.C.A.S.*, N.S. x, p. 16) dated 1190–94. He was obviously a member of a Chester family, but nothing more is known of him. The date of the present charter is approximately the same. It is in the same handwriting as **no. 244**, i.e. that of Thomas the earl's clerk, who also wrote Ranulf's charters for St. Werburgh's (**no. 228**), dated 1191–94, and for Poulton (**no. 246**), dated 1190–99. The seal, like that of **no. 244**, is Ranulf's seal as duke of Brittany, in use from 1189 to 1199.

[BERTRADA, WIDOW OF HUGH II.]

251. Agreement between Countess Bertrada and the abbot and convent of Troarn regarding the construction of a mill and fishpond on the boundary between her wood and theirs.

[1190–1200]

> Orig.: Archives de Calvados, H. 7864; cal.: d'Anisy, ii.
> 176–7.

Omnibus fidelibus notum sit huiusmodi conventionem inter abbatem Troarni et Berteleiam relictam comitis Cestrensis esse factam. Abbas et monachi facient vivarium et molendinum in divisione nemoris sui et nemoris comitisse hoc modo, quod monachi facient molendinum et vivarium totum de expensa sua, et quicquid inde fructus provenit, tamdiu monachi accipient, donec comitissa vel heredes sui medietatem expensarum eis restituant. Restituta autem expensa, in vivario utrique pari iure participabunt et scriptum suum invicem alter alteri restituet. Teste Rannulfo de Prateriis, Philippo fratre suo, Hascuillo filio Rannulfi, Willelmo de Escafou, Willelmo Barba Aprilis clerico comitisse.

> At head, divided: 'Cirographum'.
> SEAL: white, on tag, damaged; a figure with hand raised
> in benediction; presumably the seal of the abbot.

It is difficult to date this document accurately, and there is no indication of the location of the land in question, but presumably it was in the neighbourhood of Troarn. Bertrada, the widow of Earl Hugh II, was only 25 years old when her husband died, and lived until 1227. The present agreement appears to date from circa 1190–1200. Ranulf of Praers accounted to the Norman exchequer in 1198 (*Rot. Scacc. Norm.*, ii. 358). He witnessed a charter of Roger Malbank, which was confirmed by Roger's son John in 1202 (ibid., ff. 77v.–78), and issued a charter for Troarn with the assent of his son Hasculf (MS. Paris lat. 10086, f. 55) at about the same time. Ranulf, Philip and Hasculf were also active in Lincolnshire between 1191 and 1196 (*H.K.F.*, p. 144). William of Eschafou accounted to the exchequer in 1195 (*Rot. Scacc. Norm.*, i. 240, 242). William Barbe d'Averill, the countess's clerk, was the son of Ralph Barbe d'Averill, who witnessed a charter of Earl Hugh in 1162–67 (Warner and Ellis, no. 51).

252. Notification to his constables, castellans and bailiffs of Coventry of his grant to William Marshall of the land formerly held by a certain 'Liegrus' and a meadow below Caludon.

[? 1190–1200]

Bodleian Library, Dugdale MS. 18, f. 6; B.L. Harl. MS. 4748, f. 3v. (abstract without address).

Ranulphus comes Cestrie omnibus constabulariis et castellanis et ballivis suis Coventrie salutem. Sciatis me dedisse Willelmo Marescallo et heredibus suis[1] terram que fuit Liegri,[2] et pratum sub Caluedon tenendam libere[1] in feodo et hereditate. Quare volo *etc.*

1. *Text based on Dugdale MS*; et heredibus suis *and* tenendam libere *supplied from Harl. MS.*
2. Liegr̄, *Dugdale MS.*; Liegri *Harl. MS.*

This heavily abbreviated fragment is hard to place and assess. The address to his constables, etc., reads like a charter of Ranulf II, but Caludon (in Wyken, outside Coventry) only makes an appearance under Ranulf III, and William Marshall is almost certainly identical with the William Marshall of Sutton who occurs c.1200 (**nos. 253, 254**). All efforts to identify the mysterious 'Liegrus' have failed. The charter in its defective form cannot be satisfactorily dated, but it probably falls in the period 1190–1200.

253.   Gift to William Marshall of Sutton of forty acres between Coventry and his land in Asthill.

[c.1200]

Halstead, *Succinct Genealogies*, p. 451.

Ranulphus comes Cestrie omnibus tam futuris quam presentibus salutem. Notum sit vobis omnibus me dedisse Willelmo Mareschallo de Sutton pro homagio et servitio suo quadraginta acras terre inter Coventreyam et terram suam de Esthull cum pannagio et cum omnibus aliis libertatibus, tenendas ei et heredibus suis in feudo et hereditate de me et de meis heredibus libere et quiete et honorifice, reddendo ab illo et heredibus suis mihi et meis heredibus annuatim in nativitate sancti Iohannis Baptiste quedam calcaria deaurata pro omni servitio. Et quod ipse Willelmus vel heredes sui terram illam essartent[1] si voluerint, vel eam teneant cum nemore quod est in terra illa. Et ut hec donatio mea perpetue firmitatis robur obtineat, presenti scripto et sigilli mei munimine eam confirmavi. Testibus hiis Hugone de Colonciis,[2] Petro Roaud, Iuhello Berengero,[3] Gaufrido Farsi,[4] Iuhello de Lovigneio, Philippo de Oreby, Bartholomeo abbate, Richardo Pisce,[5] Willelmo de Serlant, Willelmo de Verdun, Petro clerico et multis aliis.

SEAL: lion seal on heater shield; legend SIGILLUM RANULPHI COMITIS CESTRIE.

1.   ellarcent *ed.*
2.   Colone *ed.*
3.   Benegero *ed.*
4.   Farly *ed.*
5.   Pilse *ed.*

By 1204 the lands of Hugh de Coulances (Calvados, arr. and cant. Vire) were escheat, he having gone over to the allegiance of the king of France, and the large number of Norman witnesses who did likewise indicates that this grant was made by 1203. William of Verdun was dead by 1204 or 1205 (*P.R.S.*, N.S. xviii, p. 111). For the career of William of Serland, see *H.K.F.*, p. 339. William Marshall is almost certainly identical with the man of that name who was sued by Margery of Coventry in 1194 for disseising her of her daughter's inheritance (*H.K.F.*, p. 98); he was dead by 1208–9 (*Dugdale Society, Feet of Fines*, no. 174).

254.   Permission to William Marshall of Sutton to give all tithes from his demesne and other lands at Asthill (Coventry) to maintain a chaplain in his chapel at Asthill, rendering a pound of incense yearly to the church of St. Michael in Coventry.

[c.1200]

Halstead, *Succinct Genealogies*, p. 451.

Ranulphus comes Cestrie omnibus ad quos presens scriptum pervenerit, salutem et amorem. Sciatis me concessisse et hac presenti carta confirmasse Willelmo Mareschallo de Suttonia et heredibus suis, ut donent omnes decimationes de dominio suo de Esthull et de omnibus terris et assarcis, quas eis dedi apud predictum Esthull, uno capellano, qui serviat in capella sua de Esthull imperpetuum, pro anima patris mei et antecessorum suorum, reddendo annuatim unam libram thuris ecclesie sancti Michaelis de Coventrey ad Pascha nomine impensionis. His testibus Philippo de Orebi, Petro Roaud, Petro de sancto Hillario, Iuhello de Lovigneio, Iuhello Berenger, et multis aliis apud Rigidum Pontem.

Halstead is not always reliable, but there is no reason to reject the present document. Judging by the witnesses, the date must be close to that of no. **253.**

255. Grant to Robert Marshall of Stiviehall (nr. Coventry) of 40 acres for his homage and service.

[1181–1210]

Stratford-upon-Avon, Shakespeare's Birthplace, Arthur Gregory's cartulary, f. 139.

Ranulphus comes Cestrie omnibus hominibus suis tam presentibus quam futuris salutem. Sciatis me dedisse et concessisse et hac presenti carta confirmasse Roberto Marescallo de Stivechale pro homagio et servicio suo xl. acras terre, scilicet iiii. inter rivum de Smalwell et terram quam Willelmus Ode[1] tenuit, et triginta acras et v. in exarto inter Callewod et Burchley,[1] et unam acram iuxta parcum meum et exartum quem Alexander capellanus tenuit propinquiorem terre predicti Roberti de Styvechale, cum omnibus pertinenciis predictarum acrarum sibi et heredibus suis de me et heredibus meis tenendas et habendas libere, quiete, honorifice, reddendo inde michi annuatim et heredibus meis de se et heredibus suis unam marcam argenti ad quattuor terminos anni pro omni servicio ad me vel ad meos pertinente, scilicet ad festum sancti Iohannis Baptiste quadraginta denarios et ad festum sancte Marie in Martio xl. denarios et ad festum sancti Andree xl. denarios et ad festum sancti Michaelis xl. denarios. Et preterea concessi ei clausuram de nemore meo omnibus predictis acris rationabiliter per visum forestariorum meorum. Hiis testibus.[2]

1. Readings unclear and uncertain MS.
2. Names of witnesses omitted MS.

This charter cannot be closely dated, but a grant by Robert Marshall's widow Margery (*Langley cart.*, no. 191), has been dated after 1210, and Alexander the chaplain does not appear after the time of Earl Hugh II (**no. 169**). It looks, therefore, as though it falls in the earlier part of Ranulf III's tenure of the earldom. Robert Marshall's relationship, if any, to William Marshall of Sutton (**nos. 253, 254**) cannot be established, but a relationship is not unlikely.

256.   Grant to his citizens of Chester of all the liberties and customs enjoyed by them under his predecessors, especially freedom from inquest (*recognitio*) and assize (*proportamentum*) in the city of Chester, together with other specified rights.

Chester, [1191–1194]

> Orig.: Chester City Record Office, Archives of Chester Corporation, no. 4. Enrolment from inspeximus: P.R.O., CHES 2/36, m. 5. Ed.: *8th Rep. Hist. MSS. Comm.*, p. 356 (no. 4); Morris, *Chester in the Plantagenet and Tudor Reigns*, p. 482.

Rannulfus comes Cestrie constabulario, dapifero, iusticiario, ballivis et omnibus baronibus et omnibus hominibus suis Francis et Anglis tam futuris quam presentibus salutem. Notum sit vobis omnibus me dedisse et concessisse et presenti carta mea confirmasse omnibus civibus meis de Cestria omnes libertates et omnes liberas consuetudines, quas illi unquam melius et liberius aut quietius habuerunt temporibus aliquorum predecessorum meorum, et nominatim quiet-antiam et relaxationem recognitionis et proportamenti in civitate Cestrie in perpetuum.

Et quod, si civis aliquis de predicta civitate mea moriatur, eius testamentum rationabiliter factum ratum et firmum habeatur, ubicumque ipse moriatur.

Et quod, si civis fecerit emptionem aliquam de clara die et coram testibus, et sequela postea venerit de Francis vel de Anglis, qui rationabiliter possint emptum disratiocinare, civis qui illam emptionem fecerit, quietus sit de me et de ballivis meis, perdendo tantummodo et reddendo quod emerit, si aliter non possit vendicanti satisfacere. Si vero sequela evenerit de Walense, qui possit rationabiliter rem emptam disratiocinare, precium rei empte civi reddat, quod idem civis rationabiliter poterit demonstrare se dedisse pro re empta.

Et quod, si civis in civitate predicta de catallis suis cuiquam comodaverit, liceat ei namum capere in ipsa civitate pro catallis suis recuperandis sine licencia postulata a vicecomite vel ab aliis ballivis meis.

Et si aliquis civis de predicta civitate in servicio meo occisus fuerit, de catallis suis fiat ac si ipse rationabile testamentum fecisset.

Has omnes libertates predictas et liberas consuetudines predictis civibus dedi et concessi et presenti carta mea confirmavi eis et heredibus suis, habendas et tenendas de me et de meis heredibus libere et quiete et pacifice in perpetuum. Et prohibeo ne quis eos inde disturbet aut heredes eorum super forisfacturam meam de xx. libris. Hiis testibus Rogero constabulario Cestrie, Radulfo de Monte Alto senescallo Cestrie, Radulfo de Mesnilwarin, Willelmo et Roberto Patric, Philippo de Orrebi, Ricardo et Willelmo de Boidele, Ricardo Phitone, Liulpho de Twamlawa, Rannulfo de Davenham, Warino de Vernun, Roberto filio Picoti, Petro clerico comitis, Ricardo Pisce, Herberto de Pulford, Willelmo de Verdun, Thoma clerico, et multis aliis apud Cestriam.

SEAL: on cords, small fragment of equestrian seal.

This is the oldest surviving charter of liberties for the citizens of Chester, though the text makes plain that they had enjoyed similar liberties under Ranulf III's predecessors. Though the text is not explicit, it seems probable that the clauses beginning with the concession that the testament of any citizen should hold good wherever he died, were additional liberties granted by Ranulf himself. The charter was dated 1199 by Fergusson Irvine (*Ches. Sheaf*, no. 9390), largely on the ground that Ranulf was no longer using the title duke of Brittany, but there is ample evidence that he used the simple title earl of Chester during his marriage to Constance of Brittany (1188–1199). The appearance among the witnesses of William Patric and Ralph of Montalt, both of whom died in 1199, sufficiently indicates that 1199 is the latest date; but the charter may well be earlier. The fact that Roger the constable does not use the name Lacy suggests that it was issued before 1194, and William de Verdun may have been dead by 1195 (*P.R.S.*, N.S. vii, p. 195). Though the evidence is inconclusive, it seems probable that the charter falls between 1191 and 1194; the witnesses are compatible with this date, and the equestrian seal seems to be that in use while Ranulf was duke of Brittany and earl of Richmond.

257. Grant to his citizens of Chester of a gild merchant with all the liberties they enjoyed in that gild in the time of his predecessors.

Chester, [1191–1194]

Orig.: Chester City Record Office, Archives of Chester Corporation, no. 3. Transcr.: B.L. Harl. MS. 2060, f. 34v. (old p. 61). Facsimile: *Guide to the Charters, Plate and Insignia of the City of Chester*, p. 14. Ed.: *8th Rep. Hist. MSS. Comm.*, p. 356 (no. 3); Morris, *Chester in the Plantagenet and Tudor Reigns*, p. 482.

Rannulfus comes Cestrie constabulario suo et dapifero, iusticiario et vicecomiti et omnibus baronibus et ballivis suis et omnibus hominibus suis Francis et Anglis tam futuris quam presentibus salutem. Notum sit vobis omnibus me dedisse et concessisse et presenti carta mea confirmasse omnibus civibus meis de Cestria gildam suam mercalem cum omnibus libertatibus et liberis consuetudinibus, quas illi unquam melius et liberius et quietius habuerunt temporibus antecessorum meorum in predicta gilda. Et prohibeo super forisfacturam meam x. librarum ne aliquis eos inde disturbet. Testibus hiis Rogero constabulario Cestrie, Radulfo de Monte Alto senescallo Cestrie, Radulfo de Mesnilwarin, Willelmo et Roberto Patric, Philippo de Orrebi, Ricardo et Willelmo de Boidele, Ricardo Phitone, Liulpho de Tuamlowa, Rannulfo de Davenham, Warino de Vernun, Roberto filio Picoti, Petro clerico comitis, Ricardo Pisce, Herberto de Pulford, Willelmo de Verdun, Thoma clerico comitis presencium scriptore, et multis aliis apud Cestriam.

SEAL: on cords, equestrian figure much repaired on obverse and reverse, legend wanting.

The witnesses of this charter are identical with those of **no. 256**, and both are in the handwriting of Thomas, the earl's clerk. Why it was decided to draft a separate charter for the grant of a gild merchant, is impossible to say; but there seems no doubt that both charters were issued at the same time.

258. Grant to the citizens of Chester and their heirs that no-one coming by land or by sea should buy or sell any merchandise in the city, except with their consent, save at the fairs on the nativity of St. John the Baptist and at Michaelmas.

[1208–1217, probably 1216]

Orig.: Chester City Record Office, Archives of Chester
Corporation, no. 2. Ed.: *8th Rep. Hist. MSS. Comm.*,
Appendix, p. 356; Morris, *Chester in the Plantagenet and
Tudor Reigns*, p. 482. Noted from royal inspeximus of
1239; *Cal. Ch. Rolls*, i. 247, and ii. 487. See also *Guide to
the Charters, Plate and Insignia of the City of Chester*, p.
15.

Rannulfus comes Cestrie constabulario, dapifero, iusticiario, vic(ecomiti),
baronibus, militibus, ballivis et omnibus hominibus suis presentibus et futuris
salutem. Sciatis me concessisse et presenti carta mea confirmasse dominicis
hominibus meis Cestrie et eorum heredibus, quod nullus aliquod genus mercimonii, quod ad civitatem Cestrie per mare aut per terram venerit, emat aut
vendat, nisi ipsi et eorum heredes aut per eorum gratum, nisi in nundinis assisis
in nativitate sancti Iohannis Baptiste et in festo sancti Michaelis. Quare volo
quod predicti homines mei et eorum heredes habeant et teneant antedictam
libertatem de me et de heredibus meis inperpetuum libere, quiete, honorifice et
pacifice. Et prohibeo super forisfacturam meam decem librarum ad opus meum
capiendarum, ne aliquis eos super dicta libertate impediat aut gravet. Testibus
domino H. tunc abbate Cestrie, Philippo de Orrebi tunc iusticiario Cestrie,
Guarino de Vernun, Guillelmo de Venables, Petro clerico, Rogero de Meinilgarin, Hugone et Thoma dispensariis, Aluredo de Suligny, Guillelmo pincerna,
Normanno Pantuf, Ada de Yeland, David de Malo Passu, Josceram de
Hellesby, Ricardo de Kingesleghe, Hugone et Galfrido de Duttona, magistro
Hugone, et multis aliis.

SEAL: missing.

This grant may be regarded as supplementary to the rights conveyed to the
citizens of Chester in **no. 256**. It has been dated 1215–16 on rather slender
evidence (*Ches. Sheaf*, no. 9417), but must fall between 1208, when Hugh
became abbot of St. Werburgh's, and 1217. It is, however, worth noting that the
witness Adam of Yealand was one of the hostages taken in January 1216 in a
transaction where Earl Ranulf seems to be acting on behalf of King John
(*L.P.R.*, p. 258). This may account for his presence in Ranulf's entourage; in
which case the date 1216 is not out of the question.

259. Grant to the abbey of Montmorel (dioc. Avranches) of the plot of land
which Walter the Tailor formerly held in St. James-de-Beuvron.

St. James, [1191–1194]

Orig.: destroyed, 1944. Transcr.: MS. Paris lat. 10073 (transcripts from archives of St. Lô), f. 32v. Abstracts: Paris, fr. nouv. acq. 21812, f. 369; Morice, *Histoire de Bretagne, Preuves*, i. col. 707; Round, *C.D.F.*, no. 786. Ed.: Dubosc, *Cartulaire de Mont-Morel*, pp. 270–1 (from original).

Ranulfus dux Britannie, comes Cestrie et de Richemont,[1] universis ad quos presens pagina pervenerit salutem. Universitati vestre notum facio me dei amore et pro salute animarum antecessorum meorum omnium et mee necnon et successorum meorum dedisse deo et ecclesie beate Marie de Muntmorel et canonicis ibidem sub regulari disciplina[2] deo servientibus in puram et perpetuam elemosinam placiam que fuit Gauteri Taillatoris in villa sancti Iacobi super Beverun, quietam et solutam ab omni servicio seculari et ab omni exactione. Et ut hec donatio mea rata et inconcussa[3] permaneat, nec in posterum pro tractu temporis valeat irritari, sigilli mei munimine et presentis scripti auctoritate eam duxi roborandam. Testibus Baudewino Wac, Guillelmo de Verdun, Fulcone de Servun, Guillelmo Grimaud, Rogero de Cestria fratre comitis, Rogero constabulario Cestrie, Eudone de Thoria, et aliis pluribus apud sanctum Iacobum super Beverun.

SEAL: fragmentary, a figure on horseback on obverse and reverse.

1. Richemundie *ed.*
2. sub reg. disc. *only in Dubosc.*
3. inconvulsa *Dubosc.*

Ranulf III was hereditary castellan of St. James, on the border of Normandy and Brittany. The fact that Roger the constable of Chester does not bear the name Lacy indicates that the charter was issued in the period 1191–94. As Ranulf was commander of Richard I's army in Normandy in 1194, it is possible that it dates from that time. William de Verdun may have been dead by 1195 (*P.R.S.*, N.S. vii, p. 195), and was certainly dead some time before 1203 when Walter de Verdun fined as heir for his lands (*ibid.*, xviii, p. 111). Baldwin Wake was probably dead by 1198 (*Rot. Scacc. Norm.*, ii. 385, 476, 477) and certainly before 1200 (*H.K.F.*, p. 170). Roger of Chester, the earl's brother, who also witnessed a charter of about the same period for St. Werburgh's abbey (**no. 227**), was an illegitimate son of Earl Hugh, but little otherwise is known of him. He is described in 1193–94 (*P.R.S.*, N.S. v, p. 162) as 'successor' of Henry de Lacy of Pontefract, to whom Ranulf II had granted Lowdham and East Bridgeford some time around 1150 (**no. 69**).

260. Confirmation of Henry and Juliana de Nuers' gift of Preston (Preston Brook, near Dutton, Cheshire) to Hugh Dutton.

Frodsham, [1191–1194]

Tabley MSS., Sir Peter Leycester's Liber C, f. 139v. and f. 155 (from the evidence of Dutton of Dutton); Shakerley MSS., Liber C, f. 228; Chester, Booth of Twemlow, Liber K, f. 39 (abbreviated); B.L. Harl. MS. 2074, f. 181v. (new f. 78v.). Brief reference: Orm., i. 644, 739.

Rannulfus comes Cestrie constabulario, dapifero suo, iusticiario suo et vicecomiti, baronibus et ballivis et omnibus hominibus suis Francis et Anglis tam futuris quam presentibus salutem. Sciatis me concessisse et presenti carta mea confirmasse donationem quam Henricus de Nuers et Juliana uxor eius fecerunt Hugoni de Duttona de terra de Prestona, salvo in omnibus servitio meo. Testibus hiis Rogero constabulario Cestrie, Philippo de Orrebi, Ricardo Pisce, Ricardo Phitone, Ada de Duttona, Roberto de Wivilla, Radulfo filio Rogeri, Hugone dispensario, Alano de Boidel, Willelmo de Camvilla, Iohanne Burdun, Eutropio, magistro, Radulfo medico, Ranulfo clerico de Froddesham, Thoma clerico comitis presentium scriptore, Alano minitro,[1] et multis aliis apud Froddesham.

SEAL: 'a man on horsebacke'.

1. muniero, *Shakerley and Harl. MSS.*

Henry de Nuers was a landholder in Northamptonshire who also acquired land in Oxfordshire through his wife Juliana (*H.K.F.*, p. 248). It is not clear how they acquired land in Cheshire. Their disposal of their land at Preston to Hugh of Dutton for 5 marks and a black palfrey, witnessed by Gerard de Nuers and other Northamptonshire witnesses, is recorded in Leycester's Liber C, f. 155. For the Dutton family, see *E.C.C.*, no. 9 (pp. 20–22). Around 1184–85 Hugh married the daughter of Hamo de Mascy (Liber C, f. 154). The date of the present charter is not easy to establish, but presumably it falls between 1191, when Roger succeeded his father John as constable of Cheshire, and 1194, when he inherited the Lacy estates of Clitheroe and Pontefract and adopted the surname of Lacy.

261. Gift in marriage of Helen, daughter of Jordan of Cheadle, to Geoffrey of Dutton, with all her inheritance.

[1191–1203, probably 1191–1194]

Orig.: Cheshire Record Office, Cholmondeley Deeds, Box X, Bdle. 12/1 (severely defaced by damp and barely legible). Transcr.: B.L. Harl. MS. 338 (from charters of Sir John Savage, 1599), f. 13v. (abbreviated text).

Ranulfus comes Cestrie omnibus tam futuris quam presentibus, ad quos littere presentes pervenerint, salutem. Notum sit vobis omnibus [me dedisse et concessisse] Gaufrido de Duttona pro homagio s[uo] et servicio Helenam filiam Iordani de Chedle cum tota hereditate sua ducendam in uxorem, et tenendam libere et quiete [hereditatem suam] cum omnibus ad ipsam pertinentibus, faciendo ser[vici]um quod ad terram ipsam pertinet [. . . . . .] mihi et heredibus meis. Et ut hoc ratum et [inconcussum perman]eat, presenti scripto et sigillo meo idipsum confirmavi. Testibus hiis Rogero conestabulario Cestrie, Eustachio fratre suo, Petro Rouaud, Bartholomeo abbate, Thoma dispensatore, Hamone de Masceio, Guarino de Vernun, Willelmo de Boidele, Hugone de Duttun, Adam de Duttun, Liulfo vicecomite, Ricardo de Kingesle, Gralam de Lostoc, et multis aliis.

SEAL: missing.

For this charter, see *E.C.C.*, p. 32. Geoffrey of Dutton was the youngest brother of Hugh and Adam of Dutton, who witness the charter, and by this marriage founder of the family of Dutton of Cheadle. Roger the constable's omission of the surname Lacy suggests that the charter may date from before 1194; in any case it must date from before 1204 when the French witnesses, Pierre Rouaut and Barthelémy l'Abbé, withdrew to France. Liulf of Twemlow was sheriff throughout the period beginning with Roger the constable's succession in 1190.

262.   Confirmation of Richard Bacon's foundation charter for Rocester abbey, with recital of places there specified. [Spurious]

Nottingham, [1191–1194]

Northants Record Office, Lamport Hall, Finch Hatton MS. 215 (B. 79), ff. 191–192; B.L. Harl. MS. 4028, f. 230 (both from ancient parchment roll in possession of Francis Trentham of Rocester, 1615); Harl. MS. 3868, ff. 25v.–26. Ed.: *Mon.*, vi. 411.

Universis sancte matris ecclesie filiis ad quos presens pagina pervenerit, Ranulfus comes Cestrie salutem in domino. Noverit universitas vestra me concessisse et hac carta mea confirmasse donationem quam Ricardus Bacoun fecit deo et beate Marie et canonicis sancte Marie de Roucestre de tota villa de Roucestre et de Combrigge cum omnibus dominicis suis in Roucestre, Combrigge et Watton et de omnibus villanis suis et eorum sequelis et suis catallis et cum omnibus et omnimodis suis pertinentiis, et de una bovata terre in Bredle et quatuor bovatis terre in Waterfalle, et de omnibus libertatibus et liberalibus consuetudinibus in Roucestre, Combrigge, Northulle, Wotton, Denstun, Quikesulle, Rossintone, Waterfalle et Bredelege, una cum advocacione ecclesie eiusdem ville de Roucestre et capellarum suarum Bredelege et Waterfall, et de octo carucatis et duabus bovatis terre et de tertia parte duorum molendinorum in Bruggefordea. Unde ego Ranulfus comes Cestrie et heredes mei dictam villam de Roucestre Combrigge cum omnibus dominicis suis in Roucestre, Combrigge et Wotton, cum omnibus suis villanis, suis sequelis et catallis, cum omnibus libertatibus et liberalibus consuetudinibus in Roucestre, Combrigge, Wottone, Northulle, Denstun, Quicksall, Rossintone, Waterfall, Caltone et Bredlege, una cum advocacione ecclesie eiusdem ville de Roucestre et capellarum suarum Bredleyge et Waterfall, cum omnibus pertinentiis suis in Roucestre, Combrigge, Watton, Northulle, Denstone, Quickesulle, Rossintone, Waterfall, Caltone et Bredleyge, et octo carucatas et duas bovatas terre et tertiam partem duorum molendinorum in Bruggefordia, dictis canonicis et eorum successoribus sicut nostram liberam, puram et perpetuam elemosinam contra omnes gentes warantizabimus, acquietabimus et defendemus imperpetuum. Quare volo et firmiter precipio ut ipsi ita bene et in pace, ita libere et quiete, predicta teneant sicut unquam ulla elemosina melius et liberius tenuit.[1] Et habeant omnes consuetudines, libertates suas et rectitudines et quietancias in omnibus in civitate et extra, in burgo et extra, in villa et extra, in foro et extra, in agris et pasturis et pratis, in viis et placeis et chiminis, in bosco et plano, in aquis et molendinis, in stangnis et piscaturis, in socca et sacca, in tol et theam et infangedethef[1] et weyf et wrec et aliis consuetudinibus et libertatibus. Hiis testibus Rogero constabulario Cestrie, Radulfo de Monte Alto[2] senescallo Cestrie, Simone de Kyma, Thoma dispensario, Simone de Tuschet, Willelmo de Hardredeshulle, Hugone de Novilla, Henrico de Longo Campo, Philippo de Orreby, Sansone priore de Trentham, Thoma clerico presencium scriptore, et aliis multis apud Nottingham.

1. *sic MSS.*
2. *om. MSS.*

For Richard Bacon's charter, of which this is a confirmation, see **no. 68**. Like that, the present charter is certainly not genuine as it stands, the extraordinary recital of alleged liberties and rights (including waif and wreck) in the final sentence being alone enough to condemn it. But there is nothing suspicious about the witness-list, and it is probably a much inflated version of a genuine charter. Farrer (*H.K.F.*, p. 258), who provides an identification of the numerous place-names, dates it 'prior to the year 1208', but Samson, prior of Trentham, was dead by 1203, when there was a vacancy (*Heads of Religious Houses*, p. 187), and Ralph the seneschal of Chester in 1199 (*Ches. Sheaf*, no. 9394). As

Roger the constable does not use the name of Lacy, the actual date, assuming there was a genuine charter, was probably 1191–1194. Our knowledge of Rocester is sparse, and we do not know when or in what circumstances the spurious version was produced.

263. Grant to William of Ferrers, earl of Derby, of ten librates of land in Donington (Lincs.) and five knights' fees in marriage with his sister Agnes.

[1192]

P.R.O., D.L. 41/1/35 (Inventory of Charters of de Montforts, William de Ferrers, and Thomas, earl of Lancaster).

Carta Rannulfi comitis Cestrie de decem libratis terre in Duningtona, que est de socha de Benteford, et de feodis quinque militum, scilicet feodo[1] Willelmi de Griseleya feodum unium militis, et feodo Ricardi de Vernon in Derlavestona[2] feodum unius militis, et feodo[1] Rogeri de Somervilla feodum dimidii militis, et feodo Henrici de Noers feodum duorum militum, et feodo Ricardi de Ederlingtona feodum dimidii militis, habenda in libero maritagio cum Agnete sorore ipsius comitis.

SEAL: 'cum sigillo'.

1. feodum *MS.*
2. *sic MSS; for* Herlavestona (*i.e.* Harlaston?)

This abstract is the only surviving evidence of this grant. It comes under the heading: 'Omnia tenementa subscripta data sunt, concessa et quietaclamata Willelmo de Ferariis comitis Derbie et heredibus suis'. The marriage of Ranulf III's sister Agnes took place in 1192 (*H.K.F.*, p. 10), and there is no reason to think that the marriage settlement did not occur in the same year. It may be compared with the settlements for her eldest sister Matilda (**no. 220**) and her youngest sister Hawise (**nos. 308, 309**). A similar settlement was presumably made for the fourth sister Mabel, but no evidence has survived; but provision was made later for her daughter Colette (**no. 437**). Roger of Somerville had married a daughter of Robert the butler (*pincerna*) of Chester before 1183 (*E.C.C.*, p. 5). For Henry of Nuers, see **no. 260**. Harlaston had been in the possession of the Vernons since 1154–57 (**no. 141**); Richard de Vernon died c.1212 (*H.K.F.*, p. 276).

264. Confirmation to the monks of Garendon of his father's grant of the right to send a single cart into his forest of Barrow-upon-Soar (Leics.) to collect fuel, in return for which they had surrendered to Earl Hugh the boat on the river Dee which they had been given by Ranulf II.

[c.1192]

B.L. Lansdowne MS. 415 (Register of Garendon), f. 7 (new f. 8). Ed.: Nichols, *Leicestershire*, III. ii. 809.

Rannulfus comes Cestrie conestabulario suo et dapifero, iustic(iario) et vicec(omiti), et baronibus et ballivis et omnibus hominibus suis tam futuris quam presentibus salutem. Notum sit omnibus vobis me concessisse et hac mea carta confirmasse donacionem illam quam dominus pater meus fecit deo et monachis Geroldonie, scilicet unam solam bigam errantem in foresta mea de Barua in puram et perpetuam elemosinam ad foellam suam. Et ipsi remiserunt patri meo unum batellum in aqua de De, sicut in carta ipsius exprimitur, quod dominus Rannulfus comes avus meus illis in elemosinam dederat. Et post decessum meum monachi facient pro me sicut pro quodam monacho domus sue. Quare volo et firmiter precipio quod predicti monachi predictam elemosinam in perpetuum libere et quiete et pacifice possideant, et prohibeo ne aliquis super hoc eos vexare aut molestare presumat. Testibus Willelmo comite de Ferrariis, Rogero conestabulario Cestrie, Radulfo de Monte Alto[1] senescallo Cestrie.

1. *om. MS.*

For Ranulf II's charter granting a boat on the Dee, see **no. 41.** Hugh II's charter has not survived. The present charter precedes **no. 265** by some years. Ralph the seneschal was probably killed during the Welsh attack on Mold at the beginning of 1199. Roger the constable succeeded his father in 1190 and adopted the surname Lacy in 1194. William Ferrers, earl of Derby, married Ranulf III's sister Agnes in 1192. He witnessed a few charters (e.g. **nos. 382** and **390**) at the end of Ranulf's life, c.1229–32; but at this time he is a rare witness, only attesting the marriage settlement of his wife's sisters Matilda (**no. 220**) and Hawise (**no. 308**), and it is a fair assumption that the present charter dates from about the time of his marriage. It is also interesting as another example (see **no. 169**) of the resumption (for compensation) of the gift of a boat on the Dee – is it a sign that the river was being overfished?

265. Grant to Garendon abbey of pasture for its herds in his forest at Barrow-upon-Soar (Leics.), except for his park, and of a cart a day to collect fuel; also confirmation of the gifts of Robert and William de Jorz and Thomas Despenser in his fee of Holywell Hall.

[c.1197–1207]

B.L. Lansdowne MS. 415 (Register of Garendon), f. 25
(new f. 26). Ed.: Nichols, *Leicestershire*, III. ii. 822;
Mon., v. 322 (short notice from inspeximus).

Omnibus Christi fidelibus, ad quos presens scriptum pervenerit, Ranulfus comes
Cestrie salutem. Notum sit vobis omnibus me pro dei amore et pro salute anime
patris mei et anime mee concessisse et dedisse et hac mea carta confirmasse deo
et beate Marie de Gerondona et monachis ibidem deo servientibus comunionem
pasture per forestam meam que pertinet ad feodum de Barwa, excepto parcho
meo de Baroua, in perpetuum habendam omnibus pecoribus suis cuiuscunque
generis fuerint, libere et quiete et absque omni disturbacione, et unam bigam
cotidie errantem per eandem forestam ad portandum ligna ad focum suum. Et
ego et heredes mei hanc elemosinam warantizabimus predictis monachis, et
contra omnes homines defensores astabimus. Et preterea concessi et presenti
carta confirmavi deo et beate Marie et predictis monachis donaciones quas
Robertus de Jorz et Willelmus de Jorz et Thomas dispensarius fecerunt predictis
monachis de Gerondona in feodo meo de Haliwellehaga, sicut carte ipsorum
donatorum, quas monachi inde habent, testantur. Volo itaque et firmiter
precipio quod predicti monachi omnia predicta libere et quiete et pacifice in
perpetuum possideant, et prohibeo ne aliquis eos inde vexare aut molestare
presumat. Monachi vero predicti mihi caritative concesserunt quod post
decessum meum pro me servicium facient sicut pro quodam monacho domus
sue. Hiis testibus Thoma Dispenser,[1] Willelmo Pichot.

1. *sic MS.*

The charters of Robert and William de Jorz and Thomas Despenser, here
confirmed, are preserved in the Garendon cartulary, ff 8v.–9 and ff. 18v.–19v.
(modern foliation). As the witness list is abbreviated, the present charter is
difficult to date, but it is evidently later than **no. 264.** Thomas Despenser was the
elder of that name, who was dead by 1207 (*H.K.F.*, p. 58). William Picot
witnessed Ranulf III's charters for Coventry, c.1199–1202 (**no. 311**) and for
Savigny, c.1201–04 (**no. 334**). The present charter is probably from around the
same period.

266.   Grant to David of Malpas, for £100, of the lands in Cheshire formerly
held by Robert fitz Nigel, which had been forfeited for default of service,
unless and until Robert's heirs repay the sum of £100.

[1192–1194]

Chester, Booth of Twemlow, Liber K, f. 47.

Ranulfus comes Cestrie *etc.* Sciatis quod terra quam Robertus filius Nigelli tenuit in Cestrishira infra Limam fuit seisita in manu mea per consideracionem et iudicium curie mee pro defectu servicii mei et eam per septem annos et amplius in manu mea tenui, ita quod infra predictum terminum ab aliquo non requisita fuisset. Et compertum fuit coram me in curia mea arearagium pro defectu servicii mei ad valenciam C. librarum et amplius; quas C. libras David de Malpas mihi dedit. Quapropter ego predictam terram cum omnibus pertinentiis suis memorato David in vadium liberavi, habendam et tenendam de me et heredibus meis *etc.* Et volo et firmiter precipio quod ipse David eam habeat, quousque recti heredes eiusdem terre veniant et dicto David C. libras reddant. Testibus Radulfo de Monte Alto, Willelmo de Verdun, Willelmo de Venables, Warino de Vernon.

Robert fitz Nigel, a tenant of the earl of Chester in Kegworth, Leics., and Tackley, Oxon. (*H.K.F.*, pp. 79, 242) as well as in Cheshire, died in 1185 (*R.S.L.C.*, xcii, p. 16). As Earl Ranulf says he has had his lands in his hand 'for seven years and more' the present charter cannot date from before 1192, but is probably not much later. It would seem that Robert had no direct heirs; hence the failure to do service, and the forfeiture. The recipient of his lands, David of Malpas, is a fairly frequent witness of Ranulf III's charters between 1200 and 1217, and is usually said to have been a member of the Patric family (Orm., ii. 593); but the evidence is not very strong. Robert fitz Nigel's Leicestershire lands were later conferred on Stephen of Segrave (**no. 358**).

267. Andrew son of Mabel is granted quittance of toll throughout the earl's lands, in the city of Chester and elsewhere, and from carrying writs and other customary obligations, nor shall he answer any complaint except before the earl himself or his chief justice.

Chester, [c.1194]

> Tabley MSS., Sir Peter Leycester's Liber C, pars II, f. 13v. ('ex ipsa charta originali nunc penes Petrum Daniell de Over Tabley'); B.L. Harl. MS. 2037, f. 300 (new f. 193). Ed.: Orm., i. 37 (from Liber C).

Rannulphus dux Britannie et comes Cestrie et Richemondie omnibus tam presentibus quam futuris, qui cartam istam viderint et audierint, salutem. Sciatis quod ego dedi et concessi Andree filio Mabilie et heredibus suis, ut sint liberi et quieti de me et de meis heredibus de teloneo per totam terram meam et in aqua et in terra et in civitate Cestrie et extra, et a brevibus portandis, et a prisonibus capiendis et custodiendis, et a namis capiendis, et a vigiliis faciendis nocte vel die, et a ceteris huiusmodi consuetudinibus et exactionibus, nec de querela aliqua in civitate Cestrie vel extra respondeant nisi[1] in presentia mea vel summe iusticie mee. Et super forisfacturam meam x. librarum prohibeo, ne aliquis eos de supradictis libertatibus impediat vel inquietet, sed eas libere et quiete teneant, reddendo mihi et heredibus meis annuatim vi. denarios ad festum sancti Michaelis. Hiis testibus Bertrea[2] comitisse Cestrie, Radulfo de Meinewarin, Radulfo senescallo, Hugone de Boidele et Alano fratre eius, Roaldo, Roberto camerario, Roberto Saraceno, Ranulfo Dubeldai, Nicholao filio Roberti, Thoma fratre suo, Willelmo Marmiun, Ricardo Poibel,[3] Rogero clerico, et multis aliis apud Cestriam.

> SEAL: 'A large seale of paist with the impression of the Earle on Horsebacke on both sides'.

1. *om. Liber C;* mihi *Harl. MS.*
2. Bertre *Lib. C*; Bertree *Harl. MS.*
3. Pokel *Harl. MS.*

For a grant in similar terms, see **no. 192.** Andrew son of Mabel was a member of a Chester family, like the witnesses beginning with Roald (for whom see **no. 307**), most of whom are found in city charters of the period 1190–1200 (cf. *J.C.A.S*, N.S. x, p. 16). The present charter falls within the period 1189–1199, when Ranulf III was duke of Brittany. Ralph of Montalt was dead by 1200 and was almost certainly killed during Llywelyn of Wales' assault on his castle of Mold on 6 January 1199 (*Ann. Cestr.*, p. 45; cf. Lloyd, p. 590). The reference to the earl's *summa iusticia*, or chief justice, is noteworthy. Ralph Mainwaring became chief justice about this time, but unfortunately his dates are not known. The fact that he appears here without title may indicate that the charter belongs to the first half (1190–94) rather than the latter half of the period. Mainwaring's justiciarship is usually dated 1194–1204 (*Chart. St. Werburgh*, p. iv.; *Ches. Sheaf*, no. 7804).

268.   Andrew son of Mabel is given permission to put out his nets in the river Dee next to the earl's in the trench below the bridge of Chester.

Chester, [c.1200]

> B.L. Harl. MS. 2037, f. 300 (new f. 193), from the Chester Exchequer Roll, 12 Edw. III.

Ranulfus comes Cestrie omnibus tam futuris quam presentibus salutem. Sciatis me dedisse, concessisse et hac mea carta confirmasse[1] Andree filio Mabille et heredibus suis, quod liceat eis tendere retia sua, scilicet flotreta, in fluvio de Dee in proximo loco quod[2] retia mea propria, que tenduntur in fosso subtus pontem Cestrie, reddendo ab illo et heredibus suis mihi et heredibus meis[3] annuatim vi.d. ad natale domini *etc.*[4] Testibus Radulfo de Menilwarin, Philippo de Orreby, Rogero de Camvilla,[5] Ricardo Pisce, Willelmo de Verdun, Ricardo Fiton,[6] Roberto Cuzaigno, Turdino sellario, Hugone filio Udardi, Roberto camerario, Thoma clerico, et multis aliis apud Cestriam.

1.   confirmavi *MS.*
2.   *sic MS.*
3.   *om. MS.*
4.   *The MS. copy is evidently abbreviated.*
5.   Cavil *MS.*
6.   Fith *with abbreviation sign over* h, *MS.*

For a second charter for Andrew son of Mabel, given about the same time or probably a few years earlier, see **no. 267**. The date of the present grant is not easily established, but as Ralph Mainwaring and Philip of Orreby both occur without the title of justiciar and the earl is no longer using the title duke of Brittany as in **no. 267**, it probably dates from c.1200. The last four witnesses (except Thomas the earl's clerk, who was very active around this time) are clearly Chester citizens.

269.   Confirmation to the abbey of St. Lô of the land given by Thomas Castel and Sibyl, wife of Henry Merlet.

[1194–1198]

> Orig.: archives of St. Lô, destroyed in 1944. Transcr.: MS.
> Paris fr. nouv. acq. 21814 (Delisle's transcripts), f. 555.
> Ed.: Dubosc, *Cartulaire de l'Abbaye de Saint-Lô*
> (Cartulaire de la Manche, I), pp. 37–38 (no. 21).

Notum sit omnibus tam futuris [quam presentibus quod ego][1] Ranulfus comes de Cestre[2] concessi et pre[senti scripto] et sigilli mei munimine confirmavi pro amore dei et pro salute anime mee et antecessorum meorum abbatie sancti Laudi et canonicis ibidem deo servientibus in perpetuam elemosinam donationem Thome Castel et Sibille uxoris Henrici Merlet, scilicet boscum et planam terram de Solerio iuxta fossata circumdancia illum boscum et xvi. acras terre extra fossata in plana terra versus Boscum Ale, sicut carta prenominati Thome Castel et carta predicte Sibille uxoris Henrici Merlet testantur, quas cartas predicti canonici habent. Testibus his Hugone de Longo Campo, Willelmo filio Hamonis, Willelmo de Petrafita, Willelmo de Bavent, Philippo de Longavilla, Iohanne de Praaus, Iohanne de Scaiol, Ricardo Peisson, Henrico le Depenser,[3] Ricardo de Croile, Thoma Cogeri, Thoma picerna,[3] et multis aliis.

SEAL: missing.

1. According to Dubosc, the first two lines were mutilated by vermin.
2. *sic ed.*
3. *sic ed.*

This and the charter of Thomas Castel (*Cartulaire*, p. 37, no. 20) are dated 'about 1185' by Dubosc, but, to judge from the witnesses, this is certainly too early. Richard Peisson (Pisce) is a fairly frequent witness from 1190 to 1203, but not, so far as I can establish, earlier. Richard of Croile witnessed **no. 203**, and William of Bavent is mentioned in 1198 (*Rot. Scacc. Norm.*, ii. 411), by which time William de Pierrefite was dead (*ibid.*, 365). For John de Scaiol, or Escaiol, see *E.C.C.*, no. 16(1). The charter was almost certainly given in Normandy and, taking the evidence as a whole, can fairly confidently be dated 1194–1198. Thomas *pincerna* is not connected with the Cheshire and Lancashire Butlers, but was probably a member of the family which provided officials in the Bessin.

270.   Hugh Boydell of Dodleston is granted his road at Lachford and the passage of the Mersey between Runcorn and Thelwall; no cart is to use either without his consent.

[1194–1200]

> Tabley MSS., Sir Peter Leycester's Liber C, f. 289v. (from Mr. Blackborne of Lachford's Deedes, 1666). Ed.: Orm., i. 603, note c.

Ranulfus comes Cestrie – salutem. Notum sit vobis me concessisse Hugoni de Boydell cheminum suum de Lachford – cum passagio aque de Mersey inter Runcorne et Thelwall – et quod nulla biga per predictum cheminum et passagium transeat, nisi per predictum Hugonem et heredes suos.

Hugh Boydell was the eldest son of Helte de Boydell (**no. 330**), who died in 1180, and he himself died about the turn of the twelfth and thirteenth centuries (*Chart. St. Werburgh*, p. 92). In spite of its fragmentary character and lack of witnesses, the present grant can therefore be dated fairly closely. Furthermore, there is evidence (*E.C.C.*, p. 10) that Lachford was held by William Sampson, until he resigned it into the hands of Hugh Boydell, his lord, at some date during the justiciarship of Ralph Mainwaring (c.1194–1204), and it seems obvious that the present charter would not have been sought and given until after Lachford reverted to Hugh's direct control. The road from Warrington via Lachford to Northwich and the passage of the Mersey were valuable rights, the tolls from the latter alone being worth 13s. 4d. a year, according to inquisitions taken in the reign of Edward III (Orm., i. 602, 604), and the earl's confirmation of them was well worth having.

271. Grant of Merton (Cheshire) to Ranulf of Merton, the earl's usher (*hostiarius*), for the service of keeping one of the earl's horses, and confirmation to the same of his office of usher in the earl's household, receiving two horses and three oxen annually at the earl's expense; for which concessions Ranulf gave the earl two greyhounds called Lym and Libekar.

Weaverham, [1194–1202]

P.R.O., CHES 29/20 (Plea Rolls) *die veneris proxime post festum sancti Swithini 1 Edw. II*, m. 26 (A); Shakerley MSS., Liber C, f. 137 (B); B.L. Harl. MS. 2074, p. 170 (f. 67 new) (C). Printed: Orm., ii. 176 (incomplete), from Harl. 2074.

Ranulphus comes Cestrie constabulario, baronibus, vic(ecomiti), ministris et ballivis, et omnibus suis fidelibus tam Anglis quam Francis, clericis et laicis, salutem. Sciatis me concessisse et confirmasse Ranulpho de Mertona filio Ranulphi, hostiario fideli meo, Mertonam cum boscis[1] et cum omnibus aliis provenientibus[2] ad Mertonam pertinentibus, habendam et tenendam illam tenuram sibi et heredibus suis de me et heredibus meis in feodo et hereditate libere et quiete, bene et in pace, imperpetuum,[3] per servicium[4] quod fecit patri meo et mihi postea, ad nutriendum unum cabellum mihi et heredibus meis singulis annis, quando sibi fuit missus, pro omnibus serviciis secularibus, placitis, querelis, et demandis, ita quod nullus eum implaceat inde nec implaceari permittat. Preterea concessi et confirmavi pro me et heredibus meis eidem Ranulpho et heredibus suis suum officium in domo meo esse hostiarium, cum duobus caballis et tribus bobis per annum sibi et valetto[5] super custum meum proprium. Pro hac autem concessione et confirmacione idem Ranulphus dedit mihi in gersuma duos lepores nomine Lym[6] et Libekar. Hiis testibus domina Bertrea comitissa,[7] domino Radulpho Meingarin iusticiario Cestrie,[8] domino Rogero de Lascy tunc constabulario Cestrie, Roberto de [Monte Alto],[9] domino Hamone de Mascy, domino Hugone de Spenser.[10] Datum apud Werham.[11]

1. *add.* planis *A*.
2. probamentis *A*.
3. *sic A, B; omitted C*.
4. pro servicio *B, C*.
5. valecto *B, C*.
6. Lynn *A*.
7. *Text ends after* comitissa *A*.
8. *Printed text ends after* Cestrie.
9. *Text reads* 'Mousund *or* Monsund' *B, C; seems probable that reference to Robert of Montalt (Mold co. Flint), steward of the earl of Chester, is intended.*
10. *sic B, C (for* dispensario).
11. *sic B, C; for* We(ve)rham?

The date must fall after 1194, when Roger the constable inherited the Lacy honours of Clitheroe and Pontefract and adopted the surname of Lacy, and before Ralph Mainwaring ceased to be justiciar in, or about, 1202 (*Ches. Sheaf*, no. 7804). If it were safe to draw any conclusion from the earl's title, it would have to be after 1199, when he ceased to be duke of Brittany. The place where the charter was issued is almost certainly Weaverham. Curiously, there is little further information about Ranulf of Merton. He had been in the service of Earl Hugh, and was evidently an old man by the time this charter was issued; perhaps he did not survive long.

272.   Confirmation of the exchange which Countess Bertrada, his mother, made with the canons of Repton.

[1194–1203]

Orig.: formerly with Sir Robert Burdett, not traced. Ed.:
The Topographer, ii, pp. 253–4; Bigsby, *History of Repton*, p. 61; Jeayes, *Derbyshire Charters*, no. 1948.

Omnibus sancte matris ecclesie filiis tam futuris quam presentibus Ranulphus comes Cestrie salutem. Sciatis me concessisse et presenti carta mea confirmasse excambium, quod domina Berta comitissa mater mea dedit ecclesie sancte Trinitatis de Rapandune et canonicis ibidem deo servientibus, scilicet culturam desuper domum Sercehaie, ubi quarrera est, in excambium terre de . . .,[1] et tunc inter cheminum et . . .,[1] que descendit de Herteshorn, exceptis curia et clauso capelle sancti Thome, que remanent predictis canonicis, et de alneto, sicut carta domine matris mee testatur. Hiis testibus Radulfo de Maisnilwarin, Simone Toschet, Petro Ruaud,[2] Thoma dispensatore, Warino de Vernon, Roberto Lancelin et R. Lancelin filio eius, Rogero de Camville, Fulcone filio Warini,[3] Petro clerico, Thoma clerico, et multis aliis.

SEAL: lion seal, legend SIGILLUM RANULFI COMITIS CESTRIE.

1. *All editions defective.*
2. Ruane *eds.*
3. Wareni *eds.*

The charter of Countess Bertha, or Bertrada, has not survived, and as the present charter is defective, the exact location of the places mentioned cannot be established. The date is between 1194 and 1203, probably earlier rather than later. Fulk fitz Warin appears to have died in 1199, when he was succeeded by his son of the same name (*P.R.S.*, N.S. xii, pp. 118, 121). For Robert Lancelyn, see **no. 245**.

273.   Grant to the canons of Repton of the right to send a cart once a day to collect fuel in his wood at Ticknall and of a fishery in the Trent extending as far as Potlock.

[1229–1232]

Orig.: formerly with Sir Robert Burdett, not traced. Ed.: *The Topographer*, ii. 253–4; Bigsby, *History of Repton*, pp. 61–2; Jeayes, *Derbyshire Charters*, no. 1954.

Omnibus Christi fidelibus presentem cartam inspecturis vel audituris Ranulphus comes Cestrie et Lincolnie salutem. Noveritis me pro salute anime mee et animarum antecessorum et successorum meorum dedisse, concessisse et hac presenti carta mea confirmasse in perpetuum deo et beate Marie et ecclesie sancte Trinitatis de Rapendon et canonicis ibidem deo servientibus unam bigam cum unico equo semel in die in bosco meo de Tikenhall errantem ad focale ad usus suos proprios portandum per visum forestarii mei de Tikenhall. Dedi etiam eisdem canonicis in perpetuum licentiam piscandi in aqua de Trente subtus domum suam, quantum terre sue extendunt versus Potlac, salva mihi et heredibus meis piscatione nostra ibidem, quando necesse habuerimus, sed quod nec ego nec heredes mei aliquid contra dictam donationem meam erga dictos canonicos potuimus exigere . . .[1] Et ne presens scriptum . . .[1] robur . . .[1] sigilli mei appositione illud munimus. Hiis testibus Willelmo de Vernon iusticiario Cestrie, Radulfo de Bray,[2] Aluredo de Suligny,[3] Iohanne de Lexinton, Galfrido de Appelby, Normanno de Suligny, Waltero Findern,[4] magistro Willelmo de Wetton,[5] Simone de Berford, Simone et Iohanne clericis, et aliis.

SEAL: obverse, a man on horseback in armour and close helmet, with a shield before him and sword in hand, legend: SIGILLUM RANULFI COMITIS CESTRIE ET LINCOLNIE; reverse, shield of arms, 3 garbs, the same circumscription.

1. *All texts defective.*
2. Wray *eds.*
3. Muligny *eds.*
4. *sic eds.*
5. *sic eds.; probably* Welton *or* Weston.

Potlock had been granted by Ranulf II to Burton abbey (**no. 115**). Simon de Bereford appears, after Ranulf III's death, as seneschal of Countess Clementia (**no. 444**).

274. Having inspected the charters of Repton and Calke priories and found them defective, he re-confirms them, setting out in detail the boundaries of their estates.

[c.1230]

Orig.: P.R.O., C.109 (Chancery Masters' Exhibits), 87A.

Omnibus Christi fidelibus presentibus et futuris presentem cartam inspecturis vel audituris Rannulfus comes Cestrie et Lincolnie salutem. Noverit universitas vestra quod, cum inspexissem cartas de fundacione ecclesie sancte Trinitatis et ecclesie sancti Egidii et religionis de Rapendona et de Calc et eas minus utiles quam oporteret invenissem, misericordia motus dedi et concessi et hac presenti carta mea confirmavi pro salute anime mee et comitis Hugonis patris mei et Bertree matris mee et omnium antecessorum et successorum meorum in puram et perpetuam elemosinam deo et sancte Marie et dicte ecclesie sancte Trinitatis de Rapendona et dicte ecclesie sancti Egidii de Kalc et canonicis in eisdem ecclesiis deo sub disciplina canonicorum regularium secundum regulam sancti Augustini in perpetuum servituris ecclesiam sancti Wistani de Rapendona cum omnibus capellis suis et omnibus aliis pertinentiis et libertatibus suis, et sedem molendini et stagni[1] sui sub curia eorum in Rapendona usque ad aquam descendentem[2] de domo Willelmi Etebred in Trente, cum attachiamento eiusdem stagni ad terram quam Reginaldus piscator aliquando tenuit, et cum tota aqua ibidem descendente, et totam terram que dicitur Flaxlandes, iacentem inter viam et aqueductum a rivulo descendente[3] de Shepesmor usque ad terram Willelmi de Belvaco, et totam culturam quarrerie de Rapendona iuxta Trente, et communam brusce de Rapendona secundum quantitatem omnium terrarum suarum in Rapendona, et terram in qua sedet horreum dictorum canonicorum in Tikenhale. Preterea dedi et concessi et hac eadem carta mea confirmavi deo et beate Marie et dictis ecclesiis sancte Trinitatis et sancti Egidii et canonicis de Rapendona et de Kalc, que modo est membrum predicte ecclesie de Rapendona, totam terram et boscum iacentes inter Schegwarebroc et Alrebroc preter magnam geilbergam cum omnibus pertinentiis suis et libertatibus et aysiamentis,[4] et sedes et attachiamenta stagnorum[5] suorum de Kalc, et terram et alnetum inter duo inferiora molendina sua et inter Bollehaghe et aqueductum, et quatuor bovatas terre cum omnibus pertinenciis suis in Tikenhale, quas Willelmus filius Swani aliquando tenuit, et duas bovatas terre cum pertinenciis suis in eadem villa, quas Alina vidua aliquando tenuit, et terram de Loftessco sicut fovea extendit se inter terram cultam et Rouheclives a veteri fovea usque ad viam descendentem[6] ad fontem de Newehaghe et sicut idem fons descendit[7] usque ad metas de Meltona et ex altera parte sicut terminus Meltone est usque ad capud de Loeftessco, et ex altera parte rivuli dicte fontis culturam que vocatur Hungrehulle et attachiamentum servorii sui de Loeftessco, et terram et servicium Nicholai quondam armigeri avi mei in Meltona cum pertinentiis suis, et novem solidos annuos de molendino meo in Rapendona ad quatuor terminos, scilicet ad festum sancti Michaelis viginti et septem denarios, ad festum sancti Andree viginti et septem denarios, ad annunciationem beate Marie viginti et septem denarios, et ad nativitatem sancti Iohannis baptiste viginti et septem denarios, et unum mesuagium in Wadingtona cum pertinentiis suis ex opposito domus persone ex altera parte vie. Insuper dedi et concessi predictis canonicis curiam suam plenariam, preterquam de furtis et de propriis hominibus meis, et tres carettatas de bosco meo de Sudwode in qualibet septimana. Has autem donaciones, concessiones, libertates cum omnibus pertinenciis suis in villis et extra villas in puram et perpetuam elemosinam liberas et quietas ab omni seculari servicio et exactione et demanda ego et heredes mei predictis canonicis contra omnes gentes warantizabimus in perpetuum. Et ut omnia ista rata et inconcussa in perpetuum permaneant, ea presenti pagina et sigilli mei apposicione corroboravi. Hiis testibus Willelmo de Cantelupo, Willelmo de Vernona, Baldwino de Ver, Simon et Iohanne clericis, Iohanne de Stapenhulle, Radulfo de Tikenhale, Willelmo filio Ricardi de Meysham, Galfrido de Stantona, et aliis.

> SEAL: knight on horseback, galloping, in closed helmet with shield of arms, 3 garbs, legend (largely perished) . . . OMIT . . .; reverse, shield of 3 garbs, 2 and 1, legend SECRETUM RANULFI COMITIS CESTRIE ET LINCOLNIE

1. sta(n)gni *orig.*
2. decendentem *orig.*
3. decendente *orig.*
4. aysiametis *orig.*
5. sta(n)gnorum *orig.*
6. decendentem *orig.*
7. decendit *orig.*

The grants found defective and here renewed are presumably those of Countess Matilda of the church of St. Wistan (**no. 120**) and of a quarry at Repton (**no. 119**), and Hugh II's confirmation (**no. 147**) of his father's charter (**no. 45**), but it also covers gifts not mentioned in any of these. The main defect appears to be that the boundaries were not set out specifically enough in the earlier charters. The last four witnesses of Ranulf III's charter are local Derbyshire men. The names of the others point to a date late in his life, probably c.1230.

275. Charter freeing the monks of Basingwerk from toll throughout his lands.

[1194–1204]

> P.R.O., C.53 (Chancery Charter Rolls), no. 18, m. 6.
> Ed.: *Cal. Ch. Rolls*, ii. 290.

Ranulphus comes Cestrie iusticiario, vicecomiti, prepositis, ministris et omnibus fidelibus et hominibus suis salutem. Sciatis me in omni terra mea monachos de Basingwerk pro anime mee salute et antecessorum meorum a tolneto imperpetuum quietos clamasse. Quare volo et firmiter precipio ne super hoc quod eis pro dei amore et mea et antecessorum meorum salute indulsi aliquis eis ad mei dampnum et iniuriam atque contemptum molestiam inferre presumat. Hiis testibus R. iusticiario, R. vicecomite Cestrie, R. Lancelin, Roaldo, Rogero Herre, et aliis multis.

This charter was presumably issued during the justiciarship of Ralph Main-waring (c.1194–1204). Two charters for Robert Lancelyn (**nos. 244, 245**) were issued at this time, and one was witnessed by Ralph the sheriff. This is Ralph *vicomte* of the Bessin, who died c.1202 (*Rot. Scacc. Norm.*, ii. 533), but the R. *vicecomes* of the present charter may conceivably be Richard (de Pierrepont), sheriff of the city of Chester, for whom see *E.C.C.*, p. 28. The evidence is inconclusive and does not make it possible to limit the date more narrowly.

276. Charter for the free men of Wirral, freeing them from providing food for the earl's serjeants, except six foresters on foot, but in time of war they are to find twelve serjeants and support them at their own cost. [Spurious]

Chester [1194–1208]

> P.R.O. C.66 (Chancery Patent Rolls), no. 120, m. 10; CHES 34/1 (Plea Rolls), m. 2v. ('die martis proxima post assumpcionis beate Marie', 27 Edw. III); also cited without text *ibid*. m. 5, 5v., 6, and CHES 29/33 (Plea Rolls), m. 20v. Ed.: *Cal. Pat. Rolls, 1292–1301*, p. 525.

Rannulfus comes Cestrie constabulario suo et dapifero, iusticiario, vic(ecomite), baronibus et ballivis et omnibus fidelibus suis tam futuris quam presentibus salutem. Notum sit vobis omnibus me concessisse et hac carta mea confirmasse omnibus liberis hominibus manentibus in Wirhallia et in ea terras habentibus de me et meis heredibus quietanciam de servientibus pascendis eis et eorum heredibus, ita quod ipsi et eorum heredes et homines sui et terre sue de Wirhallia imperpetuum sint quieti de servientibus pascendis, nisi solummodo de sex forestariis peditibus sine omni quo et sine omni alia secta. Et forestarii illi per totam Wirhalliam pascentur exceptis maneriis abbatis Cestrie, scilicet Estham et Brumburg et Ireby et Suttona. Et si aliquod negocium in terra mea emerserit, propter quod oporteat servientes tenere, predicti homines de Wir-hallia invenient duodecim servientes et eos tenebunt ad custum suum, quamdiu negocium terre durabit. Ipsi eciam posse suum facient de terra mea defendenda et in pace tenenda, et iuraberunt quod forestam meam pro posse suo legaliter servabunt, et quod nec in terra mea nec in foresta mea forisfacient nec forisfieri permittent, et si scierint aliquem in eis forisfacere, ipsi corpus eius, si possunt, capient et illud reddent michi vel iusticiario meo, et si eum capere non possunt, ipsi illud monstrabunt michi vel iusticiario meo vel ballivo meo de patria ipsa. Hiis testibus Galfrido abbate Cestrie, Philippo de Orreby, Hamone de Mascy, Warino de Vernon, Willelmo de Venables, Thoma et Henrico dispensatoribus, Petro clerico, David clerico de Malo Passu, Ricardo clerico, et multis aliis apud Cestriam.

This charter, if genuine, falls in the time of Abbot Geoffrey of Chester, i.e. 1194–1208, and should be compared with the relevant section (§11) of the Charter of Liberties of 1215 (**no. 394**). But is it genuine? The first suspicious circumstance is that it first comes to light in a later confirmation, and is otherwise only known in answer to *quo warranto* proceedings. Secondly, it repeats almost verbatim the terms of a charter of Ranulf III for St. Werburgh's abbey (**no. 230**), which unfortunately only exists in an abstract, without witnesses or date, in the abbey cartulary. Evidently the present charter can have been derived from **no. 230**, or **no. 230** can have been derived from the present charter, or both can be later fabrications. It is certainly surprising that a charter of such wide-reaching import, affecting the whole Wirral, should have lain unknown and unused for a century. It is also difficult to envisage the circumstances which would have moved Ranulf III to grant such concessions at the close of the twelfth century, and it might be thought, if it existed in 1215, that it would have been at least mentioned in the Charter of Liberties. On the other hand, it is easy to see why such a charter was desirable in the reign of Edward I and later, when the financial needs of the king (and subsequently of the Black Prince) gave rise to exorbitant demands and abuse of forest rights. Already in 1275 the men of Wirral were under pressure; in 1304 the whole community petitioned (to no avail) against a commission to enforce forest law and to raise revenue from amercements (cf. Hewitt, *Mediaeval Cheshire*, pp. 11–17). Though it cannot be proved, it is a reasonable assumption that the present charter (and perhaps also that of St. Werburgh's) was fabricated as a defence against this assault on ancient custom. In this case, it probably dates from c.1275, or perhaps from c.1290. Its terms are frequently cited later in answer to *quo warranto* proceedings, e.g. by Sir William Stanley in 1362 (Orm., ii. 355).

277. Grant to Barthélemy l'Abbé, his knight, of 100 acres of land in his park of Trévières for the service of one-tenth of a knight's fee.

Les Andelys, [1196–1197]

Rouen, Bibl. municipale, MS. 1235, ff. 64–64v. (Cartulaire de Normandie).

Rannulfus comes Cestrie omnibus tam futuris quam presentibus salutem. Notum sit vobis omnibus me dedisse Bartholomeo abbati militi meo pro homagio suo et servitio, et quia ipse est miles meus et de mea familia, centum acras terre in parco meo de Treveriis mensuratas cum pertica xxiiii. pedum, scilicet prata de Junchera apud Wedesche et ad Rameiam usque ad cheminum de Bernesch et Rubeam Maram usque ad terram Iohannis de Escaioel, et terram ultra aquam versus Angrevillam, tenendam[1] predicto Bartholomeo et heredibus suis de me et heredibus meis in feodo et hereditate libere et quiete et honorifice, integre et plenarie, in bosco et plano, in pratis, in pascuis, in mariscis, in viis, in semitis, in aquis et in omnibus eiusdem terre pertinentiis, per servitium decime partis feodi unius militis faciendum mihi et heredibus meis a memorato Bartholomeo et heredibus suis. Et ut hec donatio mea firma et inconcussa permaneat futuris temporibus, presenti scripto et sigilli mei munimine confirmavi. Hiis testibus Hugone de Colonciis et multis aliis apud Insulas Andeliaci.

1.   *sic MS.*

Ranulf was at L'Ile d'Andely in 1196 and 1197 (thereafter, after the construction of Château Gaillard, at La Roche d'Andely), and it is safe to assume that this charter was issued at this time. The places are all in the vicinity of Trévières. Bernesch is Bernesq, Rubea Mara is Rubercy; Rameia is La Ramée (commune of Trévières) and Angrevilla is Engreville (commune of Bernesq). For Hugh de Coulances, see **no. 337**; For John de Escaiol see *E.C.C.*, no. 16 (1). Barthélemy l'Abbé witnesses a number of charters of Ranulf III around this time, but drops out after the loss of Normandy in 1204.

278.   Confirmation to the monastery and canons of Newhouse (or Newsham, Lincs.) of the gifts of his men in his fee, viz. of Peter of Goxhill in Killingholme, of Ralph of Halton in Halton, of William son of Geoffrey in Newhouse, of Geoffrey of Turs in Cabourne, and of Ralph of Driby in Claxby and Normanby; at the same time the earl takes the canons into his protection and orders his bailiffs and ministers to defend and maintain them and their possessions.

Maidenwell (Lincs.), [1198–1200]

Orig.: Greenwell Deeds, not traced.[1] According to Sir Peter Leycester, Liber C, pars II, f. 14v., the charter was at that time no. EE.10 in the collection of Sir Simon D'Ewes, but he did not transcribe it. The following text is from a transcript by Dr. Hunter Blair of Newcastle-upon-Tyne.

1. The Greenwell Deeds were an artificial collection, relating for the most part to Northumbria and Durham, put together by the Rev. William Greenwell in the early years of the present century. After Greenwell's death, the collection was bought by Mr. Parker Brewis, who presented the items relating to the north of England (calendared by J. Walton, *Archaeologia Aeliana*, 4th Ser. iii, and separately, 1927) to the Newcastle Public Library. They are now on deposit in the Durham County Record Office. The residue of miscellaneous items, including the present charter, is said to have been presented to Durham; but it seems more likely that it fell into private hands, in the present instance probably those of Dr. Hunter Blair, and was disposed of at some stage through the market.

Omnibus sancte matris ecclesie filiis tam futuris quam presentibus Rannulphus comes Cestrie salutem. Notum sit vobis omnibus me divini amoris intuitu et pro salute animarum antecessorum meorum et anime mee et heredum meorum concessisse et hac carta mea confirmasse deo et ecclesie sancti Marcialis de Newhus et canonicis Premonstratensis ordinis ibidem deo servientibus donationes terrarum subscriptarum, que ab hominibus meis et de feodo meo eis rationabiliter date sunt: scilicet de dono Petri de Gousle in Kylingholm quinquaginta et quatuor acras terre, et de dono Radulfi de Haltone ecclesiam sancti Petri de Halton cum pertinenciis suis, et totam terram quam Willelmus filius Galfridi de feodo meo eis dedit in Newhus cum pertinenciis suis, et de dono Galfridi de Turs septies viginti acras terre que eis assignate sunt et mensurate in campis de Kaburne, et pasturam septingentis ovibus et totidem agnis quousque superannuati fuerint, et preterea triginti acras terre in illa planicia que iacet ante portam grangie sue, et terram illam in eodem territorio ubi sita est grangia sua cum pertinenciis eiusdem terre, et de dono Radulfi de Draibe locum qui vocatur Akerholes in campis de Claxeby et de Normannebi cum terris et pratis et pascuis et aliis pertinenciis suis.

Has terras predictas cum pertinenciis suis concessi et hac carta mea confirmavi deo et predictis canonicis de Neuhus, habendas libere et quiete in puram et perpetuam elemosinam, sicut carte donatorum testantur, et ipsi donatores et eorum heredes mihi et heredibus meis servicia ad predictas terras pertinencia facient de aliis terris suis quam de me tenent. Suscepi etiam in protectione mea et custodia et defensione predictos canonicos et homines suos et omnes res et possessiones suas, et precipio omnibus ballivis et ministris meis ut ipsos canonicos et omnia sua custodiant et manuteneant et defendant sicut mea dominica nec molestiam aut gravamen eis iniuste inferre presumant. Hiis testibus Waltero de Daiville, Waltero de Coventria, Radulfo filio Symonis, Henrico Murdac, Herberto de Orreby, Alano filio Raingoti, Willelmo de Farlesthorp, Roberto de Daiville, Radulfo Patesle, magistro Hugone de Cestria, Martino clerico, Philippo de Rye, et multis aliis apud Maidenewelle.

Newhouse, the first Premonstratensian monastery in England, was founded by Peter of Goxhill in or about 1143. The principal donations listed in the present charter were confirmed by William of Roumare, earl of Lincoln, before 1148 (*Mon*, vi. pt. 2, 865–6). It looks as though Newhouse, like other houses on the former Roumare fee, hastened to get its possessions and privileges re-confirmed after the succession of Ranulf III in 1198. Ralph of Pattesley is in evidence in 1198–1200 (*P.R.S.*, N.S., x, p. 276, and xii, p. 138), William of Farlesthorpe in 1200–1201 (*ibid.*, xiv, p. 19), and other witnesses at the same period. Although the date of the charter is not certain, it is reasonably safe to place it around 1198–1200.

279.   Grant to St. Melaine of Rennes of a rent of land situated in Normandy.

St. James-de-Beuvron, 25 December [1198–1200]

MS. Paris fr. nouv. acq. 21815 (Delisle's transcripts), f. 215; apparently from Paris fr. 22325 ('extraits de cartulaires de Bretagne'), pp. 81–2.

Rannulfus comes Cestrie omnibus tam futuris quam presentibus *etc.* Testibus hiis Hugone de Coloncis, Willelmo de Aubigneio, Radulfo de Aubigneio, Harsculpho de Soligneio, Iohanne Paganello, Petro de Sancto Hilario, Willelmo Andegavensi, Ranulfo de Praeriis, Petro Roaud, Iuhello de Lovigneio, Iuhello Berengero, Bartholomeo abbate, Philippo de Orrebi, Willelmo de Serlant, Luca de sancto Leodegario, Thoma de Coloncis, Gaufrido Farci, Iohanne de Escaioel. Apud Sanctum Iacobum die natalis Domini.

This abbreviated text, essentially only the names of the witnesses, is headed 'S. Melaine de Rennes' by Delisle and followed by a note 'Cette charte est un arrentement de terre scise en Normandie'. The long list of witnesses looks like a gathering of Earl Ranulf's Christmas court at St. James-de-Beuvron. Perhaps the most surprising feature is the presence of Philip of Orreby, the only Englishman among the Norman tenants. The date is not after 1203 and probably not more than two or three years earlier. No fewer than six of the witnesses also witnessed Ranulf's charter for the monastery of Longues dated 1200 (**no. 317**). For Barthélemy l'Abbé, see **no. 277**, witnessed by Hugh de Coulances, probably in 1196–97; for John de Escaiol, see *E.C.C.*, p. 35. Most of the other witnesses occur fairly frequently around this time. The last mention of Ranulf de Praers in the enrolments is in 1198–99 (*P.R.S.*, N.S. x, p. 141; *Rot. Scacc. Norm.*, ii. 358). It looks as though he may have died shortly afterwards, in which case the present charter may be dated 1200 at latest, but it is also fair to surmise that it was given before Ranulf ceased to be duke of Brittany after the break-up of his marriage with Constance of Brittany in October 1199.

Professor Barraclough expressed the hope shortly before his death that he might be able to locate and substitute a copy of the full charter.

280. Grant to Peter the earl's clerk of a boat for fishing on the Dee above and below the bridge of Chester and at Eaton.

[1194–1200]

> B.L. Harl. MS. 2131, f. 33 (new f. 29) and f. 35 (new f. 31); Shakerley MS. 3, p. 153; Chetham's Library, Towneley MSS., transcripts from the Vernon MSS., p. 177 (all apparently from a parchment book belonging to Sir George Booth). English abstract: *Ches. Sheaf*, no. 4212; brief notice Orm., ii. p. 15.

Ranulfus comes Cestrie omnibus tam presentibus quam futuris salutem. Sciatis me dedisse Petro clerico meo unum liberum batellum in fluvio de Dee illi et heredibus suis habendum et tenendum de me et heredibus meis in perpetuum ad piscandum in eodem fluvio subtus pontem Cestrie et supra pontem et apud Etonam, et ubique ubi aliquod aliud liberum batellum piscatur, die et nocte cum flotnettis et draghnettis et stalnettis et cum omni genere retium, et quod de piscibus quos ceperint voluntatem suam faciant, reddendo annuatim pro omni servicio tres denarios in nativitate sancti Iohannis Baptiste. Precipio itaque super forisfacturam meam decem librarum ne vicecomes Cestrie nec aliquis alius ei vel heredibus suis iniuriam aut molestiam faciat. Hiis testibus Hugone de Columbariis, Petro Rualdi, Galfrido Farisi, Bertolomeo abbate, Philippo de Orrebi, Nicholao camerario, Henrico Coucy, Willelmo de Verdun, Roberto Sarraceno, Radulfo Sarraceno, Rualdo, Thoma camerario, et multis aliis.

This is probably the earliest of the many charters in favour of Peter the clerk and his family. Ranulf seems to have been making fairly frequent grants of fishing rights about this time (**nos. 244, 250**), and the names of the witnesses indicate a date shortly before 1200. For Barthélemy l'Abbé (Bertolomeo abbate) see **no. 277.**

281. Grant to Peter the clerk of the land in Castle Street, Chester, next to that of Agnes, daughter of Ranulf Outhecarle, where his house is built, with freedom from service, suit of the portmoot, etc., and the gift of Robert son-in-law of Mary and all his brood.

[1199–1203]

> B.L. Harl. MS. 2131, f. 33v. (new f. 29v.), from Quo Warranto proceedings at Chester, 24 Edw. III; Harl. 506,

> f. 156 (new f. 78), from original with sketch of seal; Harl.
> 2077, f. 69 (old f. 113), the two latter only opening words,
> but a full list of witnesses. Ed.: *Stenton Misc.*, p. 40 (no.
> 12).

Ranulfus comes Cestrie universis clericis et laicis tam presentibus quam futuris, qui hanc cartam visuri vel audituri sunt, salutem. Noverit universitas vestra me dedisse et concessisse Petro clerico terram illam, que proxima est terre Agnetis filie Ranulfi Auchekarll, cum omnibus pertinentiis suis, ubi hospicium suum situm est in vico castelli Cestrie, terram illam et hospicium illud tenenda et habenda illi et heredibus suis de me et heredibus meis libere et quiete ab omnibus servitiis et exacionibus et vigilliis et sectis de portmotis et ab omnibus consuetudinibus, et sicut aliquis aliquod hospicium in civitate Cestrie liberius tenet aut quietius. Preterea dedi et concessi predicto Petro clerico et heredibus suis quietanciam tolneti et multure de blado suo ad victum suum et familie sue in molendinis meis Cestrie, in cuiuscumque manum fuerint. Preterea dedi et concessi predicto Petro clerico Robertum generum Marie cum tota sequella sua hereditarie, habendum et tenendum solute et quiete de me et heredibus meis. Et ut hee donaciones mee in posterum rate et inconcusse permaneant, eas presentis scripti testimonio et sigilli mei appositione roboravi. Hiis testibus Philippo de Horrebi tunc temporis senescaldo comitis, Ranulfo Praeres, Roulando Avenel, Petro Rualdi, Galfrido Farsi, Joelo de Luveni, Nicholao camerario, Willelmo de Verdun, Thoma pincerna, Geroldo hulbario, Roberto et Radulfo Sarracenis, Roberto camerario, Andrea Marmiun, et aliis.

SEAL: pendent on tag, lion seal.

This is one of the many grants, from the earl and others, which attest to Peter's important place in the Cheshire administration (*E.C.C.*, p. 46). It appears that the messuage in question had originally been acquired from John de Scagolo, or de Escaiol (ibid., no. 16), and was subsequently granted by Peter the clerk's son Patrick (**no. 283**) to St. Werburgh's (*Chart. St. Werburgh*, no. 199). The present charter dates from 1199 to 1203. Perhaps its most surprising feature is its reference to Philip of Orreby as the earl's seneschal (*senescaldus*). As the charter is certainly not later in date than 1203, and as Philip did not become justiciar until 1206 at earliest and probably 1207 (see **nos. 296, 337,** and **341**), the word *senescaldus* can scarcely be a copyist's error for *justiciarius*; in which case it is evidence of an earlier, and otherwise undocumented, stage in Philip's career. The title is not impossible. At precisely this time, in 1199, Walter of Coventry was made the earl's seneschal in Lincolnshire (*H.K.F.*, p. 156), and we are told that Richard Fitton, later justiciar, was his seneschal for the county of Richmond for eighteen years(**no. 196**). It is not impossible that Ranulf decided to give Orreby a similar position in Cheshire, though in this instance the arrangement lapsed after Orreby became justiciar.

282. Confirmation to Peter the clerk of his landholdings in the city of Chester: (i) the land adjacent to that which belonged to Agnes, the daughter of Ralph Outhecarle, whom John Gunde took in marriage, extending along Castle Street to the great road of Chester leading to the bridge (i.e. Bridge Street), beside which his stone house is situated; (ii) a plot of land he bought from the aforesaid John and Agnes; (iii) an alley giving on to Cuppin Lane which he bought from Philip son of William Gillenor; (iv) the land he bought of William Unred, where he made his garden; (v) the land Hugh Panter gave him in Castle Street reaching in breadth to the land which was Mary Drury's, with the right to make steps to the main road previously mentioned (Bridge Street) to give access to his stone house; the whole to be held with freedom from services and other liberties and his own court, except for pleas of the earl's sword, which were to be heard before the earl himself or his chief justice.

[1208–1213]

B.L. Harl. MS. 506, f. 156 (new f. 78); Harl. MS. 2077, f. 113 (new f. 69), both from original; Harl. MS. 2131, f. 33v. (new f. 29v.), from Quo Warranto proceedings at Chester, 24 Edw. III (an inflated text). Ed.: *Stenton Misc.*, pp. 41–2 (no. 13).

Rannulfus comes Cestrie constabulario, dapifero, iusticiario, vic(ecomiti), baronibus, ministris et ballivis et omnibus hominibus et amicis suis presentibus et futuris, presentem cartam inspecturis et audituris, salutem. Sciatis me dedisse, concessisse et hac presenti carta mea confirmasse dilecto et fideli meo Petro clerico et heredibus suis terras illas in civitate Cestrie quas adeptus est, scilicet totam terram iacentem a terra que fuit Agnetis filie Radulfi Outhecarle, quam Iohannes Gunnde in uxorem duxit, in vico castelli Cestrie in longtitudine usque ad magnum cheminum versus pontem Cestrie, iuxta quem domus sua lapidea sita est, quandam etiam partem terre quam prefatus Petrus emit de predictis Iohanne et Agnete, et vigullum quod emit de Philippo filio Willelmi filii Gillenore super vicum de Cupinelane, terram quoque quam emit de Willelmo Unred, ubi herbarium suum factum fuit, terram etiam quam Hugo Panteri ei me presente dedit, sicut carta quam de predicto Hugone habet testatur, scilicet totam terram iacentem a vico castelli Cestrie in latitudine usque ad terram que fuit Marie Druerie. Liceat vero illi et heredibus sive successoribus suis, cum voluerint, gradus facere versus predictum cheminum ad ingressum habendum in domum lapideam. Concedo etiam illi et successoribus suis quendam furnum in predicta terra ad furnagium capiendum et quietanciam mouture in molendinis meis Cestrie ad usus suos proprios et familie sue, in cuiuscumque manu fuerint, et illi et successoribus et hominibus suis omnibus in predictis terris ementibus aut vendentibus libertatem tolneti per aquas et per totam terram meam infra civitatem Cestrie et extra de omnibus que emerint aut vendiderint, et maxime de sale emendo in wicis meis, et quietanciam de auxiliis dandis. Dedi quoque et concessi prefato Petro et heredibus suis sive successoribus suis curiam suam liberam de omnibus placitis et querelis, nisi de placitis gladio meo pertinentibus, de quibus coram me vel coram capitali iusticiario meo respondebunt, ita quod de nullo placito respondebit neque vicecomiti meo neque alicui ballivorum meorum, nisi coram me vel capitali iusticiario meo, sicut predictum est. Do etiam illis et concedo quietanciam secte portmoti mei et iudicis inveniendi ad portmotum meum Cestrie et vigilie faciende et hospicii alicui inveniendi, et Robertum generum Marie et Gilebertum de Oneston et Simonem fratrem suum et Alanum Ulem cum omnibus eorum sequelis. Omnia vero predicta cum omnibus suis pertinentiis dedi et concessi et presenti carta mea confirmavi predicto Petro et heredibus suis sive successoribus suis, habenda et tenenda de me et heredibus meis libere, quiete, plene et pacifice, reddendo mihi et heredibus meis annuatim ad cameram meam Cestrie duos denarios in nativitate sancti Iohannis Baptiste pro omnibus servitiis et exactionibus universis mihi et heredibus meis pertinentibus.

Et prohibeo super forisfacturam meam decem librarum ne aliquis eos de aliqua predictarum libertatum sive concessionum disturbare aut vexare presumat. Hiis testibus Rogero de Montealto dapifero meo, Philippo de Orrebi tunc iusticiario meo, Warino de Vernun, Willelmo de Venables, Hamone de Mascy, Roberto Patric, Ricardo de Aldeford, Henrico de Aldethlea, Waltero de Daivilla, Hugone et Galfrido de Dutton, Iohanne de Pratellis, Henrico dispensario, Alexandro filio Radulfi, David de Malopassu, Willelmo de Haselewelle, Ricardo de Perpunt, Thoma camerario meo, Roberto et Willelmo filiis Arewey, Radulfo Saracen, Roberto Brasseley de Oxton, Thoma de Melsonesbi clerico meo, Ricardo de Roudestorn, magistro Hugone, et aliis.

SEAL: 'a lyon rampant in an escocheon'.

This charter, which is particularly interesting for the light it throws on the early topography of Chester, evidently takes the place of **no. 281**, and includes a number of acquisitions made subsequently to the land in Castle Street adjacent to that of Agnes, daughter of Ralph (not Ranulf, as in **no. 281**) Outhecarle, a name which presumably represents the pre-conquest 'housecarl' of Scandinavian England. In the meantime, also, three further bondmen have been added to Robert son-in-law of Mary. The present charter falls between Philip of Orreby's succession as justiciar in 1207 and the death of Richard of Aldford in 1213, and is another early instance (see **no. 374**) of reference to the earl's pleas of the sword. Roger of Montalt succeeded his brother Robert as *dapifer* in 1208–1212 (*H.K.F.*, p. 111). For Thomas of Melsonby, see **no. 356**.

283. Confirmation of Peter the clerk's gifts of lands and rents to his sons Patrick and Ranulf, the earl's godson, whom he has taken into his special custody and protection.

[1208–1216]

> Tabley MSS., Sir Peter Leycester's Liber C, f. 152 (from the originals of Lady Kilmorey); Shakerley MS. 3, p. 153 (from Sir George Booth's book, 1653); Chetham's Library, Towneley MSS., transcripts from the Vernon MSS., pp. 177–8; B.L. Harl. MS. 2077, f. 179 (new f. 91v.), from Sir Peter Leycester's transcript of original: Harl. MS. 2131, f. 32 (new f. 28), from Sir George Booth's collections. Engl. abstract (from Shakerley MS.): *Ches. Sheaf*, no. 4212.

Ranulfus comes Cestrie constabulario, dapifero, iusticiario, vicecomiti et omnibus baronibus suis, ministris et ballivis, et omnibus suis hominibus presentibus et futuris, presentem cartam meam inspecturis et audituris, salutem. Sciatis me concessisse et presenti carta mea confirmasse Patricio clerico meo, filio Petri clerici mei, et Ranulfo filio suo, filiolo meo, et universis aliis omnes donationes et concessiones quas ipse Petrus eis fecerit de terris et laicis redditibus omnibus, que in terra mea adeptus est, de cuiuscumque dono sint, habendas et tenendas illis et eorum heredibus, vel quibus ea dederint et assignaverint, adeo libere et quiete sicut carta Petri et carte illorum, de quorum dono eas habent, testificantur. Precipio quoque omnibus ballivis, ministris et fidelibus meis ut illos et suos et omnia sua protegant et manuteneant, custodiant et defendant sicut illos quos specialiter in custodia mea et protectione suscepi, et prohibeo super forisfacturam meam decem librarum ne eis sive suis molestias aut gravamina faciatis aut ab aliquo fieri permittatis. Hiis testibus Rogero de Monte Alto dapifero meo, Philippo de Orreby tunc iusticiario meo, Warino de Vernun, Willelmo de Venables, Roberto Patric, Hamone de Mascy, Henrico de Aldithlea, Henrico dispensario, Hugone et Galfrido de Dutton, Willelmo de Haselwell, Lidulfo de Twamlowe, Davide de Malopassu, Hugone de Pascy, Ioceramo de Hellesby, Ricardo de Kingeslegh, Henrico de Kagwurth, Ricardo de Bresci, Thoma clerico meo, Ricardo de Perpunt tunc vicecomite Cestrescire, Ricardo de Roudestorne, et multis aliis.

This charter falls between 1208, the earliest date at which Roger of Montalt succeeded to the hereditary seneschalship of Chester, and 1216, when Hugh of Pascy was killed. The description of Richard Perpunt, or Pierrepont, as sheriff of Cheshire, if correct, would support Ormerod's identification of him as successor (c.1210) of Liulf of Twemlow (Orm., i. 70); but the evidence that he was sheriff of the city is very strong (see **no. 372**), and it seems likely that Cheshire is a misreading of the abbreviation *Cestr'*. Peter the clerk's son Patrick, although described as the earl's clerk, appears very rarely as a witness (e.g. **no. 360**), and it seems probable that he left the earl's service early and took the living of Chipping Campden in Gloucestershire (*Chart. St. Werburgh*, no. 199).

284.   Grant of Onston to the earl's godson, Ranulf son of Peter the clerk.

[1208–1216]

> B.L. Harl. MS. 2074, f. 168v. (new f. 65v.), from Vernon MSS.; Harl. 2131, f. 32 (new f. 28), from Sir George Booth's transcripts, 1653; Shakerley MSS., Liber C, f. 108v.; P.R.O., CHES 2/50 (Recog. Rolls), m. 8; CHES 33/4 (Forest Rolls, 20–21 Edw. III), m. 31 (witnesses omitted); D.L. 39/1/19 (Forest Pleas, 21 Edw. III), m. 27 (witnesses omitted). Ed.: Orm., ii. 139 (abbreviated text from Harl. 2074); *36th Rep. D.K.P.R.*, p. 367 (from Recognizance Roll).

Ranulfus comes Cestrie constabulario, dapifero, iusticiario, vicecomiti et omnibus baronibus suis, ministris et ballivis, et omnibus hominibus suis presentibus et futuris presentem cartam inspecturis et audituris salutem. Sciatis me dedisse et concessisse et presenti carta mea confirmasse Ranulfo filiolo meo filio Petri clerici mei et heredibus suis, vel cui eam dare et assignare voluerit, villam de Onestona totam cum hominibus et nativis et cum omnibus pertinentiis suis, habendam et tenendam de me et heredibus meis pro homagio et servicio suo libere et quiete, plene et pacifice, iure hereditario, et quietanciam pannagii de dominicis porcis suis in foresta mea ubique, et quietanciam pannagii de porcis hominum suorum in eadem villa de Onestona manencium, et licenciam de pannagio suo de predictis hominibus suis ad opus suum capiendo, et quietanciam sibi et heredibus suis, vel cui terram illam dare et assignare voluerit, et eorum hominibus in eadem villa de Onestona manentibus de servientibus et forestariis meis pascendis, et de omnibus consuetudinibus et exactionibus, reddendo mihi et heredibus meis annuatim de ipso Ranulfo et heredibus suis, vel de eo cui eam dederit et assignaverit unam libram piperis vel sex denarios ad cameram meam Cestrie in nativitate beati Iohannis Baptiste. Hiis testibus Philippo de Orreby tunc iusticiario meo, Warino de Vernun, Willelmo de Venables, Roberto Patric, Hamone de Masceio, Willelmo de Haselwelle, Ioceramo de Hellesbi, Ricardo de Kyngesleghe, Lidulfo de Tuamlowe, Davide de Malopassu, Hugone de Pascy, Henrico de Kegworthe, Bertramo camerario, Thoma clerico meo, et multis aliis.

The hamlet of Onston (Orm., ii. 139) was attached to Thornton, which Peter the clerk had received from Richard of Aldford (**no. 285**), and like Thornton may well have been a member of the fee of Aldford. Many of the witnesses of the present charter also witnessed **no. 283**, and the dates of the two are probably little different, but it is not possible to say which is the earlier.

285. Grant to Peter the earl's clerk and his heirs, or anyone to whom he may assign the vill of Thornton, of quittance of suit of county and hundred and of pleas of the forest, of pannage for his pigs in the earl's forest, and of feeding foresters and serjeants.

[1208–1217]

> Orig.: J.R.U.L.M., Cornwall-Legh Deeds, no. 786. Facsimile: *J.C.A.S.*, N.S. i, p. 25. Transcr.: B.L. Harl. MS., f. 29v. (new f. 25v.), from original then in possession of Sir George Booth, with drawing of seal. Abstracts (without witnesses): P.R.O., CHES 33/4 (Forest Rolls), m. 31, and CHES 34/1, m. 11; D.L. 39/1/19 (Forest Pleas), m. 27. Full text in English: *Ches. Sheaf*, no. 10136.

Rannulfus comes Cestrie constabulario, dapifero, iusticiario, vicecomiti, baronibus suis et militibus et bayllivis, et omnibus hominibus suis presentibus et futuris presentem cartam inspecturis et audituris salutem. Sciatis me dedisse et concessisse Petro clerico meo et heredibus suis, aut cui assignaverit villam de Thorinthona, quietanciam de sectis comitatus et hundredi et placiti foreste, et quietanciam de pannagio de dominicis porcis suis in forestis meis, et quietanciam de forestariis et servientibus pascendis. Et ut hec donacio mea et concessio predictarum libertatum in perpetuum rata et inconcussa permaneat, tenenda et habenda illi et heredibus suis, aut cui eam assignaverit, de me et de heredibus meis, eam presentis scripti testimonio et sigilli mei apposicione corroboravi. Hiis testibus Philippo de Orreby tunc iusticiario Cestrie, Hugone abbate Cestrie, R. senescallo de Monte Alto, Willelmo de Venables, Warino de Vernona, Hamone de Mascy, Radulfo filio Simonis, Ricardo de Kingesleia, Ioceramo de Hellesbi, Gilberto Bruno, Roberto de Trohford, Hugone de Hole, et multis aliis.

SEAL: fragmentary (now sewn in bag), lion seal.

This is one of many grants in favour of Peter the clerk or members of his family. The grant of Thornton-le-Moors was made by Richard of Aldford between 1208 and 1213 (Orm., ii. 14), and Earl Ranulf here adds a number of liberties. It has been suggested (*Ches. Sheaf*, no. 10136) that his charter is more or less contemporaneous with Richard of Aldford's, but this is far from certain and it may well have been given some time later. Nevertheless it must fall after 1208, when Abbot Hugh of Chester succeeded, and before 1217 at latest. The names of the other witnesses do not help to narrow the date. The charter has usually been interpreted as a grant of Thornton, but that is due to a misreading of the text.

286.   Confirmation to Peter the clerk and his heirs of all lands and gifts he has received in Cheshire, quit of suit to county and hundred courts, portmoot, hallmoot, toll, passage, castlework, and other customs and exactions.

[1208–1217]

> P.R.O., CHES 29/59 (Plea Rolls, 22 Edw. III), m. 31v.; B.L. Harl. MS. 2131, f. 31v. (new f. 27v.), from Sir George Booth's collections; Shakerley MS. 3, p. 152; Chetham's Library, Towneley MSS., transcripts from the Vernon MSS., p. 176. Ed.: Orm., ii. 15 (abbreviated); Engl. abstract: *Ches. Sheaf*, no. 4212.

Ranulfus comes Cestrie constabulario, dapifero, iusticiario, vicecomiti, et omnibus baronibus suis, ministris et ballivis, et omnibus hominibus suis presentibus et futuris presentem cartam inspecturis et audituris salutem. Noveritis me concessisse et presenti carta mea confirmasse Petro clerico meo et heredibus suis omnes terras, donaciones et assignaciones, quas idem Petrus infra terram meam Cestrie adeptus est, de cuiuscumque dono et feodo sunt, habendas et tenendas illis et eorum heredibus, vel quibus eas dederint vel assignaverint vel vendiderint, cum omnibus pertinentiis suis solutas, liberas et quietas de omnibus sectis comitatuum, hundredorum, portmotum et halmotum, de theolonio, passagio, stallagio, frithwite, tallagio, de assisis et summonitionibus. Concedo etiam eis quietanciam de servientibus, forestariis et bedellis meis pascendis, de operationibus castellorum et pontium, et de omni consuetudine et exactione seculari et opere servili. Volo autem quod predictus Petrus et heredes sui de aliquo placito vel delicto coram aliquibus non respondeant nisi coram me vel capitali iusticiario meo, nisi placita vel delicta ad curiam ecclesiasticam pertineant. Et firmiter precipio super forisfacturam meam decem librarum omnibus ballivis, ministris et fidelibus meis, et omnibus aliis, ne eis sive suis iniuriam, molestiam aut gravamina faciant vel ab aliquo fieri permittant. Hiis testibus Philippo de Orreby tunc iusticiario Cestrie, Iohanne de Pratellis, Willelmo de Venables, Warino de Vernona, Waltero de Coventreia tunc senescallo, Hugone et Galfrido de Duttona, Patricio de Modberleghe, Roberto de Pulfordia, Willelmo de Hasewelle, Hugone de Pulfordia, et multis aliis.

The date of this charter is 1208–17. It is somewhat unusual in form and content, but this can be attributed to the esteem in which Ranulf III held Peter the clerk and his desire to grant him the maximum of liberties and exemptions. It is far more comprehensive than **no. 285** and presumably later in date.

287. Confirmation to the canons of Holy Cross, Waltham, of William of Roumare's charter, granting them five spades for digging in his marsh of Bolingbroke on the east side of the causeway between Stickney and Sibsey.

[1198–1202]

> B.L. Cott. MS. Tiberius C. ix (cartulary of Waltham abbey), f. 106.

Rannulfus comes Cestrie omnibus tam futuris quam presentibus salutem. Notum sit vobis me concessisse et presenti carta mea confirmasse deo et ecclesie sancte Crucis de Waltham et canonicis regularibus ibidem deo servientibus in puram et perpetuam elemosinam v. bescas fodientes in maresco meo de Bulingebroke ex orientali parte calceie que est inter Stikeneiam et Sibeceiam, habendas predictis canonicis in perpetuum liberas et quietas, sicut carta Willelmi de Roumara, qui bescas predictas eis dedit, testatur. Et ut hec mea concessio perpetue firmitatis robur opptineat, presentis scripti testimonio et sigilli appositione eam duxi confirmandam. Hiis testibus Ioullano priore de Espaulingis *et cetera*.

Jollanus prior of Spalding occurs between 1194 and 1198; his successor Nicholas occurs in 1202 and 1204 (*Heads of Religious Houses*, p. 109). Earl Ranulf's confirmation therefore falls between 1198, when he succeeded to the Roumare honour of Bolingbroke, and 1202 at latest. It was renewed by his sister Hawise de Quincy when she succeeded to the Bolingbroke lands after Ranulf's death in 1232 (D.L. 36/2, p. 17).

288. Confirmation to the abbey of Revesby of the site of the abbey founded by William of Roumare, earl of Lincoln, and the donations of William and his successors at Revesby, Sytheby, Thoresby and Hagnaby, and of other donations in detail.

[1198–1202]

> Lincoln, Dean and Chapter A/3/9 (Chapter Acts), ff. 32v.–33; Bodleian Library, Dodsworth MS. 102, f. 120 (brief abstract from muniments of earl of Lindsey at Grimesthorpe). Ed.: *Mon.*, v. 456 (short abstract); Stanhope, *Abstracts of the Deeds and Charters relating to Revesby Abbey*, p. 15, no. 50 B (from *Monasticon*).

Omnibus filiis sancte matris ecclesie Ranulfus comes Cestrie salutem. Sciatis me concessisse et presenti carta mea confirmasse deo et sancte Marie et monachis de sancto Laurencio de Revesbi pro salute anime mee et pro animabus omnium antecessorum et heredum meorum in puram et perpetuam elemosinam ipsam abbatiam, quam Willelmus comes Lincolnie fundavit, cum omni donatione quam predictus comes et Willelmus filius eius et Willelmus nepos predicti comitis dederunt eisdem monachis in perpetuam elemosinam, scilicet totam terram de Revesbi et Schicebi et Toresbi cum ecclesia, et omnem terram quam ipsi habuerunt in Hagnebi cum ecclesia, et cum omnibus pertinenciis predictarum villarum plenarie in bosco et plano, in pratis et pasturis, in aquis et molendinis, in marescis, in viis et semitis. Et in territorio de Midingesbi xx. et viii. acras terre et communem pasturam eiusdem ville; et in territorio de Marum terram que vocatur Leggeshage cum appendiciis suis; et in territorio de Kyrekebi centum et viginti acras terre inter silvam et marescum contingens terre monachorum, et ex alia parte silve iiii. acras terre et quandam partem silve quam monachi exstirpaverunt, cum commune pastura eiusdem ville; et in Sibeceia hermitorium Hacke, et Swinecote cum commune pastura eiusdem ville; et de dominio meo terram que vocatur Haiholme et West Feriwra cum prato adiacente, et licentiam edificandi domos in maresco ubicunque racionabiliter fieri poterint, et omnia aisiamenta sua ibi habere, prout indignerint; et in territorio de Stikeneie illam porcionem terre quam habuerunt, et communem pasturam eiusdem ville; et in maresco de Hatam mansionem quamdam que vocatur Seggedic cum croftis quos ibi fecerunt, cum communione pasture tocius marisci, et accipere ibidem omnia aisiamenta sua, prout indignerint.

Item, ex dono Willelmi Ferrerii[1] nepotis predicti comitis unam carrucatam terre in territorio de Enderbi cum omnibus pertinenciis suis, et totam villam de Stikney, quam dedit cum corpore suo, et quicquid in ea habuit cum omnibus pertinenciis suis, et homagium et servicium Alani filii Willelmi de Stikney et heredum eius, qui scilicet Alanus et heredes eius tenebant eandem villam de ipsis monachis in perpetuum per servicium trium marcarum argenti annuatim reddendarum ad vinum emendum ad missas monachorum. Et in Elefen unam mansionem que vocatur Medelham cum clausura continente lx. acras; et in maresco de Sibeceie xiiii. acras prati contiguas fossatis eorum de Hilledic ex aquilonari parte fossatorum claudendas, et omnes clausuras et omnia fossata que fecerunt in terra predicti Willelmi aut in maresco aut extra marescum; et in territorio de Midingesbi duas bovatas terre que fuerunt Rogeri filii Aki.

Preterea concessi eis ducere aquam de Bullingbroke ad abbatiam suam, et habere[2] ubicunque huiusmodi aqua vadit per terram dominii mei. Concessi eis tantum de terra mea quantum opus habent ad illam ducendam, et ubicunque vadit per terram hominum meorum, quantum ipsi dederunt aut concesserunt, tantum concedo eis et confirmo in perpetuam elemosinam. Insuper concedo eis et confirmo warrenam ubique in terra eorum et prohibeo ne aliquis heredum vel successorum meorum eis inde aliquam molestiam faciat, et in maresco de Totingtun concedo eis habere et accipere omnia aisiamenta et necessaria ad salinas suas de Wainfled et ad fratres suos de Seggdic.

Hec omnia predicta cum omnibus pertinenciis suis concessi et presenti carta confirmavi eisdem monachis tenenda et habenda bene et in pace, libere et integre, quiete et honorifice, soluta et quieta ab omni terreno servicio et seculari exaccione et placitis, querelis et omnibus occasionibus et secularibus consuetudinibus. Et omne servicium et omnes consuetudines, que pro his omnibus debentur regi aut alicui homini, ego et heredes mei acquietabimus, et hec omnia predictis monachis contra omnes homines warrantizabimus in puram et perpetuam elemosinam. Hiis testibus David comite fratre regis Scocie, Hugone Bardolf, Simone de Kyma, Philippo filio Roberti, Petro Roald, Roberto de Mortuo Mari, Willelmo de Veer, Philippo de Orrebi, Simone de Driebi, Thoma dispensatore, Simone Tuschet, Simone de Orrebi, *etc.*

1. Ferrii *MS.*
2. *add* et *MS.*

Revesby abbey was founded by William of Roumare, half-brother of Earl Ranulf II, in 1142–43. The Roumare inheritance in Lincolnshire passed to Ranulf III in 1198, and the present exhaustive charter was probably granted shortly thereafter. Hugh Bardulf died in 1202 (*P.R.S.*, N.S. xvi, p. 102), and Pierre Rouaut withdrew to Normandy in 1203–04. This gives the limit of date. Earl David of Huntingdon, brother of the king of Scotland, had married Ranulf III's sister, Matilda, in 1190 (**no. 220**).

289. Gift of Roger of Stickney, the earl's bondman, to Revesby abbey.

[1199–1204]

> Orig.: Revesby charters, Box II, no. 50. Cal.: *6th Rep.*
> *Hist. MSS. Comm.*, p. 235; Stanhope, *Abstracts of the*
> *Deeds and Charters relating to Revesby Abbey*, p. 15.

Sciant presentes et futuri, quod ego Rannulfus comes Cestrie concessi et dedi et hac presenti carta confirmavi deo et sancte Marie et abbati et conventui de Revesbi in perpetuam elemosinam Rogerum de Stikeneia servum meum, filium Thorevord de Sybeceia, cum tota secta sua et cum omnibus catallis suis, ita quod nec ego nec heredes mei habeamus ullum ius aut clamium in predicto Rogero aut in secta sua aut in catallis suis. Et ego et heredes mei warantizabimus predictum Rogerum et sectam suam et catalla sua predictis monachis de Revesbi. Hiis testibus Baldewino Wac, Philippo de Orrebi, Thoma dispensatore, Waltero de Coventre, Iohanne de Praeus, Willelmo de Verdun, Thoma de Orrebi, Norman Pantouf, Willelmo filio Ricardi de Haltona, Thoma cancellario, magistro Radulfo de Cliftona, Geroldo ostiario, Galfrido le Bretun, Thoma de Pleselei, Hugone de Pasci, Willelmo Lochard, Iohanne filio Gerardi, Alano de Kales.

SEAL on tag, a lion rampant; legend SIG RANUEIL COMIT[IS CEST]RIE.

This grant is not easy to date accurately. Baldwin Wake I died in 1200, but was succeeded by his son, Baldwin II (*H.K.F.*, p. 170), and a little later Thomas Despenser I was followed by Thomas Despenser II. In neither case is it clear which is referred to. The death of William de Verdun in 1204 indicates one terminus. The other is indicated by the appearance among the witnesses of Walter of Coventry, who first occurs as Ranulf III's seneschal in Lincolnshire in 1199 (*H.K.F.*, p. 156). It is noticeable also that Philip of Orreby, whose appointment to the justiciarship of Chester had certainly occurred by 1207 (*L.P.R.*, p. 356) and possibly by 1206, is not yet mentioned with his official title. The charter therefore probably falls between 1199 and 1204. For John of Préaux, who had been with Richard I at Jaffa in 1192 and later in Normandy, see **no. 337**. Thomas the chancellor also occurs in a charter (**no. 247**) for Poulton abbey of approximately the same date.

290.   Grant to Revesby abbey of a right of way over the marsh of Bolingbroke along the trench through the middle of the earl's marsh and the marshes of Robert of Rodes and Robert Marmion.

[1225–1226]

Bodleian Library, Dodsworth MS. 102, f. 120.

Ranulfus comes Cestrie et Lincolnie [*etc.*] concessisse monachis de Revesby in puram *etc.* ut faciant carragia sua per trencatam, que facta est per medium maresci mei de Bulingbroc et maresci domini Roberti de Rodes et maresci domini Roberti Marmiun, quod pertinet ad villam de Cuninggesbi, usque ad filum aque de Guitheme. Testibus domino Willelmo de Ferrers comite Derbie, Huberto de Burgo domino iusticiario regis Henrici, Iohanne de Laci constabulario Cestrie, Briano de Insula, Philippo de Kyma, Thoma de Muleton, Lambert filio eius, Philippo de Orrebi iusticiario Cestrie, Hugone dispensario, Waltero de Daivilla, Gilleberto Cusin seneschallo de Bulingbroc, Waltero de Covingtre, Ricardo filio eius, Henrico de Langeton, Rodeland de Wudehale, Alano filio Ywan de Meringes, *etc.*

A final concord, dated 26 November 1224, between Robert Marmion the elder and Robert Marmion the younger adjudged Coningsby to the former (*Linc. Rec. Soc., Final Concords*, i. 350). The distinguished list of witnesses does not help greatly with the dating. The famous justiciar Hubert de Burgh became earl of Kent on 19 February 1227. Since he is not described as such, the charter (of which this garbled version appears to be the only surviving copy) presumably falls before that date. Brian de l'Isle, appointed chief forester of England in 1221, was very active in the service of Henry III. Hugh Despenser succeeded his father Thomas in 1218 (*H.K.F.*, p. 59), and Philip of Kyme succeeded in 1220 (*H.K.F.*, pp. 123–4). It is probably safe to date the charter 1220–26, and if Robert Marmion's tenure of Coningsby dates only from 26 November 1224, its date can be narrowed even further to 1225–6.

291.   Confirmation to Kirkstead abbey of the gifts of William of Roumare in Sibsey, the East Fen of Bolingbroke, Wolmersty, and Edlington.

[1198–1202]

> B.L. Cott. MS. Vesp. E. xviii (Kirkstead cartulary), f. 162. (This is a parchment slip, unnumbered in the old foliation, between pp. 298 and 299).

Omnibus sancte matris ecclesie filiis tam presentibus quam futuris Ranulphus comes Cestrie salutem. Sciatis me concessisse et hac carta mea confirmasse deo et ecclesie sancte Marie et monachis de Kyrkested omnes donationes et confirmationes quas Willelmus de Roumara eis fecit, scilicet in campis de Cibecey xx. perticatas prati in latum et unum selionem, quem Rothol tenuit, et duas beschas fodientes in marisco de Bulingbroc, scilicet in Estfen, et tantum turbe in marisco versus Vulmarsti quantum sufficere potest ad duas patellas saline sue de Vulmarsti, et communem pasturam ad animalia sua que necessaria ad predictam salinam attrahere debent, et preterea communem pasturam in Wildemora, quam eis dedit Willelmus senior de Roumara, comes Lincolnie, et in villa de Edlingtona unum toftum cum octo acris terre arabilis et pratum quod vocatur Engcroft et aliud pratum quod vocatur Appeltredeila, cum communi pastura eiusdem ville et omnibus aliis aisiamentis infra predictam villam et extra, sicut carta, quam habent de dono Radulfi filii Symonis de Haingtona, testatur. Omnia predicta habebunt et tenebunt predicti monachi libere et quiete ab omni seculari servitio et consuetudine et exactione in puram et perpetuam elemosinam, in viis et semitis, in introitibus et exitibus et omnibus aliis aisiamentis, sicut carte donatorum, quas dicti monachi de eis habent, testantur. Hiis testibus Hugone abbate de Revesby, Gileberti de Gant.

The date of this charter falls between Ranulf III's succession to the Roumare inheritance of Bolingbroke in 1198 and the last known appearance of Abbot Hugh of Revesby in 1202 (*Heads of Religious Houses*, p. 140). As he had been abbot since 1172 and his successor Ralph is mentioned shortly afterwards, it is safe to conclude that he died about this time.

292.   Grant to the monastery of Kirkstead of lands in Beningworth to build a grange, with commons of pasture for their sheep and cattle, as given by Gilbert of Beningworth.

[1198–1217]

B.L. Cott. MS. Vesp. E. xviii (Kirkstead cartulary), f. 49
(new f. 28).

Omnibus sancte matris ecclesie filiis presentibus et futuris Rannulfus comes Cestrie salutem. Sciatis me concessisse et hac mea carta[1] confirmasse deo et ecclesie sancte Marie et monachis de Kyrkested in puram et perpetuam elemosinam tria tofto cum croftis suis in villa de Beningword in loco qui vocatur Pitsic, quem[2] Willelmus filius Aselini et Willelmus Pigge et Walterus filius Gode tenuerunt, ad unam grangiam edificandam et cetera edificia construenda, cum ipso rivulo de Pitsic,et unum toftum in Suthorp, quod Rogerus Canion tenuit, ad bercarias suas faciendas, et quindecies viginti acras terre arabilis ex una parte ipsius ville et quatuordecies viginti et quindecim acras et unam perticam et quinque fallas[3] terre arabilis ex altera parte ville per perticam ipsius ville. Et preterea concessi quadraginta et unam acras[4] et dimidiam prati in Sutheng et viginti acras prati in Breithesegges versus divisas de Sottebi. Concessi etiam eis communem pasturam quingentis ovibus per maius centum per totos campos predicte ville, et similiter ad averia que excolunt terram predictam, et ad unum taurum et decem vaccas cum sequela sua usque ad tercium annum perimpletum, et ad viginti porcos. Hec omnia concessi et confirmavi predictis monachis de Kyrkested habenda et tenenda libere et quiete et honorifice cum omnibus libertatibus suis, sicut in carta sua, quam de Gilberto de Beningword inde habent, continetur rationabiliter. Hiis testibus . . .[5].

1.   *om. MS.*
2.   que *MS.*
3.   fal. *MS.*
4.   acram *MS.*
5.   *witnesses omitted MS.*

This charter falls between 1198 and 1217 but, lacking witnesses, cannot be dated more closely. It is immediately preceded in the cartulary by Gilbert of Beningworth's charter, but this also is without witnesses.

293.   Gift to the monks of Kirkstead abbey of the site of their mill adjoining Little Fen and other tenements in the fields of Metheringham (Lincs.)

[? 1220–1221]

B.L. Cott. MS. Vesp. E. 18 (Kirkstead cartulary), f. 36v. (old f. 66), no. 44.

Universis sancte matris ecclesie filiis presentibus et futuris Rannulfus comes Cestrie et Lincolnie salutem. Sciatis me concessisse et hac mea carta confirmasse deo et ecclesie sancte Marie et monachis de Kyrkested in puram et perpetuam elemosinam sedem molendini sui iuxta Lithlefen in campis de Methringham et stagnum eiusdem molendini et refluvium aque et illud modicum terre quod iacet ante portam ipsius molendini et calcedam suam ultra Lithlefen, quantum de hiis omnibus pertinet ad feodum meum; similiter et totam terram et brueriam que est de feodo meo ab oriente de Lithlefen, scilicet terram lucrabilem quam homines Philippi de Kyma tenuerunt; et quicquid ipsis monachis fuit concessum et donatum de feodo meo in terris arabilibus, in pratis, in mariscis, in pascuis, in boscis et in omnibus aliis locis ante diem Natalis Domini anno incarnationis dominice mccxviii; tenenda et habenda libere et quiete secundum libertates que continentur in cartis donatorum suorum. Et sciendum quod ego et heredes mei pro defectu servicii nostri non distringemus tenementum ipsorum monachorum, quamdiu per aliud tenementum de ipso feodo districtionem facere poterimus. Hiis testibus . . .

It seems logical to date this charter shortly before or after 25 December 1218, the latest date for which gifts to the abbey were confirmed. The difficulty is that Ranulf III left on crusade at Whitsuntide 1218 (*Ann. Cestr.*, p. 51). It might therefore be safer to assume that it was given shortly after his return in 1220. An alternative would be to regard the year 1217, when Ranulf became earl of Lincoln and was engaged on military operations in Lincolnshire, as meant; but this also is not altogether satisfactory. In the circumstances the date must be left open, with a preference for 1220–1221.

294. Confirmation to the canons of Dereham of William of Roumare's gift of the right to dig four spits of land in the East Marsh of Bolingbroke.

Coventry, [1198–1203]

Orig.: P.R.O., D.L. 27/235. Transcr.: D.L. 42/2 (Coucher Book II), f. 277v.

Omnibus sancte matris ecclesie filiis, ad quos presentes littere pervenerint, Rannulfus comes Cestrie salutem. Notum sit vobis me pro dei amore et pro salute anime mee et animarum antecessorum meorum concessisse et hac carta mea confirmasse donationem, quam Willelmus de Roumara fecit deo et sancte Marie et canonicis de Derham, scilicet quatuor bescas fodientes in Estmaresco meo de Bulingbroc, habendas predictis canonicis in puram et perpetuam elemosinam, sicut carta predicti Willelmi de Roumara, quam canonici ipsi habent, testatur. Hiis testibus Radulfo de Mesnilwarin, Petro Roaud, Symone de Touschet, Willelmo Marescallo, Gileberto de Benningwurthe, Waltero de Coventreia, Roberto clerico de Benteford, Martino clerico, et multis aliis apud Coventreiam.

> SEAL: lion seal, device complete, legend defaced and broken; reverse blank.

Ranulf III succeeded to the honour of Bolingbroke in 1198 on the death of William of Roumare III. Walter of Coventry appears as seneschal of the earl's lands in Lincolnshire in 1199 (*H.K.F.*, p. 156). Pierre Rouaut was still in Ranulf's service in 1203, but withdrew to France after the loss of Normandy, probably in 1204 (*Ches. Sheaf*, no. 2419).

295. Confirmation to Gilbert of Beningworth of the lands which he and his ancestors held of William of Roumare.

Great Tew, [1198–1203]

> Orig.: B.L. Cott. MS. Nero C. iii, f. 183. Transcr.: P.R.O., D.L. 42/2 (Coucher Book II), f. 445v. Ed.: *The Genealogist*, N.S. xv, p. 143 (no. 12) (from Coucher Book).

Ranulfus comes Cestrie omnibus tam futuris quam presentibus salutem. Notum sit vobis me concessisse et presenti carta mea confirmasse Gisleberto de Beningwurthe et heredibus suis totam terram, quam antecessores sui et ipse tenuerunt de Willelmo de Roumara et antecessoribus suis, tenendam de me et de heredibus meis predicto Gisleberto et heredibus suis in feodo et hereditate per servicium sex militum, sicut carte Willelmi de Roumara, quas idem Gislebertus habet, testantur. Hiis testibus Petro Roaud, Rogero de Canvilla, Willelmo Marescallo, Iuhello de Lovingneio, Iuhello Berengario, Luca de sancto Leodegario, Bartholomeo abbate, Petro clerico, Willelmo de Verdun, Ricardo clerico, et multis aliis apud Tiwam.

The date must be approximately the same as that of **no. 294.** It looks as though, on succeeding to the honour of Bolingbroke in 1198, Ranulf III issued a series of confirmations of grants of his predecessor, William of Roumare. For Tew (Great Tew, Oxon.), where the charter was issued, see **no. 337.** For Barthélemy l'Abbé, see **no. 277.** William of Verdun was dead by 1205 (*P.R.S.*, N.S. xviii, p. 111), in which year further confirmations (**nos. 296, 297**) were made to Gilbert of Beningworth. A noticeable feature of the charter is the number of French witnesses.

296. Grant to Gilbert of Beningworth of the land which had belonged to Richard of Warwick, acquired through his wife Sara, Richard's daughter.

[1205]

> Orig.: P.R.O., D.L. 25 (Ancient Deeds, Series L), no. 3073. Transcr.: P.R.O., D.L. 42/2 (Coucher Book II), f. 445v. Abstract (from Coucher Book): Central Reference Library, Manchester, Towneley MSS. no. 8, p. 1086; *The Genealogist*, N.S. xv, p. 143 (no. 13).

Rannulphus comes Cestrie omnibus hominibus et amicis suis et omnibus, ad quos presens scriptum pervenerit, salutem. Sciatis me concessisse et hac carta mea confirmasse Gisleberto de Benningwrtha totam terram, que fuit Ricardi de Warewico, tanquam ius uxoris sue, filie predicti Ricardi de Warewico, habendam et tenendam de me et heredibus meis per tale servicium ut Ricardus de Warewico illam tenuit. Hiis testibus Philippo de Orrebi, Iohanne de Pratellis, Waltero de Coventreia, Rogero de Maletot, Helia pincerna, Willelmo filio Drogonis, Thoma de Orrebi, et multis aliis.

> SEAL on tag, fragmentary: on a heater shield a lion rampant.

Gilbert of Beningworth, who succeeded his father Roger about 1189 and probably died in 1224, was a frequent witness of Ranulf III's charters. Richard of Warwick died in 1205, and on 19 April the sheriff of Lincoln was directed to put Gilbert in possession of the lands Richard had given him in Scrafield and Sturton in marriage with his daughter Sara (*H.K.F.*, p. 135). Earl Ranulf's charter almost certainly was issued contemporaneously. His grant of the lands of Gilbert's father (**no. 297**) has the same witnesses, and was evidently issued at the same time. Among the witnesses particular interest attaches to Philip of Orreby, who appears without title and therefore cannot have been justiciar in 1202, or even in 1204, as Tait argued (*Ches. Sheaf*, no. 7804). This supports the suggestion (**no. 281**) that there was a gap between Ralph Mainwaring's justiciarship and Orreby's, which probably began in 1206 or 1207.

297. Grant to Gilbert of Beningworth of the lands his father Roger held of William of Roumare, together with rights in the East Fen of Bolingbroke.

[1205]

> Orig.: P.R.O., D.L. 25 (Ancient Deeds, Series L), no. 3090. Transcr.: D.L. 42/2 (Coucher Book II), f. 450.

Abstract (from Coucher Book) *The Genealogist*, N.S. xv, p. 143 (no. 11).

Rannulphus comes Cestrie omnibus hominibus et amicis suis et omnibus tam futuris quam presentibus, ad quos presens scriptum pervenerit, salutem. Sciatis me concessisse et hac carta mea confirmasse Gisleberto de Benningwurthe omnes terras et tenuras, quas Rogerus de Benningwurthe eius pater tenuit de Willelmo de Roumara, habendas et tenendas sibi et heredibus suis de me et heredibus meis libere et quiete et honorifice in villa et extra villam, in bosco et plano, in viis et semitis, in pratis et pasturis et marescis, et in omnibus locis cum omnibus pertinenciis suis per[1] servitium decem militum. Dedi eciam predicto Gisleberto et presenti carta mea confirmavi la [. . . .][2] de viginti beschis in Estfen, maresco meo de Bolingbroc, ei et heredibus suis habendas et tenendas de me et heredibus meis libere et quiete, reddendo annuatim sexaginta solidos pro omni servicio. Hiis testibus Philippo de Orreby, Iohanne de Pratellis, Waltero de Coventreia, Rogero de Maletot, Helia pincerna, Willelmo filio Drogonis, Thoma de Orrebi, et multis aliis.

SEAL on tag, fragmentary: a lion rampant.

1.   Original rubbed and illegible; missing words supplied from D.L. 42/2.
2.   Illegible in original; space in copy.

For an earlier confirmation of his father's lands, see **no. 295**. The present charter, which specifies the service owed of ten knights and also confirms Ranulf III's additional gift of the right to dig in the East Fen for an annual payment of 60s., has the same witnesses as **no. 296**, and was almost certainly issued at the same time. It is certainly later than **no. 295**, which was probably issued around 1200, and may safely be dated 1205, like **no. 296.**

298.   Confirmation to Gilbert of Beningworth of lands in Lincolnshire inherited from his father, except for the manors of Halton, Irby, Steeping and Kingthorpe, which Earl Ranulf retained.

[1220–1224]

Peterborough, Library of Dean and Chapter, Goxhill Leiger, f. 28v., no. 111 (now deposited in Cambridge University Library); copy from Leiger, County Library, Lincoln.

Sciant presentes et futuri presentem cartam inspecturi vel audituri, quod ego Rannulfus comes Cestrie et Lincolnie concessi et hac presenti carta mea confirmavi Gileberto de Beningwurthe tenementa, que ipse de me tenet in comitatu Lincolnie de hereditate Rogeri de Beningwurthe patris sui, habenda et tenenda de me et heredibus meis ipsi Gileberto et heredibus suis, faciendo inde michi et heredibus meis servicia decem feodorum militum, computatis eis serviciis trium feodorum militum et dimidii et quartadecima parte feodi unius militis in maneriis de Hautona, Yreby, Steping et Kintorp, que maneria ex dona ipsius Gileberti in manu mea retinui. Hiis testibus Philippo de Orreby tunc iusticiario Cestrie, Philippo de Kimba, Radulfo filio Simonis, Eudone de Kalecot, Aluredo de Sulligny, Iohanne filio Philippi, Roberto de Dayvilla, Gileberto Cusin, Simone clerico, et multis aliis.

For an earlier confirmation, see **no. 297**. The evidence does not permit an accurate dating of the present charter. Ranulf III succeeded to the earldom of Lincoln on 23 May 1217. Gilbert of Beningworth died in, or shortly before, 1224 (*H.K.F.*, p. 136). Philip of Kyme succeeded his father in 1220 (*H.K.F.*, pp. 123–4). Philip of Orreby resigned the justiciarship at Easter 1229. Gilbert Cusin became seneschal of Bolingbroke (see **nos. 290** and **299**) in 1223, presumably in succession to Walter of Coventry, who had held office since 1199 at latest, but the date is not known.

299. Agreement with Gilbert of Beningworth by which Gilbert assigns seven bovates in Beningworth to Earl Ranulf for a term of eight years beginning 11 November 1223 for a sum of 40 marks.

[November 1223]

Orig.: P.R.O., D.L. 27/290. Transcr.: D.L. 42/2 (Coucher Book II), f. 446; abstract (from Coucher Book): *The Genealogist*, N.S. xv, pp. 143–4 (no. 18).

Hec est convencio facta inter dominum Ranulfum comitem Cestrie et Lincolnie et Gilbertum de Beningwrthe, scilicet quod predictus Gilbertus dimisit predicto Ranulfo comiti Cestrie et Lincolnie septem bovatas terre in Beningwrthe cum omnibus pertinenciis infra villam et extra a festo sancti Martini anno ab incarnacione domini mccxxiii. usque in viii. annos, scilicet illas duas bovatas quas Ranulfus de Northorp tenuit, et unam bovatam quam Ertusius filius Walteri tenuit, et duas bovatas quas Walterus filius Willelmi tenuit, et duas bovatas quas Ertusius filius Walteri[1] tenuit, illi et heredibus suis vel cui terram illam assignare voluerit, tenendam et habendam cum predictis hominibus libere et quiete usque ad terminum prenominatum pro quadraginta marcis argenti, quas ipse Rannulfus comes dedit predicto Gilberto pre manibus. Et predictus Gilbertus et heredes sui warantizabunt predicto Rannulfo comiti et heredibus suis et eius assignatis predictam terram cum hominibus prescriptis et omnibus aliis pertinenciis usque ad terminum predictorum octo annorum contra omnes homines. Hiis testibus domino Philippo de Orreby iusticiario Cestrie, Aluredo de Suligni, Iohanne filio Philippi, Eudone de Kaletoft, Radulfo filio Simonis, Gilberto Cusin tunc senescallo, Radulfo Hardwin, Petro de Edlingtona, Ketebern de Kales, Alano filio Reingot, Thoma de Totington, et aliis.

> Cirograph in two parts, the surviving part sealed with the seal of Gilbert of Beningworth, green wax, an equestrian figure holding sword in right hand, inscription SIGIL-LUM [GI]LL[E]BERTI DE BENINGWORC. The other part was presumably sealed with the earl's seal.

1.   Ertusius fil. Walteri *orig.*

The agreement must date within a few days of the specified term. Gilbert died shortly afterwards. His warranty was soon put to the test.In 1224 Elen of Steeping impleaded Earl Ranulf for her dower in the lands of Beningworth. Ranulf vouched Gilbert's heir, William, to warranty, but Elen won her case, and William was ordered to make an exchange to the earl for the land in question (*H.K.F*, p. 180).

300.   Confirmation of the gifts of Patrick of Mobberley to Mobberley priory.

Chester, [1198–1206]

> Orig.: sold at Sotheby's, 6 March 1984, lot 508; purchaser not traced. Ed.: Orm., i. 422 (no. 8) (from original, then in possession of William Hamper, with drawing of seal).

Omnibus sancte matris ecclesie filiis ad quos littere presentes pervenerint, Ranulfus comes Cestrie salutem. Noverit universitas vestra me pro dei amore et pro salute anime mee et animarum antecessorum meorum et successorum meorum concessisse et hac carta mea confirmasse deo et sancte Marie et sancto Wilfrido et canonicis regularibus in ecclesia de Modberlega deo servientibus omnes donationes quas Patricius de Modberlega eis fecit aut eis in posterum facturus est, tam in ecclesia de Modberlega quam in terris et salinis et in omnibus aliis rebus, et terram de Tattona quam Ricardus filius Guarnerii eis dedit, et omnia alia que a predicto Patricio vel a quocumque alio eis collata sunt vel in posterum conferenda, habenda et tenenda predictis canonicis in puram elemosinam et perpetuam, sicut rationabiles carte donatorum testabunt. Suscepi etiam predictos canonicos in protectione mea et custodia et homines et possessiones eorum, et prohibeo super forisfacturam meam x. librarum ne aliquis eos iniuste vexare aut molestare presumat. Hiis testibus Radulfo de Mesnilwarin, Liulpho de Tuamlawa, Patricio de Modberlega, Petro clerico,

Willelmo de Tabbelega et Roberto et Willelmo eius fratribus, Alexandro filio Radulfi, Roberto filio Picoti, Willelmo et Roberto filiis Arnow, Radulfo Sarraceno, Symone filio Alani, et multis aliis apud Cestriam.

> SEAL: green wax, lion seal; legend fragmentary +
> S[I]GILL[UM . . . . . . CESTR]IE.

For the small Augustinian house of Mobberley, founded by Patrick of Mobberley, see *V.C.H. Cheshire*, iii. 124. It proved unviable, and was soon annexed to Rocester abbey in Staffordshire, probably c.1240. Its foundation was dated 'about 1206' by Sir Peter Leycester (Orm., i. 411). It must at any rate have been during the pontificate of Bishop Geoffrey Muschamp (1198–1208), who granted a confirmation (Orm., i. 422–3, no. 9). The appearance as first witness of the present charter of Ralph Mainwaring, almost certainly in his capacity of justiciar, and the absence of Philip of Orreby suggest a date not later and probably earlier than 1206, but any date after 1198 would be possible.

301. Grant to Nicholas son of Baldwin of Enderby (Mavis Enderby, Lincs.) of a toft and croft in the township of Enderby.

Lincoln, [1198–1206]

> B.L. Lansdowne MS. 207A (Collectanea Gervasii Holles), f. 145 (old f. 269), and f. 153 (old f. 285), with colour wash of seal; Stowe MS. 531, f. 215 (old f. 447), with sketch of seal.

Rannulfus comes Cestrie omnibus tam futuris quam presentibus salutem. Sciatis me concessisse et dedisse et hac carta mea confirmasse Nicholao filio Baldewini de Enderby pro homagio suo et servicio unum toftum et unum croftum in villa de Enderby, que Henricus molendinarius tenuit, habenda et tenenda ei et heredibus suis de me et meis heredibus in feodo et hereditate libere et quiete cum omnibus ad predictam terram pertinentibus, reddendo annuatim mihi et heredibus meis ab illo et heredibus suis xviii. denarios, scilicet iiii. denarios et obulum ad festum sancti Michaelis, iiii. denarios et obulum ad Natale Domini, et iiii. denarios et obulum ad Pascha, et iiii. denarios et obulum ad festum Sancti Botulphi. Hiis testibus Iohanne de Pratellis, Normanno Pantulf, Henrico dispensario, Waltero de Coventreia, Philippo de Bye, Willelmo de Kene, Willelmo Malebisse, Willelmo de Hauton, Nicholao clerico de Enderby, Willelmo Scotte, Philippo de Camera, Hugone Giburello, Gaufrido de Kales, et multis aliis apud Lincolniam.

> SEAL: red wax, lion seal, only fragment of legend . . .
> IGIL . . .

Mavis Enderby was part of the Roumare honour of Bolingbroke, which passed to Ranulf III in 1198 (*H.K.F.*, p. 162), and the present charter was probably granted between that date and 1206. The witnesses, apart from the first four, were all local men. Walter of Coventry was Ranulf III's seneschal for the Roumare lands. For John de Pratellis (Préaux), see **no. 337**.

302.   Confirmation to Alan of Hareby of the lands in Miningsby and Kirkby (Lincs.) which his grandfather Ivo and Ivo's brother Colswain held before him, and which Robert the chamberlain of Pontefract had recognized as his right in the earl's court at Bolingbroke.

Belchford, [1198–1206]

P.R.O., D.L. 42/2 (Coucher Book II), f. 236.

Ranulphus comes Cestrie omnibus tam futuris quam presentibus salutem. Notum sit vobis me concessisse et hac carta mea confirmasse Alano de Hareby filio Walteri septem bovatas terre in Mithingesbi et in Kirkeby cum omnibus pertinenciis suis, illas scilicet que fuerunt Ivonis avi predicti Alani et Colsuani fratris eiusdem Ivonis, habendas et tenendas memorato Alano et heredibus suis de me et de heredibus meis in feodo et hereditate libere et quiete et solute per servicium quarte partis feodi unius militis pro omnibus serviciis ad eandem terram pertinentibus, sicut carta Roberti camerarii de Pontefracto cognati predicti Alani ei testatur. Qui scilicet Robertus predictam terram reddidit et recognovit dicto Alano sicut ius et hereditatem ipsius Alani in plenaria curia mea apud Bolingbroc. Hiis testibus Thoma dispensatore, Eustachio de Cestria, Radulpho filio Simonis, Philippo de Orrebi, Willelmo Picot, Alano de Martona, Waltero de Coventreia, Philippo de Kales, Willelmo filio Drogonis, Rogero de Maletot, Helya pincerna, Willelmo de Kales, Roberto de Bolonia, Alano de Stikenai, Iohanne filio Gerardi, et multis aliis apud Bentefordam.

This charter must fall after 1198 when Ranulf III succeeded to the Roumare honour of Bolingbroke. The charter of Robert chamberlain of Pontefract, recognizing Alan of Hareby's rights, is still extant (D.L. Ancient Deeds, Series L, no. 2362), and has been printed by Stenton (*Danelaw Charters*, p. 370). As Philip of Orreby was still not justiciar of Chester, the earl's charter presumably falls before 1206; but otherwise the long list of witnesses, which looks as though it reflects a meeting of the earl's 'full court', does not help to fix the date more closely. Eustace of Chester was a brother of Roger de Lacy, the constable of Chester, and presumably an illegitimate son of John the constable; he had two other brothers, Richard and Geoffrey, who are often found in association with him (*E.C.C.*, pp. 18, 20; *Ches. Sheaf*, nos. 10142, 10150).

303. Grant to Thomas, son of Alger of Fleet (Lincs.) of nine acres in Long Bennington (Lincs.), which William of St. John gave to his father.

[? 1198–1207]

> Orig.: Westminster Abbey muniments, no. 541. Ed.: Madox, *Formulare Anglicanum*, p. 187 (no. 310), from original.

Rannulfus comes Cestrie omnibus tam presentibus quam futuris, ad quos presens scriptum pervenerit, salutem. Notum sit vobis omnibus me concessisse et dedisse Thome filio Algeri de Flete pro homagio suo et servicio novem bovatas terre in Beningtona et duo tofta cum pertinenciis suis, illas scilicet novem bovatas terre cum duobus toftis quas Willelmus de Sancto Iohanne dedit Algero patri predicti Thome, illi et heredibus suis tenenda[1] de me et heredibus meis in feodo et hereditate libere et quiete, reddendo annuatim mihi et heredibus meis ab illo et heredibus suis unam marcam argenti ad quatuor terminos, scilicet xl. denarios ad festum sancti Michaelis et xl. denarios ad Natale Domini et xl. denarios ad Pascha et xl. denarios ad nativitatem sancti Iohannis Baptiste. Et ut hec mea donacio rata et inconcussa permaneat, eam presenti scripto et sigillo meo confirmavi. Hiis testibus Philippo de Orrebi, Waltero de Coventreia, Thoma dispensatore, Radulfo de Stubbetona, Willelmo de Sancto Paulo, Iordano fratre eius, Ricardo de Scaudefordia, Waltero de Suindbeia, Willelmo de Weburgia, Hugone filio Samsonis, et multis aliis.

> SEAL: on tag, yellow wax; lion seal; legend SIGILLUM RANULFI COMITIS CESTRIE.

1. *sic orig.*

For Alger of Fleet, see *Book of Seals*, no. 185; he appears on the Pipe Roll between 1165 and 1186. His son Thomas later gave the above nine bovates in Long Bennington to Savigny (**no. 442**). Long Bennington had come into the hands of William of St. John as second husband of Olive, daughter of Count Stephen of Brittany (*Books of Seals*, p. 173). The present charter presumably dates from after 1186, and if Walter of Coventry only began to function as Ranulf III's seneschal in Lincolnshire after 1198 (*H.K.F.*, p. 156), from considerably later. Philip of Orreby is not yet named as justiciar, and Thomas Despenser (I) apparently died in 1207 (*ibid.*, p. 58). William of St. Paul last appears on the Pipe Roll in 1203–04 (*P.R.S.*, N.S. xviii, p. 169). Though perhaps earlier, the charter appears to date from between 1198 and 1207.

304.   Confirmation to the Gilbertine priory of Alvingham (Lincs.) of the lands
and pastures given by Gilbert of Turs in Cabourne.

[1198–1217]

Bodleian Library, MS. Laud misc. 642 (cartulary of
Alvingham), f. 158.

Omnibus Christi fidelibus tam futuris quam presentibus Ranulphus comes
Cestrie salutem. Notum sit vobis me divini amoris intuitu et pro salute
animarum antecessorum meorum et anime mee et heredum meorum concessisse et presenti carta mea confirmasse deo et beate Marie et conventui de
Alvingham terras et pasturas quas Gilbertus de Thurs eis dedit in territorio de
Kaburn, quod est de feodo meo, scilicet quatuor bovatas terre arabilis
continentes octoginta acras terre arabilis, scilicet quadraginta acras ex una parte
ville et quadraginta acras ex alia parte ville, in eisdem locis assignatas sicut
continetur in cartis predicti Gileberti de Thurs, quas inde habent, et tres toftos,
videlicet unum toftum quem habuit Rogerus filius Thori, et alium toftum quem
habuit Galfridus post Thomam fratrem eius totum et integrum ex aquilonali
parte publice strate, et tercium toftum quem habuit Osbertus pelliparius, et
pasturam quingentis ovibus et decem animalibus et decem porcis, et pasturam
centum agnis annuatim in campis de Kaburn seminatis per quindecim dies
continuos postquam separati fuerint a matribus, cum libero introitu et exitu ex
utraque parte ville ad communem pasturam. Hec omnia predicta concessi et
hac carta mea confirmavi deo et predicto conventui, habenda et tenenda in
puram et perpetuam elemosinam libere et quiete cum omnibus pertinentiis et
libertatibus suis, que in cartis predicti Gilberti, quas habent de eo, continentur.
Et predictus Gilbertus et heredes sui mihi et heredibus meis servicia pro
predictis terris facient de aliis terris suis, quas de me tenet idem Gilbertus et
heredes sui. Hiis testibus . . .

The relevant charters of Gilbert of Turs had previously been confirmed by
William of Roumare (*ibid.*, ff. 157v.–158), indicating that the lands in question
were held of the Roumare fee. In fact, Geoffrey of Turs held three knights' fees
of William of Roumare in 1166 (*H.K.F.*, p. 96), without much doubt the three
knights' fees in Cabourne which Ranulf III conferred on Robert de Quincy in
marriage with his sister Hawise, probably in 1199–1200 (**no. 308**). It can fairly be
concluded that the present charter only dates from after 1198, when the
Roumare inheritance passed into Ranulf's hands, and before 1217. Gilbert of
Turs appears to have survived until 1233. In 1234 his widow demanded against
Roger, prior of Alvingham, a third part of the four bovates specified in the
present charter, possibly as dower, but did not persist with her claim (*H.K.F.*, p.
97).

305. Confirmation to the nuns of Stixwould of all that William of Roumare gave them, viz. the church of Hundleby (Lincs.), the service of the tenement of Joscelin of Hundleby, and two spades digging in the marsh of Bolingbroke; also the gifts of Turpin of Billinghay, Thomas of Welton, Peter son of Alan of Woodhall and Alan son of Walter of Kirkby.

[1198–1217]

B.L. Add. MS. 46701 (Stixwould cartulary), f. 108.

Omnibus sancte matris ecclesie filiis Ranulfus comes Cestrie salutem. Notum vobis facio me concessisse et presenti carta mea confirmasse deo et beate Marie et sanctimonialibus de Stykeswold omnia illa que Willelmus de Rumara eis dedit, scilicet ecclesiam de Hundelby cum pertinenciis suis et servicium tocius tenementi Gocelini de Hundelby et duas bescas fodientes in marisco de Bulingbroc. Preterea concessi eis et confirmavi molendinum de Hundelby quod Turpinus de Bilinghey et Thomas de Weltuna et Petrus filius Alani de Wdhalle eis dederunt, et dimidiam bovatam terre in territorio de Hundelby quam Thomas de Weltuna eis dedit, et aliam dimidiam bovatam terre in territorio de Hundelby quam Alanus filius Walteri de Kyrkeby eis dedit. Hec omnia predicta concessi et presenti carta mea confirmavi prenominatis sanctimonialibus in perpetuum libere et quiete possidenda in puram et perpetuam elemoysinam, soluta et quieta ab omni terreno servicio et seculari exaccione, sicut carte donatorum testantur. Hiis testibus.

This charter must follow Ranulf III's succession to the honour of Bolingbroke after the death of William of Roumare in 1198, but cannot otherwise be dated closely. Thomas of Welton was involved in a lawsuit in 1200 (*H.K.F.*, p. 159). The outside limit is 1217, when Ranulf became earl of Lincoln, but the date is probably nearer to 1198.

306. Confirmation of Robert Bardulf's gift of a piece of land at Nantwich to the canons of Lilleshall to build a salthouse.

[1199]

Trentham, Duke of Sutherland's Trustees, Lilleshall cartulary (now deposited in British Library as B.L. Add. MS. 50121), p. 64; Bodleian Library, MS. Top. Salop d. 3, f. 18 (brief abstract).

Omnibus sancte matris ecclesie filiis, ad quos presentes littere pervenerint, Ranulfus comes Cestrie salutem. Notum vobis facio me pro dei amore et salute anime mee et antecessorum et successorum meorum concessisse et hac carta

confirmasse deo et beate Marie et canonicis de Lylleshulle ibidem deo servientibus donationem quam Robertus Bardulf eis fecit de quadam placea in Wicho
Mauban ad faciendam liberam salinam, tenendam predictis canonicis in liberam
et puram et perpetuam elemosinam, sicut carta predicti R., quam ipsi canonici
habent, testatur. Preterea suscepi predictos canonicos et omnes res et possessiones suas in protectione mea et custodia. Precipio etiam omnibus ballivis et
ministris meis, quod predictos canonicos et omnes res et possessiones eorum
manuteneant et defendant ab omni exactione et iniuria sicut meos dominicos
canonicos. Concedo etiam dictis canonicis et presenti carta mea confirmo omnia
que rationabiliter poterunt in posterum in terra mea adipisci, et sint quieti et
liberi ipsi et omnia catalla et tenementa eorum ab omni seculari servitio et
exactione per totam Cestresiriam, quantum ad me pertinet. Hiis testibus.

Robert Bardulf married Aenora, one of the daughters and co-heiresses of the
last baron of Malbank, William II (*E.C.C.*, p. 13; *H.K,F.*, pp. 16–17, 264–5);
hence his interest in Nantwich (Wich Malbank). His grant to Lilleshall, for the
soul (among others) of William Malbank, is entered in the cartulary (p. 61), but
also without witnesses, and was confirmed by King John in a charter (ibid., pp.
45–6) dated Les Andelys on 30 August 1199. It is reasonable to assume that Earl
Ranulf's confirmation was no later in date, and may even have been given at the
same time, as he also was at Les Andelys in 1199.

307.   Grant to William Munitor of the custody of the earl's garden and orchard
at Chester, drawing an allowance for one man. He is also to have his
'resting tree' and the remainder of the apples after the first shaking of the
trees, and the right to make a garden in the castle moat, finding in return
an adequate supply of cabbage every year for the earl's household from
Michaelmas to Lent, and leeks for the whole of Lent.

[c.1199]

Orig.: Chester, City Record Office, CR. 63/2, no. 120.
Transcr.: P.R.O., CHES 2/70 (Recog. Rolls, 20–21 Rich.
II), m. 3v. Brief abstract: *Cal. Close Rolls, 1247–51*, p.
341; Orm., ii. 547; *R.S.L.C.*, ciii, p. 32 (no. 85); *Ches.
Sheaf*, no. 3735. Ed.: *36th Rep. D.K.P.R.*, p. 357.

Ranulfus comes Cestrie omnibus tam presentibus quam futuris salutem. Notum
sit vobis omnibus me dedisse concessisse et hac presenti carta mea confirmasse
Willelmo Munitori custodiam gardini mei et orti mei de Cestria cum mesuagiis et
suis pertinenciis, habendam ei et heredibus suis in feodo et hereditate de me et
heredibus meis, et liberacionem suam in domo mea de Cestria ad unum
hominem, quicunque sit, in domo mea de Cestria. Concedo eciam predicto

Willelmo et heredibus suis suum restingtre et residuum pomorum meorum post excucionem arborum gardini mei, et gardinum faciendum in fossa castelli mei de Cestria. Et predictus Willelmus et heredes sui in domo mea de Cestria invenient michi et heredibus meis sufficienter caules a festo sancti Michaelis singulis annis usque ad quadragesimam et porros tota quadragesima pro omnibus serviciis et demandis. Hiis testibus Ranulfo de Meyngaring, Philippo de Orreby, Roberto filio Pigoti, Roberto Patric, Petro clerico, Rowaldo de Cestria, et aliis.

> SEAL: on cords, blue and white, fragmentary; obverse, knight on horseback, sword in right hand, legend . . . CE . . . TRIE; reverse, knight on horse, galloping, shield in left hand, pennant in right hand, legend . . .M RANUL-FUS DUX BR . . .

This interesting and unusual charter seems to date from shortly before 1200, and it is interesting that the earl uses his seal as duke of Brittany although his title in the address is simply earl of Chester. We can only speculate about William's 'resting tree' – perhaps he lay down under it to recover from his labours? The precise form and meaning of the name or office *munitor* is also not clear. It appears also in the form *minutor* and was later rendered *Myntour*, meaning miner (*R.S.L.C.*, ciii, pp. 15, 32), but it has also been translated 'blood-letter' or surgeon, or barber-surgeon, or simply barber. It was almost certainly a family name, or patronymic, rather than an occupational name, at this time, and the family, like that of the witness, Rowaldus de Cestria, was clearly domiciled in the city of Chester. William was succeeded as the earl's gardener by Geoffrey *munitor*, presumably his son (*Cal. Close Rolls, 1247–51*, p. 341), and Geoffrey and his descendants appear fairly frequently in city charters. Conceivably Alan *munitrus* or *munirus*, who witnessed two of Ranulf III's charters of approximately the same date (**nos. 245, 260**), may have been a member of the same family. Rowaldus was in no way connected with Pierre Rouaut, a frequent witness of Ranulf III's charters at this period, who was a member of a well-known Norman family and who went over to the allegiance of the king of France by 1204. Rather, he is probably identical with a Rualt who witnessed a charter of the prioress of St. Mary's, Chester, about 1200 (*J.C.A.S.*, N.S. x, p. 16). This Rualt had a son Alan (ibid., p. 18), and his widow Margaret granted land in Chester to Philip of Orreby about 1225 (*R.S.L.C.*, ciii, pp. 14–15, no. 6). Significantly William *minator* was one of the witnesses of her grant.

308. Grant to Robert de Quincy, in marriage with the earl's sister Hawise, of land to the value of £10 in Sibsey (Lincs.) and three knights' fees in Cabourne.

[1199–1200]

Orig.: P.R.O., D.L.25 (Ancient Deeds, Series L), no. 42.
Engl. abstract: *35th Rep. D.K.P.R.*, App., p. 8.

Rannulphus comes Cestrie omnibus hominibus et amicis suis ad quos presens scriptum pervenerit, salutem. Sciatis me concessisse et dedisse et presenti carta mea confirmasse Roberto de Quenci decem libratas terre in Sibecai in liberum maritagium cum Hawisia sorore mea, habendas et tenendas sibi et heredibus suis de me et heredibus meis libere et quiete et honorifice cum omnibus pertinenciis et aisiamentis tante terre in eadem villa pertinentibus. Et si eidem Roberto assedero alibi de hereditate mea decem libratas terre in loco competenti, predicta terra de Sibecai ad me revertetur. Preterea concessi et dedi eidem Roberto cum eadem Hawisia in liberum maritagium tria feoda militum in Caburna, que scilicet Gillebertus de Turs tenuit de me. Hiis testibus comite David, Willelmo comite de Derebia, Philippo de Orrebi, Roberto de Basingham, Ricardi de Lindeseia, Willelmo de Trumpingtona, Henrico de Braibroch, Willelmo de Schelfordia, David Giffard, Willelmo Picoti, Hugone, Thoma, Henrico dispensariis, Waltero de Covintreia, Waltero de Daivilla, Nicholao filio Alani, Willelmo, Roberto de Stantona, et multis aliis.

SEAL on tag, fragmentary. Lion seal, brown wax; all that
remains of legend is   +   SIGI . . . Reverse blank.

The present charter is one of three relating to the marriage and marriage settlement of Hawise, the fourth and youngest sister of Ranulf III. The second, a gift of ten librates of land in Waddington, Lincs. (**no. 309**), is a blatant forgery, dating probably from after Ranulf's death, and may be ignored here. The third is more pertinent. This is a grant of 100 librates of land by Saher de Quincy, earl of Winchester, to Robert his son and heir, to be given as a marriage portion to Hawise, 'the wife of the said Robert' (Orm., i. 28). This charter has the same witnesses as the present charter, implying that both were issued simultaneously; and since Saher was not made earl of Winchester until 1207, it would follow that the present charter was not issued until 1207 or later. It would also follow that Hawise's marriage dated from this time.

This is not plausible. As Hawise's father, Earl Hugh, died in 1181, she must have been at least 27 years old by this date. Her eldest sister married in 1190 (**no. 220**) and the third sister Agnes in 1192 (**no. 263**), and it is hard to believe that she remained single until 1207 or later. A further complication is the identity of her husband. The older authorities simply assumed that she married Saher de Quincy's eldest son, who predeceased his father in 1217.More recently, this view has been challenged and it has been argued (*Medievalia et Humanistica*, xi, pp. 8–9) that her husband was not this Robert, but his uncle, the younger brother of Saher. If this was the case, Saher's charter referred to above is a clear forgery. There are also difficulties with the witnesses. Although most are recorded considerably later than 1207, Richard of Lindsey was apparently dead by 1201

(*H.K.F.*, pp. 145, 378), and it is noteworthy that Philip of Orreby, who became justiciar in 1206 or 1207 (**no. 296**), appears without an official title. Finally, it is worth recalling that Hawise's daughter Margaret married John de Lacy in 1221 (*Ann. Cestr.*, p. 50). Although a child-marriage cannot be ruled out, it is not easy, in view of this fact, to believe that Hawise's own marriage only took place in or after 1207.

Taking these facts into account, it is difficult to accept Saher de Quincy's charter at face value. The same considerations do not necessarily apply to the present charter. The places granted are found in Hawise's possession during her widowhood (*H.K.F.*, pp. 97, 164), and there is nothing inherently improbable about the terms of Ranulf III's settlement. Its date can also be determined fairly accurately. A chance reference in the Pipe Roll of 1193–94 (*P.R.S.*, N.S. v, p. 175) to the purchase of a cloak (*penula*) and a fur (*roserellum*) for Hawise and her governess (*magistra sua*) is a clear indication that she was still unmarried at that time. In fact, her marriage cannot have taken place before 1198, as Sibsey and Cabourne, which Ranulf bestowed as her marriage portion, only came into his hands in that year, when he succeeded to the inheritance of William of Roumare. On the other hand, if Richard of Lindsey was dead by 1201, as noted above, his death sets an outside limit and suggests that the marriage took place in 1199 or 1200. This is plausible enough on all counts, and it is perhaps indicative of the importance of the occasion that the first two witnesses of Ranulf's charter should be the husbands of Hawise's elder sisters.

309. Grant to Hawise his sister in free marriage of ten librates of land in Waddington (Lincs.). [Spurious]

[1217–1218]

P.R.O., D.L. 36/3 (Cart. Misc.), f. 63, no. 203.

Ranulphus comes Cestrie et Lincolnie omnibus presentibus et futuris has literas visuris et audituris salutem. Noverit universitas vestra me dedisse et concessisse et hac presenti carta mea confirmasse domine Hawisie sorori mee decem libratas terre in villa de Wardintona in liberum maritagium, scilicet unam virgatam terre quam Ricardus filius Ysabele tenuit, et unam virgatam terre quam Willelmus filius Siwat tenuit, et unam virgatam terre quam Folquicus filius Isabele tenuit, et unam virgatam terre quam Simon filius Iohannis et Osbertus filius Hugonis tenuerunt, et unam virgatam terre quam Osbertus filius Ulfkill et Walterus le Poter tenuerunt, et unam virgatam terre quam Ricardus filius Murielle et Simon Werm tenuerunt, et unam virgatam terre quam Willelmus forestarius tenuit, et unam virgatam terre quam Aluredus Werm tenuit, et unam virgatam terre quam Willelmus filius Beatric tenuit, et unam virgatam terre quam Galfridus filius

Ysabelle tenuit, et unam virgatam terre quam Rogerus Ruffus tenuit, et unam virgatam terre quam Iohannes le Poter tenuit, et unam virgatam terre quam Willelmus filius Folquici et Willelmus Prat tenuerunt, et quoddam cotagium quod Radulfus filius Aeliz tenuit, et unum cotagium quod Radulfus bercarius tenuit, et unum cotagium quod Simon filius Girardi tenuit, et unum cotagium quod Rogerus le Pindere tenuit, et unum cotagium quod Radulfus filius Hugonis tenuit, et unum cotagium quod Robertus textor tenuit et unum cotagium quod Walterus filius Lete tenuit, et unum cotagium quod Henricus filius Girardi tenuit, et unum cotagium quod Reginaldo Blakeman tenuit, et unum cotagium quod Willelmus filius Hugonis tenuit, cum omnibus hominibus predictis et cum universa illorum sequela. Et preterea duas carucatas terre in Lundesinlande et in assarto supra hidem iacentes, proximior loco terre que fuit Ricardi de Suttona versus boscum de [L]avendona,[1] et viginti[2] acras prati in Russeye, et servicium trium militum quod Gilbertus de Turribus mihi facere solebat, habendum et tenendum predicte Hawisie et heredibus suis, qui de se exibunt, ita libere et ita quiete et ita salute in bosco et in plano et in pratis et in pascuis et in omnibus aliis locis, sicut aliquod maritagium potest melius et liberius dari vel concedi. Et ut hec mea donacio rata sit et stabilis, presens scriptum sigillo meo confirmavi. Hiis testibus domino comite David, Philippo de Orreby, Henrico de Aldidelega, Ricardo Phitun, Waltero de Covintre, Iohanne de Arderne, Warino de Vernun, Willelmo de Venabulis, Willelmo de Bello, David de Rsseby, Roberto filio Roberti, Roberto de Belteford, Ricardo de Suttona, Radulfo filio Simonis, Simone de Olne, Ricardo clerico de Olne, Simone Yuelchild, Radulfo de Lotebiria et aliis.

1.   *MS. partially defaced.*
2.   vinginti *MS.*

This charter, like others relating to the marriage of Ranulf III's sister Hawise (**no. 308**), is not easy to evaluate. The existing text, apparently hitherto unknown, is not the original, but is written in a hand of c.1300, and there are a number of anomalies and suspicious features. In the first place, the description of Ranulf as earl of Chester and Lincoln raises difficulties. As Ranulf only became earl of Lincoln in 1217, it is hard to reconcile with the fact that Hawise's daughter Margaret married John de Lacy in 1221 (*Ann. Cestr.*, p. 50). Furthermore, the first witness, Earl David of Huntingdon, who had married Ranulf's eldest sister Matilda in 1190 (**no. 220**), although he remained alive until 1219, was deprived of his earldom in 1215 or 1216 (*Complete Peerage*, v. 646). These facts alone are sufficient, on the face of it, to condemn the charter. In addition, the appearance of Philip of Orreby as a witness without his title of justiciar would be very unusual after 1208. The form of the charter is also suspicious, as is the list of witnesses. Philip of Orreby, Henry of Audley, Richard Fitton, Walter of Coventry, John of Ardern, Warin of Vernon and William Venables were all frequent witnesses of Ranulf III's charters after 1217, and there is no difficulty about explaining their inclusion; but the last ten names occur nowhere else, and were almost certainly brought in as tenants or near neighbours of Hawise. Furthermore, it is highly unusual, if not otherwise unknown, for a gift in free marriage to recite one by one every virgate and cottage conveyed, with the names of the servile tenants. On the other hand, it is not easy to see the purpose of the forgery, if it was one, but the most likely explanation is that Hawise had no good title to lands in Waddington, and needed to provide one. There is no evidence, apart from the present charter, that she had any interest there. Waddington was traditionally the dower of the countesses of Chester, passing from Matilda, who held it in 1185, on her death in 1189 to Bertrada, widow of Hugh II, and after Bertrada's death in 1227, to Clementia, widow of Ranulf III, who had livery in 1232 (*H.K.F.*, pp. 174, 199–200). Hawise may conceivably have staked out a claim between 1227 and 1232, but it is more likely that she did so some time during the complicated partitioning of the Chester inheritance, which went on almost continuously from 1232 to 1243. Whether she made it good, we do not know; but the implication is that the present charter probably dates from c.1240.

310. Conveyance to his 'dearest sister' Hawise de Quincy, of the county of Lincoln, so far as in him lay, to hold of the king as countess.

[May–October 1232]

> Orig.: B.L. Cott. Charter xxiv, 16 (damaged). Transcr.: P.R.O., D.L. 42/2 (Coucher Book II), f. 477v. (old f. 500); D.L. 42/149, f. 102v. (old p. 144); also in abbreviated form, B.L. Add. MS. 6032, f. 39 (old p. 75); MS. Stowe 531, ff. 238–238v.; Bodleian Library, Dugdale MS. 18, f. 80. Ed.: Dugdale, *Baronage*, i. 102 (from original); *Collectanea*, vii. p. 130: *The Genealogist*, i. 313; Brooke, *A Catalogue and Succession of the Kings, Princes, Dukes, Marquesses, Earles* etc., pp. 316–7; Orm., i. 28 (from Coucher Book); Nichols, *Leicestershire*, II. i. xv, p. 39 (with facsimile of seal, pl. xii, fig. 9).

Rannulphus comes Cestrie et Lincolnie omnibus presentibus et futuris presentem cartam inspecturis vel audituris salutem in domino. Ad universitatis vestre noticiam volo pervenire me dedisse, concessisse et hac presenti carta mea confirmasse domine Hawise de Quency sorori mee karissime comitatum Lincolnie, scilicet quantum ad`me pertinuit, ut inde comitissa existat, habendum et tenendum de domino meo rege Anglie[1] eidem Hawise et heredibus suis libere, quiete, plene pacifice et integre iure hereditario cum[1] omnibus pertinenciis suis et cum omnibus libertatibus ad predictum comitatum pertinentibus. Et ut presens scriptum perpetuitatis robur optineat, illud sigilli mei apposicione roborare dignum duxi. Hiis testibus venerabilibus patribus P. Wintoniensi et Alexandro Coventrensi et Lichfeldensi episcopis, R. Marescallo comite Pen-brokie, W. de Ferrariis comite Derbie, Stephano de Segrava iusticiario Anglie, Simone de Monteforti, Willelmo de Ferariis, Philippo de Albiniaco, Henrico de Aldithleia, Willelmo de Cantilupo et aliis.

> SEAL: obverse equestrian,   +   SIGILLUM RANUL-
> PHI COMITIS CESTRIE ET LINCOLNIE; reverse
> three garbs on a heater shield, SECRETUM RANULPHI
> CO: CESTRIE ET LINCOLNIE.

1. domino meo rege Anglie *and* pacifice . . . cum *illegible in original and supplied from D.L. 42/149.*

This well-known and frequently printed charter has usually been dated from April 1231, presumably from the death of Richard Marshall's predecessor, William Marshall, on 6 or 24 April 1231, to the death of Ranulf III on 28 October 1232. The latter date is certainly too late since the king recognized Hawise's title on 27 October. The former date is too early, since it appears that Ranulf III was continuously in Normandy and Brittany, engaged in military operations, from 2 May 1230, when he landed at St. Malo, to the beginning of August 1231, when he joined the king at Painscastle in Wales, but quickly proceeded to Chester, where he arrived on 21 August (*Ann. Cestr.*, p. 59). It is, however, evident from the witnesses of the present charter that it was not given at Chester, but in all probability at or in the vicinity of the king's court. It appears that Ranulf's will was proved on 6 May 1232, at a time when a tournament had to be postponed because of his infirmity (*Cal. Pat. Rolls, 1225–32*, p. 473), and this would be a likely occasion to transfer the county of Lincoln to his sister. But it is possible that the transfer did not take place until a few days before his death, which took place at Wallingford, i.e. where he would be likely to be in touch with such witnesses as Peter des Roches, bishop of Winchester, and the earl of Pembroke. In either case, it can safely be attributed to 1232.

311.   Confirmation to his burgesses of Coventry of the liberties held in the time of his predecessors and grant of the rights specified in his charter.

Coventry, [1199–1202]

> Orig.: Coventry Record Office B1. Ed.: *Archaeological Journal* xv, p. 242; Cunningham, *The Growth of English Industry and Commerce*, i. 616 (without witnesses); Coss, no. 15. Noted but not printed by Dugdale, *Warwickshire*,

p. 88; Ballard, *British Borough Charters, 1042–1216*, p. 27; Dibben, *Coventry City Charters*, p. 8.

For a full text of this document, see Coss, *The Early Records of Medieval Coventry*, pp. 22–3 (no. 15).

> SEAL: on cord, green wax; lion on heater shield; legend perished.

If Robert of Montalt succeeded to the office of seneschal in 1199 and was succeeded by Roger of Montalt in 1204 (*Ches. Sheaf*, nos. 7804, 9394, 10003), the date of the present charter can be fixed fairly narrowly. Moreover, the presence of Norman witnesses, who withdrew to France after King John's loss of Normandy, indicates a date before 1204. The charter is modelled fairly closely on that of Ranulf II, or on the confirmation of it by King Henry II (**no. 112**), and a comparison between them is instructive. As Ranulf III was in Normandy during the final phase of the French war, the date is more likely to be c.1199–1200 than later.

312. Grant to Nicholas son of Liulf of the site of the mill in the earl's park at Coventry, which his brother Simon held from Earl Hugh.

[1199–1202]

> B.L. Harl. MS. 7, ff. 115v.–116. Ed.: *Langley cart.*, no. 223.

Ranulfus comes Cestrie omnibus tam futuris quam presentibus salutem. Notum sit vobis me concessisse et hac carta mea confirmasse Nicholao filio Liolphi sedem molendini de parco meo de Coventre, quod Simon frater predicti Nicholai tenuit de comite Hugone patre meo ad faciendum ibi[1] molendinum,[2] tenendam predicto Nicholao et heredibus suis cum omnibus pe tinenciis[3] eiusdem molendini, reddendo annuatim[4] Stephano de Nerbona dimidiam marcam argenti pro omni servicio et exaccione. Et pro hac[5] concessione dedit mihi predictus Nicholaus duas marcas et dimidiam. Hiis testibus Willelmo de Hardrideshull, Symone de Ensotge,[6] Willelmo de Sagio, Willelmo Mayestro, Philippo de Orrebi,[7] Rogero de Buschervile, Milone Barba Aprillis, Willelmo de Verdun, et multis aliis.

1. et sede ille *MS. The MS is very indifferent, and there is clearly some muddle in the transcription.*
2. *add* et *MS.*
3. *add* suis *MS.*
4. annatim *MS.*

5. hoc *MS.*
6. *sic MS.*
7. Orriell *MS; correct reading almost certainly* Orrebi.

Nicholas son of Liulf succeeded to his father's lands in Coventry in 1181 (**no. 195**), and his brother Simon purchased the mill in the earl's park some years earlier (**no. 156**). It is not clear whether it is this mill that is referred to in the present charter, or that which he was authorized to make at Alderford (**no. 154**). Evidently he pre-deceased his elder brother. The present grant probably dates from 1199–1202, i.e. much the same time as Ranulf III's charter for the burgesses of Coventry (**no. 311**), which also was witnessed by Roger of Buscherville and William of Hartshill (Hardredeshulle). William de Sagio is presumably identical with William de Sais, or de Sees, who died in 1202 or 1203 (*H.K.F.*, p. 141), and William of Verdun was dead by 1205 at latest (*P.R.S.*, N.S. xviii, p. 111).

313.   Grant to Roger, the constable of Chester, of a free boat for fishing on the river Dee above and below the bridge of Chester and specifically at Eaton.

Chester, [1199–1203]

> Orig.: B.L. Harl. Charter 52A 17. Transcr.: P.R.O., D.L. 42/1 (Coucher Book I), f. 41; B.L. Harl. MS. 2060, f. 59 (new f. 33v.) Ed.: *Book of Seals*, p. 277 (no. 408).

Rannulfus comes Cestrie omnibus tam futuris quam presentibus ad quos presens scriptum pervenerit salutem. Notum sit vobis omnibus me dedisse et concessisse et presenti carta mea confirmasse Rogero conestabulario meo unum liberum batellum in fluvio de De apud Cestriam, tenendum illi et heredibus suis de me et de meis heredibus libere et quiete per quedam calcaria deaurata annuatim reddenda in nativitate sancti Iohannis Baptiste. Et concedo ei et heredibus suis quod faciant piscari cum predicto batello suo subtus pontem Cestrie et supra pontem Cestrie et nominatim apud Ettonam die ac nocte cum flonettis et draghenettis et stalnettis, et cum omnibus generibus retium cum quibus aliquid aliud liberiorum batellorum de Cestria piscatur, et ubique ubi aliquid liberorum batellorum piscatur, et quod faciant voluntatem suam de piscibus quos ceperint. Et prohibeo super forisfacturam meam decem librarum ne aliquis ipsum aut heredes suos super hoc vexare aut disturbare presummat. Hiis testibus Roberto de Monte Alto senescallo Cestrie, Radulfo de Mesnilwarin, Thoma dispensatore, Petro Roaud, Philippo de Orrebi, fratre Roberto filio Ricardi, Adam de Dottona et Hugone de Duttona, Petro clerico, et multis aliis apud Cestriam.

SEAL: on tag, 'demolished'.

The date of this grant is left unnecessarily wide in *Book of Seals*, p. 277. It must fall after 1199, when Robert of Montalt succeeded his brother Ralph as steward (*Ches. Sheaf*, no. 9394), and not later than 1204, when Pierre Rouaut withdrew to France (*ibid.*, no. 2419). Brother Robert fitz Richard is identical with Robert *thesaurarius*, prior of the Hospitallers in England; he was a younger brother of John the constable and uncle of Roger the constable. For Adam and Hugh Dutton, see *E.C.C.*, no. 9.

314.   Confirmation of Philip of Orreby's gift to Trentham priory of the free boat on the Dee, which the earl had previously given him.

Martilly, [1199–1203]

> P.R.O., CHES 2/26 (Recog. Rolls, 14–15 Edw. III, m. 3; Bodleian Library, Dodsworth MS. 31, f. 93; MS. Top. Cheshire b. I, p. 135; Chester, Booth of Twemlow, Liber D, f. 141. Abbr. texts: B.L. Harl. MS. 2039, f. 159 (new f. 154) and Harl. 2079, f. 63 (new f. 32). All above, except Recog. Roll, are taken from the Cheshire Domesday and are imperfect; only Recog. Roll has full witness list. Ed.: *Mon.*, vi. 397 (no. 3) (allegedly from autograph in College of Arms, but text as in Domesday enrolment); *Hist. Coll. of Staffordshire*, xi. 305; *36th Rep. D.K.P.R.*, p. 369 (from Recog. Roll).

Ranulfus comes Cestrie omnibus tam futuris quam presentibus, ad quos presens pagina pervenerit, salutem. Notum sit vobis me concessisse et presenti carta mea confirmasse donacionem quam Philippus de Orreby fecit deo et ecclesie beate Marie et omnium sanctorum de Trentham et canonicis ibidem deo servientibus, scilicet unum batellum super aquam de Dee apud Cestriam, quod ibi dedi predicto Philippo et ipse illud dedit deo et predicte ecclesie et canonicis de Trentham. Et ut hec donacio rata et inviolabilis permaneat, presentis scripti testimonio et sigilli mei munimine illam corroboravi. Hiis testibus[1] Ranulfo de Praers, Rogero de Goviz, Willelmo Bacun, Luca de sancto Leodegario, magistro Radulfo de Cliftona, Martino clerico, Nicholao camerario, Thoma pincerna, Willelmo Locardo, et multis aliis apud Martilliacum.

1.   Witnesses from Recog. Roll; other inaccurate texts ignored.

As Trentham had already been granted a boat on the Dee by Hugh II (**no. 151**), the present gift presumably provided the canons with a second boat. Ranulf III's preceding grant to Philip of Orreby, the well-known justiciar, has not survived. It must have been relatively early in his career. The names of the witnesses indicate that the present charter falls in the period 1198–1203. Roger de Goviz (Gouvix, Calvados, canton de Bretteville-sur-Laize, s. of Caen), who was pardoned 56s. of a debt of £4. 16. 0d. on the king's instruction in 1195 'on account of his poverty' (*Rot. Scacc. Norm.*, i. 191), occurs a number of times on the roll for 1198 (*ibid.*, ii. 317, 335, 343, 397). For Ranulf de Praers, who was active in Lincolnshire and Normandy c.1190–1200, see **no. 251**. William Bacon confirmed his father's gift of Plainseuvre to Savigny about 1200 (MS. Paris lat. nouv. acq. 2500, p. 364), and witnessed a charter of Ranulf III for Aunay dated 1201 (**no. 332**). The same charter was witnessed by Nicholas the chamberlain, who also attested a charter for Longues (**no. 317**) dated 1200 and two charters of approximately the same period for Peter the clerk (**nos. 280, 281**). Lucas of St. Leger also witnessed the charter for Longues, as well as charters for St. Melaine of Rennes (**no. 279**) and for Gilbert of Beningworth (**no. 295**), the latter dating from 1198–1203. Thomas the butler (*pincerna*) attested a charter c.1200 granting land in Chester to Peter the clerk (**no. 281**), as well as Ranulf III's confirmation (c.1194–1202) of his father's gift of Prestbury to St. Werburgh's abbey (**no. 229**) and a charter for St. Lô (**no. 269**). Martin the clerk, who occurs in the Pipe Rolls for 1194–95 and 1200–1201 (*P.R.S.*, N.S. vi, p. 250, and xiv, p. 197), witnessed charters for Newhouse (**no. 278**) and Dereham (**no. 294**). William Locard and Master Ralph of Clifton witnessed a charter of Ranulf III for Revesby (**no. 289**). The latter was also engaged in 1199 in litigation over land in Clifton Campville, Staffs. (*H.K.F.*, p. 273). These indications point to a date around 1200. Martilly, where the present charter was issued, lies on the outskirts of Vire. As this was one of Ranulf III's more frequent Norman places of residence, his presence there does not help greatly with dating; but Ranulf is known to have been at Vire in 1203 (*Rot. Scacc. Norm.*, ii. 531, 537), and this is perhaps the most likely date for the present charter.

315.   Remission to the canons of Trentham of the obligation to provide one foot soldier to serve in Wales.

[1211–1212]

Orig.: allegedly in P.R.O., Cartae Miscellaneae, 303, vol. 15 [sic], not located. Ed.: *Hist. Coll. of Staffordshire*, xi. 333.

Omnibus sancte matris ecclesie filiis presentibus et futuris presentem cartam inspecturis vel audituris Ranulphus comes Cestrie salutem. Noverit universitas vestra me pro anima comitis Hugonis patris mei et pro salute anime mee et antecessorum meorum et successorum remisisse et in perpetuum quietum clamasse de me et de heredibus meis deo et beate Marie et domui de Trentham et canonicis ibidem deo servientibus in puram et perpetuam elemosinam servicium unius peditis, quod in exercitu facere debuerunt pro terra sua de Wal. Et ut hec mea concessio et quieta clamatio perpetue firmitatis robur obtineat, eam presenti scripto et sigillo meo confirmavi. Hiis testibus Philippo de Orreby tunc iusticiario Cestrie, Rogero de Montealto tunc dapifero meo, Henrico de Aldideley, Petro clerico meo, Hugone et Thoma et Henrico dispensariis,[1] Waltero de Damvilla, Alfredo de Suleny, Warino de Vernun, W. de Venabulis, Hamone de Masci, Normanno Panton, Ricardo Phitton, Roberto de Cowdray, Roberto de Hardreshull, Roberto de Say, Roberto de Damvilla, Hugone et Galfrido de Dutton, Joceramo[2] de Hellesbi, Ricardo de Kingeslee, et multis aliis.

1. *Possibly another witness follows after* dispensariis.
2. Jorcamb *ed.*

The date of this charter is probably 1211, or possibly 1212. Roger of Montalt had followed his brother Robert as steward shortly before then (*E.C.C.*, p. 17) and Henry of Audley probably became a major Cheshire landholder about the same time (**no. 395**). The occasion was probably the campaign against Llywelyn of Wales, launched in 1211, when a great army was mobilized at Chester (*Ann. Cestr.*, p. 49), or the renewed campaign of the following year (Lloyd, pp. 634, 639); the array of barons in the long witness list suggests a gathering of Ranulf III's contingent.

316. Confirmation to Robert le Scot of his 17 acres of assarted land in Alwardsich and a messuage in Coventry.

[1199–1213]

B.L. Harl. MS. 7, f. 98. Ed. *Langley cart.*, no. 179.

Ranulfus comes Cestrie omnibus hominibus suis tam presentibus quam futuris salutem. Sciatis me dedisse et concessisse et hac mea presenti carta confirmasse Roberto le Scot pro homagio suo et servicio decem et septem acras terre de essarto in Alwardsica, quas predictus Robertus essartavit, cum omnibus per-tinenciis predictarum acrarum, et preterea quiddam mesuagium in Coventre cum pertinenciis, habendas et tenendas sibi et heredibus suis de me et heredibus meis iure hereditario libero, quiete, honorifice in bosco et plano, pratis et pascuis, et in omnibus locis, cum husbota et haibota, reddendo mihi inde annuatim et heredibus meis de se et heredibus suis xii. denarios ad nativitatem beati Iohannis Baptiste pro omni servicio et consuetudine et demanda mihi vel heredibus meis pertinentibus. Hiis testibus Thoma dispensatore, Willelmo Picoti,[1] Waltero de Coventre, Milone Barba Aprilis, Nicholao filio Lidulfi, Anketillo Locard, Lidulfo de Spanna, Vitale de Folkehull, et multis aliis.

1. P(er)icot(i) *MS.*

The land of Robert le Scot at Alwardsich is mentioned in the forged charter of Hugh II (**no. 179**). The date of the present charter seems to fall between 1199 and 1213. William Picot, a son of Gilbert Picot (*H.K.F.*, p. 71), a frequent witness under Hugh II, witnessed Ranulf III's charter for the burgesses of Coventry (**no. 311**), and a number of other charters (**nos. 265, 302, 334, 351**) c.1199–1210. Liulf of Spon (Spanna) occurs from 1196 (Coss, no. 10), and was dead by 1214 (*ibid.*, p. 65). Walter of Coventry was in the earl's service from 1199 (*H.K.F.*, p. 156). For Nicholas son of Liulf, see **no. 195**, and for Anschetil Locard see **no. 146**.

317. Assignation to the monks of Longues of certain specified tenements in place of the three measures of corn he had allotted from his manor of Trevières to make bread for celebrating Mass.

[1200]

> Archives de Calvados, H. 6295 (cartulaire de l'abbaye de Longues), f. 53v; noted *Bulletin de la Société des Antiquaires de Normandie*, vol. 46, p. 196.

Universis sancte matris ecclesie filiis, ad quos presens scriptum pervenerit, Rannulfus comes Cestrie salutem. Noverit universitas[1] vestra me caritatis intuitu et pro salute mei et meorum[2] sancte Marie de Longis et monachis eiusdem loci dedisse tres sextaria frumenti in meo manerio de Treveris ad faciendum inde panem in celebratione missarum in puram et perpetuam elemosinam. Pro his autem tribus sextariis frumenti assignavi predictis monachis has terras, scilicet campum meum in mortuis terris et campum meum de Vallicula et unam virgatam et dimidiam virgatam in quinque curtis virgatis. Quod ut firmum et inconcussum permaneat in perpetuum, presentis carte et sigilli mei munimine confirmavi. His testibus Petro Ruaudo, Bartholomeo abbate, Iuhello de Lovigni, Henrico de Reveris,[3] Johanne Paganello, Willemo de Treveris, Willemo de Livzeio, Iohanne de Escaiolo, Nicholao camerario, Luca de sancto Leodegario, Roberto de Hamarz, et multis aliis. Actum est hoc anno[4] ab incarnatione domini MCC.

1. unniversitas *MS.*
2. *sic MS.*; antecessorum et successorum *probably omitted.*
3. *sic MS.*; *probably for* Treveris.
4. *om. MS.*

The lands granted are at Trevières. The witnesses are a representative selection of the earl's Norman tenants, not a few of whom were also active in Cheshire. John de Escaiol held land in Chester itself (*E.C.C.*, pp. 34–5, no. 16). Pierre Rouaut, Joel de Louvigny and Nicholas the chamberlain are found witnessing together another land transaction in Chester about 1200 (**no. 281**).

318. Agreement between Earl Ranulf and William de Fougères settling a dispute over the marriage portion of Clementia de Fougères, Ranulf's wife, and between William and Clementia's brother, Geoffrey.

7 October [1200]

Original cyrograph (badly torn): B.L. Harl. Ch. 52A 15. Transcr. (from original 'penes Simon Dewes EE num. 12, anno 1649'): Harl. MS. 2060, f. 35v. (old p. 63); Tabley MSS., Sir Peter Leycester's Liber C, pars II, ff. 15–16. Ed.: B. de Broussillon, *La Maison de Laval*, v. 12 (from original); Orm., i. 39–40 (from Liber C); *Book of Seals*, pp. 171–2 (no. 236) (defective copy from original).

Sciant omnes ad quos presentes littere pervenerint, quod contentio, que fuit inter R. comitem Cestrie et Willelmum de Filgeriis super maritagio Clemencie de Filgeriis uxoris predicti comitis et proneptis predicti Willelmi, hoc modo pacificata est, scilicet quod predictus Willelmus reddidit Gaufrido de Filgeriis pronepoti suo ad dandum in maritagio cum Clemencia sorore sua predicto comiti totam terram quam Radulfus de Filgeriis habuit in valle Moretonii, et sicut de ea seisitus fuit anno et die quo eam dedit Alano de Dinan in maritagio cum predicta Clemencia, excepto dominio abbatie Savingneii et exceptis lx. solidis Andegavensium, quod idem Radulfus dedit Aeline nepti sue, que est monialis apud Moretonium, habendos quamdiu ipsa vixerit per manum servientis de Romeingneio, et post decessum ipsius monialis revertentur predicte C. et heredibus suis. Et preterea dabit predictus W. predicto comiti centum libras Andegavensium annuatim a natali domini, quod est anno verbi incarnati millesimo ducentesimo primo, usque ad quinque annos, in nativitate sancti Iohannis Baptiste solvendas. Preterea concessit predictus W. predicto comiti unum maritagium in denariis par taillie de Augusto, habendum per totam terram Filgeriarum, excepta villa Filgeriarum, que combusta erat.

Inter predictum vero W. de Filgeriis et Gaufridum pronepotem suum hec est conventio per consilium amicorum eiusdem G. facta, videlicet quod predictus W. totam terram de Filgeriis, sicut Radulfus de Filgeriis eam illi commisit fideliter custodiendam, tenebit a predicto natali usque in quinque annos. Et si quis ei super hoc contraire aut eum vexare voluerit, predictus comes et Willelmus de Humetis et alii amici Gaufridi et homines terre Filgeriarum, qui hanc conventionem fideliter tenendam iuraverunt, predicto W. erunt auxiliantes et consulentes pro posse suo. Completis autem quinque annis predictis, prefatus W. reddet predicto G. pronepoti suo totam terram Filgeriarum sine contradictione, sicut Radulfus de Filgeriis eam illi commisit custodiendam fideliter. Quam cum reddiderit, idem G., quando a predicto W. requisitus fuerit de iure suo terre Filgeriarum, per consilium amicorum utriusque partis et hominum terre Filgeriarum illi faciet quod facere debebit. Et si per consilium amicorum suorum et hominum terre inter se concordari non poterint, per iudicium curie domini Britannie sine dilatione illi faciet quod facere debebit. Et si alteruter illorum contra hoc venire voluerit, tam homines terre Filgeriarum quam amici utriusque partis auxiliantes erunt illi, qui hanc conventionem tenere voluerit, et nocentes ei, qui eam tenere recusaverit.

Si autem contigerit C. uxorem predicti comitis decedere infra quinque annos predictos, ipse comes dicto Willelmo de Filgeriis terram de valle Moretonii quiete reddet, si de predicta C. heredem non habuerit. Et si Galfridus de Filgeriis infra predictos quinque annos decesserit, idem Willelmus terram Filgeriarum integre et sine contradictione aliqua et absque termino Clemencie et [sponse ei]us[1] reddet, et ipsa C. et sponsus eius tenebunt predicto Willelmo conventionem, quam G. de Filgeriis et amici sui ei tenere debebant. Amplius Willelmus [de Filgeriis de omni]bus, quoscumque posuerit in castello Filgeriarum infra quinque annos, iurare faciet, quod si ipsum in fata quiescere contigerit, ipsi [omnes remanebu]nt Gaufrido de Filgeriis vel predicte C. sorori sue, si ipsa ei superstes fuerit. Et in hac conventione remanserunt [W. de Filgeriis predicto] maneria in Anglia, scilicet Tuiford et Westkintona, que Radulfus de Filgeriis frater eius illi dedit pro homagio suo et ser[vicio, sicut carte dicti R]adulfi legitime testantur. Et insuper eidem Willelmo remanet manerium de Belingtona, quod fuit maritagium [matris sue et eum] contingit iure hereditario ex parte matris sue.

Has conventiones fecit Willelmus de Filgeriis ad scaccarium apud [Cadomum cum Ranulfo comite Cestrie] et C. uxore eius et cum Willelmo de Humetis, quem idem comes et C. uxor sua loco suo assignaverunt, [spondentes se quicquid ipse] super hoc ageret ratum habituri, in presencia Samsonis abbatis Cadomi et Hugonis de Chancumb et [. . . . . . et][2] Guiterii de Mota et decani sancti Iuliani, tunc iusticiariorum domini regis. Has conven[tiones in perpetuum tenendas iuraverunt] tam predictus comes Cestrie quam Willelmus de Filgeriis, et ex parte comitis iuraverunt isti: Hugo [de Colonciis,[3] Ranulfus] de Praeriis, Petrus de sancto Hilario, Petrus Roaud. Ex parte Willelmi de Filgeriis iurave[runt isti:[2] Guido de Lav]al, Herveius de Vitreio, Gaufridus de sancto Bricio, Willelmus de sancto Bricio, et hoc ipsum iu[raverunt . . . . . .[2] et] Ricardus de Fontenai. Ut autem hee conventiones firme et inconcusse permaneant, [presentes littere sunt impressione] sigillorum comitis Cestrie et conestabularii Normannie et Willelmi de Filgeriis et Alani filii comitis et Guidonis de Laval confirmate. Actum est autem hoc nonis Octobris anno incarnationis domini MCC.

> SEALS: three seals survive pendent on green and white cords: (1) equestrian seal of Guy de Laval; (2) equestrian seal, unidentified, no legend; (3) shield of arms of William of Fougères.

1. At this point original is torn. Words in square brackets are supplied from the seventeenth-century transcripts, or occasionally from the context.
2. Two or more names missing.
3. Possibly another name follows here.

The origin of this complicated agreement lies in the fact that Ralf de Fougères, grandfather of Geoffrey and Clementia de Fougères, who outlived their fathers and died on 16 May 1194, decided to commit the custody of the whole territory of Fougères to his brother William, probably because Geoffrey was a minor at the time. This meant that any disposal on behalf of Clementia, on her marriage, had to obtain William's assent. A further complication was that William claimed certain lands, including the manor of Long Bennington in Lincolnshire, as his own inheritance from his mother Olive. When Ranulf married Clementia in 1200, Long Bennington was part of the marriage portion which her brother Geoffrey conveyed to Earl Ranulf at the time (Orm., i. 39). Whether Geoffrey was entitled to make such a settlement without reference to William is probably doubtful. In any case William evidently protested, and the present agreement was the result. It presumably lost any validity with the loss of Normandy in 1204, and Ranulf appears simply to have taken possession of Long Bennington (**no. 334**), no doubt to compensate for the Norman part of his wife's dowry which he lost.

319. Confirmation to the abbey of Plessis-Grimoult (dioc. Bayeux) of the gifts of Philippa of Rosel.

Semilly [? Martilly], [c.1200]

> Archives de Calvados, Cartulaire du Plessis-Grimoult, vol. I, f. 310v., no. 524 (A), and vol. III, ff. 142v.–143, no. 1267 (B). Short abstract (French): d'Anisy, ii. 88 (no. 524).

Omnibus sancte matris ecclesie filiis ad quos presens pagina pervenerit, Rannulfus comes Cestrie salutem. Ad universitatis vestre volo venire noticiam me concessisse et presenti carta mea confirmasse deo et ecclesie sancti Stephani de Plessicio et canonicis sub regulari disciplina ibidem deo servientibus omnes donationes quas Philippa de Rosello, filia Hugonis de Rosello, eis fecit de feodo meo, scilicet ecclesias que sunt de feodo eiusdem Philippe in episcopatu Baiocarum, possidendas integre et quiete cum omnibus decimis et pertinentiis suis, scilicet ecclesiam sancte Marie de Atreio cum omnibus decimis et terris et appendiciis eiusdem ecclesie, et ecclesiam sancti Vigoris de Meseretis cum omnibus terris et decimis et appendiciis suis, et capellam sancti Laurentii de Alnetis, et ecclesias de Rosello, videlicet ecclesiam sancti Petri et ecclesiam sancti Martini, cum decimis et terris et pratis et elemosinis ad easdem ecclesias pertinentibus; et preterea quinque acras terre quas Hugo de Rosello, pater predicte Philippe, dedit predictis canonicis apud Glatigne, et decimam molendini de Meseretis et mansuram Rogeri clerici cum virgulto et terra adiacente, et Philippa prenominata omnino dimisit calumpniam quam habebat super predictam mansuram; et terram quam Rogerus clericus de predicta Philippa tenebat apud Rosel, scilicet novem acras terre, quam terram sepedicta Philippa in manu Henrici Baiocensis episcopi resignavit, qui, presente eadem Philippa et assensum prebente, terram illam cum omnibus pertinentiis suis tam in blado quam in denariis et regardis et aliis rebus dictis canonicis in perpetuam elemosinam libere et quiete possidendam tradidit.

Preterea concessi et confirmavi eisdem canonicis mansuram de La Bretonera, que est inter domum Ricardi Berenger et mariscum fabri de Rosel, et duas percas terre que sunt in capite virgulti Philippi Normanni, assensu et concessione eiusdem Philippi, et medietatem campi Villule, cuius alteram partem possident monachi de Alneto, et apud Atreium totum tenementum Willerini filii Radulfi filii Durandi, et clausum quod est inter cimiterium et terram que fuit Putois. Concedo etiam et confirmo eisdem canonicis donationem illam quam eis fecit Rogerus Escote, assensu et concessione fratrum suorum Willelmi Roselli et Willerini Escote, de campo de Cruce, qui est ante domum Rogeri Drogun, quem Philippa de Rosel dederat predicto Rogero pro servicio suo. Omnes predictas terras et ecclesias et donationes concedo et confirmo sepedictis canonicis in perpetuum possidendas libere et quiete, sicut carte supradicte Philippe testantur. Hiis testibus Drogone abbate sancti Severi, Radulfo archidiacono Baiocensi, Gaufrido fratre suo, Roberto de Biuvilla decano, Hugone de Coulonciis, Rannulfo de Praeris, Petro Roaud, Gaufrido de sancto Bricio, Hugone de Noiers monacho sancti Severi, et aliis multis apud Similleium.[1]

1.   B is dated at Martilly (apud Martilleium). There are a number of small differences in the two texts, but they are inconsequential and have been ignored.

For Philippa of Rosel, whose gifts to Plessis are here confirmed, see Wiffen, *Historical Memoirs of the House of Russell*, i. 70–81, who also prints most of Philippa's surviving charters in an Appendix (pp. 527–531). She was married three times (to Robert Patric, Ralph de Hamars and Hugh de Clinchamp), and had a long life, being still alive, according to Wiffen, after Philip Augustus's conquest of Normandy in 1204. She was a substantial benefactress of Plessis, her first grant (Wiffen, App. no. xi) dating from c.1165, 'while she was a maiden', and also made gifts to the abbey of Ardennes (**no. 320**). Ranulf III's confirmation of her gifts to Plessis has apparently not previously been printed. It is, in effect, substantially a confirmation of the charter she gave, 'marito carens et libera ab omni matrimonio' (Wiffen, App. xii), shortly before her marriage to Robert Patric, probably in 1170; but there is no doubt that it is many years later in date. The witnesses Hugh de Coulances, Ranulf de Praers, Pierre Rouaut and Geoffrey de St. Brice occur fairly frequently on the Norman Rolls and Pipe

Rolls between 1196 and 1199, and all four witnessed the agreement of 7 October 1200 between Ranulf III and William of Fougères (**no. 318**). This gives an approximate date for the present charter, which must in any case fall before 1204, by which time Hugh, Pierre and Geoffrey de St. Brice adhered to the king of France.

320. Confirmation of the gift by Philippa of Rosel of ten and a half acres of land from her domain at Grouchy to the abbey of Ardennes.

[? 1200–1201]

Orig.: Archives de Calvados, H. 322; cal.: d'Anisy, i. 3 (no. 14); *Inventaire sommaire des Archives départementales, Calvados, Série H*, t. I, p. 200; noted Round, *C.D.F.*, p. 182n.

Omnibus Christi fidelibus, ad quos presens scriptum pervenerit, ego Ranulfus comes Cestrie salutem in Christo. Noverit universitas vestra Philippam de Rosello de assensu Aaliz matris sue dedisse deo et ecclesie sancte Marie de Ardena apud Groceium de proprio dominico suo decem acras et dimidiam terre in perpetuam elemosinam pro salute anime sue et pro quadraginta et duabus libris Andegavensium, quas abbas et canonici predicte ecclesie inde ei in caritate donaverunt. Et ego predictus Ranulfus hanc donationem predicte Philippe gratam et ratam habui et sicut capitalis dominus pro salute anime mee in puram et perpetuam elemosinam cum omni integritate sua, sicut carta ipsius Philippe quam canonici Ardene inde habent, testatur, presenti carta mea fideliter confirmavi.

Fragment of seal on tag; one-sided, on face a lion rampant.

For Philippa of Rosel, see **no. 319**. Her donation to Ardennes was originally made in the exchequer at Caen in 1176 (d'Anisy, i. 2, no. 3; printed by Wiffen, *Historical Memoirs of the House of Russell*, i. 530, no. xv), but a controversy over the land in question subsequently arose between the parties 'anno iterum Iohannis regis Anglie primo' (1199–1200), which was settled before the king's justices at Caen. It seems probable that Ranulf III's confirmation was issued at the instance of the canons shortly after the settlement. Unfortunately, the only internal evidence of date is the lion seal, which seems to have been in use from 1189 to 1217.

321.   Conferment on William Neville and his wife Amabilia of the territory of Longdendale, with extensive rights and liberties, including freedom from finding a judger for the earl's court at Macclesfield, provided that William, if he is in the province, will appear when summoned before the earl or his itinerant justice at Macclesfield, and if not, that his steward will appear in his place.

[1200–1203]

P.R.O., C.66 (Chancery Patent Rolls), no. 150, m. 13.
Ed.: *Cal. Pat. Rolls, 1317–21*, p. 245.

Ranulfus comes Cestrie dapifero, iusticiario, vic(ecomiti), baronibus et omnibus ballivis et hominibus suis Francis et Anglis tam futuris quam presentibus salutem. Notum sit omnibus vobis me concessisse et hac carta confirmasse Willelmo de Nevilla et Amabili uxori sue, et heredibus quos predicta Amabilia habuerit de predicto Willelmo, terram de Longedenedale libere et quiete in boscis, in planis, in pascuis, et in omnibus libertatibus que pertinent eidem terre, tenendam de me et heredibus meis per servicium dimidii militis pro omnibus serviciis, cum soc et sac et tol et tem et infangenthef, et cum iusticia faciente de latronibus qui deprehensi fuerint in eadem terra de hominibus suis, cum igne et aqua et duello, et quietus de haiis faciendis in foresto meo apud Maclesfeld. Et de iudice quem invenire deberet de illa predicta terra, sit ille quietus, ita quod ipse Willelmus predictus per rationabilem summonicionem, si ipse fuerit in partibus illius provincie, apparebit coram domino comite vel iusticiario eius errantis[1] apud Maclesfeld, et si forte predictus Willelmus non fuerit in illa provincia, dapifer suus in loco eius in presencia domini comitis vel iusticiario eius errantis appareat per hanc predictam summonicionem. Testibus hiis Radulfo de Maineware, Warino de Vernun, Thoma dispensatore, Petro Roaud, Roberto de Stokeport, Waltero fratre suo, Hugone de Boidel, Ricardo de Vernun, Ricardo Pisce, Adam filio Orm, Liolfo vicecomite, Anketino de Brikesart, et multis aliis.

1. *sic MS.*

William Neville held land near Oldham on the Lancashire side of Longdendale (*L.P.R.*, pp. 157, 238). He married Amabilia, daughter and coheiress of Adam fitz Swain and widow of Alexander de Crevequeur, shortly before 1202 (*ibid.*, p. 171), and died in 1211, when he was succeeded by Thomas de Burgh, husband of his daughter and heiress, Sarah (*E.C.C.*, p. 43). Of the witnesses, Robert of Stockport died in 1206 (*L.P.R.*, p. 208) and Hugh of Boydell before 1208 (*Chart. St. Werburgh*, p. 75). As Pierre Rouaut withdrew to France after the loss of Normandy, the present charter presumably falls between the date of William Neville's marriage (unfortunately not precisely known) and 1204. Whether it is a genuine charter of Ranulf III remains open to doubt, but it has certainly a better claim to authenticity than the parallel charter of Hugh II (**no. 170**). Nevertheless the grant of duel and the ordeal of fire and water is suspicious, and there is no other reference to the earl's justice on eyre. On the other hand, Longdendale was a wild and desolate piece of country, a natural resort for thieves and malefactors, and it is not altogether surprising that William was granted justice over thieves caught there. On the whole, it is probably safe to accept the charter as genuine. Nothing is known of the previous history of Longdendale. In the Domesday survey it appeared under the name Tengestvisie as part of the earl's demesne (*D.S.C.*, p. 114), and presumably remained so down to the time of the present charter; but it was waste and woodland and of no real value.

322. Remits to the monks of Combe the forinsec service due from the hide of land which Gerard of Camville gave them.

[1200–1204]

B.L. Cott. MS. Vitell. A. 1 (Register of Combe), f. 120; Bodleian Library, Dugdale MS. 12, p. 148 (from register in Cott. Vitell. D. 18, of which only fragments now remain).

Omnibus *etc.* Ranulfus comes Cestrie salutem in domino. Noverit universitas vestra me divine caritatis intuitu dedisse et de me et de heredibus meis imperpetuum remisisse deo et sancte Marie et monachis de Cumba in puram et perpetuam elemosinam forinsecum servicium pertinens ad illam hydam terre cum pertinentiis, quam Girardus de Camvilla eis dedit[1] et carta sua confirmavit, ita quod nec ego nec heredes mei predictis monachis super predicto forinseco servitio aliquam molestiam facemus.[2] In cuius rei testimonium presentem cartam sigillo meo munitam eisdem habere feci. Hiis testibus[3] Stephano de Segrave, Waltero de Dayvilla, Aluredo de Sullingny, Walkelino de Ardena, Hugone Phytun, Ricardo de Aula, Simone et Petro clericis.

1. Remainder of text, to witness clause, omitted in Dugdale MS.
2. sic MS.
3. Witnesses omitted in Cott. Vitell. A. 1.

The Cistercian abbey of Combe in Warwickshire was founded in 1150 by Richard de Camville, who died in 1176 and was succeeded by his son Gerard (*P.R.S.*, xxv, p. 46). Gerard died before 15 January 1215 (*H.K.F.*, p. 221) after a long and adventurous career. His gift to Combe of a hide of land in Vauercort (Warkworth, Northants.), which Richard fitz Walter held of his father and himself, precedes the present charter in the abbey register, and there is no reason to doubt that it is the hide referred to here. As the witness Alured de Suligny died in 1204 (*H.K.F.*, p. 41), it is possible to date the present charter within fairly close limits.

323.   Licence to the monks of Combe to acquire lands and revenues in Coventry and elsewhere in his lands.

[1200–1217]

> B.L. Cott. MS. Vitell. A. 1 (Register of Combe, seriously injured by fire), f. 32; Bodleian Library, Dugdale MS. 12, p. 158.

Sciant omnes ad quos presentes littere pervenerint, quod ego Ranulfus comes Cestrie licenciam specialem et generalem dedi et concessi monachis de Cumba, quod ipsi sine contradictione mei heredum vel successorum meorum licite valeant terras et redditus in Coventre et in omni terra potestatis mee sibi appropriare et in perpetuum pacifice possidere. Pro quibus terris et redditibus sic sibi appropriatis et in posterum appropriandis renuncio pro me, heredibus et successoribus meis curie sectam, hominum scutagium, equorum tolnetum,[1] et omne servicium seculare. Quare volo[2] et precipio omnibus hominibus et ballivis meis q[uod monachos predictos][3] et eorum servientes in nullo de predictis serviciis molestant vel gravent seu fieri permittant, sed eosdem et eorum omnia catalla ac [tenementa][3] protegant, manuteneant et defendant.

1. *Both MSS. read* cur' sect' hom' scutag' equorum toln'. *The meaning is by no means clear, and it is possible that there is a word missing before* cur'.
2. *Dugdale's text ends here.*
3. *MS. torn and faded.*

Both manuscripts are defective, and neither gives the witnesses. It is therefore impossible to give more than a very general date. The terms of the charter are also unusual; but, assuming it is genuine and assuming that the earl's title is correctly given, it must fall before 1217 and, less certainly, after 1200. In any case, it is clearly a charter of Ranulf III.

324.   Confirmation to Martin of Washingborough, his clerk, of the gift made to him in the earl's court at Bolingbroke by William le Grant of Blyton of two bovates at Kirkby and the bondmen Alan son of Ingelais and Hugh Moderles with their issue.

[c.1200]

> Orig.: Lincoln, Dean and Chapter, 73/1/18. Transcr.: D. and C. A/1/6 (Reg. Linc.), no. 1797. Ed.: *Linc. Rec. Soc.*, xli (*Registrum Antiquissimum*, vi), pp. 96–7, no. 1866. Facsimile: *Linc. Rec. Soc.*, xlii, pl. xix.

Sciant omnes tam presentes quam futuri, quod ego Rannulfus comes Cestrie concessi et presenti carta mea confirmavi Martino de Wassinburc clerico meo et heredibus suis concessionem et donationem, quam Willelmus le Grant de Blitun fecit per concessionem et assensum heredum suorum in curia mea apud Bulingbroc predicto Martino et heredibus suis pro homagio suo et servitio, scilicet duas bovatas terre in territorio de Kirkebi cum toftis et croftis, cum pratis et pasturis, et cum omnibus[1] ad predictos bovatas terre pertinentibus, scilicet cum Alano filio Ingelais et cum tota secta sua et cum Hugone Moderles et tota secta sua, et cum omnibus pertinentiis earundem duarum bovatarum, quarum scilicet Sewinus tenuit unam et Reginaldus faber tenuit aliam, tenendas predicto Martino et heredibus suis de memorato Willelmo le Grant et heredibus suis in feodo et hereditate libere et quiete et honorifice ab omni servitio et consuetudine, reddendo annuatim ab eodem Martino et heredibus suis predicto Willelmo et heredibus suis unam libram piperis ad festum sancti Botulfi pro omni servitio tam forinseco quam alio, vel sex denarios pro libra piperis, et in optione memorati Martini et heredum eius erit utrum reddat libram piperis vel sex denarios. Et has bovatas duas terre predictus Willelmus le Grant et heredes sui sepedicto Martino et heredibus suis, vel quibuscumque voluerit eas concedere et dare, contra omnes homines in soca de Bolinbroc warantizabunt. Quod, ut ratum et inconcussum permaneat in posterum, presentis scripti testimonio et sigilli mei patrocinio confirmavi. Testibus hiis Freelin Malesmains, Iohanne de Pratellis, Nicholao filio Alani, Radulfo Recucon, Philippo de Keles, Iohanne de Wassinburc, et aliis quampluribus.

SEAL: on tag, sewn up in leather bag.

1. *sic orig.; probably a slip for* hominibus, *as in William le Grant's charter, on which this confirmation is based.*

Martin of Washingborough does not occur otherwise under this name, but may be identical with the Martin the clerk who witnessed **nos. 278, 294** and **314** around 1200. Freelin Malesmains is almost certainly identical with Frederick Malesmains (elsewhere Freehericus), who accounted for the farm of Pontorson in 1198 (*Rot. Scacc. Norm.*, ii. 289) and witnessed a Norman charter dated 1203 (**no. 333**) together with Ralph Recuchon and John de Préaux. These dates point to the approximate date of the present confirmation, which must fall after Ranulf III's succession to the soke of Bolingbroke in 1198. William le Grant's charter (printed *Linc. Rec. Soc.*, xli, p. 95, no. 1865) has a different set of witnesses and must be earlier in date, suggesting that the date of the present charter is c.1200.

325. Confirmation to the church of Lincoln of two bovates in East Kirkby (Lincs.), given by William le Grant of Blyton.

[c.1200–1205]

Lincoln, Dean and Chapter A/1/5 (Registrum Antiquissimum), f. 117v., no. 623; A/1/6 (Reg. Linc.), no. 1799.
Ed.: *Linc. Rec. Soc.* xli, p. 94.

Universis sancte matris ecclesie filiis ad quos presens scriptum pervenerit,
Rannulfus comes Cestrie salutem. Noverit universitas vestra me divine pietatis
intuitu concessisse deo et ecclesie beate Marie Lincolnie duas bovatas terre in
Kyrkeby cum hominibus, pratis et paschuis, et omnibus rebus et libertatibus ad
easdem duas bovatas terre pertinentibus, quas Willelmus Grant de me tenuit in
eadem villa, in puram, liberam et perpetuam elemosinam possidendas de me et
heredibus meis, sicut carta Willelmi Grant testatur. Ut autem hec mea concessio
perpetue firmitatis robur optineat, presens scriptum sigilli mei munimine
roboravi. Hiis testibus Waltero de Daivilla, Willelmo filio Droconis, Helya
pincerna, Rogero de Maletot, Alano de Hareby capellano, Roberto de Bolonia,
Alano de Stikenia, et multis aliis.

William le Grant's charter, which is in fact a confirmation of a gift by his tenant,
Martin the clerk of Washingborough, is printed *L.R.S.*, xli, p. 93, no. 1862. Earl
Ranulf had already confirmed William's gift to Martin of the two bovates in
question (**no. 324**). As William le Grant's charter must be earlier in date, and
Kirkby was part of the Bolingbroke inheritance acquired by Earl Ranulf in 1198,
the date of the present charter must be c.1200 or perhaps a little later.

326.   Grant to the church and to the common of the canons of Lincoln of a
bovate in Hundleby, which Nicholas Bec held of him, reserving to himself
a toft which Colswain held.

[1198–1217, probably 1200–1210]

Lincoln, Dean and Chapter, A/1/5 (Registrum Antiquissimum), f. 118, no. 624; A/1/6 (Reg. Linc.), no. 1792. Ed.:
Linc. Rec. Soc., xli, pp. 97–8 (no. 1867).

Omnibus Christi fidelibus ad quos presens scriptum pervenerit, Ranulfus comes
Cestrie salutem. Noverit universitas vestra me pro animabus patris mei et matris
mee et omnium antecessorum et successorum meorum dedisse et concessisse et
presenti carta mea confirmasse deo et beate Marie et commune canonicorum
Lincolniensis ecclesie unam bovatam terre in territorio de Hundeby cum toftis et
croftis, que Nicholaus Bec de me tenuit, habendam et tenendam cum omnibus
pertinenciis suis infra villam et extra villam in puram et liberam et perpetuam
elemosinam, solutam et quietam ab omni seculari servitio et exactione, salvo
mihi et heredibus meis uno tofto, quod ad predictam bovatam pertinuit, quod
Colswainus tenuit, quod in manu mea retinui. Et ego Ranulfus comes et heredes

mei warentizabimus memoratis canonicis prefatam bovatam cum toftis et croftis et omnibus pertinenciis suis, excepto crofto quod Colswainus tenuit, sicut dictum est, contra omnes homines in perpetuum. Ut autem hec mea donatio firma et stabilis permaneat, eam presenti scripto et sigilli mei appositione corroboravi. Hiis testibus Waltero de Coventreia tunc senescallo meo, Radulfo filio Symonis, Gilberto de Welle, Philippo de Be, Henrico dispensatore, Amando, Alano de Martona, Thoma ostriciario, Henrico de Totingtona, Roberto de Bolonia, Thoma de Pleseleia, Radulfo Carbunel, Alano filio Raingoti, et aliis.

Hundleby was part of the Bolingbroke lands acquired by Ranulf III in 1198 and Walter of Coventry was his steward there. For a charter for Ralph Carbonel of Halton, perhaps dating from 1200–1210, see **no. 331**; Thomas the falconer (*ostriciario*) is also found holding land in Halton in 1202–3 (*Lincs. Records, Final Concords*, p. 51). This charter probably belongs to the same period, but cannot be safely dated more closely than 1198–1217.

327. Confirmation to the canons of Lincoln of the lands given to them by Adam of Suligny in Swaby and Huttoft (Lincs.).

[1207–1217]

P.R.O., D.L. 36/2 (Cart. Misc.), f. 34. Transcr.: D.L. 42/2 (Coucher Book II), f. 481v.

Omnibus Christi fidelibus ad quos presens scriptum pervenerit, Ranulfus comes Cestrie salutem. Noverit universitas vestra nos divine pietatis intuitu concessisse et presenti carta nostra confirmasse deo et beate Marie et commune canonicorum Lincolniensis ecclesie donationem quam Adam de Suleni dedit eidem commune in liberam et puram et perpetuam elemosinam, scilicet totam terram quam Widfare tenuit in Swabi et in territorio eiusdem ville cum pertinentiis, et quoddam pratum in pratis de Hotoft, videlicet Northdaile, quod iacet inter pratum monachorum de Parco Lude et pratum Rogeri de Farlestorpe, et toftum quod fuit Alani filii Auch apud Havedich, et pasturam ad centum oves in pastura de Hotoft. Quare volumus et firmiter precipimus quod predicti canonici prenominatas terras cum omnibus pertinentiis suis bene et in pace et honorifice habeant et teneant in puram et perpetuam elemosinam, liberam, solutam et quietam ab omni seculari servitio et exactione. Ut autem hec nostra concessio et confirmatio futuris temporibus perpetuam obtineant firmitatem, eas presenti scripto et sigilli nostri appositione corroboravimus. Hiis testibus Philippo iusticiario nostro, Waltero de Coventreia senescallo nostro.

SEAL: missing.

There is no serious reason to reject this charter, but the short witness clause is very unusual and it is surprising that no record of any sort is found among the extensive Lincoln archives. The charter is written in the same hand as text A1 of **no. 328** and, like that, may have been produced for ratification by Ranulf III but, for one reason or another, not ratified. Nevertheless Adam of Suligny's grant was confirmed by his immediate lord, Hasculf de Praers (*H.K.F.*, p. 144). The present confirmation, if actually made, cannot be dated closely, but probably falls between 1207 and 1217.

328. Confirmation to the church and canons of Lincoln of the gifts made from his fee in Theddlethorpe, Mablethorpe, Reston, Thurlby, Huttoft, Swaby, Langton, Sausthorpe, Keal, Benniworth, Hagworthingham, Claxby, Hameringham, Edlington, Horsington, Skegness and Scamblesby (all in Lincolnshire).

Winchester, [1208–1211]

Orig.: P.R.O., D.L. 36/2 (Cart. Misc.), f. 25 (A1); Lincoln, Dean and Chapter, Dij/91/3/1 (A2). Copies (not collated) of A1 in D.L. 42/2 (Coucher Book II), ff. 482v.–483, and of A2 in Dij/91/3/2 and 3/3. Ed. (A2): *Linc. Rec. Soc.*, xli (*Registrum Antiquissimum*, vi), pp. 82–5 (no. 1850) with facsimile in *Linc. Rec. Soc.*, xlii, pl. xv.

Omnibus Christi fidelibus, ad quos presens scriptum pervenerit, Ranulfus comes Cestrie salutem. Noverit universitas vestra me concessisse divine pietatis intuitu et presenti carta mea confirmasse deo et beate Marie et commune canonicorum Lincolniensis ecclesie pro salute anime mee et omnium antecessorum et successorum meorum omnes terras, quas habent de feodo meo, in puram et perpetuam elemosinam in perpetuum possidendas: videlicet, ex dono Gilberti de Suttona unam bovatam terre in Tedletorpe; ex dono Ade Muterii unum clausum in Middeldeila et preterea unum toftum et quindecim acras per particulas; ex dono Gilberti filii Haraldi unum toftum et tres acras et dimidiam; ex dono Roberti Bacheler unam acram in Sumeretwra; ex dono Roberti de Lekeburne unam bovatam et dimidiam, sex acris minus; ex dono eiusdem Roberti decem et septem acras in Silkescroft; ex dono Ricardi filii Roberti de Sumercotes dimidiam bovatam; ex dono Alani filii Alani sex acras in Wengdeiles; ex dono Ricardi de Cuninghesholme dimidiam bovatam, sex acris minus; ex dono Gilberti filii Haraldi dimidiam bovatam, novem acris minus, et unum toftum et croftum, que fuerunt Willelmi filii Grunkel. Hec supradicte terre in Tedletorpe. Ex dono Rogeri filii Durandi dimidiam bovatam, octava parte minus, et preterea septem acras in Malbertorpe; ex dono Ricardi filii

Goslani unum toftum et duas acras in Ristona; ex dono Radulfi filii Eudonis de Billesbi unum toftum et unum croftum in Turlebi et preterea unum toftum et tres acras in Hotoft; ex dono Symonis de Swabi unum toftum et dimidiam bovatam in Swabi; ex dono Osberti de Langetona unum toftum et duas bovatas in Langetona; ex dono Roberti de Saustorpe unum toftum in Saustorpe et unum toftum in Dalbi; ex dono Gilberti de Beningworthe unum toftum in Keles; item ex dono Arnaldi fratris Bone et confirmatione eiusdem Gilberti unum toftum et dimidiam bovatam in Beningworthe; ex dono Hugonis filii Roberti unum toftum et duas bovatas in Hagworthingham; ex dono Henrici filii Alani de Claxebi unum toftum et dimidiam bovatam et quatuor acras in Claxebi; ex dono Willelmi de Claxebi in eadem villa tria tofta et viginti et quatuor acras per plures particulas; item ex dono eiusdem Willelmi et Walteri clerici duo tofta et viginti acras similiter in Claxebi per particulas; ex dono Galfridi de Hameringham duo tofta et duodecim acras in Hameringham; ex dono Radulfi filii Symonis de Edlinctona unum toftum et duas acras in Edlinctona; ex dono Ranulfi de Midlei unum toftum in Horsinctona; ex dono Symonis filii Symonis unum toftum et duas bovatas in Skeghenesse; ex dono Symonis de Scamlesbi unum toftum et duas acras in Scamlesbi. Et volo et concedo ut predicti canonici Lincolnienses habeant et teneant in puram et perpetuam elemosinam omnes predictas terras cum omnibus pertinentiis suis in pratis, in pascuis et mariscis et omnibus libertatibus et aisiamentis infra villam et extra, liberas, solutas et quietas ab omni seculari servitio et exactione de me et heredibus meis in perpetuum. Ut autem hec mea concessio et confirmatio perpetuam obtineant firmitatem, eas presenti scripto et sigilli mei patrocinio corroboravi. Hiis testibus[1] Rogero de Lascy constabulario Cestrie, Philippo de Orreby tunc[2] iusticiario Cestrie, Waltero de Coventreia tunc senescallo meo, Symone de Dribi, Willelmo de Welle, Radulfo filio Symonis, Willelmo filio Walteri, Stephano de Segrava, Symone de Sais, Roberto de Lecheburne, Willelmo filio Warnerii,[3] Iacobo Brand, Willelmo nepote Warnerii,[3] Petro de Ponte, et multis aliis apud Wintoniam.

SEAL: missing (A1 and A2).

1. *The remainder, i.e. the list of witnesses, added in A1 in a second, cursive 'chancery' hand.*
2. *Added above line, A1.*
3. *sic A1;* Warn[eri] *A2.*

This long and elaborate charter is an interesting example of the procedure for securing a confirmation. The text of A1, down to and including 'Hiis testibus' is written by the same hand as **no. 327,** and was evidently produced by or for the canons of Lincoln for ratification by the earl. To this draft, after it had been accepted by the earl, one of his clerks appended the names of the witnesses in a small, cursive hand. This text should be regarded as the original charter, and has been made the basis of the present edition; A2, written in an ornate script of an ecclesiastical character, was evidently a fair copy, produced by the canons for their own use and preserved in the cathedral archives, and was authenticated by the addition of the earl's seal. This is therefore another example (see **nos. 229, 328, 444**) of a charter existing in two exemplifications, both authentic.

The date of the charter must fall before the death of Roger de Lacy in 1211, and probably after 1208. The dating at Winchester is very unusual, and presumably represents some occasion when Earl Ranulf was in attendance upon King John, but I have been unable to trace any evidence of his presence at Winchester later than January 1205 (*P.R.S.*, N.S. xvii, p. 111). William son of Warner, William nephew of Warner, James Brand and Peter de Ponte (Attebrig) were all citizens of Lincoln at this time (Hill, *Medieval Lincoln*, pp. 158, 398), and Peter de Ponte was particularly prominent (*ibid.*, p. 395). It is surprising to find them at Winchester; presumably they were a delegation sent by the canons.

329.   Confirmation to Andrew son of John of Edlington of his land in Edlington (Lincs.)

[1200–1205]

P.R.O., D.L. 42/2 (Coucher Book II), f. 44v.

Sciant omnes ad quos presens scriptum pervenerit, quod ego Ranulfus comes Cestrie concessi et hac carta mea confirmavi Andree filio Iohannis de Edelingtona totam terram quam Radulfus filius Simonis de Hamingtona ei dedit in territorio de Edelingtona, sicut carta eiusdem Radulfi, quam predictus Andreas de eo habet, testatur, tenendam ei et heredibus suis in feodo et hereditate de me et heredibus meis libere et quiete, reddendo annuatim mihi et heredibus meis dimidiam libram piperis ad festum sancti Iohannis Baptiste pro omni servicio. Testibus hiis Waltero de Pincebeche, Waltero de Coventreia, Iohanne filio Radulfi, Hugone de Sais, Roberto de Fenna, Iacobo de Rupe, et multis aliis.

Andrew is mentioned in 1212 as holding 2½ acres in Edlington for a payment of half-a-pound of pepper (*H.K.F.*, p. 148), but this confirmation, to judge from the names of the witnesses, is somewhat earlier. Hugh de Sais is mentioned in 1203–4 (*H.K.F.*, p. 141), Walter of Pinchbeck occurs on the Lincolnshire Pipe Roll between 1196–7 and 1205–6, and Walter of Coventry was Ranulf III's seneschal in the soke of Bolingbroke from 1199. This suggests an approximate date of 1200–05.

330. Confirmation to the nuns of Bullington (Lincs.) of the gifts of Helte and Idonea Boydell and two acres of meadow given by Alan Boydell. [Spurious]

[1200–1205]

Orig.: B.L. Harl. Charter 52A. 18. Short abstract: B.L. Add. MS. 6118, f. 392. Engl. summary: *H.K.F.*, p. 176.

Omnibus Christi fidelibus, ad quos presens scriptum pervenerit, Rannulphus comes Cestrie salutem. Sciatis me concessisse et hac carta mea confirmasse deo et beate Marie et monialibus de Bolinton, clericis et laicis, ibidem deo servientibus donaciones quas Heute de Boydel et Idonea uxor sua, Hugo et Alanus eorum filii, eis fecerunt, scilicet totam terram ex orientali parte bosci de Nubele, que vocatur Houpelande, et aquam de Barlingis, quantum ad eorum feodum pertinet, et aquam[1] de Gosholme usque ad metas de Appeleia, et mariscum cum prato, quod est inter aquam et boscum, usque ad easdem metas, et fossatum suum, quod fecerunt ab aqua de Barlingis usque ad parcum, Simonis filii Willelmi, et liberam viam eundi et redeundi pacifice ab abbatia usque ad aquam de Barling, et de aqua ad abbatiam, cum quadrigis et equo et pede ad predictum eius mariscum custodiendum, falcandum et parandum et trahendum, et duas acras prati in Miclehale propinquiores prato Simonis de Kyma, quas scilicet Alanus Boydel eis dedit in perpetuam elemosinam. Hec omnia predicta dedi, concessi et hac carta mea confirmavi predictis monialibus clericis et laicis ibidem deo servientibus. Hanc donacionem in perpetuam elemosinam ratam do et concedo liberam et quietam ab omni seculari servicio, sicut carte predictorum donatorum, quas inde habent, testantur, et ab omni consuetudine, geldo et denegello vel auxilio. Et hoc sit pro animabus patris mei et matris mee et antecessorum meorum et mea. Hiis testibus Simone de Kyma, Waltero Dayville, Philippo de Kyma, Roberto de Amundavilla, et ceteris.

1. aqua *orig.*

This document is written in a 14th-century book-hand. It could conceivably be a copy, but the fact that it has a fold at the foot with slits for the seal (missing) suggests that it is a deliberate forgery. Moreover, the formulation is distinctly irregular. The purpose was probably to define (or re-define) more precisely the boundaries of the land given in the fenland between Newball, Barlings and Apley. On the other hand, the expanded version may well have been based on a genuine charter of Ranulf III, dating from the beginning of the 13th century. Walter of Dayville is a very frequent witness of Ranulf III's charters, attesting no fewer than 30 down to the time of the earl's death, but none, so far as I have been able to establish, before c.1200. Robert of Amundeville succeeded to his father's lands in 1194 or 1195 (*P.R.S.*, N.S. vi, p. 25), but was evidently not yet of age, since the archbishop of Canterbury was given custody of his lands and the right to marry him without disparagement (*ibid.*, vii, p. 172). Simon of Kyme was the son of Philip of Kyme, who died before November 1194; he himself died in 1220 and was succeeded by his son Philip, who witnesses the present charter (*H.K.F.*, pp. 122–4). Farrer (ibid., p. 176) dates it c.1205 for no stated reason; but the original charter, from which the present text derives, may safely be dated 1200–1205. For an earlier confirmation of Helte de Boydell's gifts, see **no. 128**.

[BERTRADA, WIDOW OF HUGH II.]

331.   Confirmation to Ralph Carbonel of Halton (Halton Holegate, Lincs.) of half a knight's fee which he holds in Halton.

[c.1200–1210]

> Orig.: P.R.O., D.L. 25 (Ancient Deeds, Series L), no. 41.
> Transcr.: D.L. 42/2 (Coucher Book II), f. 285v.; Central Reference Library, Manchester, Towneley MS. 8, p. 1085 (from Coucher). Ed.: Orm., i. 27 (from Coucher Book).

Omnibus hoc scriptum audituris et visuris Brettreya comitissa Cestrie salutem. Noverit universitas vestra me concessisse et hac mea presenti carta confirmasse Radulfo Carbunel de Haltuna et heredibus suis pro humagio et servicio suo feodum dimidii militis quod tenet de me in Haltona pro tribus solidis annuatim michi et heredibus meis ad duos terminos reddendis de illo et de heredibus suis pro omni servicio et exaccione, scilicet ad nativitatem sancti Iohannis baptiste decem et octo denarios, at Natale decem et octo denarios. In huius autem rei testimonium presenti scripto sigillum meum apposui. Hiis testibus Radulfo filio Simonis, Simone de Seis, Andrea filio Willelmi, Willelmo de Maletoft, Willelmo de Haghe, Ricardo de Duningtun, Ricardo de Harderna, Alano filio Raingoti, et aliis.

SEAL: on tag, vesicular, female figure, legend defaced.

Ralph Carbonel witnessed a charter for Lincoln cathedral (**no. 326**) together with Ralph son of Simon and Alan son of Raingot c.1200. The present charter is not easy to date, but is probably of much the same time or a little later. William of Maletoft is mentioned in 1198 (*Rot. Scacc. Norm.*, ii. 339) and Andrew son of William in 1204–05 and 1205–06 (*P.R.S.*, N.S. xix, p. 253, and xx, p. 28). Simon de Sais witnessed a charter for Lincoln c.1208–1211 (**no. 328**). The interest of Hugh II's widow, Countess Bertraya or Bertrada, in Halton is not otherwise known; it was probably part of her dower, but this was mainly in Donington and Belchford (*H.K.F.*, p. 174).

332. Grant to the monks of Aunay (dioc. Bayeux) of exemption from tolls and customs and all other exactions throughout the lands subject to his dominion.

Brecy, [1201]

Orig.: Archives de Calvados, H. 677. Ed.: Round, *C.D.F.*, p. 189 (no. 538) (abbreviated text). Calendared: d'Anisy, i. 52 (no. 54).

Ranulfus comes Cestrie omnibus senescallis et baillivis et servientibus suis, et omnibus Christi fidelibus ad quos presens carta pervenerit, salutem. Noverit universitas vestra me pietatis et caritatis intuitu pro salute anime mee et antecessorum et heredum meorum dedisse et concessisse et presente[1] carta sigilli mei munimine roborata confirmasse deo et beate Marie de Alneto et monachis eiusdem loci liberam omnino quietantiam ab omni teloneo et passagio et consuetudine et omnimodi exactione in vendendis et emendis et transferendis et commutandis omnibus que ipsi vel homines sui assecurare poterunt propria esse dictorum monachorum in feriis et mercatis meis et in omnibus locis et terris dominationi mee subiectis. Quare volo et firmiter precipio quod dicti monachi prescriptam libertatem et quietantiam plenarie habeant et possideant in puram et perpetuam elemosinam liberam omnino et quietam. Prohibeo etiam super forisfactum meum centum solidorum, ne aliquis meorum aliquo tempore aliquo loco aliqua occasione dictos monachos super his disturbare vel molestare presumat. Actum fuit hoc apud Breceium anno ab incarnatione domini MCCI. Testibus [hiis Radulfo de][2] Clincampo, Willelmo Bacon, Nicholao Chamberlenge, Silvano de Clincampo, Ricardo Bacon, [. . . . . . et multis ali]is.[3]

SEAL: on tag, missing.

1. *sic orig.*
2. *Tear in original;* Radulfo de *supplied from Lechaudé d'Anisy.*
3. *Original torn and defective; one witness missing.*

Professor Barraclough did not provide notes for this charter.

333. Grant to the abbey of Aunay (dioc. Bayeux) of the tenement in the park of Trévières formerly held by Ranulf Columbel, and a rent of 8s. of Anjou to be taken from the 25s. a year which William Wake paid from the fee he held in the park of Trévières.

[1203]

Orig.: Archives de Calvados H. 1190. Cal.: d'Anisy, i. 52(no. 55).

Notum sit presentibus et futuris quod ego Rannulfus comes Cestrie dedi et concessi et presente[1] carta sigilli mei munimine roborata confirmavi deo et beate Marie de Alneto et monachis ibidem deo servientibus totum tenementum, quod Rannulfus Columbel tenebat de me in parco meo de Treveriis, cum omnibus pertinentiis suis, et octo solidos Andegavensium de viginti quinque solidis Andegavensium, quos Willelmus Wac reddebat michi annuatim de feodo quod tenebat de me in parco meo de Treveriis. Hanc autem donationem feci deo et dictis monachis anno ab incarnatione domini mcciii. pro salute anime mee et omnium antecessorum et heredum meorum in puram et perpetuam elemosinam liberam omnino et quietam, uno die per annos singulos ad pietanciam mona-chorum assignatam. Testibus hiis Petro Rualdo, Radulfo Recuchon, Iohanne de Pratellis, Frederico Malis Manibus, Henrico dispensatore, Iohanne de Escagel, Willelmo de Lambala.

SEAL: on tag, missing.

1. *sic orig.*

Pierre Rouaut is a very frequent witness during the 1190s, down to 1204, when he went over to the allegiance of the king of France. For Ralph Recuchon, see **no. 244**; for John de Préaux, see **no. 337**; for John de Escagel, or Escaiol, who held land in Chester, see *E.C.C.*, p. 35.

334. Notification that he has taken the abbey of Savigny and its possessions in England and in Normandy into his protection and confirming its landhold-ings in Long Bennington (Lincs.), with the consent of his wife, Clementia.

Waddington, [1201–1204]

Two originals: Paris, Archives nationales, L. 967, no. 95; Westminster abbey muniments, no. 502 (A). Cal.: Round, *C.D.F.*, p. 308 (no. 858).

Omnibus Christi fidelibus tam futuris quam presentibus, ad quos presens scriptum pervenerit, Rannulfus comes Cestrie salutem. Notum sit vobis omnibus, me suscepisse in manu et custodia et protectione mea abbatiam de Savigneio et monachos et fratres et homines et res et possessiones eorum tam in Normannia quam in Anglia, sicut mea dominica. Et sciatis me pro dei amore et pro salute anime mee et antecessorum et amicorum meorum per consensum et voluntatem Clementie sponse mee concessisse et dedisse deo et beate Marie de Savigneio et monachis ibidem deo servientibus unam carrucatam terre in dominico meo Haie de Beningtona cum pratis congruentibus assignatis et cum communione pasturarum et mariscorum pertinente ad tantum terre in eadem villa, et cum omnibus aliis eiusdem terre pertinenciis per metas et divisas illas, per quas Walterus de Coventreia senescallus meus terram illam eis liberavit, die qua eis eam dedi. Et preterea concessi et dedi eisdem totum tenementum, quod Walterus de Sonderbi tenuit in Beningtona, et toftum, quod Malgerus filius Gaufridi tenuit in eadem villa, cum una bovata terre et pertinenciis suis. Hec omnia predicta concessi et dedi prefatis monachis in puram et perpetuam elemosinam, tenenda de me et heredibus meis libere quiete et honorifice,soluta et quieta ab omni seculari servicio et demanda, ita quod in eis nichil penitus mihi retineo nec heredibus meis nisi orationes tantum, hoc tamen adiecto, quod una carrucata terre in predicta villa de Beningtona, quam predicti monachi pridem tenuerunt, reddendo annuatim unam marcam argenti, a predictis monachis mihi et heredibus meis quieta remanebit in perpetuum, et similiter sepedicti monachi de illa marca argenti in perpetuum quieti permanebunt. Ut autem hec mea donatio perpetue firmitatis robur optineat, eam presenti scripto et sigilli mei munimine duxi roborandam. Hiis testibus domina Bertraya comitissa Cestrie, Thoma dispensatore, Radulfo filio Simonis, Willelmo Picot, Waltero de Coventreia, Gaufrido de sancto Bricio, Iuhello de Lovingneio, Iohanne de Pratellis, Petro clerico de Cestria, et multis aliis. Datum apud Wadingtonam.[1]

SEAL: missing from Paris exemplification; Westminster exemplification, red wax, on a heater shield a lion.

1. The Paris exemplification is torn and affected by water stains. Inconsequential variations between the two texts have been ignored.

Ranulf married Clementia de Fougères, widow of Alan de Dinan, as his second wife, in 1200. Part of her marriage portion, apart from lands in Normandy, was the manor of Long Bennington (Orm., i. 39), but a dispute almost immediately broke out over the marriage settlement with William de Fougères, Clementia's great-uncle, who claimed Long Bennington as the inheritance of his mother, Olive, daughter of Count Stephen of Brittany (**no. 318**). In a charter given at Bennington on 27 May 1201 and witnessed (among others) by Ralph de Tutford (Twyford), his seneschal in England, and by William of Foston and William Brown (Brunus) his reeves, William gave to Savigny the tenement of Walter of Sonderby and the toft of Malger son of Geoffrey (Paris, Arch. nat. L. 968, no. 226). The present charter, repeating these gifts, is evidently later in date. It is probably explained by the failure of William and of Clementia's brother, Geoffrey of Fougères, to abide by the settlement, in consequence of which Ranulf took over the obligation to the abbey of Savigny, at the same time adding a further gift of one carucate on his own behalf. His charter must date before 1204, when Geoffrey de St. Brice was deprived of his English lands, having gone over to the allegiance of the king of France (*P.R.S.*, N.S. xiv, p. 197). Some years later Ranulf made a further gift of land in Bennington to Savigny as an 'increment' to his previous grant (**no. 335**), and Clementia confirmed his gifts in her widowhood (**no. 442**).

335.   Grant to the abbey of Savigny of one rood of land in Long Bennington (Lincs.) in increment of its existing holding, and also 11½ acres of land and six roods of meadow.

[1220–1226]

Orig.: sold at Sotheby's, c.1950, lot 111; not traced. Facsimile in Sotheby's catalogue, Plate V. Transcr.: Madox, *Formulare Anglicanum*, p. 255 (no. 433) (from original, then in archives of Westminster abbey).

Omnibus sancte matris ecclesie filiis presentibus et futuris Ranulfus comes Cestrie et Lincolnie salutem. Noveritis me assensu et consensu Clemencie uxoris mee dedisse et concessisse et hac presenti carta mea confirmasse deo et ecclesie sancte Trinitatis sancteque Marie de Savigneio et monachis ibidem deo servientibus pro salute anime mee et omnium antecessorum et successorum et parentorum meorum unam rodam terre in villa de Binigtona ad incrementum curie predictorum monachorum ex occidentali parte in puram et perpetuam elemosinam solutam et quietam ab omni seculari servicio et exactione. Preterea dedi et concessi predictis monachis in puram et perpetuam elemosinam xi. acras terre et dimidiam et sex rodas prati in haya de Binigtona iuxta terras, quas prius eis dedi in predicta haya in exscambium xi. acrarum et dimidie terre et sex rodarum prati quas predicti monachi mihi exscambiaverunt in campis de Binigtona et Fostona, scilicet super Wildholm vii. seillones, super Haydit i. seillonem, ad crucem del Hay ii. seillones, super Hayhil ii. seillones, ad Siket de Fostona i. seillonem, ad Hubbegate i. seillonem, ad Storcholm i. seillonem et culturam ad Clivisende, et in pratis de Binigtona ex orientali parte de Riholm vi. rodas prati. Concessi etiam predictis monachis claudere predictam hayam sicut cursus aque se proportat propter semitam ammovendam. Hiis testibus H. abbate Cestrie, P. de Orrebi tunc iusticiario Cestrie, Alphredo de Soleni, Gileberto Cusin, Iohanne clerico, Galfrido Cunein, Galfrido clerico, Iohanne de Stupetona, et multis aliis.

SEAL: on tag, perfect; equestrian figure galloping to the right, closed helmet, short sword in right hand, shield in left; legend + SIGILLUM RANULFI COMITIS CESTRIE ET LINCOLNIE.

This gift is a supplement or increment to the grant made, also with the consent of Countess Clementia, a number of years previously (**no. 334**). Its date falls between 1220 and 1226.

336. Gift to St. James's abbey, Northampton, of a mill and land at Heyford, pertaining to the manor of Bugbrooke (Northants.)

[1201–1207]

> B.L. Cott. MS. Tiberius E. v. (Cartulary of St. James's, damaged in Cottonian fire, 1731), f. 31v; short abstract from cartulary, Bodleian Library, MS. Top. Northants. c. V, f. 305. Cited Bridges, *Hist. and Antiq. of Northants.*, i. 501.

Ranulfus comes Cestrie omnibus hominibus et amicis suis tam futuris quam presentibus, ad quos presens scriptum pervenerit, salutem. Notum vobis facio me divini amoris intuitu et pro salute animarum antecessorum meorum et anime mee concessisse et dedisse et carta mea confirmasse deo et abbacie sancti Iacobi de Norhampton et canonicis sub regulari disciplina ibi deo servientibus molendinum de Heiford, que pertinet ad Buchebroc, et quandam virgatam terre cum pertinenciis suis in eadem villa, et essartam[1] que vocatur[2] Rochelanda, habendam et tenendam in perpetuam et puram elemosinam libere[3] et quiete ab omni seculari servicio et exaccione. Et ut hec mea donacio perpetue firmitatis robur optineat, eam presenti scripto et sigilli mei apposicione duxi roborandam. Hiis testibus Iohanne de Pratellis, Waltero de Daivilla, Waltero de Coventreia, Eustachio de Watford, Ricardo de Bosevilla, Roberto Lupo, Stephano de Segrave, Willelmo de Se land,[4] Thoma clerico presentis latore[5] et multis aliis.[6]

1. essarta *MS.*
2. vocantur *MS.*
3. libera *MS.*
4. *sic MS.*; *the name is not decipherable.*
5. *sic MS.*
6. *Last two words torn away MS.*

This is another case of a single benefaction to a monastery for which there is no obvious explanation. According to Bridges (*loc. cit.*) the earl's charter is a confirmation of gifts by John le Lou, William de Caines and Richard fitz Hugh, but this is the only charter of Ranulf III in the cartulary. The manor of Bugbrooke had been a part of the honour of Mortain, and the earl of Chester's title was disputed (*H.K.F.*, p. 226). The issue was raised in 1194, and was apparently not settled in the earl's favour until 1208–9. This, no doubt, did not prevent Ranulf III from disposing of lands pertaining to the manor, but it perhaps provides some indication of the date of the present charter. Richard Bovill died in 1206 or 1207 at latest (*P.R.S.*, N.S. xxii, p. 156). Eustace of Watford appears almost annually on the Northamptonshire Pipe Roll from 1193 to 1207, when he makes his last appearance. Stephen of Segrave appears to have succeeded his father Gilbert in 1201 (*P.R.S.*, N.S. xiv, p. 236). As John de Préaux was continuously in Normandy with Richard I in 1198 and 1199, the charter can hardly fall before 1200. For Robert Lupus see introduction to the Pipe Roll for 1208, p. xiv.

337.   Grant of Tew to John de Préaux, excepting the land formerly held by Hugh of Coulances, for the service of a fourth part of a knight's fee.

[1205]

P.R.O., C.66 (Chancery Patent Rolls), no. 148, m. 25, and no. 179, m. 10; printed *Cal. Pat. Rolls, 1317–21*, p. 26, and *1330–34*, p. 332.

Ranulphus comes Cestrie omnibus hominibus et amicis suis, et omnibus ad quos presens pagina pervenerit, salutem. Sciatis me concessisse et dedisse et hac carta mea confirmasse Iohanni de Pratellis pro homagio et servicio suo totam terram quam habebam in Tiwa cum capitali mesuagio meo et donacione ecclesie eiusdem ville et cum omnibus eiusdem terre pertinentiis in eadem villa et extra villam, scilicet in pratis et pascuis et in hominibus et in omnibus rebus eidem terre pertinentibus, excepta terra que fuit Hugonis de Colonciis in eadem villa, habenda et tenenda sibi et heredibus suis de me et heredibus meis in feodo et hereditate libere et quiete, pacifice et honorifice, faciendo inde michi et heredibus meis ille et heredes sui servicium quarte partis feodi unius militis. Hiis testibus Hugone comite de Laci, Philippo de Orreby, Thoma dispensario, Waltero de Coventre, Hugone Malebisse,[1] Normanno Pantull, Willelmo de Verdun, Aluredo de Suligni, Henrico Murdach, Henrico dispensario, Hugone dispensario, Thoma dispensario, Philippo del Bye, Willelmo de Venables, Guarino de Vernun, Willelmo pincerna senescallo de Monte Alto, Thoma clerico, Pagano de Chaurcis, et multis aliis.

1.   Malebille *MSS.*

John de Pratellis, whose family seat was at Préaux, near Rouen, was very active in the service of Richard I and John. Great Tew, in Oxfordshire, had been given to Ranulf II by Stephen, but was taken into the King's hands in 1167 (*H.K.F.*, p. 240). About 1196 Richard I restored it to Ranulf III. The present charter, conferring it on John de Préaux, was confirmed by King John in 1206, and must date from 1205. Hugh Lacy was earl of Ulster from 1205 to 1210. Hugh of

Coulances (dép. Calvados, arr. Vire) had gone over to the allegiance of the king of France in 1204. William de Verdun died in 1205, in which year his brother Walter claimed his inheritance (*P.R.S.*, N.S. xviii, p. 111), and Alured de Suligny died about the same time (*H.K.F.*, p. 41). The three dispensers, Henry, Hugh and Thomas, were the sons of the *Thomas dispensarius* named earlier in the witness list, and it seems that the title had now become a patronymic. Of the other witnesses Philip del Bye also occurs in **nos. 301** and **326.** William *pincerna* is presumably William le Boteler of Warrington, who also witnessed Ranulf III's charter of liberties in 1215 (**no. 394**), but the description of him as 'seneschal of Mold', if it is not a mistake, is very surprising. Roger of Montalt succeeded his brother Robert in the hereditary stewardship in 1204 (*Ches. Sheaf*, no. 7804), and the probability is that his name was accidentally omitted by the copyist before the word *senescallo*. It will be noticed that Philip of Orreby is not yet justiciar.

338.   Grant to Richard son of Robert of a virgate of land at Olney, and half a virgate pertaining to the earl's mill, and six acres of assarts in the wood of Hyde.

Oxford, [c.1205]

Halstead, *Succinct Genealogies*, p. 452.

Ranulphus comes Cestrie omnibus hominibus et amicis suis, et omnibus ad quos presens scriptum pervenerit, salutem. Notum sit vobis me concessisse et dedisse et hac carta mea confirmasse Richardo de Sutton, filio Roberti, pro homagio suo et servitio unam virgatam terre in Olneya, quam Gaufridus filius Osberti tenuit, cum messuagio et prato ad eandem virgatam pertinentibus, et dimidiam virgatam terre, que ad molendinum meum pertinuit, cum messuagio et prato et pertinentiis suis, et sex acras de assarco in bosco de Hyda, scilicet propinquiores domui quam Richardus Arneburgerus tenuit in bosco quod vocabatur Hydehai, et pratum quod nominatur Hydemor, tenenda ei et heredibus suis de me et heredibus meis in feudo et hereditate libere et quiete, cum husbote et haibote, et cum quietantia de passuagio,[1] et cum omnibus libertatibus et liberis consuetudinibus predicte terre pertinentibus, reddendo annuatim mihi et heredibus meis quedam calcaria deaurata ad festum sancti Petri ad Vinculam[2] pro omni servitio. His testibus Philippo de Oreby, Iohanne de Pratellis,[3] Waltero de Coventry, Henrico Despenser, Normanno Pantulf,[4] Alveredo[5] de Soligneio, Willelmo de Verdun,[6] Willelmo filio Drogonis,[7] Petro clerico, et multis aliis apud Oxoniam.

1.   passuagio *ed.*
2.   Vinclam *ed.*

3. Pracell *ed.*
4. Normando Panci. *There follows* Henrico Mordaunt; *this name has been omitted, as almost certainly it was added by Halstead.*
5. Avernedo *ed.*
6. Verdi *ed.*
7. Drogoni *ed.*

This charter has been associated with Olney near Coventry on the authority of Halstead (p. 392), but Halstead is not always to be trusted (see note 4), and it is possible that he inserted 'de Sutton' ('Richardo de Sutton filio Roberti'), which fits badly between 'Richardo' and 'filio Roberti', in order to establish a connection with Amice, daughter of Sir William of Olney, lord of Asthill (near Coventry) and allegedly son of Sir Richard Sutton, who married William Mordaunt. There is, in fact, little doubt that the charter refers to Olney, Bucks., which appears to have escheated to the crown after Hugh II's rebellion in 1173 and was restored to Ranulf III after 1195 (*V.C.H. Bucks.*, iv. 433) and before 1205–06 (*H.K.F.*, p. 19). There is a Hyde at Olney, Bucks. (*V.C.H. Bucks.*, iv. 432) and a mill (*H.K.F.*, p. 18), but neither at Olney, Coventry. Furthermore, the dating of the charter at Oxford points to Buckinghamshire, rather than Coventry. Apart from Halstead's emendations, it appears to be genuine. Many of the witnesses are identical with those of Ranulf III's grant of Great Tew in Oxfordshire to John de Préaux (**no. 337**), and the date of the two charters is probably much the same. It should be noted that Philip of Orreby is not yet designated justiciar.

339. Confirmation to the monks of Fountains of all their lands and possessions of his fee in Richmondshire, of which they had seisin when he recovered seisin of the lands of Richmondshire.

Richmond, [1205–1212]

> B.L. Cott. MS. Tiberius C. 12, (Fountains cartulary) f. 320v. (A); Add. MS. 18276, f. 45 (B), Ed.: Clay, *Early Yorkshire Charters*, iv. 78–9; abstract in W.T. Lancaster, *Abstracts of Charters in the Chartulary of the Cistercian Abbey of Fountains*, p. 198.

Ranulfus comes Cestrie omnibus hominibus suis et amicis tam presentibus quam futuris salutem. Sciatis me concessisse et hac presenti carta mea confirmasse deo et monachis ecclesie sancte Marie de Fontibus omnes terras et possessiones et quicquid habent de feodo meo in Richesmundesire,[1] unde saisinam habuerunt, quando saisinam terrarum Richesmundesire[1] recuperavi,[2] habendas et tenendas sicut carte eorum quas inde[3] habent testantur. Quare precipio omnibus ballivis meis et servientibus meis de Richesmundesire,[1] ut nullum gravamen vel

molestiam prefatis monachis inferant, sed eos et homines et res eorum manuteneant et defendant. Hiis testibus[4] Hairum filio Hervi, Brian filio Alani,
Radulfus de Multona, Roberto de Strengestona, Hugone de Magnebi, Willelmo
filio Petri de Richesmundesir, Radulfo de Hukerbi.

1. Richmundeshire *B*.
2. recuperam *B*.
3. eorum *repeated A*.
4. Hiis testibus *om. A; witnesses omitted B*.

Following his marriage to Constance of Brittany in 1188, Ranulf had been earl of
Richmond in his wife's name; but after his divorce in 1199, the honour passed to
her third husband, Guy of Thouars, and after Guy's defection to Philip Augustus
in 1203, to Robert, earl of Leicester. Robert died in October 1204, and in March
1205 the lands, fees and liberties of the honour of Richmond, except nine and
three-quarters knights' fees which Roald, constable of Richmond, and Henry
son of Hervey held, were given to Ranulf. The present charter evidently follows
this recovery of seisin. It is dated by Clay, (*op. cit.*) 1205–12, and probably falls
earlier, rather than later, in the period. The place where it was given is not
stated; but as all the witnesses are northern barons, and there are no Cheshire
names among them, it is a fair assumption that it was issued at Richmond.

340.   Ratification of exchange between Warin of Vernon and his wife Auda,
and Aenora Malbank, of Cheshire estates in Haslington, Henhull,
Hurleston, Acton and Woolstanwood for land in Great Brickhill, Newhall
and Aston, Bucks.

[1205–1214]

B.L. Harl. MS. 2077, f. 95 (new f. 62), from collections of
Samson Erdwicke 'in parvo libro papiro de la ligne de les
Vernons'; Bodleian Library, Rawlinson MS. B.144 (from
same).

Ranulfus comes Cestrie Warino de Vernon et Aude uxori eius [. . . . . .]
Escambium quod Aenora Maubach eis fecit, scilicet quicquid habet in Heselin-
ton et Henul et in Hurdleston et in Acton et in Wolstonwode pro portione
eorum in Brichul, Nova Aula et Eston. [. . . . . .] Testibus Philippo de Orreby,
Willelmo de Venables, Petro clerico, Liulfo de Twamlawe, Ricardo de Kingesleghe, Ioceramo de Hellesbie, David de Malo Passu, Willelmo eius filio,
Ricardo filio Liulfi.

The charter, of which this fragmentary notice is all that survives, arises out of the
partition of the inheritance of William Malbank, the last baron of Nantwich,

between his three surviving daughters, Philippa, Aenora, and Auda, who married Warin de Vernon of Shipbrook (*H.K.F.*, p. 264). As the witness list cannot altogether be trusted,[1] it is not easy to date. But Aenora Malbank seems to have pursued a definite policy of divesting herself of her Cheshire estates and consolidating her holding in the old Malbank inheritance in Buckinghamshire; hence her sale of all her residual lands in Cheshire to Henry of Audley in or about 1214 (**no. 395**). The present charter must almost certainly have preceded this sale, and the fact that she made the transaction in her own name suggests that it was after the death of her husband Robert Bardolf, which probably occurred before 1210, or at least after 1205, when he withdrew to the allegiance of the king of France and left his wife in charge in England (*Bedfordshire Historical Record Society*, x, p. 303).

---

1. In particular, it seems likely that Philip of Orreby's title of justiciar may have been dropped inadvertently; if true, this would affect the possible date.

341.   Confirmation to Robert, son of Robert of Stockport, of Marple and Wybersley as his heritage, with a piece of land in Upton and a burgage in Macclesfield, to be held by forest service, saving to the earl the eyries of hawks, sparrowhawks and falcons and the hunting in the woods belonging to the said lands.

Macclesfield, [1206]

> Bodleian Library, MS. Top. Cheshire b. I (Watson's Cheshire collections), p. 125 ('from the original at Marple'); P.R.O., CHES 2/275 (Recog. Rolls, 5 and 6 James I), m. 1d. Ed.: (from original): Watson, *Memoirs of the Earls of Warren*, ii. 224; (from enrolment) *39th Rep. D.K.P.R.*, p. 251. Abstract: Orm., iii. 839; Engl. trans.: Earwaker, *East Cheshire*, ii. 48 (from Watson).

Ranulfus comes Cestrie constabulario suo et dapifero, iusticiario, vic(ecomiti), baronibus et ballivis et omnibus hominibus suis salutem. Sciatis me concessisse et reddidisse et hac carta mea confirmasse Roberto filio Roberti de Stokeport tanquam ius suum et hereditatem Merpel et Wibreslegam cum omnibus pertinentiis suis in bosco et plano, in pratis et pasturis, in viis et semitis, et aquis et mariscis, et in omnibus rebus eisdem terris pertinentibus, et terram quam Walterus de predicto Roberto tenuit in Uptona, et unum burgagium in Macclefeld, habenda et tenenda dicto Roberto et heredibus suis de me et heredibus meis in feodo et hereditate libere et quiete et integre per servicium forestarie pro omni servicio, salvis mihi et heredibus meis aeiriis accipitrum et nisorum et falconum et venacione in boscis ad predictas terras pertinentibus. Et predictus

Robertus et heredes sui et eorum homines habebunt sibi necessaria in predictis boscis sine vastatione et destructione foreste mee. Hiis testibus Philippo de Orreby, Roberto Patric, Thoma dispensatore, Warino de Vernon, Rogero de Mesnilwarin, Petro clerico, Ricardo Phitun, David de Malo Passu, Herberto de Orrebi, Iordano de Bredbiri, Iohanne Phitun, Ricardo de Daveneporte, Rogero de Dunes, Willelmo de Stanlega, Ricardo de Suttona, et multis aliis apud Macclefeld.

Robert of Stockport died in 1205 or 1206 (*E.C.C.*, p. 32), and the present charter, confirming Marple and Wybersley to his son 'as his right and inheritance', is not much later in date. As Philip of Orreby is not yet justiciar, it provides further evidence (see **no. 400**) against Tait's attempt (*Ches. Sheaf*, no. 7804) to put back the date of Orreby's justiciarship to 1202, and support for Farrer's view that he became justiciar in 1207. Marple and Wybersley were the holding assigned to one of the eight foresters of the extensive forest of Macclesfield (Orm., iii. 538–9). The witnesses Roger of Dunes or Downes (*ibid.*, p. 781), Williams of Stanley (*Ibid.*, p. 832), and Richard of Sutton (omitted in Ormerod's pedigree, p. 761) were also foresters; Richard of Davenport (**no. 348**) was master-forester.

342. Confirmation of the grant of his grandfather Ranulf II to the monks of Coventry of the right to send two carts twice daily, except on feast days, to his wood to take what they need for repairs, fuel and hedging, by view of his foresters.

[1206–1208]

P.R.O., E.164/21 (Exchequer, King's Remembrancer, Misc. Books), f. 76v. (Coventry Register; C.53 (Chancery Charter Rolls), no. 135, m. 4; B.L. Add. MS. 32100 (from original inspeximus of Edw. III), f. 61; Bodleian Library, Dugdale MS. 12, f. 239 (from Register). Ed.: *Cal. Ch. Rolls*, v. 103 (no. 15); Coss, no. 16.

For a full text of this document, see Coss, *The Early Records of Medieval Coventry*, pp. 23–4 (no. 16).

For Ranulf II's alleged charter, which this reproduces almost verbatim, see **no. 113**. The omission here of the words 'Francis et Anglis' in the address points to a date after 1204. In fact, as Orreby became justiciar in 1206 at earliest (**no. 296**) and William of Warenne was dead by 1208 (*P.R.S.*, N.S. xxiv, p. 50), it is possible to narrow the date still further. William of Ardern is also said to have been dead by 1208 (*Book of Seals*, p. 33). For John de Préaux, see **no. 337**; for Nicholas son of Liulf, see **no. 195**.

343.   Grant to the monks of Coventry of an estimated 280 acres of woodland and waste in Exhall and Keresley in exchange for one of the two carts permitted to gather fuel in his wood at Coventry. [Spurious]

[1208–1215]

> P.R.O., E.164/21 (Exchequer, King's Remembrancer, Misc. Books), f. 76v. (Coventry Register); C.53 (Chancery Charter Rolls), no. 135 (inspeximus of Edw. III), m. 4; B.L. Add. MS. 32100, f. 61v. (from inspeximus); Bodleian Library, Dugdale MS. 12, f. 239 (from register). Ed.: *Cal. Ch. Rolls*, v. 104 (no. 16); Coss, no. 17; mentioned Dugdale, *Warwickshire*, pp. 80, 102.

For a full text of this document, see Coss, *The Early Records of Medieval Coventry*, p. 24 (no. 17).

In an apparently genuine charter of 1206–8 (**no. 342**), Ranulf III granted the monks of Coventry the right to send two carts twice daily to his woods to collect such timber as they needed for repairs, fuel and hedging. Subsequently, he is said to have given them 280 acres of woodland and waste in lieu of one of these carts. Of the three charters dealing with this exchange two (**nos. 344, 345**) are later fabrications, and the present charter, as it stands, is also undoubtedly a forgery. It is, however, just possible – though by no means certain – that it may be based on a genuine charter. It seems unlikely, in the first place, that the monks simply invented the exchange. Secondly, the way the grant is described – 'a certain portion' of the earl's wood 'estimated' at 280 acres, but not otherwise specified except that it lies somewhere within the boundaries of Exhall and Keresley – is hardly the formulation a forger would have chosen. It therefore seems possible that Ranulf III authorized the exchange, probably some time between 1208 and 1215. If so, the forger then elaborated his charter, first by adding specific boundaries, and then by setting out in detail the right of the monks to enclose, cultivate, etc., the land 'in perpetuity', when and as they wished, without interference from the earl's heirs and tenants. This reference to the earl's heirs and tenants (repeated in the final clause of the charter) points to the date of the forgery, either around 1250, when Prior William was actively laying hands on woodlands and waste around Coventry at the expense of the local freeholders and tenants (J. Lancaster, *Medieval Coventry – a City Divided?* p. 18), but more probably between 1334 and 1346, when Queen Isabella (as the earl's heir) and the tenants combined to challenge the prior throughout the manor of Coventry from Keresley to Exhall (*ibid.*, pp. 8, 56–7). The latter view is supported by the fact that the monks obtained a royal confirmation of their charters in 1348, containing this and a number of other forgeries; it was evidently obtained to ward off the attack and substantiate the priory's alleged rights. Not surprisingly, many of the charters it recites must be viewed with suspicion.

344. Declaration setting out in detail the boundaries of the 280 acres of woodland and waste, to be measured by a perch of 25 feet, which he has granted in free alms to the monks of Coventry. [Spurious]

[1208–1215]

P.R.O., C.53 (Chancery Charter Rolls), no. 135, m. 4;
B.L. Add. MS. 32100, f. 61v.–62. Ed.: *Cal. Ch. Rolls*, v.
104 (no. 17); Coss, no. 18.

For a full text of this document, see Coss, *The Early Records of Medieval Coventry*, p. 24–5 (no. 18).

This is not a genuine charter of Ranulf III. The address, with the constable and *dapifer* following the barons, justiciar and sheriff, is quite irregular. The witness-list, implying a date c.1208–1215, has been put together from **nos. 342** and **343**. Presumably the explanation for it is that the boundaries set out in **no. 343** were not precise enough or needed bringing up to date. Its actual date is uncertain, but it was probably one of the charters fabricated, c.1340, when the prior's position in Coventry and the surrounding countryside was under attack.

345. Release and remission to the prior and monks of Coventry of any and every right he or his predecessors possessed in the 280 acres of woodland and waste he had made over to them, so that neither he nor his heirs and assigns would ever be able to claim any right in them in future. [Spurious]

[1208–1215]

P.R.O., C.53 (Chancery Charter Rolls), no. 135, m. 4;
B.L. Add. MS. 32100, f. 62. Ed.: *Cal. Ch. Rolls.*, v. 104
(no. 18); Coss, no. 19.

For a full text of this document, see Coss, *The Early Records of Medieval Coventry*, p. 25 (no. 19).

This charter is an obvious forgery. The address to the earl's tenants and the reference to his assigns are anachronistic. The concluding malediction is ludicrously misplaced. As in **no. 344**, the names of the witnesses have been taken over from **nos. 342** and **343**. The purpose and date of the forgery are revealed by the clause prohibiting the earl's heirs or assigns from ever in future vindicating any rights in the land in question. This is a clear reference to Queen Isabella's challenge to the prior's rights and points to a date around 1340.

346.   Grant to the hospital of St. John the Baptist at Coventry of 12 acres of assarted land outside Coventry.

[1181–1217]

P.R.O., E.164/21 (Exchequer, King's Remembrancer, Misc. Books), f. 173 (Coventry Register). Ed.: Coss, no. 20.

For a full text of this document, see Coss, *The Early Records of Medieval Coventry*, pp. 25–6 (no. 20).

The hospital of St. John was founded by Edmund, archdeacon of Coventry (1161–75), with the assent of Prior Lawrence (d.1179) on the priory's fee (*V.C.H. Warws.*, ii. 109); the present grant suggests that it was subject to the priory. The charter in its abbreviated form cannot be dated, but is presumably before 1217. For the Dayville interest in Coventry, see *H.K.F.*, pp. 282–3.

347.   Grant to the hospital of St. John the Baptist at Coventry of seven acres of assarted land outside Coventry.

P.R.O., E.164/21 (Exchequer, King's Remembrancer, Misc. Books), f.173 (Coventry Register). Ed.: Coss, no. 20.

For a full text of this document, see Coss, *The Early Records of Medieval Coventry*, pp. 25–6 (no. 20).

This grant succeeds **no. 346**, to which it refers, but cannot otherwise be dated closely.

348.   Grant to Richard Davenport of freedom from suit in the county court of Cheshire and the hundred court of Northwich, and freedom from pleas in Middlewich; also from finding judgers for the aforesaid courts, and freedom from jury duties.

Leek, [1207–1213]

Orig.: J.R.U.L.M., Bromley-Davenport Muniments, Deeds, Davenports of Davenport (ii); Transcr.: P.R.O., Chester 34/1, m. 2, and Chester 34/4 (Quo Warranto 15

Hen. VII), m. 28; B.L. Harl. 2038, f. 86 (new f. 92), and Add. MS. 6032, f. 44 (new f. 23v.); Bodleian Library, Dodsworth MS. 31, f. 16 (from Quo Warranto); Shakerley MS. 3, p. 15 (also from enrolment). Ed.: Orm., iii. 62 (from original); Engl. transl.: *Ches. Sheaf.* no. 10168.

Ranulphus comes Cestrie constabulario, dapifero, iusticiario, vic(ecomiti), et omnibus baronibus suis, ministris et balivis, et omnibus hominibus suis presentem cartam visuris vel audituris salutem. Sciatis me dedisse et concesscisse[1] et presenti carta mea confirmasse Ricardo de Daunepord et heredibus suis in perpetuum de me et de heredibus meis quietanciam secte comitatus mei Cestrie et hundredi mei de Norwyko et placitorum meorum de Medio Wyko, et quietanciam iudicis inveniendi ad predictum comitatum et ad hundredum, et quietum de iureys, reddendo mihi et heredibus meis annuatim ad cameram meam Cestrie quedam calcaria deaurata vel sex denarios in nativitate beati Iohannis baptiste. Hiis testibus Philippo de Oreby tunc iusticiario meo, Hugone dispensario, Petro clerico, Warino de Vernon, Willelmo de Venablis, Roberto Patric, Hamone de Mascy, Ricardo de Aldeford, Lydulfo de Twamlaue, Ricardo Phiton, et multis aliis, apud Lech.

SEAL, on tag; broken, device and legend perished.[2]

1. sic orig.
2. According to a note referred to by Ormerod (iii. 64), and a confirmation by the Black Prince in 1353 (*Ches. Sheaf*, no. 10168) the seal was accidentally broken by a clerk, when the charter was being exhibited in the Black Prince's court, and was then joined together and sewn in parchment to preserve it.

The recipient of the present charter was grandson of the Richard Davenport upon whom Earl Hugh II conferred the head forestership of the forest of Leek and Macclesfield (**no. 176**). It must date from some time between Philip of Orreby's accession to the justiciarship, probably in 1207, and the death of Richard of Aldford in 1213. For suit of court and the duty of finding 'judgers' or 'doomsmen', with the duty of declaring law and custom, see Stewart-Brown, *Calendar of County Court, City Court and Eyre Rolls of Chester*, pp. xxxii–xxxviii.

349. Grant of liberties to the borough of Leek.

[1207–1215]

P.R.O., CHES 29/25 (Plea Rolls, 6 Edw. II), m. 37; B.L. Harl. MS. 1985, f. 189v. (from Plea Roll). Engl. transl.: Sleigh, *History of the Ancient Parish of Leek,* p. 16; cf. Ballard, *British Borough Charters 1042–1216*, p. xxix.

Ranulphus comes Cestrie omnibus tam futuris quam presentibus, ad quos presens scriptum pervenerit, salutem. Notum sit vobis me dedisse et concessisse et presenti carta mea confirmasse liberis burgensibus meis manentibus in burgo meo de Lech has libertates subscriptas, scilicet quod quilibet predictorum burgensium habeat dimidiam acram terre ad mansuram suam et unam acram in campis, et in foresta mea de Lech maeremium ad edificia sua et boscum ad focum suum per visum forestariorum meorum, et pasturam communem ad omne genus pecudum in pastura ad manerium meum de Lech pertinente.

Et quod predicti burgenses mei de Lech per totum Cestrisiram sint liberi et quieti de tolneio in aquis, in villis et in omnibus locis, et etiam in civitate Cestrie, de omnibus marchandisis, excepto sale in Wychis. Et quod quieti sint de pasnagio per totam communam manerii mei de Lech, et quod blada sua ad molendina mea molant statim post illud quod erit in tremina et ad vicesimum granum.

Et quod omnes qui ad forum et ad nundinas predicti burgi mei convenerint, quieti sint per idem tolneium quod in aliis liberis mercatis datur in comitatu Staffordie.

Et burgenses predicti per primos tres annos quieti erunt de firma, et post tres annos elapsos reddet quilibet eorum duodecim denarios de firma per annum pro omni servicio mihi pertinente, et quietus erit de omni misericordia, que ad predictam villam pertinet, pro duodecim denariis.

Et predicti burgenses per semetipsos prepositum sibi facient per assensum et consilium meum aut ballivi mei.

Et liceat cuilibet burgensi burgagium suum dare aut vendere cuicumque voluerit, nisi religioni, salvo tolneio, scilicet quatuor denariis, et salvo redditu meo.

Et volo quod predicti burgenses mei sint tam liberi ut sunt liberiores burgenses de aliquo burgo de Staffordesiria. Hiis testibus Philippo de Orreby tunc iusticiario meo, Henrico de Aldytheleghe, Warino de Vernon, Willelmo de Venables, Hamone de Masci, Petro clerico, Liulpho vicecomite, Ricardo Phiton, et multis aliis.

This charter falls after 1207, when Ranulf III was granted a market and fair at his manor of Leek (*H.K.F.*, p. 256), but is not otherwise easy to date. Liulf of Twemlow seems to have ceased to function as sheriff by 1215, if not earlier (*E.C.C.*, p. 46). For Henry of Audley (Aldithley), see **no. 395.**

350. Confirmation to Norton priory of the gifts of William fitz Nigel, the constable, and his heirs, and of two houses in Chester on the eastern side of St. Michael's church, and grant of freedom from shires and hundreds, and all other exactions and secular services.

[1207–1217]

P.R.O., E.40 (Exchequer, Ancient Deeds, Series A), no. 203.

Ranulfus comes Cestrie constabulario, iustic(iario), baronibus, vicecom(iti), ministris et balivis, et omnibus hominibus suis Francis et Anglis salutem. Sciatis me concessisse et presenti carta mea confirmasse deo et ecclesie beate Marie de Nortona et canonicis ibidem deo regulariter servientibus quicquid Willelmus filius Nigelli constabularius Cestrie et heredes sui eis dederunt et concesserunt et cartis suis confirmaverunt in omnibus terris et in omnibus locis, prout carte eorum testantur. Concedo etiam eidem ecclesie duas mansuras in Cestria, que sunt de meo feodo, quas ipsi canonici emerunt, que sunt iuxta ecclesiam sancti Michaelis ex parte orientali, liberas, solutas et quietas ab omnibus secularibus serviciis et exactionibus. Volo autem et precipio quod tota terra predictorum canonicorum et ipsi et homines sui, ubicumque fuerint et manserint in mea baliva, sint liberi, soluti et quieti de syris et hundredis, placitis et querelis, et omnibus ausiliis[1] et geldis et castellorum operationibus, et de omnibus exactionibus et secularibus serviciis et omnibus aliis rebus in perpetuum, sicut elemosina sancte ecclesie[2] data, ita etiam ut predicti canonici de omnibus terris et hominibus suis mihi aut alicui meorum non resspondeant,[1] nisi solummodo de servicio dei et oracionibus faciendis pro salute anime mee et omnium fidelium. Prohibeo etiam ne servientes mei ullo modo presumant per terras et homines predictorum canonicorum, ubicumque manserint, cibum capere vel hospitari vel aliquam molestiam illis vel hominibus suis inferre. Hiis testibus Philippo de Horrebi iusticiario Cestrie, Gwarino de Vernona, Iohanne de Preaus, Thoma dispensatore, Henrico fratre eius, Normanno Pantou, Willelmo de Heseleie, Thoma de Horrebi, Petro clerico comitis, Ranulfo persona de Frodesham, Thoma clerico comitis, Ioceram de Helhesbi, Ricardo de Kingesleie, Radulfo de Suleni, et multis aliis.

SEAL: missing.

1. *sic orig.*
2. *om. orig.*

Ranulf II freed Norton priory from gelds, castlework and other exactions (**no. 81**), and many phrases from his charter are reproduced verbatim in the present confirmation; but, surprisingly, Ranulf III's confirmation is the only other earl's charter for Norton that survives. The writing is the same as that of Prior Ranulf's charter for Adam of Dutton (c.1195–1205), reproduced in facsimile in *E.C.C.*, no. 11, and the document was evidently produced by the canons, but there is no reason to doubt its authenticity. Its date falls between 1207 and 1217, but cannot be more accurately determined.

351.   Grant to William son of Gerard of 128 acres in the assarts beyond Quorndon (Leics.) and other small parcels of land in the vicinity.

[1207–1217]

Orig.: Huntington Library, San Marino, Calif., Hastings MSS., Quorndon no. 376 (HAD 1748). Ed.: *Hist. MSS. Comm., Report on the MSS. of R.R. Hastings*, i. 67.

Rannulfus comes Cestrie omnibus presentibus et futuris salutem. Sciatis me dedisse et concessisse et hac carta mea concessisse Guillelmo filio Gerardi pro homagio et servicio suo sexcies viginti acras et octo in essartis meis ultra Querendonam, mensuratas per perthicam sexdecim pedum, scilicet totam terram meam de Suinehaga, que iacet inter Stanwalbroc et inter terram Petri filii Nicholai in Littlehaga et inter predictum Stanwalbroc et meam culturam, quam habeo in Sui[nehaga in latit]udine,[1] sicut mete apparent, quas homines mei fecerunt, quando perambulaverunt alam terra[rum][1] inter me et illum, et inter Monifalgate et sepem meam de parco meo de Querendona in longtitudine, salvis mihi duabus acris, que iacent propinquiores sepi mee de parco meo,mensuratis per perthicam sexdecim pedum, quas ad opus meum retineo, et totam terram meam, quam habui in Haverwic, que terra perficit dictas sexcies viginti acras et octo. Preterea dedi eidem W. filio Gerardi duas virgatas terre in Querendona, quas scilicet Hervisius filius Cecilie et Rogerus Dod de me tenuerunt, Hervisius unam et Rogerus aliam, cum eisdem hominibus et sequela illorum, et insuper unam acram iuxta Stanwach ad edificium suum faciendum, habendas et tenendas illi et heredibus suis de me et heredibus meis libere et quiete et honorifice et integre, cum omnibus que ad dictam terram infra villam et extra pertinere debeat, reddendo inde mihi et heredibus meis annuatim unum par calcarium deauratorum vel sex denarios in festo sancti Martini pro omni servicio et exactione seculari. Testibus Philippo de Orrebi [tunc][2] iusticiario Cestrie, Hugone dispensario, Guillelmo Picot, Thoma et Henrico, Roberto, Galfrido dispensariis, Steph[ano de Segrava, Hasculfo de S][1]uligneio, Normanno Pantuf, Magistro Hugone[3] de Cestria, Hugone Martel, et aliis multis.

SEAL: on cords, lion seal, device complete, legend missing.

1.   orig. torn and defective.
2.   Tear in original.
3.   Name omitted, orig.

It seems unlikely, but is not impossible, that William son of Gerard was the same William who held lands at Saham (Saughall Massie) in Wirral (**no. 352**). This holding was confirmed by Ranulf III between 1207 and 1217, and the present charter must have been issued during the same time-span.

352. Confirmation to William son of Gerard of four bovates of land in Saham (Saughall Massie) in Wirral, which he had received from Alan of Tatton and Petronilla his wife for his homage and service.

[1207–1217]

Orig.: J.R.U.L.M., Rylands Charter 1783. Ed.: Tyson, *Handlist of Charters, Deeds and Similar Documents in the possession of the John Rylands Library*, ii. 125.

Rannulfus comes Cestrie constabulario, dapifero, iusticiario, vicecomiti et omnibus baronibus et fidelibus suis, ministris et baillivis, et omnibus ad quos presens scriptum pervenerit salutem. Sciatis me concessisse et presenti carta mea confirmasse Willelmo filio Gerardi et heredibus suis quatuor bovatas terre in Saham in Wirhallia cum omnibus pertinenciis suis, et Ricardum et Siwardum, qui terram illam tenuerunt, cum eorum sequela tota, quas Alanus de Tattona et Petronilla uxor sua ei pro humagio suo dederunt et carta sua confirmaverunt, faciendo predictis Alano et Petronille et eorum heredibus servicium annuum, quod in eorum cartis continetur, quas ipse Willelmus de eis habere meruit. Hiis testibus Philippo de Orreby tunc iusticiario meo, Petro clerico meo, Iohanne de Pratellis, Normanno Pantulf, Willelmo de Haselwelle, Alano de Waleia, Roberto Lancelin, Willelmo de Dunvilla, Roberto de Pulle, Turstano Banastre, Hugone de Corona, Gileberto de Bernestona, Hugone de Rabi, Matheo de Thorintona, et multis aliis.

SEAL: on tag, lion seal.

The descent of the Gerards, as Ormerod observed (ii. 129) is 'beset with difficulties', but it would seem that the recipient of the present grant is the first, speculation apart, of whom we have definite knowledge. He was probably the father of the William fitz Gerard who married Emma, daughter and coheiress of Richard Kingsley and founded the family's fortunes.[1] There is also no evidence of the interest of Alan of Tatton (Orm., i. 439) in Saughall Massie. The long list of local Wirral witnesses unfortunately does not help to fix the date of this charter, but it must fall between 1207 and 1217.

1. Ormerod (ii. 131) makes him Emma's husband, but the dates virtually exclude this possibility.

353. Charter for William son of Gerard, granting him housebot, haybot and furbot in all his lands, and quittance from suit of county and hundred courts. [Spurious]

[c.1210–1215]

P.R.O., CHES 29/31 (Plea Rolls, 11 Edw. II), m. 4v; CHES 33/4 (Forest Rolls, 20–21 Edw. III), m. 32v; D.L. 39/1/19 (Forest Pleas, 21 Edw. III), m. 28v. From enrolment, B.L. Harl. MS. 2038, f. 64v. (old f. 54v.)

Sciant presentes et futuri quod ego Ranulfus comes Cestrie dedi et concessi et hac presenti carta mea confirmavi Willelmo filio Gerardi libertates, scilicet housbote et haybote et furbote, in omnibus terris meis ubicumque terram habuit sive habere poterit, altum vel validum sine visu forestariorum, preterea adquietacionem curie sectacionis et de comitatu et de hundredo et de omnimodis placitis, atque licenciam, terram perquirendi in omnibus terris meis sine calumpnia de me vel heredum meorum, habendas et tenendas de me et heredibus meis sibi et heredibus suis libere, quiete, pacifice et hereditarie pro omni servicio seculari et exaccione ac demanda, salvo servicio carte sue feoffacionis. Et ego dictus Ranulfus et heredes mei dictas libertates predicto Willelmo et heredibus suis vel assignatis suis contra omnes gentes warantizabimus, adquietabimus et defendemus. Et ut hec mea donacio, concessio et confirmacio rata et stabilis imperpetuum permaneat, presens scriptum sigilli mei impressione roboravi. Hiis testibus domino Rogero de Monte Alto, domino Philippo de Herreby, domino Hugone dapifero, domino Warino de Vernoun, Hamone de Mascy, Willelmo de Venables, Normanno Pantun, David clerico de Malpas, Ricardo de Kyngesleya, et aliis.

Like many charters found only in later pleadings, this is of very doubtful authenticity. The form and language are distinctly irregular (*sectacionis, feoffacionis, adquietabimus, altum et validum*). The reference to 'assigns' is anachronistic, if the supposed date of the charter is c.1210–15. The title or prefix *dominus* becomes common c.1230, but is virtually unknown (except in the case of abbots) twenty years earlier. It is difficult to establish the supposed date. As Philip of Orreby appears without the title justiciar, it is presumably earlier than 1208 at latest; but Roger of Montalt only succeeded his brother Robert c.1211 (*E.C.C.*, p. 17; *H.K.F.*, p. 111). Hugh *dapifer* (in all manuscripts) is almost certainly a mistake for Hugh *dispensarius*. Taking all considerations into account, the charter must be written off as a fourteenth-century forgery.

354. Confirmation of Hugh de Pascy's gift to Joel of Norbury, son of Traher, of 25 acres in the wood of Norbury.

[1207–1217]

Orig.: Cheshire Record Office, Cholmondeley Deeds, Box B, no. 377.

R. comes Cestrie omnibus presentibus et futuris ad quos presens scriptum pervenerit, salutem. Sciatis me ratam et gratam habere et presenti carta confirmare donacionem quam Hugo de Pasci fecit Iohaelo de Norbiri filio Traher et heredibus suis de viginti et quinque acris terre in nemore de Norbiri, scilicet inter Norbiri et Wenneslegh, habendis et tenendis in feodo et hereditate libere et quiete cum omnibus pertinenciis, libertatibus et aisiamentis ad predictam terram pertinentibus, sicut carta predicti Hugonis de Pascy, quam idem Iohael inde habet, testatur. Testibus Philippo de Orrebi tunc iusticiario Cestrie, Guarino de Vernona, Guillelmo de Venabulis, Rogero de Meinilguarin, Hugone dispensatore, Iohanne de Ardene, P. clerico domini comitis, David de Malo Passu, Ricardo de Rodestorn, Ricardo de Kagwurde, Guillelmo clerico, Fulcone, et multis aliis.

SEAL: on tag, missing.

The early history of Norbury (Orm., iii. 462) is almost totally deficient and, apart from this hitherto unpublished charter, nothing appears to be known of Joel son of Traher. It also appears to be the only known evidence that Hugh of Pascy was a landholder in Cheshire. He was killed during the civil war in 1216 (*Ann. Cestr.*, p. 50), but the present confirmation could have been made before or after his death, and can only be dated very approximately between 1207 and 1217. Hugh's charter is also in the Cholmondeley deeds (Box B, no. 376); it is interesting because it is sealed on the reverse with the earl's counterseal.

355. Agreement between Earl Ranulf and Robert of Legbourne, by which the latter, in return for the earl's paying his debt of 110 marks to the Jews of Lincoln, conveyed to the earl his lands of Raithby and Hallington (Lincs.) for a term of 20 years, beginning on 3 May 1208.

Lincoln, [1208]

P.R.O., D.L. 42/2 (Coucher Book II), f. 249v. (Bolingbroke no. 87).

Sciant omnes tam futuri quam presentes quod hec est conventio facta inter

Ranulphum comitem Cestrie et Robertum de Lecheburun, scilicet quod predictus Robertus pro centum et decem marcis argenti, de quibus dictus comes eum adquietavit versus Iudeos Lincolnie, tradidit predicto comiti totas terras suas de Retheby et de Halingtona cum omnibus redditibus earundem terrarum tam in hominibus quam in terris et cum omnibus pertinenciis suis in villa et extra villam habendas et tenendas ab invencione sancte crucis proxima postquam Henricus filius domini Iohannis regis Anglie natus fuit apud Wintoniam usque in viginti annos completos, salvo servicio Thome Manselli, scilicet unam marcam argenti per annum. Et si contigat ecclesiam de Rethebi vacare infra dictos viginti annos, dictus comes eam dabit cui eam dare voluerit, salva donacione eiusdem ecclesie predicto Roberto et heredibus suis post predictum terminum completum. Et predictus Robertus et heredes sui has dictas terras warantizabimus predicto comiti et heredibus suis, vel cui eas assignare voluerit, de dote et de omnibus aliis rebus usque ad terminum predictum. Si vero Iudeus aliquis aut Christianus debita petierit a predicto Roberto vel heredibus suis infra dictum terminum, ipse Robertus et heredes sui super alias terras suas capient ea reddenda, ut nulla districtio propter hoc fiat super terras predictas, quas dictus Robertus tradidit predicto comiti. Completo autem termino viginti annorum, predicte terre ad predictum Robertum et ad heredes suos revertentur quiete de predicto comite et heredibus suis. Et ut hec convencio firmiter et legaliter teneatur et observetur, ego Robertus de Lecheburun eam presenti scripto et sigilli mei apposicione confirmavi. Hiis testibus Gisleberto de Beningwurthe, Gaufrido de Saucensemara, Philippo de Orreby, Iordano de Brakenberga, Henrico de Aldithelega, Waltero de Daivilla, Waltero de Coventreia, Helya pincerna, Hugone de Sais, Stephano de Segrava, Willelmo filio Warini, et multis aliis apud Lincolniam.

The agreement was presumably made on, or shortly before, 3 May 1208. For Robert of Legbourne, see *H.K.F.*, pp. 107–8. Gilbert of Beningworth's son, William, married the eldest daughter of Geoffrey de Saucesmare (ibid., p. 180). The appearance of Philip of Orreby without the title justiciar is noteworthy. If trustworthy, it is further evidence (see **nos. 296, 337, 341**) that he did not become justiciar before 1208.

356.   Confirmation of Richard of Aldford's grant of Gawsworth to Herbert of Orreby and his wife Lucia.

Chester, [1208–1213]

London, College of Arms, MS. 1 D. 14, p. 269 ('ex evidenciis Edwardi Fyton de Gouseworth militis'). Short notice (in English): *Ches. Sheaf*, no. 4512.

Ranulphus comes Cestrie omnibus presentibus et futuris ad quos presens scriptum pervenerit, salutem. Sciatis me concessisse et presenti carta mea confirmasse Hereberto de Orreby et Lucie uxori sue Gousewrthe cum pertinentiis, illis et heredibus suis habendum et tenendum ita libere et quiete sicut continetur in carta Ricardi de Aldeford, quam de eo habent. Testibus Philippo de Orreby, Henrico de Aldithleghe, Iohanne de Pratellis, Hamone de Mascy, Willelmo de Venabulis, Willelmo de Haselwell, Lidulfo de Tuamlowe, Thoma clerico de Malsoneby, et multis aliis apud Cestriam.

Nothing is known of the descent of Gawsworth between its conferment on Hugh son of Bigod by Ranulf II (**no. 43**) and the charter of Richard of Aldford which is here confirmed. Richard died in 1213 (*Ches. Sheaf*, no. 10136), and the fee of Aldford was then granted to John of Ardern (**no. 374**), from whose heirs Gawsworth continued to be held. Herbert of Orreby was a member of the same Lincolnshire family as the famous justiciar, Philip of Orreby, perhaps (as Ormerod surmised) Philip's younger brother, and it is possible that his wife Lucia was granddaughter and heiress of Hugh son of Bigod; but the descent is far from clear, and Ormerod's pedigree (iii. 548) must be treated, as Farrer pointed out (*H.K.F.*, p. 99), with considerable reserve. Richard of Aldford's charter was witnessed, among others, by Philip of Orreby as justiciar (Orm., iii. 547), and therefore presumably falls within the period 1207–13. The date of Earl Ranulf's confirmation cannot be accurately determined, and it is impossible to say for certain whether it was given before or after Richard of Aldford's death, but probably it falls in the same period.[1] Thomas the clerk, of Melsonby, who witnesses another charter of 1208–13 (**no. 282**) as *clericus meus*, was presumably identical with the Thomas who occurs twice as chancellor (**nos. 247, 289**), and had an important place in Ranulf III's administration down to c.1210. Melsonby is in Yorkshire (N.R.), and Thomas perhaps entered Ranulf's service when he was earl of Richmond.

1. The existing text is evidently abbreviated, and the dating is confused by the fact that the copyist has left out Philip of Orreby's designation as justiciar.

357.   Charter disafforesting Thomas Despenser's fee of Barrow (co. Chester) and granting him exemption from puture and permission to take all wild animals found within the fee.

[1208–1214]

Orig.: Cheshire Record Office, Cholmondeley Deeds, Box G, no. 2. Transcr.: P.R.O., D.L. 39/1/19 (Forest Pleas, 21 Edw. III), m. 27; Chester 33/4 (Forest Rolls, 21 Edw. III), m. 19 (incomplete) and m. 31; B.L. Harl. MS. 2074 (from inspeximus of Edward VI), f. 143v. (old f.

239v.). Cited (without text) Bodleian Library, Rawlinson
MS. B. 114, p. 112, 'ex originali charta Ranulfi comitis
Cestriae penes vicecomitem Rocksavage'. Brief abstract:
Orm., ii. 339 (from Harl. 2074), and *Ches. Sheaf*, no.
6762.

R. comes Cestrie universis presentibus et futuris salutem. Sciatis me defores-
tasse totam terram et feodum Thome dispensatoris de Barewa cum omnibus
pertinenciis eiusdem ville in bosco, in plano, et in omnibus aliis locis. Quietam
etiam clamavi totam terram dictam et feodum de Barewa a potura servientum,
ita quod nulli servientes nec forestarii poturam in predicta terra vel feodo
exigere poterunt. Concessi etiam prefato Thome dispensario libertatem capiendi
omne genus bestiarum silvestrium in terram aut feodum de Barewe intrancium.
Supradictam libertatem memorato T. dispensatori et heredibus suis concessi et
dedi adeo liberam sicut liberior esse poterit, habendam et tenendam de me et
heredibus meis inperpetuum. Et ut hec mea concessio perpetuam habeat
firmitatem, eam hac carta mea et sigillo meo roboravi. Testibus H. abbate
Cestrie, R. de Monte Alto senescallo Cestrie, Philippo de Orreby tunc iusticiario Cestrie, Gwillelmo de Venabulis, Gwarrino de Vernona, Hamone de
Masci, Rogero de Meinilgarin, Roberto Patric, Hugone despensatore, Gualtero
de Daivilla, Iohanne de Ardene, Hugone de Duttun, Petro clerico, Hugone de
Pasci, David de Malo Passu, Joceram de Hellesby, Ricardo filio Liuf, Ricardo de
Kingesleghe, Henrico de Wevre, Galfrido de Duttun, Gwarino filio Gwarini de
Vernona, et multis aliis.

Barrow (later divided into the manors of Great and Little Barrow) was situated
in the forest of Mondrem and Mara, and was from the time of the Domesday
survey part of the fee of the constables of Chester. There is no record of how or
when it came into the hands of the Despensers. Thomas Despenser, the
beneficiary of the present grant, died in 1218 and was succeeded by his younger
brother Hugh, one of the witnesses (*H.K.F.*, p. 59). The present charter must
fall between the election of Abbot Hugh in 1208 and the death of Hugh de Pascy,
who was killed in 1216 (*Ann. Cestr.*, p. 50). If it were possible to identify R. de
Monte Alto, the steward, it might be possible to narrow the date, but in any case
it is unlikely to be after 1214, and is perhaps a little earlier.

358.   Grant to Stephen of Segrave of all his land in Kegworth (Leics.) of the fee
of Robert son of Nigel, namely eight virgates, and of his holding in the
field of Langley, except for the advowson of the church, which the earl
retains; to be held free of all service except scutage at the rate of 3s. when
the scutage on a knight's fee is 20s.

[1208–1214]

Orig.: Berkeley Castle, Gloucs., Fitzhardinge charters,
no. 152. Short abstracts: B.L. Harl. MS. 4748 (Segrave
cartulary), f. 8v., no. lix, and f. 9, no. lix. From Segrave
cartulary, Nichols, *Leicestershire*, II. i. 110, and III. ii.
349; Engl. abstract: Jeayes, *Berkeley Charters*, p. 54 (from
orig.).

Rannulfus comes Cestrie omnibus tam presentibus quam futuris, ad quos
presens scriptum pervenerit, salutem. Notum sit vobis me concessisse et dedisse
Stephano de Segrave pro homagio et servicio suo totam terram, quam habui in
villa de Cagwurth de feodo Roberti filii Nigelli, scilicet servicium octo virgat-
arum terre in eadem villa cum homagiis et serviciis liberum tenencium de eodem
feodo, et quicquid habui in campo de Langleia cum omnibus pertinenciis
eiusdem terre in bosco et in plano et in omnibus aliis locis, excepta advocatione
ecclesie, quam mihi retineo. Et hec omnia predicta dedi et concessi predicto
Stephano, habenda et tenenda sibi et heredibus suis de me et de heredibus meis
libere et quiete ab omnibus serviciis, faciendo forinsecum servicium quod ad
predictam terram pertinet, scilicet quod, quando feodum militis reddit viginti
solidos de scutagio, tunc reddet ipse de predicta terra tres solidos. Et ut hec
donatio mea firma permaneat et stabilis, eam presenti scripto et sigillo meo
confirmavi. Hiis testibus Philippo de Orreby tunc iusticiario Cestrie, Hugone
dispensario, Waltero de Dayvilla, Roberto Patric, Aluredo de Soleigneio,
Thoma de Tuschet, Roberto de Hardreshulle, Henrico de Cagwurth, Roberto
Samsone, et multis aliis.

SEAL: obverse, lion seal; reverse, gem counterseal, a
man seated on a chair, legend: SE[CRETUM SIGIL-
LUM] COMITIS CESTRIE.

Robert fitz Nigel died in 1185 (**no. 266**) without direct heirs, and it appears that
his land in Kegworth escheated to the earl. The present charter, of which Robert
Patric is a witness, must be earlier in date than **no. 359**, by which time Robert
was dead and his heir William was in the earl's custody. As Philip of Orreby did
not become justiciar before 1207 (**nos. 296, 341**) or even 1208 (**no. 355**), it was
probably granted in the period 1208–1214, and was thus one of the earlier of the
numerous grants made to Stephen of Segrave in the course of his long and
successful career. For the advocacy of the church of Kegworth, which Earl
Ranulf here retains for his own use, see **nos. 359** and **360.** It was later made over
to Stephen (**no. 361**), but probably not until after 1217.

359. Grant of the church of Kegworth (Leics.) to his clerk, Ralph Vernon, one
half by reason of the wardship of William Patric, a boy in the earl's

keeping, and the other half the patronage of which Robert Neville and Matilda his wife had remitted to the earl in his court at Chester.

[1215–1216]

> Orig.: Berkeley Castle, Gloucs., Fitzhardinge charters, no. 150. Short notice in Segrave cartulary (B.L. Harl. MS. 4748), f. 8v., no. lii. References: Nichols, *Leicestershire*, II. i. 110, and III. ii. 349 (from Segrave cartulary); Jeayes, *Berkeley Charters*, p. 53 (Engl. abstract, incomplete list of witnesses.)

Omnibus sancte matris ecclesie filiis presentibus et futuris presentem cartam inspecturis et audituris Rannulfus comes Cestrie eternam in domino salutem. Noverit universitas vestra me mere pietatis intuitu et pro salute anime mee et pro animabus antecessorum meorum et successorum, quantum ad patronum pertinet, dedisse et concessisse et presenti carta mea confirmasse Radulfo de Vernona clerico meo ecclesiam de Kagworthia totam cum omnibus pertinenciis et libertatibus suis, habendam et tenendam in puram et perpetuam elemosinam, unam scilicet medietatem racione custodie Willelmi Patricii pueri in custodia mea tunc existentis, et alteram medietatem, ad quam Thomas Patricius admissus fuit et institutus ad presentationem Roberti de Nevilla et Matillidis de Spuz uxoris sue, cuius etiam medietatis ius patronatus predicti Roberti et Matildis mihi et heredibus meis de se et de heredibus suis cum feudis militum ad eos pertinentibus in curia mea apud Cestriam in perpetuum remiserunt et quietum clamaverunt. Et ut hec mea concessio perpetue firmitatis robur optineat, eam presenti scripto et sigillo meo corroboravi. Hiis testibus domino H. abbate Cestrie, domino R. abbate de Deulecresse, Philippo de Orrebi tunc iusticiario meo, Henrico de Aldithlea, Willelmo de Venables, Hugone dispensario, Thoma dispensario, Iohanne de Arderna, Waltero de Daivilla, Aluredo de Sulingni, Hamone de Masci, Rogero et Rannulfo de Meisnilwarin, Petro clerico meo, Jocelino capellano meo, Willelmo clerico meo, magistro Hugone clerico meo, Ricardo de Roudestorne clerico, Patricio et Simone clericis, magistro Simone de Cestria persona de Dunintona, Hugone capellano, et multis aliis.

SEAL: fragment, unidentified.

The tangled story of the advowson, or patronage, of the church of Kegworth can be disentangled in part with the help of an entry in the register of Bishop Hugh of Welles (ed. Phillimore, *Canterbury and York Society*, i, p. 37). It begins with the death without heirs of Robert fitz Nigel, the earl's tenant-in-chief in Kegworth, in 1185 (**no. 266**). The succession seems to have been claimed in part by Robert's nephew, William of Halstead (*H.K.F.*, p. 79), who (according to the episcopal register) claimed the right of patronage in a moiety of the church, and also by a certain Ala, mother of Genteschin le Poher, and by Matilda, the wife of

Robert Neville (*H.K.F.*, p. 242), who are here said to have quitclaimed their right to Earl Ranulf. The origin of the Patric interest in Kegworth and in the other moiety of the church is not clear, but it may have been conferred by Ranulf III after 1185. It seems evident that Ranulf was determined to sweep aside these partial claims and bring the patronage of the whole church into his own hands; indeed, he reserved it for himself when granting Robert fitz Nigel's lands in Kegworth to Stephen of Segrave in 1208–14 (**no. 358**).

The present charter, conferring the whole church on Ralph Vernon as rector or parson, dates from 1215 or 1216. According to the statement in Hugh of Welles' register, the claim of William of Halstead, who lodged a formal appeal, was disallowed because he was under the sentence of excommunication promulgated on 7 July 1215 against the barons in revolt against King John, and Earl Ranulf's presentation was held to be valid, 'quia capitalis dominus est feodi'. In any case, the appearance as a witness of the abbot of Dieulacres shows that the charter must be later than 1214, and it is earlier than Ranulf's elevation to the earldom of Lincoln in 1217. Ralph Vernon, who was a minor and had to obtain a dispensation from the papal legate, cardinal Guala, was the son of Warin de Vernon (*H.K.F.*, p. 88), and his appointment may well have been a favour to his father, one of Earl Ranulf's close associates. It is interesting that Richard of Kegworth (**no. 360**) was already vicar in residence with an annual stipend of one bezant; Ralph was clearly non-resident.

360. Grant to Richard of Kegworth, his clerk, of half of the church of Kegworth, which Ralph Vernon, the parson of the said church, had granted to him at the earl's petition.

[1215–1216]

> Orig.: B.L. Add. Charter 20397. Short abstract: B.L. Harl. MS. 4748 (Segrave cartulary), f. 8v. no. liii. Noted from Segrave cartulary: Nichols, *Leicestershire*, II. i. 110, and III. ii. 349.

Universis sancte matris ecclesie filiis presentibus et futuris presentem cartam inspecturis et audituris Ranulphus comes Cestrie, patronus ecclesie de Kagwrthe, eternam in domino salutem. Noverit universitas vestra me mere pietatis intuitu et pro salute anime mee et antecessorum meorum et successorum, quantum ad patronum pertinet, concessisse et presenti carta mea confirmasse Ricardo de Kagwrthe clerico meo medietatem ecclesie de Kagwrthe cum omnibus pertinenciis et aisiamentis et libertatibus suis, quam Radulfus de Vernun eiusdem ecclesie persona ad peticionem meam ei concessit et carta sua confirmavit, habendam et tenendam ipsi Ricardo inperpetuum adeo libere et quiete sicut continetur in carta predicti Radulfi de Vernun, quam ipse Ricardus de ea habet. Et ut hec mea concessio perpetue firmitatis robur optineat, eam presenti scripto et sigillo meo dignum duxi communire. Hiis testibus domino H. abbate Cestrie, domino R. abbate de Deulecresse, Philippo de Orrebi tunc iusticiario meo, Warino de Vernun, Willelmo de Venables, Hamone de Masci, Rogero et Rannulfo de Meisnilwarin, Henrico de Adithlea, Iohanne de Arderna, Hugone et Thoma dispensariis, Waltero de Daivilla, Aluredo de Sulingni, Petro clerico meo, magistro H. et Willelmo de Stoke et Ricardo de Roudestorne clericis meis, magistro Simone de Cestria persona de Dunintona, magistro Thoma de sancto Nicholao, Patricio et Simone clericis, Hugone capellano, magistro Iohanne capellano de Barrua, et multis aliis.

SEAL: missing.

Richard of Kegworth was already vicar when Ranulf III gave the church of Kegworth to Ralph Vernon (**no. 359**), and it is hard to think of any reason why he should not have been given a moiety of the church at that time, if that was the intention, particularly as the names of the witnesses indicate that the two charters must have been issued within a few days of each other.

No fewer than 21 out of the 24 witnesses of the present charter also witnessed **no. 359**, the only difference among the lay witnesses being the addition of Warin de Vernon, probably representing the interests of his son Ralph, and it is hard to think that this formidable array was assembled on two separate occasions. The witness list is also interesting for the very full picture it gives of Ranulf III's clerical establishment. The *Jocelino capellano meo* of **no. 359** (the only witness of that charter who does not appear in **no. 360**) was almost certainly identical with the *Jocio capellano domini comitis* of **no. 412**; Patrick the clerk was the son of the famous Peter the clerk (**no. 283**). Richard of Kegworth himself later appears as *camerarius* (**no. 409**).

361.   Grant to Stephen de Segrave of the advowson of the church of Kegworth (Leics.)

[1217–1232]

B.L. Harl. MS. 4748 (Segrave cartulary), f. 8, no. 1. Ed.: Nichols, *Leicestershire,* II. i. 110 and III. ii. 349.

Carta dicti comitis [*sc.* Ranulfi] facta Stephano de Segrave de advocatione dicte ecclesie [*sc.* de Kegworth], pertinente ad terram que fuit Roberti filii Nigelli, in eadem villa, tenendam sibi et heredibus suis dictam terram cum advocatione predicta de dicto comite et heredibus suis in augmentum tenementi sui in

Segrave, per servitium iiii^te partis feodi militis pro eisdem terris pro omnibus servitiis.

When Ranulf III granted Stephen of Segrave the land formerly of Robert fitz Nigel in Kegworth, he retained the advowson of the church for himself (**no. 358**). The present abstract in the Segrave cartulary is the only surviving evidence of his decision to make it over to Stephen of Segrave. It cannot be dated at all closely, but the notification sent to Richard of Kegworth (**no. 362**) indicates that it falls after 1217.

362. Letter notifying Richard of Kegworth that he had granted Stephen of Segrave the advowson of Kegworth church and ordering him to have Stephen as his patron in future.

[1217–1232]

> Orig.: Berkeley Castle, Gloucs., Fitzhardinge charters, no. 153. Brief abstract: B.L. Harl. MS. 4748 (Segrave cartulary), f. 8v.,no. 1v. Ed.: from Segrave cartulary, J. Nichols, *Leicestershire* III. ii. 349; from original, Jeayes, *Berkeley Charters*, p. 54.

Ranulfus comes Cestrie et Lincolnie dilecto et fideli suo, Ricardo de Kegwrth clerico, salutem. Sciatis me dedisse dilecto meo domino Stephano de Segrave advocationem ecclesie de Kegwrth, pertinentem ad terram que fuit Roberti filii Nigelli in eadem villa de Kegwrth. Quare vobis mando, quatinus decetero illum pro patrono vestro habeatis. Et in huius rei testimonium presentes litteris moris patentes sigillo meo munitas vobis mitto. Valete.

For the grant of the advowson to Stephen of Segrave, see **no. 361.** This letter presumably followed shortly after, but neither this nor **no. 361** can be closely dated.

363. Grant to Stephen of Segrave of Bretby (co. Derby) which Simon of Kyme once held, in exchange for the lands formerly given him in Great Tew (Oxon.), which he has restored to the earl.

[1225–1228]

> Orig.: Berkeley Castle, Gloucs., Fitzhardinge charters, no. 154. Cal.: Jeayes, *Berkeley Charters*, p. 54.

Ranulphus comes Cestrie et Lincolnie omnibus presentibus et futuris presentem cartam inspecturis vel audituris salutem. Sciatis me dedisse et concessisse et hac presenti carta mea confirmasse Stephano de Segrave pro homagio et servicio suo villam de Bretteby cum pertinenciis, quam Simon de Kymba aliquando de me tenuit in comitatu Derbeye, habendam et tenendam de me et de heredibus meis eidem Stephano et heredibus suis libere et quiete, plene et pacifice, cum boscis et cum omnibus aliis aisiamentis et libertatibus ad dictam terram pertinentibus infra villam et extra, faciendo inde mihi et heredibus meis ipse Stephanus et heredes sui servicium quarte partis unius militis pro omnibus serviciis et demandis universis. Et pro hac donacione et concessione mea mihi reddidit et quieteclamavit predictus Stephanus totam terram illam cum pertinenciis, quam ei prius dederam in Tywa in comitatu Oxonie. Ego siquidem et heredes mei predicto Stephano et heredibus suis dictam terram de Bretteby cum pertinenciis contra omnes gentes warantizabimus. Hiis testibus Philippo de Orreby iusticiario Cestrie, Baldewino de Ver, Radulpho de Bray, Willelmo de Vernon, Nicholao de Litteris, Iohanne Guboud, Simone et Iohanne clericis, et multis aliis.

      SEAL: missing.

Simon of Kyme died in 1220 (*H.K.F.*, p. 123), and his son and heir, Philip of Kyme, sold Bretby to Earl Ranulf for £100 some time between that date and 1226 (Jeayes, *op. cit.*, p. 53, no. 151). This charter is the only evidence that Stephen of Segrave held land in Great Tew, but it is safe to assume that it was the tenement subsequently given to Baldwin de Vere (**no. 425**). The present charter was confirmed by Henry III in 1228 (*Cal. Ch. Rolls*, i. 185) and falls in all probability between 1225 or 1226 and that date.

364.   Quitclaim to Stephen of Segrave of all suits which he and his men of Bretby, Rosliston and Cotes (Derbys.) were accustomed to do at his wapentakes of Repton and Gresley.

                         [1229–1232]

      Orig.: in possession of Rev. William Gresley, 1804; not traced. Abstracts in B.L. Harl. MS. 4748 (Segrave cartulary), f. 20. Ed.: Nichols, *Leicestershire*, III. ii. 982 (from original but abbreviated); Engl. transl.: Jeayes, *Charters and Muniments of the Gresley Family*, p. 16 (no. 46), and Jeayes, *Derbyshire Charters*, no. 1955 (witnesses incomplete).

Rannulphus comes Cestrie et Lincolnie omnibus *etc.* Relaxavi et quietas clamavi domino Stephano de Sedgrava et heredibus suis omnes sectas, quas ipsi et homines sui de Bretteby, Rostlaveston et de Cotes facere debuerunt et solebant ad wapentaca mea de Rapendon et Gresle. Testibus Willelmo de Vernon iusticiario Cestrie, Willelmo de Cantelupo, Fulcone filio Warini, Baldwino de Vere, Radulfo de Bray, Iohanne de Atya, Ricardo de Biran, Waltero de Byseboc, Ricardo de Vernon, Ricardo de Arderne, Iohanne clerico, et aliis.

As Bretby was only acquired by Stephen of Segrave shortly before 1228 (**no. 363**), the present quittance must have been granted towards the end of Ranulf III's life. Jeayes dates it, without reason given, c.1232. It falls in any case after William Vernon became justiciar in April 1229. The text as given is heavily abbreviated, but the list of witnesses is complete.

365–70. Various grants to Stephen of Segrave and his son Gilbert.

[1217–1232]

> B.L. Harl. MS. 4748 (Segrave cartulary), ff. 3v., 8, 9, 10v., 13, 15v., 22; Leicestershire entries ed. by Nichols, *Leicestershire*, II. i, App. no. xiii, pp. 109, 110, 112, 114, 117.

365. Carta Ranulphi comitis Cestrie facta Stephano de Segrave et heredibus suis de duabus carucatis terre et dimidia cum pertinentiis in Segrave, quas idem Stephanus et antecessores sui tenuerunt de dicto comite per servitium xiii. s. pro omnibus servitiis per annum, tenendis de cetero de eodem comite et heredibus suis per servitium iiii.^{te} partis unius militis apud Cestriam.[1]

366. Carta dicti comitis [*sc.* Ranulfi] facta Stephano de Segrave et heredibus suis de vii.^{xx} acris terre cum pertinentiis in Calwedon, tenendis de eodem comite et heredibus suis per servitium unius spervarii sor ad advincula sancti Petri pro omnibus servitiis.

366a. Carta dicti comitis facta eidem Stephano et heredibus suis de eadem terra, tenenda de eodem comite et heredibus suis cum communa pasture pro dominicis averiis suis et hominum suorum de Calwedon in bosco dicti comitis de Coventre per annuum servitium unius spervarii sor vel xii. d. ad festum predictum pro omni servitio.

367. Carta Ranulphi comitis Cestrie et Lincolnie facta predicto Stephano et heredibus suis de tota terra sua in Montsorell extra bailiam castri cum homagio et servitio et sequelis hominum ibidem manentium et cum furno eiusdem ville, et de communa pasture habenda in bosco de Querndon et in omnibus aliis locis pro averiis et porcis hominum predictorum, quieta de omni pannagio et demanda, sicut habere solebant quando fuerunt in manu dicti comitis, cum libero introitu et exitu, tenendis in augmentum feodi quod de ipso comite tenet in Segrave, faciendo pro dictis duabus terris de Segrave et Montsorell servitium iiii.^{te} partis feodi militis pro omni servitio.

368. Carta Ranulphi comitis Cestrie et Lincolnie facta Stephano de Segrave et heredibus suis de quadam placea unius acre in bosco suo de Aldermannes-hagh ad edificia ibidem facienda, cum pastura ad xx. vaccas et unum taurum et earum exitum, quamdiu idem exitus fuerit infra etatem trium annorum, per boscum suum, ubi homines sui de Querndon habent communam pasturam ad averia sua, tenenda de eodem comite et heredi-bus suis in augmentum tenementi, quod de eodem comite tenet in Montesorell.

369. Carta quieteclamancie Ranulphi comitis Cestrie et Lincolnie facta predicto Stephano et heredibus suis et hominibus suis manentibus super duas carucatas et et unam bovatam terre de feodo suo in Kegworth de clau-sura parci de Querndon.[2]

370. Carta Ranulphi comitis Cestrie et Lincolnie facta Gilberto de Segrave et heredibus suis de tota terra sua in Blyburg et Tunstall, tenenda de eodem comite et heredibus suis per homagium et per servitium iiii.^{te} partis unius militis pro omni servitio.

1. There is another brief abstract of this charter, apparently from the original, in Bodleian Library, Dugdale MS. 18, f. 16; but it adds nothing to the above notice.
2. This charter has been broken up topographically by the compiler of the cartulary. Entries in the same words cover 3 carucates in Segrave, 2½ carucates in Cotes-on-Soar, and 2 carucates in Diseworth; they are not reproduced here.

Apart from the charters otherwise noted (**nos. 358, 361, 363, 364**), the so-called Segrave cartulary, more accurately 'The Red Book of the Lordship of Segrave' (B.L. Harl. MS. 4748), gives abstracts of the many and various acquisitions made by Stephen of Segrave, the famous justiciar of Henry III. As they omit the names of witnesses and cannot be relied upon to distinguish between Ranulf III's title as earl of Chester and as earl of Chester and Lincoln, they cannot be dated closely; but it is probably safe to say that none falls before 1207–8, when Stephen succeeded his father, Gilbert of Segrave, and, with the possible exception of **no. 365**, all probably fall after 1217. Of the gifts listed, the most substantial is that of all the earl's land in Mountsorrel outside the castle bailey (**no. 367**), together with pasture in the wood of Quorndon, in augmentation of Stephen's fee in Seagrave. The two fees were to be held for the service of one-quarter of a knight's fee, the service previously fixed for Seagrave alone (**no. 365**), implying that Mountsorrel was granted free of extra service. The subsequent grant of an acre in Aldermanshay with pasture for twenty cows and one bull (**no. 368**) was an augmentation of the tenure in Mountsorrel, and once again appears to have been given without additional service. The land granted in Caludon, in Wyken, near Coventry (**no. 366**), was subsequently found in the hands of Stephen's son and heir, Gilbert of Segrave (*H.K.F.*, p. 282); this grant also was augmented by rights of pasture in the earl's wood of Coventry (**no. 366a**). Gilbert of Segrave himself received the lands formerly held by Hugh de Cauz in Blyborough and Dunstall, Lincs. (**no. 370**); this was probably c.1230, but the date cannot be accurately established.

371. Grant of liberties to the burgesses of Frodsham.

Chester, [1208–1215]

> P.R.O., C.53 (Chancery Charter Rolls), no. 162, m. 4; CHES 33/4 (Forest Rolls, 20–21 Edw. III), m. 26; D.L. 39/1/19 (Forest Pleas, 21 Edw. III), m. 17v.: B.L. Harl. MS. 2074, f. 168v. (new f. 65v.); Harl. MS. 2079, f. 98 (new f. 64); Harl. MS. 2115, f. 170v. (new f. 151v.); Harl. MS. 2149, f. 110 (new f. 120); Shakerley MSS. (*penes* Sir Arthur Bryant) Liber C, f. 109 (all from enrolment). Ed.: *Cal. Ch. Rolls*, v. 318; Orm., ii. 46–7.

Rannulfus comes Cestrie constabulario suo et dapifero, iusticiario, vicecomiti, baronibus, ballivis et ministris suis omnibus, et omnibus hominibus suis tam futuris quam presentibus salutem. Notum sit vobis omnibus me concessisse et hac carta mea confirmasse burgensibus meis in burgo de Frodesham manentibus et mansuris, quod unusquisque illorum habeat unum liberum burgagium in eodem burgo et unam acram terre in campis, reddendo inde annuatim duodecim denarios pro omni servicio.

Concedo eciam eisdem burgensibus quietanciam de tolneio per totam terram meam tam per aquam quam per terram, nisi de sale tantum, et quod pro nullo placito exeant foras de burgo ipso, nisi pro placitis ad gladium meum pertinentibus, et de omnibus aliis placitis iudicabuntur in ipso burgo per prepositum meum et per vicinos suos. Et si aliquis eorum inciderit in misericordiam meam pro aliquo forisfacto inter illos iudicato, quietus erit de misericordia illa per duodecim denarios, excepta forisfactura a nona diei sabbati usque ad horam primam diei lune; de qua scilicet forisfactura mihi contingunt sexaginta solidi et obolus aureus.

Concessi eciam memoratis burgensibus pasturam pecoribus suis in foresta mea et in marisco meo et in omnibus locis in quibus liberi homines mei pasturam habent, et quod habeant de foresta mea quod eis opus fuerit ad edificandum per visum forestariorum meorum.

Quare volo et firmiter precipio quod predicti burgenses et eorum heredes hec predicta habeant et teneant de me et heredibus meis libere et quiete et pacifice et plenarie, salvis mihi et heredibus meis pasnagio meo et sequela molendinorum meorum et furni mei. Et precipio omnibus ballivis meis et ministris quod predictos burgenses meos custodiant et protegant et manuteneant in predictis libertatibus et liberis consuetudinibus, et quod nullus eos super hiis vexare aut disturbare presumat super forisfacturam decem librarum. Hiis testibus Philippo de Orrebi iusticiario Cestrie, Harsculfo de Salingneio, Iohanne de Pratellis, Thoma Paganello, Petro clerico, Ricardo de Perrepunt vicecomite Cestrie, Thoma camerario Cestrie, Alexandro filio Radulfi, Josceramo de Hellesby, et multis aliis apud Cestriam.

This charter probably falls between 1208 and 1215. Hasculf of Suligny, elsewhere described as lord of Dol in Brittany, is said to have crossed over to England, presumably after Philip Augustus's conquest of Normandy, 'on account of the anger of the king of France' (Morice, *Hist. de Bretagne, Preuves* i, p. 770). He and Thomas Painel (*Paganellus*), with their following, were sent to Guernsey in 1206–7 (*P.R.S.*, N.S. xxii, p. 145), and again in 1208–9 (*ibid.*, xxiv, p. 172). For Richard of Pierrepont, sheriff of the city of Chester from c.1210 to 1215, or later, see **no. 372**. The somewhat restricted liberties granted to the burgesses of Frodsham may be compared with those for Leek (**no. 349**) and Salford (**no. 435**). The charter is another early instance (see **nos. 282** and **374**) of the reservation of the earl's pleas of the sword.

372.   Quittance to Richard Pierrepont of freedom from finding a doomsman in the portmoot of Chester for the land lying between that of Richard son of Ralph and that of Nicholas Kent.

[1208–1217]

B.L. Harl. MS. 2063 (from a 'little blacke box in the great

box of auncient deeds and evidences, 1667'), f. 69v. (old f. 148).

Rannulfus comes Cestrie constabulario, dapifero, iusticiario, vic(ecomite), baronibus, civibus suis Cestrie et ballivis suis, omnibusque presentem paginam inspecturis salutem. Sciatis me dedisse et concessisse et presenti carta mea confirmasse Ricardo de Perepunt quietanciam iudicis in portmoto meo Cestrie de terra illa que est inter terras Ricardi filii Radulfi et Nicholai de Kent,[1] illi et heredibus suis de me et heredibus meis, reddendo annuatim unum denarium de landgable in festo sancti Iohannes Baptiste. Testibus Philippo de Orreby tunc iusticiario Cestrie, Petro clerico meo, Halia pincerna, David de Malpas, Lidulfo de Tuamlaw, Ricardo filio suo, Ricardo filio Radulfi, Turstan filio Iohannis, Roberto filio Ernwi, Roberto Bras, Hamone filio With,[2] Radulfo Tardi, Roberto de Hokenhulle, Colberto de Oxton, Rogero clerico, Radulfo sarraceno, Udardo filio Matthei, Thoma camerario Cestrie, Ricardo de Rodestorn clerico, et multis aliis.

SEAL, appended on strings. Lion seal, perfect. Legend:
+ SIGILLUM · RANVLFI · COMITIS · CESTRIE.

1. Bent *MS.*
2. Wid(e) *MS.*

Richard Pierrepont, or de Perpunt, is mentioned a number of times (**nos. 249, 283, 371**; *Ches. Sheaf*, no. 4212 (5); *E.C.C.*, no. 12) as *vicecomes Cestrie* around 1210–1215. As the present charter shows, he had a landholding in Chester, and he also held land in Alvanley which he sold to Philip of Orreby (*E.C.C.*, p. 37) and two salthouses in Northwich which Earl Ranulf gave after his death to Hilton abbey, Staffs. (**no. 423**). But he was not a Cheshire man, and it seems probable that Ranulf III recruited him, like Philip of Orreby, into his service from Lincolnshire. On the authority of Ormerod (i. 70) he has usually been included in the list of sheriffs of Cheshire as successor to Liulf of Twemlow, who witnesses the present charter, and he has also been identified with Liulf's son, Richard. But neither identification is tenable, since Liulf the sheriff and Richard *vicecomes Cestrie* occur together in a charter for St. Werburgh's (**no. 232**), and another charter (*Chart. St. Werburgh*, p. 409) is witnessed simultaneously by Richard son of Liulf and Richard sheriff of Chester. The conclusion we must draw (cf. *Ches. Sheaf*, no. 6661) is that Richard de Perpunt was sheriff of the city, not of the county, of Chester, perhaps in succession to William Gamberell (*E.C.C.*, p. 28). The use of his counterseal as sheriff to warrant a private deed conveying land in Chester (*J.C.A.S.*, N.S. x, p. 19) is a good indication of his official position.

The date at which he held office cannot be accurately established, but it does not seem to extend much before 1210 or much after 1220. The present charter probably falls within approximately the same timespan, but before Ranulf III became earl of Lincoln in 1217. To judge from the witness list, it was probably given in the portmoot of Chester, since the last ten or twelve witnesses are well known citizens of Chester, most of whom are named in contemporary city deeds (nos. 2, 3, 5, 6) printed in *J.C.A.S.*, N.S. x, pp. 16–19. Thomas *camerarius* founded the Chester family of Chamberlain, frequent benefactors of St. Werburgh's abbey (*Chart. St. Werburgh*, nos. 463, 621, 622, 629, etc.), but since he is referred to elsewhere as *camerario meo* (**no. 282**) and as *camerarius domini comitis* (*E.C.C.*, no. 12) it is clear that he was actually filling the office and that the name had not yet become a patronymic.

373.   Grant to William of Barrow, the earl's reeve in Chester, of twelve acres of land between Little Saughall and Blakney wood on the bank of the Dee.

[1208–1217]

> B.L. Harl. MS. 2099, f. 516 (new f. 133) from original in the hands of James Doe of Saughall, 1656, with drawing of seal; P.R.O., CHES 2/62 (Recog. Roll, 13–14 Rich. II), m. 2 dorso. Ed.: *36th Rep. D.K.P.R.*, p. 22 (from Recognizance Roll); mentioned (without references)   .
> Orm., ii. 339, 511.

Ranulphus comes Cestrie constabulario, dapifero, iusticiario, vicecomiti et omnibus baronibus suis, ministris et ballivis, et omnibus hominibus suis et amicis presentibus et futuris salutem. Sciatis me dedisse et concessisse et presenti carta mea confirmasse Willelmo de Barwa preposito meo de Cestria et heredibus suis duodecim acras terre iacentes inter Parvam Salechale et nemus de Blakene super ripam de Dee, habendas et tenendas de me et heredibus meis pro homagio et servicio suo libere, quiete, plene et pacifice iure hereditario cum omnibus pertinentiis et libertatibus suis in bosco, in plano, in pasturis, in piscariis, in aquis, in terra arabili et non arabili, reddendo mihi et heredibus meis annuatim de predicto Willelmo et heredibus suis duos vomeres[1] ad festum sancti Michaelis pro omnibus serviciis et exactionibus universis. Hiis testibus Philippo de Orreby tunc iusticiario Cestrie, Petro clerico meo, Waltero de Daivilla, Henrico de Alditlea, Warino de Vernona, Willelmo de Venables, Hamone de Masceio, Willelmo de Haselwelle, Alexandro filio Radulfi, Thoma camerario Cestrie, Ricardo de Raudestorn clerico, Davido[2] molendinario, Willelmo munitore,[3] Ricardo clerico, et multis aliis.

SEAL: on tag, lion seal, legend missing.

1.   denarios, *Harl. MS.*   2.   Tovido *Recog. Roll.*
3.   minatore *Harl. MS.*

The date of the present charter falls between 1208, by which time Philip of Orreby was justiciar of Chester (**nos. 341, 355**), and 1217. For Thomas, chamberlain of Chester, see **no. 372**; besides this charter he witnessed two others, one for the burgesses of Frodsham (**no. 371**) and the other for Peter the clerk (**no. 282**), which fall in the same period. For William Munitor, see **no. 307**. Alexander son of Ralph is identical with Alexander, the tutor of Ranulf III (*Chart. St. Werburgh*, p. 281), who had married the granddaughter of Alan Savage of Storeton as early as the end of Hugh II's earldom (**no. 188**), and must have been an old man by this time. Perhaps the most interesting feature of this charter is the description of William of Barrow (who does not seem otherwise to be known) as the earl's reeve (*prepositus*) of Chester. This is, of course, a common office, but it has apparently not hitherto been noticed at Chester; it indicates that the city, in spite of the liberties Ranulf III granted to the citizens (**no. 256**), was still in effect a seignorial borough where, as at Frodsham (**no. 371**), the earl's reeve was in control. At Leek, on the other hand (**no. 349**), and at Salford (**no. 435**) the burgesses had the right to elect the reeve (*prepositus*) themselves, though in the former case with the earl's advice and assent.

374. Conferment upon John of Ardern of the fee of Aldford with soc and sac and other franchises, and freedom from suit of court, except only pleas of the earl's sword, for the service of two knights' fees with the bounds of Cheshire. [Spurious]

[1213–1217]

> P.R.O., CHES 34/3 (Quo Warranto, 15 Henr. VII), m. 17, and m. 41v.; hence B.L. Harl. 2074, f. 70 (old f. 173); Harl. 2115, f. 152 (old f. 178); Add MS. 6082, f. 57 (new f. 30); Add. MS. 19517, f. 5 (new f. 3); Shakerley MSS., Liber C., f. 160v.; Tabley MSS., Sir Peter Leycester's Liber D., p. 150. Ed.: Orm., ii. 754–5 (abbreviated).

Ranulfus comes Cestrie constabulario, dapifero, iusticiario, vic(ecomiti), baronibus, militibus, ballivis, et omnibus fidelibus presentibus et futuris presentem cartam inspecturis et audituris salutem. Sciatis me dedisse, concessisse et hac presenti carta mea confirmasse Iohanni de Arderne militi meo pro homagio et servitio suo totum feudum de Audeforde cum omnibus pertinentiis suis, *cum sok et sak, tholl et them et infangtheif et outfangtheif, et cum libertate duelli habendi in curia sua, et cum iuisio ignis et agne*, et cum omnibus libertatibus et aisiamentis infra villam et extra villam, *et cum advocatione ecclesiarum et capellarum, et cum omnibus predicto feodo de Audeforde pertinentibus, scilicet cum serviciis, consuetudinibus et demandis mihi et heredibus meis pertinentibus, videlicet in putura servientium suorum per totum feodum de Audeforde, quam scilicet puturam de eodem feodo habui pro servientibus meis, et cum clausura haie, quam scilicet clausuram de predicto feodo de Audeforde habui ad haiam meam de Macclesfelde claudendam, et cum scirevestothe, stretewarde, revegelde, frithmote, et cum tolneto dee toto feodo de Audeforde cum pertinentiis per totam Cestrescire, tam infra nundinas quam extra*, habendum et tenendum sibi et heredibus suis, *vel suis assignatis*, de me et heredibus meis in feodo et hereditate libere et quiete, plene et pacifice, *hereditarie* et integre, in bosco, in plano, in pratis, in pascuis, in viis, in semitis, in aquis, in stagnis, in molendinis, *in vivariis, in piscariis, in moris, in mariscis, in turbariis, in feodis militum et liberorum hominum, in dominicis, in nativis*, et in omnibus serviciis, consuetudinibus et demandis predicto feodo de Audeforde pertinentibus. Concessi etiam eidem Iohanni de Arderne et heredibus suis, *sive eius assignatis*, ut teneant predictum feodum de Audeforde cum pertinenciis de me et heredibus meis liberum et quietum de secte comitatus et hundredorum et de wichemot et de auxilio vicecomitis *et de assissis et superassissis et summonicionibus*, et de secta placitorum foreste, et de omnibus placitis et querelis mihi et heredibus meis pertinentibus, exceptis tantum placitis ad gladium meum pertinentibus, faciendo inde de se et heredibus suis *vel assignatis suis* mihi et heredibus meis servicium duorum *feodorum* militum infra divisas Cestrisirie pro omnibus serviciis, exactionibus et demandis mihi et heredibus meis pertinentibus. Et ego Ranulfus et heredes mei prefato Iohanni de Arderne et heredibus suis *vel assignatis suis* dictum feodum de Audeforde cum pertinenciis et cum libertatibus prenominatis contra omnes homines et feminas warantizabimus. Hiis testibus Philippo de Orrebie tunc iusticiario meo, Rogero de Monte Alto senescallo meo, Henrico de Audelegh, Warino de Vernon, Willelmo de Venables, Hamone de Mascy, Rogero de Meingarin, Roberto Patric, Waltero de Deyvilla, Petro clerico meo, Hugone, Thoma, Henrico, Roberto et Galfrido dispensariis.

This charter, as it stands, is a gross forgery, similar in many ways to the more notorious Combermere forgeries (**nos. 240, 241**). It is, however, almost certainly based upon a genuine charter of Ranulf III, interpolated and expanded at the time of the royal inquest into the liberties claimed and exercised to cover every possible infraction charged by the king's justices against John of Ardern's distant successor, Sir John Stanley. If the more obvious interpolations (printed in italics in the preceding text) are eliminated, it is not difficult to restore a reasonably convincing version of the original charter. This has been dated 1208–1215 (*Ches. Sheaf*, no. 6603). In fact, it must fall after the death of the previous holder of the fee, Richard of Aldford, in 1213 (**no. 356**). It has been surmised (Orm., ii. 76) that John of Ardern was son-in-law of Richard of Aldford, and succeeded in this capacity, but direct evidence is lacking. The reference to the pleas of the earl's sword is interesting; as is known, they are reserved in Ranulf III's charter of liberties (**no. 394 §1**), but this is an unusually early mention.

375. Grant of protection to Dieulacres abbey, and order to maintain and protect it and everything pertaining to it.

[1214–1216]

P.R.O., C.53 (Chancery Charter Rolls), no. 117; C.66 (Chancery Patent Rolls), nos. 421, m. 26, and 519, m. 21; Salt Library, Stafford, Dieulacres roll, no. 6; Bodleian Library, MS. Top, Gen. c: 26, p. 168 (from Rudyard cartulary); Top. Cheshire b. I, p. 137; Dodsworth MS. 41, f. 95. Ed.: *Cal. Ch. Rolls*, iv. 154 (no. 11); *D.C.*, p. 355 (no. 169).

Ranulfus comes Cestrie constabulario suo, dapifero, iusticiario, vicecomiti, baronibus et omnibus ballivis et hominibus suis Francis et Anglis tam present-ibus quam futuris salutem. Sciatis quod abbatia de Deulacresse et monachi eiusdem loci et homines sui et omnes terre et possessiones sue sunt in mea manu et custodia et protectione. Quare volo et firmiter precipio quod predictam abbatiam et homines suos et terras et omnia, que ad eam pertinent, manu-teneatis et custodiatis et protegatis sicut res meas dominicas, nullam eis iniuriam vel contumeliam facientes vel ab aliquo fieri permittentes, et sitis eis in auxilio ad manutenendum rectitudines suas, quas habere debent, ne pro defectu auxilii et consilii aliquid de rectitudinibus vel rectis consuetudinibus suis amittant. Et si quis eis vel hominibus aut rebus suis in aliquo forisfacere presumpserit, sine dilatione plenariam iusticiam eis fieri faciatis. Et sint quieti de syris et hundredis et placitis et querelis et auxiliis et consuetudinibus et omni terreno servitio et seculari exactione. Et prohibeo ne ipsi vel homines sui ponantur in placitum de ulla re nisi coram me vel coram capitali iusticia mea, supra decem libras forisfacture. Hiis testibus Thoma dispensatore et Roberto fratre eius, Roberto de Coudray, Alfredo de Suleni, Iohanne de Erderne, Roberto de Daiville, Hugone de Paschi, et multis aliis.

This is the earliest of four grants, or putative grants, of protection for Dieulacres abbey from Ranulf III and, like no. **379**, must date from between the foundation of the monastery in 1214 and the death of Hugh de Pascy in 1216.

376. Grant of protection to Dieulacres abbey and exemption from tallages and all other aids and dues. [Spurious]

[1214–1216]

P.R.O., C.53 (Chancery Charter Rolls), no. 117; C.66 (Chancery Patent Rolls), no. 421, m. 26, and no. 519, m.

21; Bodleian Library, Dodsworth MS. 41, f. 95. Ed.: *Cal. Ch. Rolls*, iv. 154 (no. 12); *Hist. Coll. of Staffordshire*, 1913, p. 315.

Ranulfus comes Cestrie constabulario suo, iusticiario vicecomiti et omnibus ballivis et hominibus suis salutem. Sciatis quod abbatia mea de Deulacres, quam ego fundavi, et monachi eiusdem loci et homines sui et omnes terre et possessiones sue et omnia tenementa sua et hominum suorum in mea sunt manu et protectione et custodia. Quare volo et precipio quod predictam abbatiam et homines suos et terra eorundem impetratas et impetrandas, et omnia que ad eam pertinent, manuteneatis, custodiatis et protegatis sicut res meas proprias et dominicas. Et sint quieti de syris et hundredis, placitis et querelis, tallagiis, passagiis, pontagiis, multuris in omnibus molendinis meis, pannagio in omnibus nemoribus meis, sallinis, muragiis, tolnetis et omnibus auxiliis, misionibus seu posicionibus, consuetudinibus et demandis, que aliquo casu ab eis seu hominibus suis a quibuscumque imposterum exigi poterunt pro terris impetratis vel etiam impetrandis. In cuius rei testimonium huic scripto sigillum meum apposui. Hiis testibus Thoma dispensatore et Roberto fratre eius, Roberto de Coudray, Alfredo de Suleni, Iohanne de Erderne, Roberto de Dayvile, Hugone de Paschi, Petro et Ricardo de Kegworth clericis, et aliis.

This, the second of Ranulf III's putative grants of protection for Dieulacres, is of dubious authenticity. The witnesses, except for the addition of the two clerks, Peter and Richard, at the end, are identical with those of **no. 375**, and it is highly improbable that Ranulf would have granted two similar charters in so short a space of time. The present charter looks like an inflated and interpolated text; thus e.g. the insertion of 'et omnia tenementa sua et hominum suorum' in the first sentence. The omission from the address of the seneschal and barons is highly unusual, and suggests careless copying by a monastic scribe. The use of the words 'impetratis et impetrandis' (instead of 'perquisitis vel perquirendis', as in **no. 377**) is ecclesiastical usage. The most striking feature, however, is the inflation of the list of quittances to include pontage, pannage, multure, murage, etc. Most of these exemptions were only acquired after Ranulf became earl of Lincoln in 1217 – e.g. **no. 387** (multure), **no. 384** (pannage) – and their presence in a charter ostensibly dated 1214–1216 is highly suspicious. It is difficult to know when and why this inflated version was produced; but it is almost certainly not a genuine charter of Ranulf III.

377.   Grant of protection for his abbey of Dieulacres, which he built, and freedom from any plea except before him or his chief justice.

Chester, [May 1217 – June 1218]

Orig.: Shakerley Deeds Y. iii. xi. Transcr.: P.R.O., C.53 (Chancery Charter Rolls), no. 117; C.66 (Chancery Patent Rolls), no. 421, m. 26, and no. 519, m. 20; Bodleian Library, MS. Top. Gen. c. 26, p. 169 (from Rudyard cartulary); Dodsworth MS. 41, f. 95 (probably from William Vernon of Shakerley). Short abstract: B.L. Harl. MS. 2060, f. 28 (old p. 48). Ed.: *Mon.*, v. 628; *Cal. Ch. Rolls*, iv. 154–5; *D.C.*, p. 355 (no. 170).

Ranulphus comes Cestrie et Lincolnie cónstabulario suo et dapifero, iusticiario, vicecomiti, baronibus et ceteris suis baillivis, et omnibus hominibus suis Francis et Anglis tam presentibus quam futuris salutem. Sciatis quod abbatia mea de Deulacresse, quam construxi, et monachi mei, qui ibidem sunt, in mea sunt protectione et custodia, et quod eisdem omnes homines et terras et possessiones, quas nunc habent vel inposterum in toto comitatu Cestrie dono meo et hominum meorum vel aliis iustis modis adquirere possunt, concedo et confirmo pro me et heredibus meis, ita quod nec ego nec heredes mei in omnibus hominibus et terris dictorum monacorum meorum nunc perquisitis vel in posterum perquirendis aliquam vendicationem habere possumus, sed in liberam puram et perpetuam elemosinam pacifice possideant. Quare volo et firmiter precipio, quod predictam abbatiam et homines suos et terras, et omnia que ad eam pertinent, manuteneatis et custodiatis et protegatis sicut res meas dominicas, nullam eis iniuriam vel molestiam facientes vel ab aliquo fieri permittentes, et sitis eis in auxilio ad manutenendum rectitudines suas, quas habere debent, ne pro defectu auxilii vel consilii rectitudines suas vel de rectis consuetudinibus suis aliquid amittant. Et si quis eis vel hominibus aut rebus suis in aliquo forisfacere presumpserit, sine dilatione plenariam iusticiam eis fieri faciatis. Et sint quieti de siris et de hundredis, ut nullus vicecomes eos implacitare presumat in hundredis, et placitis et querelis et auxiliis et exercitu et consuetudinibus et omni terreno servitio et seculari exactione. Et prohibeo ne ipsi vel homines sui ponantur in placitum de aliqua re supra decem libras forisfacture, nisi coram me vel capitali iusticiario meo. Hiis testibus Philippo de Orrebi tunc iusticiario meo, R. de Monte Alto senescallo, Willelmo de Venabulis, H. de Mascy, Ricardo de Aldeford, Roberto Patric, Warino de Vernun, Petro clerico, Ricardo Roudistorn clerico, et multis aliis apud Cestriam, me presente.

SEAL: green wax, pendent on tag, lion seal.

This charter should be compared with **no. 375**, granted before Ranulf became earl of Lincoln in 1217, on which it is clearly based. It is the only known instance of the use of the lion seal after Ranulf became earl of Lincoln, and its use suggests that the charter dates from between his elevation to the earldom on 23 May 1217 and his departure for the Holy Land at Whitsuntide 1218. If that is the case, it seems possible that he did not yet have a seal incorporating his new title and that the famous seal with three garbs (Orm., i. 41) was not introduced until after his return in August 1220.

378.   Grant of protection for Dieulacres abbey.

[? 1220–1221]

> Bodleian Library, MS. Top, Gen. c. 26,p. 166 (copied
> from Rudyard cartulary). Abbreviated abstracts: Bod-
> leian Library, Dodsworth MS. 61, f. 94; B.L. Harl. MS.
> 2060, f. 24v. (old f. 41); Chester, Booth of Twemlow,
> Liber D. f. 56. Ed.: *D.C.*, p. 354 (no. 167).

Ranulfus comes Cestrie et Lincolnie constabulario suo et dapifero, vicecomiti, baronibus et ballivis suis, et omnibus hominibus suis tam presentibus quam futuris salutem. Sciatis me in honore dei et beate Marie semper virginis et sancte Benedicti abbatis et omnium sanctorum dei pro salute anime mee et omnium antecessorum et successorum meorum quandam abbatiam, que vocatur Dieulencres, de ordine Cisterciensi fundasse. Abbatia igitur illa et monachi et conversi et homines et illorum[1] res omnes et omnes terre et possessiones et omnia ad eam pertinencia sunt in mea manu, custodia et protectione. Quare volo et firmiter precipio quod predictam abbatiam et homines ipsius et terras et omnia, que ad ipsam pertinent, manuteneatis et custodiatis et protegatis et defendatis in omnibus, nullam eis iniuriam vel molestiam facientes vel ab aliquo fieri permittentes, et sitis eis in auxilium ad manutenendum rectitudines et libertates, quas habere debent, ne pro defectu auxilii vestri vel consilii de rectitudinibus aut libertatibus suis aliquid amittant. Et si quis eis vel hominibus vel rebus suis in aliquo forisfacere presumpserit, sine dilatione eisdem plenariam iusticiam faciatis. Et prohibeo ne ipsi vel homines sui ponantur in placitum de aliqua re supra libras forisfacture decem, nisi coram me ipso vel coram capitali iusticiario meo. His testibus domino abbate Cestrie, Philippo de Orreby tunc iusticiario meo, Iohanne constabulario, Rogero senescallo, Henrico de Aldithele, Willelmo de Venabules, Hamone de Mascy, Warino de Vernoun, Rogero de Meinwarin, Radulfo filio Symonis, Iohanne de Ardern, Ioceramo de Hellesby, Petro clerico domini comitis, David de Malopassu, Ricardo de Kingeslee, et multis aliis.

1.   illas *MSS.*

This charter is the fourth (and last) of the charters of protection granted by Ranulf III to the monks of Dieulacres, and it has been suggested (*Ches. Sheaf*, no. 7842) that it was given shortly after his return from the crusade in August 1220. This is not impossible. Unlike **no. 376**, there is nothing particularly unusual or suspicious about the text (unless it is the reference to St. Benedict and All Saints in the dedication, which is certainly unusual), and although the monks had got a perfectly good protection in **no. 377**, it is understandable that they may have wished for a charter under Ranulf's new seal as earl of Chester and Lincoln. It may therefore be given the benefit of the doubt; but it is noticeable that the monks did not see fit to get this charter confirmed and enrolled on the Chancery Rolls, and the only authority for it seems to be the Dieulacres cartulary, which is certainly not always a reliable source.

379. Grant to the abbey of Dieulacres of the vill of Byley and freedom from shire and hundred, from military duties and all other demands.

[1214–1216]

> Orig.: Shakerley Deeds (*penes* Sir Arthur Bryant) Y. i. xvii. Transcr.: Salt Library, Stafford, Dieulacres roll, no. 23; Bodleian Library, MS. Top. Cheshire b. I, p. 137; Dodsworth MS. 31, f. 164v.–165; P.R.O., C.53 (Chancery Charter Rolls), no. 117; C.66 (Chancery Patent Rolls), no. 421, m. 26, and no. 519, m. 20. Ed.: *Cal. Ch. Rolls*, iv. 155 (no. 14); *Hist. Coll. of Staffordshire*, 1913, p. 315.

Rannulfus comes Cestrie omnibus presentibus et futuris salutem. Sciatis me concessisse et presenti carta confirmasse abbati et monachis meis de Deulacresse totam villam de Bivelehe cum omnibus pertinentiis suis in villa et extra villam habendam et tenendam in perpetuum libere et quiete sicut liberam elemosinam, prout carte donatorum, venditorum et exchambiatorum, quas inde habent, testantur. Et preterea eisdem dedi et concessi et presenti carta confirmavi quietentiam exercitus et syre et hundredi et omnium placitorum et pouture servientium et omnium demendarum et consuetudinum ad me et heredes meos spectantium. Hiis testibus Philippo de Orreby tunc iusticiario Cestrie, Rogero de Monte Alto senescallo Cestrie, Willelmo de Venables, Warino de Vernun, Henrico de Alditelegh, Rogero de Meidinlwarin, Hamone de Mascy, Hugone et Thoma dispensariis, Waltero de Deivilla, Petro clerico meo, Aluredo de Suligni, Hugone de Pascy, Lidulfo de Tuamlowe, Ricardo filio suo, magistro Hugone, Ricardo de Kegwrthe clerico, et multis aliis.

SEAL: pendent on tag, lion seal, green wax.

Richard of Aldford had given Byley, near Middlewich, to Poulton abbey, and his gift was confirmed by Ranulf III (**no. 248**). Thereafter there appear to have been a number of smaller gifts, exchanges and purchases (*D.C.*, nos. 98–102, 117–121), and when the abbey of Poulton was transferred in 1214 to Dieulacres, near Leek in Staffordshire, these were all confirmed to Ranulf III's new foundation. The date of his confirmation must fall between May 1214, when the removal took place, and the summer of 1216, when Hugh de Pascy was killed (*Ann. Cestr.*, p. 50). The charter is also interesting as indicating that Liulf of Twemlow, who had been sheriff since c.1190, had ceased by now to hold the office.

380.   Confirmation to the abbey of Dieulacres of the vill of Byley. [? Spurious]

[1229–1232]

> Bodleian Library, MS. Top. Gen. c. 26, p. 109 (transcript
> of Rudyard cartulary). Abbreviated abstracts: B.L. Harl.
> MS. 2060, f. 25v. (old f. 43); Chester, Booth of Twemlow,
> Liber D, f. 62.   Ed.: *D.C.*, p. 327 (no. 65) (abbreviated).

Ranulfus comes Cestrie et Lincolnie omnibus presentibus et futuris salutem. Sciatis me concessisse et presenti carta mea confirmasse abbati et monachis meis de Dieulacres totam villam de Bifle cum omnibus pertinenciis suis in villa et extra villam, habendam et tenendam in perpetuum libere et quiete sicut liberam elemosinam, prout carte donatorum, venditorum et escambiatorum, quas inde habent, testantur. Et preterea eisdem dedi et concessi et presenti carta confirmavi quietanciam exercitus et syre et hundredi et omnium placitorum et puture servientium et omnium demandarum et consuetudinum ad me et heredes meos spectantium. His testibus W.[1] abbate Cestrie et K.[2] abbate Gerevalle, Willelmo de Vernoun tunc iusticiario Cestrie, Ricardo Fitun, Radulfo de Bray, Ricardo Birun, Iohanne de Laxington, Simone clerico, Ricardo de Arderne, et multis aliis.

1.   Willelmo, *Bodl. MS. and D.C.*; W° *Harl. MS.*
2.   *Only in Harl. MS.*

The text of this charter is an exact copy of that of **no. 379**, and this raises the question of its authenticity. If the first witness is Abbot William of Chester, as the Dieulacres cartulary and the Harleian manuscript state, it is certainly a forgery, since Abbot William died on 26 September 1228 and William Vernon only became justiciar at Easter 1229. But W. may possibly stand for William's successor, Abbot Walter Pinchbeck. If the charter is genuine, the explanation may be that it was thought desirable to have a confirmation from Ranulf as earl of Chester and Lincoln, whereas in **no. 379** he was still only earl of Chester. But Ranulf had been earl of Lincoln since 1217, and it is hard to understand why the monks waited a dozen years before asking for a new charter, particularly in view of Ranulf's partiality for Dieulacres. This is not the only Dieulacres charter which is suspect, and it is probably safest to view it with caution.

381.   Confirmation of the salthouse in Middlewich given to Dieulacres abbey by William Mainwaring and quittance of toll and suit at the wichmoot.

[1214–1217]

> P.R.O., C.53 (Chancery Charter Rolls), no. 117, m. 43;

C.66 (Chancery Patent Rolls), no. 421, m. 27, and no. 519, m. 21; Salt Library, Stafford, Dieulacres roll, no. 27; Bodleian Library, MS. Top. Cheshire b. I, p. 137; Dodsworth MS. 31, f. 163v.; B.L. Harl. MS. 2060, f. 26v. (witnesses only). Ed.: *Cal. Ch. Rolls*, iv. 153 (no. 8); *Hist. Coll. of Staffordshire*, 1913, p. 314.

Universis Christi fidelibus presentem cartam inspecturis et audituris Rannulfus comes Cestrie salutem. Noveritis me concessisse et presenti carta mea confirmasse abbati et monachis meis de Deulacresse in puram et perpetuam elemosinam salinam illam in Medio Wyco, quam Willelmus de Meisnilwarin eis caritative dedit, liberam et solutam et quietam de tholneto et de secta de wychmot et de omnibus secularibus consuetudinibus et exactionibus, habendam et tenendam imperpetuum cum sale de die veneris. Concessi etiam et presenti carta mea confirmavi predictis abbati et monachis et hominibus in domibus suis salem bullientes salsam capiendam de omnibus fossis, sicut eis magis expedire noverint. Hiis testibus Philippo de Orreby tunc iusticiario meo, Henrico de Aldithlea, Petro clerico meo, Warino de Vernoun, Willelmo de Venables, Hugone et Thoma et Henrico et Roberto et Galfrido dispensariis, Waltero de Daivilla, Roberto de Coudray, Aluredo de Suligny, et multis aliis.

William Mainwaring was younger brother of Roger Mainwaring (*D.C.*, no. 163), eldest son and heir of Ralph Mainwaring, the justiciar, by Amicia, a natural daughter of Earl Hugh (**no. 193**). For his gift of a salthouse, see *D.C.*, no. 124. Earl Ranulf's confirmation of his gift, attested by the five Despenser brothers, dates from 1214–17, and provides interesting detail about the operation of the salt industry. As in the case of **no. 382**, a second version of this charter, with a new list of witnesses, was produced c.1230. An abbreviated text is printed in *D.C.*, no. 304. It is not reproduced here as, apart from the witness-list, it is identical with the charter of 1214–17. The witness-list – *Willelmo abbate Cestrie, E. abbate Gerevallis, Willelmo de Vernon tunc iusticiario Cestrie, Ricardo Fitun, Radulfo de Bray, Ricardo Birun, Iohanne de Laxington, Simone clerico, Ricardo de Arderne, et multis aliis* – is used in another spurious charter (**no. 380**), and seems to have been taken from the genuine charter (**no. 393**) by which Earl Ranulf gave his heart for burial at Dieulacres, just as the list of witnesses on the spurious version of **no. 382** was in all probability taken from the earl's grant of Wetwood (**no. 390**). The reason for these forgeries is not clear, but it is evident that the Dieulacres charters as a whole must be viewed with caution, except in the few instances where the originals survive.

382. Grant to the monks of Dieulacres of land at Rudyard, on which to build their abbey.

[1217–1222]

Salt Library, Stafford, Dieulacres roll, no. 1. Ed.: *D.C.*,
p. 363.

Universis sancte matris ecclesie filiis presentibus et futuris, hanc cartam
inspecturis vel audituris, Ranulfus comes Cestrie et Lincolnie salutem. Noveritis
me pro salute anime mee et antecessorum meorum dedisse in puram et
perpetuam elemosinam deo et beate Marie et monachis apud Deulacres deo
servientibus terram de Rodeiard cum omnibus pertinentiis suis ad construendam
ibidem abbatiam, scilicet per istas divisas: per aquam de Luddebeche, que currit
inter Rudiard et Leck, usque ad domum Radulfi Bec, et inde usque ad
Merebroc, et a Merebroc usque ad Quamendehul, et inde deorsum per domum
Dodni, usque ad sepulcrum Thoni, et inde usque ad Falingbroc, et per Falinbroc
usque ad Fulhe et inde usque ad Luddebeche. Quare volo et firmiter precipio
quod dicti monachi mei de Deulacres habeant et teneant in perpetuum predictam terram ad fundandam abbatiam suam eis collatam libere, quiete, pacifice et
honorifice sicud[1] liberam et puram elemosinam, cum omnibus pertinentiis suis et
libertatibus in bosco, in plano, in pratis, in pasturis, in stangnis[1] et molendinis, in
moris et marescis,[1] in viis et semitis, et in omnibus locis et cum eisiamentis,[1] que
in predicta terra sunt vel fieri possunt, ita quod predicta terra cum suis
pertinentiis sit omnino extra forestam et libera penitus ab omni exactione
seculari, sicut aliqua elemosina potest esse liberior. Et ut hec, mea donatio
stabilis sit in perpetuum, eam hac carta mea et sigilli mei impressione roboravi.
Testibus H. tunc abbate Cestrie, Philippo[2] de Orreby tunc iusticiario Cestrie,
magistro Hugone, qui hanc cartam scripsit, et multis aliis.

1. *sic MS.*   2.   Petro *MS.*

As in other instances (**nos. 379** and **381**), there is a second version of this charter,
entered on the Charter Roll (no. 117) and on the Patent Roll (nos. 421 and 519).
It is not printed here, since (apart from petty spelling variations) it is word for
word identical with the present charter, except for a totally different witness list,
as follows: *Willelmo de Ferariis comite Derbeye, Iohanne comite de Huntedonia,
Iohanne constabulario Cestrie, Willelmo de Cantelu, Willelmo de Vernun tunc
iusticiario, Baldewino de Ver, Waltero de Deyvilla, Radulfo de Brey, Ricardo de
Burun, Iohanne de Laxingtona, Simone clerico, Ricardo de Arderne, et aliis.* The
monks of Dieulacres seem to have felt the need to update their charters, often to
the justiciarship of William of Vernon (1229–33); but in this instance the result is
a barefaced forgery. The absurdity of making a grant of land to the monks to
build their abbey fifteen years at least after its foundation is obvious. In the time
of Abbot Hugh (1208–26), on the other hand, it makes sense, and it seems
probable that the original charter dates from shortly after Earl Ranulf's return
from Damietta in August 1220, when he seems to have taken the building of the
abbey seriously in hand (*Ann. Cestr.*, p. 53), but it may also date from before his
departure in 1218. For Master Hugh, who was a fairly frequent witness in this
period, see **no. 231**.

383. Grant to the monks of Dieulacres of freedom from toll on salt and whatever else they bought or sold in the whole of his territory.

[1217–1226]

> P.R.O., C.53 (Chancery Charter Rolls), no. 117, m. 43; C.66 (Chancery Patent Rolls), no. 421, m. 27, and no. 519, m. 21; Salt Library, Stafford, Dieulacres roll (unnumbered, on dorse); Bodleian Library, MS. Top. Gen. c. 26, p. 163 (from Rudyard cartulary); MS. Top. Cheshire b. I, p. 137; Dodsworth MS. 31, f. 164. Ed.: *Cal. Ch. Rolls*, iv. 154 (no. 10); *D.C.*, p. 353 (no. 164) (abbreviated text).

Ranulfus comes Cestrie et Lincolnie omnibus hominibus salutem.[1] Sciatis me pro dei amore et salute anime mee dedisse et hac carta mea confirmasse in puram et perpetuam elemosinam deo et sancte Marie et monachis de Deulacresse quietanciam de tolneto per totam terram meam de sale et de omnibus aliis rebus quas emerint aut vendiderint, tam per aquam quam per terram. Quare firmiter precipio ne aliquis ab eis aut de hominibus suis tolnetum exigat nec propter tolnetum eos vexare aut molestare presumat. Hiis testibus H. abbate Cestrie, Philippo de Orreby tunc iusticiario Cestrie, Willelmo de Venables, Warino de Vernun, Rogero de Menilwarin, Radulfo filio Simonis, Iohanne de Arderna, et multis aliis.

1. The address is almost certainly abbreviated.

This grant was made between 1217 and 1226. Ralph son of Simon of Pulford made gifts to Poulton (*D.C.*, nos. 82, 101) shortly before the house was transferred to Dieulacres.

384. Acquittance for Dieulacres abbey from paying pannage for its pigs in all his woods.

[1218–1229]

> P.R.O., D.L. 39/1/19 (Forest Pleas, 21 Edw. III), m. 28; CHES 17/12 (Eyre Rolls, 16 Edw. I), m. 9v.; CHES 33/4, m. 32; CHES 34/1, m. 13; B.L. Harl. MS. 2072, f. 11v. (from CHES 17/12); Bodleian Library, MS. Top. Gen. c. 26, p. 167 (from Rudyard cartulary); Salt Library, Stafford, Dieulacres roll (entry unnumbered). Ed.: *D.C.*, p. 354 (no. 168) (abbreviated text); *Chetham Soc.*, N.S. lxxxiv, p. 239 (incomplete text from CHES 17/12).

Universis sancte matris ecclesie filiis presentem cartam inspecturis vel audituris Ranulfus comes Cestrie et Lincolnie salutem. Noverit universitas vestra me dedisse et concessisse et presenti carta mea confirmasse deo et beate Marie et monachis meis de Deulacresse quietanciam pannagii de omnibus propriis porcis suis per omnia nemora mea. Volo igitur et precipio quod predicti monachi mei hanc libertatem habeant in puram et liberam et perpetuam elemosinam, et ut hec mea donacio rata et inconcussa permaneat, eam sigillo meo roboravi. Hiis testibus Philippo de Orreby tunc iusticiario Cestrie, Henrico de Aldithleghe, Willelmo de Vernon, Ricardo Fiton, Hugone dispensatore, Ioceram de Hellesby, Ricardo de Kyngesleghe, et multis aliis.

This charter falls between 1218, when Hugh Despenser succeeded his brother Thomas, and 1229, when Philip of Orreby resigned the justiciarship.

385.   Grant to Dieulacres abbey of the mills of Leek and Hulme in exchange for 'Ruhtonestede' and its possessions in Leeds and Bingley and in the land in Lindsey which was William son of Drew's.

[1220–1222]

> Bodleian Library, MS. Top. Gen. c. 26 (transcript of Rudyard cartulary), p. 36. Brief abstracts: B.L. Harl. MS. 2060, f. 24v. (old f. 41); Chester, Booth of Twemlow, Liber D, f. 58.   Ed.: *D.C.*, p. 310 (no. 2).

Ranulfus comes Cestrie et Lincolnie omnibus presentibus et futuris presentem cartam inspecturis vel audituris salutem. Sciatis me dedisse, concessisse et hac presenti carta mea confirmasse abbati et conventui de Deulacres molendina de Lech et de Hulm cum pertinentiis in escambium de Ruhtonestede et omnium que habebant ex dono meo in Ledes et Bingleye et in terra que fuit Willelmi filii Drui in Lyndseya, habenda et tenenda ipsis abbati et conventui in perpetuum cum tota sequela sua et cum omnibus pertinentiis et libertatibus suis, adeo libere, integre et quiete, sicut ego et antecessores mei unquam liberius, plenius et quietius habuimus. Si quis autem de sequela predictorum molendinorum indebite se subtraxerit vel alibi molere presumpserit quam ad prefata molendina, volo et firmiter precipio super forisfacturam meam quod ballivi mei eum compellant ad debitam sequelam in predictis molendinis faciendam. Volo etiam quod homines mei de manerio de Lech faciant opera molendinorum et stagnorum sicut facere solebant. Et ut hec mea donacio perpetue firmitatis robur obtineat, illam presenti scripto et sigilli mei apposicione corroboravi. His testibus Philippo de Orreby tunc iusticiario Cestrie, Galfrido de Dutton, Herberto de Orreby, Willelmo de Malopassu, Willelmo de Meynigwaryn, Ricardo de Sondbach, Jocio capellano, Ricardo de Arderne, Symone clerico, et multis aliis.

The manors of Leeds and Bingley in Yorkshire were acquired by Ranulf III in 1217 or 1218 as a result of the default of Maurice of Ghent (*J.C.A.S.*, lviii, p. 107), and it was probably at that time that he gave the monks of Dieulacres unspecified land or rights there. Later Bingley was given to William Cantilupe junior (**no. 416**), and it seems possible that the present exchange was made in connection with that gift. The charter must fall before the death of Jocius the earl's chaplain at the end of 1222 (**no. 412**) and almost certainly after Earl Ranulf's return from a crusade in August 1220. William son of Dreu appears to have been dead by 1217 (*H.K.F.*, p. 91). For Herbert of Orreby, see **no. 356**. 'Ruhtonestede' has not been identified.

386. Grant of the church of Leek to Dieulacres abbey.

[1220–1223]

> B.L. Harl. MS. 2060, f. 28v. (with description of seal, apparently from original); Bodleian Library MS. Top. Gen. c. 26, p. 37 (from Rudyard cartulary); Salt Library, Stafford, Dieulacres roll, no. 16; P.R.O.,C.53 (Chancery Charter Rolls), no. 117, m. 43; C.66 (Chancery Patent Rolls), no. 421, m. 27, and no. 519, m. 21.   Ed.: *Cal. Ch. Rolls*, iv. 153 (no. 6); *D.C.*, p. 311 (no. 3) (abbreviated).

Universis sancte matris ecclesie filiis presentibus et futuris hanc cartam inspecturis et audituris Ranulfus comes Cestrie et Lincolnie salutem. Noveritis me pro salute anime mee et antecessorum meorum concessisse et hac presenti carta mea confirmasse deo et beate Marie et monachis meis ordinis Cisterciensis apud Deulacresse deo servientibus ecclesiam de Leech cum omnibus ad eam pertinentibus in puram et perpetuam elemosinam, ita libere et quiete possiden-dam sicut aliqua elemosina liberius et melius conferri potest, ita quod in ea vel in pertinenciis suis nihil retineo preter oraciones et elemosinas. Hiis testibus H. abbate Cestrie, Philippo de Orreby tunc iusticiario Cestrie, Rogero de Monte Alto senescallo Cestrie, Willelmo de Venabulis, Guarino de Vernun, Rogero de Menilgarin, Hugone dispensario, magistro Hugone, et multis aliis.

> SEAL: 'a man on horseback, on the back on an escocheon 3 garbs'.

This grant was confirmed by Bishop William of Chester (1215–23). Hugh Despenser succeeded his brother Thomas in 1218, and as Earl Ranulf left on crusade on Whitsuntide that year, it is reasonably safe to conclude that this charter was not granted until after his return in August 1220.

387.   Grant to the monks of Dieulacres of freedom from toll on their corn ground in his mills in Cheshire.

[1220–1225]

> Bodleian Library, MS. Top. Gen. c. 26, p. 80 (from
> Rudyard cartulary); MS. Top. Cheshire b. I, p. 38 (from
> MS. of John of Arden entitled *Baronagium Cestrie,*
> apparently from original); B.L. Harl. MS. 2060, f. 24 (old
> f. 41); Chester, Booth of Twemlow, Liber D, f. 56
> (abbreviated texts). Ed.: *D.C.*, p. 328 (no. 70) (abbre-
> viated text).

Universis sancte matris ecclesie filiis presentibus et futuris has litteras visuris vel audituris Ranulfus comes Cestrie et Lincolnie salutem. Noverit universitas vestra me dedisse et concessisse et hac presenti carta mea confirmasse pro salute anime mee et antecessorum et successorum meorum deo et beate Marie et monachis meis de Deulacresse in puram et perpetuam elemosinam quietantiam tolneti de blado suo proprio in molendinis meis de Cestria, et quod molet, quotiescunque venerit, post bladum quod erit in tramea in adventu bladi sui. Hanc vero libertatem quiete, plene et pacifice in perpetuum sine omni contradictione et vexatione habeant. Et ut hec mea donatio firmitatis robur obtineat, eam sigilli mei testimonio roboravi. His testibus Hugone[1] abbate Cestrie, Philippo de Orreby tunc iusticiario Cestrie, Petro clerico domini comitis, Roberto Bray,[2] Rogero Herre,[3] Hamone, Hugone filiis Buchardi, Iohanne filio Normanni, Ricardo clerico de Kegworth, Ricardo clerico de Ruestone,[4] et multis aliis.

> SEAL: 'in a scutcheon 3 garbs, inscrip.: SECRETUM
> RANULPHI COM: CESTR: ET LINC: On the other
> side a man on horseback'.

1. H. *Top. Ch. and Top. Gen.*; W. *ed.*
2. *Following witnesses only in Harl. 2060 and Twemlow Liber D.*
3. Hert *Harl. MS.*, herede *Liber D.*
4. *For* Rodestorn, *i.e.* Rostherne.

This charter dates from 1220 to 1225. The witnesses Roger Herre, Hugh son of Buchard, John son of Norman, Richard of Kegworth and Richard of Rostherne all occur in Chester city deeds of this period (*J.C.A.S.*, N.S. x, pp. 18–19), and it looks as though the charter was given at Chester, possibly in the portmoot.

388.   Grant to his abbey of Dieulacres of William of Foston with his progeny and of four bovates which he held in Foston (Lincs.).

[1220–1226]

Bodleian Library, Dodsworth MS. 88, f. 65v. (source not stated).

Omnibus sancte matris ecclesie filiis presentibus et futuris has litteras visuris vel audituris Rannulfus comes Cestrie et Lincolnie salutem. Noverit universitas vestra me assensu et voluntate spontanea Clementie sponse mee dedisse et concessisse et hac presenti carta mea confirmavi[1] deo et sancte Marie et abbacie mee de Deulacrese in puram et perpetuam elemosinam Willelmum de Foston cum tota sequela sua et quatuor bovatas terre, quas idem Willelmus tenuit de me in predicta villa de Foston, cum tofto et crofto et prato et cum omnibus pertinenciis et aisiamentis et libertatibus ad predictas bovatas terre pertinentibus. Et ut hec donacio mea rata et inconcussa permaneat, eam presentis scripti testimonio et sigilli mei apposicione corroboravi. Hiis testibus H. abbate Cestrie, Philippo de Orrebi tunc iusticiario Cestrie, Aphredo de Soleni, Gilberto Cosin, Iohanne clerico, Galfrido Conein,[1] et multis aliis.

1. *sic MS.*

This grant to Dieulacres is very surprising, as there is no other evidence of the abbey's interest in Lincolnshire, and it does not appear in the Dieulacres cartulary. Foston, in the immediate vicinity of Long Bennington, was part of Countess Clementia's marriage portion (hence the insistence that she had assented to the gift of her own free will), and many years previously land here had been given at her wish to the abbey of Savigny (**no. 334**). The present grant has the same witnesses as Ranulf's confirmation of land in Bennington to Savigny (**no. 335**), and must have been issued at the same time. The date falls before the death of Abbot Hugh Grylle of Chester in 1226, and almost certainly after 1220. But it is very doubtful whether the gift had any lasting effect, in view of the fact that, after Ranulf III's death, Countess Clementia gave William of Foston's son, Thomas, and the same land to Savigny (**no. 443**).

389. Gift to Dieulacres abbey of land at Cockshut Hay (2 km. west of Rudyard), and freedom from toll and all services for their salthouse in Middlewich.

[1221–1226]

Salt Library, Stafford, Dieulacres roll, no. 26; Bodleian Library, MS. Top. Gen. c. 26, p. 53; B.L. Harl. MS. 2060, f. 27 (abbr. text from original in custody of Somerford Oldfield, 1631); Chester, Booth of Twemlow, Liber D, f. 65 (identical with preceding). Ed.: *D.C.*, p. 315 (no. 21) (abbreviated text).

Universis sancte matris ecclesie filiis presentibus et futuris hanc cartam inspecturis vel audituris Ranulfus comes Cestrie et Lincolnie salutem. Noveritis me pro salute anime mee et antecessorum meorum dedisse in puram et perpetuam elemosinam deo et beate Marie et monachis meis ordinis Cisterciensis apud Deulacresse deo servientibus quatuor bovatas terre, que vocatur Cockstuth,[1] cum omnibus pertinentiis suis et libertatibus in bosco, in plano, in pratis, in pasturis, in stagnis, in molendinis, in moris et in mariscis, in viis, in semitis, et in omnibus locis et cum omnibus aisiamentis, que in predicta terra sunt vel fieri possunt, libere et quiete et honorifice sicut liberam et puram elemosinam, et sit predicta terra cum pertinentiis libera penitus ab omni seculari exactione et sit omnino extra forestam, sicut aliqua elemosina esse potest liberior. Et preterea dedi predictis monachis meis libertatem saline, quam habent in Medio Wico, ita quod sit libera a tolneto et ab omni servicio et exactione, sicut aliqua salina liberior et melior esse poterit. Hanc autem libertatem dedi dictis monachis meis in liberam et perpetuam elemosinam, et ut hec mea donacio stabilis sit in perpetuum, eam hac carta mea et sigilli mei impressione roboravi. His testibus H.[2] abbate Cestrie, Philippo de Orreby iusticiario[3] meo Cestrie,[4] Rogero senescallo Cestrie, Willelmo de Venables, Guarino de Vernoun, Rogero de Meinguarin, Hugone dispensario, Petro clerico domino comitis, et multis aliis.

1. Cocsute *Salt. Libr. roll*; Cocksuth *Booth of Twemlow*; Cocsuche, *MS. Top. Ch.*
2. Hugone *Salt. Libr. Roll*; H. abbate Cestrie *om. MS. Top. Gen. and ed.*
3. tunc iusticiario *MS. Top. Gen. and ed.*
4. *om.* Cestrie, *add* Willelmo abbate Cestrie *MS. Top. Gen. and ed.*

The salthouse at Middlewich is presumably that given by William Mainwaring (**no. 381**). Hugh Despenser succeeded his brother Thomas, who died in 1218 (*H.K.F.*, p. 59), and it is reasonable to suppose that the present charter falls after that date; but as Earl Ranulf was absent on crusade from June 1218 to August 1220, its date probably falls between his return and the death of Abbot Hugh Grylle in July 1226. Here, as in a number of other instances, the cartulary substitutes Abbot William for Abbot Hugh, but the cartulary text is unreliable and must be rejected.

390.   Grant to the monks of Dieulacres of Gonedon and Wetwood with the whole wood and pasture, reserving only the sparrowhawks, if there are any there, and also of commons with the earl's men in the pasture to the south of Gonedon.

[1229–1232]

Bodleian Library, MS. Top. Gen. c. 26, p. 56 (from Rudyard cartulary). Brief abstracts with witnesses: B.L. Harl. MS. 2060, f. 24v.; Chester, Booth of Twemlow, Liber D, f. 58 and f. 241. Ed.: *D.C.*, p. 316 (no. 24).

Universis sancte matris ecclesie filiis presentibus et futuris presentem cartam inspecturis vel audituris Ranulfus comes Cestrie et Lincolnie salutem. Sciatis nos concessisse et dedisse et hac presenti carta nostra confirmasse deo et beate Marie et abbatie nostre de Deulacres et monachis ibidem deo servientibus pro salute anime mee et antecessorum et successorum meorum Gonedunam et Wethwode cum toto bosco et plano et pastura per has divisas, scilicet per rivum qui currit in parte occidentali iuxta Horlapeltrolee[1] usque in Fulee, et de Fulee ascendendo usque ad Wildboarsegreave per rivum descendentem inde iuxta Snichmylee usque ad Trussewey, que est divisa ville de Heytone, et ita de Trussewey per cheminum de Gunedun in longum usque ad predictum rivum iuxta Horlapol-trole.[1] Has vero predictas terras cum bosco et plano et pastura infra predictas divisas contentas concessimus et dedimus predicte abbatie nostre de Deulacres et dictis monachis in puram et liberam et perpetuam elemosinam de nobis et heredibus nostris in perpetuum, tenendas cum omnibus aisiamentis que ibi sunt vel fieri possunt, in perpetuum defensum eis habendum, ita quod nullus cum eis, nisi per illos, ibi aliquam habeant communiam, salvis nobis et heredibus nostris venacionem spervariis,[2] si tamen ibi fuerint, per custodiam forestariorum de Deulacres, ita quod forestarii nostri nihil omnino se intromittant. Preterea concessimus dicte abbatie nostre de Deulacres et dictis monachis nostris in perpetuum communem pasturam totius Gonedone versus partes australes, et insuper communem pasturam inter Merebroc et rivum qui currit de Gonedone descendendo usque in Fulee, et in aliis locis ubi homines nostri communicant, ita quod homines nostri et monachi nostri communes pasturas in communi habeant. Hiis testibus Willelmo de Ferariis comite Derbeye, Iohanne comite de Huntedune, Iohanne constabulario Cestrie, Willelmo de Cantelupo, Willelmo de Vernun tunc iusticiario Cestrie, Baldewino de Ver,[3] Waltero de Deyvilla, Radulfo de Bray, Ricardo de Burun,[3] Ricardo de Arderne et aliis.

1. *D.C. reads* Horlapelbroke.
2. *sic MS.; probably should read* spervariis ad venacionem.
3. *These witnesses omitted D.C.*

The grant was made during the justiciarship of William Vernon. The land in question appears to lie 1–2 miles north-east of the modern Rudyard Reservoir, in the vicinity of Heaton and Gun End, and not at Wetwood, south-west of Stoke-on-Trent.

391. Grant in free alms to the monks of Dieulacres of the church of Sandbach.

[1229–1232]

P.R.O., C.53 (Chancery Charter Rolls), no. 117, m. 43; C.66 (Chancery Patent Rolls), no. 421, m. 27, and no. 519, m. 21; Salt Library, Stafford, Dieulacres roll, no. 27;

Bodleian Library, Dodsworth MS. 31, f. 163; MS. Top.
Cheshire b. I, p. 137. Ed.: *Cal. Ch. Rolls*, iv. 153 (no. 7).

Omnibus sancte matris ecclesie filiis presentem cartam inspecturis vel audituris
Ranulfus comes Cestrie et Lincolnie salutem. Sciatis me divine potestatis intuitu
et pro salute anime mee, quantum ad patronum pertinet, dedisse, concessisse et
hac presenti carta mea confirmasse in puram et perpetuam elemosinam deo et
beate Marie et monachis apud Deulacresse deo servientibus ecclesiam de
Sondbache cum omnibus pertinentiis suis, habendam et tenendam sibi in
proprios usus imperpetuum, ita quod nec ego nec heredes mei in predicta
ecclesia cum pertinentiis aliquid exigemus preter orationes. Et ut hec mea
donacio et concessio rata permaneat et inconcussa presens scriptum sigillo meo
roboravi. Hiis testibus domino Waltero abbate Cestrie, domino Willelmo de
Vernon iusticiario Cestrie, Willelmo de Cantilupo, Fulcone filio Warini,
Radulfo de Bray, Baldewino de Ver, Ricardo Fiton, Ricardo de Buron, Simone
clerico et aliis.

Earl Ranulf's grant was made between 1229 and 1232. In some respects it may be
called a mixed blessing. In 1224 there had been a lawsuit between the earl and
Richard of Sandbach over the patronage of the church. Earl Ranulf won his
case, but the dispute dragged on and was re-opened by Richard's heir, Roger of
Sandbach, against the monks of Dieulacres in 1253, and only settled in 1280 after
the abbey had made a payment of 100s. (Orm., iii. 96).

392.   Instructions that, wherever his body was buried on his death, his heart
was to be taken to Dieulacres for burial.

[1229–1232]

B.L. Harl. MS. 6128 (Visitation of Staffordshire, 1583), f.
97 (only full text). Abbreviated abstracts (from original):
B.L. Add. MS. 6032, f. 196 (new f. 98); Bodleian Library,
Dodsworth MS. 82, f. 110v; MS. Top. Cheshire b. I, p.
130; Chester, Booth of Twemlow, Liber A, f. 55. Ed.:
Orm., i. 40 (from abbreviated abstract).

Universis sancte matris ecclesie filiis presentibus et futuris presentem cartam
inspecturis vel audituris Ranulfus comes Cestrie et Lincolnie salutem in domino.
Sciatis me dedisse deo et sancte Marie de Deulacresse et monachis ibidem deo
servientibus cor meum post obitum meum ibidem sepeliendum, ubicumque
corpus meum sepeliri contigerit. Quare volo et firmiter precipio quod, ubicumque vitam meam finiri contigerit aut ubicumque corpus meum tumulatum fuerit,
quod heredes mei et homines mei cor meum ad abbatiam meam de Deulacresse,

quam ego ipse fundavi, absque omni impedimento et contradictione asportent condendum ibidem. Et ne hac mea donatio irritari valeat imposterum seu impediri, ego eam hac carta mea et sigilli mei apposicione roboravi. His testibus W.[1] abbate Cestrie, Edmundo[2] abbate Gerevallis, Willelmo de Vernun tunc iusticiario Cestrie,[3] Ricardo Fiton, Radulfo de Bray, Ricardo Byrun, Iohanne de Laxington, Simone clerico, Ricardo de Arden, et multis aliis.

> SEAL: obverse: equestrian figure, brandishing sword in right hand, in left a shield. Reverse: on a shield three garbs, 2 and 1. 'Both rounde about: SIG. RAN. COM. CESTRIE ET LINC'.

1. *Harl. 6128 and Add. 6032 have* Willelmus *(sic).*
2. *Only in Harl. 6128; doubtful reading, though ed. seems clear.*
3. *Following witnesses only in Harl. 6128.*

William of Vernon succeeded Philip of Orreby as justiciar in April 1229 (*Ann. Cestr.*, p. 56). None of the other witnesses helps with the dating, but the charter is clearly earlier (but perhaps not much earlier) than **no. 393**. Ranulf's concern about his health and premonition of death seem to have followed his return from Normandy in the autumn of 1231, and the present charter probably belongs to the first half of 1232.

393. Gift to Dieulacres abbey, with his heart which he has given to be buried there, of the whole manor of Leek with all its liberties and appurtenances.

[1232, probably October]

> P.R.O., C.53 (Chancery Charter Rolls), no. 117; C.66 (Chancery Patent Rolls), no. 421, m. 27, and no. 519, m. 21 (in each case two enrolments); Salt Library, Stafford, Dieulacres roll, no. 2. Abbr. transcr.: B.L. Harl. MS. 2060, f. 28v. (old p. 49); Bodleian Library, Dodsworth MS. 31, f. 162v. Ed. (from Salt Library roll): *D.C.*, pp. 363–4.

Ranulphus comes Cestrie et Lincolnie universis Christi fidelibus presentem cartam visuris vel audituris salutem. Noverit universitas vestra me pro salute anime mee animarumque antecessorum et successorum meorum dedisse, concessisse et hac presenti carta mea confirmasse deo et beate Marie et abbati et conventui abbatie mee de Deulacresse totum manerium de Lech cum omnibus pertinentiis et libertatibus suis simul cum corde meo, quod ibidem legavi sepeliendum, habendum et tenendum sibi et successoribus suis bene, quiete, integre et pacifice in liberam, puram et perpetuam elemosinam absque ullo retenemento et quietum ab omni servicio et exactione seculari. Ego vero et heredes mei predictum manerium cum pertinentiis suis memoratis abbati et conventui contra omnes gentes warantizabimus imperpetuum. Et ut hec mea donacio perpetue firmitatis robur optineat, eam presentis pagine testimonio et sigilli mei impressione roboravi. Hiis testibus venerabilibus patribus Petro Wyntoniensi, Alexandro Coventrensi et Lychefeldensi episcopis, Iohanne de Lascy constabulario Cestrie, Stephano de Segrava, Fulcone filio Warini, Henrico de Aldithlega, Willelmo de Cantilupo iuniore, Waltero de Dayvilla, Baldewino de Ver, Ricardo de Arderne, Simone et Iohanne clericis, et aliis.

The royal confirmation, from which this text of Ranulf's charter is taken, was issued at Reading on 25 October 1232, one day before Ranulf's death at Wallingford, and it is probable that the present charter is very little earlier in date. Peter des Roches, the famous bishop of Winchester, and Stephen de Segrave, the justiciar of England, witnessed another charter (**no. 310**) probably given on his deathbed. For Ranulf's gift of his heart to Dieulacres, see **no. 392**.

394.   The Magna Carta of Cheshire, or the Charter of Liberties granted at the petition of the barons of Cheshire, the same liberties to be conceded by the barons to their own knights and free tenants.

[June–September 1215]

> B.L. Harl. MS. 2071, f. 18v., from an original sealed exemplar, collated with a second copy in the same hand, of which 'both the seales were worne away' (A); Harl. 2155, f. 63, 'transcribed out of a little parchment book in quarto in the Duchy Office at Grayes Inne, page 107' (B); Harl. 1965 (St. Werburgh's Register), f. 8 (C); Harl. 2062, f. 3 (D); P.R.O., C.66 (Chancery Patent Rolls, 28 Edw. I), no. 120, m. 22, confirming an earlier inspeximus dated 27 August 1265 (E); D.L. 39/1/19 (Forest Pleas), source not specified, but apparently not from E (F). Ed.: Orm., ii. 53–54; Tait, *Chart. St. Werburgh*, pp. 101–107.

Ranulfus comes Cestrie constabulario, dapifero, iusticiario, vicecomiti, baronibus et ballivis et omnibus hominibus suis et amicis presentibus et futuris presentem cartam inspecturis et audituris salutem.[1] Sciatis me cruce signatum[2] pro amore dei et ad peticionem baronum meorum Cestresirie[3] concessisse eis et heredibus suis de me et heredibus meis omnes libertates in presenti carta subscriptas in perpetuum tenendas et habendas, scilicet:

1.   [4]Quod unusquisque eorum curiam suam habeat liberam de omnibus placitis et querelis in curia mea motis exceptis placitis ad gladium meum pertinentibus, et quod si quis hominum suorum pro aliquo delicto captus fuerit, per dominum suum sine redemptione replegietur, ita quod dominus suus eum perducat ad tres comitatus et eum quietum reducat,[5] nisi sacraber eum sequatur.

2.   Et si aliquis adventitius, qui fidelis sit, in terris eorum venerit et ei placuerit ibidem morari, liceat baroni ipsum habere et retinere, salvis mihi advocariis qui sponte ad me venerint et aliis qui pro transgressu aliunde ad dignitatem meam venerint, et non eis.

3.   Et unusquisque baronum, dum opus fuerit, in werra[6] plenarie faciat servicium tot feodorum militum quot tenet, et eorum milites et libere tenentes loricas aut haubergella habeant et feoda sua per corpora sua defendant, licet milites non sint. Et si aliquis eorum talis sit quod terram suam per corpus suum defendere non possit, alium sufficientem loco suo ponere possit.[7] Nec ego nativos eorum ad arma iurare faciam, sed nativos suos, qui per Ranulfum de Davenham[8] ad advocationem meam venerunt, et alios nativos suos, quos suos esse rationabiliter monstrare poterunt, ipsis quietas concedo.

4.   Et si vicecomes meus aut aliquis serviens in curia mea aliquem hominum suorum inculpaverit, per thwertnic[9] se defendere poterit propter sirevestoth[10] quod reddunt, nisi secta eum sequatur.

5.   Concedo etiam eis quietanciam[11] de garbis et de oblacionibus, quas servientes mei et bedelli exigere solebant. Et quod si aliquis iudex aut sectarius hundredi aut comitatus in curia mea in misericordia inciderit, per duos solidos quietus sit iudex de misericordia et sectarius per duodecim denarios.

6.   Concedo etiam eis libertatem assartandi terras suas infra divisas agriculture sue in foresta, et si landa aut terra infra divisas ville sue fuerit, que prius culta fuit, ibi nemus non crescat, liceat eis illam colere sine herbergacione, et liceat eis husbote[12] et haybote[13] in nemore suo capere de omni genere bosci sine visu forestarii, et mortuum boscum suum dare aut vendere cui voluerint. Et homines eorum non implacitentur [14] de foresta pro supradicto, nisi cum manuopere[15] inveniantur.

7.   Et unusquisque eorum omnia maneria sua dominica in comitatu et hundredo per unum senescallum presentatum[16] defendere possit.

8.   Concedo etiam quod, mortuo viro, uxor sua per quadraginta dies pacem habeat in domo sua. Et heres suus, si etatem habuerit, per rationabile relevium hereditatem suam habeat, scilicet feodum[17] militis per centum solidos. Neque domina neque heres maritetur ubi disparigetur,[18] set per gratum et assensum generis sui maritetur. Et eorum legata teneantur.

9.   Et nullus eorum nativum suum amittat occasione, si in civitate Cestrie venerit, nisi ibi manserit per unum annum et unum diem sine calumpnia.

10.   Et propter grave servicium quod in Cestresiria faciunt, nullus eorum extra Limam[19] servicium mihi faciet,[20] nisi per gratum suum et ad custum meum. Et si milites mei de Anglia summoniti fuerint, qui mihi wardam apud Cestriam debent, et venti sint ad wardam suam faciendam, et exercitus aliunde inimicorum meorum non sit in presenti, nec opus fuerit, bene licet baronibus meis [21] interim ad domos suas redire et requiescere. Et si exercitus inimicorum meorum promptus fuerit de veniendo in terram meam in Cestresiria, vel si castellum assessum fuerit, predicti barones cum[22] exercitu suo et nisu suo[23] statim ad summonitionem meam venient ad removendum exercitum illum ad posse suum. Et cum exercitus ille de terra mea recessus fuerit, predicti barones cum exercitu suo ad terras suas redire poterunt et requiescere, dum milites de Anglia wardam suam faciunt et opus de eis non fuerit, salvis mihi serviciis suis, que facere debent.

11.   Concedo etiam eis quod in tempore pacis tantum duodecim servientes itinerantes habeantur in terra mea cum uno equo, qui sit magistri servientis, qui etiam prebendam non habeat a Pascha usque ad festum sancti Michaelis, nisi per gratiam, et ut ipsi servientes comedant cibum qualem in domibus hominum invenerint, sine emptione alterius cibi ad opus eorum, nec in aliquibus dominicis baronum comedant. Et in tempore guerre[24] per consilium meum aut iusticiarii mei et ipsorum, ponantur servientes sufficientes ad terram meam custodiendam, prout opus fuerit.

12.   Et sciendum est quod predicti barones peticiones subscriptas, quas a me requirebant, omnino mihi et heredibus meis de se et heredibus suis remiserunt, ita quod nihil in eis de cetero clamare poterunt, nisi per gratiam et misericordiam meam; scilicet, senescallus peticionem de wrec et de pisce in terram suam per mare deiecto, et de bersare in foresta mea ad tres arcus, et de percursu canum suorum; et alii peticionem de agistiamento porcorum in foresta mea et de bersare ad tres arcus in foresta mea, vel ad cursus leporariorum suorum in foresta in eundo versus Cestriam per summonitionem vel in redeundo; et petitionem de misericordia iudicum de Wich triginta bullonum[25] salis, set erunt misericordia et leges in Wich tales quales prius fuerunt.

13.   Concedo igitur et presenti carta mea confirmo de me et heredibus meis communibus militibus omnibus et libere tenentibus totius Cestresirie et eorum heredibus omnes predictas libertates habendas et tenendas de baronibus meis et de ceteris dominis suis, quicumque sint, sicut ipsi barones et milites et ceteri libere tenentes eas de me tenent.

Hiis testibus[26] Hugone abbate sancte Werburge Cestrie, Philippo de Orrebi[27] tunc tempore iusticiario Cestrie, Henrico de Aldithelega, Waltero Deyville,

Hugone dispensario, Thoma dispensario, Willelmo pincerna, Waltero de Coventria, Ricardo Phitun, Roberto de Coudrey,[28] Ivone de Kaletoft, Roberto de Say, Normanno de Paunton,[29] Roberto dispensario, Roberto Deyville,[30] Matheo de Vernun, Hamone de Venables, Roberto de Masci,[31] Alano de Waley, Hugone de Culumbe,[32] Roberto de Pulfort, Petro clerico, Hugone de Pasci,[33] Joceralmo de Helesby, Ricardo de Bresci,[34] Ricardo de Kingesle, Philippo de Therven, Lithulfo de Thwamlawe, Ricardo de Perpunt, et toto comitatu Cestrie.

1. omnibus presentem cartam inspecturis, *C, D.*
2. *om. C, D. Here, as elsewhere, the cartulary version is abbreviated; such abbreviations will not normally be noted.*
3. Cestreshirie *B*; Cestreshyrie *E. Similar variations in spelling occur later; they will not be recorded.*
4. *The paragraph numbers have been added for reference.*
5. habeat *F.*
6. guerra *F.*
7. poterit *C, D:* posset *B.*
8. Davennam *B, E:* Daveliham *C, D.*
9. thiuertuic *B;* thwertuick *C, D;* twertnic *E.*
10. sirretestoth *A:* shirifetothe *B;* sirresestoht *E;* sirresitow *F.*
11. acquietanciam *F.*
12. housbote *B.*
13. haibote *A.*
14. placitentur *C, D.*
15. manum opere *A, E;* mannum opere *C, D.*
16. presentem *B, F.*
17. feoudum *A, E.*
18. disparagetur *B, F.*
19. Lymam *A, E.*
20. faciat *B.*
21. *om. A, C, D, E.*
22. *add* toto *B, C, D.*
23. a visu suo *B, F;* visu suo *E; om. C, D.*
24. werre *A, C, D, E.*
25. bullionibus *B.*
26. *witnesses omitted C, D.*
27. Orreby *E.*
28. Koudrey *E.*
29. Pant' *or* Pantulf *A*, le Painter *B.*
30. Devieile *A*, Daivill *B.*
31. Mascy *E.*
32. Columbe *E.*
33. Pascy *E.*
34. Brescy *E.*

This famous document, a counterpart to King John's Magna Carta, has long been available in print. It was published in the seventeenth century by Sir Peter Leycester and by Sir William Dugdale, and James Tait has provided a modern edition with a full commentary (*Chart. St. Werburgh*, pp. 101–107). There is also a large number of early manuscript copies, but all, so far as I have been able to establish, derive from the inspeximus of 1265 (text E) and have no independent value. They have therefore been ignored. It is perhaps surprising that no original text is known to have survived, since, if we are to believe Randle Holme, Ranulf III's charter of liberties was issued, like Magna Carta itself, in more than one exemplification. Unfortunately Holme, though he claims to have had two sealed copies before him, gives no indication of their source. Leycester's text, on the other hand, derives from the same source as Harl. MS. 2155 (text B), which was itself a copy. In general text A has been preferred, since it claims to be copied directly from an original exemplar; but a careful collation reveals no substantial variations between the different sources, except for the versions in the Chester cartulary (texts C and D), which are heavily abbreviated.

While Tait is technically correct in stating that Ranulf III's charter could have been granted at any time between 4 March 1215, when he took the Cross, and the death of the witness Hugh Pascy between May and October 1216 (*Ann. Cestr.*, p. 50), the similarity of many of the clauses to Magna Carta leaves no reasonable doubt that it was granted after King John issued the latter on 19 June 1215. It is more difficult to decide exactly when. After the renewal of civil war in August 1215, Ranulf joined the king as one of his foremost supporters. Tait has suggested (*Chart. St. Werburgh*, p. 108) that he was forced to 'buy off' his own barons to get a free hand. It is perhaps more likely that his charter was a direct reaction to the granting of Magna Carta on the part of barons who were already discontented, particularly if, as the evidence indicates (*J.C.A.S.*, lviii, pp. 110–112), Ranulf had been actively building up his own power to their detriment. The fact that he took the Cross in March, thus placing himself under the protection of the Church, indicates that he was anticipating trouble. It is even possible that the barons' petition, which unfortunately does not survive, was formulated in the early weeks of 1215, at the same time as the English barons made known their demands to King John. On the whole, the evidence suggests that Ranulf's charter falls between June and September 1215, rather than later. It was evidently issued at Chester in a full meeting of the county court.

395.   Confirmation of Aenora Malbank's conveyance to Henry of Audley of all the land she held in Cheshire within the Lyme.

[1217–1218]

> B.L. Harl. MS. 506, f. 14 (new f. 7); Harl. MS. 1535, f. 16 (new f. 44v.); Harl. MS. 2077, f. 99 (new f. 64); Chester, Booth of Twemlow, Liber A, f. 32; Bodleian Library, Dodsworth MS. 82, f. 107 (from Booth's Liber A). Notice: Orm., iii. 391.

Ranulfus comes Cestrie et Lincolnie omnibus ad quos presens scriptum pervenerit salutem. Notum sit vobis me concessisse et hac presenti carta mea confirmasse Henrico de Aldithleghe totam terram de Cestresira, quam tenet de domina Aenora de Maubanc, habendam et tenendam sibi et heredibus suis libere et quiete, sicut carta predicte domine Aenore de Maubanc, quam inde habet, testatur. Ut hec autem mea concessio et confirmacio rata et stabilis permaneat, eam presenti scripto et sigilli mei apposicione corroboravi. Hiis testibus Philippo de Orrebi tunc iusticiario Cestrie, Iohanne de Pratellis, Normanno de Pantou, Alvaredo de Suleyni, Waltero de Daivilla, Roberto fratre eius, Thoma de Orrebi, Roberto de Preus, Liulfo de Twamlowe, Ricardo de Kingeslegh, Ricardo de Bresci, Henrico de Blakenhall, et aliis.

Aenora Malbank was one of the four daughters and co-heiresses of William Malbank (II), the last of the Norman barons of Wich Malbank, or Nantwich. Her charter for Henry of Audley, granting all her lands 'in Cestresiria infra Lymam' for a payment of 100 marks and an annual rent of 40s. (Orm., iii. 390), was enrolled on the Cheshire 'Domesday Roll' on 22 April 1214 (*Ches. Sheaf*, no. 4698). The date of Earl Ranulf's confirmation is not clear, but falls almost certainly before Ranulf's departure on crusade in Whitweek 1218. Richard of Brescy and six other witnesses of the present charter witnessed Ranulf's 'charter of liberties' (**no. 394**) in 1215.

396. Confirmation of Ranulf III's gifts to Henry of Audley of Newhall (Cheshire), formerly in the possession of Hugh de Pascy, and Alstonfield (Staffs.) with the rents of Tunstall, Chatterley, Chell, Thursfield, Bradwell and Normacot; also the earl's right in the mill below his garden in Coventry and the mill of 'Altregeder', with eighteen bondmen by name.

[1217–1227]

P.R.O., C.53 (Chancery Charter Rolls), no. 18, m. 6.
Ed.: *Cal. Ch. Rolls*, i. 36; briefly noticed Orm., iii. 391, and *H.K.F.*, p. 262.

Henricus rex *etc.* salutem. Sciatis nos concessisse et hac presenti carta nostra confirmasse dilecto et fideli nostro Henrico de Aldithele omnes terras et tenementa subscripta, videlicet ex dono Rannulfi comitis Cestrie et Lincolnie totam terram de Nova Aula, que fuit Hugonis de Pascy, cum omnibus pertinentiis suis et totam terram de Alstanesfeld cum pertinentiis suis. Ex dono eiusdem comitis totum redditum de Tunstalle, Chaderlyhe, Chelle, Thurinodesfelde, Bradewulle, Normannecote. Ex dono eiusdem comitis quicquid idem comes habuit in molendino sub gardino ipsius comitis de Covintreia et molendino de Altregeder cum omnibus pertinentiis suis, et Hugonem de Atlekeieghe, Swanum filium Ragenille, Simonem de Peclem, Rannulfum de Raveneshurst, Siwardum filium Swen, magistrum Ricardum, Thomam de Holtona, Simonem de Henlige, Ricardum fabrum, Radulfum Wylaf, Willelmum Wylaf, Avrin Wylaf, Simonem de Assartis, Robertum filium Siwardi, Rogerum de Ernhale, Galfridum de Ernhale, Walterum Kyde, Rogerum Everardi.

Henry III's confirmation, which is the only surviving evidence of the above gifts, is dated 2 May 1227. Ranulf's charter or charters must therefore have fallen in the period 1217–1227. Hugh de Pascy was slain in 1216 (*Ann. Cestr.*, p. 50). This is the only evidence of his enfeoffment at Newhall, part of the barony of Wich Malbank which passed on partition to the portion of Aenora, or Eleanor, Malbank (Orm., iii. 390), who disposed of it c.1214 to Henry of Audley (**no. 395**). Alstonfield also was a part of the Malbank honour (*H.K.F.*, p. 261). It looks therefore as though Eleanor may have conveyed her Staffordshire estates to Henry of Audley, at the same time as she sold her Cheshire lands, in which case Ranulf III's charter may possibly have been granted at the same time as **no. 395**. The account in *Hist. Coll. of Staffordshire*, N.S. xii, pp. 36–43, is not entirely reliable.

397.   Writ to the justiciar of Chester to take action in a plea of mort d'ancestor between Robert son of Ranulf Grosvenor and Robert son of Robert Grosvenor concerning land in Budworth, and to summon Alice, wife of William of Stretton, formerly wife of Robert Grosvenor, grandfather of Robert son of Ranulf, to answer about her dowry.

[c.1217–1224]

London, College of Arms, MS. 1 D. 14, p. 211; B.L. Harl. MS. 2074, f. 158Cv.; Harl. MS. 2079, f. 13 (new f. 6); Add. MS. 6032, p. 234 (new f. 116); Bodleian Library, Dodsworth MS. 31, f. 85; Chester, Booth of Twemlow, Liber D, f. 135. All apparently from Cheshire Domesday Roll. English abstract: Orm., ii. 211; *Ches. Sheaf*, no. 4711 (16).

Ranulfus comes Cestrie et Lincolnie iusticiario suo Cestrie salutem. Monstravit mihi Robertus filius Ranulfi le Grosvenour quod quedam iurata per breve meum de morte antecessoris capta fuit in comitatu meo Cestrie inter Robertum filium Roberti le Grosvenour avi sui et illum de Buddeworth de terra de Buddeworth, que fuit quondam dicti Roberti avi sui; unde ipse Robertus filius Ranulfi queritur quod Alicia quondam uxor dicti avi sui dotem inde habuit iniuste. Quare vobis mando quatenus recordum dicte iurate coram nobis venire faciatis et predictam Aliciam et Willelmum de Stretton virum suum per bonos summonitores *etc.*

The parties to this suit were descendants of Robert Grosvenor, to whom Earl Hugh II had granted Budworth some time between 1162 and 1173 (**no. 163**). The elder Robert and Ranulf Grosvenor were evidently his sons, the former the uncle of Robert son of Ranulf, but the details of the suit cannot be determined. In view of the date of Hugh II's charter, Alice, the relict of the first Robert, must have been an old woman by the time Ranulf III became earl of Lincoln, and this argues for a date not long after 1217 for the present lawsuit, but there is no sure way of determining its date. Of William of Stretton (near Budworth), Alice's second husband, nothing further seems to be known (Orm., i. 663).

398. Confirmation to Bardney abbey of land in Bucknall (Lincs.) given by Roger of Milly.

[1217–1229]

B.L. Cott. MS. Vesp. E. xx (Bardney cartulary), f. 109v. (new f. 115v.). Brief reference: *H.K.F.*, p. 167.

Ranulphus comes Cestrie et Lincolnie omnibus presentibus et futuris presentem cartam inspecturis vel audituris salutem. Noverit universitas vestra me divine caritatis intuitu et pro salute anime mee et antecessorum meorum concessisse et presenti carta confirmasse deo et sancto Oswaldo et monachis de Bardneio ibidem deo servientibus totam terram quam Rogerus de Milay eis dedit et incartavit in villa de Bukenale, quam Simon pater Walteri capellani de Thimelbi tenuit, scilicet duas bovatas terre cum omnibus pertinenciis suis, habendam et tenendam de ipso Rogero et heredibus suis libere, quiete, plene et pacifice in puram et perpetuam elemosinam, prout carta ipsius Rogeri, quam inde habent, testatur. Preterea concessi et hac presenti carta confirmavi dictis monachis quietanciam sequele Alani de Luceby et heredum suorum de wapentaco de Bulingbroch. Et ut hec mea concessio et confirmacio rata et stabilis permaneat et inconcussa, eam presenti scripto et sigilli mei apposicione confirmavi. Hiis testibus Philippo de Orrebi tunc iusticiario Cestrie *etc.*

Roger of Milly died before 1219 (*H.K.F.*, p. 184). His charter is entered on f. 89 (new f. 94) of the cartulary, but does not help with dating.

399.   Grant of protection for the lands and possessions of Bardney abbey.

[1217–1232]

B.L. Cott. MS. Vesp. E. xx (Bardney cartulary), f. 78 (new f. 83).

R. comes Cestrie et Lincolnie omnibus balivis et hominibus suis, ad quos presens scriptum pervenerit, salutem. Sciatis me suscepisse in protectione mea et in manutenemento meo domum sancti Oswaldi de Bardneio et monachos ibidem deo servientes cum possessionibus et rebus suis. Quare vobis mando quatinus dictam domum cum dictis monachis, possessionibus et rebus suis protegatis et manuteneatis, sicut illos qui in mea protectione sunt. Preterea dictis monachis remisi et, quantum ad me pertinet, quietam clamavi demandam, quam eis feci de quodam pellicio et de quodam pari botarum annuus redditus,[1] salvo heredibus Roberti le Marin[2] iure suo, cum terram suam habuerint. Et in huius rei testimonium presens scriptum sigillo meo munitum eis habere feci. Valete.

1. *sic MS.*   2. *Name uncertain.*

The ancient abbey of Bardney was destroyed during the Danish invasions and refounded by Gilbert of Gant about the end of the eleventh century. Thereafter it appears to have remained in Gant patronage. The date and circumstances in which Ranulf III took it into his protection have not been determined, but may well have been shortly after he succeeded Gilbert of Gant, who had been made earl of Lincoln by Louis of France in 1216, as earl of Lincoln in 1217.

400.   Grant to Robert son of Salomon, in exchange for the fee he had in the earl's kitchen, of a rent of 20s. from Dernhall mill and 20s. from Macclesfield mill, also freedom from suit at the hundred court of Edisbury in respect of his land at Tiverton, and a grant of Withington and the land his father and grandfather held at Goulceby in Lindsey, for which gift he has surrendered to the earl the lands his father and grandfather held at Tessy and Aubigny in Normandy.

[1217–1229]

J.R.U.L.M., Mainwaring Charter 11 (14th-century transcript, not original); B.L. Harl. MS. 2074, f. 183v. (new f. 80v), from ancient copy in parchment in possession of William Vernon of Shakerley, 1649; Harl. MS. 2079, f. 160 (new f. 103), 'this coppy I had of Mr Smallwood, 1653 September'; Bodleian Library,

Dodsworth MS. 31, f. 168v.–169 (source not specified);
Chester, Booth of Twemlow, Liber D, f. 214.

Ranulfus comes Cestrie et Lincolnie omnibus presentibus et futuris presentem cartam inspecturis et audituris salutem. Sciatis me concessisse et dedisse et hac presenti carta mea confirmasse Roberto filio Salamonis in escambium totius feodi sui, quod habuit in coquina mea, viginti solidos de redditu annuo in molendino meo de Darnhale, percipiendos illi et heredibus suis de me et heredibus meis per manus firmariorum meorum vel illorum qui molendinum illud tenebunt ad quatuor terminos anni, scilicet ad festum sancti Michaelis quinque solidos, ad Natale Domini quinque solidos, ad Pascha quinque solidos, et in festo nativitatis sancti Iohannis Baptiste quinque solidos. Preterea dedi et concessi eidem Roberto et heredibus suis quietanciam hundredi de Edesbury et puture servientum meorum illi et heredibus suis et omnibus hominibus suis in terra sua de Tevertona manentibus. Et pro hac donacione et concessione mea predictus Robertus remisit et quietum clamavit imperpetuum de se et heredibus suis totum iamdictum feodum suum, quod habuit in coquina mea, ita quod nec ipse nec heredes eius in predicto feodo aliquid iuris vel clamei exigere vel clamare poterint.

Dedi etiam et concessi et hac presenti carta mea confirmavi eidem Roberto et heredibus suis Wythintonam cum omnibus pertinenciis et libertatibus suis et in molendino meo de Macclesfeld viginti solidos annuatim percipiendos, quousque illi assignavero viginti solidos in terra, et preterea totam terram quam pater suus et avus suus tenuerunt in Golgisby in Lyndeseya cum pertinenciis suis, tenendas et habendas illi et heredibus suis de me et heredibus meis libere, quiete, plene et hereditarie, reddendo inde annuatim mihi et heredibus meis de se et heredibus suis quedam calcaria deaurata vel quatuor denarios ad festum sancti Iohannis Baptiste pro omnibus serviciis et exactionibus mihi et heredibus meis de predictis terris pertinentibus. Et pro hac concessione et donacione mea idem Robertus remisit et quietam clamavit mihi et heredibus meis de se et heredibus suis totam terram quam pater et avus suus de me tenuerunt in Normannia, scilicet in Tessy et Aubigneium, ita quod nec ipse nec heredes eius in predicta terra aliquid iuris vel clamei exigere vel vendicare poterunt. Hiis testibus Iohanne constabulario Cestrie, Philippo de Orreby iusticiario Cestrie, Rogero dapifero Cestrie, Warino de Vernoun, Willelmo de Venables, Hamone de Mascy, Rogero de Maynwarin, Iohanne filio Philippi, Willelmo filio David, Radulfo filio Simonis, et aliis.

Although briefly cited by Ormerod (ii. 277 and iii. 720) and by Earwaker (*East Cheshire*, ii. 375), this somewhat unusual charter does not appear to have been printed previously. Curiously, neither Ormerod nor Earwaker mentions the cook's fee. References in the charters to the cook are, in fact, rare. Much earlier, Herbert the cook and his son Wimund are mentioned (**no. 80**), and it is evident from the context that they were actually engaged in the kitchen. In the present instance the cook's fee is obviously a considerable holding, and there is little doubt that the actual duties were performed by a deputy or deputies. Unfortunately we know no more about it, nor about Robert son of Salomon. Ormerod (iii. 720 note) conjectured that he was a Norman, but many families held lands in England and Normandy, and Robert's grandfather was already a landholder in Lincolnshire, probably in the time of Henry II. The date of the present charter is also difficult to estimate. It must fall after 1217 and before 1229, when Orreby ceased to be justiciar. As Normandy in this period was in the hands of the king of France, it is hard to account for Ranulf's interest in Robert's Norman lands. The only likely time would be 1224–27, when England and France were at war; but it would be hazardous to hang any conjecture on as slender a thread as this.

401.   Confirmation of Richard Putra's gift to Ranulf Mainwaring of the whole of Great Warford, which was part of the demesne of Roger Mainwaring.

[1217–1229]

> Tabley MSS., Sir Peter Leycester's Liber B, f. 1 ('extracted out of a very ancient Coppy of a Deede now in possession of Mr.Massey of Podington, 1662').

Ranulphus comes Cestrie et Lincolnie . . . dedi . . . Ranulpho Mainwaringe rationabile donum quod Ricardus Putra ei fecit de tota villa magne Werford, que fuit de dominico Rogeri de Mainwaringe cum toto molendino . . . sicut carta dicti Ricardi Putra, quam idem Ranulfus inde habet, rationabiliter testatur . . . Testibus Philippo de Orreby tunc iusticiario Cestrie, *etc.*

This charter, of which only this brief extract survives, cannot be dated more closely than 1217–1229. Nothing appears otherwise to be known of Richard Putra. Ranulf Mainwaring was younger brother of Roger Mainwaring, elder son of Ralph Mainwaring, the justiciar (Orm., iii. 226, 229); both witnessed with their father a charter for the nuns of Chester (**no. 225**) as early as 1200–1203. Great Warford was part of the lordship of Ralph Mainwaring before the end of the twelfth century (Orm., iii. 584), but little else is known of its early history. According to Leycester (*loc. cit.*), Ranulf Mainwaring gave it to his son Laurence about 1270; but if he was alive in 1200, this is not very plausible.

402.   Quittance to Hugh Cholmondeley of suit of court in the county court of Chester and the hundred of Dudeston (now Broxton) and of providing a judger for his lands in Cholmondeley.

[1217–1229]

Orig.: Cheshire Record Office, Cholmondeley Deeds, Box A, no. 1. Enrolments: P.R.O., CHES 34/1, m. 7, and CHES 34/4, m. 30. Short abstracts: B.L. 338 [*sic*], f. 29v. (from original, with drawing of seal); Tabley MSS., Sir Peter Leycester's Liber A, f. 146, and Chester, Booth of Twemlow, Liber H, f. 105 (both with description of seal). Other abstracts (abbreviated): Booth of Twemlow, Liber D, f. 132; Shakerley MS. 3, p. 16; B.L. Harl. MS. 2074, f. 158v.; Harl. MS. 2115, f. 163v.; Chetham's Library, Towneley MSS., transcripts from the Vernon MSS., pp. 28–29. Short notice: Orm., ii. 630; abstract in English from original, *Ches. Sheaf*, no. 10307.

Omnibus presentibus et futuris has literas visuris et audituris Rannulfus comes Cestrie et Lincolnie salutem. Sciatis me concessisse et hac presenti carta mea confirmasse Hugone de Chelmundele et heredibus suis de me et heredibus meis quietanciam secte comitatus Cestrie et hundredi de Dudeston et de uno iudice, quem nobis debuit de terra sua de Chelmundele. Quare volumus et firmiter precipimus quod predictus Hugo et heredes sui quieti sint de predicta secta et de predicto iudice de me et heredibus meis in perpetuum. Et in huius rei testimonium hoc scriptum sigillo meo roboravi. Hiis testibus Philippo de Orreby tunc iusticiario Cestrie, Iohanne constabulario Cestrie, Henrico de Alditheleghe, Iohanne de Ardene, Warino de Vernun, Waltero de Coventreia, Willelmo de Venables, Hamone de Venables,[1] Hamone de Mascy, Hugone et Galfrido dispensariis, Stephano de Sadgrave, Thoma Tusket, Ricardo Phitun, Willelmo de Vernun, Willelmo de Malo Passu, Willelmo clerico de Stoke, et multis aliis.

SEAL (now missing): 3 garbs in an escutcheon, legend:
+ S. SECR . . . M RANVLFI COM: CESTRIE ET LI
. . .

---

1. This name is almost certainly a scribal error, a conflation of the preceding and succeeding witnesses. There is no known Hamon de Venables.

This grant must fall within the justiciarship of Philip of Orreby (i.e. before April 1229), but cannot otherwise be dated closely. Walter of Coventry, who had been Earl Ranulf's seneschal in Lincolnshire, was dead by 1227 (Coss, no. 21); but the witness of the present charter may well be his successor. The dates of Hugh Cholmondeley are not known, but he was apparently still living as late as 1244 (*Chart. St. Werburgh*, pp. 408, 410).

403. Grant to Richard, son of Robert of Frodsham, of the land which belonged to Ranulf, formerly the earl's reeve in Frodsham.

[1217–1232]

P.R.O., CHES 29/43 (Plea Rolls, 6 Edw. III), m. 19v.

. . . Ranulphus quondam comes Cestrie et Lincolnie per cartam suam dedisset Ricardo filio Roberti de Frodesham totam terram cum pertinentiis, que fuit Ranulphi quondam prepositi ipsius comitis in Frodesham, habendam et tenendam sibi et heredibus suis de ipso comite et heredibus suis, reddendo annuatim eidem comiti et heredibus suis viginti solidos ad certos terminos et duos porcos de consuetudine in festo sancti Martini.

This notice, from a pleading in the county court at Chester in 1332, is the only surviving evidence of this grant, but it evidently follows closely the wording of Earl Ranulf's charter. It can only be dated between Ranulf's appointment as earl of Lincoln and his death. There is no Richard son of Robert in Ormerod's pedigree (Orm., ii. 48), although a Richard appears c.1232; but the pedigree is not very reliable. Ranulf the reeve witnessed a charter of Philip of Orreby for Peter of Frodsham (Cheshire Record Office, Cholmondeley Deeds, Box F, no. 1), but unfortunately it cannot be closely dated.

404. Writ to Richard Fitton, ordering him to give Alexander of Multon seisin of the lands he held at the beginning of the war.

[1218]

Printed: Stenton, *Rolls of the Justices in Eyre for Yorkshire, 1218–19*, Selden Society, lvi, case 34, p. 15.

Rannulfus comes Cestrie et Lincolnie dilecto et fideli suo Ricardo Fitun salutem. Mandatum regis suscepi in hec verba: H. dei gratia *etc.* dilecto sibi R. comiti Cestrie et Lincolnie salutem. Precipio tibi, quod sine dilatione talem saisinam habere faciatis Alexandro de Muletona, talem saisinam de terra sua in balliva vestra, qualem habuit in inicione guerre, nisi aliquam prius *etc.* Quare vobis mando, ut talem saisinam *etc.*

Ranulf was created earl of Lincoln on 23 May 1217, and the war ended on 12 September. The indications are that this writ, unfortunately only extant in abbreviated form, was issued not much later, probably early in 1218. Richard Fitton was one of the witnesses to Earl Ranulf's charter of liberties (**no. 394**) in 1215.

405. Grant to the burgesses of Chipping Campden (Gloucs.), freeing them and all comers to his market there of toll, and setting a penalty of 12d. if any burgess fell into his mercy, unless he had shed blood or committed a felony.

[1218–1232]

P.R.O., C.53 (Chancery Charter Rolls), no. 41, m. 4; C.56 (Chancery Confirmation Rolls), no. 95, m. 3 (confirmation of preceding). Ed.: *Cal. Ch. Rolls*, i. 340; noted in Ballard, *British Borough Charters*, ii. 264.

Rex archiepiscopis *etc.* salutem. Concessionem quam Hugo de Gundevilla fecit burgensibus de Campedena de burgagiis in burgo de Campedena et concessionem quam Rannulfus quondam comes Cestrie fecit eisdem burgensibus, de eo quod ipsi et omnes qui venient ad forum suum de Campedena sint quieti de theloneo, et quod si aliquis liberorum burgensium suorum de Campedena inciderit in misericordiam suam, quietus sit pro duodecim denariis nisi fecerit sanguinem aut feloniam.

The early charters of Chipping Campden have perished, and this short notice in Henry III's confirmation of 1249 is the only surviving evidence of Ranulf III's charter. The history of Chipping Campden after the time of Ranulf II (**no. 59**) is obscure, but it has been suggested (*Trans. Bristol and Gloucs. Arch. Soc.*, ix, pp. 139, 142) that it was forfeited after Hugh II's rebellion in 1173, and given to Hugh de Gondeville, and only restored after his death. It was certainly in Ranulf III's possession by 1199, and in 1218 he was granted an annual fair on 25–27 July (*Rot. Litt. Clausarum*, i. 361). The charter referred to in the present confirmation evidently followed after that, and probably not long after, but the exact date cannot be established.

406. Grant to Robert, son of Thurstan Woodford, of a croft called Woodford, which his father held.

[1220–1225]

B.L. Harl. MS. 2060, f. 93 (old f. 178); Harl. MS. 2064, f. 13v. (both from Leiger Book of Vale Royal, now lost, f. 14). Engl. transl.: *R.S.L.C.*, lxviii, p. 30.

Omnibus presentibus et futuris presentem cartam inspecturis vel audituris Ranulfus comes Cestrie et Lincolnie salutem. Sciatis me dedisse et concessisse et hac presenti carta mea confirmasse Roberto filio Thurstani de Wodeford pro

homagio et servicio suo unum croftum terre que vocatur Wodesford cum
pertinentiis omnibus, que predictus Thurstanus pater suus de me tenuit, in
longtitudine de Assebroke usque ad fossatum de Bruere et in latitudine a vado le
Vernun usque ad culturam de Smaldene, habendam et tenendam eidem Roberto
et heredibus suis de me et heredibus meis libere et quiete, integre et honorifice,
reddendo inde annuatim mihi et heredibus meis de ipso Roberto et heredibus
suis quinque solidos et unum porcum racionabilem ad pacandum, scilicet ad
Natale ii.s. vi.d. et ad festum sancti Iohannis Baptiste ii.s. vi.d. et ad festum
sancti Martini dictum porcum pro omni servicio et exaccione quacumque; pro
quo porco quietus erit de pasnagio de porcis suis propriis in bosco meo. Et ego et
heredes mei dicto Roberto et heredibus suis dictam terram cum pertinenciis per
predictum servicium contra omnes gentes warantizabimus. Hiis testibus Philippo
de Orreby tunc iusticiario Cestrie, Ricardo filio Liulfi, Ricardo de Kyngeslee,
Iocerano de Helesby, Ricardo de Kagwrth, Petro de Frodesham, Ricardo de
Arderne, Simone clerico, et multis aliis.

The date of this charter can only be approximately fixed, but it is certainly earlier
than **no. 407** for the same recipient. The appearance of Richard son of Liulf (of
Twemlow) in second place among the witnesses after Philip of Orreby suggests
that he may have been sheriff, although not named as such. If so, the date is
probably 1220–25, as his shrievalty (though the dates have not been established)
certainly falls in the earlier part of Ranulf III's tenure as earl of Chester and
Lincoln; he occurs as sheriff in 1221–23 (**no. 408**). The manor or estate of
Woodford lay within the boundaries of Over (Orm., ii. 182), but seems to have
disappeared.

407.   Grant to Robert son of Thurstan of Woodford of a parcel of land in
exchange for his fields at Woodford occupied by the earl's park of
Darnhall.

[1225–1230]

B.L. Harl. MS. 2060, f. 179 (new f. 93v.); Harl. MS. 2064,
f. 13v. (both from Leiger Book, now lost, of Vale Royal,
f. 14); Engl. transl.: *R.S.L.C.*, lxviii, p. 30.

Ranulfus comes Cestrie et Lincolnie omnibus presentem cartam inspecturis et
audituris salutem. Sciatis me dedisse et concessisse et hac presenti carta mea
confirmasse Roberto filio Thurstani de Wodeford pro homagio et servicio suo
quendam terram cum pertinenciis infra has divisas, scilicet de Wyldemareford
usque Heppedene in latitudine et de Heppedene usque le Wytesyche in
longtitudine, et de Wytesych usque ad cheminum de Wyldemarefort, in excambium pratorum suorum de Wodeford per vivarium meum de Dernehale

occupatorum, habendam et tenendam de me et heredibus meis eidem Roberto et heredibus suis libere et quiete in feudo et hereditate, reddendo inde de Wodeford annuatim mihi et heredibus meis de ipso Roberto et heredibus suis quinque solidos et unum porcum racionabilem ad pacandum, ad Natale ii.s. et vi.d. et ad festum sancti Iohannis Baptiste ii.s. et vi.d. et ad festum sancti Martini dictum porcum pro omni servicio et exaccione quacumque. In cuius rei testimonium presentem cartam sigillo meo munitam ei habere feci. Hiis testibus Philippo de Orreby tunc iusticiario Cestrie, Willelmo de Malo Passu, Ricardo de Sondbach tunc vicecomite Cestrie, Ricardo de Kingesle, Petro de Frodesham, Stephano de Merton, Roberto Grosso Venatore, Willelmo de Weure, Godefrido de la[1] Lawe, Rogero de London, Petro clerico domini comitis, Willelmo de Wode, Roberto . . .[2]

1. Witness-list in Harl. 2060 ends here.
2. sic MS.; witness-list incomplete.

The main interest of this charter is the reference to the earl's park[1] at Darnhall. This appears to have been a favourite country residence in Cheshire of Ranulf III and Earl John the Scot, who died here in 1237 (*Ann. Cestr.*, p. 60); it was later given by Edward I to his new foundation of Vale Royal. Ranulf III, who at the same time was building up the estate of his park at Macclesfield (**no. 410**), was clearly intent on expanding and no doubt improving it: hence his interest in the present exchange with Robert, son of Thurstan, so far as can be seen a very minor person with a smallholding of only one croft in Woodford (**no. 406**), about whom nothing else is known. The date of the charter appears to be c.1225–30, or perhaps a little later. Richard of Sandbach occurs as sheriff in 1229–30 (Orm., i. 70) and seems to have been the last sheriff under Ranulf III, but this would be a very late date for Peter the earl's clerk, whose latest occurrences otherwise (**nos. 387, 389**) do not extend much beyond 1226 (*E.C.C.*, p. 46).

1. Vivarium also means fishpond (or 'stew'), and is often used in this sense, but clearly has the wider connotation of park in this instance.

408. Grant of the wood of Marple and Wybersley and specified liberties in the forest to William Vernon for the service already owed of finding a forester.

[1221–1223]

Sudbury Hall, Derbyshire, Lord Vernon's muniments, Box xxix, Addenda III, 3 (14th-century transcript on paper); Bodleian Library, MS. Top. Cheshire b. I, p. 165 (from an exemplification under the great seal, 1 Mary); B.L. Harl. MS. 2072, f. 9 (abbreviated text without

witnesses from Macclesfield forest pleas); P.R.O., CHES
17/12 (Eyre Rolls, 15 Edw. I), m. 7. Ed.: *Chetham Soc.*,
N.S. lxxxiv, pp. 229–30 (from Chester 17/12, abbreviated
without witnesses).

Ranulphus comes Cestrie et Lincolnie omnibus presentibus et futuris hoc
scriptum visuris vel audituris salutem. Sciatis me dedisse et hac presenti carta
mea confirmasse Willelmo de Vernun pro homagio et servicio suo totum boscum
de Merpille et Wyberisleghe cum omnibus pertinenciis et libertatibus suis
liberum et quietum, et omnes aerias espervariorum in predicto bosco. Et
preterea concessi eidem Willelmo de Vernun in predicto bosco agistamenta
omnium porcorum suorum cum toto pannagio sine vexacione et impedimento.
Preterea dedi predicto Willelmo de Vernun licenciam assartandi in predictis
boscis de Merpille et Wyberisleghe, ubicumque voluerit pro libito suo. Preterea
dedi et concessi dicto Willelmo totum boscum meum cum pastura usque
Bluntesbroc et agistamenta porcorum et pannagium cum aisiamentis de boscis
ad averia sua sine vexacione et impedimento. Dedi eciam ei acquietanciam de
placitis foreste. Hec omnia predicta, scilicet boscos, aerias espervariorum, et
assartiones et agistamenta porcorum, pannagium et pasturam, dedi et concessi
predicto Willelmo de Vernun, habenda et tenenda sibi et heredibus suis de me et
heredibus meis libere et quiete, integre et honorifice in omnibus locis cum
omnibus libertatibus sine impedimento forestariorum et ballivorum meorum,
per idem servicium forestarie quod predictus Willelmus mihi facere solebat pro
terra sua de Merpille et Wyberisleghe antequam ei hanc libertatem concess-
issem, scilicet unum forestarium inveniendi pro omnibus serviciis et demandis,
salvis mihi et heredibus meis in predictis terris et boscis venacione et aeriis
ostrorum et placitis que pertinent ad gladium. Et prohibeo ne quis eum vel
heredes suos implacitet vel impediat de predictis libertatibus super forisfacturam
decem librarum. Et ut hec mea donacio rata sit et inconcussa permaneat, hoc
presens scriptum sigillo meo corroboravi. Hiis testibus[1] Philippo de Orreby tunc
iusticiario Cestrie, Hugone expensatore,[2] Henrico de Aldeleghe, Waltero de
Coventreia tunc senescallo, Ricardo Phyton, Hasculfo de Suliny, Ricardo filio
Lydulphi tunc vicecomite, Philippo de Orreby iuniore, Roberto de Vernon,
Roberto de Cok,[3] Willelmo de Parles,[4] Ricardo do Coventreia, Willelmo clerico
domini comitis, et multis aliis.

1. *Witnesses only in Sudbury MS. and in Top. Ch. b.I.*
2. *sic MSS.*
3. Tok *Sudbury MS.*
4. *sic in both MSS.*

Marple and Wybersley had been granted to Robert of Stockport in or about 1206
(**no. 341**) and he conveyed them to his sister Margaret and her husband William
Vernon on terms similar to those of the present charter at an unspecified date
after 1208 (Orm., iii. 839). Ranulf III's grant of the adjacent wood evidently
supplements this acquisition. Although some of the extensive forest liberties

claimed look suspiciously like later additions, there is no reason to suppose that the charter as it stands is not substantially genuine. As Hugh Despenser (here very exceptionally 'expensator') did not succeed his brother Thomas until 1218 (*H.K.F.*, p. 59), it can safely be dated after Earl Ranulf's return from crusade in 1220 and probably not later than 1222 or 1223, by which time Walter of Coventry had been superseded as the earl's seneschal in Lincolnshire by Gilbert Cusin (**no. 299**). Richard of Coventry was Walter's younger son (*H.K.F.*, p. 147). The dates of Richard son of Liulf as sheriff have not been established, and the present charter is valuable evidence of his tenure.

409. Grant to Vivian Davenport of the master serjeanty of Macclesfield, which Adam of Sutton held, in exchange for the land of Wilwich, which he restored to the earl.

[1221–1225]

> Orig.: J.R.U.L.M., Bromley-Davenport Muniments, Deeds, Davenports of Davenport (iii). Transcr.: P.R.O., Chester 34/4 (Quo Warranto 15 Hen. VII), m. 28; B.L. Harl. MS. 2038, f. 86v. (new f. 92v.); Harl. 2074, f. 181v. (new f. 78v.); Bodleian Library, Dodsworth MS. 31, f. 15; Chetham's Library, Towneley's transcripts from Vernon MSS., p. 24; Shakerley MS. 3, p. 14. Ed.: Orm., iii. 62, note b (inaccurate).

Rannulfus comes Cestrie et Lincolnie universis presentibus et futuris salutem. Sciatis me concessisse et dedisse et hac carta mea confirmasse Viviano de Daveneport magistralem servienciam de Maclesfelde, illam scilicet quam Adam de Suttona tenuit, habendam et tenendam illi et heredibus suis in escambium terre sue de Wilewic, quam mihi reddidit cum omnibus pertinenciis suis, ita scilicet quod, si idem Vivianus vel aliquis heredum suorum forisfaciat, unde non possit vel nolit pati esgardum curie mee, balliam dictam amittat in perpetuum, et etiam terra sua tota,[1] quam de me tenet in capite, incurrat. Hiis testibus domino Hugone abbate Cestrie, Philippo de Orreby tunc iusticiario, Henrico de Audithele, Rogero de Mainelwarin, Aluredo de Sulinny, Thoma de Orreby, Herberto de Orreby, Ricardo de Cagwrth tunc camerario, magistro Hugone, et multis aliis.

> SEAL, on tag: six garbs, three, two, one, on heater shield; legend gone.

1. *altered from* terram suam totam *in orig.*

Vivian Davenport was the son of Richard Davenport, who was granted quittance of suit of hundred and county by Ranulf III between 1207 and 1213 (**no. 348**), but the date when he succeeded his father is not known. The present charter almost certainly falls between Ranulf III's return from Damietta in August 1220 and the death of Abbot Hugh of Chester in July 1226, and probably nearer the later date, at which time Ranulf is known to have been particularly interested in the area Newcastle–Leek–Macclesfield, probably in connection with the building and endowing of his new foundation of Dieulacres (*Ann. Cestr.*, p. 53). Hilton abbey was forced at this time to hand over part of its land at Rushton for incorporation in Ranulf's new park of Newcastle-under-Lyme (**no.423**). Vivian Davenport's surrender of Wilwich was also involuntary. An inquisition taken about 1250 (Orm., iii. 62, note c) reports at length how he was compelled 'against his will' to exchange 'the park and vivaries of Macclesfield, otherwise called Wilwich', for the serjeanty of Macclesfield, and how later Earl John deprived him of puture in certain lands within the serjeanty. This probably explains the unusually severe terms of the present grant, namely that if Vivian was unwilling to suffer the judgement of the earl's court, he would lose his bailiwick in perpetuity and place at risk all the lands he held of the earl in chief. Such a clause is entirely unprecedented, and probably indicates Ranulf's awareness of Vivian's discontent with the enforced transaction. It is also further evidence, if evidence were needed, of Ranulf's imperiousness. It is also possible (Orm., iii. 757) that Adam of Sutton, whose grandfather had been invested with the forestership by Hugh II (**no. 197**), was arbitrarily deprived to make way for Vivian Davenport's appointment.

410.   Release to Vivian Davenport of the rent of 3s. which he rendered for Hysebelesbothes and the land of Peter the Smith in exchange for Hysebelesbothes, which he has quitclaimed to the earl.

[1225–1229]

> Orig.: J.R.U.L.M., Bromley-Davenport Muniments, Deeds, Davenports of Davenport. Transcr. (incomplete): B.L. Harl. MS. 2074, f. 182 (new f. 79). Ed.: Orm., iii, 63, note 1 (from Harl, 2074).

R. comes Cestrie et Lincolnie omnibus presentibus et futuris presentem cartam inspecturis et audituris salutem.[1] Sciatis me relaxasse et quietos clamasse in perpetuum de me et heredibus meis Viviano de Daveneport et heredibus suis tres solidos de redditu, quos idem Vivianus reddere solebat mihi pro Hysebelesbothes et pro terra Petri fabri, in escambium de Ysebelesbothes, quem mihi et heredibus[2] de se et suis heredibus quietum clamavit a bosco de Willewiche usque aquam, reddendo annuatim mihi et heredibus meis de se et heredibus suis quatuor sagittas barbatas ad festum Omnium Sanctorum pro omni servicio et

exactione quacumque de terra predicti Petri fabri, quam eidem et heredibus suis
quietam clamavi. Hiis testibus Philippo de Orrebi iusticiario meo tunc temporis,
Willelmo de Vernon, Ricardo Phiton, Iohanne filio Philippi, Roberto de
Stokeport, Iordano de Bredburi, Iohanne Fiton, Henrico de Wrthe, Thoma de
Teteswrthe, Ricardo de Wibbenburi, et aliis.

> SEAL: on tag, now missing; according to Harl. 2074, 'a
> heater shield with three garbs, 2 and 1, inscription gone.'

1. *After* salutem, *concluding first line,* No, *presumably first syllable of* Notum, *apparently changed
    to the direct notification* Sciatis.
2. meis *omitted MS.?*

This charter clearly belongs to the period when Ranulf III was assembling land
for his park at Macclesfield at the expense, among others, of Vivian Davenport
(**no. 409**), and probably dates from about the same time or a little later.
Isbelsbooths has disappeared, but the description of its location as extending
from Wilwich wood to 'the water', shows it was adjacent to Wilwich (also no
longer identifiable as such), which Vivian was also forced to surrender. William
Vernon succeeded Philip of Orreby as justiciar in 1229; Richard of Wybunbury
was sheriff c.1233. The date of the charter cannot be closely fixed, but the
comparison with **no. 409** suggests that it falls between 1225 and 1229.

411.   Agreement with Llywelyn, prince of North Wales, for the marriage of
Llywelyn's daughter Helen with John the Scot, Ranulf's nephew and heir,
and the terms of the marriage settlement.

[1222]

> Original cyrograph: B.L. Cott. Charter xxiv, 17. Tran-
> scripts (abbreviated): Bodleian Library, Dugdale MS. 15,
> f. 147; B.L. Harl. MS. 2044, f. 30 (old f. 5), both 'ex
> authographo penes Somerford Oldfeild de Somerford in
> comitatu Cestrie, anno 1647'; Harl. 2079, f. 32 ('This I had
> from Mr. Vernon, but the Welch testes are mistaken in
> names'). Ed.: Orm., i. 43. Abstracts: Dugdale, *Warwick-
> shire*, p. 543; Owen, *Catalogue of the Manuscripts relating
> to Wales in the British Museum*, iii. 526.

Hec est convencio facta inter dominum Rannulphum comitem Cestrie et
Lincolnie et dominum Lewelinum principem Norwallie, videlicet quod Iohannes
de Scotia nepos predicti comitis de sorore sua primogenita ducet in uxorem
Helenam filiam ipsius Lewelini, ita quod dictus Lewelinus dabit dicto Iohanni in
liberum maritagium totum manerium de Budiford in Warewikisira et manerium

de Sutthele in comitatu Wigornie cum omnibus pertinenciis suis, sicut dominus
rex Iohannes ea illi dedit in liberum maritagium, et totum manerium de
Welintona in comitatu Salopesbirie cum omnibus pertinenciis suis infra villam et
extra, habenda et tenenda dicto Iohanni et heredibus suis ex dicta Helena
provenientibus, sicut idem Lewelinus ea aliquo tempore melius et integrius
tenuit. Et preterea dabit eidem Iohanni mille marcas argenti, ita quod die
desponsacionis, scilicet in octabo assumpcionis beate Marie, faciet dominus
Lewelinus memorato Iohanni plenariam seisinam dictorum maneriorum cum
omnibus ad ea pertinentibus, et cum omnibus munimentis que dominus Lewelinus habet de dictis maneriis tam de domino rege quam de aliis; et
nichilominus eodem die cartam suam et cartam domine Iohanne uxoris sue
eidem Iohanni habere faciet, et eodem die ei solvet quingentas marcas argenti,
et alias quingentas marcas solvet ei in festo sancti Michaelis proximo sequenti.
Et si forte contigerit quod dominus Lewelinus propter calumpniam heredum
Thome de Erdintona vel alio casu manerium de Welintona predictis Iohanni et
Helene uxori[1] sue et illorum heredibus guarantizare nequiverit, dominus
Lewelinus faciet eis racionabile et competens escambium in comitatu Salopesberie, nisi forte dominus R. comes Cestrie et Lincolnie prece vel pecunia possit
illorum calumpniam pacificare, et tunc quicquid ad pacificandam[1] dictam
calumpniam idem comes erogaverit, dictus Lewelinus solvet illud plenarie.
Dictus vero Iohannes dicto desponsacionis die[1] assignabit dicte Helene nomine
dotis centum libratas terre, et si forte aliquis casus contigerit quod dicti comes et
Lewelinus ad predictum diem desponsacionis faciende interesse nequiverint,
nichilominus alio die per eorundem comune consilium statuendo fiat despon-
sacio. Et hanc convencionem firmiter et bona fide tenendam Iohannes de Scotia
et Helena in manu domini Reineri episcopi de sancto Asaph affidarunt, et
dominus comes supradictus et Lewelinus eam iuramentis suis et sigillis suis una
cum multis de eorundem fidelibus confirmarunt. Testibus domino Reinero
episcopo de sancto Asaph, domino H. abbate Cestrie, domino H. de Lasci
comite Ultonie, P. de Orrebi iusticiario Cestrie, H. de Aldidele, Gualtero de
Daivilla, Ricardo Phiton, Edeneuet Vaghan, Ennion filio Righerit, Goronou
filio Edeneuet, Heilin filio Keuret, Heilin filio Idhit, magistro Estruit, magistro
Ada, David clerico Lewelini, magistro H. et Simone clericis domini comitis, et
multis aliis.

> SEAL of Llywelyn: obverse, to the right equestrian figure
> in armour, horse galloping; legend defaced. Reverse:
> antique oval intaglio gem, a boar passant to the right
> under a tree; legend SIGILLUM SECRETUM
> LEWLINI.

1. *MS. torn and illegible; word supplied.*

The marriage of John the Scot and Helen sealed the peace which Ranulf
concluded with Llywelyn of Wales in 1218, shortly before he set out on crusade,

and which was renewed after his return in 1220 (*Ann. Cestr.*, p. 50). The marriage took place in 1222, presumably on 22 August as foreseen in the agreement, but the marriage settlement was clearly drawn up earlier in the year. Only the part of the cyrograph sealed by Llywelyn, i.e. Ranulf III's copy, survives. The manors of Bidford (Warwick) and Suckley (Worcs.), here conveyed to John the Scot, had been conferred on Llywelyn in 1215 (Lloyd, p. 647). It is not clear when or how he obtained Wellington (Salop.), which had been granted to Thomas of Erdington, sheriff of Shropshire, in 1212 (*P.R.S.*, N.S. xvii, p. 112), but presumably after Thomas's death, which appears to have occurred in 1218 (*Cal. Pat. Rolls, 1216–25*, p. 168). Evidently Thomas's heirs still contested possession. Of the witnesses Reiner, who had been bishop of St. Asaph since 1186, had frequently played a mediatory role; he was now an old man, and died in 1224 (Lloyd, p. 689). Ednyfed Fychan (*Edeneuet Vaghan*) was Llywelyn's leading counsellor and seneschal (Lloyd, p. 684), whose place was taken after his death in 1246 by his son Goronwy (*Goronou*). The clerks Ystrwyth (*Estruit*), Adam and David were all active on Llywelyn's behalf (Lloyd, p. 685). The other Welsh witnesses – Heilin ap Cywryd (*Keuret*), Heilin ap Iddig (*Idhit*), and Einion ap Rhydderch (*Righerit*) – have not been identified.

412.   Grant to the nuns of Polesworth of ten marks annually from his rent at Coventry, until he was able to assign them the same amount in a fixed place, out of which the nuns were to pay two marks a year to the monks of Barberie.

[1222]

P.R.O., C.54 (Chancery Close Rolls), no. 147, m. 39 dorso. Ed.: *Cal. Close Rolls, 1327–30*, p. 357; Coss, no. 21.

For a full text of this document, see Coss, *The Early Records of Medieval Coventry*, pp. 26–7 (no. 21).

It has been suggested (J. Lancaster, *Medieval Coventry – a City Divided?*, p. 34 and note 16) that Ranulf III's grant to Polesworth was in some way compensation for injuries inflicted in the time of Stephen, the implication apparently being that R(obert) the father of R(obert) Marmion, for the salvation of whose soul the gift was made, was Robert II, who was killed in 1114 (**no. 75**). The truth is a good deal simpler. Polesworth, like Barberie in Calvados, was a Marmion foundation. On 13 November 1221, Earl Ranulf contracted to pay £400 for the wardship and marriage of Robert Marmion, son and heir of Robert Marmion senior, who died in 1218 (*Cal. Pat. Rolls, 1216–25*, p. 319). Evidently his gift was made for the soul of his ward's father, Robert IV. It seems to fall in 1222. Jocius, the earl's chaplain, was prebendary of Underdown in Bridgnorth. This prebend was vacant by 12 December 1222 (*ibid.*, p. 359). Assuming that the vacancy was due to Jocius's death, the date of Ranulf's charter can be fixed within narrow limits.

413.   Grant to the nuns of Greenfield (Lincs.) of freedom from suit at his court of Greetham for the lands in Haugh, Wainfleet, Ulceby, Bilsby, Swaby, Thoresby, Huttoft, Claythorpe, Fairford and Newton, which they hold of the honour of Greetham.

[1217–1232, possibly c. 1223]

> Orig.: B.L. Harl. Charter 52 A 16. Transcripts (from orig.): B.L. Harl. MS. 2060, f. 36 (old p. 64); Tabley MSS., Sir Peter Leycester's Liber C, pars II, f. 14. Ed.: (with facsimile of seal): Nichols, *Leicestershire*, II. i. App. xv, p. 39 (abbreviated); mentioned by Stenton, *Danelaw Charters*, p. cviii.

Rannulfus comes Cestrie et Lincolnie omnibus senescallis suis, ballivis et ministris suis salutem. Sciatis me divine caritatis intuitu et pro salute anime mee et animarum antecessorum et heredum meorum remisisse et in perpetuum quiete clamasse de me et de heredibus meis domui de Grenefeld et monialibus ibidem deo servientibus sectas omnes de curia mea de Graham de tenementis omnibus subscriptis, que de feodo meo tenent de honore de Graham; scilicet de quinquaginta quinque acris terre arabilis et de quinque acris prati in Haga de dono Amfridi de Haga; et de quinque acris terre in Haga de dono Thome Burgevin et Agnetis uxoris sue; et de duobus toftis in villa de Wainflode de dono Philippo de Praeres; et de undecim acris terre arabilis et quadam cultura, que vocatur Butrecalewange, in Ulesbi de dono ipsius Philippi de Praeres; et de una acra terre et duobus sellionibus in Suabi de dono Henrici filii Gilberti; et de una acra terre in Suabi de dono Willelmi Burgevin; et de uno tofto et de una acra terre in Suabi de dono Gilberti le Noreis, et de pastura ad viginti quatuor oves et ad tria animalia de dono ipsius Gilberti; et de duabus acris terre in Suabi de dono Philippi filii Gilberti; et de quinque acris et dimidia terre arabilis et dimidia perticata de marisco in Suabi de dono Roberti filii Haldani; et de duabus acris et dimidia in Suabi de dono Roberti filii sacerdotis; et triginta tribus acris terre in Thoresbi de dono Willelmi filii Otueri; et una bovata terre in Farford de dono Allani de Wdetorpe; et de una deila prati in Hotoft de dono Radulfi de Bilesbi; et de una acra terre in marisco de Clactorpe de dono Philippi de Clactorpe; et de duodecim denariis redditus de uno tofto in Clactorpe de dono Radulfi de Grendale; et de una salina et quinque acris prati in Neotona de dono Pycoti de Houtona; et de tredecim acris et dimidia in Haga de dono Willelmi Burgevin.

Quare vobis mando et firmiter precipio quatinus propter huiusmodi occasionem vel exactionem dictam domum vel dictas moniales non molestetis nec vexetis in aliquo. Et in[1] huius rei testimonium presens scriptum sigillo meo munitum eis feci. Hiis testibus Alexandro de Poingtona, Radulfo filio Symonis, Eudone de Caletoft, Iohanne de Atie, Alveredo de Suleny, Roberto de Campania, Gilberto Cusin, Allano filio Rengot, Symone clerico, Willelmo Cusin, et multis aliis.

> SEAL: pendent on parchment tag, creamy white, fine condition but imperfect at lower end; 3¼ ins. when perfect. Obverse: equestrian, the earl in armour, hauberk of mail, surcoat, flat-topped helmet with visor closed, sword, shield of arms; horse caparisoned, galloping; arms, three garbs, two and one; legend + SIGI . . . COM . . . . . . NIE. Reverse: small, round counter-seal, 1½ ins.; shield of arms, as in obverse; legend + SECRETUM RANULFI COMITIS CESTRIE ET LINCOLNIE.

1. om. orig.

This charter is not easily dated, but it is perhaps worth noting that five of the witnesses (Ralph son of Simon, Eudes of Caltoft, Alured de Suligny, Gilbert Cusin, and Alan son of Reingot) witnessed an agreement between Earl Ranulf and Gilbert of Beningworth (**no. 299**) in 1223. Gilbert Cusin succeeded Walter of Coventry as seneschal of Bolingbroke about 1220–1221. Alexander of Pointon is a witness of **nos. 418, 419** and **421**. For William son of Otuer's gift of land at Thoresby, see **no. 127**.

414. Agreement in the king's court at Westminster between Earl Ranulf and the prior of Kenilworth, by which the latter recognized the earl's right of advowson in half the church of Stoke, near Coventry, and in return the earl gave the prior and church of Kenilworth two virgates of land in 'Sheperung'.

13 November [1223]

> B.L. Cott. MS. Vesp. E. xxiv (cartulary of Stone), f. 2v.
> Ed.: *Cal. Ch. Rolls*, i. 204; noted *H.K.F.*, p. 281.

Hec est finalis concordia facta in curia domini regis apud Westmonasterium in crastino sancti Martini anno regni regis Henrici filii regis Iohannis viii . . .[1] inter Ranulfum comitem Cestrie petentem et W. priorem de Kenillwurd tenentem . . . de advocacione medietatis ecclesie de Stokes, unde placitum fuit inter eos in prefata curia, scilicet quod predictus prior recognovit advocacionem ipsi comiti et heredibus suis in perpetuum, et predictus comes Ranulfus pro deo et salute animarum antecessorum suorum dedit et concessit ipsi priori duas virgatas terre cum pertinenciis in Sheperung, scilicet dimidiam virgatam terre cum pertinenciis quam Henricus Vivien tenuit, et dimidiam virgatam cum pertinenciis quam Willelmus filius Willelmi tenuit, et quartam partem unius virgate terre cum pertinenciis quam Ricardus molendarius tenuit, et quartam partem unius virgate terre cum pertinenciis quam Robertus de Schulton tenuit, et quartam partem unius virgate terre cum pertinenciis quam Reginaldus filius Roberti molendinarii tenuit, et quartam partem unius virgate terre cum pertinenciis quam Ricardus filius Wydonis tenuit, habendas et tenendas ipsi priori et successoribus suis et ecclesie sue de Kenillwurd de predicto comite Ranulfo et heredibus suis in puram et perpetuam elemosinam, liberam et quietam ab omni servicio seculari et exactione.

1.   Names of justices and other irrelevant matter omitted.

I have tentatively accepted the editor of *The Calendar of Charter Rolls's* and Farrer's identification of Stoke with Stoke, near Coventry, presumably because of the nearness of Kenilworth; but definite evidence is lacking, and Shepering has not been located. Stenton, *Rolls of the Justices in Eyre for Gloucestershire (Selden Society*, lix, no. 1055), identifies it even less plausibly with Stoke-on-Trent.

415.   Letter to King Henry III, assuring him of the loyalty and good will of Fawkes de Breauté and of his own intention to help the king overcome the dangers threatening his land, and announcing that he has persuaded Llywelyn, prince of North Wales, to conclude a truce of one month.

Chester, [4–14 August, 1224]

P.R.O., Ancient Correspondence II, no. 161 (copy endorsed 'Transcriptum responsi comitis Cestrie'). Ed.: Shirley, *Royal and other Historical Letters Illustrative of the Reign of Henry III*, i. (no. 204); Engl. abstract, Edwards, *Calendar of Ancient Correspondence concerning Wales*, p. 14.

Domino regi *etc.*

Litteras excellentie vestre recepi die dominica proxima post festum beati Petri ad Vincula apud Cestriam per venerabilem patrem A. Coventrensem episcopum et fratrem I. monachum de Wareduna, per quas mihi significastis, quod bene scivi occasionem quare ad castrum de Bedeford obsidendum divertistis, et qualiter dominus Falkesius de Breaute inde respondit.

Ad quod dominationi vestre significo, quod dictam occasionem simul cum dicto responso satis audivi, sicut plures alii audierunt. Super hoc autem quod vobis placuit mihi significare de domino Falkesio de Breaute, quod pro viribus suis, ut audistis, dampna vobis machinari conabatur, pro certo sciatis quod hoc nunquam scivi nec perpendere potui, immo bene vidi et perpendi quod ipse de ira vestra tristis existens et dolens, semper, postquam versus illum irati fuistis et commoti, paciente se tenuit et sine aliquo dampno vobis vel alicui de terra vestra inferendo, sicut ille qui semper desideravit et desiderat gratiam vestram, si placet, per auxilium amicorum recuperare et predictam iram vestram pro posse suo sedare.

Super hoc etiam quod mihi significastis et me vestri gratia rogastis, ut nunc constanter et fideliter vobis assistendo, dampna, si que terre vestre de partibus meis viderentur imminere, elidere curarem et avertere, dominationi vestre significo, quod de fideliter et constanter vobis et antecessoribus vestris assistendo et serviendo semper affectum habui, et ad omnia dampna vestra impedienda pro posse meo fideli libenter curam apponam.

Audito siquidem mandato vestro, statim cum Lewelino principe Norwallie colloquium habui, quem simul et plures de magnatibus suis valde commotos inveni, eo quod de dampnis multociens, ut dicunt, eis illatis nullas emendationes receperunt. Et tamen ita cum illo locutus sum, quod pacem terris vestris tenebit et a suis teneri faciet a predicta die dominica in unum mensem, quare bene intelligo quod nuncii vestri, qui iam, ut audivi, ad illum venerunt, treugas capient usque ad aliquem terminum.

Et quia per litteras vestras mihi significastis quod, nisi dicta causa esset, mihi mandavissetis, quod ad vos sine dilacione venirem, hoc audito et dictis terris vestris taliter assecuratis, omittere nolui quin ad vos venirem, et versus vos venio ad cicius quod potero. Bene valeat et crescat semper excellencia vestra.

The years 1223 and 1224 were a time of unrest, or incipient unrest in England, coupled with the threat of invasion from Wales, arising largely from resentment at the growing influence of the justiciar, Hubert de Burgh, over Henry III (still a minor until 1227), among those, including Earl Ranulf, the bishop of Winchester, and the doughty Norman warrior Fawkes de Breauté, who had loyally supported the royal cause in the troubled months after the death of King John. Ranulf's letter belongs to the last stage of this crisis after the outlawry of Fawkes in June 1224 and the siege of his castle of Bedford. Fawkes himself fled to Wales and Chester, leaving his brother William in command at Bedford. As the present letter shows, both Ranulf and Llywelyn interceded on his behalf, but in vain, and he was driven into exile, where he died in 1226. The danger, from the royal point of view, was that Ranulf and Llywelyn would make common cause with him. Hence the king's letter to Ranulf, which reached him at Chester on 4 August 1224, to which Ranulf's letter is the reply. It must have been written between 4

August and the capitulation of Bedford on 14 August, and Ranulf's decision to place his support behind Henry, and use his influence with Llywelyn on the king's behalf, brought the crisis to a close. Nevertheless, the firmness of tone of Ranulf's letter is notable. When he writes to the king of 'your lands' and his own lands, the impression left, despite his deference and courtesy, is of one power speaking on terms of equality to another, and he has no hesitation in rejecting Henry's charges against Fawkes.

416.   Grant to William Cantilupe junior of the whole of Bingley (Yorks.) for the service of half a knight's fee.

[1224–1227]

P.R.O., C.53 (Chancery Charter Rolls), no. 24, m. 11; Bodleian Library, Dodsworth MS. 128, f. 45v. (from enrolment, incomplete). Ed.: *Cal. Ch. Rolls*, i. 115.

Randulfus comes Cestrie et Lincolnie omnibus presentibus et futuris presentem cartam inspecturis et audituris salutem. Sciatis me dedisse et concessisse et hac presenti carta mea confirmasse Willelmo de Cantilupo iuniori pro homagio et servicio suo totam villam de Bingelay cum omnibus pertinentiis suis in dominicis et in serviciis, in liberis et rusticis, et in omnibus libertatibus et aisiamentis ad eandem tam infra villam quam extra pertinentibus, habendam et tenendam de me et heredibus meis illi et heredibus suis adeo libere, plene et quiete sicut ego eam unquam plenius, liberius et quietius habui vel tenui, salvis mihi et heredibus meis feodis militum que extrinsecus sunt ad predictam terram pertinentem, faciendo inde mihi et heredibus meis de illo et heredibus suis servicium dimidii militis pro omni servicio et exactione mihi et heredibus meis de predicta terra pertinente. Et ego et heredes mei dicto Willelmo et heredibus suis dictam terram contra omnes homines et feminas warantizabimus. In cuius rei testimonium presentem cartam sigillo meo munitam ei habere feci. Hiis testibus Philippo de Orreby tunc iusticiario Cestrie, Hugone dispensatore, Waltero de Dayvilla, Emerico de Sacy, Ricardo Fitun, Willelmo de Vernun, Eudone Kaletot, Radulfo de Carevilla, Philippo de Orreby iuniore, Radulfo de Say, Ricardo de Covintreia, Willelmo de Benigworthe, Simone clerico, et multis aliis.

William Cantilupe junior was the son of King John's seneschal, and from the late or middle 1220s a regular member of Earl Ranulf's entourage, accompanying him to France in 1230 (*Cal. Pat. Rolls, 1225–32*, p. 360), and frequently witnessing charters. Ranulf had acquired the manor of Bingley in 1217 (*J.C.A.S.*, lviii, p. 107), and had subsequently given the monks of Dieulacres lands or rights there. These were resumed in 1220–22 (**no. 385**), perhaps to prepare the way for the grant to William Cantilupe. The date of the grant is not easily established, but the witnesses indicate that it followed shortly thereafter. Philip of Orreby junior predeceased his father and died before 1227 (*Ches. Sheaf*, no. 4711), and Richard of Coventry, son of Ranulf's seneschal in Lincolnshire (*Chart. St. Werburgh*, no. 245), seems to have succeeded his father at approximately the same time (Coss, no. 21). William of Beningworth succeeded his father Gilbert in, or perhaps shortly before 1224 (*H.K.F.*, p. 180). Eudo of Caltoft witnessed an agreement between Earl Ranulf and Gilbert of Beningworth (**no. 299**) in 1223, and a charter for Gilbert perhaps a year or two earlier (**no. 298**). Emeric de Sacy was sent to Poitou on royal business in October 1221 (*Cal. Pat. Rolls, 1216–25*, p. 303), and Ralph de Careville, 'who came with the earl of Chester', had letters of protection in 1230 (*Cal. Pat. Rolls, 1225–32*, p. 377). Cumulatively, this evidence seems to suggest a date of approximately 1224–27 for the present charter, which is preserved in an enrolment of 26 February 1230.

417–21.   Series of five agreements between Ranulf and specified groups of free men, by which the latter quitclaimed to the earl their rights in 500 acres of common pasture in the West Fen of Bolingbroke.

[1225–1226]

Orig.: (i) P.R.O., D.L. 27/270, between Ranulf III and 55 named persons, sealed with 54 seals, of which 7 are now missing; (ii) D.L. 25/2422, between Ranulf III and 14 named persons, sealed with 12 seals, of which now 2 are detached and one is missing; (iii) D.L. 27/271, between Roger of Huntingfield and his men of Toft and Ranulf III, sealed with Roger's seal and 9 others; (iv) D.L., 27/272, between Oliver de Vallibus and his men of Frieston and Butterwick, sealed with Oliver's seal and 13 others (5 missing), women's seals being doubled; (v) D.L. 25/2423, between Ranulf III and four named men, sealed with 4 seals.[1] Transcripts of all in order given: D.L. 42/2 (Coucher Book II), f. 261–263.

---

1. *As the terms of all five lengthy agreements are identical, except for small verbal variants, only the first is reproduced verbatim here, but the names of the free men are appended in each instance as follows in the original Latin.* (ii) Petrum filium Ricardi, Hugonem filium Oukes, Gilbertum filium Willelmi, Reginaldum nepotem Tholy, Willelmum nepotem Tholy, Willelmum filium Reginaldi, Henricum filium Hervici, Iohannem filium Wydonis, Iohannem Lonk, Hubertum filium Leverini, Rogerum filium Pygoti, Willelmum Red, Benne Crun et Ricardum filium Reginaldi; (iii) *Roger of Huntingfield and* Iohannes de Huntingfelde, Hugo filius Eudonis, Reginaldus filius Yun, Robertus de Rabedic; Iohannes filius Benedicti, Alanus de Hypetoft, Katerina filia Iohannis; (iv) Oliver de Vallibus *and his free men of Frieston and Butterwick*, viz. Alexander de Pointona, Nigellus de Pincebec, Iohannes de Edlingtona, Willelmus de Farceaus,

Willelmus de Rupe, Gilbertus cocus, Ricardus filius Wydonis, Walterus de Turno, Rogerus filius Ricardi, Robertus filius Matildis, Alanus niger, Thomas Gybert, Iohannes de Kynedamme, Alanus de Rupe, Thomas de Gartona, Wido filius Iohannis, Alardus filius Oukes, Iohannes filius Eudonis, Galfridus filius Ysabelle, Radulfus Ysoud; (v) Iohannem filium Ade, Iohannem Oiller, Robertum Stif, Iohannem filium Willelmi.

Sciant presentes et futuri quod ita convenit inter homines de Frestona et de Butterwyke – scilicet Willelmum filium Hervici, Alanum filium Roberti, Ricardum filium Willelmi, Radulfum filium Thome, David de Rupe, Radulfum filium Gilberti, Ranulphum filium Willelmi, Willelmum filium Aylwini, Ricardum filium Elwyni, Willelmum Herre, Willelmum filium Wydonis, Reginaldum de Rupe, Willelmum filium Thome, Hugonem de Willueby, Willelmum filium Malgeri, Antonium filium Alani, Iacobum filium Thome, Hervicum filium Haraldi, Baldricum filium Rogeri, Ricardum filium Iohannis, Hubertum cappentarium, Adam cambrarium, Eudonem filium Reginaldi, Willelmum filium Hobbe, Iordanum filium Warneri, Wydonem filium Walteri, Thomam filium Hugonis, Clementem filium Walteri, Iohannem filium Hugonis, Galfridum Ruffum, Willelmum de Ponte, Radulfum filium Godrici, Alanum Kyte, Ricardum Galle, Robertum filium Leverici, Iohannem filium Arlildi, Mabillam que fuit uxor Malgeri, Thomam filium Ade, Willelmum Westrensem, Iohannem filium Willelmi, Iohannem filium Abrahe, Reginaldum filium Gudonis, Rogerum filium Alardi, Martinum filium Galfridi, Radulfum filium Hervici, Rogerum fabrum, Iohannem filium Emme, Warinum de Rapedic, Gilbertum de Fenna, Hubertum de Rypa, Willelmum filium Stephani, Ricardum filium Heyne, Alanum Herre, Reginaldum filium Gudonis et Willelmum Lamb – petentes communam pasture in Westfen ex una parte, et Ranulphum comitem Cestrie et Lincolnie tenentem ex altera parte, scilicet quod predicti homines de Frestona et de Butterwyke concesserunt et pro se et heredibus suis quietum clamaverunt dicto Ranulpho comiti Cestrie et Lincolnie totum ius suum et clamium, quod habuerunt in quingentis acris terre in eodem marisco cum pertinenciis mensuratis per percam viginti pedum, et quod predicte quingente acre terre clauduntur fossatis de latitudine et profunditate ad placitum suum, ita quod predicte quingente acre terre plenarie sint contente infra dicta fossata, fossatis non computatis domino comiti infra predictas quingentas acras terre, ita scilicet quod habeatur inter fossata predicte terre et aquam de Wyma ex una parte, et inter fossata dicte terre et maram que appellatur Phylnorthemere ex altera parte, quedam via in latitudine sexdecim percarum mensuratarum per percam viginti pedum.

Concesserunt eciam et quiete clamaverunt predicti homines de Frestona et de Butterwyke dicto Ranulpho comiti Cestrie et Lincolnie et heredibus suis totum ius suum et clamium quod habuerunt in placea que iacet inter fossatum de Stiwordcroft et fossatum monachorum de Revesby, que clausa est per fossatum inter dicta duo fossata versus occidentem, ita quod predicte quingente acre terre et predicta placea quiete remaneant imperpetuum domino comiti et heredibus suis de omni demanda tam de communa quam de aliis. Et pro hac concessione concessit dominus comes pro se et heredibus suis quod predicti homines de Frestona et de Butterwyk habeant communam pasture ad averia sua propria de predictis villis et turbarie et falcarie, sicut habere consueverunt in marisco appellato Westfen ad estoveria sua in predictis villis cum libero introitu et exitu, faciendo ei servicium quod facere consueverunt, scilicet de quolibet homine domum tenente ubi ignis ardet, duos denarios in die sancti Martini, reddendos servienti domini comitis in predictis villis pro omnibus serviciis et exactionibus. Concessit eciam predictus dominus comes pro se et heredibus suis quod, si aliquod averiorum predictorum hominum de Frestona et de Butterwyke venerit infra dictas quingentas acras terre vel infra dictam placeam inter fossatum de Stiwordecroft et fossatum monachorum de Revesby, sine occasione deponatur et non imparcetur.

Et ad maiorem huius rei securitatem huic scripto facto in modum cirographi dicti homines de Freston et de Butterwyke sigilla sua apposuerunt, et alteri parti huius scripti facti in modum cirographi apposuit dominus comes Cestrie et Lincolnie sigillum suum. Hiis testibus Gilberto de Gant, Willelmo de Albeniaco, Thoma de Muletona, Philippo de Kyma, Willelmo de Welle, Stephano de Setgrave, Radulfo de Bray, Willelmo de Vernun, Iordano de Gysseby, Gilberto Cusin, Willelmo de Wyllueby et Alexandro de Hybbetoft.

SEAL: 54 seals, of which 7 missing.[1]

1. Here, and in the other four agreements, only the tenants' half of the two-part cirograph with their seals survives; the part sealed with the earl's seal is no longer extant.

This group of charters, to which attention was drawn in *H.S.L.C.*, ciii, p. 31, deserves separate study, especially if taken in conjunction with other charters and agreements of a similar character and date. It can safely be assumed that all five were issued more or less simultaneously. This is shown not only by the virtual identity of the texts, but also by the fact that all have the same twelve witnesses,[1] and it is probable that they were issued in consequence of a judgement in favour of the earl in the king's court. A similar judgement regarding alleged rights of common pasture in the North Fen was given in his favour in the king's court at Lincoln on 13 October 1226 ('a die sancti Michaelis in quindecim dies anno regni regis H. filii Iohannis decimo'),[2] and the present agreements probably belong to the same period, or perhaps a little earlier.[3]

The key sentence in the agreements is that in which it is recognized that Earl Ranulf may enclose the 500 acres in which his rights have been acknowledged with ditches of a breadth and depth at his pleasure ('quod predicte quingente acras terre clauduntur fossatis de latitudine et profunditate ad placitum suum'). This seems to imply an intention to undertake the work of draining the fen on a considerable scale, and, if so, it appears to contradict the prevailing view (Darby, *The Medieval Fenland*, pp. 52, 79) that drainage, except in a small, piecemeal way by individual farmers, did not get under way before the close of the fifteenth century. It also suggests that Ranulf III was an early entrepreneur with a deliberate policy of large-scale reclamation. Indeed, there is a good deal of evidence that he was consolidating his holdings and buying up land in the fens, presumably as a preliminary to reclamation, at this time. Thus, in addition to securing rights in the North Fen, he succeeded in 1226 (Easter term 10 Henry III) in securing the release by Abbot Henry and the convent of Kirkstead of their alleged rights of common pasture 'in all the marshes and meres of the soke of Bolingbroke' (D.L. 41/2/20), and a series of agreements with individuals shows the same policy. These (all recorded in the Coucher Book) include the purchase from Alexander of Pointon of all his lands in Wrangle and Leake (East Fen) for 700 marks (f. 274), and the quittance by Alexander of 'the five spades I have of his gift in the marshes of the North Fen', (f. 274v.); land from Alexander son of Philip of Keles (f. 254) and from Emma, daughter of Anketinus de Kales (f. 243v.) in East Keal and West Keal; the surrender by Gilbert of Beningworth of 'all his rights in twenty spades in the marsh of Toynton' (f. 243v.), and the sale back by the latter (who seems to have been chronically in debt) of his manors of Little Steeping for 200 marks and of Halton Holegate and Kingthorpe for £200 sterling and the payment by the earl of 170 marks owing to Elias son of Martina, Jew of Lincoln (f. 285). All this points to a policy of land accumulation in the Fenland and eventual reclamation, which appears to have been one of Ranulf III's projects at this time. The successful challenge to the traditional rights of the small peasant freemen in the West Fen was clearly part of the same policy. The names of the freemen in the five agreements give, incidentally, an unusually good conspectus of a segment of this class, so characteristic of the Danelaw.

1. **Nos. 418, 420** and **421** also add Alexander of Poynton and Nigel of Pinchbeck. **Nos. 417, 420** and **421** read (correctly) Aesseby or Eysseby (i.e. Ashby by Partney, Lincs.) for Gysseby.
2. The text is in the Coucher Book (D.L. 42/2), ff. 283v.–284, and an abstract in Boyd & Massingberd, *Lincolnshire Records: Abstracts of Final Concords*, pp. 190–1, no. 112. The suit was between the earl and, as here, a long list of defendants 'de communa in marisco ipsius comitis in Northfen', in which the defendants denied that the earl had any commons in their lands or that they had done him service. On a grand assize they recognized the whole marsh to be the earl's right and remitted it to him, in return for which Earl Ranulf remitted his claim for 200 marks damages, which he said they had inflicted on him. The similarity between this agreement and the present agreements is obvious.
3. There is no reason why the agreements about the West Fen and the North Fen should be simultaneous, and Earl Ranulf may have obtained a judgement regarding the former before seeking a similar judgement about the latter. If William d'Aubigny (de Alben[iaco] or de Albin[iaco] of the present charters) is William earl of Arundel, son of Earl Ranulf's sister Mabel, who died in 1224, this must be the case; but it seems unlikely that his title would have been omitted in that case, or that he would have taken second place in the witness-list after Gilbert of Gant. On the other hand, it is possible that the reference to him without title belongs to the period before he succeeded his father as earl in April 1221, but it could not be much earlier, as Earl Ranulf only returned from crusade in August 1220 (*Ann. Cestr.*, p. 51). There was, however, another William de Albiniaco, who was appointed justice on 16 February 1225 (*Cal. Pat. Rolls, 1216–1225*, p. 568), and is elsewhere described as William d'Aubigny of Belvoir, and the witness of the present agreements is more likely to be he; in which case any difficulties about the date disappear.

422. Confirmation to Grimsby abbey of the gifts of Earl Ranulf II and of Gilbert of Turs's gift of seven virgates.

[1227–1230]

London, College of Arms, MS. Vincent 120, p. 74; Chetham's Library, Towneley MSS., transcripts from the Vernon MSS., pp. 339–40.

Ranulfus comes Cestrie et Lincolnie omnibus Christi fidelibus ad quos presens scriptum pervenerit, salutem in domino. Sciatis me concessisse et hac presenti carta mea confirmasse deo et ecclesie sancti Augustini de Grimesby et canonicis ibidem deo servientibus pro salute anime mee, patris et matris mee *etc.* quartam partem illius manerii quam Hugo[1] de sancto Paulo tenuit de Ranulfo avo meo *etc.*, quam Ranulfus comes Cestrie avus meus eis donavit et Hugo pater meus confirmavit, ut per cartam inde patet, quam canonici tunc habuerunt, et septem virgatas terre *etc.*, prout carta Gilberti de Turse et confirmatio Willelmi Romare, que illi habuerunt et ostenderunt, testantur.[2] Quare volo et firmiter precipio, ut dicti canonici libere et quiete possident *etc.* Testibus Iohanne comite nepote meo, Willelmo de Cantilop,[3] Fulcone filio Waren, Baldwino de Ver, Henrico de Ferariis.

1. Henricus *Towneley MS.*　　　　2. *om. MSS.*
3. *sic MSS.*

For Hugh II's confirmation of Ranulf II's charter, see **no. 189.** Ranulf III's nephew, John the Scot, had livery of the earldom of Huntingdon on 25 April 1227. As William Cantilupe junior, Fulk fitz Warin and Baldwin de Vere all accompanied Ranulf III to France on 20 April 1230 (*Cal. Pat. Rolls, 1225–1232*, p. 360), the present charter probably falls between these two dates. A full text has not been found.

423. Grant to Hilton abbey, Staffs., of two salt houses in Northwich, which Richard of Pierrepont had formerly held, in exchange for a fishpond in his park of Newcastle.

[1227–1232]

J.R.U.L.M., Lat. MS. 319 ('out of a leiger book of ye prior of Stone given in evidence at Stafford Assizes, and is Sir Walter Astons'), f. 69.[1]

1. *In the margin*: Abbas de Hulton.

Ranulphus comes Cestrie et Lincolnie [etc. dedi et concessi][1] eis duas salinas in Norwico in excambium mote[2] in parco meo[3] de Novo Castello, quam[4] dicti monachi mihi concesserunt, illas scilicet duas salinas que[5] fuerunt Ricardi de Perpunt.

1. dedit *MS.*
2. motae *MS.*
3. suo *MS.*

4. qui *MS.*
5. qui *MS.*

The castle and manor of Newcastle-under-Lyme were granted to Ranulf III in 1215 (*Orm.*, i. 34), but he did not begin to lay down a park until considerably later, probably around the year 1225. Hilton abbey was founded by Henry of Audley in 1223 (*Mon.*, v. 715), and according to a plea of 1235 (*H.K.F.*, p. 256), the land which Ranulf III enclosed within his park was one of his gifts to the monastery. Richard of Pierrepont, sheriff of Chester, was alive in 1220 (**no. 372**) and probably later, but the date of his death is not known. Unfortunately, the present short abstract of Ranulf III's charter, which is our sole surviving source of information, has no witnesses, but it is probably safe to date it between 1227 and Ranulf's surrender of the earldom of Lincoln to his sister Hawise in 1232 (**no. 310**).

424.   Confirmation to the canons of Cockersand abbey of all the lands and holdings which they possess within his fief.

[? 1228–1232]

> B.L. Add. MS. 37769 (Cockersand cartulary), f. 17; B.L. Add. MS. 32099 (copy of preceding), f. 19v. Ed.: *Chetham Soc.*, N.S. xxxviii, p. 58.

Omnibus sancte matris ecclesie filiis ad quos presens pagina pervenerit, Rannulfus comes Cestrie salutem. Notum sit vobis me concessisse et hac carta mea confirmasse deo et beate Marie de Cokersand et canonicis Premonstratensis ordinis ibidem deo servientibus omnes terras et tenuras de feodo meo, que eis racionabiliter collate sunt, habendas et tenendas in perpetuum salvo servicio meo. Concessi etiam eis quietanciam de theloneo salis per totam terram meam, quod ipsi canonici aut ipsorum homines[1] ad usus proprios dictorum canonicorum emerint. Quare volo et firmiter precipio quod predicti canonici predicta habeant et teneant in perpetuum, et prohibeo ballivis et servientibus meis ne eos super hiis vexare aut inquietare presumant. Hiis testibus . . .[2]

1. aut *deleted MS.*

2. *Witnesses omitted MS.*

The first appearance of Cockersand (in the north of Amounderness) is as a small hospital c.1184, and it was not until about 1201, when King John confirmed the site to the Premonstratensian canons, that it was turned into a monastery (*V.C.H. Lancs.*, ii. 154). There is no evidence nor any reason to think that Ranulf III had any interest in this part of Lancashire at this time, or before 1217 at earliest. If his title in the present charter is taken literally, this creates difficulties, and it seems possible that the compiler of the cartulary took liberties with the text and that the charter belongs to the period when Ranulf was earl of Lincoln. For that reason Farrer, the editor of the cartulary, has dated it 1228–1232, when Ranulf is otherwise known to have been consolidating his position in Lancashire (**no. 433**). This seems reasonable, but is, of course, little more than surmise.

425. Grant to Baldwin de Vere for his homage and service of one half of the third part of the demesne of Great Tew (Oxon.), of 8s. rent from the Southern mill of Tew, and 17 virgates and a cottage and a half in the same village.

[c.1229]

Orig.: Northants. Record Office. Ed.: Halstead, *Succinct Genealogies*, p. 255. Royal confirmation: *Cal. Ch. Rolls*, i. 114.

Rannulphus comes Cestrie et Lincolnie omnibus presentibus et futuris presentem cartam inspecturis vel audituris salutem. Sciatis me concessisse, dedisse et hac presenti carta mea confirmasse Baldewino de Ver pro homagio et servicio suo totam medietatem tercie partis tocius dominici de Tywa et octo solidatos redditus, quos habui in molendino australi de Tywa, et decem et septem virgatas terre et unum cottagium et dimidium in eadam villa, scilicet duas virgatas terre quas Ambrosius tenuit, et duas virgatas terre quas Rogerus filius Wimarci tenuit, et duas virgatas terre quas Gilbertus frater ipsius Rogeri tenuit, et duas virgatas terre quas Willelmus de Tackele tenuit, et duas virgatas terre quas Quenilda tenuit, et unam virgatam terre quam Adhelina tenuit, et unam virgatam terre quam Hugo Palmarius tenuit, et duas virgatas terre quas Ricardus Novus homo tenuit, et unam virgatam terre quam Willelmus Baro tenuit, et unam virgatam terre quam Nicholaus Alverich tenuit, et unam virgatam terre quam Willelmus filius Ambrosii tenuit, et unum cottagium quod Robertus molendinarius tenuit, et dimidium cottagium quod Gilbertus Carufex tenuit, habenda et tenenda de me et de heredibus meis eidem Baldewino et heredibus suis libere et quiete, plene et pacifice et hereditarie, in culturis, in dominicis, pratis, pascuis, boscis, planis, viis, semitis, terris et aquis, cum omnibus predictis hominibus et eorum sequelis et consuetudinibus, et cum omnibus libertatibus et aysiamentis et omnibus aliis pertinenciis ad predictum tenementum pertinentibus infra villam et extra, faciendo inde mihi et heredibus meis ipse Baldewinus et heredes sui servicium vicecesime partis feodi unius militis pro omnibus serviciis et demandis universis. Ego vero Rannulphus et heredes mei dictum tenementum cum omnibus pertinenciis suis eidem Baldewino et heredibus suis contra omnes gentes in perpetuum warantizabimus. Et ut hec mea donacio et concessio in posterum perpetue firmitatis robur optineant, eas presenti carta et sigilli mei apposicione roboravi. Hiis testibus dominis Waltero de Dayvilla, Radulpho de Bray, Gilberto de Segrave, Waltero de Biseboc, Radulpho de Say, Ricardo de Buron, Gilberto et Rogero de Norfolche, Baldewino de Brucurt, Eustacio de Beknes, Henrico Harang, Elya pincerna, Willelmo coco, Iohanne et Willelmo de Westona clericis, et aliis.

> SEAL: on tag (only fragment now surviving); obverse: (82 mm. diameter), equestrian figure, sword in right hand, galloping, legend; + SIGILLVM. RANVLPHI. COMITIS. CESTRIE. ET. LINCOLNIE. Reverse: (40 mm. diameter), on a shield 3 garbs, legend + SECRETVM. RANVLPHI. COMITIS. CESTRIE. ET. LINCOLNIE.

The lands in Great Tew here granted to Baldwin de Vere were almost certainly those surrendered to Earl Ranulf by Stephen of Segrave some time between 1225 and 1229 (**no. 363**). The present grant was confirmed by Henry III on 18 February 1230 and was probably made not a great deal earlier. Baldwin de Vere occurs frequently as a witness in Ranulf III's later years, and if it could be assumed that this charter marks the time when he entered into Ranulf's service, it would provide a date *post quem* for other charters in which he appears. For the subsequent history of the de Vere holding in Tew, see *H.K.F.*, p. 241.

426. Confirmation to Spalding priory of the gifts of Countess Lucy.

[1229–1232]

> P.R.O., C.53 (Chancery Charter Rolls), no. 117 m. 37; B.L. Add. MS. 35296 (Spalding register), f. 9v; Add. MS. 5844 (Cole's transcript of preceding), f. 76v. (old f. 148). Ed.: *Mon.*, iii. 217; *The Genealogist*, N.S. v, p. 71 (no. 42); *Cal. Ch. Rolls*, iv. 166 (no. 15).

Universis sancte matris ecclesie filiis Ranulfus comes Cestrie et Lincolnie salutem. Noverit universitas vestra me divine pietatis intuitu et pro salute anime mee et animarum antecessorum et successorum meorum concessisse et presenti scripto confirmasse deo et beate Marie et sancto Nicholao de Spaldingis monachisque ibidem deo servientibus in liberam, puram et perpetuam elemosinam illas donaciones quas Lucia quondam comitisse Cestrie fecit eis, scilicet ecclesiam et manerium de Spaldingis cum omnibus pertinenciis suis. Quare volo et concedo ut predicti monachi teneant et habeant predicta libere, pacifice cum omnibus dignitatibus et omnibus que ad illa pertinent, ubicumque fuerint in bosco, in plano, in foro, extra forum, in aquis, in pascuis, in mariscis, in piscariis, in theloneis, in ecclesiis, in decimis, et omnibus aliis rebus ad predictam ecclesiam et manerium pertinentibus, sicut carta testatur, quam habent de predicta Lucia comitissa, et carta confirmacionis Willelmi de Romara predecessoris nostri, quam inde habent. Hiis testibus domino Waltero tunc abbate Cestrie, domino Willelmo de Vernun tunc iusticiario Cestrie, domino Radulfo de Bray, Petro sacerdote, Simone clerico, et aliis.

For the charter of Countess Lucy, see **no. 16**. The present confirmation falls within the period 1229–32.

427.   Grant to Spalding priory of freedom from entertaining the earl for three periods of forty days during the year.

[1229–1232]

> B.L. Add. MS. 35296 (Spalding register), f. 143.; Add.
> MS. 5844 (Cole's transcript of preceding), f. 132 (old f.
> 257).

Omnibus Christi fidelibus presens scriptum visuris vel audituris Ranulfus comes Cestrie et Lincolnie salutem. Noverit universitas vestra me divine pietatis intuitu et pro salute anime mee et pro salute animarum comitis H. patris mei et Bertree comitisse matris mee et antecessorum meorum remisisse et quiete clamasse de me et heredibus meis in perpetuum in puram et perpetuam elemosinam deo et beate Marie et sancto Nicholao et priori et conventui Spaldinge consuetudinem annuam, quam a predicto priore et conventu exigere solebam, scilicet per-hendinacionem per tres quarentenas in anno in domo de Spaldinge ad custum dicte domus, ita quod ego nec heredes mei[1] nec aliquis alius occasione mei vel heredum meorum aliquid de consuetudine vel occasione dicte consuetudinis in predicta domo de cetero exigere poterimus. Et ut hec mea remissio et quieta clamacio perpetuitatis robur optineant, presentem paginam sigilli mei apposicione roboravi. Hiis testibus domino Waltero abbate Cestrie, Willelmo de Vernoun iusticiario Cestrie, Fulcone filio Warini, Philippo de Orrebi, Ricardo Fitoun, Iohanne de Athia, Iohanne clerico, et aliis.

1. nec mei *repeated MSS.*

The connection of the earls of Chester with Spalding reaches back to Ranulf I and Countess Lucy (**no. 14**). For Ranulf III's interests as patron, see **nos. 430** and **431**, and his letters on the subject (**nos. 428, 429**) to the bishop of Lincoln. The present charter falls after the appointment of William Vernon as justiciar in succession to Philip of Orreby in April 1229 (*Ann. Cestr.*, p. 56) and before Ranulf's death in October 1232. The Countess Bertrada, Earl Ranulf's mother, had died in 1227 (*Ann. Cestr.*, p. 54).

428. Letter to Bishop Hugh of Lincoln, notifying him that he has agreed, as patron, to the candidate proposed by the abbot of St. Nicholas of Angers for the position of prior of Spalding.

[January 1230]

Lincoln, Dean and Chapter, Register of Hugh of Welles,
Roll Ia, m. 9v. Ed.: *Linc. Rec. Soc.*, ix, p. 185.

Reverendo patri in Christo et domino H. dei gratia Lincolniensi episcopo devotus filius R. comes Cestrie et Lincolnie salutem in salutis auctore. Noverit paternitas vestra, quod abbas sancti Nicholai de Andegavia ad me tanquam ad patronum prioratus sancti Nicholai de Spaldingis accessit et, petita prius a me licencia eligendi, michi presentavit in priorem eiusdem domus dominum Iohannem priorem de Kirkeby; unde, quia audivi et intelligo ipsum esse virum providum et honestum et discretum, ad hoc assensum prebens, eundem Iohannem per litteras meas patentes in priorem dicte domus de Spaldingis vobis presento, devote supplicans quatinus, si placet, hoc quod vestrum est sine difficultate et dilatione circa ipsum exequi velitis. Bene valeat paternitas vestra in domino.

The approximate dates of this and the following letter (**no. 429**) of Earl Ranulf to Bishop Hugh of Lincoln can be established by reference to the preceding account in the bishop's register (*Linc. Rec. Soc.*, ix, pp. 182–4) of the election of Simon of Hauton as prior of Spalding. Here it is stated that the above letter recommending John, prior of Monks Kirby (Leics.), was presented to the bishop by the abbot of St. Nicholas, Angers, on 10 February 1230 ('die beate Scolastice Virginis, dominica scilicet sexagesima, a. d. millesimo ducentesimo vicesimo nono'). But, as no letters of consent were presented from the convent of Spalding, the hearing was prorogued until 7 March ('dies ss. Perpetue et Felicitatis'). On the latter day, the earl's proctors, Walter de Pinchbeck, abbot of Chester, and Master Gilbert of Weston, presented the second letter from Ranulf (**no. 429**), withdrawing his support from John, while at the same time it transpired that the monks of Spalding objected strongly to his candidature, and he was persuaded to withdraw in favour of Simon. From this it follows that the present letter was written some days before 10 February, presumably towards the end of January 1230. The second letter (**no. 429**) must have been written between 10 February and 7 March, and almost certainly after the letter of the abbot of St. Nicholas, dated 16 February (*Linc. Rec. Soc.*, ix, p. 185), probably at the end of February.

For the complicated arrangements governing the appointment of the prior of Spalding, of which Earl Ranulf was hereditary patron, see **nos. 430** and **431**. The priory of Monks Kirby (Leics.), like Spalding, was a cell of St. Nicholas of Angers.

429. Letter to Bishop Hugh of Lincoln, revoking his previous letter in favour of Prior John of Kirby as prior of Spalding and notifying him that he has sent the abbot of Chester and Master Gilbert of Weston as his proctors, since he is unable personally to attend to the matter.

[16 February–7 March 1230]

Lincoln, Dean and Chapter, Register of Hugh of Welles, Roll Ia, m. 9v. Ed.: *Linc. Rec. Soc.*, ix, pp. 185–6.

Venerabili *etc.* H. Lincolniensi episcopo R. comes Cestrie *etc.* salutem *etc.* Dilecte paternitati vestre grates refero multiplices super hoc, quod ius, quod habeo in patronatu prioratus Spaldinge, firmum et stabile vultis servare. Nullo enim modo a forma compositionis inter me et abbatem Andegavie super dicto patronatu in presentia vestra facte volo recedere; unde, quia in propria persona dicto negotio intendere non possum, dilectos et fideles meos dominum W. abbatem Cestrie et magistrum G. de Westona procuratores meos constituo ad faciendum quicquid ad me pertinet secundum formam compositionis predicte. Ratum enim et gratum habeo quicquid ab eis actum fuerit in predicto negotio. Quare affectuose precor vos, quatinus, si placet, eis in hiis, que vobis ex parte mea dicent, fidem habeatis, et eo, non obstantibus litteris presentationis per abbatem Andegavie et per priorem de Kirkeby ad vos optentis, effectui mancipare velitis. Pro certo enim sciatis, quod littere ille falsa suggestione fuerant impetrate, propter quod viribus debent carere. Bene valete.

For the date of this letter, see **no. 428**. Its formulation makes it abundantly clear that the bishop of Lincoln had taken exception to Ranulf's preceding letter, presumably because in specifically presenting the prior of Kirby he had, in the bishop's view, exceeded his rights of patronage. Evidently there was some agreement, or 'form of composition', which the bishop believed Earl Ranulf had transgressed. This may explain the drawing up, two years later, of new agreements (**nos. 430, 431**) setting out in great detail the respective rights of the earl, the abbot of Angers, and the diocesan.

430. Agreement with the abbot and convent of St. Nicholas, Angers, respecting the election of the prior of Spalding, of which church the earl is patron.

[March 1232]

> Original indented cyrograph: P.R.O., D.L. 25/48; transcr.: D.L. 42/2 (Coucher Book II), f. 270. Cal.: *35th Rep. D.K.P.R.*, p. 9.

Notum sit omnibus Christi fidelibus tam presentibus quam futuris, ad quos presens scriptum pervenerit, quod, cum orta esset controversia inter nobilem virum Rannulphum comitem Cestrie et Lincolnie ex una parte et dominum abbatem et conventum sancti Nicholai Andegavensis ex altera super ordinacione prioris et prioratus Spalding e, cuius patronatum gerit dictus comes, tandem in hunc modum amicabiliter compositum est inter eos, videlicet quod cum dictum prioratum de Spalding e per mortem prioris vel aliter vacare contigerit, abbas sancti Nicholai Andegavensis, qui pro tempore fuerit, pro se et conventu suo sancti Nicholai Andegavensis per se vel per procuratorem suum et conventus Spalding e predicto comiti et heredibus suis post eum predictum prioratum vacare tempestive significabunt. Vocato siquidem tempestive et rationabiliter dicto abbate sancti Nicholai Andegavensis a conventu Spalding e apud monasterium sancti Nicholai Andegavensis, et licencia a dicto comite et heredibus suis post eum ab abbate sancti Nicholai Andegavensis et conventu de Spalding e per se vel per procuratores eorum eligendi ad dictum prioratum priorem petita et obtenta, idem abbas pro se et conventu sancti Nicholai Andegavensis vel procurator ipsorum ad dictum prioratum accedat, et tunc idem abbas pro se et conventu sancti Nicholai Andegavensis, vel procurator eorum pro eis et conventu Spalding ensi, priorem eligent idoneum ad dictum prioratum de intus vel de extra, ita tamen quod nullum eligent qui prius professionem non fecerit abbati predicto vel successoribus suis.

Electum autem in priorem dicto comiti vel heredibus suis presentabunt, qui a dicto comite vel heredibus suis receptus cum litteris ipsius comitis vel heredum suorum patentibus domino episcopo Lincolniensi presentabitur, qui circa eum quod debebit, salvo iure abbatis et conventus sancti Nicholai Andegavensis et dicti comitis et heredum suorum, exequetur, salva dicto abbati et successoribus suis in perpetuum iurisdiccione regulari in dicto prioratu tanquam abbatibus suis secundum ordinem monachalem.

Si vero dictum abbatem vel successores suos rationabiliter vocatos propter discordiam regum et regnorum Francie et Anglie vel ob alia inpedimenta contigerit non venire vel procuratorem, sicut predictum est, non mittere infra tres menses post vacacionem dicti prioratus, conventus de Spalding e nichilominus, licencia eligendi petita et obtenta, tunc eliget sibi priorem et presentabit, secundum quod premissum est, salvo iure in posterum predictorum abbatis et conventus sancti Nicholai Andegavensis de aliis prioribus eligendis, sicut superius est notatum.

Et in huius rei testimonium uterque illorum, scilicet dictus abbas pro se et conventu suo et dictus comes, sigilla sua vice mutua huic scripto modo cyrographi confecto apposuerunt. Actum anno domini M.CC. tricesimo primo mense marcio.

SEAL on tag: missing.

The priory of Spalding was founded by Countess Lucy, wife of Ranulf I, and her first husband, Ivo Taillebois, as a cell of the abbey of St. Nicholas, Angers (**no. 14**), and the earls of Chester, as successors of the founders, retained the patronage. This gave rise, as the present charter states, to controversy as to the respective rights of the abbot, the earl and the diocesan (in this case the bishop of Lincoln) in the appointment of the prior, such a controversy clearly being reflected in the letters (**nos. 428, 429**) written by Ranulf III to Bishop Hugh of Welles in 1230. The present lengthy and elaborate agreement was intended to settle such controversies, so far as the abbot and the earl were concerned. To ensure its observance, it was confirmed simultaneously by the abbots of Abingdon and Combe, the dean of Hereford and the priors of Coventry and Monks Kirby (P.R.O., D.L. 25/49). Although it took account also of the diocesan's rights, it did not satisfy the bishop of Lincoln, and the result was the drafting, two or three months later, of another elaborate agreement (**no. 431**). The present agreement is dated March 1231; it can safely be assumed that this is 1232 New Style.

431. Agreement between the bishop of Lincoln and the prior of Spalding, on the one part, and Earl Ranulf and the abbot and convent of St. Nicholas of Angers, on the other part, with respect to the election, presentation and institution of the prior of Spalding.

Brampton (Hunts.), 8 June 1232.

Original quadripartite cyrograph: P.R.O., D.L. 25/49. Transcr.: D.L. 42/2 (Coucher Book II), ff. 263v.–264v.; B.L. Add. MS. 35296 (Spalding register), ff. 11v–12v. (without witnesses). Cal.: *35th Rep. D.K.P.R.*, p. 10.

Hec est amicabilis composicio et pacis reformacio realis et perpetua facta anno gratie millesimo ducentesimo tricesimo secundo apud Bramtonam iuxta Huntindonam in ecclesia die martis proxima post octabas Pentecostes inter dominum

Lincolniensem episcopum Hugonem secundum et Simonem priorem et conventum Spaldinge ex una parte et nobilem virum Rannulphum comitem Cestrie et Lincolnie et Constancium abbatem et conventum monasterii sancti Nicholai Andegavis ex altera, sub hac forma videlicet, quod, salvo iure plene, integre et in perpetuum predicto nobili et successoribus suis, quantum ad patronum pertinet, et salvo iure episcopali in admissione et institucione priorum Spaldingensium et visitacione eiusdem prioratus et aliis ad episcopum spect-antibus integre, plene et perpetuo predicto episcopo Lincolniensi et success-oribus suis, quoad legem diocesanum et iurisdictionis episcopalis, et salvo iure predicto abbati et successoribus suis in hiis, que spectant ad observanciam regularem et disciplinam monachalem in eodem prioratu, salvis etiam iure et possessione prioris Spaldingensis, qui nunc est, et sibi succedencium, ut toto tempore vite sue, postquam ab episcopo Lincolniensi fuerint instituti, tanquam priores immobiles in spiritualibus et temporalibus et beneficiis conferendis et presentationibus ad illa et recepcione monachorum quoad habitum plenam habeant potestatem, non ammovendi absque causa canonica cognita et probata, cum dictum prioratum Spaldingensem vacare contigerit, petent idem abbas et conventus Spaldingensis, vel procurator monacus ad hoc specialis eiusdem abbatis et successorum suorum una cum conventu Spaldingensi, ipso abbate tempestive per conventum Spaldingensem ad hoc vocato apud monasterium sancti Nicholai Andegavis, a dicto comite vel heredibus suis licenciam eligendi priorem.

Qua petita, eligent dictus abbas et successores sui et conventus Spaldingensis, vel procurator monacus ad hoc specialis dicti abbatis et successorum nomine monasterii sancti Nicholai Andegavis et idem conventus Spaldingensis, priorem, et electionem ipsam cum electo, petito assensu dicti comitis vel heredum suorum, cum litteris assensum ipsius comitis vel heredum suorem continentibus episcopo Lincolniensi presentabunt. Quibus per episcopum examinatis, ipse episcopus quod suum est circa electionem ipsam et electum exequetur, et cum per dictum episcopum fuerit prior institutus, non ammovebitur nisi causa canonica cognita et probata.

Dictus abbas et successores sui, cum opus fuerit aut viderint expedire, ad dictum prioratum causa visitacionis faciende pro hiis que sunt ordinis et regule, tanquam abbas habens professiones monachorum dicte domus et alia que pertinent ad regularem observantiam in eadem, venient cum familia moderata et honesta, prout convenit honestati abbatis monasterii memorati. Quod si in adventu suo vel modo veniendi vel mora ibidem seu aliis huiusmodi honerosus extiterit vel molestus, honus immoderatum in huiusmodi per episcopum Lincolniensem censura ecclesiastica refrenabitur atque corrigetur.

Porro dictus abbas et successores sui monachos honestos, non tamen ultra quatuor, de partibus transmarinis oriundos ad domum Spaldingensem pro mora ibi facienda transmittere poterunt, plures alios illuc non missuri, quamdiu predicti quatuor ibidem commorentur. Qui, cum venerint, vivant regulariter sub iugo discipline et prioris Spaldingensis cum conventu eiusdem, ita tamen quod, cum necesse fuerit pro negociis eiusdem abbatis, in Anglia expediendis, petita prius licentia a priore Spaldingensi, liceat eis ire et redire in expensis abbatis, scilicet si alicui vel aliquibus ipsorum quatuor idem abbas vel successores sui administracionem negociorum suorum committere voluerint.

Hoc etiam adiecto, ut si tempore visitacionis memorate preter predictos quatuor dictus abbas vel successores sui aliquem vel aliquos ex causa rationabili vera et expressa in capitulo Spaldingensi decreverint ammovendum vel ammovendos, alius vel alii per ipsum abbatem et successores suos loco eius vel eorum subrogetur vel subrogentur. In eius vel eorum tamen ammocione et alterius vel aliorum subrogacione, si proprio motu abbatis vel instigacione monachorum seu aliorum queratur, color vel causa confingatur, huiuscemodi correctio et cohercio in episcopi Lincolniensis maneat potestate, salvo iure dicti comitis et heredum suorum.

Verum noviciorum tempore huius composicionis et pacis reformacionis de eadem prioratu existencium recepit idem abbas apud Spaldingas hac vice professiones, salvo sibi iure in posterum et successoribus suis recipiendi eas in ecclesia sua Andegavensi, nisi professuris gratiam facere velint, quod eorum professiones admittantur in Anglia, ita tamen quod nec per istam nec per aliam gratiam recipiendi professiones ipsi abbati vel successoribus suis preiudicium generetur in posterum, quin in dicto monasterio Andegavensi novicii Spal-dingenses professiones suas faciant ipsi abbati et successoribus suis, cum ipsi abbates voluerint. Ad quas Andegavis faciendas venient bini in tercio vel quarto conversionis sue anno ad mandatum abbatis, libere ituri et redituri absque difficultate, impedimento et contradictione abbatis vel monachorum Andegavensium, quando ipsi professi volent.

In cuius rei testimonium huic composicioni et pacis reformacioni signa dictorum episcopi et comitis, necnon abbatis et prioris habencium a conventibus suis de componendo et pacificando mandatum speciale, vice mutua[1] sunt appensa, quorum abbatis et prioris procurationes insinuate in ede sacra, scilicet in custodia prioris sancti Eadmundi, sunt deposite, donec littere de rato speciales a dictis conventibus emanaverint. Est autem presens scriptum quadripartitum, cuius una pars resedit penes dominum Lincolniensem episcopum, alia penes dominum comitem Cestrie et Lincolnie, tertia penes abbatem et conventum Andegavienses, quarta penes priorem et conventum Spaldingenses, et unicuique tria sigilla apponuntur. Hiis testibus: Roberto Lincolniensi, Iohanne Nor-hamptonie et Gileberto Huntindonie archidiaconis; Radulfo de Warvilla, magis-tro Waltero de Werministre, Willelmo de Winchecumba et Thoma de Askeby, canonicis Lincolniensibus; Rogero tunc priore, Thoma de Norfolk et Henrico, monachis beati Petri de Burgo; Radulfo de Ely et Thoma de Graingham monachis Spaldingensibus; domino Radulfo de Bray, Petro de Bramptona, Elya de Hayles et Ada de Welles capellanis; magistris Simone de Wautona, Iohanne de Histona, Willelmo de sancto Brioco, Ricardo de sancta Cruce, Thoma de Stede, Roberto de Gravele, Alexandro de Standfordia, Iohanne Maunselle, et multis aliis.

> SEALS on tags: (1) fragmentary; (2) vesica-shaped, seated ecclesiastical figure, legend illegible; (3) missing.

1. From this point original torn and partly defaced. Missing words and names supplied from transcripts in Coucher Book and Register.

This elaborate agreement should be compared with **no. 430,** only a few weeks earlier in date. Most of its provisions are concerned with delimiting the rights of the abbot of St. Nicholas, Angers, as visitor of Spalding, and asserting the ultimate authority of the bishop of Lincoln in the institution of the prior; but in some ways the most striking feature is the whittling away of the rights of the earl of Chester as patron of Spalding. These amount now to little more than the right to issue (and therefore presumably to withhold) a licence to elect a prior after any vacancy; but the earl has no voice, according to the terms of the agreement, in the choice of the person to be presented to the bishop for examination and presentation. This is part of a more general attack on lay patronage, which had enabled founders of monasteries and their successors virtually to nominate the heads of religious houses under their control. It looks as though Ranulf III had attempted to exercise some such right in 1230, when he put forward the name of the prior of Monks Kirby (**no. 428**) and clearly incurred some sort of episcopal reprimand (**no. 429**); and it seems possible that the present agreement, restoring peace between the parties, is a consequence of this or a similar dispute. Noticeable also is the repeated stipulation that the prior of Spalding, once instituted, shall be irremovable, except for a recognized canonical offence; this also looks like an attempt to stop arbitrary lay interference, if for any reason the earl found the prior unacceptable.

432. Confirmation to Nicholas de Lettes of Matilda Venables' grant of Wincham with a carucate of land in Twembrook and its appurtenances.

[c.1230]

> Tabley MSS., Sir Peter Leycester's muniments, Wincham 3 (loose transcripts), also Liber B, f. 29 (abbreviated); B.L. Harl.MS. 2007, f. 106 (from Vernon's Liber P, with description of seal). Ed.: Orm., i. 627 (brief abstract from Liber B).

Ranulfus comes Cestrie et Lincolnie omnibus presentibus et futuris presentem cartam inspecturis vel audituris salutem. Sciatis me concessisse et hac presenti carta mea confirmasse Nicholao de Delettes Wymingham cum omnibus pertinenciis suis infra villam et extra et unam carucatam terre in Tynebroc cum pertinentiis cum medietate bosci de Alreschaghe et cum communia pasture in Lindwode, scilicet ad quindecim averia et ad viginti porcos, que Matilda de Venables pro homagio et servicio suo ei dedit, habenda et tenenda eidem Nicholao et heredibus suis vel eius assignatis et heredibus assignatorum suorum de dicta Matilda et heredibus suis per servicium dimidii militis dicte Matilde et heredibus suis inde faciendum, secundum tenorem carte ipsius Matilde, quam idem Nicholaus inde habet. Et ad maiorem huius rei securitatem presentem cartam sigillo meo munitam ei habere feci. His testibus Willelmo de Vernon, Baldwino de Vere, Radulfo de Bray, Radulfo de Say, Henrico de Harang, Ricardo de Buron, Galfrido de Aplebie, Hugone Phiton, Walkelino de Arderne, Simone et Iohanne clericis, et aliis.

> SEAL: 'His seale on ye one side a man on horseback and aboute it SIGILL. RANI. CO. CESTR. ET L.: and on other side a lesser seale with 3 garbes in a scohean and about it SCORĪA RANĪ COMITE CESTR. ET LIN-COLNE'.

Wincham had been Venables property since the time of Domesday (*D.S.C.*, p. 192). According to Ormerod (*loc. cit.*) using Sir Peter Leycester's materials, it was given by William Venables of Kinderton to his sister Matilda in marriage about the reign of Richard I, and she later conveyed it to Nicholas de Elets or Lettes. This is the grant here confirmed by Ranulf III. It is dated by Ormerod 'about 1230' and this seems approximately correct. Nicholas de Lettes, who appears to have come from Nottinghamshire, witnessed a charter for Philip of Orreby (**no. 434**) at this time and another for Stanlaw (**no. 215**) a year of two earlier. His tenure was very short (see **no. 462**).

433. Agreement with Roger of Marsey for the completion by the latter of the sale to the earl of all his lands between Ribble and Mersey, and specifically of the manor of Bolton le Moors.

[1230]

> P.R.O., D.L. 42/1 (Coucher Book I), ff. 77–77v.; B.L. Harl. MS. 2063, f. 23v. (new f. 113v.); and Central Reference Library, Manchester, Towneley MS. 8, pp. 1067–8 (both abbreviated texts from Coucher Book). Ed.: Orm., i. 36.

Hec est convencio facta inter dominum Ranulfum comitem Cestrie et Lincolnie et Rogerum de Mareseye, videlicet quod dicti comes et Rogerus tradiderunt domino Radulfo de Bray in equali manu quadraginta marcas argenti et cartam quam dictus Rogerus fecit domino comiti vendicione et dimissione omnium terrarum suarum, quas habuit vel habere potuit inter Ribble et Merseye, ita scilicet quod idem Rogerus sine dilatione iturus est inter Ribbel et Merseye ad deponendum se de dicta terra et ad faciendum omnes illos, qui de ipso ibidem tenuerunt, homagia sua facere dicto domino comiti vel fidelitatem eius ballivis loco suo constitutis, et etiam ad saisinam de Boultona cum omnibus pertinenciis suis dicto comiti faciendam. Quo facto, dictus Radulfus de Bray sepedicto comiti cartam iam dictam reddet, et eidem Rogero dictas quadraginta marcas. Et si contingat quod tenentes de dictis tenuris ad hoc, quod predictum est, domino comiti faciendum per ipsum Rogerum adesse noluerint, sepedictus comes vel ballivi sui ipsos compellent ad hoc faciendum. Et dictus Rogerus ad sumptus domini comitis itinerabit una cum ballivis comitis, quousque negocium istud, secundum quod predictum est, fuerit consummatum. Et ad maiorem huius rei securitatem uterque illorum presenti scripto more cirographi concepto sigillum suum apposuit. Hiis testibus domino Waltero abbate Cestrie, domino Willelmo de Vernona iusticiario Cestrie, Radulfo de Bray, Waltero Dayville, Ricardo de Biron, Iohanne de Lexintona, Simone et Iohanne clericis.

In 1229 Henry III granted Ranulf all his land between Ribble and Mersey, including West Derby, Liverpool and Salford (*J.C.A.S.*, lviii, p. 109). The purchase of the lands of Roger of Marsey for 200 marks was presumably intended to consolidate his hold. Roger was the son of Ranulf of Marsey who died shortly before 1207 (*L.P.R.*, p. 408); his deed of sale is printed in Orm., i. 37, and has the same witnesses as the present cirograph. Both date almost certainly from 1230.

434.   Quittance to Philip of Orreby of two pigs a year for pannage from Alvanley and 14d. annually for streteward and sheriff's stuthe.

[c.1230]

Orig.: Chester City Record Office, D/CAS/1. Transcr.: B.L. Harl. MS. 2074, f. 172 (new f. 69).

Rannulfus comes Cestrie et Lincolnie omnibus presentem cartam inspecturis vel audituris salutem. Sciatis me dedisse et concessisse et hac presenti carta mea confirmasse quietanciam de me et heredibus meis Philippo de Orreby et heredibus suis de duobus porcis, quos annuatim de consuetudine pro pannagio percipere consuevi de Alvaldeleghe, et de quatuordecim denariis quos annuatim percipere solebam de eadem villa pro streteward et shirrevestude. Et in huius

donationis et quietancie testimonium hanc presentem cartam sigillo meo muni-
tam ei habere feci. Hiis testibus Fulcone filio Warini, Baldewino de Ver,
Nicholao de Litteris, Walkelino de Arderne, Willelmo de Malo Passu, Ricardo
de Sondbache, Hugone de Chelmundele, Ricardo de Kingesle, Petro de
Frodesham, magistro Gileberto de Westona, Ricardo de Arderne, Simone et
Petro clericis, et multis aliis.

SEAL: on tag, missing.

Philip of Orreby, the famous justiciar, purchased Alvanley from Richard of
Pierrepont and Robert of Alvanley some time after 1210 (Orm., ii. 75). The names
of the witnesses of the present charter indicate that it was given shortly after
Orreby's retirement from the justiciarship in 1229, probably in 1230. The first
witness, Fulk fitz Warin, married Agnes, the daughter of Orreby's son, another
Philip, who predeceased his father. It is a curious fact, by comparison with the
grants showered on Philip's contemporary, Peter the clerk, that this is the only
grant Ranulf III is specifically known to have made to his great justiciar. For
shirrevesteth, defined as a 'customary rent collected in the five hundreds of the
county of Chester', see *R.S.L.C.*, lix, pp. 133, 171.

435.   Charter for Salford, granting it the status of a free borough and setting out
the liberties of the burgesses.

[1231]

Orig.: archives of the corporation of Salford. Transcr.:
P.R.O., D.L. 41/1/13. Facsimile: Tait, *Mediaeval Man-
chester*, frontispiece. Ed.: Baines, *The County Palatine of
Lancaster*, ii. 170; English transl.: Harland, *Mamecestre*
(*Chetham Soc.*, liii, vol. i. 200–202).

Ranulfus comes Cestrie et Lincolnie omnibus presentibus et futuris presentem
cartam inspecturis vel audituris salutem. Sciatis me dedisse, concessisse et hac
presenti carta mea confirmasse, quod villa de Salford sit liber burgus et quod
burgenses in illo habitantes habeant et teneant omnes istas libertates subscriptas.

In primo, quod quilibet burgensium habeat unam acram ad burgagium suum et
reddet de quolibet burgagio suo per annum duodecim denarios pro omnibus
firmis que ad burgum illum pertinent.

Si vero prepositus ville aliquem burgensem calumpniaverit de aliquo placito et
calumpniatus non venerit ad diem nec aliquis pro eo infra Laghemote, in
forisfactura mea est de duodecim denariis.

Item, si aliquis burgensis aliquem burgensem implacitaverit de aliquo debito et ipse cognoverit debitum, prepositus ponat ei diem, scilicet octavum, et si non venerit ad diem, reddat mihi duodecim denarios pro forisfactura diei, et debitum reddat, et preposito iiii. denarios.

Si aliquis burgensis in burgo aliquem burgensem per iram percusserit vel verberaverit absque sanguinis effusione, per visum burgensium sibi pacem faciet, salvo iure meo, scilicet xii. denariis.

Item, si aliquis implacitatus fuerit in burgo de aliquo placito, non respondeat nec burgensi nec villano nec alicui alio nisi in suo Portmannemot, scilicet de placito quod ad burgum pertinet.

Si aliquis burgensis vel alius appellet aliquem burgensem de latrocinio, prefectus attachiet eum ad respondendum et stare iudicio in Portmannemote, salvo iure meo.

Item, si aliquis implacitatus fuerit de vicino suo vel de aliquo aliquo de aliquibus, que ad burgum pertineant, et tres dies secutus fuerit, si testimonium habuerit de preposito et de vicinis suis quod adversarius suus defectus sit ad hos tres dies, nullum postea det ei responsum de illo placito et alter cadat in misericordiam.

Item, nullus burgensis debet furnare panem qui sit ad vendendum, nisi ad furnum meum per rationabiles consuetudines.

Si molendinum ibi habuero, ipsi burgenses ad molendinum meum molent ad vicesimum vas, et si molendinum non habuero ibidem, molent quocumque voluerint.

Item, predicti burgenses possunt eligere prepositum de se ipsis, quem voluerint, et removere in fine anni.

Item, quilibet burgensis burgagium suum potest dare, inpignorare vel vendere cuicumque voluerit, nisi heres illud emere voluerit; sed heres propinquior erit, ad illud emendum, salvo servitio meo, ita tamen quod non vendatur in religione.

Item, burgenses possunt namare debitores suos pro debitis suis in burgo, si debitor cognoverit debitum, nisi sint tenentes de burgo. Catalla burgensium non debent namari pro alicuius debitis, nisi pro suis propriis.

Item, burgenses predicti et omnes sui de quocumque emerint vel venderint, ubicumque fuerit in dominicis meis, sive in nundinis sive in foris, erunt quieti de tolneto, salvo tolneto salis.

Quicumque fregerit assisam sive de pane sive de cervisia remanebit in forisfactura de xii. denariis tribus vicibus, et ad quartam vicem faciet assisam ville.

Ipsi autem burgenses habebunt communam liberam pasturam in bosco, in plano, in pasturis omnibus pertinentibus ville Salfordie, et quieti erunt de pannagio in ipso bosco ville de Salfordia. Iidem burgenses rationabiliter de predicto bosco capient omnia necessaria ad edificandum et ad ardendum.

Item, quilibet potest esse ad placitum pro sponsa sua et familia sua, et sponsa cuiuslibet potest firmam suam reddere preposito, faciendo quod facere debeat, et placitum sequi pro sponso suo, si ipse forsan alibi fuerit.

Burgensis, si non habuerit heredem, legare poterit burgagium suum et catalla sua, cum moriatur, ubicumque ei placuerit, salvo tamen iure meo, scilicet iiii. denariis, et salvo servitio ad ipsum burgagium pertinente, ita scilicet quod illud burgagium non alienetur in religione.

Cum burgensis moriatur, sponsa sua manebit in domo cum herede et ibi habebit necessaria, quamdiu sine marito fuerit; et ex quo maritari voluerit, discedet libere sine dote et heres ut dominus manebit in domo.

Item, cum burgensis moriatur, heres eius nullum aliud relevium dabit mihi nisi huiusmodi arma, scilicet gladium vel arcum vel lanceam.

Nullus infra wapentachium Salfordie, ut sutor, peliparius, fullo vel aliquis talis, exerceat officium suum, nisi sit in burgo, salvis libertatibus baronum.

Prefati vero burgenses dabunt firmam suam de burgagio ad quatuor anni terminos, scilicet ad natale Domini iii. denarios, ad mediam quadragesimam iii. denarios, ad festum beati Iohannis Baptiste iii. denarios, et ad festum beati Michaelis iii. denarios.

Omnia predicta placita erunt terminata coram ballivis domini comitis per visum burgensium.

Quicumque burgagium suum vendere voluerit extra religionem et a villa discedere, dabit mihi iiii. denarios et libere ibit, quocumque voluerit, cum omnibus catallis suis.

Ego vero Rannulfus et heredes mei omnes predictas libertates et consuetudines predictis burgensibus et heredibus suis contra omnes gentes in perpetuum warantizabimus, salvo mihi et heredibus meis rationabili tallagio, quando dominus rex burgos suos per Angliam talliare fecerit. In cuius rei memoriam presenti pagine sigillum meum apposui. Hiis testibus domino Willelmo iusticiario Cestrie, Simone de Monte Forti, Pagano de Chaurciis, Fulcone filio Warini, Gilberto de Segrava, Walkelino de Ardene, Ricardo de Vernun, Rogero Gernet, Rogero de Derby, Galfrido de Burun, Hugone de Birun, Simone et Iohanne clericis, et multis aliis.

> SEAL: on tag, much damaged; knight with shield in left
> hand, right arm extended, but sword missing; legend
> perished.

This charter dates after 1229, when Henry III conferred all his lands between
Ribble and Mersey, including the wapentake of Salford, on Ranulf III (no. **433**).
In all probability it dates from 1231. The second witness, Simon de Montfort, the
future earl of Leicester, returned to England with Ranulf, to claim his
inheritance, at the beginning of August 1231. Both were present with the king at
Castle Maud, Radnor, on 18 August, and it is virtually certain that Simon
accompanied Ranulf to Chester on 21 August (*Ann. Cestr.*, p. 59). The last four
witnesses, before the two clerks, are all well known Lancashire figures.
Although constituted a 'free borough', the government of Salford remained
essentially manorial, under the control of the earl's bailiffs, rather than
municipal.

436.   Truce between England and France concluded by Ranulf earl of Chester
and Peter de Dreux, duke of Brittany, and sealed with the earl's seal. In
the camp near St. Aubin, 4 July 1231.

> Orig.: Paris, Arch. nationales, J. 241, no. 34. Ed.: Teulet,
> *Layettes du Trésor des Chartes*, ii. 210 (no. 2141).

Universis presentes litteras inspecturis P. dux Britannie, comes Richemondie, et
R. comes Cestrie salutem in domino. Notum facimus quod, cum dominus H. rex
Anglie illustris mihi P. duci Britannie per litteras suas patentes potestatem
dedisset treugas ineundi cum illustri domino Ludovico rege Francie et suis pro
ipso domino rege Anglie et suis, nos duo treugas inivimus cum eodem rege
Francie et suis pro dicto rege Anglie et suis a festo beati Iohannis Baptiste nuper
preterito in tres annos.

Forma autem treugarum talis est, quod comes Marchie debet recuperare
insulam Oleronis vel, quolibet anno usque ad finem treugarum, habebit
octingentas libras Turonensium in recompensationem dicte insule, medietatem
in festo Omnium Sanctorum et medietatem in festo Ascensionis Domini. Item
comes Marchie et uxor sua et heredes sui durantibus treugis non implacitabuntur
nec vexabuntur in foro ecclesiastico nec in foro laicali de aliqua re, de qua essent
tenentes tempore quo date fuerunt treuge vel de qua tunc essent in pace; immo,
durantibus treugis, per omnia remanebunt in tali statu in quo erant ea die qua
treuge iste fuerunt inite. Et si aliquo modo vexarentur vel implacitarentur
interim, quin remanerent in eadem pace et in eodem statu ut supradictum est,
dominus rex Francie posset eos iuvare sine se mesfacere, et non teneretur extunc
in antea istas treugas observare. Insuper est ordinatum quod, si aliqui foris-

fecerint in terra dicti comitis Marchie infra treugam et in terram alicuius baronum regis Anglie redierint post forisfactum, si ille in cuius terram redierint, requisitus per dictatores, treuge emendare infra quadraginta dies noluerit, dominus rex Francie possit dictum comitem iuvare contra eum sine se meffacere et rex Anglie fautorem non iuvabit neque delinquentem. Et idem de baronibus ipsius regis Anglie observabitur. Hoc ipsum observabitur de baronibus domini regis Francie. Quod autem superius dictum est de vexatione sive implacitatione comitis Marchie sive uxoris sue vel heredum suorum, intelligitur, si rex Anglie per se vel per suos implacitaret vel vexaret vel faceret implacitari vel vexari, quia tunc dominus rex Francie posset eos iuváre sine se meffacere et non teneretur dominus rex Francie extunc in antea treugas regis Anglie observare.

Iurabunt autem treugam istam ex parte regis Anglie comes Richardus frater eius et Hubertus de Borc iusticia Anglie. Actum in castris prope sanctum Albinum anno domini MCC. tricesimo primo mense iulio in festo sancti Martini estivalis.

> SEALS: on tags; (i) torn away; (ii) circular, yellow wax; obverse: equestrian figure armed with shield and helmet, brandishing sword in right hand, legend: + SIGILLVM RANVLPHI COM . . . IS CES . . . . COLNIE; reverse: counterseal, on a roundel three garbs, two and one, legend: + SECRETVM RANVLFI COMITIS CESTRIE ET LINCOLNIE.

After the conclusion of Henry III's abortive expedition of 1230 to France and the king's return to England, command of the English forces on the Continent was left first to William earl of Pembroke, the earl marshal, and after his death in April 1231 to Earl Ranulf of Chester. With depleted forces military operations were impossible, and on July 4, 1231, Ranulf and Peter of Dreux, duke of Brittany and earl of Richmond, concluded this truce for a period of three years.[1] It was Ranulf's last active participation in continental affairs.

1. Peter of Dreux presumably took precedence over Ranulf in the negotiations because of his ducal status. It is unnecessary here to discuss his somewhat equivocal role; he quickly reverted to the allegiance of the king of France. See in summary Powicke, *The Thirteenth Century*, pp. 93–97. His seal is lost.

437. Confirmation of the grant of thirty librates of land which Earl Ranulf made in his lifetime to his niece Colette, daughter of the late earl of Arundel, as her marriage portion, to be assigned from the manor of Leeds in the county of York.

[1232]

> P.R.O., C.66 (Chancery Patent Rolls), no. 43, m. 9. Ed.:
> *Cal. Pat. Rolls, 1232–47*, pp. 2–3; Engl. abstract, *H.K.F.*,
> p. 10.

Rex concessionem et assignationem, quam Rannulfus quondam comes Cestrie et Lincolnie in vita sua fecit Colette nepti sue filie W. quondam comitis Arundell ad se maritandum de xxx. libratis terre cum pertinentiis, assignandis ei in portione Hugonis de Albiniaco, quem ipsum continget de hereditate, que fuit predicti comitis, gratam habet et acceptam, ipsamque pro se et heredibus suis concedit rex et confirmat, volens quod predicte xxx. librate terre assignentur ei in manerio de Ledes in comitatu Eboracensi.

Henry III's confirmation, from which this abstract is taken, is dated 22 November 1232, less than one month after Ranulf III's death. The text of Ranulf's grant has not survived, but it can safely be assumed that it was made, like his grant of the county of Lincoln to his sister Hawise (**no. 310**), within a few weeks of his death. Ranulf had acquired the manor of Leeds in 1217 (*J.C.A.S.*, lviii p. 107).

JOHN 'THE SCOT', EARL OF CHESTER (1232–1237)

438.   Grant to the chapel of Hilbre Island and the monks living there of 10s. from the exchequer of Chester by the hand of the chamberlain of the castle, for the maintenance of the light of St. Mary.

[1232–1237]

> B.L. Harl. 1965 (St. Werburgh's register), f. 23v. (new f. 26v.). Ed.: *Chart. St. Werburgh*, p. 299 (no. 521).

Iohannes comes Cestrie dedit capelle de Hildeburghey et monachis ibi degentibus ad luminaria sancte Marie decem solidos argenti de scacario Cestrie per manum camerarii castri ad festum sancti Martini percipiendos.

Hilbre Island (Orm., ii. 501) lies off West Kirby at the mouth of the Dee, and had been given by Robert of Rhuddlan, with the consent of Earl Hugh I, to the Norman abbey of St. Evroul (**no. 1**). Here there was a cell of monks. Later, probably c.1137–40 (*Chart. St. Werburgh*, p. 293) it passed with West Kirby from St. Evroul to St. Werburgh's (no. 132), of which it remained a cell. The light of St. Mary was presumably a lighthouse or navigational aid for mariners.

439. Grant to Henry of Yarwell of half a virgate of land in Yarwell (Northants.)

[1232–1237]

Orig.: Northants. Record Soc., Westmorland Charter 2, ix. 1.

Omnibus presentem cartam inspecturis vel audituris Iohannes de Scocia comes Cestrie et Huntedonie salutem. Sciatis me concessisse et dedisse et hac presenti carta confirmasse Henrico de Iarewelle pro homagis et servicio suo dimidiam virgatam terre cum pertinenciis in Iarewelle, illam scilicet dimidiam virgatam terre quam Alexander Yennewic aliquando tenuit in eadem villa, habendam et tenendam de me et heredibus meis illi et heredibus suis libere et quiete, plene et pacifice, cum omnibus libertatibus et aisiamentis ad predictam terram pertinentibus, tam infra villam quam extra, reddendo inde annuatim mihi et heredibus meis ille et heredes sui septem solidos sterlingorum ad quatuor terminos anni, scilicet ad Natale viginti et unum denarium,[1] ad Pascha viginti et unum denarios,ad nativitatem beati Iohannis Baptiste viginti et unum denarios et ad festum sancti Michaelis viginti et unum denarios, pro omni servicio et exactione quacumque ad predictam terram pertinente. Et ego et heredes mei predictam dimidiam virgatam terre cum pertinenciis predicto Henrico et heredibus suis contra omnes gentes in perpetuum warantizabimus. In cuius rei testimonium presentem cartam sigillo meo munitam ei habere feci. Hiis testibus Willelmo de Cantelupo iuniore, Baldewino de Pantona, Gileberto de Nuers, Petro de Westona, Roberto de Hale, Philippo Patric, Gileberto de Iarewelle, Willelmo de Dodintona, Henrico parvo, Roberto filio Petri, Ricardo de Croylandia, Willelmo, Haroldo, Petro et Hugone clericis, et aliis.

SEAL: equestrian, defaced.

1. sic orig.; later entries abbreviated (denar̄).

Yarwell was part of the honour of Huntingdon (*H.K.F.*, pp. 396–7), and all the witnesses except William of Cantilupe, and probably the two clerks Peter and Hugh, appear to be local men. I have been unable to date the grant except within the tenure of Earl John.

440. Confirmation to John de Lacy, earl of Lincoln and constable of Chester, of ten knights' fees, as held by his antecessors, to hold for the service of half a knight's fee.

[c.1233]

P.R.O., D.L. 42/1 (Coucher Book I), f. 49. Abbreviated transcripts from Coucher: B.L. Harl. MS. 2063, f. 113 (old f. 235); Shakerley MS. 3, p. 168; Chetham's Library, Towneley's transcripts from the Vernon MSS., p. 219; Central Reference Library, Manchester, Towneley MS. 8, p. 1066. Abstract: Orm., i. 697–8; Engl. abstract: *Ches. Sheaf*, no. 4212.

Sciant presentes et futuri quod ego Iohannes comes Cestrie et Huntendonie concessi, remisi, quietum clamavi et presenti carta mea confirmavi Iohanni de Lascy comiti Lincolnie et constabulario Cestrie decem feoda militum in Anglia, illa scilicet que de me tenuit et antecessores sui de antecessoribus meis tenuerunt, pro servicio dimidii feodi unius militis, quod ipse et heredes sui michi et heredibus meis facere debent pro omni servicio, habenda et tenenda eidem Iohanni de Lascy et heredibus suis de me et heredibus meis libere quiete et pacifice, ita quod ego Iohannes comes Cestrie et Huntendonie predictus nec heredes mei nichil amplius poterimus habere clamare vel exigere in dictis decem feodis militum quam servicium dimidii feodi unius militis. Hec autem predicta decem feoda militum ego et heredes mei ipsi et heredibus suis per predictum servicium contra omnes gentes imperpetuum warantizabimus. Ut autem hec mea concessio et quietaclamacio rata sit et stabilis imperpetuum, eam sigilli mei apposicione roboravi. Hiis testibus domino Henrico de Audidelegha, domino Willelmo de Cantilupo, domino Ricardo Phiton tunc iusticiario Cestrie, domino Radulfo Basset, domino Hugone Phiton, Galfrido de Appilby, Nicholao de Damenevilla, Henrico de Longo Campo, Willelmo de Longo Campo, Petro clerico, et multis aliis.

It has usually been assumed that this charter refers to the constable's hereditary barony of Halton, the ancient service of which was ten knights' fees (Tait, 'Knight Service in Cheshire', *E.H.R.*, lvii, p. 439). But the ten fees mentioned are specifically stated to be 'in England' (i.e. the constable's holding outside Cheshire). Moreover, in 1252 and later the Cheshire knights' service of the constable was assessed at 8 knights (Stewart-Brown, *Chetham Soc.*, N.S. lxxxiv, pp. xlvi, li). Conceivably, Earl John's drastic reduction to ½ knight's fee was ignored by the Crown after it annexed the earldom in 1237. Earl John made other substantial grants to John de Lacy (**no. 441**), who was clearly an important person after he succeeded to the earldom of Lincoln on 23 November 1232, at the instance of Hawise de Quincy, mother of his wife Margaret, to whom the earldom had been conveyed by her brother, Ranulf III (**no. 310**). The present charter probably dates from 1233, in which year Richard Fitton became justiciar of Chester.

441. Grant of various rents etc., in Partney, Dalby, Irby, Hameringham, Colkesby and Hemingby (all in Lincs.) to John de Lacy, earl of Lincoln and constable of Chester, in augmentation of his manor of Greetham.

[1234–1237]

P.R.O., D.L. 42/2 (Coucher Book II), f. 294.

Sciant presentes et futuri quod ego Iohannes comes Cestrie et Huntedonie dedi et concessi et hac presenti carta mea confirmavi Iohanni de Lacy comiti Lincolnie constabulario Cestrie pro humagio et servicio suo in incremento manerii de Graham cum pertinenciis, quod ei dedi, viginti quatuor solidos de tolneto de Partenay de terra Dalby, quam mater domini Hugonis de Haringtona tenet, tres solidos de quodam homine Rigkelley, quatuor denarios de prato de Hyreby, unam marcam de Roberto fabro de Hamingham pro quodam tofto, sex denarios de quodam homine de Hyreby, unum denarium de domino Iohanne de Esterby, quadraginta solidos de Haraldo filio Humfridi, sex solidos de duabus bovatis et dimidia terre in Kolkesby et de tercia parte unius bovate xxviii. solidos iiii.d.; habendos et tenendos de me et heredibus meis illi et heredibus suis simul cum predicto manerio de Graham et xxxii. solidis et vii.d. de Hemingby, cum homagiis predictorum Iohannis de Esterby, Haraldi filii Humfridi et Hugonis de Haringtona, simul cum Iocelino filio Heming et sequela sua, Hugone filio Ricardi cum sequela sua, Waltero filio Reginaldi cum sequela sua, Matilda vidua cum sequela sua, Rogero filio Roberti cum sequela sua, Allota de Cotes cum sequela sua, Gode uxore Helsi cum sequela sua, Agnete uxore Gileberti cum sequela, et simul cum tenentibus et vilenagio in Kolkelby cum sequela eorum. Ego vero Iohannes comes Cestrie predicto Iohanni comiti Lincolnie predictos redditus, homagia predicta et predictos homines cum eorum sequelis warantizabimus et heredibus suis contra omnes homines imperpetuum, secundum tenorem cirograffi confecti inter me et Hawisiam de Quency. Hiis testibus Willelmo de Raleghe, Henrico de Handeleghe, Willelmo de Cantelupo iuniore, Ricardo Fitun, Radulfo Basset, Normanno de Aray, Willelmo de Beningwrth, Coline de Danevilla, Henrico de Notingham, Henrico de Luncham, Osberto clerico, Ricardo clerico, et aliis.

Greetham had been given to John the Scot's father, Earl David of Huntingdon, on his marriage with Ranulf III's sister Matilda in 1190 (**no. 220**), and on his death passed to her with Hemingby as her *maritagium (H.K.F.*, p. 83).

Matilda died at Epiphany 1233, and Greetham evidently reverted to the earl, who then gave it (as the present charter states) to John de Lacy, who had succeeded to the earldom of Lincoln at the instance of Hawise de Quincy, mother of his wife Margaret, on 23 November 1232 (**nos. 310, 440, 457**). Hawise, who appears to have been particularly litigious (**no. 309**), evidently maintained some sort of claim in Greetham, where she was engaged in litigation with the earl of Derby in 1234 (*H.K.F.*, p. 83), and before making the present grant to John de Lacy, Earl John had to come to an agreement with her; but the cirograph setting out the arrangement has not survived. It looks, however, as though the present charter, augmenting Lacy's holding, is unlikely to have been given before 1234. It represents a fairly considerable addition to his income.

[CLEMENTIA, WIDOW OF RANULF III.]

442.   Confirmation to the abbey of Savigny of its lands in Long Bennington and Foston (Lincs.)

[? 1233–1235]

> Orig.: Westminster abbey muniments, no. 516. Transcr.:
> Madox, *Formulare Anglicanum*, pp.256–7 (no. 437), from
> original.

Sciant presentes et futuri quod ego Clemencia filia Willelmi de Filgeris, quondam sponsa Rannulfi comitis Cestrie et Lincolnie, in ligia potestate mea dedi, concessi et presenti carta mea confirmavi pro anima Rannulfi comitis Cestrie et Lincolnie et pro salute anime mee et pro animabus antecessorum et successorum meorum deo et beate Marie et abbati et conventui de Savigneio omnes terras, res et possessiones, quas habuerunt in villis de Benigtona et de Fortona[1] illo die quo dominus meus Rannulfus comes Cestrie et Lincolnie obiit, habendas et tenendas in liberam, puram et perpetuam elemosinam cum omnibus eisiamentis et omnibus libertatibus et pertinenciis suis infra villam et extra, scilicet unam carucatam terre in haya iuxta ecclesiam sancti Swithuni in escambium pro quadam carucata terre in campis de Benigtona, et unam rodam terre in villa de Benigtona ad incrementum curte predictorum monachorum ex parte occidentali, et undecim acras terre et dimidiam et sex rodas prati in haya de Benigtona iuxta terras quas habuerunt in dicta haya, in escambium undecim acrarum et dimidie terre et sex rodarum prati, quas predicti monachi michi escambiaverunt in campis de Benigtona et de Fortona,[1] scilicet super Wildholm septem seliones, super Heydich unum selionem, ad crucem de haya duos seliones, super Haihul duos seliones, ad Sichet de Fortona unum selionem, ad Hubbekate[2] unum selionem, ad Storkholm unum selionem et culturam de Cliveshende, et in pratis de Benigtona ex orientali parte de Rieholm sed rodas prati. Concessi etiam prefatis monachis claudere predictum hayum et defendere. Preterea dedi eis totum tenementum quod Walterus de Swindresby tenuit in villa de Benigtona cum omnibus libertatibus suis et pertinenciis, et toftum quod Malgerus filius Gaufridi tenuit in eadem villa cum una bovata terre et pertinenciis suis. Preterea concessi et confirmavi sepedictis abbati et conventui illas novem bovatas terre quas habent ex dono Thome filii Algeri de Flet, et remisi ad pitanciam faciendam feria quarta in capite ieiunii unam marcam argenti quam idem Thomas solebat solvere pro predicta terra.

Hec omnia predicta dedi, concessi et presenti carta confirmavi predictis monachis in puram, liberam et perpetuam elemosinam, tenenda et habenda libere et quiete, pacifice et integre, soluta et quieta ab omni seculari servicio, exactione et demanda, ita quod in eis nichil penitus michi retineo nisi orationes tantum. Et ego Clemencia et heredes mei hec omnia prenominata predictis abbati et monachis contra omnes homines et feminas in perpetuum warantizabimus. Et ut hec omnia rata et stabilia perseverent in perpetuum, ea presentis scripti testimonio et sigilli mei appositione roboravi. Hiis testibus domino Roberto tunc abbate de Cumbermare, domino Reginaldo tunc priore de Rependona, domino Iohanne subpriore de Rependona, domino Gilleberto capellano, Hamone de Turevilla, Helia pincerna, Radulfo de Akofera, Henrico de Mottr[am],[3] et aliis.

> SEAL: oval, green wax on parchment tag; obverse, a tall slender woman standing, in her left hand a bird; legend SIGILL' CLEMENCIE COMITISSE CESTRIE; reverse, oval counterseal, a bird standing, legend S' CLEMENCIE COMIT' CESTRIE ET LINCOL'.

1. *sic orig.* (*for* Fostona).
2. *sic orig.* (*for* Hubbegate).
3. *Reading doubtful.*

This charter is in effect a confirmation of the earlier charters of Ranulf III (**nos. 334, 335**), the only substantial difference being the confirmation of the gift of nine bovates by Thomas son of Alger of Fleet, who had acquired them many years earlier from William of St. John (**no. 303**). The indications are that Clementia's charter was given shortly after Ranulf's death. Robert abbot of Combermere succeeded Thomas, who was alive in 1228, and occurs 1230–32 (*V.C.H. Cheshire*, iii. 155), and Reginald prior of Repton also occurs c.1230 (*V.C.H. Derbys.*, ii. 63), but the times of their deaths or resignations are not known. As Countess Clementia survived until 1252, it is impossible to give an accurate date, but 1233–35 seems likely.

[CLEMENTIA, WIDOW OF RANULF III.]

443. Grant to the abbey of Savigny of Thomas son of William of Foston with his progeny, and of the four bovates his father held in Foston.

[? 1233–1235]

Bodleian Library, Dodsworth MS. 88, f. 65v. (source not given).

Omnibus sancte matris ecclesie filiis presentibus et futuris has litteras visuris vel audituris, Clementia filio Willelmi de Filgeriis, quondam sponsa Ranulfi comitis Cestrie et Lincolnie salutem. Noverit universitas vestra quod ego in ligia potestate mea dedi et concessi et hac presenti carta mea confirmavi deo et sancte Marie et abbati et conventui de Savigneio in puram et perpetuam elemosinam Thomam filium Willelmi de Fostun cum tota sequela sua, et quatuor bovatas terre quas dictus Willelmus pater eiusdem Thome tenuit in predicta villa de Fostun,[1] cum tofto et crofto et prato et cum omnibus pertinenciis et aisiamentis et libertatibus ad predictas quatuor bovatas terre pertinentibus. Et ut hec mea donacio rata et inconcussa permaneat, eam presentis scripti testimonio et sigilli mei apposicione corroboravi. Hiis testibus domino Roberto de Cumbermara, domino Reginaldo tunc priore de Rependon, domino Iohanne tunc suppriore de Rependona, domino Gilberto capellano, Hamone de Turevilla, Radulfo de Akofera, Helia pincerna, Henrico de Muttr,[2] et aliis.

1. Fortun *MS.*   2. *Reading uncertain.*

About 1220–26 Ranulf III had given William of Foston and the land here specified to Dieulacres abbey (**no. 388**). It looks as though Countess Clementia only waited for his death to revoke his gift and confer William's heir and land on her favourite foundation of Savigny. This charter has the same witnesses as Clementia's general confirmation of the lands of Savigny in Long Bennington and Foston (**no. 442**), and is almost certainly of the same date.

[CLEMENTIA, WIDOW OF RANULF III.]

444. Gift to the abbey of Savigny of rent and services in the land in Foston (Lincs.) held by William of Sutton, son of Roland of Sutton.

[1239–1252]

Orig. (two): Westminster abbey muniments, no. 540 (= A) and no. 545 (= A1).

Sciant omnes quod ego Clemencia comitissa Cestrie tempore viduitatis mee constituta pro salute anime mee et nobilis viri Ranulfi quondam comitis Cestrie, mariti mei, necnon et omnium antecessorum et successorum meorum dedi et concessi absque omni retenemento meo vel heredum meorum deo et abbatie Savigneii et monachis ibidem deo servientibus totum redditum et servicium, et quicquid habebam vel habere poteram ego vel heredes mei quacumque racione in tota terra quam tenuit de me in Fostona Willelmus de Suttona, filius Rollandi de Suttona, tenenda et habenda ipsis monachis in puram et perpetuam elemosinam, ab omni servicio et seculari demanda liberam[1] penitus et quietam.[1] Hanc vero donacionem meam ego et heredes mei predictis abbatie et monachis contra omnes homines et feminas warantizabimus. In cuius rei testimonium et perpetuam firmitatem presenti scripto sigillum meum apposui. Hiis testibus Willelmo de Furnesio, Simone de Cumbermara, Henrico de Bellalanda, Gaufrido de Ruffordia abbatibus, Roberto de Lexentona, Hamone de Torvilla, Ricardo de Huwelle, Ricardo de Marcham,[2] Simone de Berefordia senescallo, Roberto de Campedena clerico, Radulfo de Acovere, et multis aliis.

> SEAL (in both exemplifications): green wax, vesica; obverse, a female figure in flowing garments, bird in left hand, legend SIGILL'. CLEMENCIE COMITISSE CESTRIE; reverse, small vesica seal, a bird, legend in beaded border S. CLEMENCIS. COMIT. CESTRIE ET LINCOL +

1. *sic MSS.*   2. *sic A.*; Mutham *A1.*

This charter is another example (see **nos. 229, 328**) of a dual exemplification, perhaps explicable in the present instance by the fact that the monks of Savigny required one copy for use in England, the other for preservation in their own archives. Copy A is written in a rather stiff charter hand, A1 in a set diplomatic minuscule, identical with that of **no. 442**, and to all appearances produced by the beneficiaries. But both exemplars are authenticated with the countess's seal of green wax and are undoubtedly authentic.

To judge from the names of the witnesses this charter is considerably later in date than **nos. 442** and **443**. William abbot of Furness occurs as late as 1246 (but may, of course, have been in office earlier) and apparently did not die until 1266–67 (*V.C.H. Lancs.*, ii. 130), and Simon abbot of Combermere occurs 1237–45 (*V.C.H. Cheshire*, iii. 155). Henry abbot of Byland occurs in 1231 and thereafter in a number of fines down to 1254–55 (*V.C.H. Yorks.*, iii. 133), and a G. abbot of Rufford occurs in 1239; he followed an Abbot Simon, who was in office in 1232, and apparently survived until 1252 (*V.C.H. Notts.*, ii. 154). Robert of Campden, in all probability Clementia's personal clerk, is probably the R. de Stainsby who was instituted in 1238 (*Chart. St. Werburgh*, p. 139, no. 122), and Simon de Bereford her steward. These indications point to a date after 1239 at earliest. Whether the rather surprising gathering of abbots from very widespread regions has any significance, can only be a matter of surmise; but it might conceivably point to a date not long before Clementia's death in 1252.

445. Remission to the monks of Dieulacres of the homages and services belonging to the manor of Leek, which he has retained for himself.

[1233–1236]

> P.R.O., C.53 (Chancery Charter Rolls), no. 117; C.66 (Chancery Patent Rolls), no. 121, m. 25, and no. 519, m. 20. Ed.: *Cal. Ch. Rolls*, iv. 156 (no. 20); *Hist. Coll. of Staffordshire*, 1913, p. 316.

Omnibus presentibus et futuris Iohannes de Scotia comes Cestrie et Huntedonie salutem. Noverit universitas vestra me pro salute anime mee et pro salute omnium antecessorum et successorum meorum remisisse et quietaclamasse deo et beate Marie et abbati de Deulacresse et monachis ibidem deo servientibus in liberam puram et perpetuam elemosinam omnia homagia et servitia pertinentia ad manerium de Lek, que prius retinui ad opus meum, ita quod ego vel heredes mei in dicto manerio cum pertinentiis nichil omnino poterimus exigere, sed possideant predicti abbas et monachi sepedictum manerium de Lek cum omnibus pertinentiis et libertatibus suis absque ullo retenemento plene et pacifice, prout carta pie memorie domini Ranulphi quondam comitis Cestrie et Lincolnie avunculi mei testatur. In cuius rei testimonium presenti scripto sigillum meum apposui. Hiis testibus venerabili viro domino Alexandro Coventrensi et Lychefeldensi episcopo, Waltero abbate Cestrie, Roberto abbate de Cumbremare, Henrico de Auditheleghe, Warino de Vernun, Willelmo de Breyn, Radulfo de Camays, Radulfo de Say, Hanketino de Folevilla, et aliis.

For Ranulf III's gift to Dieulacres of the manor of Leek with all its appurtenances, see **no. 393**. After his succession in November 1232 John the Scot had evidently withheld various profitable rights. These he now restores, but we can only establish the approximate date of his charter.

446. Confirmation to Dieulacres abbey of the gifts of Ranulf III and other donors.

[1233–1237]

> Salt Library, Stafford, Dieulacres roll, no. 7; Bodleian Library, MS. Top. Gen. c.26 p. 164 (transcript of Rudyard cartulary). Short abstracts: B.L. Harl. MS. 2060, f. 24v. (old f. 41); Add. MS. 6032, f. 120 (old p. 242); Chester, Booth of Twemlow, Liber D, f. 58. Ed.: *D.C.*, p. 353 (no. 165).

Omnibus presentem cartam inspecturis vel audituris, Iohannes de Scotia comes Cestrie et Huntindonie salutem. Sciatis me pro salute pie memorie Ranulfi quondam comitis Cestrie et Lincolnie avunculi mei et pro salute anime comitis Davidis patris mei et pro salute anime mee animarumque omnium antecessorum et successorum meorum concessisse et hac presenti carta mea confirmasse deo et beate Marie et abbatie de Deulacres et monachis ibidem deo in perpetuum famulantibus omnes rationabiles donationes et libertates a dicto Ranulfo comite et ab antecessoribus suis et a quibuscunque aliis infra terram meam vel alibi illis in puram et perpetuam elemosinam collatas, sicut carte dicti Ranulfi comitis et aliorum, quas dicti loci abbas et conventus inde habent, rationabiliter testantur. Et in huius rei testimonium presenti scripto sigillum meum apponere feci. His testibus Waltero dei gracia abbate Cestrie, Roberto abbate de Cumbremara, Karolo abbate de Stanlawe, Ricardo Phitun tunc iusticiario Cestrie, Roberto de Campania, Hugone Phitun, Radulfo Basset, Franco Teutonico peregrino, Ada de Audithele, et aliis.

This charter was probably given not long after John the Scot's accession, but a close dating is not possible. This is the only mention of Frank the German (*Francus Teutonicus*), perhaps because, as the description *peregrinus* implies, he was a pilgrim, or (more likely) a chance visitor on a journey.

447.   Grant of protection to Dieulacres abbey.

[1233–1237]

> Bodleian Library, MS. Top. Gen. c. 26, p. 165 (transcript from Rudyard cartulary); abbreviated texts in B.L. Harl. MS. 2060, f. 24v. (old f. 41), Add. MS. 6032, f. 120 (old p. 242), and Chester, Booth of Twemlow, Liber D, f. 58. Ed.: *D.C.*, p. 354 (no. 166) (abbreviated text).

Iohannes de Scotia comes Cestrie et Huntundon constabulario suo, dapifero, vicecomiti, baronibus et ballivis suis et omnibus hominibus suis tam presentibus quam futuris salutem. Noveritis me pro salute anime comitis Ranulfi avunculi mei et mee animarumque antecessorum et successorum meorum specialiter suscepisse in manutenemento meo et custodia et protectione mea abbatiam de Deulacres, monachos et conversos ibidem deo servientes, homines, res, terras et possessiones, et omnia ad predictam abbatiam pertinencia. Quare volo et firmiter precipio quod dictam abbatiam et omnia ad eam pertinencia pro posse fideli manu teneatis, custodiatis, protegatis in omnibus, nullam eis iniuriam vel molestiam inferentes nec pro posse vestro eis inferri permittentes, et quod sitis eis in auxilium et consilium ad libertates suas et iura sua habenda et manutenenda in omnibus pro posse vestro fideli. Et si quis eis vel hominibus vel rebus suis in aliquo forisfacere presumpserit, sine dilacione eisdem faciatis iusticiam plenariam. Et prohibeo supra forisfacturam decem librarum ne ipsi vel homines sui ponantur in placitum de aliqua re nisi coram me ipso vel coram capitali iusticiario meo. In cuius rei testimonium presens scriptum sigillo meo munitum contuli. His testibus Waltero abbate Cestrie, Ricardo Phitun tunc iusticiario Cestrie, Willelmo de Cantelupo, Willelmo de Malopassu, Hugone Phitun, Walkelino de Arderne, Galfrido de Appleby, Simone, Petro, Hugone clericis, et aliis.

This charter is in effect a confirmation of Ranulf III's grant of protection (**no. 378**), the terms of which it largely repeats.

448.   To the citizens of Chester: confirmation of the liberties conferred by his uncle, Earl Ranulf, and the further concession that the right to buy at a discount (*capcio*) shall be limited to the earl and his justiciar, when they are in the city, and in the case of ale shall be limited to four sextaries from one brewing.

[1233–1237]

> Orig.: Chester City Record Office, Archives of Chester Corporation, no. 8. Ed.: *8th Rep. Hist. MSS. Comm.*, p. 356; Morris, *Chester in the Plantagenet and Tudor Reigns*, p. 487.

Iohannes comes Cestrie et Huntendonie constabulario suo, dapifero, iusticiario, baronibus, militibus, ballivis suis et ministris, et omnibus fidelibus suis present- ibus et futuris salutem. Sciatis me concessisse et hac presenti carta mea confirmasse omnibus civibus meis Cestrie, quod nullus mercator aliquod genus mercimonii, quod ad civitatem Cestrie per mare aut per terram venerit, emat vel vendat nisi ipsi cives mei Cestrie et eorum heredes vel per eorum gratum, nisi in nundinis assisis, scilicet in nativitate sancti Iohannis Baptiste et in festo sancti Michaelis.

Item concessi et hac presenti carta mea confirmavi eisdem civibus meis Cestrie, quod si civis fecerit empcionem aliquam et coram testibus, et sequela postea venerit de Francis vel de Anglicis qui rationabiliter possint emptum illum diracionare, civis qui empcionem illam fecerit quietus sit de me et de ballivis meis, perdendo tantummodo et reddendo quod emerit, si aliter non possit vendicanti satisfacere. Si vero sequela venerit de Walense, qui possit rationabiliter rem emptam diracionare, precium rei empte civi reddat, quod idem civis rationabiliter poterit demonstrare se dedisse pro re empta.

Item concessi et hac presenti carta mea confirmavi dictis civibus meis Cestrie gildam suam mercalem, habendam et tenendam adeo libere, quiete et honorifice sicut eam habuerunt in tempore avunculi mei domini Ranulfi comitis Cestrie et Lincolnie.

Item concessi et hac presenti carta mea confirmavi prefatis civibus meis Cestrie, quod nulla capcio fiat in civitate Cestrie preterquam ad opus domini comitis et iusticiarii sui, dum fuerint ibidem, et hoc sit tresdecim denariati pro duodecim denariis, nisi tantummodo de cervisia, scilicet quatuor sexteria ad plus de una bracina, et precium cuiusdam sextarii debet esse iiii. denarii; et nullus habeat capcionem illam cervisie preterquam dominus comes et iusticiarius, et illa capcio fiat per ordinem in circuitu, ubi fieri debet.

Preterea concessi et hac presenti carta mea confirmavi memoratis civibus meis Cestrie omnes libertates et omnes liberas consuetudines, quas illi melius et liberius aut quiecius habuerunt de avunculo meo Ranulfo comite Cestrie et Lincolnie secundum tenorem magne carte, quam eis dedit quando fuit comes Cestrie et Lincolnie. In qua carta ad maiorem securitatem eis faciendam sigillum meum simul cum sigillo avunculi mei Ranulfi comitis Cestrie et Lincolnie apposui.

Has vero prenominatas et superscriptas libertates et liberas consuetudines omnes concessi et hac presenti carta mea confirmavi dilectis et fidelibus meis, scilicet omnibus civibus meis Cestrie, habendas et tenendas illis et heredibus illorum de me et de heredibus meis inperpetuum libere et quiete, pacifice et honorifice. Quare volo et firmiter precipio quod super dictis libertatibus et liberis consuetudinibus nemo illis iniuriam faciat, impedimentum aut gravamen, super forisfacturam decem librarum, set omnes ballivi mei ipsos et eorum libertates et liberas consuetudines et iura protegant et manuteneant. Ego siquidem et heredes mei omnes prenominatas et superscriptas libertates et liberas consuetudines sepedictis civibus meis Cestrie et heredibus illorum contra omnes homines warantizabimus, et in huius rei testimonium presentem cartam sigillo meo munivi. Hiis testibus Ricardo Phiton tunc iusticiario Cestrie, Henrico de Aldithele, Hugone Phiton, Willelmo de Lai, Willelmo de Malopassu, Willelmo de Venables, Guarino de Vernon, Walkelino de Arderne, Rogero de Meingarinc, Hamone de Masci, Willelmo Patricio, Ranulfo de Praeris, Ricardo de Sinbiche, Hugone de Cholmundele, Ricardo de Kingesle, et multis aliis.

SEAL: pendent on tag, missing.

The date of this charter lies between June 1233, when Richard Fitton was appointed justiciar, and the death of John the Scot in June 1237. The only fresh privilege granted is the limitation on the amount of 'captions' the earl and the justiciar might take, viz. a discount of one penny in every thirteen pence worth of goods bought by them while in residence in the city, and four *sextaria* (a sextary being six gallons) from every brewing at a price of 4d. per sextarium (*Ches. Sheaf*, no. 9509). Otherwise the charter confirms in whole or in part the earlier grants of Ranulf III, the first paragraph **no. 258**, the second paragraph one of the main provisions of **no. 256**, and the third paragraph the grant of a gild merchant in **no. 257**. The most perplexing section is the penultimate paragraph in which Earl John confirms all the liberties granted by Ranulf III in the 'great charter' which he gave the citizens 'when he was earl of Chester and Lincoln'. No such charter is known, and the fact that Henry III only confirmed the three known charters of Ranulf III (*36th Rep. D.K.P.R.*, p. 92) strongly suggests that no such charter ever existed. The probability is that Earl John is referring to **no. 256**, but this, of course, was issued some years before Ranulf became earl of Lincoln in 1217.

449.   Confirmation to St. Werburgh's abbey of the gifts of his predecessors and their barons, together with a quittance of the payment of three loaves daily to the tower of Chester castle and of the maintenance of his serjeants in Huntington, Cheveley, Iddinshall and Wervin in time of peace and in Prestbury and Goostrey at all times.

[1233–1237]

St. George's Chapel, Windsor, MS. xi. E. 5 (inspeximus of Guncelin de Badlesmere, 1280); B.L. Harl. MS. 2071, f. 46 (old f. 32). Ed.: Orm., i. 42; *Chart. St. Werburgh*, p. 81 (no. 26).

Omnibus Christi fidelibus presens scriptum visuris vel audituris Iohannes de Scocia comes Cestrie et Huntindonie salutem in domino. Sciatis me concessisse et confirmasse deo et domui sancte Werburge de Cestria et abbati et monachis ibidem deo servientibus in puram et perpetuam elemosinam pro salute mea et comitisse mee et pro anima comitis David patris mei et comitisse Matildis matris mee et pro anima Ranulfi comitis avunculi mei et pro animabus omnium antecessorum et successorum meorum omnes donaciones et dignitates et libertates, quas comites antecessores mei et barones eis dederunt. Insuper ego ipse do, concedo et presenti scripto confirmo predictis abbati et monachis quietanciam de tribus panibus, quos solebant dare diurne ad turrim castelli mei de Cestria, et quietanciam de pultura servientium in villis suis, scilicet Huntin-dun, Chevelee, Idinghale, Wirwin tempore pacis et Presteburi et Gorestre inperpetuum. Quapropter volo et omnibus hominibus meis et amicis firmiter precipio quod predicti abbas et monachi habeant et teneant libere, quiete, bene et in pace omnes donaciones suas cum pertinenciis et dignitates et libertates suas et quietanciam de tribus panibus aliquando ad turrim Cestrie datis et quietanciam de pultura servientium, ut predictum est, et quod utantur et uti permittantur libertatibus suis secundum tenorem cartarum et confirmacionum antecessorum meorum, quas inde habent. Et prohibeo super forisfacturam meam decem librarum, ne quis super hiis prescriptis prefatos abbatem et monachos de cetero molestet, vexet vel disturbet. Et ut hec mea confirmacio, concessio et donacio firmitatis robur obtineant inperpetuum, presenti scripto sigillum meum apponi feci. Hiis testibus domino Ricardo Phitun tunc iusticiario Cestrie, dominis Warino de Vernun, Willelmo de Venables, Hamone de Mascy, Hugone de Phitun, Willelmo de Malopassu, Walkelino de Arderne, Willelmo de Boidel, Ricardo de Sondbache, Ricardo de Wibinburi tunc vicecomite Cestresirie, Hugone de Venables, H. de Struencle clerico, et aliis.

450. Grant to St. Werburgh's abbey of the tithes of his new mills in Cheshire.

[1233–1237]

> B.L. Harl. MS. 2060, f. 117 (new f. 42v.), and Harl. MS. 2071, f. 8 (new f. 21), both from original with drawing or description of seal. Ed.: *Chart. St. Werburgh*, pp. 96–7 (no. 54).

Omnibus sancte matris ecclesie filiis Iohannes de Scocia comes Cestrie et Huntingdonie salutem. Noveritis me concessisse et dedisse deo et sancte Werburge et abbati et monachis Cestrensibus pro salute anime mee et pro anima comitis Ranulfi avunculi mei et pro animabus David patris mei et Matildis matris mee et omnium antecessorum et heredum meorum in puram et perpetuam elemosinam decimas novorum molendinorum meorum de Cestriascira integre et plenarie. Quare volo et firmiter precipio quod predicti abbas et monachi predictas decimas de ipsis novis molendinis meis plene percipiant et in pace possideant. In cuius rei testimonium presenti scripto sigillum meum apponi feci. Hiis testibus domino Ricardo Phiton tunc iusticiario Cestrie, Warino de Vernon, Hamone de Mascy, Willelmo de Malopassu, Hugone Phiton, Willelmo de Lay, Hugone clerico, et aliis.

> SEAL: appended on silken cord; obverse, equestrian seal, legend + SIGILLUM . . . NIE; reverse, shield of arms, three pales, legend + SIGILLUM SECRETI.

The tithes of the earl's mills of Cheshire had been confirmed by Ranulf II (**no. 25**) and Hugh II (**no. 130**). This grant, which falls between 1233 and 1237, is supplementary. William de Lay (and all the other witnesses except the clerk Hugh) attested Earl John's charter for Chester (**no. 448**).

451.   Grant to Richard Fitton of three-quarters of the earl's demesne in Nessington (? Nassington, Northants.), together with 31 of the earl's cottars, listed by name.

[1233–1237]

Orig.: Lancashire Record Office, de Trafford Muniments, Fitton Charters bundle 5, no. 4.

Omnibus hoc scriptum visuris vel audituris Iohannes de Scocia comes Cestrie et Huntendonie salutem. Sciatis me concessisse, dedisse et hac presenti carta mea confirmasse Ricardo Phyton pro humagio suo et servicio tres partes tocius dominici mei cum pertinenciis in Nessigtona et viginti quatuor acras prati in prato meo de Arnewas propinquiores divisis prati de Nessigtona cum tota pastura que vocatur Calemers. Et preterea concessi et dedi eidem Ricardo omnes cotteros meos subscriptos, scilicet Gerandum Puppe, Willelmum Staiard, Willelmum Trulle, Thomam filium Eduse, Radulfum filium Philippi, Robertum Grossum, Emmam que fuit uxor Henrici, Nicholaum filium Herberti, Galfridum fabrum, Gilbertum fullonem, Henricum et Gregorium, Willelmum de Ailingtona, Ricardum de Rising, Galfridum de Byham, Willelmum filium Bernardi, Radulfum textorem, Martinum sutorem, Iohannem filium Margerie, Robertum de Stanfordia, Robertum carpintarium, Robertum bedellum, Hergivam viduam, Rogerum filium Eduse, Robertum filium Thome, Galfridum Coker, Bernardum filium Herberti, Bernardum bedellum, Willelmum filium Bernardi, Willelmum Cusin et Edusam filiam Willelmi Harard et quatuor solidos de virgata terre quam eadem Edusa tenuit, cum tota omnium predictorum sequela et consuetudinibus, et cum terris pratis et cotagiis omnibus que de me tenuerunt Nessigtona sine ullo retinemento, habendos et tenendos de me et heredibus meis illi et heredibus suis, vel cui assignare voluerit, libere, quiete, plene et pacifice in feudo et hereditate cum omnibus libertatibus, consuetudinibus, serviciis, et omnibus aliis aisiamentis ad predictas terras pertinentibus, et in omnibus comoditatibus que in dictis terris cum pertinenciis fieri possint, tam infra villam de Nessigtona quam extra, faciendo inde mihi et heredibus meis ille et heredes sui vel sui assignati servicium quinte partis feodi unius militis pro omnibus serviciis, exactionibus et demandis universis. Et ego et heredes mei predictas terras et homines cum omnibus pertinenciis, sicut supradictum est, dicto Ricardo et heredibus suis vel suis assignatis contra omnes gentes warantizabimus in perpetuum. In cuius rei testimonium presentem cartam sigillo meo munitam ei habere feci. Hiis testibus dominis Waltero abbate Cestrie, Henrico de Aldithele, Rogero de Monte Alto senescallo Cestrie, Willelmo de Venables, Willelmo de Malo Passu, Willelmo de Boidel, Radulfo Basset, Galfrido de Appleby, Roberto de Beaumes, Baldewino de Pantona, Anketino de Folevilla, Ada de Aldithele, Radulfo de Say, Willelmo de Lacu, Serlone de Wlawstona, Petro, Hugone, Ricardo de Coldrea clericis, et aliis multis.

SEAL: on silken cord, missing.

This grant has traditionally been referred to Hessington, which has been identified with Haslington in Cheshire (Orm., iii. 587 note). But the beautifully written charter distinguishes clearly between capital N and capital H, and there can be no doubt that the placename is *Nessigton*. This is Nassington in Northamptonshire, an ancient member of the honour of Huntingdon (*H.K.F.*, pp. 396–7). The difficulty is that there is no other evidence of a Fitton tenure in this place, but there is also none of a Fitton interest in Haslington (Orm., iii. 315). Perhaps we should assume that the holding was lost during the partition of the honour of Chester after the death of John the Scot, when Nassington was assigned to William, earl of Albemarle. It is noteworthy that Wimboldsley, which was also granted to the justiciar, Richard Fitton, by Earl John (**no. 452**), was lost after a short interval, and it looks as though the family, after riding high under John the Scot, suffered a temporary eclipse; but the circumstances are obscure. What is certain is that neither grant was more than short-lived.

452. Grant to Richard Fitton of the manor of Wimboldsley.

[1233–1237]

> Orig.: Lancashire Record Office, de Trafford Muniments, Fitton Charters bundle 5, no. 3. Transcr.: Chetham's Library, Raines' transcripts xxv, 81.

Sciant presentes et futuri, presens scriptum visuri vel audituri, quod ego Iohannes de Scocia comes Cestrie et Huntedonie dedi, concessi et hac presenti carta mea confirmavi Ricardo Phyton pro homagio et servicio suo manerium de Wynbaldeleghe cum omnibus pertinentiis suis infra villam et extra villam, habendum et tenendum de me et de heredibus meis sibi et heredibus suis vel suis assignatis[1] libere, quiete, pacifice et honorifice[2] in bosco, in plano, in pratis, in pascuis, in viis, in semitis, in aquis, in stangnis,[1] in molendinis, in vivariis, in piscariis, in moris, in marriscis,[1] in homagiis, in villenagiis, in serviciis, in omnibus aisiamentis et comodis[1] ad predictum manerium pertinentibus, reddendo inde annuatim mihi et heredibus meis de se et de heredibus suis vel de suis assingnatis[1] unum parium calcarium deauratorum vel sex denarios, scilicet ad Natale Domini, pro omni servicio, exaccione et demanda. Et ego Iohannes et heredes mei predictum manerium de Wynbaldeleghe cum omnibus pertinenciis et libertatibus, ut predictum est, eidem Ricardo et heredibus suis vel assingnatis[1] contra omnes gentes warantizabimus in perpetuum. In cuius rei testimonium presens scriptum sigillo meo munitum ei habere feci. Testibus hiis domino Waltero abbate Cestrie, Rogero de Monte Alto senescallo Cestrie, Henrico de Audideleghe, Radulfo Basset, Warino de Vernon, Hamone de Mascy, Willelmo de Venabulis, Willelmo de Malo Passu, Galfrido de Appelby, Willelmo de Lacu,

Anketillo de Folevilla, Ricardo de Sondbache, Ricardo de Kyngeleghe, Petro de Frodisham, Hugone clerico, et aliis.

SEAL: on silken cord, fragmentary and defaced.

1. *sic orig.*   2. honororifice *orig.*

This grant has sometimes been referred to Wilmslow, where the Fittons were landholders, but, as Ormerod pointed out (iii. 587 note), it can only refer to Wimboldsley in Northwich hundred. The difficulty is that there is no other evidence of a Fitton interest in Wimboldsley. Perhaps we should assume that it was forfeited, like Rushton (**no. 454**), by Richard Fitton's son, Hugh, or that it was somehow lost during the partition of the honour of Chester after John the Scot's death; but as Richard Fitton survived until 1246, this is not entirely convincing.

453.   Quittance for Richard Fitton from puture and toll throughout Cheshire and from finding judgers in the hundred of Macclesfield for the fee of Fulshaw.

[1233–1237]

> Shakerley Deeds, N. 3 (formerly at Somerford Park, now in custody of Sir Arthur Bryant), certified notary's copy from enrolment in the Portmoot of Chester, 16 October 1508; Shakerley MSS. Liber C, f. 246v.; B.L. Harl. MS. 2131, f. 37 (new f. 33), from a parchment book in quarto belonging to Sir George Booth; Harl. MS. 2074, f. 184 (new f. 81); Bodleian Library, MS. Lat. Misc. c. 66 (from Humphrey Newton's Commonplace Book), f. 10v.; in addition, many abbreviated versions, usually with shortened witness-lists. Briefly noticed (in English) Orm., iii. 587; Earwaker, *East Cheshire*, i. 43.

Omnibus presentem cartam inspecturis vel audituris Iohannes de Scocia comes Cestrie et Huntyndonie salutem. Sciatis me concessisse et dedisse et hac presenti carta mea confirmasse de me et heredibus meis Ricardo Phiton et heredibus suis quietanciam pulture servientum tocius terre sue et hominum suorum in Cestria et Cestrisciria et similiter quietanciam tolneti dicte terre sue et hominum suorum per totam terram meam Cestrie et Cestriscirie. Et preterea dedi et concessi de me et heredibus meis eidem Ricardo et heredibus suis quietanciam iudicatores inveniendi in hundredo meo de Macclesfeld de feodo de Fulshawe, quos[1] quidem ipse et antecessores sui michi et antecessoribus meis prius inde in dicto hundredo invenire consueverunt, ita quidem quod nec ego nec heredes mei a dicto Ricardo vel heredibus suis de cetero super predictis quietanciis aliquid exigemus vel exigere poterimus, sed bene volo et firmiter precipio quod ipse et heredes sui imperpetuum dictas habeant quietancias, et prohibeo super foris-facturam meam decem librarum ne quis eum vel heredes suos, terras suas vel homines suos super eisdem quietanciis gravare aut molestare presumat. Et ut hec mea concessio et donacio predictarum quietanciarum perpetue firmitatis robur obtineant, presentem cartam sigillo meo munitam ei habere feci. Hiis testibus Willelmo de Cantelupo iuniore, Roberto de Campania, Rogero de Monte Alto senescallo Cestrie, Warino de Vernun, Hamone de Mascy, Willelmo de Venables, Willelmo de Malo Passu, Ricardo de Sondbache, Ricardo de Kyngesley, Ada de Hellesby, Ricardo de Wibbenbury tunc vicecomite Cestrescire, Petro et Ricardo clericis, et aliis.

1. *Called for by sense, but MSS. have* que, quem, quam.

The fee of Fulshaw was bought by Richard Fitton, the father of the present Richard Fitton, who also acquired the manor of Fallibroome from Earl Hugh II (**no. 196**), about the end of the twelfth century, during the justiciarship of Ralph Mainwaring (Orm., iii. 586). The present grant probably falls after Fitton became justiciar in or about June 1233. Fitton subsequently gave Fulshaw to the Hospitallers (Orm., iii. 602), but as his charter cannot be dated and he lived until 1246, the gift may well have taken place in the period after the death of John the Scot.

454. Grant to Hugh Fitton of the manor of Rushton and the vills of Great and Little Eaton.

Macclesfield, [1233–1236]

> B.L. Harl. MS. 139, f. 18v. (new f. 29v.) only complete text. Abbreviated texts: B.L. Harl. MS. 2079, f. 53 (new f. 27); Add. MS. 4032, f. 96v.; Sloane MS. 1301, f. 263v.; Bodleian Library, Dodsworth MS. 31, f. 140v.; MS. Top. Cheshire b. I, p. 136; Chester, Booth of Twemlow, Liber D, f. 188. Short English abstract: Orm., ii. 238.

Iohannes de Scotia comes Cestrie at Huntendonie omnibus presentem cartam inspecturis vel audituris salutem. Sciatis me concessisse et dedisse et hac presenti carta mea confirmasse Hugoni Phiton pro homagio et servicio suo totum manerium de Ruston cum pertinentiis suis et villas de Magna Eiton et de Parva Eiton cum omnibus pertinentiis suis, habendas et tenendas de me et heredibus meis sibi et heredibus suis libere et quiete, plene et pacifice, honorifice et hereditarie, videlicet in dominicis, homagiis, villenagiis, serviciis, in boscis, in panagiis, in planis, in pratis, in pasturis, in viis, in semitis, in moris, in mariscis, in aquis, in stagnis, in molendinis, vivariis, piscariis, et cum omnibus libertatibus et aisiamentis ad predictum manerium et predictas villas iuste pertinentibus, tam infra villas quam extra, sine ullo retinemento, salvis mihi et heredibus meis placitis ad gladium meum spectantibus, faciendo inde mihi et heredibus meis ipse et heredes sui servicium sexte partis feodi unius militis pro omnibus serviciis, actionibus et demandis, et universis ad me et ad heredes meos inde spectantibus. Et pretetea concessi et dedi predicto Hugoni et heredibus suis et omnibus hominibus suis in predicto manerio et predictis villis manentibus quietanciam de omnibus placitis foreste mee de la Mare, nisi quando cum venacione in eadem foresta capta fuerint, et quietanciam pulture servientum et forestariorum, et quietanciam secte in comitatibus, hundredis, et in curia de Weverham faciende, et quietanciam assisarum, summonitionum et visuum terre faciendarum. Et prohibeo super forisfacturam meam decem librarum ne quis dictum Hugonem, heredes suos aut homines suos super aliquibus predictis de cetero gravare aut molestare presumat. Ego autem et heredes mei predictum manerium et villas predictas cum omnibus pertinentiis suis, libertatibus et quietanciis predictis predicto Hugoni et heredibus suis contra omnes gentes in perpetuum warantizabimus. In cuius rei testimonium presentem cartam sigillo meo munitam ei habere feci. Hiis testibus W. dei gratia tunc abbate Cestrie, Thoma de Furnivall, Gerardo fratre suo, Henrico de Alditheleghe, Roberto de Campania, Rogero de Monte Alto senescallo Cestrie, Hamone de Mascy, Warino de Vernon, Willelmo de Venables, Willelmo de Malo Passu, Walkelino de Arderne, Ricardo de Sandebach, Ricardo de Wibbenburi tunc vicecomite Cestresirie, Ricardo de Kingesle, Petro de Frodesham, Petro et Ricardo clericis, et pluribus aliis apud Macclesfeld.

> SEAL: green, appended on crimson lace; obverse, the earl on horseback, on his left arm a shield of 3 piles, in his right hand a drawn sword, legend + SIGILL . . . IOHANNIS HUNTENDONIE; reverse, shield of arms, 3 piles, legend SIGILLO S'C'O. REGIO.

Hugh Fitton was the son of Richard Fitton, Earl John's justiciar. His tenure of Rushton was short-lived, as he apparently forfeited it for felony, and it was resumed by the earl before 1237 (Orm., ii. 238).

455.   Permission for Hugh Fitton to make a park at Rushton.

[1233–1236]

> B.L. Lansdowne MS. 229, f. 58v. (new f. 57v.), from original; Harl. MS. 139, f. 18 (new f. 29), from a copy 'I

had of my cozin Mr. Richard Longeford de Deffryneloyd, otherwayes Wrytham, the 10 day of Januarii, a.d. 1552'.

Omnibus presentibus et futuris Iohannes de Scotia comes Cestrie et Huntedonie salutem. Noveritis me dedisse et concessisse et presenti carta confirmasse Hugoni de Phyton libertatem ad parcum faciendum et sex sautoria ad dictum parcum infra divisas suas de Ruston et de Ayton, quas ei dedi, tenendum libere et quiete sibi et heredibus suis cum omnibus aisiamentis ad dictum parcum pertinentibus sine omni impedimento mei vel heredum meorum. Et prohibeo super forisfacturam decem librarum ne quis eum vel heredes suos super predictis vexet iniuste vel impediat. In cuius rei testimonium presens scriptum sigillo meo munitum ei habere feci. Testibus hiis Warino de Vernon, Hamone de Mascy, Willelmo de Venabulis, Walkelino de Arderna, Galfrido de Appleby, Anketillo de Folevilla, Willelmo de Lacy, Petro et Hugone clericis, et aliis.

> SEAL: green wax, appended on black, red and silver lace; obverse, the earl on horseback, in his right hand a drawn sword, on his left arm a shield of arms, 3 piles; reverse, shield of arms, 3 piles.

This grant must be later than **no. 454**, but not perhaps by more than a few months.

456.   Grant to Robert of Angers of the land Walter Galiot held of him in Chester and the custody of the North Gate.

[1233–1237]

> P.R.O., CHES 29/59 (Plea Rolls), m. 7 ('die martis prox. ante festum s. Thome Apostoli, anno regni regis Edw. III 21'); B.L. Harl. MS. 2037 ('from Mr. William Vernon, 1636'), f. 193 (old f. 300), abbreviated text possibly from original.

Sciant presentes et futuri quod ego Iohannes de Scocia, comes Cestrie et Huntendonie, concessi dedi et hac mea presenti carta confirmavi Roberto de Andegavia pro humagio suo et servicio illam terram in civitate Cestrie quam Walterus Galiot de me tenuit, et custodiam porte aquilonaris eiusdem ville cum seriantia quam idem Walterus de me habuit, cum omnibus pertinenciis suis sine aliquo retenemento, tenendam et habendam de me et heredibus meis illi et heredibus suis in feodo et hereditate libere, quiete, integre et honorifice, et faciendo mihi et heredibus meis de se et heredibus suis inde servicium quod prefatus Walterus Galiot mihi facere consuevit. Ego vero et heredes mei predictam terram cum seriantia et pertinenciis prefato Roberto et heredibus suis warantizabimus imperpetuum contra omnes. In cuius rei testimonium scripto huic sigillum meum apposui. Hiis testibus dominis R. Phiton tunc iusticiario Cestrie, Radulfo Basset, Hugone Phiton,[1] Iohanne de le Mascy de Atie, Hugone de Panton, Petro Marescallo, Tevill, Hugone, Gilberto, Ricardo clericis, et aliis.

1. *This witness omitted Harl. MS.*

The serjeanty (*seriantia*) of the North Gate also included custody of the prison. A Gregory Galioth occurs in a deed of c.1220 (*J.C.A.S.*, N.S. x, p. 18), but there appears to be no other record of Walter Galiot, and Robert of Angers (or Robert the Angevin) is also unknown. John de Atye witnessed charters of Ranulf III c.1230 (**nos. 364, 413**), but this is his only appearance as John de le Mascy. For Hugh Fitton see **nos. 454** and **455**.

457.   Grant to John, earl of Lincoln and constable of Chester, of the fourth part of the manor of Leeds (Yorks.).

[1233–1237]

> P.R.O., D.L. 41/1/36, inventory of charters and documents found in Pontefract Castle relating to the Lacy family.

Item carta Iohannis de Scocia comitis Cestrie et Huntendonie facta eidem Iohanni comiti Lincolnie et constabulario Cestrie de quarta parte manerii de Ledes, illa scilicet que ad ipsum descendebat per dominum Ranulphum comitem Cestrie et Lincolnie, tenenda de ipso Iohanne comite Cestrie et heredibus suis per servicium octave partis feodi unius militis.

The manor of Leeds was assigned to Hugh d'Aubigny in the partition of the honour of Chester following the death of Ranulf III (**no. 437**), but this quarter had apparently already been granted to John de Lacy before Ranulf's death. John de Lacy, the constable of Chester, was son-in-law of Ranulf's sister, Hawise, to whom Ranulf had conveyed the county of Lincoln shortly before his death (**no. 310**); she passed on her rights almost immediately to John and his heirs by her daughter Margaret (Orm., i. 28, 697).

458.   Grant to Alexander of Bunbury of exemption from paying suit of court to his hundred court of Willaston for the vill of Stanney.

[1233–1237]

P.R.O., CHES 34/4 (Quo Warranto, 15 Henr. VII), m.
23; thence B.L. Add. MS. 6032, f. 97, and Shakerley MS.
3, p. 11. Noted: *Ches. Sheaf*, no. 6535.

Quidam Iohannes de Scocia quondam comes Cestrie per cartam suam dedit, concessit et confirmavit cuidam Alexandro de Bunbury, antecessori ipsius Iohannis, cuius heres ipse est, et heredibus suis imperpetuum quietanciam omnium sectarum hundredi sui de Wilaston de villa de Staney et omnium hominum suorum in eadem villa manencium, et quietanciam puture bidellorum suorum de prefato hundredo, et profert predictam cartam, que hoc idem testatur.

According to the Bunbury Memorandum Book (an eighteenth-century compilation now in the West Suffolk Record Office, E.18/710/1.16), a similar answer was made to a quo warranto suit in 39 Edw. III. Unfortunately, in neither case was the original charter recited. The Bunburys were landholders in Little Stanney from the twelfth century (*Chart. St. Werburgh*, p. 269). According to Sir Henry Bunbury (*The Early History of the Bunburys of Bunbury and Stanney*) the elder Alexander of Bunbury died in 1231, and the recipient of the present grant must be his son, the younger Alexander.

459. Request to the officials of the bishop of Coventry and Lichfield to admit a suitable clerk presented by Robert of Praers, who had established his right of patronage in the earl's court, to the church of Wynbunbury.

[1233–1237]

B.L. Add. MS. 6032, p. 101 (new f. 52), with sketch of seal; Harl. MS. 2039, f. 159 (new f. 154); Bodleian Library, Dodsworth MS. 31, f. 152v.; MS. Top. Cheshire b. I, p. 137; Chester, Booth of Twemlow, Liber D, f. 199. (All apparently from original with Sir Randle Mainwaring of Peover, 1612).

Iohannes de Scotia comes Cestrie et Huntingdonie dilectis amicis suis officiariis domini Coventrensis et Lichfeldensis episcopi salutem et sinceram dilectionem. Noveritis quod dominus Robertus de Praers miles per breve meum ultime presentacionis disrationavit in curia mea ius patronatus ecclesie de Wibbunbury. Quare vos precor, quatenus clericum idoneum ad eandem ecclesiam vobis ex parte dicti Roberti presentatum admittere et quod vestrum est ei inde facere velitis. Appellacionibus ante pro iure meo, quod credebam mihi competere in advocacione dicte ecclesie, ex parte mea interiectis renuncio. Valete.

SEAL: three piles joined at base; legend + SIG. IOHĪS. COM. CESTRIE.

Wybunbury was held by the Praers family of Barthomley as mesne lords under the Vernons (Orm., iii. 482). A Sir Robert occurs in the Praers pedigree (*ibid.*, p. 301) under the year 17 Henry III (1232–1233).

460.   Grant to Stephen of Segrave of all his land in Alconbury and Weston (Hunts.), together with the land granted previously to Baldwin of Ponton, for which he made an exchange in Whissendine (Rutland), except for the service of Robert of Stukeley for the lands previously given to Robert in the same townships.

[1233–1237]

B.L. Harl. MS. 4748 (Segrave cartulary), f. 24v.

Carta Iohannis de Scotia comitis Cestrie et Huntendonie facta Stephano de Segrave de tota terra sua in Alkmundebury et Weston, simul cum terra ibidem, quam dedit prius Baldewino de Paunton, pro qua fecit ei escambium in Wissyndene, et cum omnibus ad dictam terram pertinentibus, exceptis assarto et bosco de Liminich, et excepto homagio et servitio Roberto de Stivecle et heredum suorum de terris eidem Roberto prius datis in eisdem villis, tenenda eidem Stephano et heredibus suis de dicto comite et heredibus suis per servitium tertie partis feodi militis.

For the Segrave cartulary, from which this notice is taken, see **no. 365**. For Baldwin of Ponton, see *H.K.F.*, p. 314. There is no other evidence that he held lands in Whissendine (*ibid.*, p. 358), nor of his or Stephen of Segrave's tenure in Alconbury. John the Scot had made an earlier grant to Stephen of Segrave, before he became earl of Chester (Harl. MS. 4748, f. 25v.).

461.   Quittance for the monks of Stanlaw from suit of pleas of Delamere forest for their land in Wynlaton, unless they or their men are found with game or engaged in any manifest transgression, or if their animals are allowed to stray in the earl's forest beyond the monks' boundary.

[1233–1237]

B.L. Egerton MS. 3126 (Whalley cartulary), f. 194;
P.R.O., CHES 33/4 (Forest Rolls, 21 Edw. III),m. 30;

D.L. 39/1/19, m. 26. Ed.: *Chart Whalley,* ii. 471 (from
Egerton MS.)

Omnibus presentem cartam inspecturis vel audituris Iohannes de Scocia comes
Cestrie et Huntyngdonie salutem. Sciatis me concessisse et dedisse et hac
presenti carta mea de me et heredibus meis imperpetuum confirmasse¹ deo et
ecclesie beate Marie de Stanlawe et monachis ibidem deo servientibus quietanciam, de sectis placitorum foreste mee de ² la Mare de terra ipsorum monachorum in Wynlatona³ et de fine faciendo qui ad sectas illas pertinere solet, et
quietanciam de scutagio de eadem terra dictorum monachorum in Wynlatona,³
ita quod dicti monachi de cetero inde non graventur nec molestentur. Et si forte
animalia eorundem ibidem existencia casualiter ultra metas suas proprias per
escapeamentum in dictam forestam meam de die venerint et ibidem inventa
fuerint sine custodia ibidem facta, capiantur et replegientur. Et si de nocte in
eadem inventa fuerint sine custodia, hoc emendetur. Si vero cum custodia
ibidem facta de die vel de nocte inventa fuerint, hoc sine dilacione convincatur et
emendetur. Et similiter si dicti monachi vel eorum homines inventi fuerint cum
venacione vel in aliquo delicto manifesto quod ad forestam pertinet, hoc
convincatur et secundum modum delicti emendetur. Et prohibeo super forisfacturam meam ne quis dictos monachos de cetero contra hanc meam concessionem et quietanciam gravare aut molestare presumat. Et ut hec mea concessio
et quietancia de me et heredibus meis dictis monachis facta imperpetuum
perseveret, presentem cartam sigillo meo munitam eis habere feci. Hiis testibus
W.⁴ dei gratia tunc abbate Cestrie, Henrico de Audithelega, Willelmo de
Cantelupo iuniore, Ricardo Phitoun tunc iusticiario Cestrie, Roberto de
Campania, Hugone Phitoun, Ricardo de Sondbache, Hugone de Chelmundele,
Ricardo de Kyngesle, Roberto Grosso Venatore, Iohanne de Haselwelle, Petro
de Frodesham, Petro clerico, et aliis.

1. quietumclamasse *Egerton MS.*
2. *in CHES 33/4 and D.L. 39/1/19.*
3. Wynfletona *CHES 34/4 and D.L. 39/1/19.*
4. CHES 33/4 and D.L. 39/1/19 read Willelmo, *which is impossible as Abbot William died in 1228;* W. *presumably stands for Abbot Walter Pinchbeck (1228–40).*

Wynlaton or Wynfleton (Willington in Edisbury hundred) was given to Stanlaw
by Henry Despenser (**no. 214**); the monks had already received a quittance from
feeding his serjeants and foresters from Ranulf III (**no. 215**).

462.   Confirmation of Henry de Lettes' grant to William Venables of Wincham
and a carucate of land in Twembrook with its appurtenances.

[1234–1237]

Tabley MSS., Sir Peter Leycester's muniments, Wincham

8, (loose transcripts, also Liber B, f. 29 (abbreviated);
B.L. Harl. MS. 2007, f. 107 (from Vernon's Liber P).
Briefly noticed in English: Orm., i. 627.

Iohannes de Scocia comes Cestrie et Huntedonie omnibus presentibus et futuris presentem cartam inspecturis vel audituris salutem. Sciatis me concessisse et hac presenti carta mea confirmasse Willelmo de Venabulis Wymingham cum omnibus pertinenciis suis infra villam et extra et unam carucatam terre in Tynebroc cum pertinenciis cum medietate bosci de Alreschahe et cum communia pasture in Lindwode, scilicet ad quindecim averia et ad viginti porcos, que Henricus de Lettes pro homagio et servicio suo ei dedit, habenda et tenenda eidem Willelmo et heredibus suis vel eius assignatis et heredibus assignatorum suorum de dicto Henrico et heredibus suis per servicium dimidii militis dicto Henrico et heredibus suis inde faciendum, secundum tenorem carte ipsius Henrici, quam idem Willelmus inde habet. Et ad maiorem huius rei securitatem presentem cartam sigillo meo munitam eidem habere feci. His testibus domino Waltero abbate Cestrie, dominis Henrico de Aldithele, Warino de Vernon, Willelmo de Vernon, Radulfo Basset, Willelmo de Malo Passu, Walkelino de Arderne, Rogero de Mohaut senescallo Cestrie, Radulfo de Kemmeys, Willelmo de Boydel, Simone clerico, Ricardo do Kingesle, et aliis.

Wincham had been conveyed to Nicholas de Lettes by Matilda Venables in the time of Ranulf III (**no. 432**). He subsequently conveyed it to Henry de Lettes, who still held it in 1234 (Sir Peter Leycester, Liber B, f. 29) and perhaps later, but subsequently sold it by the charter here confirmed to William de Venables. John the Scot's charter repeats verbatim the words of Ranulf III's for Nicholas de Lettes, from which it is obviously taken.

463.   Grant to the monks of Combermere of pasture for 2000 sheep, 4 bulls and 24 oxen and 40 cows, and horses and other animals in his forest of Macclesfield, with other rights and privileges, saving only the earl's right of hunting. [Spurious]

Chester, [April 1234]

P.R.O., CHES 33/6 (Forest Rolls, 27–31 Edw. III), m. 49.

Omnibus sancte matris ecclesie filiis hoc presens scriptum inspecturis vel audituris Iohannes de Scocia comes Cestrie et Huntindonie salutem. Noverit universitas vestra me pro salute anime mee et antecessorum et successorum meorum dedisse, concessisse et hac presenti carta mea confirmasse deo et beate

Marie et monachis monasterii de Cumbermere et eorum successoribus seu assignatis in puram et perpetuam elemosinam pasturam sufficienter in foresta mea de Maclesfeld per totam pro duobus milibus ovium, cuiuscumque etatis voluerint. Centenarius vero numerus erit continens sexies viginti oves. Si autem plures oves ibidem habuerint, per duas legales homines meos et per duos conversos suos numerabuntur et sine forisfactura amovebuntur. Concessi etiam eisdem monachis pasturam sufficientem in predicta foresta mea viginti quatuor bobus et quadraginta vaccis cum exitu illarum trium annorum et quatuor tauris. Item concessi eisdem pasturam sufficientem exitui illarum vaccarum prius habitarum, donec sint etatis trium annorum, ita quod dicti monachi habeant omnia supradicta in dicta foresta racione istius carte et aliarum cartarum[1] Ranulphi avunculi mei, quas dicti monachi inde habent, plenius continetur. Et habeant in dicta pastura eques et equas ac alia animalia eisdem necessaria.

Concessi etiam eisdem monachis et eorum successoribus vel eorum assignatis quod possint capere in predicta foresta maeremium ad edificandum et boscum et turbarium ad ardendum ac alia estoveria eis necessaria capienda cum housebote et haybote, quandocumque et quocienscumque voluerint, sine contradiccione mei vel heredum meorum, iusticiarii, forestariorum vel aliorum ballivorum quorumcumque. Item concessi eisdem monachis et eorum successoribus sive assignatis quod nunquam de cetero ego vel heredes mei vel aliquis alius nomine meo aliquod approwiamentum quoquomodo faciemus in foresta predicta ad nocumentum seu gravamen dictorum monachorum seu ad distruccionem pasture eorundem, nisi de mera voluntate et assensu dictorum monachorum, et quod ipsi monachi et successores sui seu assignati inperpetuum habeant et teneant omnia supradicta, que habent infra metas foreste nostre de Maclesfeld, quieta de vasto et regardo, ita quod idem abbas et conventus et successores sui solum de terris infra metas et bundas dictorum monachorum in culturam redigere et de solo suo approwiare possint pro voluntate sua, modis quibus sibi magis viderint expedire, sine occasione, calumpnia vel impedimento nostri vel heredum nostrorum, iusticiarii, forestariorum, viridariorum et omnium aliorum ball-ivorum et ministrorum nostrorum quorumcumque, salvis nobis et heredibus nostris venacione infra metas et bundas monachorum predictorum. Et quod forestariis, viridariis vel aliis quibuscumque super aliquibus presentacionibus seu indictamentis ad predictos abbatem et conventum vel eorum homines aut eorum successores faciendis occasione transgrescionis de venacione nostra infra metas et bundas foreste predicte per ipsos facte seu faciende non credatur, et quod predicti abbas et conventus et eorum successores aut homines ipsorum occasione transgressionis huiusmodi non occasionentur in aliquo seu graventur, nisi cum manu opere fuerint inventi. Ut autem mea donacio et confirmacio rata et stabilis inperpetuum remanent, huic scripto sigillum meum apposui. Hiis testibus domino Waltero tunc abbate Cestrie, Iohanne tunc abbate de Deulacres, Ricardo Fyton tunc iusticiario Cestrie, Rogero de Monte Alto, Willelmo de Malo Passu, Walkelino de Arden, Hugone Fytton, Willelmo de Boydell,

Hugone et Ricardo clericis, et aliis. Datum apud Cestriam quarto [. . ...]² Aprilis anno domini M°CC° tricesimo quarto.

1. *sic MS.*; *presumably should read* sicut in aliis cartis.
2. *illegible sign*; *not* kal., id., *or* non.; *possibly* die.

This apparently hitherto unknown charter of Earl John largely repeats the rights of pasturage granted in Macclesfield forest in the charter of Ranulf III (**no. 240**), with variations in favour of the monks. Thus the 2000 sheep can now be of any age, whereas in Ranulf's charter they had to be removed after one year; instead of 16 oxen they can pasture 24; instead of 24 cows they can pasture 40; and the number of horses and mares, previously 6 and 10, is now unlimited. These and other variations suggest that this charter is later than **no. 240**, but it is hard to believe that either is genuine, although the witnesses of Earl John's charter are compatible with the alleged date. The inclusion of a dating clause is highly irregular, and in itself enough to condemn the charter as spurious.

464.   Grant to Lindores Abbey of 20s. annually from land held at farm by the earl's burgesses of Inverurie.

[1232–1237]

Ed.: *Lindores Chartulary*, pp. 20–21 (no. 17).

Omnibus has litteras visuris vel audituris I. de Scocia comes Cestre¹ et Huntedon salutem. Sciatis me dedisse et concessisse et presenti carta mea confirmasse deo et ecclesie sancte Marie et sancti Andree de Lundors et monachis ibidem deo servientibus viginti solidos sterlingorum annuatim percipiendos de terra quam burgenses mei de Inveruri tenent de me ad firmam, que iacet inter burgum de Inveruri et pontem de Balhagerdyn,² donec illos eisdem in loco certo assignavero; tenendos et habendos de me et heredibus meis in puram et perpetuam elemosinam pro salute anime domini Hugonis de Roppel ad pietanciam³ dictorum monachorum die anniversario eiusdem Hugonis. Et ego et heredes mei dictos xx. solidos dictis abbati et conventui contra omnes homines warrantizabimus. Hiis testibus dominis Henrico de Striuelyn,⁴ B. de Paunton, H. Phyton, Galfredo de Appelby, Simone de Garentuly, Henrico de Boyvilla, David de Audereye, et aliis.

1. *sic ed.*
2. Balhaggardy, north of Inverurie.
3. *recte* pictancia (pittance), but frequently in this form.
4. Stirling (brother of the earl).

465. Grant of a toft in Inverbervie to Lindores Abbey, and of another toft in Inverurie for the use of the church there.

[1232–1237]

Ed. *Lindores Chartulary*, pp. 21–2 (no. 18).

Omnibus sancte matris ecclesie filiis, ad quos presens scriptum pervenit, I. de Scocia comes Cestre[1] et Huntedon, salutem in domino. Noveritis me pro salute anime mee patris mei et matris mee et omnium antecessorum meorum et successorum dedisse concessisse et hac presenti carta mea confirmasse deo et ecclesie beate Marie de Lundors et monachis ibidem deo servientibus unum toftum in villa de Inverbervyn, illud videlicet, quod[1] fuit Utting Cachepol, iuxta[2] castrum ex parte australi, pro escambio illius tofti,[1] quem comes David pater meus eis dedit in eadem villa, et unum toftum in villa de Inveruri ad opus ecclesie eiusdem ville et capellanorum ibidem serviencium, illud[1] scilicet dimidium toftum, qui[1] fuit Roberti di Boverdyn, et unam rodam, que fuit Bernardi, et aliam rodam, que fuit Utting Ruffi; tenenda et habenda de me et heredibus meis in perpetuum libere quiete integre pacifice et honorifice cum omnibus pertinentiis libertatibus et aisiamentis ad predicta tofta pertinentibus in liberam puram et perpetuam elemosinam. In cuius rei testimonium huic scripto feci apponere[1] sigillum meum. Hiis testibus: dominis Henrico de Strivelyn, Simone de Garentuli,[3] Willelmo de Lacu, Walone de Burg, Girardo de Lindeseye, Ada de Audideleger,[4] Nicholao de Inverpephin, Roberto de Wrth clerico, et aliis.

1. *sic ed.*
2. justra *MS.*
3. Simon was 'ballivus' to Earl John before 1234.
4. *sic ed..*

466. Grant to Lindores Abbey of a toft in Dundee and a fishery in the Tay; grant that certain lands lying between those of the earl and the abbey should remain common land for ever; and grant that if the monks were to build mills on their land in the future, the earl's successors would not prevent the inhabitants of the abbey's lands from using the new mills rather than those of the earl.

Berwick, [1232–1237]

Ed.: *Lindores Chartulary*, pp. 22–3 (no. 19) (A); pp. 97–8 (no. 90) (B).

Omnibus hoc scriptum visuris vel audituris Iohannes[1] de Scocia comes Cestre[2] et Huntendun, salutem. Sciatis me dedisse et hac carta mea confirmasse deo et ecclesie sancte Marie et sancti Andree de Lundors et monachis ibidem deo servientibus et servituris unum toftum in Dunde proximum tofto sancti Clementis versus occidentem, et piscariam in They[3] proximam piscarie, quam dedi domino Henrico de Brechyn,[4] versus Portencrag[5]; tenendam[6] sibi et habendam[7] in liberam puram et perpetuam elemosinam. Concessi etiam eis, ut terra illa, que perambulata fuit inter magnam Durnach et Logindurnach coram me et domino[8] I. abbate de Lundors et aliis probis hominibus, sit in communi in perpetuum, sicut recognitum fuit per sacramenta illorum, qui terram illam perambulaverunt, et quod de cetero non fiat aliqua perambulacio inter terras meas et terras illorum, sed teneant ipsas divisas, quas habuerunt tempore patris mei et tempore meo, sine molestia et sine[9] gravamine. Volo etiam et concedo, ut, quando voluerint vel potuerint facere molendina in terris suis, nullus successorum meorum impediat homines manentes in terris ipsorum ire libere et quiete ad molendina illa cum omni secta sua et multura, quamvis solebant sequi molendina mea, quamdiu fuerunt[10] sine molendinis propriis. Testibus: domino H. de Strivelin fratre meo, domino Roberto de Campaniis, domino Hugone Phyton, domino Galfrido de Appelby[11], domino Anketill de Foleville, Petro et Rogero clericis, Hugone de Panton [12], Baldwino[13] de Anuers, Petro Pincerna. Apud Berewic.

1. I *B*.
2. *sic A, B.*
3. Tehy *B.*
4. Brehin *B.* (Henry of Brechin, an illegitimate son of John the Scot's father, Earl David, as was Henry of Stirling.)
5. Portincrag *B.* (i.e. Portincraig.)
6. tenendum *B.*
7. habendum *B.*
8. dompno *B.*
9. *om. B.*
10. fuerint *B.*
11. Appilby *B.*
12. Pantona *B.*
13. Baldwino *B.*

467. Acknowledgment of the tithes which the earl owes to Lindores Abbey from the lands of the Garioch, from the time when Simon of Garentully became his bailiff to Martinmas 1234.

[c. 1234]

Ed.: *Lindores Chartulary*, pp. 24–5 (no. 21).

Omnibus presentes litteras inspecturis vel audituris Iohannes de Scocia comes Cester[1] et Huntendun salutem. Noverit universitas vestra me teneri Iohanni abbati de Lundors et eiusdem loci humili conventui in quinquaginta et sex libris et tribus obolis sterlingorum pro decimis terre mee de Garviach[2] ad ecclesiam suam de Lundors spectantibus, computatis a tempore, quo Simon de Garentulli ballivam suam de me recepit, usque ad festum sancti Martini anno gratie MCCXXX quarto, decimis firmarum eiusdem termini in denariis eiusdem computatis simul cum sexaginta et quatuor solidis et VII denariis de mutuo michi facto. In cuius rei testimonium presentes litteras meas patentes sigillo meo signatas eis habere feci. Valete.

1. *sic ed.*
2. i.e. the Garioch.

468. Order to his bailiffs to pay the tithes due to Lindores Abbey from the lands of the Garioch from Martinmas 1234.

[?1234–7]

Ed.: *Lindores Chartulary*, p. 24 (no. 20).

I. de Scocia comes Cestre[1] et Huntendun ballivis suis de Garviach[2] salutem. Mando vobis, quatinus a termino sancti Martini anno gratie MCCXXX quarto reddatis abbati de Lundors et humili eiusdem loco coventui[1] decimas totius terre mee de Garviach ad ecclesiam suam de Lundors spectantes, sicut solvi consueverunt tempore patris mei et meo secundum tenorem carte sue, quam inde habent; et non dimittatis, quin hoc faciatis. Valete.

1. *sic ed.*
2. i.e. the Garioch.

469. Confirmation of the grants of Earl David to St. Andrews Priory.

[1232–1237]

Ed.: *St. Andrews Cartulary*, pp. 240–1.

Omnibus sancte matris ecclesie filiis presens scriptum visuris vel audituris Iohannes de Scotia comes Cestrie et de Huntedon eternam in domino salutem. Noverit universitas vestra nos divine pietatis intuitu concessisse et hac carta nostra confirmasse deo et ecclesie sancti Andree apostoli in Scocia et canonicis ibidem deo servientibus et servituris donaciones concessiones et confirmaciones quas venerabilis pater noster Comes David eisdem canonicis dedit concessit et cartis suis confirmavit videlicet totam terram de Forgrunt unde controversia vertebatur inter ipsum et eosdem canonicos cum dimidia carucata terre quam antecessores nostri dederunt ecclesie de Forgrunt in dotem per rectas divisas suas libere et quiete et honorifice ab omni consuetudine et exaccione seculari et totum canum et kuneueth de terra de Eglesgirg et servicium que homines predictorum canonicorum de dicta terra de Eglesgirg predicto patri nostro debebant. Et unum plenarium toftum in burgo nostro de Dunde liberum et quietum ab omni servicio et consuetudine et exaccione seculari et unam marcam argenti ad oblatas faciendas ad pasca de firma burgi nostri de Dunde predictis canonicis absque ulla disturbacione reddendam. Et duas carucatas terre in Kinalchmund in perpetuam elemosinam per rectas divisas suas liberas et quietas ab omni servicio et exaccione seculari, sicut in auctenticis scriptis sepe dicti Comitis David patris nostri et antecessorum nostrorum plenius continetur. Et ad huius concessionis nostre et confirmacionis perpetuam securitatem predictis canonicis faciendam presens scriptum sigilli nostri inpressione roboravimus testibus Domino Iohanne abbate de Lundors, Domino Henrico de Struvelin fratre nostro, Domino Gerardo de Lindeseya, Domino Willelmo de Lee, Domino Ada de Audelee, Domino Willelmo de Burg, Domino Symone de Garnecoll, Dompnis Petro et Samuele capellanis nostris, David de Canes, Rogero et Roberto de Wrth et Valentino clericis nostris, Nicholao de Inverpef'in et multis aliis.

GUIDE TO ABBREVIATIONS USED IN THE TEXT

For full bibliographical details of works, including those for which the references in the text are sufficiently full to make their inclusion below unnecessary, see the Bibliography.

Ann. Cestr.	*Annales Cestrienses*, ed. R.C. Christie.
B.I.H.R.	*Bulletin of the Institute of Historical Research.*
B.L.	British Library.
Book of Seals	*Sir Christopher Hatton's Book of Seals*, ed. L.C. Loyd & D.M. Stenton.
Bristol and Gloucs. Arch. Soc.	*Bristol and Gloucestershire Archaeological Society.*
Cal. Ch. Rolls	*Calendar of Charter Rolls.*
Cal. Pat. Rolls	*Calendar of Patent Rolls.*
Chart. St. Werburgh	*The Chartulary or Register of the Abbey of St. Werburgh, Chester*, ed. J. Tait.
Chart. Whalley	*The Coucher Book or Chartulary of Whalley Abbey*, ed. W.A. Hulton.
Ches. Sheaf	*Cheshire Sheaf.*
Coss	*The Early Records of Medieval Coventry*, ed. P.R. Coss.
d'Anisy	*see* Léchaudé d'Anisy in Bibliography.
D. C.	*The Chartulary of Dieulacres Abbey*, ed. G. Wrottesley.
D.K.P.R.	*Deputy Keeper of the Public Records* (e.g. *36th Rep[ort of]*)
D.S.C.	*The Domesday Survey of Cheshire*, ed. J. Tait.
E.C.C.	*Facsimiles of Early Cheshire Charters*, ed. G. Barraclough.
E.H.R.	*English Historical Review.*
Heads of Religious Houses	*The Heads of Religious Houses, England and Wales, 940–1216*, by D. Knowles & others.
Hist. Coll. of Staffordshire	*William Salt Archaeological Society: Collections for a History of Staffordshire.*
Hist. MSS. Comm.	*Historical Manuscripts Commission.*
H.K.F.	*Honors and Knights' Fees*, ed. W. Farrer.
H.S.L.C.	*Historic Society of Lancashire and Cheshire.*
J.C.A.S.	*Journal of the Chester Archaeological Society.*

Journal Brit. Arch. Assn.	*Journal of the British Archaeological Association.*
J.R.U.L.M.	John Rylands University Library of Manchester.
Langley cart.	*The Langley Cartulary*, ed. P.R. Coss.
Linc. Rec. Soc.	*Lincoln Record Society.*
Lincs. Records, Final Concords	*see* W.O. Massingberd & W.K. Boyd in Bibliography.
L.P.R.	*The Lancashire Pipe Rolls*, ed. W. Farrer.
Mon.	*Monasticon Anglicanum*, by W. Dugdale.
Nat. Lib. Wales	National Library of Wales.
N.S.	New series.
Ord. Vitalis	*Historia Ecclesiastica*, by Orderic Vitalis.
Orm.	*The History of the County Palatine and City of Chester*, by G. Ormerod.
Oxford Hist. Soc.	*Oxford Historical Society.*
P.R.O.	Public Record Office.
P.R.S.	*Pipe Roll Society.*
Regesta	*Regesta Anglo-Normannorum*, ed. H.A. Cronne & others.
Rot. Litt. Clausarum	*Rotuli Litterarum Clausarum*, ed. T.D. Hardy.
Rot. Scacc. Norm.	*Magni Rotuli Scaccarii Normanniae*, ed. T. Stapleton.
Round, *C.D.F.*	*Calendar of Documents Preserved in France*, ed. J.H. Round.
R.S.L.C.	*Record Society of Lancashire and Cheshire.*
Stenton Misc.	*A Medieval Miscellany for D.M. Stenton*, ed. P.M. Barnes & L.F. Slade.
T.R.H.S.	*Transactions of the Royal Historical Society.*
V.C.H.	*Victoria County History.*
William Salt Arch. Soc.	*William Salt Archaeological Society.*

BIBLIOGRAPHY
(including acknowledgements)

A. *Original sources.*

Professor Barraclough made use of a wide range of original sources in the preparation of this edition. In offering a list of the repositories and individuals referred to in the text, the Society would like to take the opportunity of expressing its gratitude to all those who have granted Professor Barraclough access to their collections, provided a considerable number of photocopies of documents, given permission for material to be used in this project, and generally offered assistance and co-operation. Professor Barraclough's work includes items held in the following collections and repositories:

Adlington Hall, Cheshire; Archives départementales de l'Orne, Alençon; Archives départementales du Calvados, Caen; Archives nationales, Paris; Beamont MSS., Warrington; Belvoir Castle, Leicestershire; Berkeley Castle, Gloucestershire; Bibliothèque capitulaire de Bayeux (relevant material now in the Archives du Calvados); Bibliothèque municipale, Rouen; Bibliothèque nationale, Paris; Birmingham Reference Library; Bodleian Library, Oxford; British Library (formerly British Museum Library); Sir Arthur Bryant's collection of Shakerley manuscripts; Burton-upon-Trent Museum and Art Gallery; Cambridge University Library; Cheshire Record Office; Chester City Record Office (including Booth of Twemlow material in the Earwaker papers deposited by the Chester Archaeological Society); Chetham's Library, Manchester; College of Arms, London; Coventry Record Office; Derby Public Library; Eaton Hall, near Chester; The Gentleman's Society, Spalding; Huntington Library, San Marino, California; John Rylands University Library of Manchester (formerly John Rylands Library); Lancashire Record Office, Preston; Lincoln County Library; Lincoln Dean and Chapter Library; Manchester Central Library; National Library of Wales, Aberystwyth; Northamptonshire Record Office; Northamptonshire Record Society; Peterborough Dean and Chapter Library; Public Record Office; St George's Chapel, Windsor; Salisbury Dean and Chapter Library; Salt Library, Stafford; Shakespeare's Birthplace Trust Record Office, Stratford-upon-Avon; Sudbury Hall, Derbyshire; Tabley Hall, Cheshire (relevant material now in Cheshire Record Office); Westminster Dean and Chapter Muniments; and West Suffolk Record Office, Bury St Edmunds.

Arising from his own communications since Professor Barraclough's death, the General Editor wishes to thank the following repositories and individuals for granting the Society permission to reproduce in print for the first time full versions of certain charters, and for their uniformly helpful and encouraging approach to the preparation of this volume:

The British Library, the Public Record Office, and the Bodleian Library,

Oxford, for the great majority of items falling into this category, identifiable from the detailed references at the head of each chapter;

the Archives départementales de l'Orne for **no. 132**;

the Archives départementales du Calvados for **nos. 186, 251, 317, 319, 320, 332 & 333**;

the Trustees of the Berkeley Muniments for **nos. 86, 87, 217, 358, 359, 362 & 363**;

the Bibliothèque municipale, Rouen for **nos. 181 & 277**;

the Bibliothèque nationale for **nos. 9, 10, 11, 183, 204, 259, 269 & 279**;

Birmingham Reference Library for **no. 202**;

the Syndics of Cambridge University Library for **no. 57**;

Cheshire Record Office and Cheshire County Council for **no. 401**;

Chester City Record Office for **no. 266**;

Sir Dermot de Trafford, Bart., for **nos. 451 & 452**;

the Most Hon. the Marquess of Cholmondeley for **nos. 261 & 354**;

the College of Arms, London for **nos. 189, 356 & 422**;

the Grosvenor Estate (Eaton Hall) for **no. 244**;

the Huntington Library for **nos. 82 & 351**;

the John Rylands University Library of Manchester for **nos. 131, 171, 352 & 423**;

Mrs Ann Lee (Revesby Charters deposited in the Lincolnshire Archives at Lincoln) for **no. 289**;

the Dean and Chapter Library, Peterborough, for **no. 298**;

the Shakespeare Birthplace Trust Record Office for **nos. 60, 169 & 255**;

the Dean and Chapter of Westminster for **nos. 334 & 444**.

The Society also wishes to thank:

Dr P.R. Coss and the Dugdale Society for their willingness to agree to the publication of charters **72, 154, 155, 156, 168, 312 & 316**, which appeared in print in virtually the same format in Dr Coss's edition of the *Langley Cartulary* in 1980; Dr Una Rees and the National Library of Wales for their willingness to agree to the publication of charters **61, 62, 63, 64, & 153**, which appeared in print in virtually the same format in Dr Rees's edition of the *Cartulary of Shrewsbury Abbey* in 1975; Mr A.E.B. Owen, Keeper of Manuscripts at Cambridge University Library, and Mr R.C. Yorke, Archivist of the College of Arms, for their very helpful amendments to the references to their manuscripts; and Mr Robert Bearman, Senior Archivist at the Shakespeare Birthplace Trust, for providing fuller references to his Record Office's manuscripts, viz. DR 10/1406 for the Gregory-Hood Leger Book and DR 10/1409 for Arthur Gregory's Cartulary.

The General Editor would also like to thank Dr Dorothy Clayton, Dr Peter Coss, Dr Judith Green and Dr Alan Thacker for their helpful comments, corrections and encouragement in the preparation of this volume.

B. Printed works cited.

[*Abingdon Chronicle.*] *Chronicon Monasterii de Abingdon*. Ed. J. Stevenson. 2 vols. London, Rolls Series, 1858.
Annales Cestrienses. Ed. R.C. Christie. *R.S.L.C.* xiv (1887).
Baines, E. *The History of the County Palatine and Duchy of Lancaster*. 4 vols. London, Fisher, 1836.
Baker, G. *The History and Antiquities of the County of Northampton*. 2 vols. London, 1822–41.
Ballard, A. & others (eds.) *British Borough Charters, 1042–1216*. 3 vols. Cambridge U.P., 1913–43.
Barnes, P.M. & Slade, C.F. (eds.) *A Medieval Miscellany for D.M. Stenton*. London, Pipe Roll Society, 1962.
Barraclough, G. (ed.) *Facsimiles of Early Cheshire Charters*. Oxford, Blackwell, 1957.
Beamont, W. *A History of the Castle of Halton and the Priory or Abbey of Norton*. Warrington, Percival Pearse, 1873.
Benedict of Peterborough. *Gesta Regis Henrici Secundi Benedicti Abbatis: the Chronicle of the Reigns of Henry II and Richard I, 1169–92. Ed. W. Stubbs.* 2 vols. London, Rolls Series, 1867.
Bertrand de Broussillon, Arthur, *Count. La Maison de Laval, 1020–1605*. 5 vols. Paris, 1895–1903.
Bigsby, R. *Historical and Topographical Description of Repton*. London, Woodfall & Kinder, 1854.
Boyd, W.K. & Massingberd, W.O. *Lincolnshire Records: Abstracts of Final Concords, Richard I, John and Henry III.* Ed. Massingberd, transcribed and translated by Boyd. Vol. I. London, 1896.
Bridges, J. *The History and Antiquities of Northamptonshire*. 2 vols. Oxford & London, 1762–91.
Brooke, R. *A Catalogue and Succession of the Kings, Princes, Dukes, Marquesses, Earles and Viscounts of this Realme of England*. London, 1619.
Bunbury, Sir Henry. *The Early History of the Bunburys of Bunbury and Stanney*. Privately printed, 1965.
Calendar of the Charter Rolls. 6 vols. London, HMSO, 1903–27.
Calendar of Patent Rolls. London, HMSO, 1903–
Cartularium Abbathiae de Whiteby Ordinis S. Benedicti. Ed. J.C. Atkinson. 2 vols. Durham, Surtees Society, 1879–81.
The Cartulary of Shrewsbury Abbey. Ed. U. Rees. 2 vols. Aberystwyth, National Library of Wales, 1975.
The Chartulary of Dieulacres Abbey. Ed. G. Wrottesley. *William Salt Society, Collections for a History of Staffordshire*, N.S. ix (1906).
Chartulary of the Abbey of Lindores, 1195–1479. Ed. J. Dowden. *Scottish History Society, Pubns.* xlii (1903).
The Chartulary or Register of the Abbey of St Werburgh, Chester. Ed. J. Tait. 2 vols. *Chetham Society*, N.S. lxxix, lxxxii (1920, 1923).

Clay, C.T. (ed.) *Early Yorkshire Charters*. Vols. IV-XII. Based on the manuscripts of the late W. Farrer. *Yorkshire Archaeological Society, Record Series, Extra Series*, 1935–65.

Collectanea Topographica & Genealogica. 8 vols. London, 1834–43.

The Complete Peerage. New edition, revised and much enlarged. Ed. V. Gibbs, H.A. Doubleday, etc. 13 vols. London, St Catherine Press, 1910–59.

Coss P.R. (ed.) *The Early Records of Medieval Coventry*. London, Oxford U. P. for the British Academy, 1986.

The Coucher Book or Chartulary of Whalley Abbey. Ed. W.A. Hulton. 4 vols. *Chetham Society*, x, xi, xvi, xx (1847–9).

Cunningham, W. *The Growth of English Industry and Commerce*. [*Edition not identified.*]

Darby, H.C. *The Medieval Fenland*. Cambridge U. P., 1940.

Davis, R.H.C. *The Early History of Coventry*. Oxford, Dugdale Society, 1976.

Davis, R.H.C. *King Stephen*. London, Longman, 1977.

Dibben, A.A. *Coventry City Charters*. Coventry Corporation Public Relations Department, 1969.

The Domesday Survey of Cheshire. Ed. J. Tait. *Chetham Society*, N.S. lxxv (1916).

Dubosc, F. *Cartulaire de l'Abbaye de Mont-Morel*. Saint-Lô, 1878.

Dubosc, F. *Cartulaire de la Manche*. Saint-Lô, 1878.

Dugdale, W. *The Baronage of England*. 3 vols. London, 1675–6.

Dugdale, W. *Monasticon Anglicanum*. New edition by J. Caley, H. Ellis and B. Bandinel. 6 vols. London, 1846.

Dugdale, W. *The Antiquities of Warwickshire Illustrated*. [*Edition not identified.*]

Dugdale Society, Feet of Fines. *see* Warwickshire Feet of Fines, *below*.

Earwaker, J.P. *East Cheshire, or a History of the Hundred of Macclesfield*. 2 vols. London, 1877–80.

Edwards, J.G. *Calendar of Ancient Correspondence Concerning Wales*. Board of Celtic Studies, University of Wales, History and Law Series 2. Cardiff, 1935.

Eyton, R.W. *Court, Household and Itinerary of King Henry II*. London, 1878.

Farrer, W. (ed.) *Early Yorkshire Charters*. Edinburgh, 1914–16.

Farrer, W. *Honors and Knights' Fees*. 3 vols. (vol. II only used here). London, 1923–5.

Farrer, W. (ed.) *The Lancashire Pipe Rolls* . . . transcribed and edited by Farrer, *etc*. Liverpool, Young, 1902.

Gesta Stephani Regis Anglorum. Ed. K.R. Potter. Second edition. Oxford, U. P., 1976.

Groombridge, M.J. *Guide to the Charters, Plate and Insignia of the City of Chester*. Chester, Phillipson & Golder, 1950.

Halstead, R. *Succinct Genealogies of the Noble and Ancient Houses of Alno or de Alneto* . . . *etc*. London, 1685.

Harland, J. (ed.) *Mamecestre: Being Chapters from the Early Recorded History . . . of Manchester*. *Chetham Society*, liii, lvi, lviii (1861–2).

Sir Christopher Hatton's *Book of Seals*. Ed. L.C. Loyd and D.M. Stenton. Oxford, Clarendon Press, 1950.

Hewitt, H.J. *Medieval Cheshire*. *Chetham Society*, N.S. lxxxviii (1929).

Hill, J.W.F. *Medieval Lincoln*. Cambridge U. P., 1948.

Historia et Cartularium Monasterii S. Petri Gloucestriae. Ed. W.H. Hart. 3 vols. London, Rolls Series, 1863–7.

Historical Manuscripts Commission. *Reports*. London, HMSO, 1874–

Historical Manuscripts Commission. *The Manuscripts of the Duke of Rutland Preserved at Belvoir Castle*. 4 vols. London, HMSO, 1888–1905.

Historical Manuscripts Commission. *Report on Manuscripts in Various Collections*. London, HMSO, 1901–

Historical Manuscripts Commission. *Report on the Manuscripts of R.R. Hastings of the Manor House, Ashby de la Zouche*. 4 vols. London, HMSO, 1928–47.

Inventaire Sommaire des Archives Départementales . . . Rédigé par A. Bénet. *Calvados, Archives Ecclésiastiques, Série H,* Tom. 1. Caen, 1905.

Inventaire Sommaire des Archives Départementales . . . Rédigé par L. Duval. *Orne, Archives Ecclésiastiques, Série H,* Tom. 1. Alençon, 1891.

Jeayes, I.H. *Descriptive Catalogue of Derbyshire Charters*. London & Derby, Bemrose, 1906.

Jeayes, I.H. *Descriptive Catalogue of the Charters and Muniments in the Possession of Lord Fitzhardinge at Berkeley Castle*. Bristol, Jefferies, 1892.

Jeayes, I.H. *Descriptive Catalogue of the Charters and Muniments of the Gresley Family*. London, Clark, 1895.

Knowles, D. & Hadcock, R.N. *Medieval Religious Houses: England and Wales*. New edition. London, Longman, 1971.

Knowles, D. & others, eds. *The Heads of Religious Houses, England and Wales, 940–1216*. Cambridge U. P., 1972.

Lancaster, J.C. *Medieval Coventry – a City Divided?* Coventry and Warwickshire Pamphlets, no. 11, 1981.

Lancaster, W.T. *Abstracts of the Charters and Other Documents Contained in the Chartulary of the Cistercian Abbey of Fountains*. Leeds, Whitehead, 1915.

The Langley Cartulary. Ed. P.R. Coss. Stratford-on-Avon, Shakespeare Centre, for the Dugdale Society, 1980.

Léchaudé d'Anisy, A.L. *Extrait des Chartes et Autres Actes Normands ou Anglo-Normands qui se Trouvent dans les Archives du Calvados*. 2 vols. Caen, 1834.

Lloyd, J.E. *A History of Wales from the Earliest Times to the Edwardian Conquest*. New impression. 2 vols. London, 1948.

Madox, T. (ed.) *Formulare Anglicanum: a Collection of Ancient Charters and Instruments . . . etc.* London, 1702.

Magni Rotuli Scaccarii Normanniae. Ed. T. Stapleton. 2 vols. London, 1840–4.

Morgan, M.M. *The English Lands of the Abbey of Bec*. London, Oxford U.P., 1946.

Morice, P.H. *Mémoires pour Servir de Preuves à l'Histoire Ecclésiastique et Civile de Bretagne.* 3 vols. Paris, 1742–6.

Morris, R.H. *Chester in the Plantagenet and Tudor Reigns.* Chester, 1893.

Nichols, J. *The History and Antiquities of the County of Leicester.* 4 vols. London, 1795–1815.

Orderic Vitalis. *Historia Ecclesiastica.* Ed. A. le Prévost. 5 vols. Paris, Société de l'Histoire de France, 1838–55.

Ormerod, G. *The History of the County Palatine and City of Chester.* Second edition revised and enlarged by T. Helsby. 3 vols. London, 1882.

Owen, E. *A Catalogue of the Manuscripts Relating to Wales in the British Museum.* London, Cymmrodorion Society, 1900.

Patterson, R.B. (ed.) *Earldom of Gloucester Charters.* Oxford, Clarendon Press, 1973.

Pollock, Sir F. & Maitland, F. W. *History of English Law Before the Time of Edward I.* Cambridge U. P. [*Edition not identified.*]

Powicke, F.M. *The Thirteenth Century, 1216–1307.* Oxford, Clarendon Press, 1953.

Prou, M. & Vidier, A. *Recueil des Chartes de L'Abbaye de Saint Benoît-sur-Loire.* 2 vols. Paris, 1907–32.

Regesta Regum Anglo-Normannorum 1066–1154. Ed. H.A. Cronne, H.W.C. Davis, R.H.C. Davis, *etc.* 4 vols. Oxford, Clarendon Press, 1913–69.

The Register of St Osmund (*Vetus Registrum Sarisberiense*). Ed. W.H. Rich Jones. 2 vols. London, Rolls Series, 1883–4.

Registrum Antiquissimum. – vols. 27–9, 32, 34, 41–2, 46, 51, 62, 67–8 of *Lincoln Record Society.*

Reports of the Deputy Keeper of the Public Records. London, HMSO, 1840–

Richard of Hexham. *Historia de Gestis Regis Stephani et de Bello de Standardo.* Ed. R. Howlett. In *Chronicles of the Reigns of Stephen, Henry II and Richard I* (vol. III), London, Rolls Series, 1886.

Robert of Torigni. *Chronicle.* Ed. R. Howlett. In *Chronicles of the Reign of Stephen, etc* (vol. IV), London, Rolls Series, 1889.

Roper, W.O. (ed.) *Materials for the History of the Church of Lancaster.* 2 vols. *Chetham Society,* N.S. xxvi, xxxi (1892–4).

Rotuli Litterarum Clausarum. Ed. T.D. Hardy. 2 vols. London, Record Commission, 1833–44.

Round, J.H. *Calendar of Documents Preserved in France.* London 1899.

[*St Andrews Cartulary.*] *Liber Cartarum Prioratus Sancti Andree in Scotia.* Ed. T. Thomson. Edinburgh, Bannatyne Club, 1841.

Sauvage, R.N. *L'Abbaye de Saint-Martin de Troarn.* Caen, Delasques, 1911.

Shaw, S. *The History and Antiquities of Staffordshire.* 2 vols. London, Robson, 1798–1801.

Shirley, W.W. (ed.) *Royal and Other Historical Letters Illustrative of the Reign of Henry III.* 2 vols. London, Rolls Series, 1862–6.

Sleigh, J. *A History of the Ancient Parish of Leek in Staffordshire.* Second edition. London, 1883.

Stanhope, E. *Abstracts of the Deeds and Charters Relating to Revesby Abbey, 1142–1539*. Horncastle, 1889.

Stewart-Brown, R. (ed.) *Calendar of County Court, City Court and Eyre Rolls of Chester, 1259–1297*. *Chetham Society*, N.S. lxxxiv (1925).

Stenton D.M. (ed.) *Rolls of the Justices in Eyre . . . for Gloucestershire, Warwickshire and Staffordshire, 1221, 1222*. *Selden Society* lix (1940).

Stenton, D.M. (ed.) *Rolls of the Justices in Eyre . . . for Yorkshire in 3 Henry III, 1218–19*. *Selden Society* lvi (1937).

Stenton, F.M. (ed.) *Documents Illustrative of the Social and Economic History of the Danelaw*. London, British Academy, 1920.

Stenton, F.M. *The First Century of English Feudalism, 1066–1166*. Oxford, Clarendon Press, 1932.

Tait, J. *Mediaeval Manchester and the Beginnings of Lancashire*. Manchester, 1904.

Taylor, F. *Selected Cheshire Seals, 12th–17th Century, from the Collections in the John Rylands Library*. Reprinted from the *B.J.R.L.* xxvi, no. 2, 1942.

Teulet, J.B.A.T. & others. *Inventaires et Documents . . . Layettes du Trésor des Chartes*. 5 vols. Paris, 1863–1909.

Thompson, A.H. *The Abbey of St Mary of the Meadows, Leicester*. Leicester, Archaeological Society, 1949.

Tyson, M. *Handlist of Charters, Deeds and Similar Documents in the Possession of the John Rylands Library*. Part II. Manchester U. P., 1935.

Victoria History of the County of:
  Buckingham. Ed. W. Page. 4 vols+index. London, Constable, 1905–28.
  Chester. Ed. B.E. Harris assisted by A.T. Thacker. Oxford U. P., 1979–
  Derby. Ed. W. Page. London, Constable, 1905–
  Lancaster. Ed. W. Farrer & J. Brownbill. London, Constable, 1906–
  Nottingham. Ed. W. Page. London, Constable, 1906–
  Warwick. Ed. H.A. Doubleday, W. Page & others. London, Constable, 1904–
  York. Ed. W. Page, etc. London, Constable, 1907–

Warner, G.F. & Ellis, H.J. (eds.) *Facsimiles of Royal and Other Charters in the British Museum*. London, British Museum, 1903.

Warwickshire Feet of Fines: Abstracted from the Originals in the Public Record Office by E. Stokes, *etc*. 3 vols. *Dugdale Society*, Publications nos. 11, 15, 18 (1932–43).

Watson, J. *Memoirs of the Ancient Earls of Warren and Surrey and their Descendants to the Present Time*. 2 vols. Warrington, 1782.

Wiffen, J.H. *Historical Memoirs of the House of Russell, from the Time of the Norman Conquest*. 2 vols. London, 1833.

William of Newburgh. *Historia Rerum Anglicarum*. Ed. R. Howlett. In *Chronicles of the Reign of Stephen, etc* (vols. I, II), London, Rolls Series, 1884–5.

INDEX

All references in this index of persons and places are to charter numbers, not to page numbers.

While a high proportion of place names and personal names have been identified and given their modern spellings, the rest remain cited in the forms which appear in the charters. The index does not claim (except where specifically indicated) to distinguish between different persons (and, in a few instances, places) of the same name, or to identify all instances in which the same person is referred to in the charters by different names, titles or vocational descriptions. In deciding whether 'filius de' indicates the patronymic prefix 'Fitz', or merely 'son of', Professor Barraclough's usage has been followed. The only abbreviation used in the index is 's.' for 'son'.

J., monk of Wareduna 415
Jaffa (Palestine) 289
James, s. of Thomas 417–21
Jews of Lincoln 355
Jocius *capellanus* 385, 412
John, abbot of Combermere 242
  abbot of Dieulacres 463
    Hoil 102
    Lindores 466–8
  archdeacon of Northampton 431
  camerarius 60
  capellanus 22, 34, 45, 81, 85, 88, 92, 95, 98–9,
    109, 115, 117
  de Barrua 360
  clericus 35, 227, 273–4, 335, 363–4, 388, 393,
    427, 432–3, 435
  constable of Chester 159, 163, 166, 171–2, 180,
    188, 190–2, 194, 206, 208, 227–8, 260, 302,
    313
  king of England (1199–1216) 258, 306, 311,
    320, 328, 337, 355, 359, 394, 411, 415–6, 424
  le Poter 309
  magister 37, 41, 59
  prior of Monks Kirby 428–9, 431
    Trentham 133, 148, 177, 182
  servant 107
  s. of Abraham 417–21
  s. of Adam 417–21
  s. of Arlild 417–21
  s. of Benedict 417–21
  s. of Emma 417–21
  s. of Eudo 417–21
  s. of Gerard 289, 302
  s. of Hugh 417–21
  s. of Margery 451
  s. of Norman 387
  s. of Philip 297–8, 397, 407
  s. of Ralph 329
  s. of Wido 417–21
  s. of William 417–21
  sub-prior of Repton 442–3
  the Scot, earl of Chester (1232–7) 220, 240,
    382, 390, 407, 409, 411, 422, 438–41,
    445–69
Jollanus, prior of Spalding 287
Jordan 173
  clericus 60
  s. of Warner 417–21
Jorz, Robert de 265
  William de 265
Joscelin *capellanus* 359
  castellanus 107–8, 116
  s. of Heming 441
Judith, sister of Hugh I 26
Junchera 277

Kalecot *see* Kaletoft
Kales, Alan de 289
  Alexander de 417–21
  Anketinus de 417–21
  Emma de 417–21
  Geoffrey de 301
  Ketebern de 299
  Philip de 302, 417–21
  William de 302
Kaletoft, Eudo de 298–9, 413, 416
  Ivo de 214, 394
Karolus, abbot of Stanlaw 446
Katherine, daughter of John 417–21
Keal *see* East Keal
Keckwick (Ches.) 15
Kegworth (Leics.) 266, 358–62, 369
  Henry de 283–4, 358
  Peter de 376
  Richard de 354, 359–62, 376, 379, 387, 406,
    409
Keles *see* Kales
Kemmeys, Ralph de 462
Kene, William de 301
Kenilworth (Warwicks.) 414
  prior of *see* W., prior
Kent, Nicholas 372
Keresley (Warwicks.) 343
Kersal (Lancs.) 84
Keuret *see* Cywryd
Killingholme (Lincs.) 278
Kinalchmund 469
Kinesby *see* Kingsbury
Kingeseia (Ches.?) 13, 28
Kingsbury (Warwicks.) 74, 94, 199
Kingshill (Warwicks.) 60, 169
Kingsley, Emma de 352
  Leuca de 225
  Ranulf de 137, 163, 225
  Richard de 212, 214–15, 225, 232, 258, 261,
    283–5, 315, 340, 350, 352–3, 357, 378, 384,
    394–5, 406–7, 434, 448, 452–4, 461–2
Kingthorpe (Lincs.) 298, 417–21
Kirkby (Lincs.) 288, 302, 324
  Alan de 305
  Walter de 305
Kirkstall abbey (Yorks.) 69
Kirkstead abbey (Lincs.) 103, 291–3, 417–21
  abbot of *see* Henry, abbot
Kocscelinus 53–4
Kyde, Walter 396
Kyme, Philip de 104, 165–7, 182
  Philip s. of Simon de 290, [293?], 298, 330, 363,
    417–21
  Simon de 203, 262, 288, 330, 363
    s. of William, de Kyme 34, 40, 66, 73–4, 77,